the gilmore girls companion

With love to Richard & Judy Berman, and sincere respect to Amy Sherman-Palladino, Daniel Palladino, and the entire cast and crew of *Gilmore Girls*.

命

This book is dedicated to Pamela Norman Berman, who never says "you can't do that," only "what can I do to help." *Aishiteru*.

COVER + INTERIOR DESIGN
Pamela Norman Berman
pnormandesigns@me.com

PHOTOGRAPHY: See P. 471 for photo credits.

Published by BearManor Media
bearmanormedia.com

THE GILMORE GIRLS COMPANION
AS Berman, author.
p.cm.

Includes bibliographical references and index.

ISBN 1-59393-616-8

1. Television and popular culture, 2000-2010 2. Biography.
3. Television and popular culture-history. I. Title.

10 9 8 7 6 5 4 3 2 1

What's Inside

a gift by edward herrmann

An actor's life is full of ups and downs. Sometimes the work comes so fast and heavy he can't deal with all of it. Sometimes, as the saying goes, he can't get arrested. But if he is very lucky, a project comes along that makes all the lean times seem unimportant. Such a project is like a gift. Such a gift in my life was The *Gilmore Girls*.

I had avoided episodic television for years until I read the pilot for a new show that I thought was hip, smart, funny, and an ironic turning on its head of the usual teen show format: a young girl who was less interested in boys and makeup and sex and popularity, than reading *War and Peace.*

Adults were not automatically idiots and the dialogue was sharp, funny and loaded with literary awareness. It was, in a word, intelligent. The cast was terrific, the producer/writer team eccentric and off center in the best sense, and there was every prospect that the show, with careful tending from a sympathetic network, could be a success. No one has to tell me how rare a successful television show is these days. Commercial networks have a nasty habit of pulling the plug on shows—some of them very good—within three or four episodes if some arbitrary numbers are not hit in a prescribed time limit. Not so the WB network, at least with The *Gilmore Girls*. However the decisions were made to keep the show going, and I don't pretend to know what blood was shed in that struggle, we were given a second season and the chance to build an audience.

And what an audience! Just as I write this, I am in New Haven, Conn. at the Yale Rep. doing Edward Albee's *A Delicate Balance*, a great American play at a wonderful theater. Yesterday I was asked to a "tea" at Trumbull College, a tradition at Yale where visiting scholars speak in an informal way to whoever wants to come. After a very interesting question-and-answer period about art, playwriting and the aesthetic of a creative life in America, I was surrounded by young Yale undergraduates in an outpouring of gratitude for the show, its message and the power it had of healing the usual rifts in the mother/daughter relationship of adolescence. “My mother is my best friend because of that show! Thank you, thank you, thank you!!” Of course it might have helped that the setting of Rory's college days was Yale, but the message was clear: the show had a truly positive and powerful influence on kids trying to make creative decisions about their futures at the most confusing and trying time of their lives: the infamous teen years. There is so much garbage out there encouraging kids to take the road of least resistance, and here was a show that was amazingly popular telling them to raise the bar and try for something less vulgar, something better. And doing it with grace, humor and wicked wit.

As I said, a gift. Warner Bros. Studio was a great place to work: all those ghosts of Cagney and Bogart and Errol Flynn. And the working conditions, always horrendous on a single-camera, one-hour show, were made intriguing and fun by the wonderfully funny and smart cast. We stay in touch and have great satisfaction in each others' success. The greatest joy for me, however, is the impact the show has had on a whole generation of young people who learned that, though growing up is tough at the best of times, it can be done with humor, honesty and love. The gulf between generations is far less important than is commonly supposed when people can drop the pose and talk honestly with each other. And this was the real triumph of The *Gilmore Girls*. A gift.

1
Luke's

STARS HOLLOW
FOUNDED · 1779 ·
4

8
Miss Patty's

12

4

5

WARNER BROS. LOT SHOOTING LOCATIONS

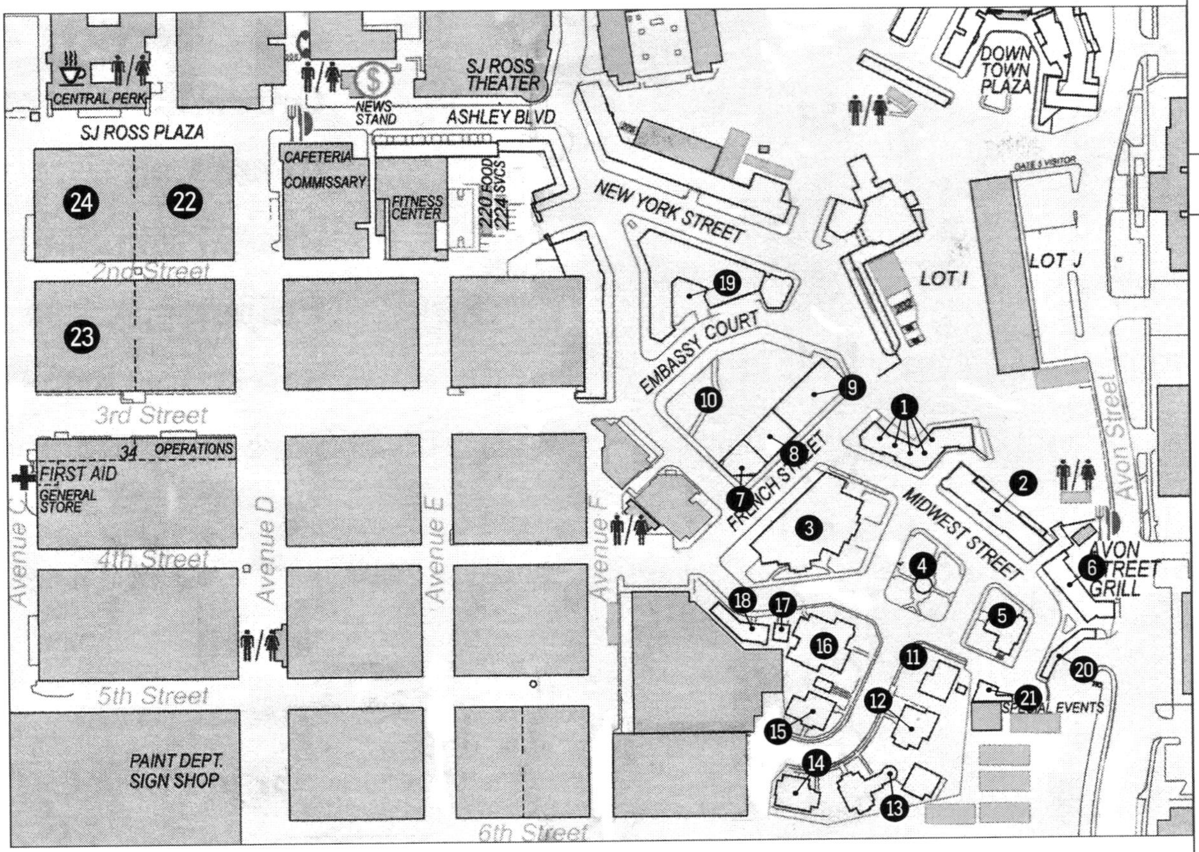

1. Luke's/Taylor's soda shoppe/flower shop/library/bank/Doose's Market stock room
2. Doose's Market/beauty shop/Antonelli's/post office/Stars Hollow Books
3. Weston's/arcade/Stars Hollow Video store/high school + classrooms/ Luke's apartment
4. Gazebo/Stars Hollow sign
5. Church/Dean's apartment/Chris' apartment
6. Bar
7. Bootsy's newsstand/Yale bar
8. Miss Patty's
9. Park/statue
10. Park/outdoor shots/Yale exterior shots
11. Kim's Antiques
12. Sookie's house/Lorelai's house
13. Babette + Morey's/Stars Hollow Historical Society/clothing store/Anna Nardini's shop
14. Lindsay's house
15. Dean's house/Cheshire Cat Inn/Black White + Read/Lord of the Rings party house/Liz + TJ's garage
16. Lane, Zack + Brian's apartment/Gilmore mansion basement/Liz + TJ's apartment/Honor's bridal suite
17. Garage w/Luke's boat
18. Jason Stiles' apartment
19. Chilton exterior
20. LeChat Club
21. Hewes Bros. gas station/Gypsy's garage
22. Lorelai's house/Chilton/Dragonfly Inn interiors
23. Independence Inn/Gilmore mansion interiors (S1) ...later became Yale
24. Stage 12: Gilmore mansion interiors

previously on **gilmore girls...**

One evening in October 2004, actor Nick Holmes urges his silver Oldsmobile Alero high into Los Angeles' Griffith Park mountains, occasionally glancing at a map he's been given for the evening's festivities. His global positioning system is useless in this area and he has a 7:30 pm call time to make for this, his first episode of *Gilmore Girls*.

He's been auditioning for the series since the pilot, first for the role of Dean, then Tristin, and finally Jess. Now he's managed to get himself through the Warner Brothers gates as Robert, the Life and Death Brigade's resident marksman for the group's "Out of Africa" adventure. Though he can't know it now, his first episode, "You Jump, I Jump, Jack," will quickly become one of the most beloved in the series.

If he can find the shooting site. Though the map's a bit dodgy, there are members of the production crew scattered about "every half-mile to encourage you in the right direction." As first-episode experiences go, this one's breathtaking. (Never mind the flat tire he'll suffer on the way back after they wrap around 3 the next morning.)

Just a few weeks later and nearly 6,000 miles away in the Hanover district of Germany, a twentysomething accountant named Cira wakes up to her 3 am alarm, fires up her computer, and begins the downloading process for the *Gilmore Girls* episode "You Jump, I Jump, Jack" that aired in the US the previous night, before settling down for another couple hours sleep. This ritual has become a way of life for people around the world. "Because of the dubbing, we usually get the episodes that air in the US a few months later," Cira says. "So when the story line became interesting, I started downloading the English episodes right after they aired."

"Aww, I miss 'Downloading Wednesdays,'" says another fan, Katka Rylichová, in the Czech Republic.

While American television programs have been eagerly consumed the world over for generations, *Gilmore Girls* is one of only a few that's driven international fans to not only seek out the latest episodes, but also to write *Gilmore* stories of their own, maintain Web sites dedicated to it and its cast, and even to learn English to bypass the slipshod dubbings and subtitles that have marred its international releases from the beginning.

What is it about this series that has kept audiences all over the world debating every nuance of every episode more than three years after the last one aired? And why do those who worked on *Gilmore Girls* still juggle their busy schedules and negotiate Los Angeles' notorious traffic to see each other several times each year?

It was questions like these, as well as the author's own love of this series, that led to the writing of *The Gilmore Girls Companion*. Before starting on this book in June 2008, I'd conducted several interviews for a forthcoming book about the making of the '70s sitcom *Soap*. While surviving members of the cast and crew were gracious and always willing to share their experiences, the nearly 30 years that had passed since it ended had faded even the keenest memories. The idea that recollections about the making of *Gilmore* would be similarly lost spurred me to make just one more phone call and to send that one-in-a-million-shot e-mail.

Though great pains were taken to reach out to everybody involved, several declined to participate. Some wanted to close that particular chapter of their life, others hinted that they were holding on to their stories for their own memoirs. Fortunately, the 40-plus people who did take the time to share their memories helped to create the most detailed behind-the-scenes account of *Gilmore Girls* to date.

Before we get started, a quick note on how names are handled in this book. Though I've stuck with the journalistic convention of referring to people by their surnames, you will find two exceptions here. Initially, this came about because balancing the names Daniel Palladino and Amy Sherman-Palladino throughout a book-length narrative proved a pretty cumbersome prospect. However, it soon occurred to me that after spending a good 153 episodes traipsing about their make-believe world, who among us really thinks of them as anything but Amy & Dan?

Primarily, this book is meant to give fans some idea of what went on behind the scenes of the series, from the first glimmer of the idea to the final episode. Though some of its hundreds of cultural references are mentioned when necessary, this is not meant to be a compendium of those, which could easily fill a book this size on their own. The decision was also made to leave out cast and crew information for each episode, as this is all available online in a variety of places. Character names are spelled as they appear on IMDB.com. Age information concerning actors, too, has also been omitted, as it can complicate things for them when they audition for roles significantly younger than they are.

When there's a reference to something that has taken place in the *Gilmore* universe, it is usually followed by numbers in parentheses, e.g., (5.18), with the first number denoting the season, and the second the episode. Quotes from the series are transcriptions; while every effort was made to ensure their accuracy, names especially are open to interpretation barring access to the final shooting scripts.

With all that sorted, let's get this party started. Though our destination is the Anywhere USA town of Stars Hollow, Conn., our story actually begins in California's San Fernando Valley. Give CatKirk a pet (carefully), slip this Kirk's Town Tours map in your pocket or purse, and take a hearty swig of Miss Patty's Founders Day Punch. It's a wild ride; you're gonna need it.

"Those stars,
so bright. This
forest, hollow..."

the road **to stars hollow**

It's May 17, 2010. A light rain falls over the Warner Brothers lot in Burbank, Calif. Most shows are on hiatus right now, which means the only people working today are mostly those moving lights and rigging sets for the ABC Family series *Pretty Little Liars.* Former *Gilmore Girls* production designer Rachel Kamerman is stuck in her office on the lot making sure that all the sets for the new series are in place.

Tours of the Warner Brothers lot, however, are in full swing. A tour guide brings his cart to a halt in front of the house once shared by Lorelai and Rory Gilmore. While he rattles off a few quick facts about the empty house to the punters taking identical pictures of the set, *Gilmore Girls* key set costumer, Valerie Campbell, slips out the back of Lorelai's house, which reveals itself to be the *front* of Sookie and Jackson's place. "Space is never wasted here," she calls over her shoulder, and off we go through the studio's Midwest Street exterior set, hunting the old ghosts of a television series that, 10 years on, refuses to die.

A couple of days before this, Campbell's birthday celebration played host to 82 guests, including several from *Gilmore Girls*: Keiko Agena (Lane), Michael DeLuise (TJ), John Cabrera (Brian), Biff Yeager (Tom), Honorine Bell (Lulu), and nearly the entire video editing team. In past years, the likes of Edward Herrmann (Richard), Sean Gunn (Kirk) and many others have attended her parties, or simply stopped by to say hi.

Gilmore Girls (or simply *Gilmore* as cast and crew inevitably refer to it) was an experience that forged strong bonds between the dozens who worked in front of the cameras and behind the scenes. It's not the first time that such on-set friendships have been compared with the fierce loyalty soldiers form in the trenches, but in the seven-year struggle to get *Gilmore Girls* on screen week after week, it fits.

Hours were long—21-hour days were not unheard of—scripts were twice the length of those for other hour-long shows, and executive producers Amy Sherman-Palladino and Daniel Palladino demanded that the lines be delivered precisely as written. Virtually every department suffered losses due to members quitting or being sacked, often for their inability to meet Amy's stringent demands. Many still recall a batch of buttons that made the rounds sporting just two words: "Yes Amy." Yet for all the long hours, emotional breakdowns and desperate searches for on-set places to grab a few minutes' sleep, nearly all admit that the seven-year insanity resulted in some of the best work and fondest memories of their careers.

Amy Sherman: Growing Up with the King of Comedy

There is an odd disconnect between actors and their audiences, only exacerbated by the hyperconnected reality of the World Wide Web. While many fans come to view their favorite actors as extensions of their own family, whipping their hero worship into a fine frenzy through sites such as Twitter and Facebook, the actors themselves inhabit a different reality entirely. For them, it's all about the hunt for the next paying gig, even as they fill the time in between with friends and the exercise of their other creative muscles.

Whether it's Keiko Agena playing bass and drums at a Japantown club in Los Angeles with her master-guitarist husband, Shin Kawasaki, or Tanc Sade (Finn) rounding up a few actors to perform in movies with a $20 budget, many spend whatever free time they have blowing off steam. And if they can keep each other entertained, so much the better.

It's a tradition as old as Tinseltown itself, and one Amy Sherman experienced growing up in her parents' home in Van Nuys, Calif., in the San Fernando Valley.

In the '60s and '70s, her father, Don Sherman, performed stand-up comedy everywhere, from Las Vegas to Australia, and wrote for a variety of big television programs including *The Love Boat*, *The Steve Allen Show* and *Laverne & Shirley*. In addition, he appeared in television hits such as *Barney Miller*, *The Monkees*, *Starsky & Hutch* and *Gimme a Break*. Many years later, these appearances would be pivotal in the creation of one of *Gilmore Girls*' most enduring characters: Kirk.

The comedian's home was the drop-in spot for many Jewish Catskills comics, all anxious to see how their material fared against other professionals. Shecky Greene and Jackie Mason were just two who spent time in the Sherman home, where Amy began to develop an appreciation for the cadence heard in the nightclubs and resort halls at that time.

Here, too, is where she probably began to cultivate her taste for the dark humor that would later pervade Stars Hollow. The Catskills comics carved out lifelong careers based on routines about their own misfortunes, Rodney Dangerfield probably the best known today. It doesn't take much to draw a line from the Borscht Belt to Old Man Twickham's regular deathbed appearances (5.18) or Kirk's creepy relationships with old women who leave him their jewelry (6.1).

While Amy was developing an ear for the spoken word, her mother, Maybin Hewes, a former dancer, had other plans for her daughter. She urged Amy to become a dancer, too, with the hopes of one day seeing her become a "hoofer in a Broadway musical," as Amy told the Jewish Journal in March 2003. Absent from the whole conversation was any suggestion that Amy would seek higher education.

Don Sherman: King of the Cruise Lines

While Amy & Dan would stand in picket lines during the first Hollywood writers strike of the 21st century, Amy's father actually discovered his calling as a cruise ship comedian as the result of a writers strike in the late 1970s. With no other work available, he leapt into his first performance for Holland America Line cruises and never looked back, working the seas 40 weeks a year. As of 2009, the 79 year old was still working, now exclusively for Celebrity cruise line, 20 weeks a year.

"One of my great regrets is that I didn't go to college," Amy told The New York Times in January 2005. "I had very little patience for school, and it was never stressed in my household." Instead, she pursued a dancing career, even as she started taking classes with the legendary LA comedy improv company The Groundlings around 1990. It was there that she met, and formed a writing relationship with, Jennifer Heath.

Together, they wrote spec scripts for the sitcoms *Roseanne* and *Anything But Love*. Amy was waiting to hear back about an audition she'd done for the part of Rumpleteazer for the touring company of the Andrew Lloyd Webber musical *Cats* when Heath rang her up to tell her *Roseanne* wanted to hire them both on the strength of their script. As Amy told the Los Angles Times in April 2001, "Once I accepted the idea, I realized, 'I don't have to diet anymore. I never have to put on toe shoes again.'"

The Age of the Showrunner

Although Amy had never seen the appeal of slaving away in an office for a living, there was no denying the attraction of being able to communicate her wit to a wider audience. Dancers were largely interchangeable, had a shelf life only slightly longer than the average NFL quarterback, and for the most part, ended up largely forgotten.

Just a few years earlier, not much better could've been said of TV writers. Amy had seen her father work his tail off writing for some of America's most influential shows, only to be left to toil in anonymity with other writing greats behind whoever the flavor-of-the-month actor was at the time. Not every writer had the talent, stamina or desire to provide for their golden years entertaining tipsy cruise-ship passengers.

Yet something crazy had happened at the beginning of the '80s, something that ran contrary to the star-based system that had prevailed in television, film and radio. The writer had emerged from the smoke-filled rooms of Hollywood to actually gain recognition, first with studio and network producers, and later (and to a lesser extent) with American audiences.

In his gripping memoir *Billion-Dollar Kiss*, TV writer Jeffrey Stepakoff pin-

Catskills Comics & the Borscht Belt

From the 1920s to the 1960s, middle- and upper-class New York Jews headed to the Catskill Mountains in upstate New York every summer to stay at resorts such as The Concord. While Jews were barred from many hotels throughout the country then, the Catskill establishments welcomed them, and in many cases were run by Jews. These places in the "Borscht Belt" also happened to feature stand-up comedy by those who would go on to dominate radio, television and the movies, including Mel Brooks, George Burns, Milton Berle, Jackie Mason and Rodney Dangerfield. *Dirty Dancing*, a movie that

gets at least one nod in *Gilmore Girls ("Hey! Nobody puts Baby in the corner"//2.6)*, is set at Kellerman's, a Catskills resort. (Kelly Bishop starred in that 1987 coming-of-age classic.)

points the beginning of this change to the 1981 premiere of police drama *Hill Street Blues*. The series was created by Steven Bochco, who would go on to bring us everything from *LA Law* to *Doogie Howser, MD* and *NYPD Blue*.

Of course there had been powerful, well-respected American television showrunners prior to 1981. Norman Lear virtually invented the mature sitcom in the 1970s with the likes of *All in the Family*, *One Day at a Time* and *Good Times*.

Yet Bochco turned the TV-writing formula on its head with *Hill Street Blues*, Stepakoff points out. "Until this time, TV writers made their two-dimensional characters move around like chess pieces. Characters were forced to service a story.... But in *Hill Street*, character motivated story, as opposed to the other way around."

While most of television remained the same through the '80s, gradually more character-based programs were added to the prime-time schedule, including *Moonlighting* and Bochco's *LA Law*.

While *Hill Street Blues* would never enjoy stellar ratings, it did capture critical acclaim, and as a consequence, a boatload of free publicity in the highly competitive, three-network landscape. With the burgeoning American cable TV market siphoning off viewers, proven showrunners were even more valuable. As Stepakoff notes, "Studio executives began to concern themselves first and foremost with the showrunner—the writing executive producer—and later with what show would actually be run."

Network executives weren't merely embracing this new model of storytelling for the hell of it. American society was undergoing its own transformation.

President Ronald Reagan might've spent most of his two terms in office telling the American people that good times were just around the corner, but many were starting to wake up from the shared delusion of prosperity. The angst caused by Vietnam, the oil shortage and the Iranian hostage crisis might've all ended, but the shameless greed and the overly-simplistic views of the religious right had begun to fester among those who saw their paychecks lagging behind the cost of living.

Maybin Hewes Returns

In 2009, Amy executive produced her then-78-year-old mother's return to the stage in *Still Struttin'* at North Hollywood's Crown City Theatre, where Hewes danced and sang such Broadway standards as "I've Got Rhythm" and "Times Like These."

The desperately poor were used to being left out of the national conversation; the blue-collar workers were not. Since the days of the whistle-stop tours of Roosevelt, working people were used to being promised the moon in exchange for their political support. Sure, there were some grumblings when the status quo continued to prevail, but at least it was nice to be courted. During the Reagan and Bush eras, Wall Street and its junk-bond kings had the administration's ear, the God-fearing were pandered to for their ability to get out the vote in Middle America, and the working classes were shown the door.

The great pockets of people now left out in the cold not only found it increasingly difficult to swallow the standard television fare that filled the airwaves, those syrupy-sweet sitcoms and rosy-hued dramas seemed to mock the very lives they now lived. When stand-up comedienne Roseanne Barr was handed the keys to her own sitcom in 1988, a few network executives at ABC not only recognized which way the wind was blowing, they were banking on it.

Roseanne and the Rise of the Domestic Diva

Any discussion about *Gilmore Girls* sooner or later must mention that other groundbreaking WB series, *Buffy the Vampire Slayer*. While a rousing game of six degrees of separation can certainly be played with these fan favorites, they also share a common ancestor: *Roseanne*.

Buffy creator Joss Whedon's first television writing gig was also on that show, another case of getting a spec script into the right hands. Like Amy, Whedon's father, Tom, knew his way around the television networks, having written for *The Golden Girls*, *Benson* and *Alice*. Joss' grandfather, John, had done the same for *The Donna Reed Show*.

Joss Whedon joined the *Roseanne* writing team in 1989 and ended up writing just a few scripts that year before leaving. While *Roseanne* is still hailed in some circles as one of the best written situation comedies in American television, in many ways it was also a model for how *not to* run a television show—something Amy and Heath would learn when they joined the writing team in 1990 at the tail end of Season 3.

Amy & Dan got their start on the sitcom *Roseanne* starring Roseanne Barr (center). Here Amy would learn to "make the small big, and the big small" when writing TV scripts.

Most accounts maintain that series star Roseanne Barr ran her show with an iron fist, relying more on intimidation than encouragement. As Amy told The AV Club in February 2005, "*Roseanne* had just fired everybody, so they were completely restaffing and they had no chicks. And we were a team, and we were cheap, and our timing was perfect. It was a very quick and easy process, which is not the norm."

Though Amy and Heath would end their official writing partnership after just one year, they each stayed on as story editors for *Roseanne*. Their script for Season 4's "A Bitter Little Pill to Swallow," in which Roseanne and TV daughter Becky (Alicia Goranson) discuss birth control, earned the show an Emmy nomination.

Despite the rough treatment that writers suffered at the hands of Barr, Amy had the opportunity to see how a real TV writers room works, where seven writers or so went over an episode outline, threw in their ideas and created a cohesive script. Even in the 1990s, many shows were cobbled together in an assembly line fashion by a dozen writers or more, the finished product less than the sum of its parts.

In *Roseanne*'s writers room, the motto was "Make the small big, and the big small," Amy told writer Susan LaTempa. "When we broke stories, we would take that small incident and blow it up and make that big, and then if there was something really big and over the top, we'd make it tiny. That's usually the way your real life works." It was a lesson that Amy would return to again and again on *Gilmore Girls*.

"If I'd got on a different show and it was more joke-driven, more, 'there are six people and they're trying to fuck each other, ha ha ha,' I don't know if I would still be writing."

—AMY ON HAVING HER FIRST WRITING JOB BE ROSEANNE (THE AV CLUB, 2/9/05)

At the best of times, producing a regular television series can be counted on to test your nerve, your scruples, and your faith in the shaky vocation you chose. When that series is particularly ambitious in what its showrunner is trying to pull off, it can be hell; even more so if the show is successful. On *Roseanne*, those who weren't fired or driven off the show pulled closer together. Two alliances Amy made would prove crucial to the creation of *Gilmore*. Writer Mike Gandolfi, still a close friend of Amy's today, would play Stars Hollow's bookstore manager Andrew. Another writer, Daniel Palladino, who she met in 1992, would become the yin to her yang, the two marrying about five years later.

It was also around this time that Amy was approached by a talent agent, Gavin Polone, who wanted to represent her. "When she was on *Roseanne*, she was hot, everybody wanted Amy," he remembers. Though she didn't sign with Polone then, fate would throw them together soon enough.

Amy & Dan: The Wilderness Years

Amy was 24 when she joined *Roseanne*, but four seasons later, she needed a change. Neither she nor Dan had any interest in knocking out script after script for half-hour comedies until a fickle Hollywood handed them their walking papers.

In September 1995, Amy wrote a script for the CBS sitcom *Can't Hurry Love*, which went the way of most TV shows in about five months, though it did afford her the opportunity to work with future *Gilmore Girls* producer Patricia Fass Palmer.

As Amy told the Los Angles Times in April 2001, she had gotten very spoiled by the quality of writing on *Roseanne*. On the shows that came after, she was the "one schmuck sitting in the room who's [saying], 'But it's not good enough yet,' and everyone else has nannies and stuff and they want to get out by 6 o'clock."

In 1996, it was on to another sitcom, Fox's *Love and Marriage* (aka *Come Fly With Me*) starring *The Closer*'s Anthony Denison. This one was yanked after just two episodes.

The seemingly "instant success" of *Gilmore Girls* came to Dan and Amy after nearly a decade spent slaving behind the scenes of several shows.

While this is the series that many point to as that long dark hour of the soul for Amy's career, it was also one where she was gathering people and ideas that would find better use years later on *Gilmore*.

Not only had Palmer produced this show, too, but also *Roseanne* writer Gandolfi had contributed his talents to the cause. A very young Adam Wylie (Paris' "winningly naive" foil Brad Langford) frequently popped up in episodes. Most importantly, it was here that Amy worked with Helen Pai, who would become one of her closest friends, sharing with her stories about her Korean upbringing. We may never learn who Lane's father is, but Pai is certainly her mother, or at least her eccentric aunt.

Years later, during the making of Amy's *The Return of Jezebel James*, *Gilmore Girls*' Gypsy, Rose Abdoo, suddenly realized she'd auditioned for *Love and Marriage* years before. It was Abdoo who pointed out one very obvious harbinger of *Gilmore Girls* in *Love and Marriage*. The husband and wife portrayed in the series are called Jack and *April Nardini*.

Amy was caught in a vicious cycle all too familiar to anybody who's tried to make it in Hollywood. Like any high-stakes gamble, there are winning streaks and losing streaks, and the latter can batter your confidence horribly. Butting heads with executives along the way hadn't helped, but was to be expected if the writer/producer cared more about the craft than kissing ass. "Amy, at the time, was somebody who had burned a lot of bridges from the shows she had done before," Polone admits.

Most are familiar with actors who spend years landing small roles on series and large roles on pilots never picked up before they become

Gavin Polone — Gilmore's Dark Horse

Ostensibly the reason people in Hollywood hate reality TV is because it screws professionals out of jobs in an industry already extremely difficult to make a living in. Some, however, will admit that series such as *Big Brother* and *Survivor* also are uncomfortably close to what they have to deal with every day. And just as in reality TV, every show has its dark horse. For *Gilmore*, that's executive producer Gavin Polone.

Today one of the most successful TV and film producers in America (if you've seen *Zombieland*, *Curb Your Enthusiasm* or *Panic Room*, you've seen one of his projects), Polone started out as a Hollywood talent agent.

In 1985, the aimless 21-year-old Polone met an International Creative Management talent agent at a party and became her assistant, according to The New York Times Magazine in February 2003. Within a couple of years, he had adopted the image of an agent that many have today: all fancy suits, Ferraris and a pony tail. After a particularly messy split with his next employer, United Talent Agency, in 1996, he went from being an agent (who lines up work for his clients) to being a manager (who manages their careers and can produce their work, potentially pocketing more than an agent's 10%).

By the time he opened his own company, Pariah, many in the industry regarded him as just that. It was not merely the fact that they believed he had aired the dirty laundry of the talent agency racket in the press during his legal battles with UTA, it was the way he dealt with others in the business. The New York Times Magazine's headline says it all: "How a Pathologically Blunt Producer Makes it in Suck-Up City."

Anybody who's dealt with Polone will tell you that he'll always give it to you straight, without the niceties. After the author's own conversation with him for this book, it's very easy to understand why he and Amy parted ways just two years into *Gilmore*. Yet it's just as easy to see that it was probably Polone's ability to tackle executives head on that bought the series time enough, and Amy & Dan control enough, to establish healthy viewer numbers for the series, thus ensuring its longevity.

established. Few realize how brutal this process is on writers. If you're an actor, there's always the chance that you'll be plucked from obscurity for a big hit because you have the right look or the right voice (or even that you look like the actor they've hired to be your mother or your child), but getting network heads or producers to read a writer's scripts or watch a recording of a show that never made it to air takes a lot longer, and is far less likely to happen.

Still, with the benefit of hindsight, *Gilmore* fans can't help but get a little giddy over familiar names and faces that popped up in Amy's life during this otherwise trying time for the writer.

In 1997, she contributed some scripts to *Over the Top*, a sitcom starring Tim Curry and Annie Potts, which again disappeared from the network schedules. Gandolfi wrote some episodes, Dan executive produced some, and the future Miss Patty, Liz Torres, showed up in several. Even Paris' Doyle, Danny Strong, appeared in a couple. Recalls Strong, the second episode "was the one that basically introduced my character into the show, and it got canceled that episode, so it was very bad luck for me."

In 1998, Amy wrote a few episodes for *Veronica's Closet* starring Kirstie Alley, executive producing some. Again she worked with Gandolfi, and even briefly overlapped with director Lee Shallat Chemel, who would end up directing most of *Gilmore*'s Season 7.

By this time, Amy & Dan were both represented by Polone, who realized that Amy had the goods as far as writing went; she simply needed to land one good series that would give her a chance to build a fanbase. What had really been holding her back, he claims, was her.

Pitching Those 'Drop Dead Gorgeous' Girls

The stereotype of the temperamental creative genius spans most cultures. Amy, according to many, is no exception.

"Look, she's a great writer," Polone says. "She would write great scripts, but then when she went into production, she would tell people to fuck themselves basically, so it didn't really work out." Despite this, Polone admits that when he went from being a talent agent with about 70 clients to a manager with only 16, Amy was one of the clients he kept.

As Amy told The New York Times in 2005, "To be really good, you have to be willing to have everybody in the world hate you. That's hard to do, because this is a small town and everybody plays golf together. And if you flip off the guy at CBS, he's going to be having lunch with Fox, NBC and ABC. And that is your reputation. And that's my reputation—I know it."

By 1999, Amy had a couple of television ideas that she was working on with Polone to pitch to the only two networks that were still speaking to her, he says—NBC and The WB. One was an hour-long show about a 15-year-old-girl in Los Angeles based on a Los Angeles Times Magazine article she had optioned; the other was a half-hour show based on her father's childhood growing up in the Bronx, only set in the present.

Polone says he had his own idea for a series, this one based on *Drop Dead Gorgeous*, a 1999 movie he'd recently produced with production partner Judy Hofflund. Written and executive produced by Lona Williams, the movie starred Kirsten Dunst as a young girl from the poor part of town competing in a beauty pageant where contestants keep dying; Ellen Barkin played her mother, who has her own history with the pageant.

"The relationship between Ellen Barkin and Kirsten Dunst in that movie was kind of interesting and I started thinking about the relationship between a mother and daughter who were close in age," he says. "I wanted to do a show about that, but not people who lived in a trailer... but where the mother kind of made it a little bit and had a good life, yet had this best friend who's her daughter.

"I came up with the teaser of the actual [*Gilmore*] pilot that was made where you see a woman at a restaurant and a guy hits on her, and she goes to the bathroom and the guy hits on her daughter, and then he realizes they're mother and daughter, which is surprising because they seem so close in age."

Polone says he first pitched the idea to Williams, but she had another movie going into production. He then pitched it to Amy. "She and I decided that she would pitch these two other ideas—the one that she had the article on and the other one about her father—and then if we were in the room and people were interested, we'd pitch my idea because she liked that, too."

Their first stop was NBC, where they pitched the LA Times story and what would become *Gilmore Girls* to executive JoAnn Alfano, and the show based on Don Sherman's childhood to another NBC exec, Shelley McCrory. Not realizing that McCrory would later buy the Don Sherman idea, Amy and Polone decided to give one of the youngest networks on the block a try, too: The WB.

Whether or not Amy truly had burned bridges in Los Angeles to the extent that Polone suggests, the television landscape had changed greatly since her heyday on *Roseanne*. The renaissance in television programming that The WB brought to American TV screens would be pivotal in giving Amy another chance to make it in Hollywood.

Getting a Foot in the Door at the Frog

However much your eyes glaze over when talk of governmental deregulation crops up, deregulation was crucial to the creation of *Gilmore Girls*.

The 1993 repeal of the FCC's Financial Interest and Syndication Rules after 23 years meant that the major television networks could once again create their own television shows rather than having to rely on independent studios and producers to make the programs they aired.

Between this new freedom and the recent success of Rupert Murdoch's launch of the Fox TV network in the US (home of *The Simpsons* and *Married...with Children* among other hits), those at moviemaking studio Warner Brothers saw an opportunity to create a network of their own. They might not be able to bring in the same viewership numbers enjoyed by the big three networks—ABC, NBC and CBS—but the creation of their own TV-production arm would mean that Warner Brothers could pocket all the ad revenue generated by its own shows, without having to pay a third-party studio to create content. It could also grab even more cash for any series it sold to TV channels in syndication.

Warner Brothers launched The WB on Jan. 11, 1995 with two hours of programming Wednesday nights on the handful of TV affiliate stations it could muster. Five days later, UPN—a joint venture between Viacom/Paramount and Chris-Craft Industries (and later CBS)—was launched. Though both networks premiered with modest ratings—a scant 2 million homes tuning in for The WB's first night—they would quickly build larger followings and separate, distinctive identities.

The WB didn't hit its stride until its 1996-1997 season, which gave it the slow-burn hit *7th Heaven*, executive produced by the legendary Aaron Spelling (*Beverly Hills 90210*). However, it was the 1997 debut of *Buffy the Vampire Slayer* that arguably put The WB on the map. In what remains one of the most ambitious series in American television, *Buffy* became the template for the successful WB series: strong, intelligent female lead characters; mature situations; unprecedented writing and sophisticated humor.

In the fall of 1999, by the time Amy and Polone found themselves at the Warner Brothers Ranch—a 32-acre area in Burbank about a mile from the Warner Brothers lot—The WB was looking for something

Dorothy Parker Thinks Here

From the book that Rory shares with Dean before falling asleep at Miss Patty's (1.9) to the poster on Rory's dorm room wall, and Amy's own Dorothy Parker Drank Here Productions company, the American writer and wit Dorothy Parker (1893-1967) is clearly more than a stab at attracting the nation's literati. (Amy changed her company's name, from the Devil's Concubine, at the last minute.)

"Genius. Love her," Amy told the Los Angeles Times in April 2001 when the subject of Parker came up. "Here's this bitter, boozy and yet incredibly witty woman. I loved not only her writing style, I loved who she was, and I loved her shortcomings.... She would take money for writing assignments and then wouldn't do them. Everything about her always made me laugh, even the way she died; I mean, she was this big gin addict and she didn't care."

Born Dorothy Rothschild in Long Branch, NJ, Parker grew up on the Upper West Side of New York. She played piano at a dance school to make ends meet until she broke into magazine writing as an editorial assistant for Vogue, before becoming a staff writer at Vanity Fair. However, it was her darkly humorous verse, short stories and whimsically wry book reviews that made her famous.

While her marriage to Edwin Parker was a dud, she became lifelong friends with Robert Benchley, who might not have had a romantic relationship with Parker, but matched her quip for quip. Parker and Benchley would go on to form the unofficial but highly influential Algonquin round table at the Algonquin Hotel in New York City (namechecked more than once in *Gilmore*). It was during these lunch dates with an ever-changing roster, including the likes of director George S Kaufman, New Yorker magazine founder Harold Ross and Harpo Marx, that Parker's fame was assured. Not for anything she wrote, mind you, but for such comments as: "You can lead a whore to culture, but you can't make her think" (when asked to use "horticulture" in a sentence). In fact, she might have been speaking for Lorelai when she wrote, "I loved them until they loved me."

new. Kevin Williamson's *Dawson's Creek* and JJ Abrams' *Felicity*, both launched the previous year, had further convinced the network that the teen market was where it wanted to be.

Not yet aware that NBC had decided to pick up the show based on Amy's father, she pitched that and the Los Angeles Times Magazine story to WB president Susanne Daniels and executive vice president Jordan Levin.

"I had been there about 45 minutes, and eyes were glazing over," Amy told The AV Club. "Everybody was thinking about their lunch, and whether they had calls to return."

"They kind of were like, 'What *else* do you have,'" Polone recalls. What happened next is pretty clear, only the details are contested. According to Polone, he pitched the mother-daughter story himself. In her book (written with journalist Cynthia Littleton) *Season Finale*, Daniels recalls it was Amy who put it out there about 45 minutes into their conversation. Both accounts agree that neither Amy nor Polone had really thought out the details beyond the simple mother-daughter pitch.

The WB was already gaining a reputation for being the place to be if you wanted to do something new and interesting. Amy and Polone had managed to get their foot in the door, but if they didn't come up with some details fast, somebody else would surely bump them out of the running.

If You're Out on the Road...

A few days later, Amy & Dan took some time off and went to Connecticut, in part because Amy wanted to see Mark Twain's house in Hartford, she told The AV Club. All the while she'd been trying to figure out who her mother and daughter characters were. Until then, she'd figured they'd be in some decent-size American city.

But during their New England trip they happened on Washington Depot, Conn., and stayed at the Mayflower Inn, walking around the town the following day. "Everybody seemed to know each other, and there was a pumpkin patch across the street. I went to a diner and people kept getting up to get their own coffee. No one was there to be waited on."

Edward Herrmann, who lives in New England, says, "Washington Depot is absolutely *nothing* like Stars Hollow; it is a weekend haven for New Yorkers." The hotel that Amy & Dan stayed at "is so fake they have resorted to those awful cutesy bronze statues in the lobby. A pile of ye olde luggage sits right next to the check-in desk."

However cloying the hotel was, Amy saw the small-town environment as one that would have been very nurturing for a 16-year-old girl who'd just run away from home, pregnant, looking for a place more in tune with who she was.

As Amy put it to The AV Club, "I thought that if a 16- or 17-year-old kid with a brand new baby was going to run away from home and try and find a place to carve out a niche for herself, I wanted her to find a very safe place, an accepting place, where the kid could be raised in an environment that was completely different from where she came from, which was very cold and gray and judgmental, with a lot of rules and pearls and debutante balls and high heels and hair spray."

From there, placing the young mother's estranged parents in the larger city of Hartford made perfect sense. As Hartford is synonymous with the insurance industry, her father naturally would be a successful insurance company executive. In the span of a couple of days, Amy had put the core of the show together.

Gilmore Girls Comes Home

While Amy was putting the story together in New England, Polone was trying to keep The WB interested in the project long enough to do a deal.

Though the production part of his career was taking off with such successes as the movie *Stir of Echoes* (co-starring a pre-Paris Liza Weil), Polone was in the unenviable position of having to cement an arrangement with The WB of 1999, which was enjoying its first golden age of programming. Polone called Levin to see if they had a deal on *Gilmore Girls*. "And Jordan was like, 'I don't think I have any money,'" Polone remembers.

Desperate to make it happen, Polone told Levin that he could keep *Gilmore* "for the next year if you don't pick it up for this year. I was making a new form of deal where they get even more time than they would normally get for the pilot if they would just buy it."

After mulling it over, Levin got back to Polone with an equally unusual funding idea. Recently, the Association of National Advertisers had launched the Family Friendly Programming Forum, a coalition of dozens of major advertisers including heavy hitter Procter & Gamble. The FFPF had set up a fund to finance "family friendly" television scripts, with the goal of bestowing a positive image on the very sponsors that usually found themselves on the front lines of any TV boycott launched by the easily offended. If any of those scripts actually were turned into a pilot, the fund would be reimbursed by the network.

Levin told Polone that he might be able to fund the *Gilmore* pilot with seed money from the fund. Polone recalls that "I said I don't know what the tone of it's going to be yet, so I don't want to commit that it's 'family,' which communicated to me something like *7th Heaven*, which was not what I wanted to do, nor would Amy. And he said, 'No, don't worry about it. They don't have any say over anything that happens.'"

So Who DID Create Gilmore Girls?

For many *Gilmore* fans, the idea that Amy might not have originated the premise of the show is heresy, and there is no denying that in subsequent years, there has been a lot of bad blood between her and Gavin Polone. Though the producer has a reputation for being gruff and hard nosed, the *Drop Dead Gorgeous* link is a tough one to discount. (If you really want your head to spin, *Drop Dead Gorgeous* creator Lona Williams actually worked on *Roseanne* as an assistant to executive producer Bruce Helford while Amy was on that show.)

Still, there's nothing so innovative about the idea of a mother and daughter who are best friends; more than a few mothers have taken this approach with their offspring. It's what Amy & Dan and the *Gilmore* team did with the premise that matters. Many, many people made the series the beloved institution that it is today; there is more than enough credit to go around.

"They liked the hand-painted look for the town of Stars Hollow, for festivals, parades, and celebrations. The banners that hung from the lamp posts were computer generated, though, in my experience, it is rare to get as much hand-painted work as I did on that show. It was really enjoyable to do."

—CASEY KASEMEIER, SIGN PAINTER

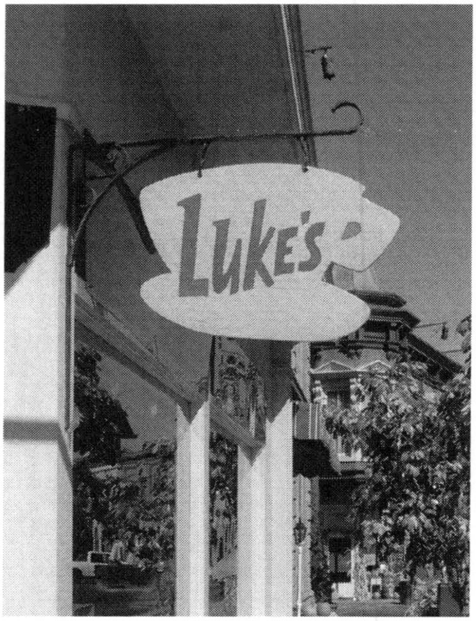

Though they still hadn't received a strong commitment from The WB, Polone went ahead lining up potential studios to shoot the pilot because he thought it would give them more leverage with the network. He focused on two: Sony and ATG, an operation backed by Hollywood super-agent Mike Ovitz. Initially interested, Sony pulled out of negotiations at the last minute because it was developing a program similar to *Gilmore*, Polone explains.

"I then tried to negotiate a deal with ATG. We got deep into negotiation and I was trying to get more money for Amy, and they eventually blew the deal over $10,000. It's interesting because that company eventually went under more or less, and they would've had a hit show that would've made them millions. They'd had all these series picked up but nothing went the distance. It all got blown over 10 grand. So we went through the process, and Amy wrote a phenomenal script, which became *Gilmore Girls*."

The Gilmore name had come from the Gilmore Bank at The Farmers Market in Los Angeles—the bank a somewhat stuffy, sober presence in a shopping area more prized for its funky atmosphere.

The WB finally agreed to pay for a pilot of *Gilmore Girls*, partially financed by the FFPF, which kicked in just under $1 million to finance eight scripts for the network, including the pilot, according to a November 2000 piece on E! Online. The average script price at the time: $75,000.

"They were picking up a bunch of pilots that year," Polone says. "And we were the lowest one on the food chain because we had no commitment against it. It was even worse than no commitment—they could even hold it for another year if they wanted to." From what he remembers, *Gilmore Girls* was the last pilot script picked to move into production.

By this time it was the end of February 2000, and Amy and Polone were scouring Los Angeles and New York for people to cast, all without even having a studio nailed down. Polone had heard from Sony that they were interested in doing *Gilmore* again but The WB had other plans. After all, one of the major selling points for Warner Brothers having a network in the first place was its ability to capture additional revenue on the studio end—thank you, deregulation.

"In the end, we were pushed very hard by The WB to deliver it to their sister company," Polone says. He remembers going to Amy and telling her that he hated the strong-arm tactics being used against them. "She, to her credit, and rightfully so, said, 'Given our situation, I don't want to cause any waves here.'"

There really was nothing else to say. *Gilmore Girls* wasn't going anywhere.

"I grew up with that feeling of, 'Gee, if you lived in a town where everyone knew who you were, wouldn't that be delightful?' Our few trips to smaller towns always fed into that. It fed into my psychotic version of the warmth and safety of a smaller environment, where people kind of gave a shit about each other."

-AMY (THE AV CLUB, 2/9/05)

The Stars Hollow town square on the Warner Brothers lot.

So this is Stars Hollow, eh?

the pilot

Having only received the go-ahead to shoot a *Gilmore Girls* pilot in February, Amy and Gavin Polone were under the gun to throw something together fast. The one thing they had going for them was one hell of a script. And from that, there was just one thing missing.

In *Season Finale*, Susanne Daniels recalls Amy coming in for a story meeting with the WB network execs to tell them where the show would be going. There she revealed that a big fight would erupt between Lorelai and her parents at the very first Friday night dinner, which would take place in the episode *after* the pilot. Giving it some thought, Daniels writes, she suggested that Amy include that fight in the pilot instead. "It seemed to me it really belonged...to reinforce the characters of Lorelai and Emily and explain why they had become so estranged, and it reinforced to Rory what a personal sacrifice it was for her mother to ask her parents for the tuition money."

A pilot script is a tricky thing, and like most endeavors, if they're pulled off expertly, it's something that's virtually seamless to the audience. It's not easy to write a script that telegraphs where a series is going to go for the next five years or more.

Yet, in that very first script, Amy introduces 11 series regulars. Just as a skilled artist may only paint a few defining lines in a street scene to stand in for the whole background, Amy gives us, with the exception of Lorelai and her immediate family, just enough about each character to make us feel as if we know them. Luke is stubborn but caring, Sookie is flaky but a good friend, Michel is rude but sincere in his own petulant way.

It would be that script that would bag *Gilmore Girls* some of its most noteworthy performers. Right now, however, Amy and Polone were looking at airing the show in eight months, and they didn't have a single actor to rehearse.

Up Fronts

In the US television world, networks host meetings between network executives, media and advertisers around the third week of May to show potential advertisers what programs they will be rolling out that fall, in the hopes that they will buy ads around them. Usually this entails the showing of clips, and question-and-answer sessions with execs and series stars.

It's a Long, Long Way to Pick a Rory

At this point, they had signed their pilot director, Lesli Linka Glatter, who had worked on such prestigious series as *NYPD Blue* and *Freaks and Geeks*. So desperate were they to get things rolling, all three insisted on sitting in on casting interviews for their two leads at the New York and LA offices.

During this time, WB network executives in Los Angeles and the Warner Brothers Productions studio in New York were sending out character breakdowns to agents simultaneously.

Alison Goodman, assistant to casting director Jeff Block and Mary Clay Boland in New York, had graduated from university with a writing degree. Though the office was casting about 20 pilots a year, she instantly fell in love with the *Gilmore Girls* script. "It became a passion piece for me," she says. So much so, she would become a writers assistant on the show years later.

The pressure to cast *Gilmore* was intense, especially as the May 2000 "up fronts" were just around the corner. The creative team was cutting it very close.

Though Goodman can't remember Alexis Bledel's head shot, "it was just one of those young, beautiful, faces," she says. "We were trying to find someone new, someone interesting."

Born in Houston, Kimberly Alexis Bledel grew up in a Spanish-speaking household, the daughter of Nanette Dozier, who grew up in Mexico, and Argentinean Martin Bledel. Most *Gilmore* fans will know the rest. Her parents convinced her to enter community theater at 8 to overcome her shyness; she was discovered by a modeling agency at 14 at the local mall, which sent her on an around-the-world excursion, earning her a decent living while getting her used to life in front of the camera.

She entered New York University's Tisch School of the Arts in 1999. "I was a film student, and must admit I found myself feeling a bit lost in a class where many of the students had been making films since they were 10 years old," she said in an interview promoting her 2009 film *Post Grad*. "I had just decided that film might be something I'd be interested in studying my senior year of high school."

Bledel enjoyed Manhattan and its surroundings, but being there for any length of time meant finding work. Fortunately, she'd retained her modeling agent, who began sending her on television auditions. "I thought maybe it would be some extra money," she told Elle Girl in November 2005. "I didn't know anything about how television works."

Warner Brothers' Goodman had been chatting with Bledel's manager off and on for years. Once Goodman and Block had the opportunity to meet her, they were stunned. "There was just something about her," Goodman says. "In person she was very shy and quiet, not this vivacious energy, just very simple and pretty."

Shy and quiet. The comparisons with Rory would come very quickly in Bledel's career, mostly because the actress *was* shy. According to *Gilmore Girls* co-workers, it's a trait that remains with her today, despite the endless magazine interviews and photo shoots that ensnare an actress on the rise.

In casting for any other type of role, this reticence might have torpedoed her chances, but this was no ordinary pilot, and Rory Gilmore was not your typical TV teen. Amy wanted "to write a smart teenage girl character who wasn't a bombshell, or a mousy loner yearning for a Prince Charming to come break her out of her shell," Daniels writes in *Season Finale*. "Amy had in mind a girl with real complexity—a kid who was fiercely independent and intellectually precious but naïve in matters of the heart."

In the DVD commentary for "You Jump, I Jump, Jack" (5.7), Amy remembers Bledel being bored, slightly ill, and anxious to keep an appointment somewhere else after their first meeting at the New York casting office. "She was so real. It was hard to find a 16-year-old girl who didn't seem jaded or Hollywoodized. All the young kids we read with resumes a mile long all walked in with their tattooed boyfriends or were making out in the parking lots because they were adults, they weren't kids anymore."

If anything, Block says, he was having the opposite problem trying to find an actress to play the 16-year-old Rory. "It's so young, a lot of actresses are not established at that age, so you're looking for that specific feel. You do a lot of prescreening to hopefully find the right person, and we did with Alexis."

The first day she walked into the casting office, "I remember immediately being struck by her beauty, and just something about that innocence that she had, and that amazing kind of person that she is," Block says. But after having her read through a couple of scenes, he thought, "Hmmm, she's not ready to come in yet. It was a little too rough."

He gave her some notes about how he thought the character should be performed, and arranged to meet her again a few days later at the office. On her return, they again worked on her performance together.

"And then he put her on tape," Goodman recalls. "He came over to my desk and said, 'You have to come and see this.'" By this time, Bledel had left for the day. "I went into this tiny little office that we used as a tape room and he showed me what she looked like on the TV. And no joke, she looked like a Botticelli angel. Her face—in person it was very pretty, very quiet—but there was something about her on camera—she lit up on TV. She looked like an angel, and we were like, 'Oh my God.'"

On her third interview, Bledel met with Amy, Polone and Glatter. "I remember she came in and she had a cold," Goodman says. "She was just not feeling it at all, but something about when we put her on camera, we just fell in love with her."

"To Amy and Gavin's and Lesli's credit, once they saw her, they really just were struck by her immediately," Block says. "They loved her right away."

Says Polone, "She'd never really done anything before. In fact, I remember looking at her resume when she came in to read after seeing girl after girl after girl in New York. She had literally on her resume some kind of hometown production of *The Wizard of Oz*. She had nothing. And she just absolutely nailed it. From that moment, both Amy and I knew she was going to get the part."

"I said, 'This is the best thing that I've read in many years. Whether you cast me in it or not, I don't care, but I just wanted to meet and congratulate you on writing something really original and fresh and funny.'"

—EDWARD HERRMANN (RICHARD) ON HIS AUDITION

Edward Herrmann: WASP, Where is Thy Sting?

When you're a working actor with any plans to remain so, you must beware the career-derailing force that is typecasting. After *Dracula*, Bela Lugosi's career was pretty much stuck in the sinister-foreigner mode, and heaven help poor consummate baddy Peter Lorre.

But there are also more subtle ways that Hollywood pigeonholes actors, placing them in the same kinds of roles over and over again. It was a phenomenon that even highly esteemed actor Edward Herrmann had experienced.

Despite a long history of playing very different roles—Klipspringer in 1974's *The Great Gatsby* with Robert Redford, oddball inventor Ezra Stiles (no relation to Jason, thank you) in *The Great Waldo Pepper*, again with Redford. Yet it was Herrmann's turn as President Franklin Roosevelt in two TV movies (1976 and 1977) called *Eleanor and Franklin* that would influence his career for many years to come.

"Casting people and producers tend to go with what they know, what they see, what has been successful," he admits. "'He did FDR. This guy can't do a drug dealer, he can't do anything else.'"

It was more than just *Eleanor and Franklin* that made Herrmann seem a good fit for WASPy characters. The actor had grown up in Grosse Pointe Farms, Mich., right on the periphery of blue blood central. Its population was less than 10,000, and it was one of five communities that captured much of the wealth produced in the heyday of Detroit's automakers.

Not that Herrmann and his family were upper crust by any means. Parents Jean and John were both from Indiana, John being the first in his family to go to college—a freshman when he was just 15. In 1940, John, then an engineer, moved to Detroit for work, and then Washington DC during the war, where Herrmann was born, before returning to Michigan. Once there, a friend helped him and his family get a little house in Grosse Pointe Farms, the actor says, "and I mean *little*."

"After I auditioned for it... I knew that they didn't have their leads. I thought, 'Oh God, I hope I don't end up with two little funny blonde girls because we won't match.'"

—KELLY BISHOP (EMILY)

Drawing a diverse group of people around them, Herrmann's parents filled the house with intelligent conversation, and the actor "grew up surrounded by a world that vaguely resembled the world Amy was creating for Emily, Richard, and their daughter and granddaughter," he says.

Though Herrmann had "a brief flirtation" with a short-lived 1975 American TV riff on *Upstairs, Downstairs* called *Beacon Hill*, it was theater and film that won his heart, so those were the projects he pursued. But by the end of the 1990s, the acting profession wasn't what it used to be. Where once an actor could make two or three movies a year for television and live comfortably, now it was another story. So Herrmann began reading scripts for pilots. When he finally came across the script for *Gilmore Girls*, he knew he'd discovered something unique.

"This one just jumped off the page to me because it was hip, it was funny, it suggested something of the world that I was living in, in Connecticut," he says. "What I really loved about it was that it turned the populist idiom upside down. Here was a girl in public high school who was bored silly with boys and makeup, and wanted to read *Les Miserables*. That, I thought, was charming."

Living in Connecticut, the actor went in to meet with Jeff Block and company at Warner Brothers' New York casting office.

"I remember that his agent was like, 'It's just going to be a meeting, he's not going to audition,'" Goodman says. "So we're like fine, he's Ed Herrmann, awesome."

While Goodman wasn't in the room when Herrmann came in, Block quickly filled her in on what had happened. Though actors of his stature seldom are required to actually audition, Herrmann had insisted on doing so. Says Goodman, "They fell in love with him for the fact that he was just like, 'OK, what do you want me to do? I'm an actor, I'll audition.'"

"I'm not good at auditions but I must've said the right thing," Herrmann says. "Amy tends to be spontaneous in her decision making often, and virtually offered me the part right there, which I thought was nice. I don't know if they had me in mind [before I auditioned] or not. I was very happy to be chosen. In my experience, it's best not to know how choices are made because you're either the first choice or the 10th."

Kelly Bishop: Finding *Gilmore's* 'Emily Post'

As if there weren't enough challenges to putting together the *Gilmore Girls* pilot, it was also being developed during a typical pilot season, which meant that the only actors it could land would be those who hadn't signed up for another show.

Many were about Italian families, riding on the coattails of *The Sopranos*, Kelly Bishop recalls. "I was looking at all the scripts; I went in on a couple of them, not with wild enthusiasm," she admits.

Finally, she picked up *Gilmore*. "I kept looking at the length of the script because a sitcom script is fairly short, and an hour-long show is about twice the size. I kept thinking is this a sitcom? It's so funny. No it can't be, just by the locations and the size of this script. This is absolutely wonderful."

A leading lady of the New York stage, Bishop swung by Warner Brothers' New York casting office in March 2000 and auditioned for Block, Amy and Polone, who taped her performance.

"It was great that they came to us instead of having to send the tape out to LA, not having met anyone," Bishop says. "That's always a little dicey. Very often they'll do that, and if they're interested, they might actually have a director's session or a producer's session where those people come back east and meet with you and put you back on tape again. That's just their process." As she remembers it, the audition consisted of Emily's first scene with Lorelai and Richard. "She says, 'Hi Mom' and I say, 'Is it Easter?' Because then when Ed came in later, he had that same line. 'Richard, look who's here. Lorelai dropped by.' And he says, 'Is it Christmas,' which I thought was terribly funny. It kind of said it all right there about the estrangement."

Though the actress felt she'd given them an excellent audition, she'd been in the business long enough to know that you never really know how things went until you receive that phone call later. The fact that Amy had seemed enthusiastic about her performance only made her more apprehensive. "I find that when they're very enthusiastic about something you've done at your audition, or they put you on tape, it's like the kiss of death. If they sit there and stare at you and you feel absolutely horrible about the reaction, then you get home and your agent is already on the phone saying, 'They loved you.' So Amy being very enthusiastic set me back a little bit."

"Amy said, 'I wanted you, I told them I wanted you, and they kept throwing names at me and saying maybe you should see some other people, and I kept saying no.' So that's Amy. I'm deeply grateful to her for that."

—KELLY BISHOP, ON WHY IT HAD TAKEN SO LONG FOR HER TO BE CAST

That concern only deepened as time passed and she heard nothing at all about how her audition had been received. Every once in a while, her agent would ring Block's office, only to hear that they were still testing people for the part. "That was the really uncomfortable time for me," she says. They were also floating the idea that she would have to fly to LA to audition for the network executives.

It was April before she finally heard she'd won the role of Emily; the pilot was slated to be shot in Toronto later that month. And all of this was happening a month before the May up fronts.

"Now I realize after the fact that they were looking at Lauren and Alexis and they were trying to get that all done," Bishop says. "They weren't going to worry about a supporting character until they had their leads."

Little did Bishop know that Lorelai *still* had yet to be cast.

Scott Patterson: Finally in the Major Leagues

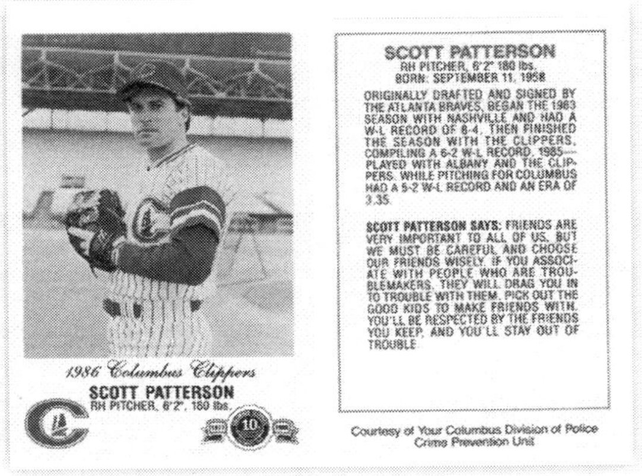

One of the unique aspects of the script was the open-ended role Amy had written for Lorelai's love interest, Luke. Where many scriptwriters hasten to outline any potential romantic liaisons in broad strokes, Amy had stuck to what she'd been saying all along: the relationship between mother and daughter was the show's focus. As a result, anybody they hired to be Luke would have plenty of time to warm to the role.

If Luke Danes was a recluse who never strayed more than a few miles from where he was born, Scott Patterson was his opposite. Born in Philadelphia, Patterson grew up in Haddonfield, NJ, the son of a boxer-turned-ad-executive and a homemaker. Frank and Hope split when Scott was 15. An accomplished high school baseball pitcher, he left the field shortly after his father left home, he told People magazine in January 2002.

In 1977, he entered Rutgers University in New Jersey, where baseball reentered his life after three years of playing guitar and questioning what he wanted to do. As he told People, "My roommate kept telling me it was a waste of God-given talent not to play, so I decided to give it a shot."

Though he soon dropped out of Rutgers, his baseball skills took him to Florida and Arizona before he was drafted into the minor leagues. From 1980 to 1987, he pitched for AAA and AA teams of the Texas Rangers, the New York Yankees and the Atlanta Braves. After he was cut from the Dodgers in 1987, he spent a year in Europe, where he met some theater students who showed him another side to life. His twenties had been about finding himself in sports, which would return him to the bench permanently in another 20 or 30 years, no matter how good he was. Acting would take as much commitment as he could give.

He moved to New York City briefly to study acting before relocating to West Hollywood in 1992. Over the next few years he would appear in several commercials and, most famously, play Elaine's "sponge-worthy" date in *Seinfeld* in 1995.

Lorelai? Lorelai?

Ultimately, *Gilmore Girls* would reap the success it did based on a strong ensemble cast. Yet the way the script was written meant that actually getting the pilot off the ground hinged on finding two female leads with what future *Gilmore* casting director Mara Casey would call "the *thing* factor." ("They have a thing. No matter what their training is, there's the *thing*.")

In the 24/7 echo chamber that is *Gilmore Girls* fandom, it's easy to forget that Lauren Graham wasn't always the pinup for young female *Gilmore* fans around the world. As Amy points out in the commentary for "You Jump, I Jump, Jack," the role of Lorelai was the last one cast.

"We actually brought three actresses in to play Lorelai," Polone remembers. (One was Nina Garbiras (*Boomtown*, *The $treet*), according to Goodman.) "And eventually the network said no to all three. Ultimately, they said we really like Lauren Graham if she'll come in and read."

The picture Graham has painted of her career at this time in various interviews is that of a struggling actress barely making ends meet, little noticed by the Hollywood power brokers. Yet unbeknownst to her, many in the industry *had* taken notice.

Born in Honolulu, Hawaii, Graham grew up in the Washington DC suburbs of Northern Virginia. After her parents split when she was five, she went to live with her father, Lawrence, a candy industry lobbyist; her mother moved to England.

Relocating to New York in the mid-1980s, she left Barnard College with a BA and graduated with a master's from Southern Methodist University in Dallas. She finally moved to Los Angeles in 1995, where she landed various guest spots on *Caroline in the City*, *Seinfeld*, and a three-episode *Law & Order* story arc ("Showtime," "Turnaround" and "D-Girl") in 1997, which also featured future *Gilmore* love interest Scott Cohen (Max). "We didn't really know each other then," Cohen says. "We had the same agent and the agent kept saying we should meet."

Cohen doesn't recall where he met Graham, exactly, but their paths would cross again at a TV critics press conference in 2000, shortly after his own triumph in NBC's fantasy miniseries, *The 10th Kingdom*. "We just hit it off as friends. I would see her in LA and we'd go for a drink or something like that, but it wasn't like I saw her all the time."

"Lauren was great. They were going, 'Oh, we'll rehearse.' And she looks at me and goes, 'We don't need to rehearse, let's shoot it! Let's go!' And we'd just do it. So we became our own little Gilmore family there."

-EMILY KURODA (MRS. KIM)

By this time, Graham had just shot the first few episodes of a new NBC comedy called *MYOB* (*Mind Your Own Business*), which was very much on the bubble with the network. She'd already worked on three other sitcoms that had died on the vine, including *Townies* with '80s movie queen Molly Ringwald (*Sixteen Candles*, *The Breakfast Club*) and Jenna Elfman, shortly before she found success on *Dharma & Greg*.

Though *MYOB* had done poorly in the ratings during its midseason Spring 2000 run, there was still a chance that NBC could bring the show back for another season, which would've tied up Graham for the foreseeable future. Yet so insistent were the network execs, the *Gilmore* crew decided to hire Graham for the pilot anyway under a "second position" contract, meaning they were screwed if *MYOB* came back again. As Daniels put it in *Season Finale*, "All of us involved had agreed that there would not be any quickie recasting over the summer.... Without Lauren Graham, we had no show."

"Lauren just nailed it in the reading," Polone says. "We made a deal, it was a very difficult deal to make, and we made our pilot."

Though Graham has politely distanced herself from her work on *Gilmore Girls* in recent years, there is little doubt that the series was as important to her at that time as it was to nearly everyone else involved. After years of doing everything from cold medicine commercials to wearing the dog mascot costume of the US FIFA World Cup, the actress was ready to find a regular gig where she could concentrate on her work rather than the perpetual hunt for new jobs to pay the rent.

The main street in Unionville, Ontario, where the *Gilmore Girls* pilot was filmed.

Says Cohen, "I remember when Lauren went off to Toronto to shoot this pilot. She was like, 'Oh, I hope it goes.'"

Graham was hired about a week before work began on the show.

Bringing Stars Hollow to Life

Considering the speed with which the creative team had brought it all together, it's amazing that nearly every actor to appear in that very first episode would stay on throughout the life of the series.

Kelly Bishop first met with Lauren for a quick read-through of their first scene together. "We didn't make any comment, either one of us, but I just felt this settling down," she says. "We both went, 'OK, this is good. This is going to work between the two of us.' Then Alexis came on set and I remember turning around and seeing this girl walk in. I looked at her and in my head I went, 'China doll! Look at that face, look at that face!' That face is to die for."

Shooting began in the Toronto suburb of Unionville in Markham, Ontario, to save on production costs. Though the show would relocate to the Warner Brothers lot once it went to series, its time in Unionville would greatly influence the Burbank sets. A dog breeder's house filled in for the Gilmore mansion; a hardware store for Luke's Diner (which would later inspire an entire backstory for Luke's place of business).

"For a while, which would've been fun, they were contemplating shooting it all in Toronto to save money," Herrmann says, which would have been an easier commute for the actor from his Connecticut home. Yet everybody knew that if the show passed muster, Warner Brothers would cut costs further by building sets on the backlot if it went to series.

As the network executives received footage from the shoot, they grew increasingly excited. When they finally decided to pick up the show for series, there was a big meeting in New York, where nearly everybody had forgotten that they still had to wait a good two weeks to see if Graham was going to be available to shoot any more episodes.

***Gilmore*'s casting team: Mara Casey (above) and Jami Rudofsky.**

The Start of Seven Years of Perfect Casting

Racing against time, the *Gilmore* team shot the pilot episode that would then be presented to The WB. If the network execs gave them the thumb's up, they'd go to a final pilot, and ultimately, to series. If not, Amy and Polone would have to find another project.

Though *Gilmore Girls* dodged its first major bullet when Graham was freed from her NBC contract, they were not so lucky with their first Sookie, Alex Borstein.

A highly respected comedienne even before her work on the animated comedy series *Family Guy*, Borstein was a regular on the sketch comedy show *MADtv*, something that would prevent her from continuing as a series regular should *Gilmore Girls* be picked up for series. Though she traded in her kitchen apron for a harp as Lorelai's Independence Inn foil Drella, Borstein's husband, Jackson Douglas—the couple had married a year before the *Gilmore* pilot—would stay on until the final episode as Stars Hollow's lovable produce seller, Jackson.

"The thing I'm most proud of is so many of the people we cast, their careers jumped off from Gilmore Girls."

—JAMI RUDOFSKY

Meanwhile, Rory's love interest, Dean Forester, had been played by actor/drummer Nathan Wetherington in the pilot presentation; among other things he'd played drums for The Blue Man Group. "It would've been a very, very different kind of Dean," Goodman says. "He was much more of a surfer/skateboarder guy."

"He's a very quiet guy and she's a spark plug, so she was around chatting everybody up. She's fun. They're both great. Totally different people."

-MICHAEL WINTERS (TAYLOR) ON AMY & DAN

Amy and Polone finally screened their pilot for the WB execs. "I thought it was so dang cute I couldn't see straight," remembers casting director Mara Casey. The network execs agreed and gave the team the go-ahead. Though they'd cleared their biggest hurdle, they now realized they had to reshoot the pilot, this time with a new Sookie and a new Dean—Wetherington didn't quite fit the part—and they had to do it all before the network up fronts, which were fast approaching.

Casey had only been in the casting business less than three years, and had recently left her previous casting employer, Jeanie Bacharach, to strike out on her own. It was Bacharach who introduced her to her casting partner, Jami Rudofsky, and Bacharach who had tipped her off about the *Gilmore* project.

Casey rang up an agent she knew who managed to get her and Rudofsky an appointment with Amy and Polone. "We got our break, I think, because they needed a casting director weeks ago and we were young and hungry," Casey says. "They said we know you guys will work your asses off, and we did."

Two weeks into their new gig, the casting directors were frantically searching for a new Sookie; they didn't even have time to consider a new Dean yet. In the same week, they would find both.

Manager Dan Spilo rang up Rudofsky. "He said, 'Listen, I know you're not there yet, but I have this kid in town from Texas and he's amazing, I promise you,'" Rudofsky recalls. "We kept saying no to him, and he said, 'He's leaving in the next couple of days, please just see him.' We had not even had one producer session with Amy, we had just been pre-reading actors and getting our ideas together of who to bring to her."

"We're like OK fine, we're not seeing Deans, but we'll read him," Casey says. A little while later, Jared Padalecki arrived at the little *Gilmore* trailer park on the Warner backlot. "He walked in the room and I thought eh, he's cute, and then he opened his mouth and it was done."

Amy often lamented the lack of good looking young male actors who can actually form a sentence. This was something Casey and Rudofsky had run into throughout their careers, especially when casting for network television. It comes down to three little words: executives want "hot." "So a lot of your hotties, especially at that age, don't have a strong theater background, or they have the luck of having great representation because of the way they look," Casey says. "They don't necessarily have the goods to match how hot they look." Padalecki knew how to talk and had the rugged good looks sure to please the suits at The WB.

"We knew he was leaving the next day so we called over to Amy's office," Rudofsky remembers. "They had already had two Deans. They had one that had to be recast, then they put a second one in the pilot presentation and they wanted him recast, so this was our third Dean."

Amy came over to their trailer, met with Padalecki for a few minutes, and stepped outside. "She looked at us and was like, 'Well that's not fair. You can't just cast someone on the first try.'" Though they were told to keep an eye out for a better Dean, Amy was convinced they'd found their guy.

"Somebody like Jared Padalecki didn't have a ton of training," Casey says. "However he has a *thing*. Sometimes people are just special and they drop down from heaven, and he's one of them."

Barely settled into their trailer, the casting team had already discovered one of Hollywood's new crop of young talent. A few days later, they would bring another to the fore.

For days on end, they'd been frantically searching for a new Sookie, sifting through head shots, lining up meetings. "We just kept reading people and reading people and reading people," Rudofsky remembers. The pair were auditioning an actress one day who told them, "You should read my friend Melissa McCarthy." McCarthy was already on their list of people signed up to interview.

"And when she came in and read for us, we were like, 'Oh my God,

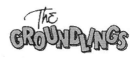

The Groundlings

Founded in 1974 by Gary Austin, The Groundlings is one of the most influential theatrical improv groups in the US, having produced such performers as Will Ferrell, Julia Sweeney (*Saturday Night Live*), Lisa Kudrow (*Friends*) and Paul Reubens (Pee-wee Herman) among others.

this is it,'" Rudofsky says. "If they don't love this girl, they're crazy.'"

At this point, McCarthy's credits didn't run much beyond some small film roles, including the 1999 Katie Holmes vehicle *Go* and 2000's *Drowning Mona* with Danny DeVito and Bette Midler. For some, her main claim to fame at that point was the fact that her cousin is actress Jenny McCarthy. In Los Angeles, however, she was fairly well known in comedy circles for her work with The Groundlings.

Recalls Casey, "Melissa came in, and I think it was literally the only audition I couldn't get through in the pre-read because I was laughing so hard. I said, 'I'm so sorry, that was just horrible on my part.'"

"She came in and brought things to the part that no one else had done," Rudofsky says. "And Melissa's physical comedy is amazing. So it just added to the character."

Soon, the pilot was reshot, and all that remained was to see if it would find the wings to make it out of pilot purgatory. The odds were squarely stacked against it.

"I've been doing this for 14 years," Rudofsky says. "Not one other pilot I've worked on has gotten picked up."

Character Sketch Richard: 'An Easy Man for Me to Understand'

Though it would take several episodes to round out his character, Edward Herrmann was delighted to be playing a man who had hidden depths, despite the fact that, at first glance, Richard wasn't too far beyond the type the actor had played previously.

"Here was Richard, this WASPy fellow, but he wasn't just any WASPy fellow. He was written with humor and an edge and an intelligence, and I thought this might be fun, especially since I don't have to—this will sound terrible, but I didn't have to work very hard to find him. He was an easy man for me to understand. I've known people like that. So I thought this will be fun because I don't have to practice with a lisp or a limp or do something wildly foreign to my nature."

1.1 Pilot

First aired: Oct. 5, 2000 // Written by Amy Sherman-Palladino // Directed by Lesli Linka Glatter

Lorelai Gilmore, 32, and her 16-year-old, super-brainy daughter, Rory, are more like friends than mother and daughter, sharing makeup and stealing each other's CDs. After trying for two years, Lorelai has finally managed to get Rory into the exclusive prep school Chilton, but the enrollment fee is more than she can swing on her salary from managing the Independence Inn. Lorelai's estranged parents, Richard and Emily, agree to give Lorelai the money in exchange for a weekly Friday night dinner with the girls and one weekly phone call updating them on Rory's school experiences and Lorelai's life. But after meeting Dean Forester, Rory has second thoughts about going to Chilton, which leads to the girls' first major fight.

! GINCHY! Joey hitting on Lorelai, then Rory, and Rory's "Are you my new daddy" response; the introduction of Kim's Antiques and Mrs. Kim; Lorelai's meeting with her parents, and the first meeting of Rory and Dean ("Oh. Rory. Me. That's me").

NOTES *'Wow, you do not look old enough to have a daughter. I mean it. And YOU do not look like a...daughter.'*

✱ Already Lorelai and Sookie are talking about opening their own inn someday. Lane mentions that her parents (*plural*) set her up with the 16-year-old son of a business associate who's going to be a doctor when he grows up. When Lorelai can't come up with the money for

"I met Helen right off the bat and heard her stories. And she's just a wonderful person to hang out with, and one of Amy's best friends. It was quite nice to have somebody to go to to hear all the real stories about what actually happened to her."

—KEIKO AGENA ON PRODUCER HELEN PAI, WHOSE LIFE WAS THE BASIS FOR LANE KIM

***Gilmore Girls* has long inspired artists around the world, as seen in this retelling of Dean and Rory's first meeting by Signe Hammar in Sweden (http://art.callher-green.com/).**

Chilton, it's actually Sookie who first suggests asking Richard and Emily for it. Lorelai is taking a business class twice a week. Dean has just moved to Stars Hollow from Chicago.

✱ Lorelai will replace her penchant for bawdy humor ("I offered to do the principal") for more veiled sexual innuendos. In fact, Lorelai's out-of-character line may be a warning shot across the bow of the Family Friendly Programming Forum to ensure episodes would be free of any kind of moral policing. Sookie will also lose her slapstick doltishness in the kitchen eventually. But all in all, what we see is what we will get for many years to come.

TODAY'S CELEBRATION The Stars Hollow hayride.

5 MINUTES How long it takes to get to Chilton from Richard and Emily's house.

40 MINUTES How long it takes to get to Chilton from Stars Hollow by bus.

AMEN, SISTER FRIEND

LORELAI [*to Sookie about Rory getting into Chilton*]: From that school she'll be able to get into any college she wants. She's going to get the education I never had and do all the things I never did, and I can resent her for it and we can finally have a normal mother-daughter relationship.

RORY: So, do you like cake?
DEAN: What?
RORY: They make really good cakes here. They're very...round.
DEAN: OK, I'll remember that.
RORY [*embarrassed*]: Good. Make a note. You wouldn't want to forget where the round cakes are.

RORY [*on how she got her name*]: [Lorelai] was lying in the hospital thinking about how men name boys after themselves all the time, you know? So, why couldn't women? Her feminism just took over. Although personally I think a lot of Demerol also went into the decision. I never talk this much.

LORELAI: ...After all, you're me.
RORY: I'm not you.
LORELAI: Really? Someone willing to throw important life experiences out the window to be with a guy? Sounds like me to me.

Amy and Polone had managed to assemble a tight team in near record time, and had essentially sold their first born to The WB thanks to Polone's make-or-break deal. Yet the network had taken an enormous gamble, too, backing a show whose "quirk factor" hadn't been seen since the days of *Green Acres* in the mid-1960s, and whose showrunner was far from a proven commodity. Still, The WB's brief was to invest in new and interesting programming to reinforce its claim to being a network to rival the big three, Fox, and especially, UPN. Though it was difficult to see it at the time, *Gilmore Girls* would be instrumental in giving it a legitimacy with critics, if not with the television viewing public, that it had never had before.

"I normally don't make a comment on the script to them, I just go and do the thing because it's a kind of superstition. I think every time I've said, 'This is a fabulous script, I love this part,' I don't get the job. I couldn't resist it though. I had to say, 'This is an amazing script. This is really terrific writing.'"

— KELLY BISHOP ON FIRST READING FOR THE PART OF EMILY

"Welcome to
our little corner
of the world"

season **one**

Despite huge obstacles—including time crunches and unprecedented business arrangements—*Gilmore Girls* was ordered to series. Quickly the producers assembled the best crew they could find to relocate the slapdash Stars Hollow of Ontario to Warner Brothers' Midwest Street, the Anytown-USA section of its backlot. Before *Gilmore Girls*, its familiar features had been seen in the films *The Music Man* (1962) and *Bonnie and Clyde* (1967), and such television series as *The Dukes of Hazzard* (1979-1985) and *Growing Pains* (1985-1992).

Though Amy would later remind people that The WB threw *Gilmore* to the wolves by putting it up against ratings beasts *Survivor* and *Friends* on Thursday nights, there were many at the network and the studio who were rooting for the show. Says Gavin Polone, "It was actually very good for the show because there were no expectations that we would ever get anything, so we could just go based on the critical reviews and the fact that it was the best show on the network."

Throughout the US, television stations that had thrown their lot in with The WB to become affiliates were bombarded with VHS copies of the *Gilmore* presentation pilot with its different Sookie and Dean, as well as the finished pilot. There was some noodling around with the name of the series, too, as it vacillated between *Gilmore Girls*, then *The Gilmore Way*, before finally coming back to the original title. (Never mind the fact that every script would carry the name *THE Gilmore Girls.*) Chris Iller, former promotions manager for Orlando, Fla.'s WB affiliate WKCF, still has some promotional art for *The Gilmore Way*.

"Sounds like a method of natural childbirth."

—LAUREN GRAHAM ON THE SERIES' ALTERNATE TITLE: "THE GILMORE WAY." (ENTERTAINMENT WEEKLY WEB SITE, 9/29/00)

In June, shortly after the May up fronts, The WB invited affiliates to a conference and after party in Santa Monica to get them pumped up about the new fall season. Iller recalls telling a friend, "I saw that girl [Lauren Graham] from the *Gilmore Girls*, she's here." From behind him came that now familiar voice: "I hear you talking about me; would you like a picture together?" The answer, naturally, was yes.

Bio ☺ Sean Gunn (Kirk Gleason)

Growing up in St. Louis with four brothers and a sister, Sean Gunn got used to competition at a very early age. While he was working in school plays and auditioning for the best acting programs, brother James became a director and screenwriter (*Slither*), Brian became a screenwriter, Matt wrote for Bill Maher, Patrick became a businessman, and Beth an attorney.

Following the usual theater route after graduating from DePaul University, Gunn appeared in everything from brother Jimmy's directorial debut, *Tromeo & Juliet*, to the *Buffy* spin-off *Angel* and *October Road*. He's also demonstrated his acting range in a handful of independent movies, most notably *The Man Who Invented the Moon*, directed by Hep Alien's Brian, John Cabrera.

For sheer performance insanity, though, it's hard to top his appearances in James Gunn's series *PG Porn*, especially as Peanuts' Peppermint Patty in *A Very Peanus Christmas*.

To much of the television-watching public, he remains Kirk. To his family and friends, he is...The Judge?

"My brother Matt gave me that nickname," Gunn says. "He says it's because I'm a judgmental bastard, but I think he says that in jest. When you come from a family of six, it's hard to describe the nuance of it, I guess. Let me preface this by saying I really see myself as being as nonjudgmental as a person can get. But I'm strongly opinionated and I have no qualms about telling you what my opinion is. I can tell you this: When he gave me the nickname, it stuck very quickly with a lot of people. They just started calling me The Judge. I take it as a sign that I have confidence, so I think that's good."

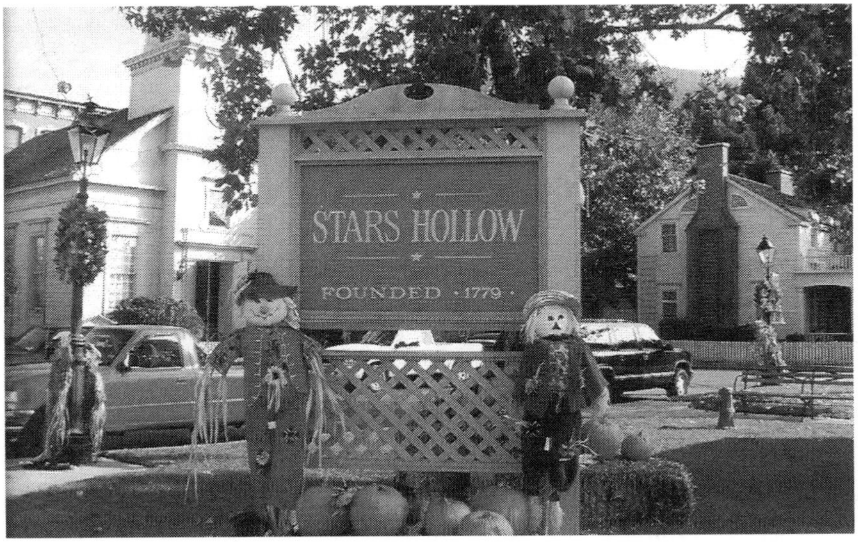

Though Iller had enjoyed the *Gilmore Girls* pilot when he saw it, he didn't see the same level of enthusiasm elsewhere at WKCF. "I don't remember a lot of my buddies being too excited because it did look like a chick show. [The tape] didn't get passed around as much, but I remember thinking it was good."

Meanwhile, less than 50 miles away, cracks were already forming at the head of the production.

Throughout her career, Amy had never pretended to be the go-along-to-get-along type. "She's a rebel," Kelly Bishop says. "She'll be a rebel all her life."

And the woman who'd told The New York Times "to be really good, you have to be willing to have everybody in the world hate you," had already begun to make good on that philosophy during production of the first few episodes of the series, Polone says.

As Susanne Daniels relates in *Season Finale*, Amy finally blew up after being bombarded with notes from WB execs concerning the scripts she was developing. Taking one phone call too many, she told the executive on the other end, "You're not my mother. I don't want to hear how disappointed in me you are, or how upset you are. If you want to fire me, fire me. But don't call me anymore!"

Guest star vs. Special Appearance By: the TV Pecking Order

Although America's Screen Actors Guild doesn't define "guest star," "special guest star" or other types of billing, it does recognize a category it calls "major role performers," according to SAG spokeswoman Pamela Greenwalt. A major role performer is a freelance performer who negotiates billing for a show that uses any of the following terms:

1) Guest Star
2) Special Guest Star
3) Starring
4) Special Appearance By...

The person who gets this billing must be hired for a minimum of five days for a half-hour show or eight days for an hour show As you would imagine, stars who negotiate any of the above billing descriptions also enjoy a higher salary than what standard day performers are paid. It works out to day-performer rate X 8 days + 10%.

Everybody was far too busy on set to worry about what was going on in the executive offices. It was the first season for an untested show, and everybody was gearing up for one hell of a production schedule.

1.2 The Lorelais' First Day at Chilton

First aired: Oct. 12, 2000// Written by Amy Sherman-Palladino// Directed by Arlene Sanford

Rory's first day at Chilton is the day from hell, from being late for school to her mother's ridiculous "laundry day" outfit. Before the day is out, she'll meet, and inspire the wrath of, Paris Eustace Geller after accidentally destroying her diorama, and come up against the leering Tristin Dugray. While Rory finally stands up to Paris at school, Lorelai cancels the DSL Internet connection Emily ordered for Rory, and tells her mother that she will decide what's best

Behind the Scenes: From Mick to Kirk

While only the second episode, "First Day" introduces Kirk, one of *Gilmore Girls*' most-beloved characters, and one who will endure until the final episode. Or *was it* the same character?

"Your guess is as good as mine," Sean Gunn says. "I think it's supposed to be the same character." True, the guy who comes to Lorelai's home to install a DSL connection is called Mick, but it's hard to ignore that he has the same quirky, pig-headed attitude that made Kirk the highlight of many future *Gilmore* scenes.

While Gunn's agent recommended that he pass on the audition for Mick because it was a co-star role, "which means the pay was next to nothing," his manager was friends with casting director Mara Casey, who had auditioned him over a year ago for *Judging Amy*, and urged him to at least read the script.

"I was like let me see the scene. If I think it's funny, I'll do it. And it was good. It's a very long scene for a co-star, too. So I did it and I liked it, but I thought I was done with the show." Amy loved Gunn tremendously, but as soon as the episode was shot, she'd already moved on to the challenge of casting the next one. Among other roles, there was that of the man who delivers the swans to the inn to consider. Casey and partner Jami Rudofsky brought in several people, but Amy kept saying, "'I don't know, I still keep hearing that kid Sean in the part,'" Rudofsky recalls. "Then she proceeded to tell us the story about how her father used to be on *Gimme a Break* because he was friends with the producers, and every week they had a small part for him. He would come in and just put on a different hat and play a different character. I said to Amy, 'This is gonna sound crazy, but remember what you told us about your father? Why don't you do that with Sean?'"

That was on a Friday, and Amy would have none of it. By Monday morning, she'd changed her tune. "Amy's idea was to bring him back as Kirk, a guy who couldn't keep one job for longer than a day, which followed through his story line throughout the years," Casey says. "[Gunn] just has that quirk factor that Amy responded to. She loved him so much, she made him a regular."

Of course Kirk changed a great deal over seven years, something that Gunn still marvels at. "Sometimes I watch the very first scene I ever did on the show and I'm like, 'God, that was pretty good; how did I get so over the top after that?'"

for her daughter. Yet at the end of the day, the girls have each other, and that's enough. For now.

GINCHY! Rory explaining her ambitions to be like Christiane Amanpour to Headmaster Charleston; Paris, Madeline and Louise pulling a Watergate on Rory's school file; everybody that Lorelai meets chiming in on her inappropriate attire; Lorelai enjoying Luke's flash of jealousy when she tells him about being asked out by a Chilton dad; and Rory's "fact off" with Paris.

NOTES *'The pressures are greater, the rules are stricter, and the expectations are higher.'*

If the opening teaser with Lorelai painting Rory's toenails on the porch wasn't a carefully calculated attempt to get buzz going on the male side of the gender divide, Lorelai's "rodeo" outfit certainly was. As Graham told Entertainment Weekly in 2000, "I've already gotten the briefing: 'Don't cut your hair and be prepared to wear [only] a bra at any time.'"

The mother-daughter dynamic (including Emily) that would make *Gilmore Girls* a hit, only briefly glimpsed in the pilot, is on full display here. The obsessive Rory ("7:15! 7:16! 7:17!"), the focused-but-flaky Lorelai ("This is the last time I buy anything just because it's furry") and the wittily acerbic Emily ("Do you need a ride or is your horse parked outside?") all make appearances.

Rory's starting Chilton a month late. Paris tells her that she's not only going to be the editor of The Franklin school newspaper next year, she's also going to be class valedictorian. While her first goal will be realized (2.5), her second will not (3.21).

Overall, an excellent start to a series. Amy's script is expertly paced, allowing relationships (Luke and Lorelai, Sookie and Jackson) to develop in their own time.

TODAY'S CELEBRATION Rory's first day at Chilton.

KIRK OF ALL TRADES DSL installer. (Even when he's Mick, he's Kirk.)

Louise (Teal Redmann, left), Madeline (Shelly Cole, center) and Paris (Liza Weil, right).

"That's why my shorts will be very short."

—LAUREN GRAHAM ON THE WB'S HOPES FOR EXPANDING GILMORE'S APPEAL TO MEN. (ENTERTAINMENT WEEKLY, 9/29/00)

YOU'VE ENTERED EMILYLAND [*About Rory*] I hate that she takes the bus. Drug dealers take the bus.

AMEN, SISTER FRIEND

RORY [*to Headmaster Charleston*]: Maybe I'll be a journalist and write books or articles about what I see. I just want to be sure that I see... something. You'll notice the debating team's also missing from my résumé.

PARIS [*reading Rory's file*]: Formerly of Stars Hollow High School.
LOUISE: Where's that?
PARIS: Drive west, make a left at the haystacks and follow the cows.
LOUISE: Oooh, a dixie chick.

MICHEL: Excuse me. There's a phone call for you, and if I'm to fetch you like a dog, I'd like a cookie and a raise.

MISS PATTY [*to students*]: Now walk smooth. That's the new *Harry Potter* on your heads. If they should drop, Harry will die and there won't be any more books.

RORY: You cannot date Luke.
LORELAI: I said nothing about dating Luke.
RORY: If you date him, you'll break up, and we'll never be able to eat there again.
LORELAI: I repeat, I said nothing about dating Luke.
RORY: Date Al from Pancake World; his food stinks.

"I think that was Amy's idea from the beginning, to have this relationship between the grandfather and the granddaughter blossom. Which was very hard on the daughter to see, this unaffected affection being expressed between her father and her daughter. That was a lovely dynamic element in the show that I really enjoyed."

— EDWARD HERRMANN (RICHARD)

1.3 Kill Me Now

First aired: Oct. 19, 2000 // Written by Joanne Waters // Directed by Adam Nimoy

Forced to choose a sport at Chilton, Rory, urged by Emily, picks golf, which Richard reluctantly teaches her at Emily's insistence. Richard and Rory bond over country club life and HL Mencken. Seeing the strained relationship between a mother and her twin brides getting married at the Independence Inn reminds Lorelai of the special relationship she has with her own daughter. As Emily points out, Lorelai is indeed afraid that Rory will fail to see her grandparents in the same poor light that Lorelai herself always has.

GINCHY! Michel's way of telling the grooms apart; the "Tiger Woods" hat that Emily gives Rory, and Rory's pride in it later on; the gradual bonding between Richard and his granddaughter. A special insanity award goes to this episode for having Lorelai and Rory fight over who has the larger boobs.

NOTES *'If Rory goes and has a good time without you, then I win.'*

Last episode, we had the first big *Gilmore* inconsistency with Lane referring to two parents; this episode, it's Richard waxing nostalgic about his late mother. (Though read another way, he could merely be saying

Behind the Scenes Lauren & Alexis' Special Chemistry

Just three episodes in, the two leads have developed an unusually effective way of working together. Despite a lack of on-screen experience, Alexis Bledel "had a way that was so natural," Kelly Bishop says. "It was just a natural instinct. But she also had a great advantage in Lauren because Lauren is such a pro and knows exactly how to get to the mark."

Just how much of a pro Bishop learned later when she happened to mention how marvelous it was that Lorelai touched her on-screen daughter so much, suggesting a deep affection. "She said, 'Some of that in the beginning was just to get [Bledel] to her mark because she wasn't tuned in to get to that mark for focus. I would put my arm around her and bring her with me.' I thought, 'God, isn't that amazing?'"

This episode, "there's one little shot that was in the opening [credits] where Lauren smooths her hair," Bishop says. "I remember the day they shot that. I thought, 'What a beautiful gesture.' That wasn't about getting her on her mark, but was by then something that Lauren was doing in terms of showing affection for her daughter. That's one of my absolute favorite few seconds of the show; I'm so glad they used that in the opening.

For all I know, it could've been that when Lauren turned and looked at her she thought her hair was slightly out of place and she smoothed it. But the way it came out was so warm—it's exactly what you would want your mother to do."

Behind the Scenes

Someone to Watch Over Me

"For the lead in a one hour television show, you just never get a rest," Edward Herrmann says. "Unless you're an old scarred-up pro who knows how to budget their time, knows how to relax a little bit and slough the tension off a bit, you can run out of energy very quickly. As [Russian acting theorist Constantin] Stanislavski says, you wipe your feet when you leave the theater."

It was apparent to many that Alexis Bledel was having trouble doing that early on. It wasn't hard to see why. Although she had traveled a bit for her modeling work, *Gilmore Girls* was totally different from anything she had done before. The pressures of learning to work with photographers and dealing with fellow models' attitudes were one thing; delivering hastily absorbed chunks of dialogue that would make the most seasoned Shakespearian actor quiver was another.

"She had a very tough time the first couple of seasons because she didn't have any acting experience to speak of," Herrmann says. "What was tough about it for her was that this series depended so heavily on the interaction between Lauren and Alexis, and they were on camera so much of the time."

Just 18, she was living alone in Los Angeles, 1,500 miles from her family in Houston. "She was not a wild liver by any means, but it would get to her," Herrmann says. So much so, the producers asked the venerable actor to keep an eye on her and make sure she was coping with the demands she was facing. "I said, 'She's burned out! You're burning her up! She's exhausted.'"

Part of the problem was that all of this responsibility and fame had come upon her during her very first time in front of the TV camera, one of her friends points out. Where most actors start out with small roles and slowly learn the ropes outside the public spotlight, Bledel had been thrown into the deep end. The normal process by which actors decide over time whether this is actually something they want to do with their lives had been denied her.

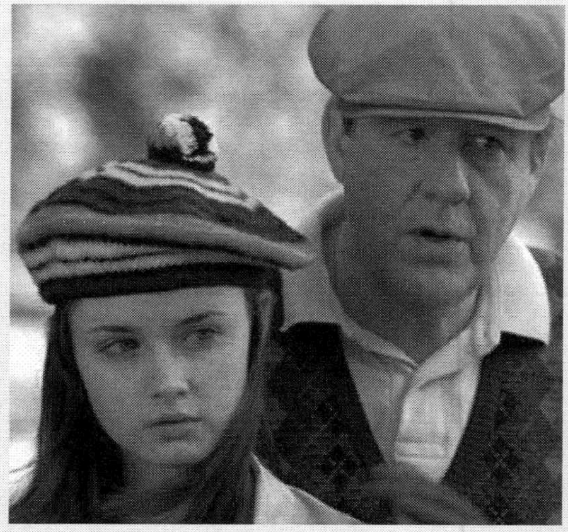

Feeling immensely protective of the actress, Herrmann would take her to the Musso & Frank Grill on Hollywood Boulevard (said to be a favorite hangout of everyone from Humphrey Bogart to Al Pacino), and generally tried to help her adjust to a situation that he knew firsthand to be extremely difficult. He adored the girl, absolutely, but he also looked after her because it was in the finest traditions of the stage.

"As a young player I gravitated toward the older actors and learned some lessons about the lead in a company," he says. "There's an actor or two who provide a kind of gravitas, a center." While you run the risk of meddling, "a word here or a word there, to mollify, or at least to let the person vent…can be very helpful."

None of this took away from the fact that Herrmann admired Bledel, and saw greatness in her. He's been known to compare her to one of the most iconic, enduring actresses of the 20th century: Audrey Hepburn.

"There is something about Audrey Hepburn, too, which is not actorish, it is simply this 'presence.' Alexis has this transparency about her—there's no character except this extraordinary presence. It's raw. Whatever is said to her has this ripple that goes *through* her. She's extraordinary."

There was no mistaking Bledel's appeal. The same, unspoiled charm Amy had spotted in New York, the same Botticelli angel quality that had so stunned the casting directors, was effortlessly transferred to the small screen in *Gilmore Girls*.

she was great in her day.) We also get the beginning of the long-running "Emily can't keep a maid" joke.

⊛ Though this is our first look at an episode without Amy's byline, there's no mistaking the underlying voice of the show's creator. The "look who's controlling" talk between Lorelai and Emily demonstrates a stunning insight into all three Gilmore women, putting audiences on notice that this is not your typical parade of stereotypical characters.

⊛ Richard is the executive vice president of the Gehrman-Driscoll Insurance Corp. in charge of its international division. This is also the first time Rory mentions wanting to go to Fez, and the European backpacking trip she and her mom are planning on once Rory graduates high school. The friendship that quickly blossoms between Rory and her grandfather triggers conflicting emotions in Lorelai, and sets Rory up for a terrible sense of betrayal when she brings Dean to her grandparents' house (2.1).

⊛ Though Richard is describing one's approach to holding a golf driver, his line about "a precise combination of confidence and humility" neatly describes all of the Gilmores at their best. When any Gilmore loses this balance, hurt feelings, if not out-and-out disaster, will ensue.

TODAY'S CELEBRATION Freaky twin double wedding.

KIRK OF ALL TRADES Swan delivery guy. (Yes, still technically not Kirk, but who's kidding who?)

EMILY'S MAID DU JOUR Emily will always be remembered as the woman who could never keep a maid. Here we get a laundry list of the *cooks* who have disappointed her. This episode, it's Sarah (though Emily calls her Mira), who actually gets a morsel of praise from her employer. Past cooks included Heidi (who had trouble closing things, including the liquor bottle), Sophia (who sang) and Anton. In future episodes, it is often implied that the maids also cook the meals.

DIRECTED BY As you might have suspected, Adam Nimoy is the son of *Star Trek*'s Spock, Leonard Nimoy. In addition to this episode of *Gilmore Girls*, he's directed episodes of everything from *NYPD Blue* to *The Practice*.

What I Kept

It's terrible fashionwise, but I kept these red shoes that they gave to Lane. I think it was one of her very first pairs of shoes, so they must be 10 years old by now, but they're the most comfortable shoes ever. And I kind of talk a little bit about this on the [DVD extras]. And then there was another sweater that I wore in the diner a lot. So I have that in my closet. The thing is that it *is* cute and I would kind of want to wear it. But I can't wear it because then I feel like people would recognize me more, it would just be a weird thing, so it just sits there in my closet.

—Keiko Agena (Lane)

AMEN, SISTER FRIEND

MICHEL [*to Lorelai*]: To me you are the teacher in the Charlie Brown cartoon.

LORELAI: Golfing was masterminded by my mother, of course. One minute we're having an excruciating family dinner and the next she's manipulating my kid into spending her Sunday with my father at the country club. Oh, I can't talk about it anymore. It's making me too upset. Tell me something happy.
SOOKIE: I can't make the strawberry shortcake.
LORELAI: Wow. You *suck* at this game.

Behind the Scenes: Growing Pains

While audiences were being treated to some strong first episodes, the rumblings at the executive level were threatening to seriously undermine the project.

"There was a lot of combat between Amy and the network and the studio," Polone recalls. It was in the middle of this episode, only the fourth of the first season, that the network and the studio were threatening to get rid of Amy.

Polone claims he went to network exec Jordan Levin and told him he'd talk to Amy. "I went to Amy and I said, 'You've gotta stop fighting with them and just do what they say or you're going to be fired, and that can't happen to you at this point in your career given where you are. If the show's a hit, you can go be however you want. And if the show fails you can go be however you want. But you're going to be kicked off and that would be the worst of all possible worlds for everything.'"

Polone's account should be tempered with the knowledge that the rift that remains between the producer and the *Gilmore Girls* creator was already starting to form around this time. However, by most accounts, "Amy wanted it Amy's way," as one person put it. While many outside of Hollywood, and indeed some within it, see this as being the tantrum-like behavior of an artist, it's difficult to appreciate the pressures Amy was under if you lack a reasonable understanding of the writer-producer's lot.

Ever since her success on *Roseanne*, Amy had watched as one project after another was canceled, and the old-boys club of network television shut their doors to somebody who refused to cater to their sometimes ill-advised, and even occasionally self-contradictory, production notes.

Though Edward Herrmann was referring to the whole decision-making process in Hollywood, he could have been referring to Amy's refusal to compromise on *Gilmore Girls* when he said, "Decisions are so often made by people who have no artistic understanding or sensitivity whatsoever—they're executives, network or studio or production company. It's been going on forever."

However at odds Amy and Polone would ultimately become, she took his advice this time and reined in her temper, he says.

From his own experience producing a television series currently in the works, Herrmann observes, "I can see already how many people want to attach themselves to it, and how all of their opinions can multiply the weight on it and crush it. So I understand Amy's reluctance to let anybody mess with her baby."

MICHEL [*explaining how he can tell the twin grooms apart*]: Yes, well, I'm very good at observing people, you know, learning their tics and traits, the sound of their voices. It's a gift.
SOOKIE: That one has a Post-It on its back.
MICHEL: Oh, well then that's Mark, the one on the right is Matt.
LORELAI: You will go and take that off of him.
MICHEL: I will not. We can't all just call everyone "sweetie" and get away with it.

EMILY: You brought us used dessert?
LORELAI: It's not used, it's left over.
EMILY: How nice. I'll just put it in the kitchen next to my half-empty box of Cheer.

1.4 The Deer-Hunters

First aired: Oct. 26, 2000//Written by Jed Seidel//Directed by Alan Myerson

Rory knew it was going to be rough starting Chilton a month late, but now it's taking its toll. When waking up late after an all-night cram session loses Rory the chance to take her test, mother and daughter give the Chilton officials hell. Funny, Rory's English teacher, Max Medina, doesn't seem to mind all that much. Meanwhile, Sookie is disheartened by a less-than-stellar review of her "magic risotto."

GINCHY! Lorelai bugging Rory while she's studying; Lane's super funky closet retreat; Rory's freakout followed by Lorelai's dressing down of "Il duce," Headmaster Charleston.

NOTES *'Wow, smart girls are mean.'*
Rory's listmaking makes its first appearance with her school supply roster. This is the first we hear of Dean's infatuation with Rory since the pilot, and the first time *Gilmore Girls* dips into a classic comedy formula that reaches back to the days of old radio shows such as *The Jack Benny Show*. One character sets up a funny past event ("Last week there was a huge debate over whether plaid scrunchies were acceptable headwear"), and another will refer to it later on ("That's the one who voted for the scrunchies"). This script goes nuts with it, working it again with the magic risotto and Rory being hit by a deer.

* This is the first we hear that Rory's wanted to go to Harvard "ever since she could crawl," something Lorelai herself questions during their deer hunt.

TODAY'S CELEBRATION The (nearly) rave magazine review of the inn, and the Shakespeare test.

THE OFFENDING 'MAGIC RISOTTO' REVIEW "The words divine, delectable and delirious don't begin to describe the delicious experience of dining at the Independence Inn. Only chef Sookie St. James can make a simple salad of hot-house tomatoes and assorted fresh herbs seem like a religious experience. Her lobster bisque is worth every sinful, cream-filled rich sip. The entrees are as heavenly as the starters. Though the much lauded risotto was perfectly fine, it was the simple handkerchief pasta with brown sage in a butter sauce that sent me through the roof." [He ordered a Riesling to wash it down with, the philistine.]

AMEN, SISTER FRIEND

PARIS: Hey, you know, not everybody can be smart. As my mother always says, *somebody* has to answer the phones.

RORY [*while Lorelai is searching in the magazine for the review*]: Jeez, who's naked?
LORELAI: Uh, Lucien Mills, food critic.
RORY: Yeah? How's his butt?

LANE: Are you all right?
RORY: I just got hit by a deer.
LANE: You hit a deer?
RORY: No! I got hit by a deer!
LANE: How do you get hit by a deer?
RORY: I was at a stop sign and he just hit me! Oh my God! [*Getting out to look for the deer.*]
LANE: Was it a four-way stop?
RORY: What does that matter?
LANE: I don't know. I don't know what to ask after you've been hit by a deer.

1.5 Cinnamon's Wake

First aired: Nov. 2, 2000 // Written by Daniel Palladino // Directed by Michael Katleman

Max manages to get Lorelai to meet him for coffee (a pre-date date), and Rory chat's up Dean at his new job at Doose's Market. Already ailing, Morey and Babette's cat, Cinnamon (first mentioned in 1.3), succumbs to the inevitable after some clams at Al's Pancake World. The resulting wake postpones Lorelai and Max's first date, but prompts Rory to tell Dean she's "interested" in him, before she runs away.

! GINCHY! Michel trying to get out of speaking to a group of French tourists; Miss Patty getting sexy to the produce and Kirk (now *officially* Kirk) busting her for eating it; Sookie helping herself behind the counter at Luke's; Babette and Morey's gathering and their tender moment afterward looking for the Big Dipper.

NOTES *'OK, our town is just weird.'*

Dean's borderline-stalking of Rory on the bus telegraphs Dean's future inability to let go of her, even after he's married (4.22).

Clutching at straws to come up with reasons they shouldn't date, Lorelai tells Max that she wants to be in The Bangles, but that doesn't mean she should "quit my job and get a guitar and ruin

Behind the Scenes: We Should All Have a Teacher Like Max Medina

If Scott Cohen looks at home in the classroom, it might be because he was a substitute teacher at PS 111 in Queens, NY, when he was in his early 20s. After teaching a Kindergarten music class temporarily, he was offered a permanent position.

"I had to think about it for a couple of days and then I lied about getting this huge movie in Mexico," he says. As much as he hated to leave behind children he'd grown to love, he realized he needed his days free if he was going to ever make it as an actor. Still, "I've always been good with kids. I have taught acting and clowning and music and all kinds of things to kids. Now I'm really interested in teaching college level acting, but I haven't quite done it yet."

"I remember touching Lauren's arm and her reacting to it," Cohen says, recalling the shooting of Max and Lorelai's coffee rendezvous. "It was just a moment and I felt, 'Wow, this is a beautifully written, beautifully done scene that really should be in a movie.' And I've always remembered it as such."

— SCOTT COHEN (MAX) RECALLING A FAVORITE SCENE FROM "CINNAMON'S WAKE"

my life to be a Bangle, does it?" Max points out that The Bangles broke up which, though technically true, is negated with a reunion concert Lorelai takes Rory and the Chilton girls to later (1.13).

The complete absence of Richard and the token appearance by Emily prove that merely five episodes in, the elder Gilmores are every bit as vital to the series as Lorelai and Rory.

TODAY'S CELEBRATION Cinnamon's wake.

KIRK OF ALL TRADES Doose's Market assistant manager.

AND INTRODUCING... ***Kirk Gleason*** Recalls Sean Gunn, "I do remember at an early table read, like the second show I did, I started saying my lines and Lauren looked up and her face lit up and she said, 'Hey!' She didn't know that it was going to be the same person. And that made me feel good. I certainly wouldn't say that anybody made me feel uncomfortable, but it's not until you keep coming back that people realize that oh, he's here to stay."

AMEN, SISTER FRIEND

EMILY: Oh wait—Rudolph Gottfried.
LORELAI: Another cousin?
EMILY: No, a Nazi that we knew. I'd forgotten. We stayed with him once in Munich. Nice old man. Interesting stories.

Making an Episode 1 The Schedule

Though some of the faces in front of and behind the camera will change over the years, the production process for *Gilmore Girls* will remain virtually unchanged.

Usually production on a season begins in July and runs straight through to April or May the following year. Like most hour-long shows, each episode of *Gilmore* is shot on an eight-day cycle, usually Wednesday to Friday of the next week. With very few exceptions, the only days off are holidays such as Thanksgiving (a four-day weekend), Christmas (two or three weeks off, similar to students' winter breaks in the US), and about two months hiatus between the end of one season and the beginning of the next. Working closely with the producers, actors can arrange brief amounts of time off to tackle other projects, usually movies.

To accommodate such a rigorous schedule, the writers, producers and video editors have to constantly be working on future episodes to meet their deadlines.

LORELAI: Mom you socialized with a Nazi? That's despicable! That's heinous!
EMILY: No dear, that was a joke.

LANE [*discussing Cinnamon's passing*]: They said that they rolled her body into a lamp.
(*Rory nods.*)
LANE: Did you laugh?
(*Rory shakes her head.*)
LANE: Did you want to?
(*Rory nods.*)

KIRK: I wasn't aware that you were *the* Miss Patty. The owner tells me that you're one of our best customers and you can put anything into that mouth that you want to. Those were his words; I could have paraphrased them.

BABETTE: I never thought a man would ever even want me.
LORELAI: I know the feeling.
BABETTE: Oh please, with that ass? Gimme a break.

"I'm constantly avoiding getting bashed. I have a callous though, so no big deal."

—TED ROONEY (MOREY) ABOUT AVOIDING HITTING HIS HEAD ON THE LOW DOORWAYS IN BABETTE + MOREY'S HOUSE

1.6 Rory's Birthday Parties

First aired: Nov. 9, 2000 // Written by Amy Sherman-Palladino // Directed by Sarah Pia Anderson

Rory's turning 17 on Friday, and she's getting two parties this year: one at her grandparents' house and one at home. While Lorelai finally feels like she's making some headway reaching her mother, Emily's turned Rory's party into another social function, inviting all of the Chilton students that make Rory's life miserable. Though Emily's ritzy soiree is a disaster, the more humble affair in Stars Hollow gives everyone some food for thought.

GINCHY! Emily's "Put a Post-It on it"; Lorelai and Emily shopping for Rory's gift; Paris and Rory both showing up to check out the new Harvard brochures; the Rory cake; Rory's choice of reading material for her grandfather and his delight with discovering he's "an autumn"; and Emily's realization that she doesn't really know Lorelai at all.

NOTES *'God, you know, you're doing the same thing to her that you always did to me. You're trying to control her, and when that doesn't work you just shut her out.'*

Christopher calls weekly and sees the girls at Christmas, and sometimes Easter. We also learn just how incestuous Connecticut's upper crust is—Richard's done business with Tristin's grandfather. Miss Patty's devastation after Rory discontinued her dance lessons sounds similar to the disappointment Amy's mother felt when Amy left dance behind for television writing.

Like all the best comedies, there is a great deal of drama holding the whole story together. Lorelai's heart-to-heart with Rory in her old room about coming out to her parents about her pregnancy ("It was the only time they ever looked small to me") is done with the perfect amount of "confidence and humility" (*see Notes for 1.3*).

Some notable firsts here include Luke's first proposal to Lorelai (sort of), the first inkling that Paris likes Tristin (and has a great deal in common with Rory), Miss Patty's last name (LaCosta), the first appearance of the bracelet Dean made for Rory, and the very first time that Richard and Emily have been to their daughter's house.

Emily's comment about Luke looking at Lorelai "like you were about to give him a lap dance" is uncharacteristically crass for Emily, and again may be a testing of the waters with the network and a dig at *Gilmore's* initial financing by the Family Friendly Programming Forum.

Easily one of the best episodes of Season 1, and a strong contender for best of the series.

What I Kept

I got some Hep Alien stuff, some T-shirts; I didn't take a brick or a rock or anything, but some swag. I have a Hep Alien coozie, which they used in some episode as background stuff. They would always check your car to make sure you weren't taking something off the lot as you would exit; they would make you pop your trunk.

—Todd Lowe (Zack)

TODAY'S CELEBRATION Rory's birthday. Twice!

YOU'VE ENTERED EMILYLAND $12 is not a present.

10 The number of generations of Gellers who've attended Harvard. This will change to five later (3.16).

AMEN, SISTER FRIEND

LUKE [*about Rory*]: She's not here yet.

LORELAI: All right. You'll have to entertain me until she arrives. OK, burger boy, dance.

LUKE: Will you marry me?

LORELAI: What?

Behind the Scenes Sally + Liz

While the *Gilmore* set had more than its fair share of wits, nearly everybody bows to the duo of Sally Struthers and Liz Torres. "When they held court, boy, whoever was the visiting director was always scratching their head about how to keep them quiet," laughs Ted Rooney (Morey). "They would just take over and everyone would start cracking up. Even if no one else was cracking up, they were cracking up at each other. They were shushed more than once, but they were fun. They're not that old school, but they're of an older school, and they just know how to tell stories and jokes and put on different hats and entertain. They're always fun to hang out with."

"As time went by, they were basically this big warm furnace of laughter and it was open to anybody," recalls Honorine Bell (Lulu). "So if you weren't feeling like you were having a good time or you were in a grouchy corner or something, you could just go over there and you were guaranteed a laugh. They're both so funny together, and they have so many stories about Studio 54 and theater in New York."

Charlene Tilton (*Dallas*) actually read for the role of Babette, too, recalls casting director Mara Casey. "But I was beside myself with excitement that Sally got that part. I think she came in from Vegas to audition because she was doing the Patsy Cline show, but Sally is just a delight. I know that *Gilmore Girls* helped facilitate additional work for her, and that makes me very happy because she's just an absolute doll. Amy is younger than I am but I believe we had the same appreciation for the stars we remember from the '60s and '70s as children."

LUKE: Just looking for something to shut you up.

LUKE: So I hear you're having a party Saturday.
RORY: Yeah. Mom's famous for her blowouts.
LORELAI: The best one was her 8th birthday.
RORY: Oh yeah, that was good.
LORELAI: The cops shut us down.
LUKE: The cops shut down an 8-year-old's birthday party?
RORY: And arrested the clown.
LUKE: I don't want to hear any more of this.

LARS: Richard, I've got Dennis on the phone and he heard the same thing I heard.
RICHARD: Well, one wrong man can always find a friend.

EMILY: You smiled. You're pleased that the ice man looked at you like a Porterhouse steak.

LORELAI: I'm smiling because you're crazy and that's what you do to crazy people to keep them calm.

THE BIRTHDAY MORNING SPEECH

LORELAI: Happy birthday, little girl.

RORY: Hey.

LORELAI: I can't believe how fast you're growing up.

RORY: Really? Feels slow.

LORELAI: Trust me, it's fast. What do you think of your life so far?

RORY: I think it's pretty good.

LORELAI: Any complaints?

RORY: I'd like that whole humidity thing to go away.

LORELAI: All right. I'll work on that.

RORY: So, do I look older?

LORELAI: Oh yeah. You walk into Denny's before 5, you've got yourself a discount.

RORY: Good deal.

LORELAI: So you know what I think?

RORY: What?

LORELAI: I think you're a great, cool kid, and the best friend a girl could have.

RORY: Right back at ya.

LORELAI: And it's so hard to believe that at exactly this time many moons ago, I was lying in exactly the same position—

Behind the Scenes: All That Food

Though there's never a shortage of food whenever the girls are around, you will seldom see them take a bite until the very end of the scene. This is because once they get to the end without having to shoot another take, it's deemed reasonably safe to eat. Otherwise, they would have to eat over and over, take after take. Aside from the obvious effects of eating this much, it would also be pretty rough on those responsible for ensuring the remaining food looks the same throughout the scene.

Graham often requested miniature tomatoes whenever she was called on to eat something in a scene because she could eat them quickly and be ready to say all those lines.

RORY: Oh boy. Here we go.

LORELAI: Only I had a huge, fat stomach and big fat ankles and I was swearing like a sailor—

RORY: On leave.

LORELAI: On leave, right! And there I was—

RORY: In labor.

LORELAI: And while some have called it the most meaningful experience of your life, to me it was something more akin to doing the splits on a crate of dynamite.

RORY: I wonder if the Waltons ever did this.

LORELAI: And I was screaming and swearing, and being surrounded as I was by a hundred prominent doctors, I just assumed there was an actual use for the cup of ice chips they gave me.

RORY: There wasn't.

LORELAI: But pelting the nurses sure was fun.

1.7 Kiss and Tell

First aired: Nov. 16, 2000//Written by Jenji Kohan//Directed by Rodman Flender

Thanksgiving is approaching and Taylor's trying to get Luke to spruce up the diner appropriately. Rory slips into Doose's Market to see Dean and gets a kiss for her troubles, which she tells Lane all about. Mrs. Kim overhears and confronts Lorelai about her daughter's immoral behavior. Trying to be the cool mom, Lorelai invites Dean over for movie night, much to Rory's embarrassment.

! GINCHY! Rory and Dean's first kiss; Lorelai's phone call to the fridge repair company; Rory and Lane in their pilgrim costumes; and Lorelai's fashion pep talk shortly before Dean arrives.

NOTES *'Cause not talking about guys and our personal lives—that's me and my mom. That is not me and Rory.'*

* Considering how celebration-crazy Stars Hollow becomes, it isn't until this episode that we get our first real taste of that mania, and surprise, surprise, it's Taylor spearheading the insanity. This is also the episode where the girls begin their "who are you kidding" consumption of enormous amounts of junk food, pissing off people the world over.

"I really always wanted a big sister when I was a kid—I was an only child. I actually had a sister who died very young, very horrible and sad, so I always grew up thinking, 'Oh my God, if I could have a sister who was my pal, and we'd look kind of alike...' So if anything, I think it would be like if I ever had a kid, I'd probably want to be a pal."

—AMY (LOS ANGELES TIMES, 4/9/01)

Luke prevents Lorelai from attacking Dean at Doose's, an interesting lead up to Luke's attitude toward the bagboy later (1.17). Lorelai admits to Luke that Dean actually reminds her a bit of Christopher.

TODAY'S CELEBRATION Thanksgiving, and Rory and Dean's first kiss/date/hangout session.

AND INTRODUCING...*Taylor Doose*

META, META, META Rory's reaction to Lorelai's blatherings about the Liz/Lucky kiss on *General Hospital* could easily be Amy letting off some steam about her own actors' behind-the-scenes struggles with delivering their lines exactly as written. Says Rory, "I think they're actors being paid to play a part so it's nice that they're living up to their obligations." Speaking of that soap opera, is it mere coincidence that the most famous couple from that long-running series was "Luke and Laura"? Sounds a little like "Luke and Lorelai"...

WRITTEN BY Jenji Kohan (sister of *Will & Grace* creator David Kohan) would only receive a writing credit for this episode of *Gilmore*, but she produced another 11. Five years later she would create the popular Mary-Louise Parker hit *Weeds*. Kohan's Facebook profile says it all: "I have created *Weeds* but mysteriously nobody knows me."

AMEN, SISTER FRIEND

LORELAI: I'm crushed. I'm bleeding. Get me a tourniquet. Oh no, they're dirty 'cause Rory wouldn't wash them with her stuff.

RORY: Lane? Lane?
LANE: What's wrong?
RORY: I got kissed! (*Rory holds up a box of cornstarch.*) And I shoplifted.

LORELAI [*On the phone to the fridge repair place*]: Yeah, can you hear that? No, no, it's higher, it's like a high-pitched kind of an "*Eeeee!*" sound. It started last week but it was lower and it only happened when we opened the door and now it's higher and it's on all the time, so I think it's really growing in confidence. OK, look, I've already told this to three other people so could you just please tell me what is wrong with this fridge? I'm not going to make the noise again. I'm not—*Eeeeee!* Look, Jerry, I don't have a lot of pride but I do have enough that I do not want to make that noise again, so could you please tell me what is wrong with the fridge or connect me with someone who can? Thank you. Hello Rusty, great. Listen, my fridge is making this weird sound. It's like a high-pitched—you know what—actually, is Jerry still there? OK, have him make the sound.

RORY: Well I don't want our first hanging out session to be with my mother either.
LORELAI: Stop saying mother like that.
RORY: Like what?
LORELAI: Like there's supposed to be another word after it.

1.8 Love & War & Snow

First aired: Dec. 14, 2000 // Written by Joan Binder Weiss // Directed by Alan Myerson

It's the annual reenactment of the Battle of Stars Hollow, and as usual Luke wants nothing to do with it. And as usual Lorelai is eagerly awaiting the first snow. Unusually, Rory is far too hung up on Dean to listen to Lane, and Lorelai finally "brings a boy home" when Max Medina finds himself stranded in the Hollow.

GINCHY! Lorelai's delight at smelling the approaching snow; Rory finding the photos of a young Lorelai and Christopher in her mother's

Making an Episode 2 The Writers Gather

Two or three times a season, Amy & Dan and the writers spend a weekend together in Las Vegas, La Jolla, Calif. or Palm Springs, discussing the overall story arc for the next six to 13 episodes in terms of what will be happening to characters that season, writer Janet Leahy says.

For the rest of the production year, the writers sequester themselves in a special writers room on the Warner Brothers lot five days a week, 10:30 am to 7 pm, to pitch different story ideas that can be woven into these larger story arcs. For example, a story arc for Season 1 sees Lorelai get engaged to Max Medina, but one of the smaller stories on the way to telling this larger one includes the return of Christopher (1.15).

Though some might think the regular hours the writers enjoy are cushy when compared with the 14-20 hour days put in by some of the cast and most of the crew, the TV writers room is its own little pressure cooker.

"You showed up and you worked and if you weren't in that room, you felt guilty about it," writer Jane Espenson says. "Absences didn't happen."

Lorelai enjoys her snow, especially after it strands Max in Stars Hollow.

room at Richard and Emily's place, and the subsequent, bittersweet paging through the photo album.

NOTES *'The world changes when it snows.'*

⊛ Our first glimpse of a town meeting in all its glory, as well as of Luke's hatred for all things public-spirited. Lane tells Rory how awkward it would be for her to be involved with Rich Blumenfeld because they're bandmates. Just wait till you get it together with Zack, Lane (5.4). Luke's father was a Battle of Stars Hollow reenactor, which may explain his attitude toward these things. Lorelai tells Max she's never brought a man to their house before.

⊛ Max nearly got married once before, but she moved to Thailand to pursue a business opportunity with Bank of America. We learn that Emily's younger sister, Hopie, is the great expatriate of the family, though later we learn Richard's mother, Trix, lives abroad.

TODAY'S CELEBRATION 224th Anniversary of the Battle of Stars Hollow.

KIRK OF ALL TRADES Battle of Stars Hollow reenactor.

EMILY'S MAID DU JOUR Anna, who must've bought the frozen pizza lurking in the Gilmore freezer. (Florence is the cook, who can't make it because of the snow.)

YOU'VE ENTERED EMILYLAND [*on the subject of frozen pizza*] Rory, that's food you eat at a carnival, or in a Turkish prison.

AMEN, SISTER FRIEND

LUKE: Tradition is a trap. It allows people to stick their head in the sand. Everything in the past was so quaint, so charming. Times were simpler. Kids didn't have sex. Neighbors knew each other. It's a freaking fairy tale. Things sucked then, too. They just sucked without indoor plumbing.

RORY [*to Lorelai*]: I know you're not a cat person, so you truly will be alone if you don't find someone.

1.9 Rory's Dance

First aired: Dec. 20, 2000// Written by Amy Sherman-Palladino// Directed by Lesli Linka Glatter

Rory's not certain of the nature of her relationship with Dean, though she succeeds in convincing him to take her to her first dance—Chilton's formal. What begins as a fairy-tale evening ends up opening old wounds between Emily and Lorelai, and creating a serious rift between Lorelai and Rory.

! GINCHY! Rory asking Dean out; Emily's repulsion at discovering Lorelai's monkey lamp, and their subsequent bonding over mashed banana on toast; Dean and Tristin's confrontation at the dance.

NOTES *'You're going to lose her just like I lost you.'*

Rory and Dean are still in that limbo between relationship and non-relationship, which they finally resolve, much to Lorelai's consternation. The Paris-Tristin-Rory triangle is pretty well spelled out in this episode, too. Paris' entourage is also coming into its own: Louise leans toward slutty, Madeline sweet but ditsy. For all

Behind the Scenes: From 'Buffy' Mayor to Stars Hollow Selectman

At the height of *Buffy the Vampire Slayer*'s popularity, it seemed like you couldn't turn around without somebody raving about actor James Marsters' portrayal of the evil-turned-tortured vampire Spike on that WB series. Though the California actor with the engaging English accent was not aligned with the forces of darkness in real life, he was mates with the man who would bring us the closest thing to a villain Stars Hollow could come up with: the wonderfully annoying Taylor Doose.

Actor Michael Winters first met Marsters at the Pacific Conservatory of the Performing Arts in Santa Monica, Calif. For 10 years, Winters taught, acted and directed there, and Marsters was a student. After Winters settled down in Seattle with its rich theater scene (*Gilmore Girls* brought him the money to make the down payment on his home years later), Marsters landed there, too, and they worked on a couple of acting projects together. In fact, the *Buffy* actor has often credited Winters with convincing him to seek his fortune in LA.

"I was whining about the fact that I was working in the theater and I couldn't afford to buy a new car," Winters says. "And in some interview I read, he said, 'Well, I didn't want to end up like that, not being able to buy a new car, so I went to LA.'"

Winters left for Hollywood shortly thereafter, and was even up for the role of Sunnydale's evil Mayor on *Buffy*, he says, but previous professional commitments scuttled it. The role went instead to Harry Groener, an old friend of Winters.

her sniping at Rory, it's Paris who's humiliated when her date, Jacob, admits he's actually her cousin, and proceeds to hit on Rory.

Dean and Rory fall asleep in Miss Patty's studio while reading *The Portable Dorothy Parker*. The subsequent firestorm this innocent act causes is a grim sign of things to come (1.16). Rory may be completely blindsided by the way Lorelai tears into her mere moments after defending her actions to Emily, but we'll soon see where Lorelai gets this from when Richard does the same thing with Lorelai (1.15).

Amy's Mom

When Miss Patty and her yoga class discover Rory and Dean asleep in her studio, check out the woman who says, "Oh my goodness, it's Lorelai's girl." That's Maybin Hewes, Amy's mom.

Considering how optimistic the episode began, the clash between mother and daughter comes completely out of left field. It's a bold declaration that despite the series' cheery beginnings, the show's creator refuses to sugarcoat what many feared would be a wholly unrealistic relationship between parent and child. And Kelly Bishop proves once again how integral she is to the series.

TODAY'S CELEBRATION Chilton's formal dance.

OY WITH THE ____, ALREADY! Sookie's clumsiness!

EMILY'S MAID DU JOUR Marta, who's responsible for locking up the Gilmore mansion while Emily stays to look after Lorelai.

AMEN, SISTER FRIEND

RORY [*describing the Chilton formal to Dean*]: Well, it's this thing where you go and they play music and you're supposed to get all dressed up and do some kind of dance, and then there's chicken.

Behind the Scenes: LA Winter Wonderland

"It was a big mess because the snow machine made so much noise, we had to [rerecord the dialogue for] all our scenes," Scott Cohen says of the snow-filled scenes he shot with Graham.

"The thing that we got grilled on all the time was make sure they're wearing their gloves and hats and coats and scarves, because it's supposed to be Connecticut, it's supposed to be cold," adds key set costumer Valerie Campbell. "Trying to get actors to put on clothes when it's 90 degrees outside and they're trying to pretend it's 0 degrees is really difficult."

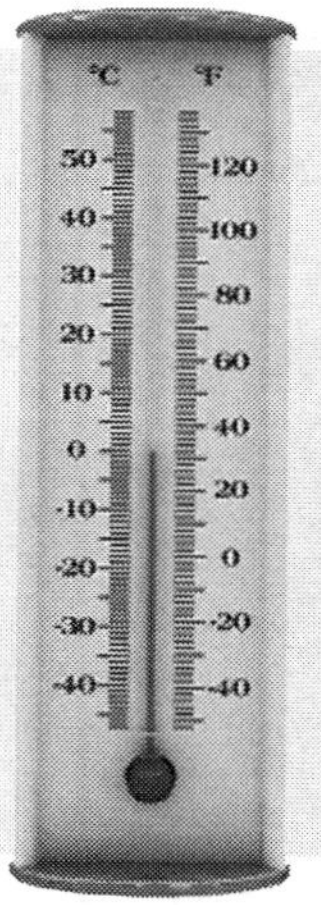

LORELAI: Come on already!
RORY: I'm primping.
LORELAI: You're 16. You have skin like a baby's ass. There's nothing to primp.

LORELAI: Hey, Dean, meet my mother, Emily Post.
EMILY: Emily *Gilmore*.

RORY: [Miss Patty] says she's done everything there is to do in show business except set fire to the hoop the dog jumps through.

EMILY: You're going to lose her. You're going to lose her just like I lost you.
LORELAI: I am not going to lose her, do you hear me? Even if I hadn't gotten pregnant, you still would have lost me. I had nothing in that house. I had no life. I had no air. You strangled me. I do not strangle Rory.
EMILY: Oh you're so perfect and I was so horrible. I put you in good schools. I gave you the best of everything. I made sure you had the finest opportunities. And I am so tired of hearing about how you were suffocated and I was so controlling. Well, if I was so controlling, why couldn't I control you running around getting pregnant and throwing your life away?

Dean and Rory enjoy the Chilton formal experience before Tristin, Paris and sleep ruin their evening.

1.10 Forgiveness and Stuff

First aired: Dec. 21, 2000 // Written by John Stephens // Directed by Bethany Rooney

Four days after the events of last episode, life sucks for the Gilmores. Lorelai and Rory aren't speaking, Emily's uninvited Lorelai to her annual Christmas party, and Richard lands in the hospital. Even as Lorelai and Rory re-examine their roles as daughters, Lorelai's relationship with Luke takes an interesting turn.

GINCHY! Luke's Santa burger and how he swings into action after Lorelai learns that her father's in the hospital; Lorelai's vision of herself through her father's eyes on the ride there; Luke's hospital phobia; the hospital room interaction between Richard and Emily; and Luke and Lorelai turning out the lights in the diner to watch the procession.

NOTES *'God, how did everything get so screwed up?'*

The (female) baby Jesus doll has been in the Stars Hollow pageant since 1965. Lorelai's brief exchange with Dean at the window about where he ranks in her enemies list—"I'm still a little hot for that crazy bomber guy who's been living in a cave for a year"—will seem particularly haunting by the beginning of Season 2, following the events of Sept. 11, 2001.

Emily's great uncle founded the hospital that Richard's been taken to. Luke tells Emily that he's kept his father's hardware store exactly as it was, though it's a diner now. It turns out that Richard suffered a bout of angina rather than a heart attack, though he's going to have to cut out red meat, heavy desserts and take some real exercise (not golf). The new baseball cap Lorelai gets Luke will become her barometer for how he feels about her at the end of the series (7.20).

"I was a child raised by a single parent—by my father—whom my teachers always found very attractive. To my knowledge, my father had several parent-teacher conferences that really were not necessary. ...I do identify with this in some way."

-LAUREN GRAHAM (CNN.COM, 1/10/01)

TODAY'S CELEBRATION The Stars Hollow Christmas pageant and Emily's Christmas party.

YOU'VE ENTERED EMILYLAND It's not "Ms. Gilmore." It's "*Mrs.* Gilmore!" "*Mrs.* Gilmore!" I'm not a Cosmo woman!

EMILY'S MAID DU JOUR Dava, who may be called upon to bring some bed sheets for Richard's hospital stay.

AMEN, SISTER FRIEND

LORELAI [*about her father*]: He lived his life the way he thought he was supposed to. He followed the rules taught to him by his nonfishing, non-Barbie-buying dad. He worked hard. He bought a nice house. He provided for my mom. All he asked in return was for his daughter to wear white dresses and go to cotillion and want the same life that he had. What a disappointment it must have been for him to get me.

EMILY: Richard Gilmore, there may be many things happening in this hospital tonight but your dying is not one of them.
RICHARD: But—
EMILY: No! I did not sign on to your dying. And it is not going to happen. Not tonight, not for a very long time. In fact, I demand to go first. Do I make myself clear?
RICHARD: Yes, Emily. You may go first.

1.11 Paris is Burning

First aired: Jan. 11, 2001 // Written by Joan Binder Weiss // Directed by David Petrarca

Lorelai and Max are enjoying their newfound couplehood (at least initially), and even Rory is warming to the idea. Yet trouble, as usual, is just around the corner. Embittered by her own crumbling home life, Paris reveals exactly who Mr. Medina was kissing in his classroom.

"She's extremely dry, which I think is hilarious. And she pulls her weight on that show, man. She had a lot of really intense, long, tongue-twisting speeches. And people loved it when we came to work because, given she always had so much stuff to do, she was ready to go, always."

–SHELLY COLE (MADELINE) ABOUT LIZA WEIL (PARIS)

GINCHY! The Skippy the hamster story; Rory's confrontation with Paris and their uneasy truce; Sookie asking Jackson out in mid-tirade.

NOTES *'You always let your emotions get in the way. That's the problem with you Lorelai—you don't think.'*

The pre-divorce squabbling of Paris' parents has spilled into the local papers, making the already irritable girl even more hateful. Max's outside-of-Chilton name for Rory is Rebecca, and Rory's for Max is... Norman? ("I'm sorry, *Psycho* was on earlier...")

Lorelai's sudden reluctance over Max, ostensibly triggered by how attached she sees Rory becoming to him, is right on schedule, according to Sookie. Two months is usually when she starts doing her "'getaway dance." Max's response to Lorelai telling him she needs space—"I want as little space as possible; 100 clowns crammed into a Volkswagen"—manages to cover actor Scott Cohen's first acting career (clowning) and his first brush with fame (as the flirtacious driver in a Volkswagen Passat commercial) in just a few words.

The final scene of Rory coming home to find Lorelai in tears, and her comforting response, will be reversed just a few episodes later (1.17).

TODAY'S CELEBRATION Does Parent's Day count as a celebration? (It does the way Lorelai and Max go about it.)

YOU'VE ENTERED EMILYLAND A mistake is when you throw out your credit card bill. A mistake is when you forget to RSVP to a dinner party. A mistake is when the gardeners miss trash day and the barrels are full for a week.

AMEN, SISTER FRIEND

RORY: Buttercup is a special dog. She's extremely skittish and tends

to react badly towards blonde haired females, brunette males, children of either sex, other animals, red clothing, cabbage or anyone in a uniform.
LORELAI [*to Luke*]: Hey, we just found the doggy version of you.

LORELAI [*in between kisses from Max*]: But what about my required reading? But I won't make the cheerleading squad! Mr. Medina, is this my extra credit work because Missy just had to take a test.

PARIS: Your mom, Mr. Medina, mouths open. I saw them. How's the coleslaw? Good?

LORELAI [*to Sookie*]: When did you become the relationship expert? You haven't been in a relationship in years. [*Realizing what she's just said*] Wow! Zero to jackass in 3.2 seconds.

1.12 Double Date

First aired: Jan. 18, 2001 // Written by Amy Sherman-Palladino // Directed by Lev. L. Spiro

Lorelai's freaking out over studying for a test about Wal-Mart for her business class; Lane wants Rory to set her up with Dean's friend, Todd; and Sookie press gangs Lorelai into keeping Jackson's cousin, Rune, company while she has her first date with Jackson. One couple quickly becomes an item, the other...not so much.

Character Sketch Mrs. Kim: 'That Lady's Scary'

Though few beyond the *Gilmore Girls* set knew it for the first couple of years, Lane Kim was actually based on Amy's best friend and *Gilmore* producer Helen Pai, who knew firsthand what it was like growing up in a Korean-American household. Though Mrs. Kim could seem tyrannical at times, Emily Kuroda and the writers each worked to reveal the velvet hand beneath the iron glove.

"She was just written as a very over-the-top, strict mother. You look at the script and you wouldn't think, 'Oh, I would give my life for my daughter,'" Kuroda says. "But when I looked at the script, that was my first impression."

Of course being told that Mrs. Kim was from Korea also suggested a certain way of speaking.

"When I went in, I did an accent. Then Amy goes, 'What are ya doing?' I said, 'Well, she's from Korea.' 'Nah, don't do that.' So I didn't do that. Mrs. Kim kind of has an accent, but it's not a Korean accent. It's very military. Every-thing-is-on-the-beat. And that's from Amy."

Bio Chad Michael Murray (Tristin Dugray)

Actors such as Lauren Graham practiced their craft in the television world for years before hitting it big on *Gilmore*. Chad Michael Murray had only been in Los Angeles for a year before landing his breakout role as Rory's foil, Tristin.

Born in Buffalo, NY, Murray and his three brothers, sister and half-brother were brought up by their father after his mother left when he was 10. Landing a scholarship to a modeling convention in Orlando, Fla., he met his agent there. After graduating from a Buffalo public school, he moved to LA, and saw his acting career take off.

After *Gilmore*, the actor had a 12-episode run in another WB hit, *Dawson's Creek*, before landing a starring role on the frog network's *One Tree Hill* starting in 2003. Six seasons into its run, Murray actually had the opportunity to write his own episode ("We Three (My Echo, My Shadow and Me"), and in 2009, to direct another ("A Hand to Take Hold of the Scene").

GINCHY! A typical, frenetic morning in the Gilmore household as the girls get ready for the day, all to the tune of XTC's "Earn Enough for Us" (arguably the best opening to an episode ever); the way Rune is revolted by Lorelai; Sookie and Jackson's date; and Lane's front yard phone call to Rory.

NOTES *'This place is too fancy, my hair is too tight and this dress is all wrong.'*

Lane tells Todd that she's recently gotten into former Velvet Underground singer Nico. Her Nico obsession will continue throughout the series. Luke seems ready to ask Lorelai out, only to be interrupted by a panicked Mrs. Kim.

TODAY'S CELEBRATION Double date times two.

OY WITH THE ___, ALREADY Sookie's clumsiness!!

META, META, META Sookie says "last looks" before she and Lorelai meet Jackson and Rune for their date. "Last looks" is usually what's called on set prior to shooting a scene, giving the costumers, hair and makeup people a final opportunity to make sure everybody's perfect.

AMEN, SISTER FRIEND

LORELAI: I can't remember any of this crap!

MICHEL: Well, not everyone is cut out to be their own boss. Maybe you are more of a worker bee, a follower, a ticket ripper, or the man at

Lorelai tries to calm Sookie down shortly before her first date with Jackson.

the concert with the orange glow stick directing you where to park.
LORELAI: You're baiting me, aren't you?
MICHEL: No, I seriously have no faith in your aptitude.

LORELAI: I'm too tall.
LUKE: Get out.
LORELAI: I'm serious.
LUKE: Doesn't [Rune] understand how great that is? You can get all the stuff from the top shelf.
LORELAI: Exactly. That is exactly what I bring to a relationship. Explain that to him, will you.

LORELAI: Look, when I was a teenager, my parents tried to keep me locked up. They tried to force me to become what they had in mind, and now I'm not talking exactly about Lane here, but in my case, it really didn't work.
MRS. KIM: You blame your parents for getting pregnant?
LORELAI: No, I just think sometimes if I'd had a little more space or someone to listen to me, things might have turned out different. Now I got lucky, because having Rory—totally the best thing that could have happened. But let's be honest, I certainly don't want Rory to turn out like me.
MRS. KIM: I don't want Lane to turn out like you, either.
LORELAI: Now I believe that's the first thing that you and I have ever agreed on.

"I would always run into this girl named Brenda Maben. One day she was like, 'Come work with me on Gilmore Girls.' I could've sworn she said Gibson Girls. I was like, 'Oh, it's a period piece.'"

—VALERIE CAMPBELL, KEY SET COSTUMER

1.13 Concert Interruptus

First aired: Feb. 15, 2001 // Written by Elaine Arata // Directed by Bruce Seth Green

While Stars Hollow is trying to raise funds to repair the bridge with a charity rummage sale, Lorelai discovers the long lost love of Luke's past and Rory is thrown to the wolves—Paris, Madeline and Louise—for a school presentation. Seeing that Rory has the opportunity to turn her tormentors into allies, Lorelai gives the girls her coveted 9th row tickets to The Bangles concert in New York City, but it's going to take more than "walking like an Egyptian" to change the Chilton girls.

GINCHY! Mrs. Caldicott's exchange with Tristin in class; Lorelai rounding up Madeline and Louise at the party; and her talk with Luke at the end. As he observes, "Remembering is not pining."

NOTES *'You know what? I think this is the best night I've ever had.'*

Paris' mother is having their house completely repainted to get rid of all signs of her father after the divorce (1.11). Miss Patty danced on the drums she's trying to get rid of at the Copa Cabana in 1969. Luke had a "very serious" girlfriend, Rachel, five or six years before; why Lorelai never knew this remains a mystery. (Sookie says it was because Rachel traveled all the time, but still...)

There's no street sign on Lorelai's street; Rory told Paris and company to turn right at the statue of Monty the rooster. Sookie tells Lorelai that she thinks Rachel ditched Luke because Stars Hollow was too small for her and Luke didn't want to leave—he wouldn't even go away for college. This will come up again when Dean tells Luke that Lorelai's not going to stay in Stars Hollow forever (5.18). Paris has been in the same class as Tristin since kindergarten; he kissed her once in 6th grade on a dare.

Bio Emily Kuroda (Mrs. Kim)

Born in Fresno, Calif., Emily Kuroda was extremely shy growing up, finally getting into theater in high school to get out of her shell, very much like Alexis Bledel.

Kuroda was perpetually discouraged by the lack of opportunities for Asian-Americans in theater and television. "When I went to [California State University-Fresno], I was in theater and I guess because I'm Asian, they said, 'Well, you have to teach.' So I was getting my teaching credentials and my masters, and this Asian-American theater group came to my college in Fresno and I said, 'Well, *they're* acting.'"

Kuroda headed off to Los Angeles in 1978 to study with that group, East-West Players. Though she would spend much of her career on stage throughout California, Seattle and New York, she also carved out a diverse television career, starting in the 1980s. Credits include *LA Law*, *MacGyver*, *Columbo* and *ER*. Yet it was on *Gilmore Girls* that Kuroda would enjoy her greatest exposure.

"What they wrote for me—it was really good writing. Asian-American actors have been computer scientists, but gosh, Keiko and I were able to blossom and grow and explore and change, and have all these layers and colors, and every day I think how lucky I am to have had that."

Paris warms to Rory slightly after having a blast at The Bangles concert.

TODAY'S CELEBRATION Stars Hollow charity rummage sale to rebuild the bridge, and a rare opportunity to see The Bangles.

OY WITH THE ___, ALREADY Sookie's clumsiness!!!

META, META, META "It was very, very hot in that room that day" is Lorelai's excuse to Rory, explaining how she was talked into organizing the rummage sale. This also describes the actual shooting conditions in Miss Patty's studio during those ubiquitous town meetings. "It just got hotter than hell in there," remembers Michael Winters.

1 MONTH How long Rory and Dean have been together.

AMEN, SISTER FRIEND

RORY [*about the charity rummage sale*]: The point of this is to get crap out of here, not to trade it in for new crap.

PARIS [*to Rory about Tristin*]: I know he's flirting with me to get to you, but at least he's flirting with me.

1.14 That Damn Donna Reed

First aired: Feb. 22, 2001 // Written by Daniel Palladino and Amy Sherman-Palladino // Directed by Michael Katleman

Lorelai volunteers to help Luke paint the diner, Rory and Dean fall out over their differing views about The Donna Reed Show, *and Richard and Emily very nearly miss their chance to go to Martha's Vineyard this year. Add our first glimpse of Rory's father and you have an instant* Gilmore Girls *classic.*

GINCHY! Lorelai and Rory's *Donna Reed* dialogue and Dean's response; Lane's CD stash and filing system; Lorelai and Sookie's discussion about Luke; Richard and Emily's reaction to Lorelai's joke about Rory becoming a maid; and the grandparents' gleeful Martha's Vineyard coup.

NOTES *'Donna Reed would have never forgotten the rolls. They're gonna make me turn in my pearls.'*

✱ This is one of those episodes that covers more ground than seems possible in a scant 42 minutes. Morey and Babette finally replace Cinnamon with a new kitten, Apricot. Rory's night at the Dells' will only be the second night mother and daughter have spent apart. When Rory mentions going away to college someday, Lorelai tells her "I will sleep on the floor in your dorm, next to your bed," which is exactly what she does years later (4.2). Dean's observation that Rory is only upset about Donna Reed because her mother thinks that way is ostensibly a throwaway line, but one that will echo throughout the series as Rory struggles to discover who she is away from her mother.

✱ Luke's Diner hasn't been painted since his father died, and probably was only painted twice then. The little detail about where his father scrawled a hardware order on the wall is a sterling example of Amy's ability to paint an entire relationship with just a single, human image. Dean's calling Rory when he's minutes away is going to backfire on him next season (2.16). Luke and Dean's brief confrontation while taking out the trash foreshadows a much uglier clash later (5.18). Christopher's first appearance tells us pretty much everything we need to know about why Lorelai split with him, and even sets up next week's

Character Sketch ✱ Lorelai + Michel

The relationship between Lorelai and Michel echoes that between Lorelai and her parents, albeit with one crucial difference: she is Michel's boss. He may grumble about her bad jokes and the way she handles a situation, but in the end, Michel has to do what he's told.

"To me, it was a love and hate relationship, the same he would have with a sister," says Yanic Truesdale. "In my view, and in my dealing with her, she was my baby sister. Someone who I have great affection for, someone who I find smart and I want to protect, yet someone who I find irritating, who needs to be guided, who doesn't know half of what I know."

drama nicely with the words "my folks are back in Connecticut." Lorelai admits to Emily that she might have feelings for Luke.

TODAY'S CELEBRATION Choosing the paint scheme for Luke's Diner and *Donna Reed* night at Morey and Babette's.

OY WITH THE __, ALREADY! Christopher saying, "I thought I'd stop by and surprise the Gilmore girls." It only happens a few times in the series, but it always sounds extremely forced when the name of the show appears in the dialogue.

THINGS WE'VE LEARNED Ted Rooney (Morey) and Sally Struthers (Babette) went to the same high school, Grant High School in Portland, Oregon. "She says one of her favorite teachers was my dad, who taught her math," Rooney says. "So when she got on *All in the Family*, I was still young and she was the famous person to come out of Grant High School. When I met her on the set, we were sitting next to each other in those directors chairs, and she said something about how hot it was. And I said, 'Yeah, not like the summers in Portland, Oregon.' She took a breath and put it all together: 'You're not Ed Rooney's son are

Character Sketch: I Am 16 Going on 27

Though actors playing younger characters than themselves on teen dramas is nothing new, *Gilmore* had its own unique dynamic because of Bledel's youth (18 when she started the show) compared with the age of Keiko Agena, who played her best friend—26 at the beginning.

"I think it was definitely weird for me," Agena says. "First of all I think that was another reason I was so relaxed when I went to the audition, because I'm so much older than this character, I didn't think they'd hire me. So that was the first surprise. Also at that time the most awkward thing was that I hadn't told a lot of people my actual age. I think it would've been better if I'd just said right off the bat that I was 26. But some people had suggested that I be a little mysterious about my age. Lame advice, but anyway I took it. So it wasn't as awkward with Alexis because Alexis knew, so it was fine. I think the weirdness was me relating to other people, but they didn't know that I wasn't very close to the age of my character."

you?' She recognized the face; the Rooney look is hard to miss. She didn't know me because when she was in school, I was 3 or 4 years old."

'SHE WAS AN UNCREDITED PRODUCER AND DIRECTOR ON HER TELEVISION SHOW… WHICH IS ACTUALLY PRETTY IMPRESSIVE' Amy gives her audience a history lesson here about Donna Reed, and one that hits a lot closer to home than some might realize today. Though there have been a handful of female television showrunners in the US, there were many in the industry who took one look at the first few *Gilmore Girls* scripts and suggested that Amy's name was a pseudonym for *West Wing* creator Aaron Sorkin. When *Gilmore* casting assistant (and later writers assistant) Alison Goodman finally met Amy, "I was like, 'You *are* real, you exist,'" she remembers. "But it was like how demeaning to Amy."

AMEN, SISTER FRIEND

LORELAI [*speaking for Donna Reed on TV*]: I just had an impure thought about your father, Alex. Funny, I don't know why I had it. It isn't the second Saturday of the month.
RORY: [*as Alex*]: Hey, I heard you had an impure thought.
LORELAI: I must now sublimate all my impure thoughts by going into the kitchen and making an endless string of perfect casseroles.

LORELAI [*about Luke*]: We're picking out paint colors tonight so it's going to be hours of "yes," "no," "yes," "no," "yes," "no," until my world-famous perseverance wears him down and he winds up in a ball on the floor crying like a girl. Wanna come watch? [*We will actually see Lorelai do something similar to Luke in 6.8.*]

LORELAI: Well OK, you're 16, you have a whole house to yourself for the evening. I expect that you're going to have your boyfriend over. But what is with the apron?
RORY: It's a long story.
LORELAI: Did it involve a sharp blow to the head?
RORY: I gotta go check on Apricot.
LORELAI: Oh my God! I just saw the pearls.

What I Kept

I kept trying to take the Marc Jacobs coat they had my character wearing, but it didn't work out. I might've gotten away with a pair of hosiery once, by accident, I swear. They're pretty serious about that. "Oh you can just send it back to us in the mail." There was none of that over there.

—Honorine Bell (Lulu)

1.15 Christopher Returns

First aired: March 1, 2001 // Written by Daniel Palladino // Directed by Michael Katleman

It's Christopher's first time in the Hollow, and he certainly gets the full experience. However, when the Haydens and the Gilmores gather for the first time in years, Friday night dinner hits a new low.

GINCHY! Christopher running the gauntlet in Stars Hollow; the uncomfortable meeting between the Haydens and the Gilmores, and Richard's stern defense of his daughter.

NOTES *'He wants things he is not ready for.'*

Lorelai and Christopher have known each other since Lorelai was 6; they both were in his new Porsche when he crashed it two hours after he received it for his 16th birthday. Dean and Luke continue their antagonistic relationship over softball. It's official: Al's Pancake World doesn't serve pancakes. (A pretty confusing town, considering the diner looks like a hardware store.)

Though Straub blames Lorelai for ruining his son's life, Christopher admits to her he never would've gotten through Princeton. It was Christopher who wanted to get married when he first got Lorelai pregnant, and he proposes to her again now, the morning after a quickie on the Gilmore porch.

TODAY'S CELEBRATION Christopher's visit to Stars Hollow and the disastrous Friday night dinner with the Gilmores and the Haydens.

KIRK OF ALL TRADES Softball heckler. (More of a hobby than a vocation.)

AND INTRODUCING...SCHNICKELFRITZ! First used by Lorelai as a name for Christopher's parents.

OY WITH THE ___, ALREADY! Discussion of where and how Rory was conceived (in this case, the porch at the Gilmore home).

AMEN, SISTER FRIEND

RICHARD [*explaining why he defended Lorelai from Straub's abuse*]: A member of my family was being attacked. The very Gilmore name was being attacked. I will not stand for that, not under any circumstances.

Al's Pancake World

Al switched to international cuisine a couple of years back, getting out of pancakes. But as Rory explains to her dad, "He would've changed the name but he had already printed like a million napkins with the original name, so he just kept it."

Bio Keiko Agena (Lane)

When she first showed up for her audition as Rory's best friend, Lane Kim, Keiko Agena was surprised to find that there were "pages and pages" of girls ready to try out. By the time she returned for a callback, it was down to her and just one other girl.

Calling on the inner tranquillity that comes from being an actor who's already employed—she was just finishing her role as Leila Foster on The WB's Keri Russell vehicle *Felicity* at the time—she breezed through her audition and landed the part. OK, she was 26 playing a 16 year old, but no one knew how far that role would take her.

Born in Honolulu, Agena grew up with three younger sisters. She left around 17 to attend Whitman College in Walla Walla, Wash. for a year, before finally alighting in LA in 1992 to visit her boyfriend. Digging what the area's Incline Theatre Group was doing, she never returned to Washington. Of course Whitman had also been running her $22,000 a year, she says. "That was a bit of a deciding factor."

Today, Agena balances her acting career with several creative outlets, including her own line of greeting cards and jewelry called Mango Pop (mangopop.com). Where many actors simply license their names for fragrances or clothes they seldom see, Agena illustrates and writes each card using cute characters with a decidedly dry sense of humor. Though these are primarily sold online, Agena's been known to sell her wares with other local artists throughout Los Angeles. She also continues to play drums (continuing the skill she picked up on *Gilmore Girls*) and bass with several bands including LA's once-a-year group Supper Club, with husband and guitarist extraordinaire Shin Kawasaki. (And based on a May 2010 show the author caught in Japantown, it's safe to say she rocks it!)

LORELAI: OK, well it doesn't really matter why you did it.

RICHARD: Yes it does matter why I did it! It matters greatly! Lorelai, what are you going to take away from this? That everything that happened in the past is suddenly fine because I defended you?

LORELAI: No.

RICHARD: That the hell that you put your mother and I through for the past 16 years is suddenly washed away? Well it's not.

LORELAI: We've all been through hell, dad.

RICHARD: I had to tell my friends, my colleagues, that my only daughter, the brightest in her class, was pregnant and was leaving school.

LORELAI: That must have been devastating.

RICHARD: And then you run away and treat us like lepers. Your mother couldn't get out of bed for a month. Did you know that? Did you?

LORELAI: No.

RICHARD: We did nothing to deserve that. Nothing to earn that!

EMILY: Rory, I know you heard a lot of talk about various disappointments this evening and I know you've heard a lot of talk about it in the past. But I want to make this very clear. You, young lady, your person and your existence, have never, ever been—not even for a second—included in that list.

1.16 Star-Crossed Lovers and Other Strangers

First aired: March 8, 2001 // Teleplay by John Stephens & Linda Loiselle Guzik // Story by Joan Binder Weiss // Directed by Lesli Linka Glatter

Birds do it, bees do it, and from the looks of things, everybody in Connecticut does it. From Tristin and Summer at Chilton to Sookie and Jackson (and even Michel) at the inn, everybody's celebrating love and hormones—even Rachel's back, much to Luke's confusion. Rory is looking forward to her three-month anniversary with Dean, which only leaves Lorelai at a loose end. Emily, however, is ready to fix that.

GINCHY! Chase Bradford, and Richard letting Lorelai sneak out of the house to get away from him; Dean's final surprise and Rory's reaction to his "I love you."

NOTES *'Tonight your daughter is celebrating her three-month anniversary. What was the last relationship you had that lasted that long?'*

It's only been a week since Richard told Lorelai how disappointed in her he is, but clearly he regrets it, letting her sneak away from Chase. Dean's reaction to Rory's inability to reciprocate his love in the junkyard is our first indication of the powder keg lurking just beneath his gentle exterior. Luke's is the first mention of the Founders Day punch, but not the last (5.18).

Though a strong episode, it also reflects the multitude of people credited with its creation (see credits above), and was probably meant to be written by Amy or Dan, or both. The next episode, written by Amy, spends most of its running time bringing us back to the Lorelai and Rory we know.

TODAY'S CELEBRATION Stars Hollow Founders Day festival, complete with annual bonfire. As Rory tells Dean, "This is a town that

Richard's Defining Moment

Though Lorelai's devastation at being yelled at by her father so soon after he defended her is almost palpable, the moment was a defining one for the elder Gilmore, Edward Herrmann says.

"It was the closest Richard ever came to actually explaining why he was so hurt and so angry," he says. "That kind of defined the direction of that intractable problem that was the engine for the rest of the series for me. How does he deal with his disappointment, his anger, his love, that Greek sort of tension? You can't change what happened, but you somehow have to pray that it makes you wiser and not more bitter.

"I think Amy had her finger on that brilliantly. I thought the basic structure of the show Amy built was just wonderful. That scene defined his dilemma with Lorelai."

Little do Dean or Rory suspect how badly their three-month anniversary date will end.

likes the celebrating." And on Friday, Dean and Rory's three-month anniversary.

TAYLOR OF ALL TRADES Recording secretary for the Stars Hollow City Council.

EMILY'S MAID DU JOUR Emily excuses herself to help Leta clean up (!).

"It was really, really hard work putting all that banter together and saying it really fast. Some of my only notes were 'Faster! Faster!' It's very difficult. It was probably the hardest job I've ever had, just for that reason."

-SHELLY COLE (MADELINE)

AMEN, SISTER FRIEND

MISS PATTY: ... So one night, cold and black with no light to guide them, they both snuck out of their homes and ran away as fast as they could. It was so dark out that they were both soon lost and it seemed as if they would never find each other. Finally, the girl dropped to her knees, tears streaming down her lovely face. "Oh, my love. Where are you? How will I find you?" Suddenly, a band of stars appeared in the sky. These stars shone so brightly they lit up the entire countryside. The girl jumped to her feet and followed the path of the stars until finally she found herself standing right where the town gazebo is today. And there, waiting for her, was her one true love, who had also been led here by the blanket of friendly stars. And that, my friends, is the story of how Stars Hollow came to be, and why we celebrate that fateful night every year at about this time. Now, we still have a little time left in our story hour. Who wants to hear about the time I danced in a cage for Tito Puente?

1.17 The Breakup, Part II

First aired: March 15, 2001 // Written by Amy Sherman-Palladino // Directed by Nick Marck

Picking up right where the last episode ended, Rory tells Lorelai that Dean broke up with her for no reason. The next day, she throws herself into her famous lists and getting things done, trying to ignore what's just happened. Rachel is settling in, serving coffee at Luke's. Luke is ready to beat up Dean, and Rory drags Lane to Madeline's party to help her forget everything. Meanwhile, Lorelai realizes she needs to square things with Max one way or the other.

GINCHY! Rory's manic, post-breakup enthusiasm to get things done; Luke's protective instincts toward Rory kicking in; Lorelai having a "Max box"; Jackson attempting to make Sookie dinner; and Tristin and Rory finding common ground.

NOTES *'You need to wallow.'*

The stuffed chicken Dean made fun of (1.7) is named Col. Clucker, has been with Rory since she was 4, and is consigned to Rory's "Dean box." This episode we see a new side to Rory's drive, especially her tunnel vision when it comes to Harvard. Lists and the Ivy League are like prayer beads to the devout, a means of comfort (and in this episode, mania) when times get tough. Paris wants to be a cancer research scientist.

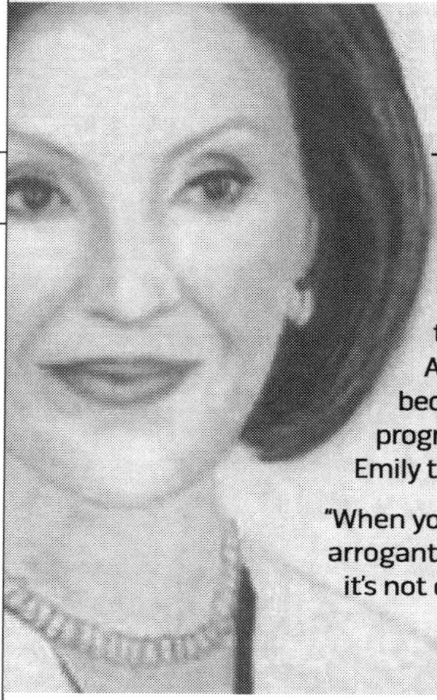

Character Sketch: Getting Into Emily's Head

Though Kelly Bishop says she didn't do too much soul searching about Emily for the first couple of years, "because I was letting the scripts tell me where Amy wanted her to go," it became clearer as the series progressed just what had made Emily the woman she is.

"When you have this kind of arrogant, demanding woman, it's not coming from a place of happiness, it's coming from a very insecure place. Then you think about how humiliated she must've been to have a daughter give birth to a child out of wedlock at the age of 16, what that said about me as a parent and about our family as leaders in the community. It would've been very embarrassing. So I think that the character is walking a tightrope in a sense. The same thing with her affection for her family. Clearly she loves her daughter and loves her granddaughter and loves her husband, but especially when it comes to her daughter, she's so disapproving because Lorelai's not doing it the way it's supposed to be done."

TODAY'S CELEBRATION Madeline's party.

15 YEARS How long Rory has known Lane.

AMEN, SISTER FRIEND

LUKE: Oh God, he's got a nerve. I mean what does he think, he's gonna do better than Rory? Is he crazy? Jeez. All right, well forget it, OK. Good riddance, adios, bien venidos, hasta la vista.
LORELAI: Could we get off the Small World ride and start cooking please?

LANE: Hi, I'm Lane.
LOUISE: As in "walk down a...?"

1.18 The Third Lorelai

First aired: March 22, 2001 // Written by Amy Sherman-Palladino // Directed by Michael Katleman

We finally see Emily faced with her Kryptonite—Richard's mother, Lorelai the First, aka Trix. Rory convinces Tristin to ask Paris out, and may be about to get her karmic reward in the form of a $250,000 trust fund from her grandmother. But a few words from Emily makes Lorelai see that financial independence could destroy her special relationship with her daughter.

GINCHY! Emily's "Stop talking to the dogs"; Rory helping Paris get ready for her date; Lorelai and Emily's inability to find cell phone reception in the tea room.

NOTES *'If she gets that money, Lorelai will never come back here. She won't have to.'*

Ever since *The Brady Bunch*'s "cousin Oliver," nothing has sent shivers up the spine of the American TV viewer more than a character mentioning "so and so's coming for a visit." Fortunately, we end up with the delightful Trix in the form of Marion Ross. And yes, she's made a remarkable recovery from death (1.2).

Trix moved to London after her husband died. She remarks on how tall Lorelai and Rory are, echoing Richard's own comments about Rory on their first Friday night dinner together (1.1). Richard informs Trix that Rory is in the top 10 percent of her class at Chilton. He and his father went to Yale. "I don't care if she demeans me and looks down

Bio ☺ Shelly Cole (Madeline Lynn)

It's rare that you meet an actor who tells you, "I would be OK if I didn't do it for the rest of my life," but Shelly Cole has seen too much to get hung up on Hollywood.

Born in Oklahoma City, OK, Cole spent her first eight years moving around a lot before settling in Texas, "until I was old enough to get the H-E-double-hockey-sticks out of Texas," she says. From there she moved to Seattle for a couple years, hitchhiked across the country, and even ended up in Alaska for six months. "I've always been an adventurous person and tried things; it's kind of kept me alive."

In October 1997 she moved to Los Angeles, acquired an agent almost immediately, and landed a television commercial for Nintendo. In August 2000, her agent sent her to a casting session for the first nonpilot episode of *Gilmore Girls*. She auditioned for casting director Mara Casey and Amy, she recalls. "I left and Mara came after me in the parking lot and said, 'Come back for a second.' They asked me to do it totally differently, just an idea that Amy had. So I did, and the next thing I know, three years go by. You come to LA, you have these stars in your eyes, and you have no idea what the business is about. I got so lucky that I got this as my first job."

Since *Gilmore*, Cole has pursued another passion between jobs: helping children in need. During the 2008 SAG strike, she started volunteering at the Mattel Children's Hospital UCLA in Los Angeles. "My job is to take their mind off of their tumors and their cancer and their plugs and cords and help them forget for a little while. It makes me realize that I've got a pretty darn good life and I'm pretty lucky. And I think lucky people should give back to the world."

Ultimately, she wants to help children deal with their world through acting. "I didn't have the awesomest upbringing. When I stumbled upon acting it was like, wow. I spent most of my childhood feeling really lost. I think eventually I'd like to move away from California and teach acting to kids. I've always had this dream about having this nonprofit program. I know what it meant to me to be able to find expression in acting.

"Funny that Madeline is one of the characters that I'm most remembered for, but I've done some very dark roles. It's really helped me exorcise some demons. I kind of had this dream someday of being able to pass that on."

on me; I don't care if she thinks I've tarnished the Gilmore name," Emily tells Richard, fed up with his mother, foreshadowing a disastrous revelation (4.16).

✱ Though Rory's matchmaking efforts with Paris and Tristin might be a way of working through her own recent breakup with Dean, she seems to be dealing with her loss a little too well.

TODAY'S CELEBRATION The arrival of Trix.

EMILY'S MAID DU JOUR She had Stella wax the floors to prevent Trix from coming in the front door.

12 How old Lorelai was when Trix last visited.

THE FIX IS IN With this episode, we've heard all three of the Gilmore women talk about "fixing" something (the other two times being in 1.14). This time it's Emily, suddenly feeling bad that she's caused Trix to rescind her trust fund offer. She tells Lorelai that she'll call Richard. "He can talk to her. He can fix it. I'll make him fix it!"

AMEN, SISTER FRIEND

LORELAI: Mother, grandma is a very old woman. I highly doubt that she's going to remember everything she ever bought you.
EMILY: She will remember down to the very last shrimp fork, and do you know why?
LORELAI: No. [*To the dog statues*] Do you guys know why?
EMILY: Because she doesn't just give you a present, she *gives* you a present. And she tells you where to put it, how to use it, what it costs—for insurance purposes, of course. And God forbid you should have a different opinion or you don't think it works in the space or you just get tired of waking up every morning with those horrifying animals staring at you!
LORELAI: [*To the dog statues*] She's just upset.
EMILY: Stop talking to the dogs!

TRIX: Well perhaps our presence in the dining room will teach your help that when one is told dinner is at 7:00, people often expect dinner at 7:00.
EMILY: But it's only five after, Mom.
TRIX: Only five after? Richard, in the event that I am kidnapped and a ransom is demanded at a certain time, I would prefer that Emily not be in charge of the drop-off.

"It's funny because I meet people and it's like, 'You're Gypsy!' And I start talking and they look at me and they're like, 'Oh, maybe you're not.' I decided Gypsy was of indeterminate origin; we didn't ever pick the country where she really came from."

—ROSE ABDOO

1.19 Emily in Wonderland

First aired: April 26, 2001 // Written by John Stephens and Linda Loiselle Guzik // Directed by Perry Lang

Rune, Lorelai's lovable blind date (1.12), is staying with Jackson after losing his job and his home. Sookie convinces Lorelai to put him up in the old potting shed behind the inn that she and Rory lived in when they first came to Stars Hollow. Little does anybody realize how much trouble that shed will cause when Emily finally sees where her daughter chose to live all those years ago. Lane is waiting to hear from

Henry, and Rachel is desperate to convince Luke she's in it for the long haul this time...or is she? Lorelai's love life might be in the toilet and her mother may be driving her crazy, but she is determined to concentrate on the one goal that seems most within reach: her own inn.

! GINCHY! Rory showing Emily around Stars Hollow, particularly her nostalgic description of the shed; the room Emily comes up with for Rory.

Bio Yanic Truesdale (Michel Gerard)

Born in Montreal, Yanic (*YahNEEK*) Truesdale was raised by a mother who was deeply into the arts, from painting and photography to having her own clothing line. "So I was raised very free, very open-minded, and my mom's vision of things is, 'You can do anything in life as long as you're happy,'" he says. But she was never one for theater or film.

As a result, being an actor was never anything that appealed to him until he found himself drawn into it during his last year of high school. One of his classmates was applying to acting school and asked him if he'd be her scene partner. "She never got accepted," he says. "But I got accepted."

The first time we see the Independence Inn's Michel Gerard, he's fobbing off a prospective guest over the phone with a bored, self-important, "No, I'm sorry, completely booked." You wouldn't think to look at him that the dapper, self-assured looking Truesdale had only been learning English over the last two years.

In 1998, he left Montreal to study at the Lee Strasberg Theatre & Film Institute in New York. In French-speaking Quebec, he'd already made something of a name for himself on television, including on the region's extremely popular series about a Quebec hockey team, *Lance et compte* (*He Shoots, He Scores*). He was actually taking a year off from a sitcom when he went to New York. "I basically learned my English there that year, and then the first year in LA, but it was pretty bad."

Actually, he was in Los Angeles 11 months in 1999 before he landed the role that would make him famous the world over. But those 11 months were a real wake-up call for an actor who was used to being a "name" in his native Montreal.

Toward the end of his first year in LA, Truesdale finally managed to sign with an agent in the valley "who no one had ever heard of." Shortly after that, someone he'd met with when he'd first come to town called him to say he'd booked Truesdale an audition for *Gilmore Girls* because he sounded right for the part. "Basically that was my first audition. I went in and I got it."

Right away, the actor had his work cut out for him. Like everybody else on the show, he was required to get his lines out exactly as written. However, he was the only actor required to do so through a thick accent. "I would often argue that a French-speaking person wouldn't use this word or that word—it was too sophisticated, too complicated, too hard to pronounce."

While he'd come up with an accent for his audition that was closer to an authentic French accent, Amy was concerned that the audience wouldn't be able to understand what was being said. The accent he ended up using was certainly not French, "but I guess to an American ear, it probably sounded fine," Truesdale says. "But it bugged me for a long, long time."

NOTES *'You had to take that little girl away. That was bad enough. But to that? To live there, in a shed, like a hobo?'*

Perhaps Michel and Emily have more in common than their tormenting of Lorelai.

* Lorelai burned all of her baby pictures when she was 7 after years of hearing how her head was unusually large. Rory tells Emily about Kim's Antiques, not only creating a compelling reason for her to spend some time in Stars Hollow, but also perpetuating the idea that Lane's parents (plural) own the store. Rachel's only recently developed the photos from the "firelight" festival (1.16); she shows Lorelai a picture of the old Dragonfly Inn, the first we see or hear of it (behind the mill and over the footbridge).

* Lorelai tells Rachel that the idea of owning her own inn has only been with her for the last couple of years, though she will lengthen that considerably later (4.22). Rory takes Emily to Teriyaki Joe's, which we never hear about again. Rachel calls Lorelai up to Luke's apartment above the diner to see her pictures of the Dragonfly Inn; this is the first time Lorelai's ever been up there. Luke facetiously tells Lorelai that he's "thinking of conquering the flower shop next door and expanding the freezer." He will actually buy the entire building next season (2.15) to prevent Taylor from acquiring that same flower shop.

TODAY'S CELEBRATION Rachel gets one of Luke's sock drawers!

AMEN, SISTER FRIEND

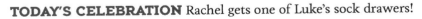

EMILY: As a child, your mother had an unusually large head.
LORELAI: The best thing about it was that she would tell me constantly. My first complete sentence was, "Big head want dolly."
RORY: I can't imagine it being that bad.
EMILY: It wasn't. It just affected her balance a little so. . .

LORELAI [*After agreeing to hire Rune*]: But I swear to God Sookie, the minute the guests start complaining or disappearing, he's out of there.

RORY [*to Emily about the potting shed*]: I know it looks small, but it's really pretty. Come on. See, we had our bed right over there, and mom put up this really pretty curtain around the tub so that it looked like a real bathroom. And we would just sit outside at night when the inn would have parties and we'd just listen to music and feed the ducks...

EMILY [*on the phone to Rory*]: N'Sync or 98 degrees?
RORY [*to Lane*]: Uh, N'Sync or 98 degrees?
LANE: What kind of sick joke is this?
RORY [*to Emily*]: I don't think I could choose.
EMILY: What about that other group? The Backside Boys?
RORY: You mean the Backstreet Boys?

1.20 PS I Lo...

First aired: May 3, 2001 // Written by Elaine Arata & Joan Binder Weiss // Directed by Lev L. Spiro

Poor Rory. She's still avoiding Dean, but Lane's been seeing him behind her back as her partner for science class. Her mother's been talking regularly with Max and is set to go out on a date with him, without telling her. Overwhelmed, she blows up at Lorelai and flees to Richard and Emily's. When Lorelai discovers the reason Dean and Rory broke up, she realizes it really is "like mother, like daughter."

Making an Episode 3 — The Writing Day Begins

Few people on a television show work straight through the hours that they're on the lot. Writers are pretty much confined to the writers room the entire time, trying to hammer out large plot points and tiny scene details destined to be rewritten by the showrunner, especially if that showrunner has as unique a voice as Amy.

"The room work was so intense and focused that it was difficult to get away for other appointments," writer Jane Espenson says. "Of course, this was nothing compared to sitcom hours, which often extend late into the night and early morning. Both Amy and I come from that world; these hours were very humane by comparison."

Writers start filling the room shortly before 10; Dan (beginning with Season 2) is usually there, and sometimes Amy, in preparation for "breaking" the episode, where the scenes are assembled and placed in the right order. "It's the best seat in the house," says *Gilmore Girls* casting-assistant-turned-writers-assistant (Season 4) Alison Goodman. "You get to sit in the room with the writers and listen to everything they say: funny, stupid, boring, great, amazing."

GINCHY! The "1-2-3" game; Lorelai buying Luke new clothes; Rory's face-off with Lorelai; Richard offering Rory a cocktail in a moment of confusion; Lorelai counseling Rory on being able to love, and her follow-through on promising Max to tell everybody they're back together.

NOTES *'I would hate to think that I raised a kid who couldn't say I love you.'* Max and Lorelai have been chatting regularly on the phone for two or three weeks. Rory's keeping track of where Dean *isn't* at any given time in a little notebook.

Though this episode has the slight flavor of a "shoe leather" episode meant to walk us to the next phase of the relationship between Lorelai and Rory, there's no questioning how effective it is. Dean finally gets some vindication, Lorelai discovers that not everything she's taught Rory has been for the best, and even the little screen time that Emily and Richard receive is effective, and as always, welcome.

TODAY'S CELEBRATION Rory's meltdown, and Lorelai and Max getting back together.

EMILY'S MAID DU JOUR Rosa.

AND HERE'S A SHOUT OUT TO OUR INTERNATIONAL FANS RICHARD: He tacked on an extra $5 just for waiting. Feel like I'm back in Prague.

YOU'VE ENTERED EMILYLAND [*to Richard*] "Oh, you're a mind reader now, how nice. We'll get you a turban and a little booth by the train station.

'A MOTHER WOULDN'T DO THIS' Initially, there were many TV viewers who didn't sit well with the whole mother-daughter friendship dynamic. They'd seen clueless mom's try this tactic in real life, and it seldom ended well. As it turned out, Amy received a lot of pushback from the network for the same reason. "In the beginning, there was a lot of 'On *Dawson's Creek* we do things this way,'" Amy told The New York Times in January 2005. "On the relationship between Rory and Lorelai, I got a lot of notes early on about motherness. 'A mother wouldn't do this.' And I said, 'This mother would.'... They're used to mothers saying, 'That's

"Because most of the stuff on TV is pretty bad, I'm really glad that Gilmore still has a following and people are still talking about it and are still jazzed about it. I can't believe it, but they are."

-EMILY KURODA (MRS. KIM)

right and that's wrong,' and Lorelai doesn't do that because she's still trying to figure out what's right and what's wrong herself."

AMEN, SISTER FRIEND

LORELAI: OK, you've been in this mood for a week now and while I love the unexpected ups and downs of motherhood, I've got to say I'm tired of Goofus and I'd like my Gallant back.
RORY: You can't just say a normal sentence, right? Just 'Hey, let's talk' is too dull for you.

EMILY [*to Rory, after she shows up at the Gilmore mansion, right before Richard and Emily are meant to leave for a boring event*]: Everything's going to be fine. Richard, say something encouraging.
RICHARD: Uh Rory, I'm sorry you're upset but I applaud your timing.

DEAN: You know, I am sick and tired of everyone blaming this thing on me. I mean, you and the whole stupid town looking at me like I'm a criminal. I say 'I love you' and she just sits there and I'm the jerk? I'm the bad guy?

Bio Scott Cohen (Max Medina)

Scott Cohen learned many things during his short time on *Gilmore Girls*, especially the power of "no."

Cohen was approached by Amy for three different episodes of the series. At the time, he wasn't really interested in doing television at all. "I remember my agent was telling me that Amy Sherman-Palladino is desperate to have me on her show. I was kind of like, 'I don't really know how she knows who I am; why does she want me so badly? It doesn't sound like a show that I'm really interested in.'"

They sent him the pilot episode, which he was very impressed by. "But I kept on saying no, and they kept on raising the money, and I kept on saying no, and they kept on raising the money, and then finally I said yes. And that was it."

Cohen's always suspected it was Lauren Graham who first sold Amy on him. Once he saw how Amy worked, creating this odd little world of Stars Hollow, they became great friends, and remain so to this day.

Born in the Bronx, Scott Cohen broke into the acting world via clowning, and still wonders how he got there. While studying acting in New York, he held many jobs—waiter, bike messenger, photographer's assistant, toy seller. In his early 20s, he fell into substitute teaching, before landing his first big film role in 1990's *Jacob's Ladder*. However, it was his role as the man-wolf in the NBC fantasy miniseries *The 10th Kingdom* in 2000 that cemented Cohen's fanbase worldwide.

"I had always acted and I had always had fun doing it, but never really thought of it as a 'career,'" he says. "I seriously think to myself now, '*is* this really a career?'"

LORELAI [*to Rory*]: You know, I'm still learning this stuff, too, and since I'm still learning, I think I haven't thought enough about what I'm supposed to be teaching you.

1.21 Love, Daisies & Troubadours

First aired: May 10, 2001// Written by Daniel Palladino // Directed by Amy Sherman-Palladino

Luke is spending every spare moment repairing things around Lorelai's house, and not hanging around Rachel. Rory wants to get back together with Dean, but Tristin has his heart set on her—cue Paris conniption fit. Lorelai and Max are fighting again, which prompts a last grand gesture.

GINCHY! Rory going to Dean's house and freaking out his sister, Clara, and her thinly veiled defense of the Troubadour in the town meeting; Rachel warning Luke not to wait too long to tell Lorelai how he feels; Dean having a Rory box; the final few seconds as Lorelai and Rory meet to share their news.

NOTES *'Big things. Big, potentially life-changing things.'*

The beginning of this one is like trying to watch an over-loaded commuter jet take off. Luke tells Lorelai that having Rachel back has only proved to him how much of a loner he is. "Maybe you have to lower your expectation bar a little bit," she tells him, only to fall prey to similar doubts herself at the beginning of Season 2. Troubadour No. 2 runs a Kinko's copy shop in Groton, Conn. To get off the subject of troubadours at the town meeting, Taylor designates the Troubadour as the official one for Stars Hollow.

We get our first mention of Ceaser (Rachel says she sent him home early), but we won't actually see him until much later (3.6, played by Christopher Grey, and 3.20 by Aris Alvarado). Luke's little confrontation with Max is our first glimpse of his obnoxious jealousy, which will flare up with Dean, and ultimately lead to a punch-up with Christopher (7.10).

Although there's always been a feeling among fans and *Gilmore Girls* writers alike that you throw Kirk into a scene when you're not sure what else to do, his delivery of the daisies is not one of those occasions. This begins Kirk's "loneliness arc," leading to his bidding on

Day of the Troubadour

Though we've seen him around the Hollow since "That Damn Donna Reed" (1.14), the Troubadour came into his own this episode with his light-hearted feud with a rival troubadour (Dave "Gruber" Allen). The producers had originally planned to get English singer-songwriter Robyn Hitchcock for the role of the Troubadour's rival, Grant-Lee Phillips says. "He and I are pals and we had been touring together, and they thought this will be great." Yet Hitchcock was in England at the time and couldn't get away. That's when he suggested Allen. Having performed often at Phillips' own long-time LA venue, Largo, Allen developed a comic persona there called "The Naked Trucker," who regularly sings humorous songs wearing little more than a hat, boots and his guitar. The Naked Trucker had also opened for Phillips' former band, Grant Lee Buffalo, in the mid-1990s. When Allen showed up in Stars Hollow, "that worked out pretty great. I knew him arriving there, and quickly made friends with all these new faces, too."

Lorelai's two worlds collide when Max meets Luke.

Sookie's basket (2.13), and finally his asking Lorelai out on a date (3.2). Of course, once we see how he treats Lulu, we understand why he's been so lonely for so long.

For the second time this season we get a reference to a pet called Skippy (1.11), this time Paris suggesting a dog called Skippy might have had her puppies on the clothes Rory loaned to her for her date with Tristin. Paris has just been named editor of The Franklin.

TODAY'S CELEBRATION Max's proposal, and Dean and Rory reunite.

KIRK OF ALL TRADES Daisy delivery guy.

OY WITH THE ___, ALREADY! Max and Lorelai discussing the type of dating they did. Too much information! And once again, quit working "Gilmore girl" into the dialogue.

JOHNNY McSHORT-AND-FAT Rory's suggestion for the name of the guy who owned the Hewes Bros. garage before Maven Hewes, a name that sounds suspiciously similar to Maybin Hewes, Amy's mom.

5 WEEKS How long it's been since Rory and Dean broke up.

6 MONTHS How long the Troubadour has been fulfilling this role in Stars Hollow.

AMEN, SISTER FRIEND

LORELAI [*explaining to Rory why she didn't throw her Dean box away*]: ... You're gonna want that stuff one day when you're old and married and looking back and thinking, 'I certainly had an interesting life.' And then you can pull out all your old boyfriend boxes. Which is good, because I threw away stuff I'd kill to have today. Look, I put it in with the Max box so they could chat and keep each other company and commiserate about how they had a Gilmore girl and lost a Gilmore girl...

LORELAI: You have crossed over into the dark side, Luke. [Just how long do you think they'd been waiting to use that *Star Wars* reference?]

LORELAI [*to Max about how a proposal should go*]: No, it has to be planned. It should be magical. There should be music playing and romantic lighting and a subtle buildup to the popping of the big question. There should be a thousand yellow daisies and candles and a horse, and I don't know what the horse is doing there unless you're riding it, which seems a little over the top, but it should be more than this.

The End...or the Beginning?

Despite the critical praise *Gilmore Girls* received in the US throughout its first season, the writers and producers had faced the age-old dilemma of not knowing if their show would be picked up for another season until well into this one.

This season had done admirably in the ratings scramble, averaging about 3.6 million US viewers per episode, with the season finale bagging a respectable 4.1 million. For comparison, one of the best-rated episodes of *Friends* from the same year ("The One After 'I Do'") attracted nearly 32 million viewers. As the 2004 *MADtv* spoof *Gabmore Girls* would observe, "Number 92 in the ratings, but that's Number 1 for The WB."

Flower Power

Though Scott Cohen saw them bring all of those daisies on set ("I was in awe of how many flowers were actually in the studio") and start to arrange them, he went back to New York before they shot Lorelai's discovery of them at the inn. Shortly after the season finale aired, he found himself in New York, this time performing on stage.

"There were about 150 or 200 members of my fan club who came to see this play in New York and they all brought yellow daisies with them," he says. "After the show ended, they all threw their daisies up on the stage, and I wasn't even the star of the play."

"I Can't Get Started"

season **two**

Gilmore Girls had experienced the best first season it could've hoped for. Though its I-Can't-Believe-it's-a-Network network and the intensity of its dialogue guaranteed that it would only ever enjoy niche popularity, critical acclaim and strong word-of-mouth had made a second season possible.

Having proved its mettle the previous season by squaring off against the likes of *Survivor* and *Friends*, *Gilmore Girls* was moved to Tuesday nights. "The fact that *Gilmore Girls* beat *Friends* in female teens this May sweep and is building Emmy buzz has been extremely gratifying for a freshman series," Jordan Levin said in a press release at the time.

"When they moved it from that time slot to Tuesday night, the show really picked up," Polone says.

The cast and crew of *Gilmore Girls* spent their entire first season digging in and hoping they wouldn't be canceled. Now it seemed they might be here to stay. The first sign? Bye bye to the *Gilmore Girls* trailer park.

"The first season we were all in trailers, so we had this dinky trailer that we worked out of, and Amy & Dan had another trailer next to us," casting director Jami Rudofsky recalls. "The second season, they're like, 'We're moving you to new offices.' And we got *real* offices."

Amy, too, got a real office—more a pink-and-red boudoir, complete with a large cardboard cutout of *Angel* star David Boreanaz and a (now) official creative partner in Dan. He'd proved his writing ability during the first season; now he shared the title of executive producer.

The trust and respect between husband and wife had been apparent from the start. Though Amy would always garner the most attention on *Gilmore*, Dan would often run the writers room when she was attending to something else, and she inevitably backed up any decisions he made. It's telling that the only DVD commentary available (for Season Five's "You Jump, I Jump, Jack") begins with the pair of them yacking away, and ends with Dan wrapping it up on his own, several minutes after Amy has inexplicably disappeared from the recording session.

2.1 Sadie, Sadie...

First aired: Oct. 9, 2001 // Written and directed by Amy Sherman-Palladino

Lane's being shipped off to Korea for an indefinite stay, Lorelai's said yes to Max, and Rory's high marks at Chilton are the subject of a special dinner at her grandparents' house. But an unexpected dinner guest creates a huge rift between parents, grandparents and each other.

! GINCHY! The way Lorelai lets Rory know she said yes to Max, and Emily and Richard's reactions; Jackson fleeing in terror from the kitchen on hearing Lorelai is engaged; Emily learning of Lorelai's engagement and her terse talk with Richard right after.

NOTES *'Dad looks at you... and has a terrible Lorelai flashback.'*

* Lane is still going on about her very plural parents, informing Rory that the two of them were in their room plotting.

* Rory's finished in the top 3 percent of her class at Chilton. Sookie's reference to the musical *Funny Girl* ("Sadie, Sadie, married lady...") will be echoed in Season 7 when Christopher makes it the focus of his romantic drive-in movie gesture (7.4). (It also happened to be one of Graham's favorite musicals growing up.) Both times it is an evocation of something close to Lorelai's heart in a situation she knows is wrong. This time she will avoid making a big mistake, next time she won't be so lucky.

The ugly scene that takes place between Dean and the rest of the Gilmore clan is painful to watch, but also a great leap forward for the series. If Rory is indeed on the "hero's journey" (as will come up tangentially in the Joseph Campbell references in 4.17), she's now broken away from the second of the three pillars that have kept her a child (let's not forget her handling of Emily in 1.6.). Rory will split with Lorelai in Season 5. She will also get a good taste of Dean's humiliation when she meets Logan's family (5.19). Emily ordering Richard to apologize to Rory after discovering Lorelai's engagement *makes* this episode. There is the feeling that this was meant to be a season finale rather than a season opener, which has a lot to do with its power.

OY WITH THE ___, ALREADY! Bootsy. Sorry Boots, but you're just not Stars Hollow. And the phrase "Gilmore girl" ("Well Dean, all I can say is that tonight you officially became a Gilmore girl"). Nothing is as jarringly uncool as namechecking your own show.

What I Kept

I have all my scripts.

—Scott Cohen
(Max Medina)

Behind the Scenes
Heart Troubles

Even in Stars Hollow, reality has a way of intruding. While all of Stars Hollow hit the town center to celebrate the forthcoming nuptials of Lorelai and Max on screen, things were not nearly so wonderful just off camera.

From the first days of *Gilmore Girls* right up until a couple of years before it ended, the series had been a close studio lot neighbor to ABC's hit *The Drew Carey Show*. With the exception of the show's star, most of the actors from that sitcom would hang around the *Gilmore Girls* wardrobe trailer between rehearsals.

However, one August night in 2001, the *Drew Carey* folks were nowhere to be seen, recalls key set costumer Valerie Campbell. "I think their entire crew had wrapped and gone home and they were rewriting some script pages or going over some notes or something." Campbell and Brenda Maben were busy getting a few little girls into their dresses for their night scene on the bench with Scott Patterson.

All of the sudden, an ambulance pulls up and carries Drew Carey out on a stretcher. Carey had been suffering from chest pains that night and later underwent an angioplasty and stent insertion.

"It was really surreal," Campbell says. "Luckily he was OK, but at the time nobody within our group said anything. It was this really odd 'Okaaaay.'"

TODAY'S CELEBRATION Rory landing in the top 3 percent of her class. And let the ritual humiliation of Dean commence.

EMILY'S MAID DU JOUR Antonia, maker of homemade Beefaroni and Twinkies.

HYUNG-HYUNG Lane's Korean name.

AMEN, SISTER FRIEND

RICHARD: You know, when I was 10 years old, I knew exactly where I wanted to work.
LORELAI: That's because you were always picked last for dodgeball.
RICHARD: I knew I wanted to go to Yale and put on a nice suit every day and be a very important man in a very powerful firm. And I knew I wanted to travel and see the world.

Behind the Scenes: The Big One

Cast and crew were still tackling the season premiere when news reports began coming in from the opposite coast on Sept. 11, 2001.

"I was about to go to the set when 9/11 happened," remembers Scott Cohen, who lived in New York City with his family about 10 blocks from the World Trade Center. That day, his wife and son were in the city. For all the long hours that the cast regularly put in, for all the pains that were taken to deliver every line spot on, the producers halted it all when they realized that one of their own was being swept up in this event.

"They were so amazing to me," Cohen says. "I mean the entire day, it was as if they got all of Warner Brothers to break through communications systems to get me on the phone with my wife and my son. They made sure that I had contact with them, they made sure that I was OK, they made sure that they were going to get me home as quickly as they could. They were like, 'We don't need to shoot anything, let's just get you home. We'll get you on the first flight.'"

Only later would Cohen discover that his wife had seen the doomed planes fly overhead, and his son, who attended a school 15 blocks from the World Trade Center, saw the toppling of the towers.

Back in Burbank, the producers were trying to get Cohen on the Warner Brothers corporate jet so that he could go home and be with his family. By this time, however, nearly every American aircraft had been grounded by the FAA.

"It was one of the only times in my life that I just felt like these people really, really care," Cohen says. "It might not have just been about me. I'm sure it was about 9/11 and everybody needed to come together."

Cohen was no stranger to the absurd feeling that actors sometimes experience, when the fantasy world in which they exist overlaps uncomfortably with reality, but this...

"I was living in this fantasy world of Stars Hollow while I'm watching on TV the World Trade Center being destroyed."

EMILY: I want you to call Rory tomorrow and apologize.

RICHARD: What?

EMILY: I want you to call her and tell her you're sorry. That you weren't feeling well and you think that Dean is a lovely boy and he's welcome here anytime.

RICHARD: Have you gone insane? Under no circumstance will I–

EMILY: Our daughter is getting married. She's getting married and she didn't tell us. When Rory decides to get married, I'd like her to tell us. Call her tomorrow.

2.2 Hammers and Veils

First aired: Oct. 9, 2001 // Written by Amy Sherman-Palladino // Directed by Michael Katleman

While Richard has made peace with Rory, Emily is freezing Lorelai out, barely registering the news of Lorelai's engagement when she hears it. Rory suddenly discovers that she's behind on extracurricular activities and panics Rory-style. It all ends with a Stars Hollow extravaganza that feels just the tiniest bit hollow.

GINCHY! The girly hammer Lorelai gives Rory; Lorelai's imitation of Dean pining for her; Luke sitting down by the little girls at the engagement party; and Emily and Lorelai's final scene together.

NOTES *'There's nothing like a family to screw up a family.'*

Lorelai's getting married in three months, putting the date at the beginning of January (presumably after Max's return from his University of Toronto gig). She also mentions that she gave her parents her address when she moved out, which puts Emily's earlier comments about how terrible Lorelai was for running away with Rory in a new light. Her parents knew where to find her if they really wanted to be a part of their lives.

Paris says she'll have a life after graduating from Harvard, a worldview that will prove devastating later (3.16). Lorelai hits Emily with both barrels on her inability to keep a maid, including the wonderful line "these are women from countries that have dictatorships and civil wars and death squads, and all of that they survived, but five minutes working for Emily Gilmore and people are begging for Castro." The next time the subject of Emily and repressive regimes comes up (5.21), it won't be quite so private.

"I remember the first episode I did, which was the Habitat for Humanity thing, they wouldn't let me use the power saw. I did have a saw in my hand and I was sawing a piece of wood, but I thought it was so ridiculous that a power saw was sitting right there. It was probably because Alexis was coming up to talk to me. They didn't care about me, I was a day player, but they didn't want any chips flying at her."

–BIFF YEAGER (TOM)

[*] Jackson's "I'm not ready for marriage" freakout is the first of many future explosions over pivotal moments in his life, especially where it concerns their future children. Once more Emily reminds Lorelai that she has a big head (1.19).

TODAY'S CELEBRATION Max & Lorelai's engagement party.

EMILY'S MAID DU JOUR Marina.

1,500 How many calories Michel allows himself daily.

PARIS' VOLUNTEERING TRACK RECORD SINCE THE FOURTH GRADE

—Handed out cookies at the local children's hospital

—Led study groups

—Was a camp counselor

—Organized a senior illiteracy program

—Worked a suicide hotline

—Volunteered at a runaway center

—Adopted dolphins

—Taught sign language

—Trained seeing-eye dogs.

AMEN, SISTER FRIEND

EMILY [*responding to Lorelai's wedding news*]: Well, I think that's very nice. I certainly hope we'll be in town for it, but if not I promise we'll send a nice gift. Now excuse me, I'm going to check on the roast.

LUKE: Well, there's nothing like a wedding to screw up a family.
LORELAI: Actually, in my case, there's nothing like a family to screw up a family.

LUKE: And then after all that planning, the reception will still be a disaster because no matter what you do or how carefully you plan, halfway through one of those nauseating Bette Midler ballads, someone's getting drunk, someone's sleeping with someone else's wife, and someone's chicken kiev is landing on the cake.

What I Kept

I have a beach cruiser, and Warner Brothers had painted it for me. You know on old-school motor bikes you have a plate in there with your name on it? A whole bunch of them made a nameplate for me and painted it. One guy cut the metal, another guy put holes in it, another guy painted it. It was a really, really sweet gift from those guys. It says "Tanc," and underneath it is an army tank, and on the back of it hangs an Australian flag. That was a really sweet thing for them to do. I still ride it now. That bike means more to me than my Corolla, that's for sure. I live in Venice [Calif.], so it's really cruisy around here. I ride my beach cruiser everywhere with a little basket on the back. I buy my groceries, I go down to the farmers market and just kind of hang out. I probably spend as much time on the cruiser as I do in my car.

—Tanc Sade
(Finn)

Making an Episode 4 'Breaking' an Episode

Frequently, Amy and the writers will chew over ideas for individual scenes, big picture possibilities, and even things completely unrelated to the episode that might someday be useful in another story arc. The writers assistant's job: Get it all down in their laptop.

"It's almost like transcribing six people talking at the same time about insignificant stuff and the most important stuff, and trying to figure out what that is, and keeping it in some kind of story format," explains writers assistant Alison Goodman.

Meanwhile, Amy, like a medium channeling spirits that only she can see, is actually speaking in the voices of the individual *Gilmore Girls* characters. "And I don't mean like Seth MacFarlane," Goodman says, referring to the voice actor famous for the cartoon *Family Guy*. (MacFarlane actually turns up as Lorelai's annoying fellow college graduate Zach in 2.21.) "But you know who she is when she's speaking. And it's typing as fast as that woman talks in conversation. She'll have Emily and Lorelai conversations, then she'll say, 'Read it back to me!' And I'm like, 'Oh shit!'"

Over the course of several hours, five or six whiteboards in the room—they are on wheels so you can turn them around and write on both sides—will be completely filled in Dan's inch-tall writing as everybody pitches their ideas for how an episode should go. It's the lion's den, everything's fair game: the writers' personal relationships, childhood traumas—one writer's night terrors are even given to Kirk (4.22).

Once the "big picture" of the episode's been worked out on the whiteboards and the writers assistant's copied it all down in their laptop, the boards are erased, refilled this time with every detail about the episode they all can think of, writer Janet Leahy says.

"The show was built on small details which linked the characters' lives, and the lion's share of these details were pitched in the room. We would fill nearly six boards with the smallest of writing. If anyone came in from the outside, it looked a little insane. But once those details were in place, it made the outline enormously easy to type up.... No story point was missing from the boards, and some dialogue was on there as well."

By this time, Amy has returned to the writers room, where whoever has been chosen to write that episode (or the co-producer if this is an episode that Amy or Dan is to write) will use the whiteboards to orally pitch Amy the story, Leahy says.

"She has a tremendous ear and could hear if a story was working or not, and had an amazing knack for coming up with quick solutions. It was also very helpful for the writers to get up and pitch an entire episode, something I believe helped prepare writers to go to the networks and pitch their own pilots."

One of Amy's greatest talents, Goodman says, is being able to glance at the whiteboards and see which acts are not working in an episode. "She could look at it like it was a puzzle and see what was missing. She would say, 'We're missing a beat in Act 3—let's have Taylor come in.'"

***Gilmore* writers (left to right) Jane Espenson, Janet Leahy and Sheila R Lawrence.**

RORY [*to Dean, about bailing on the book sale*]: We can get a pizza and go on Amazon. You'll be just as bored watching me ordering books, I promise.

RORY: I can't hang out or kick back. I need to find a retarded kid and teach him how to play softball. Oh God, listen to me, I am horrible. I am under-qualified and horrible.

LORELAI: I don't know how to tell you things Mom. I don't know if you've noticed this or not, but we don't communicate very well. When something good happens to me, I'm just afraid you're gonna make me feel bad about it. And when something bad happens to me, I'm always afraid you'll say, 'I told you so.' I'm not sure if that's always fair, and I'm sure I share part of the blame for this circle we get into, but you think your words don't have any effect on me, but they do.

2.3 Red Light on the Wedding Night

First aired: Oct. 16, 2001 // Written by Daniel Palladino // Directed by Gail Mancuso

As much as Lorelai wants to be excited by her approaching wedding, she's just not feeling it. To be fair, even Dean has a better insight into Lorelai than her husband-to-be. Meanwhile, Taylor Doose is working his magic, bringing Stars

Behind the Scenes Stars Hollow: Every Day a Celebration

For a small town snuggly under the iron-fisted rule of Taylor Doose and a network of gossips, Stars Hollow sure does know how to kick up its heels. Whether it's Revolutionary War reenactments or townwide wedding celebrations, if you turn on an episode of *Gilmore Girls*, it's bound to be one where the inhabitants are in a celebratory mood.

"Every festival scene was fun," says key set costumer Valerie Campbell. "You just never knew what was going to happen when you got to set, how amazing it was going to look."

"I just thought it was such a sweet little make believe town," Keiko Agena says. "How did this little town have so much money to throw a festival every week? I loved all our strange excuses to decorate the town."

Just as the fictional Stars Hollow had its bout with the pickle stench problem, parts of Midwest Street on the Warner Brothers lot had its own little olfactory challenges from time to time. The year that assistant director trainee Mindee Clem Forman was there, they had gotten in fake pumpkins for the area's fall festival. "The year before, they'd gotten all these pumpkins to be around for the Stars Hollow autumn festival and they had all rotted; the stench was kind of overpowering."

Regardless of what was being celebrated, if it was a festival in Stars Hollow, especially at night, you could bet that the icing on the cake would always be the gazebo.

Says Rose Abdoo, "When they used to put all of the little lights around it for the winter festivals, or festoon it with fall leaves, it was so beautiful."

Hollow its first traffic light, a sign of things to come.

GINCHY! Rory suggesting a quote from Mussolini ("We have buried the putrid corpse of liberty") for the wedding program, and Lorelai loving it; Dean imparting his wisdom about the girls to Max; the crosswalk with its big yellow button; Emily's memories of her pre-wedding jitters and the effect it has on her fellow party people; Max telling Lorelai what everybody else is thinking ("You need to think about someone other than yourself for a few minutes a day"); the scene of Luke and Lorelai standing silently under the chuppah; and the girls stuck at the stoplight.

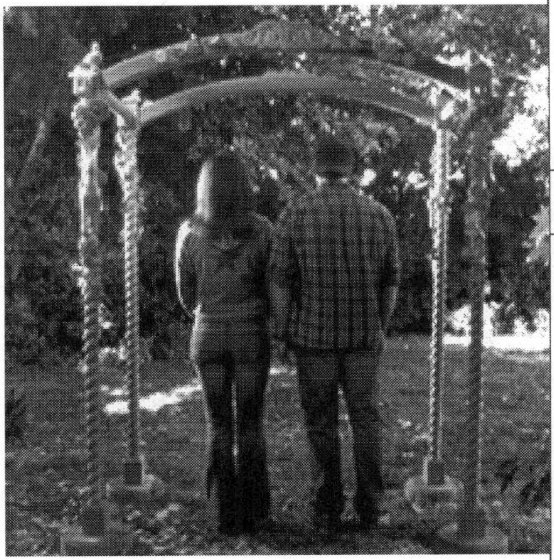

Luke and Lorelai take a moment to live in the moment.

NOTES *'It won't just be the 'me and you secret special clubhouse no boys allowed' thing anymore.'*

We can already see that this marriage is doomed—the girls are only just now bringing Max in on one of their movie nights. Leave it to Dean to be the voice of experience here.

Lorelai's bachelorette party takes place a week before the wedding. Miss Patty's married three men, but has married four times. Emily married Richard 34 years ago. Michel ends up sitting at a table with a drag queen Celine Dion, our first glimpse into his Celine fixation.

Another "shoe leather" episode designed to get us from point A to B, yet one with a few excellent scenes. We've known this was coming, Lorelai's known it was coming, and even Max has gotten a clue by now. Watching the collapse of the Max/Lorelai relationship is akin to having a tooth pulled.

TODAY'S CELEBRATION Dean and Rory's getting-back-together anniversary, and the installation of Stars Hollow's first traffic light and metered crosswalk. And arguably, Lorelai's liberation.

AND HERE'S A SHOUT OUT TO OUR INTERNATIONAL FANS

RORY [*to Lorelai, who's woken her up to ask her what she's doing*]: Taking back Poland.

LUKE [*about Taylor's traffic light putsch*]: It's like Hitler's Germany.

SOOKIE [*about Rory, confirming that she's a model to get her into an over-18 bar*]: She's very big in Germany.

SCHNICKELFRITZ ALERT! Michel's being one at Lorelai's bachelorette party.

AND INTRODUCING... ***The chuppah*** The wooden archway thing Luke built for the wedding will be around for a little while to come.

AMEN, SISTER FRIEND

DEAN [*explaining the Gilmore rules to Max*]: Oh yeah. Like don't ever use the last of the Parmesan cheese. And never get into a heavy discussion late at night 'cause that's when they're at their crankiest. Oh, and uh, go with their bits.
MAX: Their bits?
DEAN: Yeah, like if you're eating pizza with them and Lorelai decides that the pepperoni is angry at the mushrooms because the mushrooms have an attitude, and then she holds up a pepperoni and the pepperoni asks for your opinion, don't just laugh. Answer the pepperoni.

LUKE: I mean, people grow and evolve their whole lives. The chances that you're gonna grow and evolve at the same rate as someone else...too slim to take. The minute you say, 'I do,' you're sticking yourself in a tiny little box for the rest of your life. But hey, at least you had a party first, right?

Character Sketch 'I Would Rather Be Hated...'

Thanks to the expert writing and Kelly Bishop's marvelous performance, we seldom hate Emily Gilmore, but there are certainly times when we'd like to give her a good slap. Yet it's Emily's acerbic nature that makes the role so fulfilling, Bishop says.

"I would rather be hated because I was believed than do a wimpy performance of a character that was unpleasant. I get a kick out of playing these women because I don't like them either. In my playing them, I'm sort of mocking them at the same time.

"I've certainly met a few women like this, and I can't tell you how many people came up to me in that first year and said, 'Oh, you're just like my aunt.' Or, 'Gosh, I didn't know you'd met my grandmother.' So there are a lot of those women out there. The ones that broke my heart were those who said, 'You remind me of my wife.' I'd want to say, 'Oh you poor thing, I'm so sorry!'"

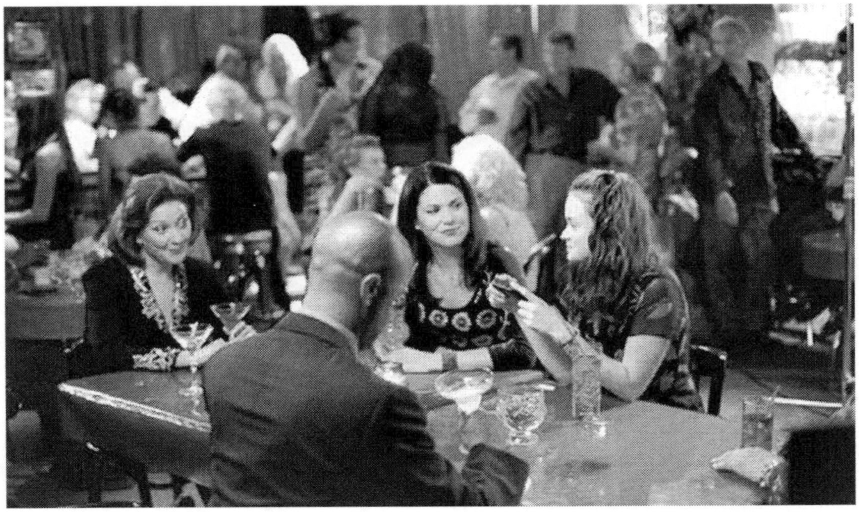

Emily proves herself a romantic during Lorelai's bachelorette party.

[And later...]

LUKE: I guess if you can find that one person, you know, who's willing to put up with all your crap, and doesn't want to change you or dress you or, you know, make you eat French food, then marriage can be all right. But that's only if you find that person.

2.4 The Road Trip to Harvard

First aired: Oct. 23, 2001 // Written by Daniel Palladino // Directed by Jamie Babbit

The girls Thelma and Louise it around New England, ending up at an insanely tacky B&B, before hitting Harvard, where Rory fits right in. Realizing she can't run from the truth forever, Lorelai lets those most important to her know the wedding will not take place, and sets her sights on taking a big step of another kind.

! GINCHY! Lorelai's snide remarks in the guest book ("satanic forces are at work here," or "sat and forever am at work here," if you prefer); Rory fitting in at Harvard; and the final scenes between Luke and Lorelai.

NOTES *'The point of this is to be spontaneous.'*

* Lorelai plans to hit a funky bed and breakfast in Portsmouth, NH, run by her friend Donald; what they find is The Cheshire Cat. Lorelai tells the other guests her children's books are *Goodnight, Spoon* and *The Horse that Wanted to Bark*.

Rory and Lorelai finally see Harvard.

What *Gilmore* Means to Me:

I first began to watch *Gilmore Girls* a few episodes into the first season, beginning with "Rory's Birthday Parties." From there, I got hooked completely. I told my mom about the show, and we both began to watch and enjoy it together; we got so involved with the characters and their stories. My aunt and cousin watched it together, too, and we still have the DVDs to watch whenever we want. It was a terrific show, possibly the best TV show I have ever seen, and I still remember it today.

—Chris Hadley, *Louisiana*

* Lane returns from Korea. The highlight? It's music bootleg heaven!

* Lorelai tells Luke she's decided to keep the chuppah as a decorative archway for the yard because he made it for her.

* For those who like to speculate about product placement on *Gilmore Girls*, (*cough*) Harvard.

* Amy & Dan's stay in Washington Depot, Conn., reportedly inspired Stars Hollow, and there's a good chance that LeDawn's Cheshire Cat B&B is probably inspired by the Mayflower Inn, where they stayed. However much grief Lorelai gives Rory about her way of coping with crises—making lists and acting simply to act—Lorelai does the same thing, as witness the final jolt that gets her moving on the road to the Dragonfly Inn.

TODAY'S CELEBRATION Rory and Lorelai's trip to Harvard and (for Luke) the Lorelai/Max breakup.

SCHNICKELFRITZ ALERT! Luke says he was a "pickleschnitz" about Max.

ANGIE & TRISH Lorelai and Rory's Harvard names.

AMEN, SISTER FRIEND

RORY: Thirteen million volumes? I've read like, what, 300 books in my entire life and I'm already 16? Do you know how long it would take me to read 13 million books?

LORELAI: But honey, you don't have to read every one of them. *Tuesdays with Morrie?* Skip that. *Who Moved My Cheese?* Just stuff you already know.

LORELAI: Ginchy! [*A sound of approval as she tries to pass for a Harvard student.*]

2.5 Nick & Nora/Sid & Nancy

First aired: Oct. 30, 2001 // Written by Amy Sherman-Palladino // Directed by Michael Katleman

It's a new school year and already Paris is promising to make Rory's life a living hell on the school newspaper, The Franklin. *Luke's nephew, Jess, has moved in with him, much to the annoyance of Stars Hollow. But this breath of fresh air might be just what Rory needs.*

GINCHY! Luke threatening the scouts; the evilness that is Paris; Rory's interview with Max; Luke casually shoving Jess into the lake; Luke laying down the law to Jess and Jess' reaction; Jess giving Rory her book back...annotated.

NOTES *'In life there will be people that you don't like, but that you have to coexist with.'*

You sure this isn't the season premiere because man it feels like one. Luke suddenly has a sister *and* a 17-year-old nephew. Jess' father, who worked at a Der Wienerschnitzel hot dog concession, ditched Liz about two years ago. By the time Jess finally tracks down his father, Jimmy (3.21), he's still working at a hot dog stand. Luke and Liz lost their mother when they were kids; Liz skipped town with Jess' dad while their father was sick.

Rory's never quite met anyone like Jess before.

We get the first Luke and Lorelai fight, and probably one of the reasons Luke fails to tell her about April in Season 6. This won't be the last time they fall out over Jess.

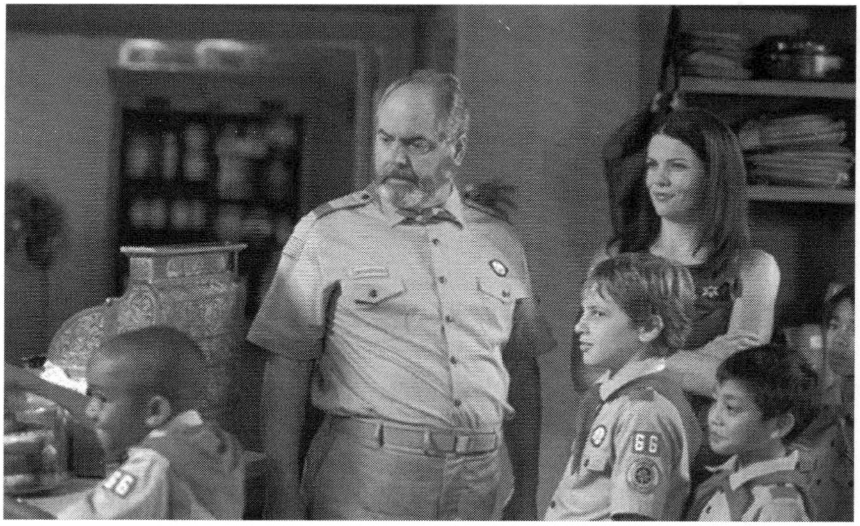

Taylor's influence extends to the next generation of Stars Hollow.

Gilmore Girls + Unrequited Love

Although Max would be far more histrionic in his heartbreak over Lorelai's desertion in other episodes, it was his brief exchange with Rory after the tape recorder's been turned off ("I just want you to know, I really wanted to be your stepfather...") that probably hit audiences the hardest.

"I think this is one of the things that was so beautiful about *Gilmore Girls*," Scott Cohen says. "That unrequited love was such an important part of that story; it was so intense and you felt the passion of that feeling all the time. We shot all these romantic scenes between me and Lorelai, but you always knew that it was not going to be. There was this whole sense of this Anna Karenina/Russian literature/unrequited love feeling. It's beautiful."

Just a question, but how is it that Stars Hollow High says the Pledge of Allegiance in six different languages? Where are these multi-ethnic children...and their parents?

The money Taylor accuses Jess of taking is out of a donation cup for repairing the same bridge the rummage sale was for (1.13). Though we're never told as much, there's a good chance that this is the same bridge Luke pushes Jess off of.

TODAY'S CELEBRATION Celebratory dinner for Jess moving to Stars Hollow.

OY WITH THE ___, ALREADY! Jess being a smart ass. Sure, he's supposed to be a troubled soul, but the way he spoke to Lorelai—jeez!

INTRODUCING...*Jess Mariano* Luke's nephew will turn Stars Hollow upside down as he tries to turn the head of one Miss Rory Gilmore.

AMEN, SISTER FRIEND

RORY [*to Paris*]: And no matter how many crappy, stupid, useless assignments you throw at me, I'm not going to quit and I'm not going to back down. So you can go home tonight and think about the fact that no matter what you do and no matter how evil you are, at the end of the year, on my high school transcript, it's going to say that I worked on The Franklin. So, if you'll excuse me, I have some reading to do on the origins of concrete.

LORELAI [*about her fight with Luke*]: Rory, this was a bad one, OK? This was not Nick and Nora, this was Sid and Nancy, and I'm not going in there.

RORY: I just want you to know, I really wanted you to be my stepfather.
MAX: I just want you to know, I really wanted to be your stepfather.

LUKE: But me raising a kid? I don't even like kids. They're always sticky, you know, like they've got jam on their hands. Even if there's no jam in the house, somehow they've always got jam on their hands. I'm not the right guy to deal with that. I have no patience for jam hands.

2.6 Presenting Lorelai Gilmore

First aired: Nov. 6, 2001 // Written by Sheila R Lawrence // Directed by Chris Long

Emily's losing serious points in the high society world (thank you, Richard!), but bringing Rory out officially at the debutante ball may reverse things nicely. Everyone rallies around the debutante but Richard, who falls apart under secret pressures of his own.

GINCHY! Richard's impassioned speech at the ball; Jess dressed like Luke wiping down the tables; and Lorelai going over to "hang" with her mother.

Bio Mädchen Amick (Sherry Tinsdale)

Though Mädchen Amick's uber-organized Sherry inspired plenty of ire among *Gilmore* fans who didn't take kindly to her messing things up between Lorelai and Christopher, the actress had her own loyal fanbase thanks to her time as Shelly Johnson on the macabre David Lynch series *Twin Peaks*, and in the follow-up film *Twin Peaks: Fire Walk with Me*. Not that she was alone in that: Sherilyn Fenn (Sasha/Anna Nardini) was also a *Twin Peaks* regular.

Born in Reno, Amick moved to LA at 16; she landed the *Twin Peaks* role a year later. By 1999, she had a brief but memorable story arc on The WB's *Dawson's Creek* as Nicole Kennedy, the Hollywood exec who dashes Dawson's hopes for the movie he's making by telling him how trite it is, before being revealed as the new girlfriend of Dawson's father.

Since *Gilmore*, Amick has turned up on a number of popular shows in multi-episode roles including *ER*, *Joey*, *Gossip Girl* and *Damages*.

NOTES *'That should've been you up there. Nothing's turning out the way it was supposed to.'*

Two episodes in a row we see two seemingly rock-solid relationships get rocky. Last time it was Luke and Lorelai, this time Richard and Emily. Richard's condescending dismissal of Emily's foundation efforts will lead to greater consequences later (6.9). Emily's still burning through maids at a pretty good clip, but judging by the humor with which she explains it to her friends, you can certainly see where Lorelai gets her own sparkling wit.

Christopher brings Rory the *Compact Oxford English Dictionary* he tried to buy her before (1.15), and tells Lorelai his new job in Boston has him

Making an Episode 5: Creating the Script

Once the general pitch of an episode's been approved by Amy, the writers assistant takes everything from the whiteboards, every idea that's been floated, every piece of dialogue that's been suggested, and works that into her "final notes" report.

The final notes are then handed off to the writer of that particular episode—usually chosen toward the end of this process. The writer then transforms it into a detailed outline, which will be gone over in detail by Amy & Dan, Janet Leahy says. After that, the writer's sent off to bang out the script.

"The document was so detailed that you could literally paste it into Final Draft and convert it into the script," writer Jane Espenson says. "By the time a writer began their solo work, the episode was very much determined. There was less guesswork, less chance of having a script go off the rails.

"I missed the chance to sometimes let a scene become something unexpected, but there was also something nice about the democratic way the staff would work together, weaving in our own personal experiences as we did the scene work as a group. And you certainly never felt you were writing your way into the wilderness. The primary duty of the episode writer was adding the vast amount of dialogue that the show called for."

The rest of the writers will remain in the writers room, continuing to hash out ideas for the next episodes.

"Amy was always all over the place," writers assistant Alison Goodman says. "But very much decisions were made by what she wanted. If there was a question, I would ask her and get back to the writers."

After several days, the writer will turn in their first draft. Amy gives the writer any notes she has on things that need to be tweaked in the script. "At some point, Amy would take over the script, as is usual for a showrunner," Espenson says.

Whatever show a writer works on, one of the hardest things to get used to is the fact that no matter how well you write, the showrunner is pretty much certain to rewrite just about everything. It's how shows retain their unique voice. The only aspect that really varies is how each showrunner handles this process.

"After coming from *Buffy* where Joss [Whedon] tended to lead you through many rewrites until you got it right, it was hard having material taken away for rewriting," Espenson admits. "But looking back, Amy's voice is so distinctive and she was able to generate these enormous scenes so quickly and helping tech companies scale back and stay in business.

✱ There's something very chilling in the way Richard tells Emily and Lorelai he's being phased out. Knowing Amy & Dan's passion for classic television and film, there's a possibility that this is a reference to the 1955 Kraft Television Theatre episode *Patterns*, which launched the television career of its writer, *Twilight Zone* creator Rod Serling.

✱ Richard proudly told Dean (2.1), "I knew I wanted to go to Yale, and put on a nice suit every day and be a very important man in a very powerful firm." Now, humbled by his work situation, he says, "I want to

deftly, this really was the most efficient system for making the show."

Amy stays very late at the studio many nights each week, rewriting large chunks of every script, even as she's fielding inquiries from the studio and network bosses, producers' concerns and writer ideas. If she's directing an episode that week, she might have to stay even later or early into the morning.

"The vast majority of dialogue in every episode was written by Amy personally," Espenson says. "The speed and volume was astounding. I'm sure there must have been evenings in which she would generate 20 pages of dialogue after a long day on set. She went above and beyond to make sure every episode had the perfect *Gilmore* tone."

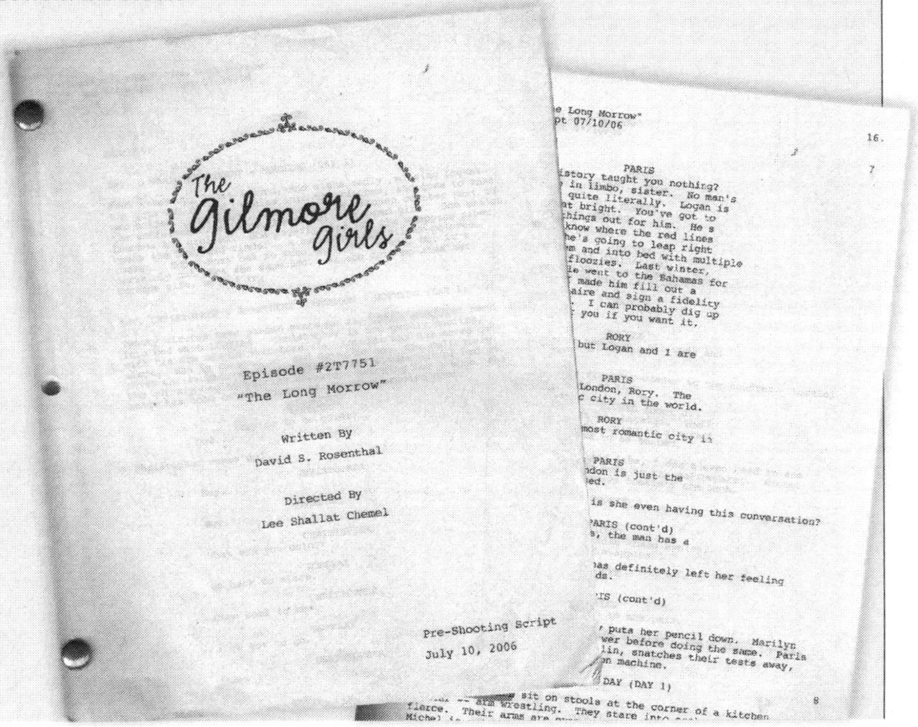

get up every morning and put on my suit and go to my office and do my work, like I've done every day for the past 30 years. That's what I want to do. That's the only thing I want to do."

Rory takes her first steps into her grandparents' world.

✱ Just when Lorelai's coming around to the idea of making things work with Christopher, he reveals he's living with a woman, Sherry, in Boston, who prompted his recent change for the better. Easily the most depressing episode to date.

EMILY'S MAID DU JOUR Leisal, who Lorelai graciously allows to hide in the kitchen. (She only made it through the evening.)

YOU'VE ENTERED EMILYLAND I wanted my granddaughter to be presented to society in a beautiful, elegant ballroom, not a Shakey's.

TODAY'S CELEBRATION Daughters of the Daughters of the American Revolution Debutante Ball.

AMEN, SISTER FRIEND

LORELAI [*to Christopher*]: Now I know you would rather sit through *Endless Love* than ever be a part of this scene again. But this is very important to your daughter and she has never asked you for anything, and although no one's keeping track, it would seem that your constant nonpresence in her life and your lack of ever showing up when you say

Bio Liz Torres (Miss Patty)

Like Miss Patty, Liz Torres has, indeed, "done everything there is to do in show business except set fire to the hoop the dog jumps through." Born in the Bronx, Torres took New York City's nightclub circuit by storm, before gaining national exposure in 1971 on *The Tonight Show*. From there, she was a regular fixture on '70s television, including on *The Mary Tyler Moore Show* spin-off *Phyllis* and several episodes of *All in the Family* alongside fellow Stars Hollow gossip Sally Struthers.

Behind the Scenes A Day in the Life of Kelly Bishop

One doesn't roll out of bed and instantly strike the perfect balance between glamour, vulnerability and hard-nosed stubbornness; you have to work up to being Emily Gilmore.

Kelly Bishop was always the first actor at work "because they did give me two hours for makeup and hair, which I wanted," she explains. "So I was usually in by 6 in the morning, and we generally went until 9 or 10 at night. So I would do makeup, camera blocking and then we'd shoot scene, scene, scene. We did have a full hour lunch break, and then we'd just start up again. It was long, and I'm not one to read a book while I'm doing something—I find I get too lost in the story of a book. So I would do crossword puzzles—that's another place that Ed [Herrmann] and I latched on to each other. We spent a lot of time doing the Times crossword puzzle together.

"I wasn't really good about visiting my friends out there. I was always afraid somebody would say, 'Oh come have dinner,' and give me directions. It would then be like 55 minutes to get there, and I didn't want to do it. I really kept tight to myself.

"I lived in an apartment complex that was very close to the studio, and I just went back and forth. I'd go down, I'd do my work, and I'd go right back to the apartment. If I had an early morning the next day, I'd prepare the coffee and take off my makeup and get myself all together, do a little bit of e-mail, and then just go to bed. I let it control me when I was out there."

you're going to, or calling when you say you're going to, or basically doing anything when you say you're going to, would tend to indicate that you owe her big time. Now, before you say no, I want you to take a minute and remember you have a great daughter who needs you, and she has a mother who will hunt you down like a half-priced Kate Spade purse if you disappoint her.

RORY: At one point Miss Patty thought Dean was gonna get hurt; she made me sit in the corner and watch.
LORELAI: Hey! Nobody puts Baby in the corner. [A nice reference from *Dirty Dancing*, which starred Kelly Bishop.]

RICHARD: Alan Parker was phased out. I now have his office, I now have his parking space. Do you know what happens from here? I lose more accounts, slowly but surely. They will put a younger man on them with me to be trained by the best. And then one day they'll call and ask me to let that young man take a meeting without me, just to see how fast he's learning. And then suddenly that young man is given that account. And this happens again and again and again until I'm nothing but a symbolic figurehead that they roll out for banquets and group pictures. And then one day, Emily, I will be asked to leave.

2.7 Like Mother, Like Daughter

First aired: Nov. 13, 2001 // Written by Joan Binder Weiss // Directed by Dennis Erdman

Rory's guidance counselor tells her she needs to "mix it up" with other students if she wants a referral for college; Lorelai's told to do the same by Headmaster Charleston. The result: Rory gets shanghaied into the Chilton Puffs sorority and Lorelai joins the Boosters and puts on a charity fashion show at the inn. Special guest model: Emily!

GINCHY! Rory's daily book luggage, and her telling off of Headmaster Charleston when she gets caught ringing the initiation bell; Emily and Lorelai's mother-daughter runway performance at the fashion show.

NOTES *'Talk to some kids, I'll hang out with their moms, and we'll get into Harvard, take over the world, then buy Chilton and turn it into a rave club.'*

Last episode it was Richard being dragged to events he had no interest in, this time it's Rory and Lorelai. Rory tells the guidance counselor the only time she's been late to class is when she was hit by a deer (1.4). "It's a big story for me, I'm surprised I don't tell it better."

"I pledge myself to the Puffs, loyal I'll always be. A P to start, two Fs at the end, and a U sitting in between."

—THE CHILTON PUFFS INITIATION PLEDGE

There are 10 sororities at Chilton, the Chilton Puffs has been the top one for 50 years. Paris' mother and aunt were both Puffs. Former US Supreme Court Justice Sandra Day O'Connor was "Puffed" in 1946 and became president in 1947. Every Puff has snuck into the headmaster's office at night to ring the 120-year-old Chilton bell three times and recite the following: "I pledge myself to the Puffs, loyal I'll always be. A P to start, two Fs at the end, and a U sitting in between." Technically Rory wasn't Puffed as she only rings it twice before she's caught by Headmaster Charleston.

TODAY'S CELEBRATION The Chilton Booster Club's Annual Fall Festival Fundraiser, and the (almost) initiation of Rory into the Puffs.

KIRK OF ALL TRADES Lorelai's Jeep repair guy.

EMILY'S MAID DU JOUR Unnamed.

YOU'VE ENTERED EMILYLAND Animals eat outside. Human beings eat inside with napkins and utensils.

YOU'VE ENTERED RORYLAND Loners are those guys that you see walking around wearing, I don't know, out-of-date clothing, bell bottoms, and they tend to carry a duffel bag with God knows what inside. That's a loner.

INTRODUCING... *The Chilton Puffs*

SCHNICKELFRITZ ALERT! Old Headmaster Schnickelfritz Charleston.

AND HERE'S A SHOUT OUT TO OUR INTERNATIONAL FANS

RORY: Lorelai Gilmore. Nope, doesn't sound model-ey enough. You need something that stands out more. How about Waffle? We could call you Waffle and say you're from Belgium?

AMEN, SISTER FRIEND

LORELAI [*after roping Emily into being a model for the fashion show*]: Waffle's very happy.

EMILY: Funny isn't it?
LORELAI: What's funny?
EMILY: How nicely you seem to be fitting into the world that you ran away from.

Bio Michael Winters (Taylor Doose)

After you've watched Michael Winters as Taylor Doose for a while, his 2007 turn as US vice president Dick Cheney in the ACT Theatre's production of David Hare's *Stuff Happens* isn't that much of a stretch. "I have a great picture of me with this sort of bland smile on my face and little devil horns" from that production, he says. "I thought I'd use that for my Christmas card some year."

Born in Norfolk, Va. (his father was in the Navy), Winters moved to Ohio when he was 2, and went to school at Northwestern University in Chicago. Since then, he's lived on the West Coast, moving to Seattle (where he eventually settled) in 1988. He likes to say he got into acting in second grade playing Joseph in his school's Christmas play because he was the tallest kid in the class, though he admits it was his high school drama teacher, fresh out of the air force, who made him want to pursue the actor's life. "He would grab the football players and make them come and audition for the plays."

Despite appearing on several major series, including *Friends*, *Ally McBeal*, *Frasier* and *Law & Order*, Winters' first love remains the stage. "There's not much attention given to the acting of the performances [in TV], that's your job," he says. "They're more concerned with camera placement and camera moves and lighting and continuity. There's a big time pressure on television to get this stuff done today."

Bio Milo Ventimiglia (Jess Mariano)

For someone perceived as being quiet and reserved, Milo Ventimiglia has a knack for being seen. In just the last few years, he's appeared in *Rocky Balboa* (2006) as the son of Sylvester Stallone's iconic boxer, 12 episodes of the NBC series *American Dreams*, and most notably as superhero Peter Petrelli in several seasons of *Heroes*.

Born in Orange County, Calif., he studied at the American Conservatory Theater on a scholarship, and attended UCLA. Though he guest starred on several shows before *Gilmore Girls*, it was that series that launched him into stardom. Not content to be just another network hunk, Ventimiglia has used his success to propel himself and his friends into several creative ventures, including the creation of a comic book series for Top Cow called *Rest* with friend Russ Cundiff, published in collaboration with their production company, Divide Pictures. Divide has also produced several online video projects, and even a line of T-shirts. Divide also keeps in close contact with fans via the Divide Social Club (www.dividesocialclub.com).

Co-star Liza Weil told YM magazine that Ventimiglia was instrumental in getting some of the younger cast members to go out after work. "We always wanted to, but Alexis works so much and it's tough to rally ourselves at the weekend. Recently, we've been out for food or to the movies, and he's the catalyst for that. We get recognized more when we travel in packs—the other day Alexis and I were in a restaurant and this woman came up and said, 'You're not supposed to be friends!' Alexis explained that it's just television."

PARIS [*to Rory*]: Well, how nice it must be to be you. Maybe someday I'll stumble into a Disney movie and suddenly be transported into your body, and after living there a while, I'll finally realize the beauty of myself. But until that moment, I'm going to go in there and I'm going to become a Puff. Now get out of my way.

2.8 The Ins & Outs of Inns

First aired: Nov. 20, 2001 // Written by Daniel Palladino // Directed by Michael Katleman

A sudden change in plans means that Lorelai and Sookie might be forced to move ahead with their dreams to open their own inn, which sends Lorelai into an emotional tailspin. Meanwhile, Emily is having a portrait of Rory painted to hang in Richard's study, and Jess is stirring up trouble for Luke. But is he really the complete jerk he seems to be?

GINCHY! Jess' "crime scene" outside Doose's Market; Mia pretending not to understand Michel; and her recollections of Lorelai's arrival at the inn at the beginning, undercut by her meeting with Emily.

NOTES *'The inn is where Rory took her first step. It's where I took my first step. It's more of a home to me, more than my parents' house ever was.'*

✱ Lorelai and Sookie discover that Fran of Weston's bakery owns the Dragonfly Inn—it was her parents' business. When Lorelai and Rory bought their house, the best name they could come up with for it was "The Crap Shack." The way Luke explains how he went into business on his own and learned by trial and error explains a lot about his character, and his insecurities.

✱ This is our first glimpse of Mia, owner of the Independence Inn, who now lives in Santa Barbara. She tells the girls that Luke used to be a skateboarder and wore a *Star Trek* T-shirt for quite a while.

✱ Once she realizes that Mia wants to sell the Independence Inn, Lorelai gets cold feet about opening one of her own, and lays into Sookie about her lack of reliability. This is the first fight she's had with Sookie, she tells Emily. And while Sookie and Lorelai make up this time, it's not the last time that Lorelai will come down on Sookie for her flightiness (4.14).

Lane, Who's Your Daddy?

One of the enduring enigmas of *Gilmore Girls* is a question Keiko Agena's heard many, many, many times. "Where's Lane's dad?! I have no idea," she says. "I certainly made up different theories along the way. I do know at the very beginning I said 'parents' a few times, and then I stopped saying parents and just started saying mom.

"I think I made up this story that he was teaching somewhere in some foreign country doing ministry work. You'd think he'd show up by my wedding, but that didn't happen. I have no idea where my dad went. I was crossing my fingers that I'd get a script delivered at my front door one day and it would say Lane Kim's dad in there, but it never came." Emily Kuroda, too, always held out hope of meeting Mrs. Kim's erstwhile husband. "I was actually going to do a play in DC and Amy called and said, 'We want you for a couple of episodes.' I said I'm doing a play in DC, I'll come back early. And she goes, 'No, you can't go.' What do you mean? I already told them I would do it. And then she finally said, 'Because Lane's going to get married!' I said, 'Ohhhh. OK, I'll have to drop out of the play.' Then I thought for sure I was going to find out about Mr. Kim, but no."

* In the scene where Emily meets Mia, Kelly Bishop, once again, does more with a few (admittedly well-crafted) lines than most actors accomplish in an hour of screen time.

TODAY'S CELEBRATION The "what's to be done with Jess" town meeting.

EMILY'S MAID DU JOUR Marisella. (Technically she's the cook, but most of Emily's maids seem to be multipurpose servants.)

TAYLOR OF ALL TRADES Taylor speaks for the Stars Hollow Business Association, the Stars Hollow Tourist Board, the Stars Hollow Neighborhood Watch organization, and the Stars Hollow Citizens for a Clean Stars Hollow council.

THE CRIMES OF JESS MARIANO

—Creating a fake crime scene outside Doose's Market
—Stealing money from the Save the Bridge fund
—Swiping Babette's gnome, Pierpont
—Hooting at one of Miss Patty's dance classes
—Removing a garden hose from Fran's yard
—Setting off the fire alarm at Stars Hollow High

From the Editing Room 1 Take A Shot

Though the writing of *Gilmore* was her main concern, Amy knew precisely how she wanted each episode to look.

First, she didn't like insert shots, editor Raul Davalos says. "Even if Lauren and Alexis are looking at a photograph, rarely would we cut to the photograph they're looking at. 'Oh look, this is you wearing your bunny outfit.' We never cut to the photograph of Alexis wearing the bunny outfit."

You have only to look at the ugly-baby picture in "The Bracebridge Dinner" (2.10) to see how not seeing the photo actually heightens the comedy.

Gilmore also avoided those "choker" close-ups, the ones that go from the eyebrows to the Adam's apple. Not only are such shots claustrophobic for the audience, but they also are less interesting overall to look at. Concentrate on the churning emotions in Lorelai's face during her drunken toast at Lane's wedding (6.19), for instance, and you miss the awkward body language that doesn't just tell us she's sad and drunk, but also utterly vulnerable.

On *Gilmore*, "If it's a close-up, it would be from the top of the head to the middle of the chest," Davalos says. "Otherwise, Amy was a big fan of the cowboy shot," so named because it resembles shots in old westerns where it's wide enough to see the gun below the belt.

—Controlling the weather and writing the screenplay to the Mariah Carey movie *Glitter* (Lorelai's accusations).

OY WITH THE ___, ALREADY! Bootsy. And not just because he stomped on Luke's clay hand imprint in the first grade. (Three kids saw him!)

AMEN, SISTER FRIEND

MIA: There was a phony murder?
LORELAI: Yeah, the town's too dull to work up a real murder.

LORELAI: I'm good at doing what I have to do. When I had to get a job, I got it. When I had to find a house for us and a life for us, I got it. When I had to get Rory into Chilton, I did it. But I don't have to leave the Independence Inn. I don't have to go into business for myself. I don't have to walk out on that limb and risk everything I've worked for.

MIA: When Lorelai showed up on my porch that day with a tiny baby in her arms, I thought to myself, what if this were my daughter, and she was cold and scared and needed a place to live? What would I want for her? And then I thought, I'd want her to find somebody to take her in and make her safe and help her find her way.
EMILY: That's funny. I would've wanted her to find someone who would send her home.

2.9 Run Away, Little Boy

First aired: Nov. 27, 2001 // Written by John Stephens // Directed by Danny Leiner

Loves past and future are in the air. A mysterious ice cream maker has appeared as a wedding present for Lorelai and Max. After a pep talk from Sookie, Lorelai decides to move on by going out with Paul from her business class. Rory is aiding the course of true love between Henry and Lane, while playing Juliet to Tristin's Romeo in the school play. Now if only Rory can keep Dean and Tristin away from each other so that her boyfriend doesn't learn the secret that she and her leading man share.

GINCHY! Lane's weird relationship with Henry; Rory practicing how she's going to tell Dean that she kissed Tristin, and Lorelai pretend-

Morey and His Shades

"They always made me wear my sun-glasses," Ted Rooney remembers. "I would take them off 'ac-cidentally' and hope that no one would notice. But there was always somebody, and it was their job to check. 'Ted, your glasses! Ted, glasses!' Even Sally [Struthers] would try to help with it. At one point we're in this banquet scene, indoors obviously, not near the sun at all, and she says, 'Don't you think Ted shouldn't be wearing his glasses now? It doesn't make sense. He's indoors and everything. I know it's part of his character, but come on, that's crazy.' And they came back, 'No, he needs to wear his glasses.'"

ing to be Dean; Rory's "I've always wanted a little brother" and Luke's wanting to move the children away from Lorelai after meeting Paul.

NOTES *'It's called closure, hon.'*

✱ We get the first appearance of that wonderful Paris bait, Brad Langford, who is quickly passed over for the part of Romeo. In addition to Celine Dion, Michel has a thing for Destiny's Child.

✱ Lorelai's costuming skills are developing nicely (1.9, 1.10). She's now making costumes for Rory's production of *Romeo & Juliet*. Lane still has two parents, according to Rory.

✱ Just a couple episodes before, Lorelai awkwardly told Luke not to date one of the Chilton moms he met at the fashion show. This time, Luke mercilessly teases Lorelai about how young her "casual" date, Paul, looks. "Why are you so mad at me," she asks.

✱ Just when it looks certain that Brad Langford will have to fill in for Tristin, we learn he's changed schools. Fret not, he will return (2.14).

✱ It's only established at the beginning of this episode that Tristin's been hanging around a couple of troublemakers, making his trouble with the law and his banishment to military school smack of a network trying to free up Chad Michael Murray so he can go off in search of other projects. Though it's clear that his *One Tree Hill* character, Lucas Scott, is not meant to be Tristin, you can't help noticing that the series is set in North Carolina, the same place Tristin's military school is supposed to be.

What I Kept

Amy would give us reading gifts and things like that, and mostly it was just products and stuff, but I still have some of that. But that's cosmetics, so that doesn't really count.

—Kelly Bishop (Emily Gilmore)

TODAY'S CELEBRATION More of a performance, really. *Romeo & Juliet*, and Lorelai being open for business again, datingwise.

720 SQUARE FEET The size of Miss Patty's dance studio (according to the *fictional* MissPatty.net).

MISSPATTY.NET In her search for places to rehearse their scene from *Romeo & Juliet*, Paris discovers this Web site, a domain that remains in the tight little grasp of Warner Brothers. MissPatty.com is a real estate company in Bangkok, and MissPatti.com....is a school of dance!

12 The number of blueberries Michel allows himself to have in his pancakes.

Bio Liza Weil (Paris Geller)

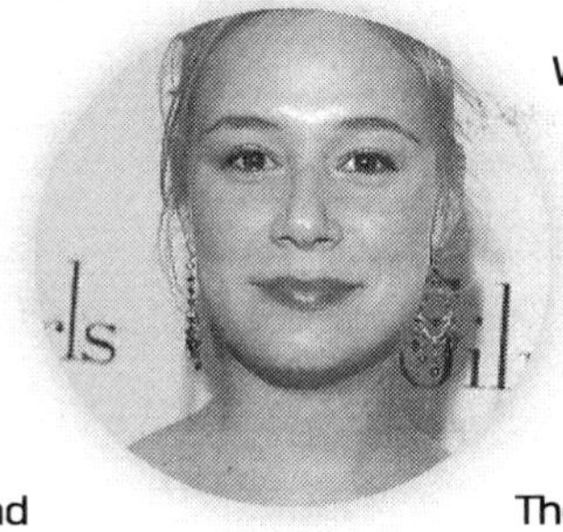

Far from the insane overachieving student she plays, Liza Weil told Seventeen magazine that she was the "worst student ever." She failed English during her last year of high school and had to go to summer school to make up for it, according to the Denver Post.

Weil was born in New Jersey to Lisa and Marc Weil, who toured Europe with their comedy troupe The Madhouse Company of London. (Her father only missed out on working with Monty Python co-founder John Cleese because he couldn't afford the cost of the flight, she told the Denver Post.)

When she was 7, the Weil family settled in Lansdale, Pa., and Liza commuted back and forth to New York City for auditions. She landed her first TV role in 1994 with *The Adventures of Pete & Pete* episode "Yellow Fever," in which she appeared with her mother.

Though Weil originally auditioned for the part of Rory, Amy loved the actress so much, she created the part of Paris just for her. "There is some of me in Paris," she admitted to Seventeen. "Both of us can be hyperfocused and passionate about things. But Paris has a very exaggerated version of my neurosis."

AMEN, SISTER FRIEND

PARIS [*to Rory*]: You're Juliet. You're the best public speaker here, you've definitely got that waif thing down, and you'll look great dead.

PARIS: Rory, sorry to interrupt. Hi Henry. But see, we're all standing over there trying to map out a game plan and a rehearsal schedule, and I'm sure whatever the two of you are talking about over here is so much more fascinating and important and, well gosh, let's just say it, fun. But I'd really like to get an 'A' on this assignment, and in order to do that I'm afraid you're gonna have to discuss your sock hops and your clambakes some other time, OK? Thanks.

SOOKIE [*to Lorelai, explaining Luke's actions*]: He has had to watch you go from one guy to another, and then the engagement, and then the engagement was off, and patiently he's waited. And now in walks this kid and he says, "My God, will she date anyone else in the world before she'll date me?"

LORELAI: I don't have very many people in my life who are in my life permanently forever. They will always be there for me. I will always be there for them, you know? There's Rory and Sookie, and this town and ... you. I mean, at least I think I've got–
LUKE: You do.

2.10 The Bracebridge Dinner

First aired: Dec. 11, 2001 // Written by Daniel Palladino // Directed by Chris Long

Lorelai and Sookie are preparing a lavish 19th century dinner at the Independence Inn for the Trelling Paper Co. when the winter weather strands the guests of honor in Chicago. Since it's all paid for anyway, they decide to invite everyone in Stars Hollow for a night to remember. But why is Jess acting up as the winter break draws near, why doesn't Lorelai tell Rory about Christopher's invitation to stay with him and Sherry, and why is Richard suddenly so happy?

Lorelai, Rory...and SnowBjork.

! GINCHY! The ugly-baby Christmas card and where it turns up after dinner; the magical sleigh rides through Stars Hollow; Luke thinking he's discovered "the secret of parenting"; Richard's sudden joie de vie; Rory watching Emily and Lorelai mirroring each other as they get ready for bed.

NOTES *'An out-of-control, over-the-top slumber party.'*

* Paris mentions her Portuguese nanny for the first time, though confusingly says that her parents are out of town. Did they get back together (1.11)?

* Poor Dean. He finally got rid of Tristin last episode, only to have Jess, who's only been in town about two months, start in on him in this one. Ostensibly this is because Dean broke up a fight between him and Chuck Presby at school, but it's pretty clear there's another reason. Rory convinces her mom to invite Richard and Emily to the shindig to help cheer her grandpa up over his work troubles (2.6).

* The CEO of Richard's insurance firm finally gets a name, but we won't actually meet Floyd until later (4.13). The way Richard unburdens himself to Emily is touching, humorous and above all, convincing. He also points out something about Emily *to* Emily that we normally associate with Rory. "You like order, you like lists, you like to know where you're going or what's coming. You like all things planned."

TODAY'S CELEBRATION Why the Bracebridge dinner, of course, or the snowman building competition if you're a Stars Hollow event purist. Oddly, Jess is right—the girls' snowwoman *does* look like Bjork.

THE GUEST LIST Morey and Babette, Lane and Mrs. Kim, Richard and Emily, Dean and Clara, Luke and Jess, Bootsy, Taylor, Paris, Michel.

KIRK OF ALL TRADES Servant at the Bracebridge Dinner.

OY WITH THE ___, ALREADY! Bootsy! (Someone get him out of here *please*!)

AND HERE'S A SHOUT OUT TO OUR INTERNATIONAL FANS Richard recounting a beautiful moonlit night in Prague on the Charles Bridge ruined by some kids blasting a Cher song on their boombox. No worries. Richard stood proudly and hummed Mozart's "Prague Symphony," dispatching the kids and earning a few bucks from a couple of tourists to boot.

AMEN, SISTER FRIEND

LUKE [*letting Lorelai in on the secret of parenting*]: You visualize the reality you want and then, if necessary, you lie to bring it about.

Rory [*pulling back her covers*]: Mom!
LORELAI: What, honey?
RORY: You put the picture of the ugly baby in my bed?
LORELAI: I didn't, I swear. That ugly baby is stalking us. Run away!
RORY: Poor baby, it's not his fault.
LORELAI: I think it's a she.
RORY: Poor baby, you picked the wrong parents.

LORELAI: Hey Mom. You didn't make it back to the room last night. Did you get lucky?
EMILY: Could you be any cruder?
LORELAI: Yeah, I can be cruder. Hey mom, did you get la-?

What I Kept

I do have a couple of the scripts. I have the last script that Amy wrote, and I think the last script of the last season. I have the Kirk doll that I made. Remember when he was the guard for the maze and he was on the stilts? I made a maze guard outfit for it!

—Valerie Campbell (key set costumer)

2.11 Secrets and Loans

First aired: Jan. 22, 2002 // Written by Linda Loiselle Guzik // Directed by Nicole Holofcener

It's served them well, but Chez Lorelai is succumbing to the ravages of termites, and its owner has no idea where she's going to find the $2,000 to get rid of the *bugs and the $15,000 to fix it. Though Rory thinks she's helping, she only makes matters worse when she tells Emily, despite Lorelai telling her not to.*

GINCHY! Jackson's pajamas; Mrs. Kim kicking Rory out of the antique shop because she's a termite "carrier."

NOTES *'Mom, our house is falling down.'*

Aside from her other community accomplishments, Lorelai played Tevye in the Stars Hollow Community Theater production of *Fiddler on the Roof*, earning 5 and a half stars from the Stars Hollow Gazette. Little did she know that Kirk would be taking the same role years later in the elementary school production of the same play (5.15).

Jackson has quite the family. We've already met cousin Rune, and now we learn of another cousin who runs a copy company that puts pictures on pajamas.

Lorelai has a quick phone conversation with a Mr. Rygalski at the bank, the first attempt to work the name of Helen Pai's husband, Dave Rygalski, into the series. We'll have to wait until next season to meet Lane's almost-boyfriend by that name in the form of Adam Brody (3.3).

740/760 Rory's PSAT scores (verbal/math)

730/750 Paris' PSAT scores (verbal/math)

HEY, FAMILY FRIENDLY FORUM! Michel tells Lorelai that women in Thailand do a trick with a ping-pong ball "that is a real crowd-pleaser."

KIRK OF ALL TRADES Termite/home repair expert.

TODAY'S CELEBRATION The Gilmore home is saved!

AMEN, SISTER FRIEND

LORELAI: You know, I think if we put Paris and my mother in a room together, the world would implode.

2.12 Richard in Stars Hollow

First aired: Jan. 29, 2002 // Written by Frank Lombardi // Directed by Steve Gomer

Richard's slowly going crazy adjusting to his new retirement, and he's driving Emily up the wall with him. When Lorelai agrees to show him around Stars

Giving the Troubadour a Voice

"There was an episode where we did a cover of 'Be True to Your School,' the Beach Boys song," Grant-Lee Phillips (the Troubadour) says. "It starts off with me singing it and strumming it and then Lorelai walks into frame. I'm still in frame, I have to keep strumming and mouthing it but you can't hear me. So, in order to make that realistic, you have to have some sort of metronome. I cut an earlier version of it on the set with no one talking so you have all the ambience you naturally would have. I'm playing at the top of the scene. They come in, talk for a bit, they exit, then cut back to the troubadour still playing, but I, in fact, had not been playing. Just crazy stuff. I think it all stemmed from what is the most entertaining way to go about this, and figure out a way to make it happen. I think it's a credit to the ambition and idealism of the show."

Behind the Scenes: Jackson + the Wrestler Pajamas

The lengths to which cast and crew went for the sake of a single gag is one of the noblest, yet craziest hallmarks of *Gilmore Girls*. The saga of Jackson's wrestler pajamas is just one example among many.

One evening Brenda Maben and Valerie Campbell were waiting for the script for "Secrets and Loans" when Maben got a call from producer Patricia Fass Palmer, Campbell recalls. Palmer says, "I just wanna give you a head's up. They want pajamas for the first scene up tomorrow morning with Jackson as a youth wrestling, as if they're from his high school."

And that's pretty much how things happened. It was after 5 pm—it was already dark—and the wardrobe department suddenly had to come up with the impossible. "Occasionally on that show we'd have to scramble and whoever could do whatever would do it," Campbell says. "Even if you'd never done it before, you learned."

Maben put down the phone, grabbed Campbell, and said, "Uh, I need you." While Maben planned it out, Campbell rang up Jackson Douglas. Though the actor was nearby in Los Angeles, it turned out all of the photos from his high school years were tucked away at his family home in Seattle. Douglas' father e-mailed him some of the pictures, which he then forwarded to Campbell. They now had Jackson's face as a high school kid. Now came the tricky bit.

"California," one of the show's grips, happened to have a teenage nephew who was a wrestler, so there was a good supply of high school wrestling photos...on the other side of town. His sister braved the horrendous traffic to bring them to the lot. (She happened to be a big fan of *Gilmore Girls*, so everyone was happy.)

There were now two elements in hand, but the clock was ticking and they still didn't have a pair of Jackson's embarrassing PJs.

Campbell hit the Web looking for more wrestling pictures that she could download and manipulate, just in case those they'd received from California didn't work. As a last ditch effort, she called her husband and had him find her old high school yearbook, just in case. At last, it seemed they were looking pretty good on photos. There was just one more problem: "We needed white pajamas. We couldn't find white pajamas in the stores at that time; they just weren't available." Either the writers were going to have to come up with another sight gag, or they were going to have to get creative in a hurry.

Fortunately, Maben found just what they needed in her closet at home at the other end of town. From there she hit the local Kinko's copying center to print out the various photos they had before heading to her final stop: The Wizard. It was at this popular Hollywood screen-printing company that she ironed on as many of the wrestling images as she could, before zipping back to the Warner Brothers lot shortly before call time. If Maben managed to catch more than a couple hours of sleep, Campbell would be amazed.

"We got the images on the pajamas, got them on set just in time and everybody was like 'Wow!' I think that maybe that was our biggest mistake, being able to do that. We set the bar with that. At that point, we pretty much could not get out of doing anything then."

Hollow for the day, she discovers that her father still sees her as a child. Paris is determined that The Franklin will win the Oppenheimer Award for Excellence in School Journalism...by exposing the "seedy underbelly" of Stars Hollow! Rory, however, may have beaten her to the punch by inadvertently getting nearly everything at the Stars Hollow Video Store restricted.

GINCHY! Emily's desperation to get Lorelai to take Richard for the day; Rory showing Richard the books stashed around her room; the brinkmanship between Richard and Dean over the car and Richard's parting words to Lorelai; Jess' "surprise" for anyone who rents *Bambi* or *Dumbo*.

NOTES *'I am a grown woman and you will treat me the way you treat people who have invited you to their house or you will not be invited again.'*

The last time we saw Emily truly shaken up was during Trix's visit (1.18). Though Richard is never as rude as his mother, he has a similar way of driving Emily out of her mind.

As maddening as Taylor's overbearing attitude can be, there's something almost touching about the way he envisions Rory as the embodiment of purity. This episode she's his hero for sparking the censorship of videos; later he makes her his "Ice Cream Queen" to promote his new ice cream and candy store (4.1).

Al's Pancake World has the best egg fu young in Stars Hollow.

Rory tells Richard that she started the "Harvard obsession board" in her room a few years ago, but things got kicked up a notch when the student store had a two-for-one flag sale when they visited the campus (2.4). Richard has had to face up to many things during his day in Stars Hollow, but this is probably the final straw for Rory's Yale-educated grandfather. The seeds for the Gilmores' calculated visit to Yale (3.8) are sown here. Having Dean show up again after their disastrous meeting (2.1), and to give Rory a car he deems unsafe, only makes things worse.

Dean's father sells stereo systems. Richard asking Dean how tall he is clearly runs in the family—he remarks on Rory's height early on (1.1), and his mother makes a similar observation when seeing both Rory and Lorelai (1.18). Richard points out to Lorelai that she has never once invited him to her house, placing a different spin on the Gilmores' visit for Rory's birthday party (1.6).

From start to finish this is Edward Herrmann's episode, from the annoying way he treats Lorelai to his tenderness toward Rory, and his comedic battle with Dean. His parting words to his daughter, and the

Richard, Lorelai & the Ties that Strangle

This episode would not be the last time that father and daughter would clash; their inability to see eye-to-eye was one of the driving forces of the series. Yet, as Edward Herrmann points out, "There can't be that wonderful or terrible moment between father and daughter when things are pulled up in a Greek cathartic explosion and things are resolved, or not resolved.

"If the father can at last tell his daughter how much he loves her and the daughter can at last come home and be embraced, the characters could move on. But that can't happen, because if you do that, you lose the tension, the frisson between these two people. A television series keeps characters in a kind of stasis, and ours was a seven-year stage production! The wonder of the show was that it kept one's interest for so long without the characters essentially moving on."

Richard informs Lorelai that grapefruit is brain food.

final shot of the episode, are heartbreaking.

META, META, META Lorelai tells Michel to “call Gandolfi’s and order a case of champagne,” a tribute to Amy's longtime friend and Stars Hollow book store manager Mike Gandolfi (Andrew).

TODAY’S CELEBRATION The unveiling of...the Rory Curtain. Also, Rory gets her car and Richard sees Lorelai in action at the inn.

KIRK OF ALL TRADES Stars Hollow Video clerk.

TAYLOR OF ALL TRADES Stars Hollow Video owner.

EMILY’S MAID DU JOUR Heloise.

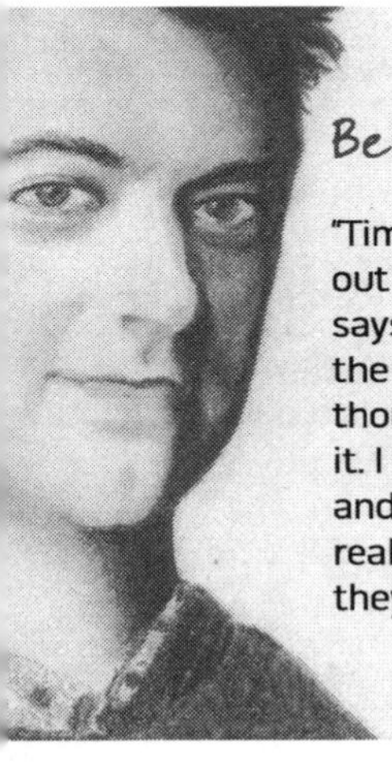

Behind the Scenes Kirk at the Video Store

“Timing was something that I had to figure out on my feet pretty early on,” Sean Gunn says. “I remember when I was working in the video store and I had a moment that I thought was really funny the way I was doing it. I was taking a bit of a pause to exhale and do this kind of sigh that I thought was really hilarious. Then when I watched it back, they edited out the pause so it wasn’t funny. It taught me, or reiterated to me, that my timing had to be both spot on and I didn’t have any extra time to mess with. If I thought something took a few extra beats, that really wasn’t an option. I had to figure out how to time it correctly and barrel through the dialogue, which was tricky but a great acting exercise.”

"There was a line where I said, 'I miss my home,' so I decided to do it like I was coming from someplace else, like she missed her village far away, not just being at her house. I guess it worked because Amy was like, 'Yeah, that's Gypsy.'"

-ROSE ABDOO (GYPSY)

EVERY WEDNESDAY AT 3 When Emily gets her hair done.

6247 Lorelai's Stars Hollow Video card number

AND INTRODUCING...*Gypsy* Our first glimpse of Gypsy also happened to be the scene Rose Abdoo performed for her audition, she says. "At the time, I didn't know I was going to be part of the town; I just thought it was a one-day thing." During the actress' first days on set, it was series veteran Edward Herrmann who eased her nervousness tremendously. "He was so kind to me and we kind of bonded because we both had a Michigan connection. We also talked about theater. He just totally put me at ease, and that was the scene where he kept saying 'check the car again.'"

AMEN, SISTER FRIEND

EMILY: I can't calm down! I can't turn around without him being there, following me, staring at me.
LORELAI: Well, he likes you.
EMILY: Don't be cute, do not be cute! The man is driving me insane. I am going to go insane, and if you don't help me, I will take you with me!

PARIS: According to the papers, there's been a huge increase in the number of families fleeing the major cities in favor of small towns. Hundreds of thousands of city-slicking yuppies carting the trophy wife

Bio David Sutcliffe (Christopher Hayden)

Like Yanic Truesdale, David Sutcliffe is a native of Canada, born in Saskatoon and educated at the University of Toronto.

He moved to Los Angeles (with a short stint in New York City) to pursue his acting career, making appearances in *Will & Grace*, *Friends*, *CSI* and *Providence*, before landing the role of Rory's father, Christopher.

After *Gilmore*, he snagged the recurring role of Kevin Nelson on *Private Practice*. Like his on-screen love interest, Lauren Graham, he also appeared on the *World Series of Poker* in 2005.

In 2006, People magazine caught up with him right before Season 7 kicked off. At the time, Sutcliffe was just getting into...ballroom dancing? "I signed up for the introductory course, which was like a four-week thing," he told the magazine. "By the end of it, I was hooked. I love it. It's sort of flirty, but it's not sexual. I can't quit until I've got it down and I can really dance." One more reason Emily preferred Christopher to Luke?

and the asthmatic kids off to small towns in search of the simple life. Milk a cow, pet a pig, find yourself, all that kind of crap.

PARIS [*summing up Stars Hollow*]: Nothing, not even a cigarette butt on the ground, I can't believe it. This town would make Frank Capra wanna throw up.

RICHARD [*to Lorelai*]: I am an annoyance to my wife and a burden to my daughter. Suddenly I realize what it feels like to be obsolete. I hope that you never have to learn what that feels like.

2.13 A-Tisket, A-Tasket

First aired: Feb. 5, 2002 // Written by Amy Sherman-Palladino // Directed by Robert Berlinger

The annual "Bid on a Basket" fundraiser is in full swing. Though a tad Donna Reedish, it's one of those traditions that makes Stars Hollow the quirky American town the girls love. So why is it causing so much trouble this year? Jackson's mad at Sookie, Jess outbids Dean for Rory's basket (and Rory loses the bracelet Dean gave her), and Miss Patty is trying to get Lorelai a man. Lane's faring no better as Henry finally realizes that Mrs. Kim will make any date with her impossible. And when Lorelai finds Emily in her corner, she goes against her better judgment and gives Jess something she never thought she would—a chance.

GINCHY! Miss Patty carrying a picture of Lorelai for her matchmaking efforts; Jackson going from moving in with Sookie to proposing; Lane and her mother commiserating over the loss of Henry, the Korean, church-going doctor-to-be; Lorelai's disgust at the way Emily backs her up over Rory and Jess; and Rory calling Jess.

NOTES *'He has his eye on her and he's trouble.'*

Last time it was Jackson dragging his heels about advancing his relationship with Sookie (2.1). Now Sookie's the one who's been putting off discussing moving in together.

Jess takes Rory to the bridge from which Luke pushed him (2.5) for their picnic.

There's something oddly touching about the way Lorelai explains her fondness for the romantic idea behind the basket fundraiser; she speaks

Favorite Scenes: Sean Gunn

"This is the first episode I did that I really started to love the character," Sean Gunn says. "It's still probably my favorite scene that I did in the whole span. It was the first time that, even though it was ridiculous, you got the idea that Kirk was a real guy, that he wasn't just this punch line. At the end of the episode he went home and had this life that seemed really kind of sad and dreary to me. That was really fun because I felt like that was the first scene that took some chops beyond just timing. I think the character changed a little bit after that."

of it with the same sentimental fascination she has with snow.

While every *Gilmore* boyfriend inspires its fans and haters, the final moments of this episode between Rory and Jess on the phone is a clear example of what Amy & Dan were brilliant at. Few TV writers have matched the Palladinos' talent for portraying young love.

TODAY'S CELEBRATION The "Bid on a Basket" fundraiser.

$90 What Jess pays for Rory's basket at the auction.

$35 What Kirk pays for Sookie's basket.

$52.50 What Luke pays for Lorelai's basket.

$250 What Jackson ends up paying Kirk for Sookie's basket. (He's paying it off in weekly installments of crinkle-cut carrots.)

12 The number of brothers and sisters Kirk has.

YOU'VE ENTERED EMILYLAND [*explaining that Richard's joined a cigar club*]: Twice a week he comes home smelling like a flophouse.

Bio Ted Rooney (Morey Dell)

Early on, Ted Rooney quickly discovered the value of a good imagination. "My mom would often get stories like, 'I think one of your sons is underneath a bush picking flowers and singing to himself,'" he remembers. "'Oh, that would be Ted.'"

After playing basketball in Germany for a while, Rooney came back and pursued acting, including some off-Broadway work in New York City, before moving to California.

"I'm one of those guys that does the small guest roles, that slides below the radar, that nobody really recognizes, and makes a living. That actor is a dying breed right now. A lot of the guys that I've known at auditions are not showing up anymore; they're back to whatever they used to do."

In other words, a character actor, yet one who has appeared on many shows that enjoy a strong following: *Lost, Seinfeld, ER, Roswell, Malcolm in the Middle, 7th Heaven, Weeds*... and a *Star Trek* spinoff.

As the seventh of nine children, Rooney had that once-in-a-lifetime opportunity to be the other "Seven of Nine" on *Star Trek Voyager* when he played the alien Varn. "I saw that my outfit sold online, too. I was tempted because it fit me perfectly. It was handmade out of leather, and I thought for a couple of Halloween events, it would be kind of cool."

For his *Gilmore Girls* audition, Rooney cut short a vacation in Mexico and "was in and out in probably 20 seconds. I said a couple lines, walked out, went back on vacation. So I was very surprised to hear that I actually got the part. I think it was when I walked in the room, they thought, 'Oh, *that'll* be funny!'"

Bio Sally Struthers (Babette Dell)

Like on-screen husband Ted Rooney, Sally Struthers was born in Portland, Oregon. Discovering her on the irreverent *Smothers Brothers Comedy Hour*, famed producer Norman Lear cast her as Gloria Bunker Stivic on *All in the Family* in 1971. After winning two Emmys on that show, she hasn't stopped working since. (The character Gloria even had her own self-titled show later on.)

In addition to copious amounts of cartoon voice work for everything from *TaleSpin* to *Fred Flintstone and Friends*, she's rarely been off the stage. Anyone who grew up in the US in the 1980s can also attest to the work she did for the Christian Children's Fund, which aimed to help support impoverished children in the developing world.

AMEN, SISTER FRIEND

KIRK: I don't need you to buy me another basket. I won this one. You can't just come by and take it away. Just because you have a girlfriend and she made this basket for you doesn't give you the right to bully those of us who don't have girlfriends or anybody to make a basket for them.
JACKSON: I swear, you better be as pathetic as you sound.
KIRK: Oh, trust me

EMILY: And Rory, how's that boyfriend of yours?
RORY [*still fuming over Dean discussing their fight with her mom*]: Apparently very chatty.

What I Kept

I don't think I kept anything. But keep in mind we thought we were going to go back. So perhaps I would've taken something, I don't know. But I don't have anything.

—Yanic Truesdale (Michel)

2.14 It Should've Been Lorelai

First aired: Feb. 12, 2002 // Written by Daniel Palladino // Directed by Lesli Linka Glatter

Lane's on house arrest after the Henry fiasco, Rory and Paris are debate partners at Chilton, and Christopher's brought Sherry to the Hollow. Emily is crushed to see Christopher moving on without her daughter; Lorelai has her own issues with it all.

GINCHY! Lane's phone-stalking of Rory around town; Paris grilling Lorelai over Rory's milk-laden cereal; Brad's reaction to Paris on stage; the elaborate way Rory gets Lane's Belle & Sebastian CD to her; and Christopher's angry reaction to Lorelai's little speech.

NOTES *'He's always been crazy about you but you've always kept him at arm's length. You keep everyone at arm's length.'*

Dean's saving up for a new motorcycle that we'll never see. Brad, who apparently changed schools after his first run-in with Paris during *Romeo & Juliet* (2.9), returns for the assisted-suicide debate.

This is the first time Lorelai and Rory get to meet Sherry, and oddly, the first time Christopher meets Sookie. This might also be the first time we really, really get to see Lorelai's selfish side. Though she didn't handle the Max issue well, what we saw then was blind panic. Her reaction to Sherry insinuating herself into Rory's life, on the other hand, is the first flash of the selfishness that will make Lorelai such an interesting character throughout the series. The fact that Christopher points out how she kept him and Max apart when it looked like there would be a wedding is particularly interesting.

Sherry is the East Coast sales rep for L'Oreal Cosmetics. Christopher's now driving a Volvo. Sherry's last relationship lasted 11 years with no marriage. She tells Rory that she wants at least two kids, and was even considering single parenthood before she met Christopher. Her feelings on this subject will take a dramatic turn in a few years (5.6).

TODAY'S CELEBRATION The Chilton assisted-suicide debate.

META, META, META Paris telling Rory that she only speaks 135 words per minute (compared with Paris' 178 wpm) is a cheeky riff on the show's own trademark fast-talking.

WEDNESDAY NIGHTS AT 7 When Christopher calls Rory.

AGE 2 How old Kirk was when Mrs. Kim met him.

8 MONTHS How long Christopher and Sherry have been together.

YOU'VE ENTERED EMILYLAND You know historical homes are infested with mold, don't you? It gets inside the walls and grows out of sight and shoots off spores that slowly kill you and your family.

AMEN, SISTER FRIEND

PARIS: I was listening to the CD I burned of the cassettes I made of our mock debates against the make-believe team and I realized that you were not talking fast enough.

LORELAI [*what she says to piss off Christopher*]: I was just thinking, you know, all these years, no matter what my relationship status has been, whether I've been dating or hibernating or whatever, I think I've always had you in the back of my mind, you know. The prospect of us being together. But this prospect was sort of indefinitely on hold while you found yourself and got your personal life together so that you could really be there for me, and especially for Rory. But you and I have been so linked in my mind that I think I have unconsciously sabotaged every decent relationship I've had, including the one with Max, because I was waiting for you, and I shouldn't have been. And now that I see that, and I see you settling down with Sherry, I think I can move beyond it.

Bio Rose Abdoo (Gypsy)

Though many *Gilmore* regulars grew to love the show's unique little quirks, a small number were fans of the series before they ever got there. Rose Abdoo counts herself among them. "I would always watch it, so sometimes if I would do an episode, I'd be at the table read going, '*That's* what's going to happen?!' I was participating as a fan and a townsperson."

Born in Chicago, she came up in the business through the improvisation scene, spending four years with the famed Second City group, working alongside several notable performers including Stephen Colbert, Chris Farley and Amy Sedaris. Though it was fellow Chicagoan Mara Casey, a casting director for *Gilmore*, who first approached her about trying out for the show, Abdoo actually read for the part of Sookie for the pilot.

When it came time to audition for Gypsy, Abdoo says, "There were a lot of people at that audition, and I remember thinking I've gotta look like an auto mechanic, what am I going to wear? My friend that I was living with, she had a watch with a really wide wristband, and I was like yeah, that's what an auto mechanic would wear. And I thought you know what, I'm going to put my hair in pigtails, and I made the decision that every time I did Gypsy, I want my hair to be the same. But that day of the audition I thought she should be a little bit of a tomboy."

During her time on *Gilmore*, Abdoo also enjoyed success among young audiences as Senorita Rodriguez on the Disney Channel hit *That's So Raven*. One of the more challenging aspects of her career was her transition from doing improvisational work to scripted television and film. "I always said that in Chicago, when I did Second City, I was always 'the actress at Second City.' And then I'd do a legitimate play and they'd be like, 'she's that improviser from down the street.'"

2.15 Lost and Found

First aired: Feb. 26, 2002 // Written by Amy Sherman-Palladino // Directed by Gail Mancuso

Luke's had it with living in his cramped apartment above the diner now that Jess is there; Lorelai is doing her best to get along with Jess, who's cleaning her gutters; and Rory's discovered that she's lost the bracelet Dean gave her. Luke and Jess both seem bent on "taking a chance" to shed their Unabomber tendencies, in their own unique ways.

GINCHY! Jess driving Luke crazy with his "then we can hold hands and skip afterwards" retort to Luke's remodeling plans; the plans for town domination that Taylor seems to let slip to Luke; Lorelai's "you little jerk" speech to Jess; Luke taking the sledgehammer to his old place and then hitting Jess with his own "we'll hold hands and skip afterwards" bit.

NOTES *'You might wanna reevaluate how madly in love she is. I wouldn't start calling him son yet.'*

Lorelai's hurting from her failed attempt to clean their rain gutters. As she told Luke at the "Bid on a Basket" event (2.13), she'd been hoping the Collins kids would buy her basket and end up cleaning them.

Clearly Lorelai's learned nothing from her furry alarm clock (1.2) as she now has one that wakes you up to the barnyard animal sound of your choice.

Dean notices that Rory's not wearing the bracelet he gave her, which she lost when she was at the bridge with Jess (2.13) two weeks ago. Jess sneaks into her room and slips it under her bed.

TODAY'S CELEBRATION "Buy a Book" fundraiser at the library.

TAYLOR OF ALL TRADES Owner of the apartment (and the building) that Luke wants to rent. He owns 10 buildings! He also has his eye on the flower shop next to Luke's Diner for a collectible plate store.

1.5 INCHES The grass height at all of Taylor's properties.

$100,00 What Luke pays for the building next to the diner to keep Taylor from moving in there.

AMEN, SISTER FRIEND

RORY [*to Jess*]: You come over. You seem to have a very firm grasp of the English language. You put together several full sentences, even using a couple of words that contain two or more syllables, and then my mother appears and suddenly we need a thought bubble over your head to understand what you're thinking. Can you tell me why that is?

LUKE [*to Lorelai about Taylor*]: He's systematically buying up the town. He's gonna turn it into Taylorville where everyone'll wear cardigans and have the same grass height.

LUKE: I knew I just had to do something, and I had your voice going round and round in my head.
LORELAI: Yeah, it's kinda like the "Small World" song.

2.16 There's the Rub

First aired: April 9, 2002 // Written by Sheila R Lawrence // Directed by Amy Sherman-Palladino

Can you say relax? Luke is expanding his apartment above the diner so he can finally get a bit of peace living with Jess, Lorelai's been lured into spending the weekend at the relaxing Grove Park Spa (OK, with her mother, but still), and Rory's all set for a relaxing weekend of doing laundry and eating Indian food. What could possibly go wrong?

GINCHY! Madeline and Louise processing Paris' request for help on a Friday night; pretty much every spa scene; Paris saving Rory from Dean's wrath; Lorelai convincing Emily to steal the robe; Dean and Lorelai saying "Rory wouldn't lie," and neither of them believing it anymore.

NOTES *'Why can't we have what you and Rory have?'*

Paris' dad has moved back home after realizing how much it would cost to divorce her mother.

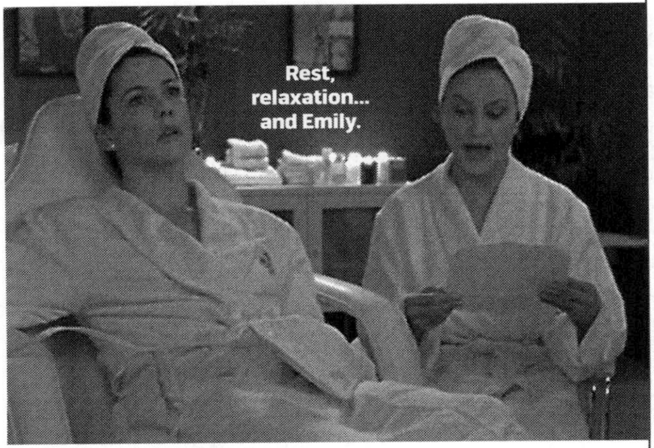
Rest, relaxation... and Emily.

"We always had a festival in Stars Hollow every episode, so we worked all night most of those nights. We always had little side games going. The crew at one point got into electric airplanes. At lunch, everybody would be flying their airplanes through Stars Hollow. We got into horseshoes for a while. We were hardcore into karaoke. That was a really big deal with our show."

–PATTY MALCOLM, LAUREN GRAHAM'S STAND-IN

Behind the Scenes Writing 'The Rub'

"We definitely were drawn to the idea of putting Lorelai and Emily in an intimate situation where they're vulnerable and can't escape, so that they have no choice but to join forces," says this episode's writer, Sheila R. Lawrence. "An evil health spa seemed like the perfect solution! (Plus, we were hoping it would mean that we could write off massages as research.)"

In the episode, "Just as Lorelai's starting to let herself really enjoy being with her mom like this, Emily defensively pulls back. Not only that, she blames Lorelai for pushing her to do things outside her comfort zone, like eat in a bar. That came directly from an incident with my own mom, where the details were very different, but the feelings were absolutely the same."

Though beloved *Barney Miller* star Hal Linden portrays the "silver fox" who hits on Emily at the bar, Lawrence says it was actually '70s heartthrob Chad Everett (*Medical Center*) who they thought of as the prototype for the character, who ended up actually being called Chad.

"Dan Palladino went so far as to bring in one of his albums, so we had his picture staring at us in the writers room while we were breaking the episode. And, as a tidbit that's probably only interesting to my immediate family, my brother played the bartender in those scenes."

This is one of those "it's going in the vault" episodes; every minute nearly perfect. In 42 minutes we get a quantum leap in Emily and Lorelai's relationship, an amazing use of Kelly Bishop, a brilliant three-hander between Paris, Rory and Jess, and an unexpected evolution in Rory's character.

Lorelai's masseur, Kip, is actually Graham's personal assistant, Gary Riotto. (He'll crop up again as a customer in 7.16.)

TODAY'S CELEBRATION Lorelai and Emily's spa vacation.

YOU'VE ENTERED EMILYLAND I certainly don't eat at bars. Hookers eat at bars!

AMEN, SISTER FRIEND

LORELAI: Mom, you signed us up for a couple's massage.
EMILY: So?
LORELAI: A couple's massage is for a couple, not a couple of people.
EMILY: It's more efficient this way. We'll both be finished at the same time.
LORELAI: Mom, do you know what most people who get these massages do about five minutes after it's over? They have sex, together, probably while wearing their robes.

PARIS [*on phone to her nanny after being invited by Rory to stay for dinner*]: Hola, es Paris. Voy a comer la cena de cas de Rory. Hay mucho mac and cheese!

PARIS: Typical guy response. Worship Kerouac and Bukowski, God forbid you'd pick up anything by Jane Austen.
JESS: Hey, I've read Jane Austen.
PARIS: You have?
JESS: Yeah, and I think she would've liked Bukowski.

2.17 Dead Uncles and Vegetables

First aired: April 16, 2002 // Written by Daniel Palladino // Directed by Jamie Babbit

Luke's arranging a funeral for his Uncle Louie, Emily is nudging Sookie down the aisle of a wedding she can never afford, and Taylor Doose's market faces some stiff competition from a familiar face.

GINCHY! Rory constantly forcing Jess to help Luke in the diner; the delight Lorelai takes in running Luke's; Luke's response to Emily's "What do you think of the Romanovs?"; the town reminiscing about what a bastard Louie was; and Rory delighted by her success at drawing Jess into town events.

NOTES *'I don't wanna take away your fun, I just want you to be careful. See, you've entered Emilyland.'*

Apparently Emily having her DAR meetings at the inn wasn't a throwaway gag after she co-signed Lorelai's loan to rebuild their house (2.11).

The more we hear about Uncle Louie, the more we realize that he was very much like Luke. It seems that Luke realizes this, too. While there's always been something between him and Lorelai, this may be what lights the fire to get him thinking about settling down. The possibility of the two of them getting together is one not lost on Emily, either.

TODAY'S CELEBRATION The DAR meeting, and the funeral for Luke's Uncle Louie.

TAYLOR LEFT ME TWISTIN' The song that the Troubadour wrote

Emily's Defining Moment

Though Emily is beloved for her ability to cut anyone down to size with a few well-chosen words, it is her drive to do what she thinks is right that makes her so intriguing. Kelly Bishop found a scene in this episode between Emily and Lorelai particularly revealing.

"I remember sitting on the end of the bed and I was actually admitting to her how envious I was of the relationship that she and Rory had. And she was trying to say to me, 'But you have to let them be free.' And I was saying, 'But that's not the way I was raised. I wasn't taught that you become *friends*.'

"Emily was very anxious in that moment because she was trying to do it perfectly right, the way she had obviously taken it from her mother. Like a good little girl, dressed just right and doing the right thing. And here she is, this crazy rebel daughter. That's a moment when she's truly trying to understand Lorelai and to understand this relationship, but it's really almost a lament she has: 'That's not what I was taught, that's not the way I grew up.' I found it a very vulnerable moment. I loved it, actually."

about how Taylor waited before he jumped to his aide against the other troubadour (1.21).

85 How old Uncle Louie was when he kicked it.

AND HERE'S A SHOUT OUT TO OUR INTERNATIONAL FANS

Sookie downloading "wedding stuff" from Prague. "And did you know it's not called Czechoslovakia anymore? It's just Czech Republic. Slovakia is its own separate thing. It's weird, isn't it?"

Says Czech Republic-based fan Katka Rylichová, "There´s lots of Czech Republic and Prague references in *Gilmore Girls*. People here thought it was added in translation and didn´t believe that it was in the original. I wonder why there were so many references; it's not like anyone knew that Czech Republic exists when I was in the US."

"There are things that I learned on Gilmore Girls that I have brought into my recording process. You have a scene or two and it's make-or-break time; I really thrive on that level of urgency. Like when you're in a play, you can't go, 'Can we try that one more time?' People take plenty of takes sometimes when it requires it, but you don't want to be that one dude who screws it up for everyone."

-GRANT-LEE PHILLIPS (THE TROUBADOUR)

AMEN, SISTER FRIEND

LORELAI [*to Luke, after he asks her if she knows how to make coffee*]: I am Cathy Coffee, mister, the bastard offspring of Mrs. Folger and Juan Valdez.

TAYLOR [*to the vegetable seller*]: Wait a minute, I know you. You're that long-haired freak that wanted to be town troubadour even though that weird, brown-corduroy-jacket-wearing freak was already it.

LORELAI: I don't wanna take away your fun, I just want you to be careful. See, you've entered Emilyland.
SOOKIE: Emilyland?
LORELAI: It's an upside-down world where the Horchow House is considered low-rent and diamonds less than 24 carats are Cracker Jack trinkets and Bentleys are for losers who can't afford a Rolls.

LORELAI: Come on, scrambled's better. Give it a shot. Say you want two scrambled eggs on toast, please?
CUSTOMER: OK, young lady, two scrambled eggs on toast.
LORELAI: Adam and Eve on a raft and wreck 'em! That's real live diner talk, see? The wreck 'em is the scrambled part.

2.18 Back in the Saddle Again

First aired: April 23, 2002 // Written by Linda Loiselle Guzik // Directed by Kevin Dowling

Rory and the Chilton kids are tasked with designing a consumer product, and rope Richard into being their adviser; Michel's mom is in town and Dean is getting a little too needy. What begins as a cynical cash grab over a new type of first aid kit becomes something more important to Richard's own sense of self-worth.

GINCHY! Paris' pitch for the first aid kit; the meeting of the StyleAid Corp.; and that last, heartbreaking scene.

NOTES *'Emily, I am in the middle of something here and I don't expect you to understand it.'*

Richard's new passion for antique cars is a nod to Edward Herrmann's own collection of classic automobiles. Emily and Richard have been married 35 years; that's also how long Richard says he's been in the business world.

Dean and Rory's awkward relationship takes a sadder turn, but will get even more depressing over the next two seasons.

TODAY'S CELEBRATION Richard's emergence from a short-lived retirement.

EMILY'S MAID DU JOUR Elsa.

Bio Scout Taylor-Compton (Clara Forester)

Like so many on *Gilmore Girls*, Desariee Starr "Scout" Taylor-Compton's handful of appearances as Dean's little sister, Clara, offer a delight inversely proportional to her scant screen time.

Born in Long Beach, Calif., Taylor-Compton told her parents at a very early age that she wanted to be on TV. After some false starts, her mother managed to get her into the student film scene. Once she had an agent, she started out making commercials before appearing on such TV hits as *ER* and *Ally McBeal*.

Since then, the actress has popped up in a slew of movies and TV shows, including several in the horror genre. Like on-screen big brother Jared Padalecki's tussle with Jason in the *Friday the 13th* remake, Taylor-Compton tackled another '80s killer in Rob Zombie's *Halloween* (2007) and its sequel. (She actually auditioned for *Friday the 13th!*) Though horror movies are a time-tested launching pad for young actors, many are quick to point out that Taylor-Compton having a mortician for a father might also have something to do with it.

SUSIE ST. JAMES The name on Sookie's wedding invitations.

18 Michel's age when he left France.

SALES What four aptitude tests have told Lane that her career should be.

THE PRODUCT PITCHES
—Lipstick Lo-Jack: Louise and Madeline's solution to lost makeup.
—Locker robot: Madeline's off-the-cuff thought for a homework help buddy.
—Tricked out first-aid kits: Paris' cynical suggestion for getting teens to buy cheaply produced medical supplies turns into the StyleAid Corp.
—What actually wins the contest: The locker alarm.

YOU'VE ENTERED EMILYLAND [*On people who go to psychiatrists*] Disturbed people, deviants, people with multiple personalities who see things and hear people talking to them and roam the streets talking to themselves and licking parking meters.

AMEN, SISTER FRIEND
RORY: Who knows how to [*build a robot*]?
MADELINE: I don't know. He looks like he should know.
BRAD: I've never built a robot.
LOUISE: But you've tried, haven't you?
BRAD: Yes, I have.

PARIS [*pitching her locker first aid kit*]: Monday morning, Muffin wakes up and looks in the mirror. "Oh no, I have a zit on my face. I'll just look down when I walk so hunky football player won't notice." And bam — Muffin smacks right into the cafeteria wall. Ouch, that's gotta hurt.

What's Up With Madeline?

"I guess a little part of my personality is Madeline, but I decided that Madeline really didn't think about a lot of things," Shelly Cole says. "She thought about weird things, but I always thought that Madeline was in her own little happy world. In that little world there are butterflies and fairies flying around and they have soup there and they have striped socks. That's a really small part of my personality. But I always played her like that because it was the most fun. Like oh, a light bulb goes on over her head and she just says whatever she's thinking. She was a really odd character to maintain over the years."

2.19 Teach Me Tonight

First aired: April 30, 2002 // Written by Amy Sherman-Palladino // Directed by Steven Robman

Jess is in serious danger of repeating his junior year of high school. Yet how could one night of tutoring Jess land Rory in the hospital with a fractured wrist? While both Rory's car and Luke and Lorelai's relationship are destroyed, the crisis does end the tiff between Lorelai and Christopher. But where does Sherry fit into all of this?

GINCHY! Luke and Jess' brief exchange after the accident on the bridge; and *a film by kirk* (Miss Patty did the choreography).

NOTES *'That little punk nephew of yours almost killed my kid tonight!'*
Taylor's shown *The Yearling* at the movie-in-the-square event for the last three years. Lorelai and Christopher haven't talked since she pissed him off with her little speech (2.14). Jess' small-town crime wave continues with missing baseballs at the school and a missing ladder at Doose's Market.

When Jess points out that being a Christiane Amanpour-like foreign correspondent sounds a little rough for Rory, she immediately freaks out about what would happen if she couldn't realize that dream. Already the seeds have been sewn for her later career implosion (5.21). When Lorelai shows up at the hospital, she's every bit Emily's daughter; compare her behavior with Emily's hospital flipout in 1.10.

TODAY'S CELEBRATION Movie-in-the-square night.

KIRK OF ALL TRADES Movie director. (His hero, Akira Kurosawa. Sorry, he meant *Who's the Boss* director Asaad Kelada.)

AMEN, SISTER FRIEND
LUKE: Hey, I am sorry about Rory. You know I care more about her than I do myself, but at least you know where Rory is and at least you know that she's OK. Now I have to find Jess and I have to make sure that he's OK, and if that cuts into your screaming time, well that's just too damn bad!
LORELAI: Go to hell!
LUKE: Right back at ya!

Bio Teal Redmann (Louise Grant)

With her Clara Bow looks and smoky voice, Teal Redmann was always going to land roles like the flirtatious Louise Grant and, more famously, Jim Brass' wayward daughter, Ellie, on the original *CSI*.

Born in Minnesota, Redmann moved to Los Angeles at 17 (though her first modeling gig came at the age of 2). In addition to *Gilmore*, she's appeared on *Boston Public*, in Disney's TV movie *Double Teamed*, and the 2003 flick *Dumb and Dumberer: When Harry Met Lloyd*.

2.20 Help Wanted

First aired: May 7, 2002 // Written by Allan Heinberg // Directed by Chris Long

For the first time in living memory, Luke's Diner is closed, and Lorelai and Rory both know why. While Lorelai struggles to get her father's new company off to a good start, Rory does a slow burn over how everybody blames Jess for the accident and refuses to acknowledge her own culpability.

GINCHY! Dean reading Rory's letter and how quickly he forgives her; Lane finally getting to play the drums...in the dark; and Rory and Luke's final scene.

NOTES *'Pain is your body's way of saying, 'I'm not OK now, but I will be soon.'*

After 20 years as Richard's secretary, Margie refuses to come to work for him at The Gilmore Group.

From shopping for school supplies with Rory (1.4) to shopping with Emily for Rory's birthday present (1.6), Lorelai bonds with her family through shopping; this episode's office supply hunt continues the tradition.

Though Rory's guilty conscience over the way everybody sees Jess is interesting, this feels more like a filler episode.

TODAY'S CELEBRATION The opening of The Gilmore Group, Richard's new international insurance consulting firm (as of last week).

KIRK OF ALL TRADES Though he never actually lands the gig, he sure tries to get hired by Sophie's music store. (He *is* licensed to carry a gun.)

AMEN, SISTER FRIEND

LANE [*to Sophie, trying to get access to the drums*]: I can't go home until you say yes. I have to rock, I have to! Please, I'm so begging you—let me rock!

RORY: I'm sick of this. I'm sick of everyone treating me like I'm some kind of mindless idiot being led around by a guy.

LORELAI: I'm sorry but when my daughter comes home broken I get to hate the guy who broke her. That's how it works. He's gone, I win. You are wearing a cast and I get to hate him forever!

Emily's Jewelry

At some point during the second season, Kelly Bishop began pointing out to Amy and the producers that somebody in Emily's position would have some piece of jewelry that's important to her, probably a necklace. Since the actress is allergic to costume jewelry and she realized that they were not going to spend a few grand on a gold necklace for the character, she took care of the matter herself.

While visiting family out of town, she bought a necklace for Emily. "So that gold necklace you almost always see me in, that's mine," she says. "And all the rings and the earrings, that's all my jewelry because I didn't want to end up with a rash. But once something becomes a costume, I don't wear it."

She's worn that necklace twice since *Gilmore*, both times in plays. "It's this rather heavy gold necklace, which I could be enjoying any time I want, but I only wear it as a costume."

2.21 Lorelai's Graduation Day

First aired: May 14, 2002 // Written by Daniel Palladino // Directed by Jamie Babbit

After three years, Lorelai's finally graduating from her business class. Counter to her wishes, Rory's invited Richard and Emily to the event, and counter to everyone's wishes, Rory's taken the bus to New York City to find Jess.

! GINCHY! Lorelai riffing off a barely awake Jackson; Rory's "Salute to Vegetables" story (she was broccoli); pretty much every scene of Rory in New York; the final scene between Lorelai and Rory.

NOTES *'No more finals, no more studying, no more school, the pressure's off.'*

✱ Lane's taken to practicing her drumming with Lorelai's pots and pans. As sweet and helpful as people think Rory is, she's also every bit as willful as her mother. If Lorelai tells her not to do something, you can bet she will go ahead and do it anyway, whether it's blabbing about how she got her cast to Emily (last episode) or about their termite problem (2.11). This time it's telling her grandparents about Lorelai's graduation.

✱ Rory's "If all else fails you can marry rich" line is a completely accidental bit of foreshadowing for what is to come (7.21). Paris is already plotting to run for student council.

✱ Liza, the soon-to-be ex of Zach at Lorelai's graduation, is played by Alicia Bergman, who played Gemmy Nardini in Amy's *Love and Marriage*

Lane & Her Drums

"I was really excited when they told me I was going to get drum lessons," Keiko Agena remembers. "I still play the drums a little now, which is something I never would've done if it wasn't for the show." Of course having a professional guitarist for a husband means she's not likely to lose those skills anytime soon. "Sometimes after a bunch of Tsingtao beers I'll get on the drum set for a little bit, which has been a lot of fun."

"Why did you come here?"

Bio ☺ Biff Yeager (Tom)

Biff Yeager as Taylor Doose? It could've happened. Our Tom the contractor read for the role back when they were making the pilot. "I didn't get that part, and actually I'm kinda glad because [Michael Winters] did a hell of a lot with that role. Then about seven or eight months later they called me in for Tom." The only thing that the casting directors told him: "Read fast."

Yeager has spent more than 30 years working in television and film, appearing in everything from *Seinfeld* and *Hill Street Blues* to *Star Trek The Next Generation* and *Straight to Hell*, a movie that merged the acting (!) talents of The Clash's Joe Strummer and The Pogues. Like many in the business, he traces his passion for acting back to school. In this case, kindergarten. "I played an elephant and there were seven other animals on the stage, and they were all too scared to do their lines, so I got up and did everybody's."

Growing up in Long Island, NY, he spent the first part of his life doing ornamental work with iron (and occasionally getting in trouble) before realizing acting was what he wanted to do. Aside from his acting work, he's also had at least one script optioned, and directed a few short movies himself.

"I thought one of the reasons I never got too much further was I never networked, which is what you really have to do," Yeager says. "You have to get out to parties and really meet people and I never did that. If a job came in, it came in; if it didn't, it didn't. Maybe lazy is what people would call it."

sitcom. (Last name sound familiar?) Zach is played by Seth MacFarlane, creator of the animated comedy *Family Guy*, which stars Alex Borstein (aka Drella/Miss Celine/the original Sookie).

TODAY'S CELEBRATION Lorelai's graduation and Rory's goodbye to Jess.

EMILY'S MAID DU JOUR Beatrice, an English maid who, among other things, prepares a proper English tea, except for forgetting to doily line the plates.

WHAT'S IN LORELAI'S GRAD BASKET FROM CHRISTOPHER
—$25 US savings bond
—Youth hostel card
—Copies of *What Color Is Your Parachute* and *The Portable Nietzsche*
—*The Graduate* DVD
—Armed forces application
—Disposable camera
—A pearl necklace.

THINGS WE'VE LEARNED Emily's filmmaker, Raul, is named after longtime *Gilmore* video editor Raul Davalos.

AMEN, SISTER FRIEND

JESS: Why did you come here?

RORY: What?

JESS: I said why did you come here?

RORY: Well—

JESS: I mean, you ditched school and everything. That's so not you. Why'd you do it?

RORY: Because you didn't say goodbye.

JESS: Oh. Bye, Rory.

RORY: Bye, Jess.

2.22 I Can't Get Started

First aired: May 21, 2002 // Written by Amy Sherman-Palladino and John Stephens // Directed by Amy Sherman-Palladino

Sookie and Jackson are getting married, Rory is Paris' running mate for the student council presidential elections, and Christopher and Lorelai are on the verge of getting back together. What could be a better time to inject a little trouble into the air?

GINCHY! Emily harping on about their "pity invite" to Sookie's wedding; Sookie's pre-wedding freakout; that killer final scene of the girls standing side by side, both at an emotional crossroads.

NOTES *'It's nobody's fault. It just isn't it.'*

Paris telling Rory to be her running mate to better her chances of getting into Harvard is one more step on the road to Paris' ultimate humiliation (3.16).

Behind the Scenes: Gilmore's Pacing

Gilmore Girls' unusual story structure is an important element in the series' infinite rewatchability, according to *Gilmore* writer Janet Leahy. "Something else that made the storytelling fresh was when a story was finished being told, it may not have been the end of the episode. This, too, made for better storytelling. In other words, one of your plots could end in the third act, and so we would begin a new story right there. The show would always have a climax in the last act, dramatically and comedically, but it would not necessarily be the one you'd expect. Often it made you want to tune in next week to see what happens."

"I can't get started..."

✱ Rory kisses Jess for the first time, then runs away. A perfect recreation of her first kiss with Dean (1.7), though way more complicated.

✱ One of the strongest episodes since Season 1, both comedically and dramatically, and a hell of a cliffhanger for a season finale. How could Lorelai ever tell Christopher to abandon Sherry's baby?

TODAY'S CELEBRATION Sookie and Jackson's wedding, Rory and Paris' electoral triumph, and for the Luke and Lorelai fans out there, the collapse of the Lorelai and Christopher relationship.

EMILY'S MAID DU JOUR Inger, played by Alexis Bledel's stand-in, Inger Jackson.

AND INTRODUCING... *'Oy with the poodles, already!"* The phrase that launched a thousand eBay items.

Bio Melissa McCarthy (Sookie St. James)

One of the members of *Gilmore's* large Chicago contingent (including Sean Gunn, Rose Abdoo and casting director Mara Casey), Melissa McCarthy is also one of the few people on the series whose talents were only partially seen on camera. A longtime member of LA's Groundlings improvisational comedy troupe, McCarthy's comic timing is impeccable (search for her name and "Marbles" on YouTube to get some idea of her range).

Though born in Plainfield, Ill., McCarthy didn't fully indulge her interests in performance until she moved to New York City, where a friend convinced her to start hitting the city's comedy clubs during their open-mic nights. Once she found her footing doing stream-of-consciousness comedy, she spent the next five or six years working in New York's theater scene. When she moved to LA, she fell in love with The Groundlings, finding an environment that encouraged her fast-on-the-draw ability to improvise while giving her the opportunity to write and hone her skills with other like-minded performers.

Since *Gilmore*, McCarthy has continued to build a successful TV career, first with the series *Samantha Who?*, and most recently *Mike & Molly*.

AMY AS DIRECTOR Amy's people skills weren't always ideal; the phrase "Amy wanted things Amy's way" has been repeated too often to mention. Yet few would deny that her at-times-abrasive demeanor served to make *Gilmore* a high-quality, consistent series. Though always full of praise for the fine stable of directors who brought their skills to Stars Hollow, Amy, like most showrunners, took the reins when she felt an episode required expert handling.

"I give myself a couple of episodes a year where I know that if I don't get it, it wasn't going to work," she told The AV Club in February 2005. "It's not because somebody else fucked it up.... I get physically ill when I go into the editing booth and I see a very specifically structured, written scene, and my stage directions have been ignored and the dialogue is sloppy and they didn't go enough times and the paces are off."

AMEN, SISTER FRIEND

LUKE: Lorelai, what is it exactly that you want me to do? I'm not mad, I'm not holding a grudge, I heard your apology, I feel I'm being polite, I listened to your doughnut bit, I got you your coffee. What would make you happy?
LORELAI: I want Luke back.
LUKE: He's standing right here.
LORELAI: No, he's not.

PARIS: Everyone in the whole school hates me. Oh yeah, they think I'm the best for the job, but they don't want to go to the mall with me so they won't vote for me, and that means I'm going to lose.
RORY: Well, how is my running with you gonna change anything?
PARIS: Because people think you're nice. You're quiet, you say excuse me, you look like little birds help you get dressed in the morning. People don't fear you.

KIRK [*to Luke about his new suit*]: I got it for Sookie's wedding. I read an article in the paper recently that said that weddings are an excellent place to meet women.
LUKE: Well, if it was in the paper, it must be true.

What *Gilmore* Means to Me

I was 32 when my mother died in January 2010—the same age as Lorelai at the start of the show. My mother was nearly 56, close in age to Emily. And as I began my process of letting go of my own relationship with my mother, I simultaneously watched Lorelai and Emily begin their journey toward re-establishing their own. In many ways I felt validated. I was not crazy, nor was I ungrateful, nor was I a bad daughter. I was a woman who loved her mother deeply, but struggled to speak of this love in a language that my mother could understand. Somehow, Lorelai and Emily helped me to finally get what years of therapy could not—that no matter how hard you try to love someone, nothing you can do or say will change who they are. It took the death of my mother for me to really understand and appreciate *Gilmore Girls*, and the relationship I had with my mother.

—Laura,
Bethlehem, Pa.

KIRK: I hope so, 'cause I'm so damn lonely not even Animal Planet does it for me anymore.

LUKE [*to Jess*]: You know what people told me when I said you were coming here to live with me? They told me I was crazy, they told me I was insane, they told me to start writing letters to Jodie Foster, but I ignored them. I was so sure that I knew what I was doing and then you showed up and you know what happened? You proved them right. I was crazy, and now after all that has happened, after all the chaos and havoc that you have wreaked, you're seriously standing there wearing a T-shirt with a picture of a butt with hands that are flipping *me* off, telling me you wanna come back?

Oh Those Lines!!

Gilmore Girls + the Word-Perfect Rule

To the television audience, *Gilmore Girls* is known primarily for the speed of its dialogue. To actors, it's notorious for its creator's insistence on delivering every single word precisely as written.

"There was lots of fast talking, and even for old pros like Kelly and myself, it was tough," Edward Herrmann admits. He would be able to modify the odd dangling participle if Amy happened to be on set. If she wasn't, there was no changing a letter.

Guest stars had a particularly rough time of it, Kelly Bishop says. "There was a lot of quiet panic with our guests at times." As the social face of the Gilmore family, Emily found herself dealing with everybody from exchange students to debutantes-in-training, which meant Bishop frequently found herself acting opposite many who were new to *Gilmore*.

Olivia Hack (Rory's dormmate Tana) points out, "When you actually booked that show, they'd send you a letter with your first script that they require it to be performed exactly as written, so they're not fooling around from the get-go."

"Many guest actors would come on and they would have a meltdown because they couldn't do it," dialogue coach George Anthony Bell recalls. "It's just the pressure of having to get it completely right, and then to deliver it at a rapid speed. All you're thinking about are the lines and how to get them out."

Few people on either side of the camera were as universally loved and appreciated as Bell. Despite her own appreciation of the man, Emily Kuroda says, "You do a take and you hear him say, 'She said 'and,' not 'but' on that take.' And they're marking it down. And I'm like, 'Aw, man!'"

For those like Katie Walder (Janet) coming from a soap opera background, the word-perfect aspect of the show was particularly challenging. "On a soap, you have one take and you just get out the gist of it. Then they'd be, 'OK, next scene.' That's why people get a bad rap on soaps. It's only because you have one take to do it."

Considering the long hours and rigorous performance requirements that the actors shouldered daily,

This season, mother and daughter were forced to do some major growing up, and with them, the series grew up, too. Though *Gilmore* would hang on to its trademark quirkiness for years to come, Season 2 gradually phased out some of the setup/punchline qualities that pervaded the first season. Compare the end of Season 1 to the final episode this time around and you can appreciate just how complicated the lives of Lorelai and Rory have become in just a year's time.

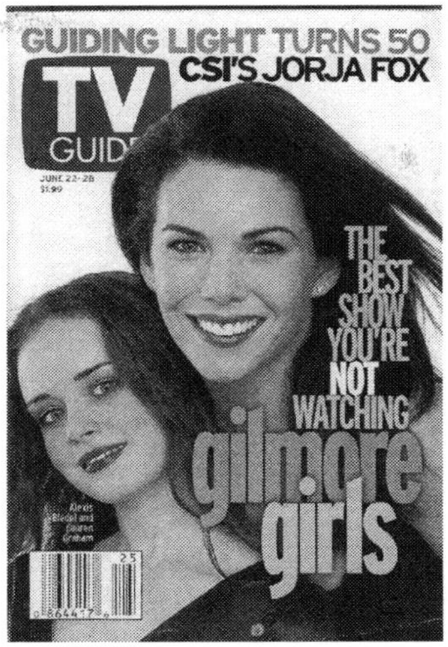

it's hardly surprising that tempers occasionally ran hot. For Herrmann, who had built a highly respected career delivering some of the best-written lines in the English language, *Gilmore*'s insistence on word-perfect delivery occasionally tried his patience. "There were times when I'd really get upset. The insistence on a particular word order that I didn't think was even grammatically correct, and nobody was around to change it; it would drive me nuts.

"Finally, Lauren began saying, 'Oh God, Ed, don't take it so seriously—just change it!' I said, 'Yeah, but you're the star of the show. I'm just this little wee person.' 'Yeah, right,' would be the inevitable reply." These little exchanges would often help him get through these situations. "Finally, you just have to take a breath and make it work."

The writers were also affected by this insistence on script fidelity. "I tried to be very precise with the words and rhythms I used in my scripts," Jane Espenson says. "Rory, Lorelai, Paris... they have extremely specific voices and they engaged in very quick and punchy exchanges. In that situation, you even end up switching out words just to get one fewer syllable into a line."

"Many guest actors would come on and they would have a meltdown because they couldn't do it..."

— DIALOGUE COACH GEORGE ANTHONY BELL ON THE SPEEDY DIALOGUE CHALLENGE

Yet, when Amy & Dan departed at the end of Season 6 and the new *Gilmore* regime did away with the word-perfect requirement, the actors soon came to appreciate what they'd had. "I missed her," Kuroda says of Amy. "I really did. Her wacky energy, her insistence on being word perfect, and fast! Talk fast! I miss that!"

"On some shows where the writing isn't nearly as precise or demanding, you can virtually ad lib your way through it," Herrmann says. "But the fact that Amy insisted on crossing the t's and dotting the i's—often to good effect, but sometimes to not such good effect—it really made you focus and not get sloppy."

"Rory's Feeling a Little Territorial Today"

season **three**

With its cliffhanger Season 2 finale, *Gilmore Girls* seemed primed for its best year to date. Yet in the production offices, tempers that had been guarded in order to weather the program's growing pains now were being vented daily.

While the author would've welcomed the opportunity to speak with Amy & Dan or the other producers involved in *Gilmore*, the only executive who consented to speak about the show also happened to be the one with the worst feelings about his time on it—executive producer Gavin Polone. (Though many who shared their experiences working with Amy for the book admitted she had an abrasive side, they also pointed out how much pressure she was under from network executives to change the elements of the show that actually made it so unique.)

"She would just surround herself with her flunkies," Polone says. "Everything was such a loyalty test. Afterward, there are so many people I've apologized to for how I treated them, including Lauren. Everything was 'off with their head,' and I fired so many first ADs and writers. And later, people like [writer] Jenji Kohan and people who were very successful, apologizing afterward, almost like making amends to all these people I had to fire. It was a real painful experience to have to work under that environment. The thing about it that was so interesting was that [Amy] just wasn't like that in the beginning."

Temperamental artists are not rare in Hollywood, of course. Amy had served under Roseanne Barr, after all. And most people in the business know the classic formula by heart: "People such as Orson Welles were notoriously difficult to work with; Welles was a genius; I'm hard to work with; therefore I'm a genius, too." There was only one thing that made Amy even more annoying to those she worked with. In her case, the formula appeared to be correct.

'Please Don't Even Talk About Washington...'

While most fans took Rory's summer trip to the nation's capital as simply an excuse to explain her absence from Stars Hollow while Jess got chummy with Shane at the beginning of Season 3, some behind the camera say we were actually supposed to get some scenes of Rory in DC. The idea was to show our aspiring journalist meeting her long-time idol, CNN's Christiane Amanpour, there. What allegedly scuppered this proposed meeting was the studio's refusal to come up with the money for a skeleton crew to shoot the scenes on location. Rory would have to wait for the series' final episode to meet Amanpour, and then it would only be in the lobby of the Dragonfly.

3.1 Lazy-Hazy-Crazy Days

First aired: Sept. 24, 2002 // Written and directed by Amy Sherman-Palladino

Lorelai's dreaming about having Luke's twins, Paris finds love (or at least a date) in Washington DC, and Emily and Richard finally understand that their daughter isn't getting back together with Christopher. Yet too many questions remain unanswered as the girls struggle to sort out their love lives in their quest for "the whole package."

! GINCHY! Barbara Boxer sicking Paris on Rep. Doug Ose; Lorelai's defense of Dean in her conversation with Rory; Emily and Richard fighting over Christopher's leaving Lorelai; the weird way Lorelai (or "Mimi") makes up with Luke after all the ugliness over Jess last season.

NOTES *'You don't have to make every decision right now.'*

* Luke telling Lorelai "the reference is enough, you'll learn that one day" in her dream is a fun little nod to Amy & Dan's continuous inser-

Paris contemplates being this close to power (and Jamie) in Washington DC.

tion of odd pop cultural and historical references throughout the series. Lorelai's dream about Luke making her breakfast will actually come true a couple years later (5.4).

✱ Jess has stolen the odd bit of gym equipment and faked a murder scene in the past, but Taylor landing in a wheelchair after somebody left a banana peel on his doorstep may actually be a step toward something far more serious.

✱ Paris' debate partner, Jamie, Princeton man though he may be, will soon play the Dean to Paris' Rory—a smitten boy who will never be able to keep up with her on an intellectual level. Rory's answer to Paris' question, "How do you know if a guy is right for you" gives her the chance to verbalize what we know she's been struggling with since Jess blew into town. Rory's throwaway line about Paris needing a new therapist will come back to haunt her next season (4.2). Lorelai and Rory have refused to speak with Christopher since he went back to Sherry (2.22).

✱ Once again, Richard and Emily lift a reasonably fine episode to greater heights with the few minutes they're on screen. Richard continues to be extremely consistent with his attitude toward both Lorelai and Christopher.

✱ Rory's famous list making surfaces once more, and will ultimately teach her that list making alone is worthless when you're trying to tackle matters of the heart.

Gavin Polone Leaves

The strained relationship between Amy and executive producer Gavin Polone reached its nadir at the table read for this episode, Polone says.

"I remember leaving the table read and going out to my car and calling my lawyer. I said, 'I'm willing to give up money but I've got to get away from here. I can't be around these people anymore. From that point on, I never watched another episode of the show. I don't remember how much money it was, maybe it was $5,000 an episode or something, but during the negotiation there was the opportunity for me to make some extra money if I continued to consult. For some reason Amy wanted that, and we weren't getting along. I said I'll give up the money, I don't care."

TODAY'S CELEBRATION The First Annual Stars Hollow End of Summer Madness Festival.

SID & NANCY OR LEOPOLD & LOEB The names of Lorelai's twins in her dream.

KIRK OF ALL TRADES Purveyor of his own skin-care line called "Hay There," based on the "secret of the cows."

CALLING ALL LAWMAKERS Even without knowing much about Amy & Dan, most *Gilmore* fans realize that they were extremely interested in politics. This episode marked the first coup in this regard when the casting office managed to get Democratic California Sen. Barbara Boxer in front of the camera. "The whole point is we needed a senator or congressman, and I'll be really honest with you: I didn't know the difference between senators and congressmen back then," says casting director Jami Rudofsky. "It was such a learning experience for me. We got the list

The 21½-Hour Day

Already notorious in the business for being the show that keeps many of its cast and crew working 14 hours on a good day, *Gilmore* work days occasionally ran even longer. During the making of this episode, they would surpass even that.

The first day wasn't so bad, and actually had two notable people watching Amy direct, an event that always drew those who wanted to get a glimpse of how the *Gilmore* magic was made. One was actor Fred Savage (*The Wonder Years*), the other, Jackson Douglas.

"The next day is the day we did a 21½hour day," recalls key set costumer Valerie Campbell. Part of that had to do with shooting the End of Summer Madness festival. In the morning they shot the barbershop quartet performing around the gazebo, but had to send them home midday because they were running into serious overtime. Unfortunately, Amy wanted to see them in the background of other shots. After a bit of planning, the wardrobe department quickly had the barbershop costumes washed, dried, and put them on some of the background actors.

Meanwhile, "Jackson comes in and Fred comes in a little bit later. Fred stays maybe four or five hours, he leaves. We're still shooting after 14 hours. Normally you'd go home after 14. We then continued to shoot a crazy amount of time.

"Throughout the day we go up to Jackson: 'Jackson, why don't you go home. You're just observing, you're not even getting paid.' He's like, 'Nah, I'm going to be there till the end. Not like Fred Savage.' From then on I kept going up to him and saying, 'Where's Fred Savage, Jackson?!'

"Needless to say that Jackson ended up directing episodes of *Gilmore Girls*, where Fred Savage did not."

Bio Jackson Douglas (Jackson Belleville)

Poor Jackson Douglas. He was all set to play the love interest to his real-life wife, Alex Borstein—they'd only been married about a year—when her *MADtv* contract yanked her out of the role of Sookie shortly after the presentation pilot was shot. Fortunately, he landed an excellent sparring partner/on-screen wife in Melissa McCarthy.

Considering how often we see Douglas on *Gilmore*, there is maddeningly little public information available on the fellow. What we are left with is his admirable ability to make Jackson Belleville, a somewhat-whiny produce merchant on the printed page, a lovable addition to Stars Hollow's cavalcade of lunatics. We salute you, Jackson Douglas, whoever you are.

of every senator and congressman's offices and just started calling people and sending out faxes. Actually, a lot of people responded."

AMEN, SISTER FRIEND

PARIS: Oh man, I can't believe this! I finally get asked out on a date and I missed it.

LORELAI: I always thought if he could just get it together, grow up, maybe we could do it. Maybe we could really be a family in the stupid, traditional Dan Quayle, golden retriever, grow old together, wear matching jogging suits kind of way. And then he did get it together—he became that guy. . . and he gets to be that guy with her. Chris is gonna have a baby with his girlfriend. He's gonna marry her. . .and he's gonna be there for her while she's pregnant, and he's gonna be there with her while her child grows up, and he's gonna be there for her while she does ...whatever it is she does. And I am in exactly the same place that I was in before.

3.2 Haunted Leg

First aired: Oct. 1, 2002 // Written by Amy Sherman-Palladino // Directed by Chris Long

The awkwardness just keeps on coming for Lorelai and Rory. Christopher's trying to make up with Lorelai, Rory is trying to get over Jess and focus on Dean, and Emily is struggling to understand why Rory and her parents can't be one big happy family. Throw in Kirk asking Lorelai out on a date, and a haunted leg is the least of Lorelai's troubles.

GINCHY! Kirk asking Lorelai out and Rory's response; Luke's glee as he tells Lorelai that Kirk asked him for advice before asking her out;

Emily kicking Christopher out of her house; and Rory and Jess' final scene together.

NOTES *'We must learn that our actions have consequences.'*

Already strained from their aborted swearing in as Puffs (2.7), Rory and Paris' relationship with Francie is going to get a whole lot worse. Jessica Kiper, who plays Jess' summertime fling Shane, went on to become a popular addition to the American reality TV series *Survivor* starting in 2008.

TODAY'S CELEBRATION Paris and Rory's swearing in as student body government president and vice president.

EMILY'S MAID DU JOUR Sarah, who has to remember that the big bell is the door and the small bell is the oven. Sarah also is the rarest of the rare—a maid who actually returns (5.5) with the same name, and is played by the same actress, Christy Keefe.

From the Editing Room 2 Two Cameras

Often in a show that uses two cameras (confusingly called a "one-camera" show in the industry parlance), you set up two cameras on Person A: one for a close-up shot, the other for a wider shot. After that, you turn both cameras around to Person B in the scene, and record their part of the dialogue. *Gilmore* preferred to do it another way, says editor Raul Davalos.

"The best way to do it is using what is called dueling over-the-shoulder shots. You have one angle on Luke, with a little bit of Lauren's shoulder, and then a complementary angle in the other direction. In other words, Lauren with a little bit of Luke's shoulder, matching the size of their heads. That way, if it's a great performance, you can keep the performance because you're just cutting from one camera to the other. If you shoot both angles toward Lauren, you have to mix that performance with the performance of Luke when you turned around and shot in the other direction.

"So Amy was very keen on this, once she started directing herself, to enable the actors to perform as they would in the theater. We would have a camera on her and a camera on him, and this would preserve both of their performances.

"That also helped a lot if they were sitting down at a table and they're sipping coffee. Matching that stuff is a nightmare. No matter what you'd say, they'd never pick up the coffee cup on the same line or at the same time, from one take to the other. So you would have her saying, 'Rory's going to Yale,' then she'd take a sip of coffee. Then on the next take, she takes a sip of coffee and says, 'Rory's going to Yale.' They have so much to remember and they tried very hard to match themselves, but it's really hard. Especially when you're doing a page and a half at once. So having these dueling angles really helped to maintain the performances."

YOU'VE ENTERED EMILYLAND [*commenting on Shauna Christy's shooting of her philandering husband*]: At least she had a husband to kill.

¾ OF AN INCH The maximum Chilton skirts have been permitted to be raised for 30 years.

AMEN, SISTER FRIEND

LORELAI [*to Rory, complaining about her cold*]: I mean, I'd like to have a good illness, something different, impressive. Just once I'd like to be able to say, 'Yeah, I'm not feeling so good, my leg is haunted.'

KIRK [*after asking Lorelai out*]: By the way, I think you might be the prettiest girl I've ever seen, outside of a really filthy magazine.

RORY [*to Christopher*]: No, I always understand and I don't wanna understand! I don't even really wanna talk about this right now. I've got mom, that's all I need. Go be somebody else's dad!

LORELAI: Christopher, is Sherry still pregnant?
CHRISTOPHER: Of course she is.
LORELAI: Are you still with her?
CHRISTOPHER: Yes.
LORELAI: Are you gonna marry her?
CHRISTOPHER: Yes.
LORELAI: Then honey, we are where we are. Accept it.

JESS [*to Rory*]: I'm sorry, did I hear from you at all this summer? Did I just happen to miss the thousands of phone calls you made to me, or did the postman happen to lose all those letters you wrote to me? You kiss me, you tell me not to say anything—very flattering, by the way—you go off to Washington, then nothing. Then you come back here all put out because I didn't just sit around and wait for you like Dean would've done? And yeah, what about Dean? Are you still with him? 'Cause last time I checked, you were, and I haven't heard anything to the contrary. Plus, the two of you walking around the other day like some damn Andy Hardy movie. Seemed to me like you're still pretty together. I half expected you to break into a barn and put on a show.

What I Kept

I wanted to get that Kim's Antiques sign, but I didn't. Every year, because we didn't know if we were going to get picked up again, Keiko and I would sit there and Keiko would go, "I'll have *that* sign and you can have that sign." I don't know if she ever got the sign she was pointing at, but I didn't get my sign.

—Emily Kuroda (Mrs. Kim)

3.3 Application Anxiety

First aired: Oct. 8, 2002 // Written by Daniel Palladino // Directed by Gail Mancuso

The long dreamed of application to Harvard has finally arrived at Rory's house, but between Emily and the adviser at the college application seminar, she's lost all confidence in her ability to get into the prestigious school. Though a visit to a Harvard alum puts her slightly at ease, neither she nor Lorelai can ignore the fact that, one way or the other, they will soon have to part.

! GINCHY! The seminar panelists shooting down everything Rory's done to get into Harvard; Luke fielding ice cream requests from a procession of children; the Springsteens' "other daughter"; and Taylor's bizarre soda shoppe diorama.

Says Lorelai, "Over my dead body is Kate Hudson getting your spot" at Harvard.

NOTES *'As far as I'm concerned, you should pack your bags.'*

* Paris jumps in to save the panel when Rory quietly implodes. Rory will return the favor when they both appear on C-SPAN, but with far more awkward results (3.16).

* Taylor has jettisoned his dreams of opening a decorative plate shop next to Luke's (2.15), and instead has his heart set on a soda and candy store.

* Any series can indulge in continuity with its major plot points, but here the Springsteen family quizzing each other at lunch inspires Lorelai to say, "Very Kennedyesque," referring to something Emily told the girls nearly two years ago (1.18).

* Though Lorelai and Rory have been planning for Rory to go to Harvard for years, this is the first time that it's hit both of them that they will soon be separated, to say nothing of Rory's separation from Dean. With Taylor already putting up a sign for his soda shoppe and Jackson asking if he can move his collection of antique tools into Rory's room, Stars Hollow seems to be on the verge of some major changes.

TODAY'S CELEBRATION a) The arrival of the Harvard application,

Bio Grant-Lee Phillips (The Troubadour)

Grant-Lee Phillips is the perfect television minstrel—a soulful voice contained in a sweetheart of a guy. In other words, a musician with plenty of street cred with the Generation Xers who's no more likely to set fire to the sets than the craft services people.

Born in the Stockton, Calif., Bryan Phillips mastered the guitar in his teens, and relocated to LA at 19. After dropping out of UCLA and failing to connect with the prevailing glam rock scene at the time, the singer-songwriter formed the iconic Grant Lee Buffalo in 1991. The band married Phillips' Neil Youngesque song style with an alternative rock edge that made the group a minor sensation on college campuses throughout the country. After they broke up in 1998, Phillips continued to work on his solo career. As far back as his early 20s, Phillips "was looking for a way to do it all," he says, taking film classes for more than a year before deciding to pursue music.

After *Gilmore*, Phillips ended up scoring Amy's ill-fated 2008 follow up, *The Return of Jezebel James*. "Aside from that, we've bowled a few games and kept in touch. I'm a much better guitar player than I am a bowler."

b) Rory and Lorelai's dinner with Harvard graduate Darren Springsteen, Class of '74, or c) All of the above. (Essay question to follow; do *not* choose Hilary Clinton as your subject.)

$100 A MONTH What Lane earns waxing end tables at Kim's Antiques.

KIRK OF ALL TRADES Angling for a position at either Luke's skateboard and soda bottle shop or Taylor's soda shop.

AND INTRODUCING...*Dave Rygalski* Named after the very musically inclined husband of Helen Pai. Dave Rygalskis real and imagined will play pivotal roles in the formation of Hep Alien later this season.

AMEN, SISTER FRIEND

PARIS: Personal anecdote. When I was 12 and I was writing the first of my trial essays in practice for the day I'd write my real essay, I chose Hillary Clinton. Then I realized every braindead bint in a skirt would be writing about Hillary, but it was good to clear the pipes.

EMILY [*to Lorelai*]: With the dot-com bust and the job market dwindling and the stock market going up and down like a yo-yo, everyone and his brother knows the best chance for success and financial security is not just to go to college, but to go to a top college....I was watching TV

"I would imagine this is the case with other actors who have done the show, but you act in that really fast-pace style long enough and it starts to get into your brain. You have to really think about it when you're in other audition situations. That you don't just rocket through everything you audition for, which happened to me on several occasions, I will admit."

-JOHN CABRERA (BRIAN)

and that insipid Kate Hudson was talking about going to a university. If she decides to go to Harvard, she'll get right in over Rory, who we know is more qualified.

"You just do more homework and you're a little more prepared, although there are people [on Gilmore] that can just pick up the sides, not having looked at them, glance over them a little bit, then do it. I don't know how they do that."

-KELLY BISHOP, ON BEING A NEW YORK STAGE ACTOR ON GILMORE

[Later]

LORELAI [*to Rory*]: And jobs are dropping and dot-com bombing and something's acting like a yo-yo, I don't know what but it's not good! And over my dead body is Kate Hudson getting your spot, let me just say that right now!

RORY: Mom, you're freaking out!

LORELAI: Yes, I'm freaking out!

RORY: Well, you can't freak out, *I'm* freaking out! [*Rory's cell phone rings*] Hello?

PARIS: What the hell did Romaine mean when he was going on about weeding out the hyper-intense in the interview process? He stopped just short of calling me by name. I'm losing it!

3.4 One's Got Class and the Other One Dyes

First aired: Oct. 15, 2002 // Written by Daniel Palladino // Directed by Steven Robman

Desperate to come clean with her mother about the new love in her life—her band—Lane decides to first declare her independence by dyeing her hair purple, with Rory's help, of course. Luke and Lorelai get lured into giving a talk at Stars Hollow High by the PTA, and Jess and Luke have an uncomfortably frank discussion about the women in their lives.

Behind the Scenes: The Great Flyover

Working on *Gilmore Girls* had its fair share of complications to begin with, and that's before you took the nearby airport into account. "That was something that surprised me working there," says Todd Lowe (Zack). "It's pretty close to the Burbank Airport, so any time there's an airplane flying over you can't shoot because it's not going to match if you're cutting back and forth to people—you're going to hear this airplane in the background. For example, Rory talks and the noise is not there and they come back to you and it's there.

"Even inside the house you can hear it. The sound guy's waiting there and finally he gives the signal to start the cameras up to speed, and by the time we get ready to take it, the airplane will be gone."

❗ GINCHY! Every scene the band is in; Lorelai's "Oh, by the way, Jess had a girl in the closet"; and Jess throwing Luke's situation with Lorelai back in his face.

NOTES *'I've spent my whole life compromising and being the good little girl and not doing what I want.'*

✖ Lane's band has already learned four songs, though when they convinced Sophie to let them practice at the music shop is unclear. (Doesn't matter, it's not working out.) She's still borrowing the drums from Sophie until she can earn some money to pay for them.

✖ This is the first time we actually learn that Lorelai got her GED after dropping out because of her pregnancy.

✖ Jess and Luke's complicated relationship takes an interesting turn here as the former finally gives voice to the fact that both of them have the same problem—they're both in love with Gilmore women. This little talk will reach its coda when Luke finally decides to do something about it (4.20), and will be echoed slightly more uncomfortably when Dean weighs in on a similar situation (5.18).

TODAY'S CELEBRATION Luke and Lorelai giving a talk about their success to the students at Stars Hollow High, and Lane's "independence day."

KIRK OF ALL TRADES We learn from Lane that Kirk once had a band called The Kirk Gleason Five, before Mrs. Kim shut it down and ruined the band Queen for him permanently.

AND INTRODUCING..._Lane's Band 1.0_ Brian, Zack and Dave are in the house, but Adam Brody already has *The OC* look in his eyes. He'll be moving on to that show before too long.

STATE HIGH HURDLES CHAMPION 1985 That would be Stars Hollow High's own "Butch" Danes.

SNOOPY Brian has a tattoo of him, apparently. ●————————

💡 THINGS WE'VE LEARNED John Cabrera and a couple of animator friends of his did the animatics (computer animation on which movie scenes are based) for *Slither*, the 2006 tongue-in-cheek horror movie directed by Sean Gunn's brother, James. "In the end, what ended up being shot, what ended up being edited, looks strikingly similar to what we created," Cabrera says. "I knew they were going to use it as a guide, but they really kept to it. I was very proud when I saw the screening of the film."

AMEN, SISTER FRIEND

MRS. KIM [*presenting Lane with college applications*]: They're all good religious programs, and I've already thrown out the ones that let boys and girls sit in the cafeteria together: the party schools.

JESS: Hey, the girls that I like don't give a damn about me! And unlike some other people I know, I'm not gonna sit around hoping that they change their minds and suddenly notice me.
LUKE: What's that supposed to mean?
JESS: You fixed any neighbors' porches lately? Or you go on a picnic or you get rooked into giving a ridiculous speech at a high school?
LUKE: Shut up.
JESS: At least I've got a little self-esteem.
LUKE: Shut up.
JESS: I'm not playing golden retriever, hoping one day she'll turn around and fall in my arms. If she doesn't wanna be with me, then fine!

"I saw Jon Hamm [who played Peyton Sanders] at the Emmys the other day and I was like, 'You know you owe it all to me.' He played the most thankless boyfriend on Gilmore Girls, a date that never really happens. And I remember thinking at the time, 'What is this gorgeous tall guy doing without his own TV show?'"

–LAUREN GRAHAM, VANITY FAIR, 9/10/10

3.5 Eight O'clock at the Oasis

First aired: Oct. 22, 2002 // Written by Justin Tanner // Directed by Joe Ann Fogle

In just a few days, two men have dropped into Lorelai's life. Her sweet-but-goofy new neighbor, Dwight, has somehow talked her into watering his new lawn while he's away on business. Then she pursues the dashing-but-boring Peyton Sanders after meeting him at one of Emily's auctions, only to have her disastrous date create a new rift between her and her parents.

GINCHY! Luke and Jess' reaction to the woman nursing her baby in the diner; Richard telling Lorelai that if her mother wants the first cup of tea, she'll get the first cup of tea.

NOTES *'You don't know until you try, right?'*

It's hard not to read Dwight as the writers' take on all the *Gilmore* fans who've daydreamed about finding a sweet little small town like Stars Hollow. His screeching wife, Doris, (heard only on his answering machine), is the ubiquitous Alex Borstein (Drella, the first Sookie and Miss Celine).

Rory tells Jess that Dean's on his way over to fix her sprinkler disaster.

✱ Though a distractingly uneven episode, this one contains one of the best insights into the psyches of Richard and Emily we will ever get with Richard's "tea" explanation (see "Amen, Sister Friend").

TODAY'S CELEBRATION Society Matron's League Auction and Lorelai's first date with Peyton.

HEY, FAMILY FRIENDLY FORUM! LORELAI [*after Luke, upset by a nursing mother, points out that his establishment is a diner, not a peep show*]: Hey, consider making it a combo. You could charge more for your cheeseburgers. Of course, no one would ever feel the same ordering a glass of milk again, but...

THE COBRA The nickname given to Emily by Natalie for cajoling the auctioneer to turn up despite not feeling well.

AND HERE'S A SHOUT OUT TO OUR INTERNATIONAL FANS Rory now wants to go to Amsterdam.

THING'S WE'VE LEARNED When Richard is getting so heated up on the phone with Lorelai, Lauren Graham stand-in Patty Malcolm was the one acting on the other end of the line to inspire that anger. "Edward [Herrmann] always treated me like a fellow actor, he never treated me as a stand-in," Malcolm says. "We had the most amazing scene and I was just giving it to him. Afterwards, he thanked me for giving him a lot to respond to. I was like Thank *you*. What you gave me was one of the most exciting things I've done in my life. I remember I skipped to my car, I was so excited. This was the best day ever; I did a scene with Ed Herrmann!"

AMEN, SISTER FRIEND

EMILY: I must say I was very impressed with the selection this year. I even wound up purchasing a couple of pieces for myself.

RICHARD: Yes, how nice to have yet another chair you can't sit in.

EMILY: It's 100 years old.

RICHARD: Wonderful. We can put it next to the 200-year-old footstool you can't put your foot on.

EMILY: Oh Richard, please.

RICHARD: I'm only teasing, Emily. It is one of the great pleasures of my life to be able to surround you with a house full of useless objects. No, I'm never happier than when we're standing in the corner staring at our furniture.

[Richard, trying to explain to Lorelai why her ditching of Peyton could mess things up for Emily, proceeds to tell her about one of Emily's fellow DAR members. The unfortunate woman bounced a check a couple of years before and was no longer given the first cup of tea at DAR meetings. Since then, Emily has been given the first cup of tea.]

RICHARD: Of course it sounds insane! It *is* insane. That is not the point.

LORELAI: OK, then what's the point?

RICHARD: The point is your mother is upset and I don't want her to be upset. Now, you may not understand her world, I may not understand her world, but it is her world, and in her world it is very, very important

Bio Jared Padalecki (Dean Forester)

Along with Milo Ventimiglia, Adam Brody and Chad Michael Murray, Jared Padalecki was one of the breakout stars of *Gilmore*, going on to reach superstardom in the role of Sam Winchester on The CW series *Supernatural*.

Born in San Antonio, Texas, Padalecki was actually attending the University of Texas–Austin when he landed the role of Dean, which forced him to quit. Not that falling into acting was accidental—he'd been taking acting classes since the age of 12.

Though Dean had a hell of a time on *Gilmore* being jerked around by girlfriend Rory, he faced even greater obstacles in his movie roles. While still on the show, he joined *Gilmore* rival Chad Michael Murray (Tristin) in the 2005 remake of the horror flick *House of Wax*, before going toe-to-toe with '80s killer Jason in the 2009 reboot of *Friday the 13th*.

that she have the first cup of tea. And I don't care about your independence or what you told your mother or anything else you have to say. If my wife wants the first cup of tea, she's going to have the first cup of tea!

3.6 Take the Deviled Eggs...

First aired: Nov. 5, 2002 // Written by Daniel Palladino // Directed by Jamie Babbit

Though Sherry invited Rory to her baby shower in Boston, both of the girls get roped into attending. Jess is behind the wheel again, this time with a car he bought from Gypsy. Where did he get the money, and what nefarious use will the girls find for the deviled eggs Sherry foists on them?

GINCHY! Taylor's run-in with the town's clerics; Rory getting through a karaoke rendition of "Baby Face" without using the word "baby"; the town loner's disastrous protest; and the egging of Jess' car.

NOTES *'I guess being in dad's world automatically means being in Sherry's.'*

Despite the detente between Christopher and the girls since Sherry got pregnant (2.22), he e-mailed Rory a month or so ago and they've been in touch ever since.

Christopher Grey played Ceaser this time around; Aris Alvarado won't take over the role until 3.20.

Though the Hayden bundle of joy will be spelled Gigi in many a fan fiction, Sherry herself tells us this episode that "GG" is, in fact, short for the two g's in "Georgia."

When Rory got into Chilton, Emily informed her that it was just minutes from Richard and Emily's house. This time around, Sherry informs Lorelai and Rory that Harvard is less than three miles from her house, and starts pushing for Rory to spend time there.

TODAY'S CELEBRATION Sherry's baby shower.

KIRK OF ALL TRADES Though not technically a job, Kirk fancies himself "sort of a car aficionado."

DIRK SQUAREJAW Jess invites Luke to call him this after confessing that he is the all-American boy, complete with job at Wal-Mart.

Gypsy's A1 Secret

"I have a lot of respect for auto mechanics now and their abs because when you roll out from beneath a car and sit up, it's not that easy to do over and over again," Rose Abdoo says. "I remember that day, they said, 'Oh Rose, we're not going to gross you out in the truck—[the oil] will be A1 Steak Sauce.' Well, by the end of the day I was like, 'I don't think I can ever smell A1 Steak Sauce again as long as I live.' It's super sticky; I think it might've been better if it had been motor oil."

What does Christopher see in this woman?

SQUEEGY BECKINHEIM & TOOKIE CLOTHESPIN Two names that Lorelai gave stores, resulting in even more catalogs being sent to their house.

AMEN, SISTER FRIEND

TAYLOR: Well, that's not indicated here, but it doesn't matter, because protesting is not allowed in the town square, period. It's un-American.

LUKE: You mean like the Revolutionary War?

BABETTE: And Rosa Parks?

TAYLOR: That's different. They were against the British and buses. No one likes the British or buses.

"I had a lot of friends who said to me, 'I didn't realize there were Jews in Stars Hollow.'"

-ALAN BLUMENFELD (RABBI BARANS)

TAYLOR: So it's hardball, huh? Well, the council gave you special permission to run bingo out of that building. We could withdraw it.

RABBI: At your peril.

TAYLOR: Meaning?

RABBI: You're gonna tell my little old ladies, my bubbies, you're shutting down their bingo?

TAYLOR: I'm not afraid of your bubbies, Rabbi.

REVEREND: Oh God, thank you for letting me be in the room when Taylor said that.

3.7 They Shoot Gilmores, Don't They?

First aired: Nov. 12, 2002 // Written by Amy Sherman-Palladino // Directed by Kenny Ortega

Every year, Stars Hollow holds a 24-hour dance marathon, and every year Kirk wins it. When Lorelai convinces Rory to be her dance partner this year, she thinks that's all going to change. Little does she know that this quaint little Stars Hollow event will have a direct impact on Sookie and Jackson's child-bearing plans, and Rory and Dean's already fragile relationship. Only Lane sees the contest end better than it began, as Mrs. Kim meets, and seemingly approves of, her beloved Dave Rygalski.

GINCHY! Oh where to begin? Dean's initiation into girls' time-honored practice of calling (and hanging up on) boys they like; an exhausted Lorelai and Rory trying to keep going on the dance floor; Luke sounding out Lorelai on having more kids; Dave getting on Mrs. Kim's good side; Dean's breakup with Rory; and the business-like way Jess handles the aftermath.

The VERY Limited Edition Gilmore Girls Cookbook

Before you start to salivate, understand that the *Dragonfly Inn Kitchen Cookbook* is a very limited edition book: there is only one in existence.

As a wedding present for *Gilmore* first assistant director James Moran who was marrying a chef, key set costumer Valerie Campbell set out to make by hand a one-of-a-kind cookbook, featuring recipes supplied by every member of the cast, crew and production, with the exceptions of Amy & Dan.

"I ended up binding them by department, so I had all the actors in one section, all the grips, all the electrics, all the camera people. Then I did little crazy drawings on top of certain ones. In between areas where there was a space, instead of leaving that space there, I drew a cartoon ad for one of the businesses in the town."

Some of the recipes to be found within its pages include:

—Sean Gunn's Banana Quesadilla's

—Jared Padalecki's Grilled Chicken

—Lauren's Vodka Grahamlicious

—Alexis' Roasted Pork Tenderloin Stuffed with Poblano Chiles.

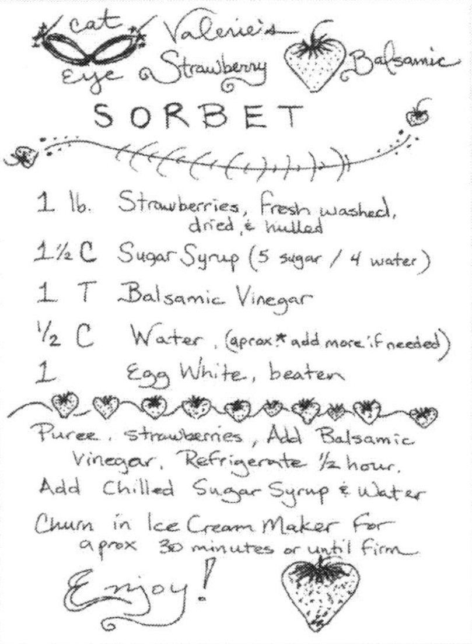
Cat Eye Valerie's Strawberry Balsamic
SORBET
1 lb. Strawberries, fresh washed, dried & hulled
1½ C Sugar Syrup (5 sugar / 4 water)
1 T Balsamic Vinegar
½ C Water (aprox* add more if needed)
1 Egg White, beaten
Puree strawberries, Add Balsamic Vinegar. Refrigerate ½ hour.
Add Chilled Sugar Syrup & Water
Churn in Ice Cream Maker for aprox 30 minutes or until firm
Enjoy!

'It Was So Wrong!'

Before shooting the scene with Louise and Madeline making out with a couple of guys against the lockers, the director "came up to us and was like, 'OK, you guys have to be completely making out with someone,'" Shelly Cole recalls. "We're like, 'Ohhhkay.' 'We haven't hired anybody for you to make out with, so you have to pick somebody out of the background actors.'

"So they just grabbed these five guys that we had never seen before, they line them up against the wall, and they make us point out the ones we want to make out with! It was so wrong!! Are you kidding? It was so humiliating for these poor guys to have to stand up against the wall and to be chosen out of a lineup to go make out on screen. Not like making out with us was some big deal, but to have a featured thing so they can get an extra bump in pay (they got to have a featured extra role), we had to choose the fate of these poor guys."

NOTES *'Rory's feeling a little territorial today.'*

✱ Two vital bits of information about the bridge that's been a constant focus of Stars Hollow charity drives: They've been raising money to restore it for eight years now, and the Tennessee Williams lookalike contest last month brought in enough to complete the effort. (The dance competition is to raise money for a tarp to throw over the bridge.)

✱ Dean's inability to grasp Lane's practice of calling up Dave and hanging up on him is just a symptom of his inability to understand Rory; he gets quite an education this episode. This is all a sharp contrast to the smug Dean who once gave Max Medina pointers on understanding the girls (2.3).

✱ Kenny Ortega is an inspired choice for directing the dance marathon episode. Already a legend for choreographing such classics as *Dirty Dancing* (starring Kelly Bishop) and *Xanadu*, Ortega would enjoy a strong resurgence after *Gilmore* directing such hits as *High School Musical 1-3* and *This Is It*, the Michael Jackson performance movie that made headlines after the singer's death. A serious contender for best episode of the series.

TODAY'S CELEBRATION The 24-hour dance marathon, the 75th anniversary of The Franklin, and the end of Rory and Dean's relationship (again).

KIRK OF ALL TRADES Dance marathon champion.

FOUR IN FOUR Jackson tells Sookie he wants four kids in four years.

3 How many months it's been since Paris and Jamie's first date.

AMEN, SISTER FRIEND

PARIS. Why are we working Saturday, Paris? What's so special about the 75th issue, Paris? Why does my head feel so light and yet not float away, Paris?

TAYLOR: You would kick Tiny Tim's crutch out from under him, wouldn't you?
LUKE: If he asks for a free cup of coffee, gimpy's going down.

RORY [*about Kirk*]: He has no career, no girlfriend, no pet, no car. He lives with his mother, she won't even let him have his own key. The only thing he does have in his whole lonely, pathetic existence is this marathon. If we win, if we take him down, if we take away that last little piece of dignity, then we leave him with nothing.
LORELAI: I wonder if he'll cry.

DEAN: Oh please! You've been into him since he got to town, and I have spent weeks—months, actually—trying to convince myself that it wasn't true, that everything was fine between us. But now I know that I was an idiot. You're into him and he's into you, and Shane, who by the way, should be listening to this 'cause it's so damn obvious.

"The beauty of Gilmore Girls is there were some incredibly funny moments, but if you got it, you got it, and if you didn't, we're moving on. So people got different things from the show, but they had to pay attention."

-KELLY BISHOP (EMILY)

Behind the Scenes Dance Marathon

As the *Gilmore* producers grew more confident with their cast and crew, they became more ambitious with what they filmed. After this, we get "The Festival of Living Art" (4.7) and the LDB's outing in "You Jump, I Jump, Jack" (5.7).

Shot on location at a high school gym near the Warner Brothers lot over the course of three or four days, the dance marathon was "very painful because there was so much to shoot," recalls key set costumer Valerie Campbell.

"I just remember having endless things we were doing, one after another after another. It was as if *we* were doing the dance marathon."

Even something as simple as pinning paper number tags on the backs of the dance contestants ended up being more work than many fans probably realized. "The numbers with the pins were tearing the dresses, so we're trying to fix the dresses between shooting and have them not blow off. Of course the dancing was fun."

RORY: What's obvious? What did I do?
DEAN: Everyone can see, Rory! Everyone. And I'm tired, but I'm over it, so go ahead, go. Be together. There's nothing standing in your way now, 'cause I'm out.

3.8 Let the Games Begin

First aired: Nov. 19, 2002 // Teleplay by Amy Sherman-Palladino // Story by Amy Sherman-Palladino and Sheila R Lawrence // Directed by Steven Robman

Rory and Jess are together, much to the confusion of Luke. Meanwhile, Richard convinces Emily and the girls to come on a road trip with him to Yale, ostensibly so he can attend a reunion of the a cappella singing group The Whiffenpoofs. Yet when they learn his true reason for it all, even Emily has a hard time forgiving him for his duplicity.

GINCHY! Lorelai's Frank Lloyd Wright story; Luke laying down the law to Jess; Richard and Emily reminiscing about their Yale courtship; the entire Yale interview fiasco, including Rory's common-sense reason for being upset; and as always with an Amy-written episode, the final scene.

NOTES *'This is part of Grandpa's evil plan to take over my life, abolish my free will, pull me into the Gilmore world, dress me in pearls and ruin my life.'*
One of the more amusing suggestions made by people behind the

scenes about Emily's penchant for hiring and firing maids was that it was actually a reflection of Amy's own practices when it came to the crew.

Richard had already given Pennilyn Lott his class pin when Emily broke them up; this is not the last we'll hear of the woman (4.9). He proposed to Emily at a bench on the Yale grounds—there's a trash can there now.

Lorelai discovers that Emily very nearly wasn't her mother, an interesting riff on the Stars Hollow kids pointing out that if she had waited until later to have Rory with another man, it wouldn't have been Rory (3.4).

TODAY'S CELEBRATION Rory's (surprise) Yale interview.

EMILY'S MAID DU JOUR Liliana, who seems intent on besieging Emily with walnuts.

GLORIA ESTEFAN The only role model Rory could think of at her Yale interview.

AMEN, SISTER FRIEND

LORELAI: You know what, I've spent a lot of time and energy fighting the whole Jess thing. Rory's made her choice, I want her to be happy. I'm just hoping for the best at this point.
LUKE: Very romantic.
LORELAI: Says the man who yelled "Finally!" at the end of *Love Story*.

RORY: I'm sure you and I can figure out a fun thing to do while they're off at dinner, some cool road trip thing.
LORELAI: In New Haven?
RORY: Well, yeah.
LORELAI: Sweetie, have you ever been to New Haven?
RORY: No.
LORELAI: Take a look at the coffee pot tomorrow before I clean it; that's New Haven.

RORY [*about Jess*]: OK. Now let's say he's in the house and there's a fire, and you can either save him or your shoes—which is it?
LORELAI: That depends. Did he start the fire?

"People were always warm to me [on the show] but they did warm up a little bit more when I became a regular. That's like being a ball player and being called up to the big leagues. It's different and everybody treats you different. I'm sure that they'd love to say that they don't but they do. You just get more respect when you're a regular. Except Sally Struthers, who treats everybody the same no matter who they are."

—SEAN GUNN (KIRK)

What's Up With These Titles?

Though *Gilmore Girls'* episode titles started out fairly straightforward, the Palladinos' penchant for obscure references soon infected those, too.

"We TV writers, we used to name these scripts, and no one outside of the office or the studio or networks would ever see the titles," Dan told the Chicago Tribune in February 2006. But once DirecTV and cable systems started placing the episode titles on the nation's TV screens, there was an added incentive to be inventive with them.

LORELAI: You know, they're together now.

LUKE: What?

LORELAI: Oh yeah. 'I have to get a part for my car,' 'I'm going to go study'—that's kid code for 'Meet me at the previously agreed upon location far away from my clueless uncle.'

LUKE: You're kidding me, right? You don't really think that—damn, they are! They're together. They used the kid code and now they're together!

3.9 A Deep-Fried Korean Thanksgiving

First aired: Nov. 26, 2002 // Written by Daniel Palladino // Directed by Kenny Ortega

Known, though they are, for being able to eat several times their body weight in junk food, the girls are faced with their greatest challenge yet: four Thanksgiving feasts in one day! Between bites, Kirk gets a pet, Rory spills the beans about where she's applied for college, and Lane and Dave grow closer.

GINCHY! Catkirk!; Lane and Dave's subterfuge to lay the groundwork for dating; Jackson's entrance with the turkey; the offense Richard takes at the only French Lorelai knows, and the amusement of his French guests.

NOTES *'How are we going to eat four Thanksgiving dinners?'*

When Lorelai thinks Sookie's kidding about Emily standing behind her, she quips that Joseph Stalin is standing behind Sookie. Stalin will reenter their lives again in a couple of years (5.21).

The girls have missed the last two Friday night dinners since Richard pulled his Yale stunt last episode; Emily and Richard will be out of town all through December.

No secrets are safe at dinner when the Gilmores are involved. Last time around, Richard reluctantly revealed to the diners at the Bracebridge dinner that he had retired (2.10). This time, it's Rory and her secretly applying to Yale.

What is it with Dean? He had a short pissing contest with Luke not so long ago (1.14), he nearly starts a fight with Jess this episode, and later still he'll really hit Luke where it hurts (5.18).

Bio Adam Brody (Dave Rygalski)

They don't come much smoother than Dave Rygalski worming his way into Mrs. Kim's good graces (3.7). It was Adam Brody's mix of straight-up geek appeal and confident charm that made it work.

Brody's charm was probably best summed up by Deanna Kizis in a May 2004 Elle magazine article, "The Geek Shall Inherit the Earth": "Brody fools us into thinking he's our own discovery, a catch whose appeal eludes lesser women."

Born in San Diego to a lawyer father and graphic artist mom, Brody spent his teens trying to live the California surfer-slacker dream, until a Quentin Tarantino-like stint working at a Blockbuster video store got him to thinking about pursuing that other California dream: acting.

Shortly after moving to Los Angeles, he went from parking cars at the Beverly Hills Hotel to landing a series of roles on several shows, including *Judging Amy* (as "Barry Gilmore"), *Smallville* and the TV movie *Growing Up Brady*, before finally hitting the Hollow. Though many were certain Dave Rygalski was the one first destined to become Mr. Lane Kim, it wasn't long before Brody found a larger profile role as the nerdy-but-desirable Seth Cohen on Fox's *The OC*.

TODAY'S CELEBRATION Thanksgiving...times four.

OY WITH THE ____, ALREADY! Dean's tough talk. Sure, he's been through the wringer with Rory and Jess, but his ominous talk rarely leads to actual fisticuffs.

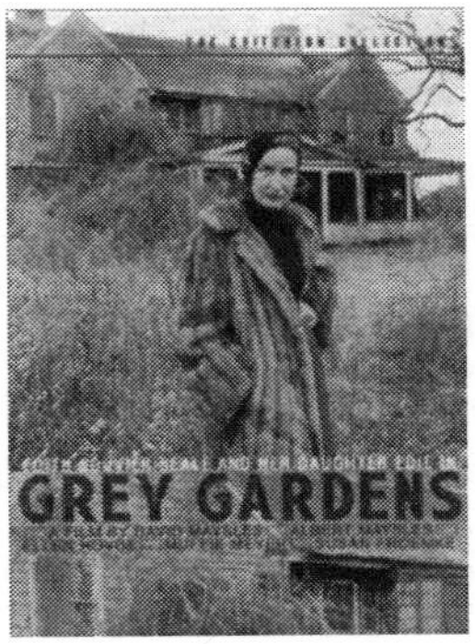

'GREY GARDENS' The "cold open" for this episode finds the girls watching the 1975 documentary *Grey Gardens* about Big Edie and Little Edie Beale. Aside from being a reflection of Amy & Dan's love of this documentary about a quirky mother and daughter who live together in a dilapidated mansion, it's hard to miss the similarities between the relationships of the Beales and Emily and Lorelai (rather than Lorelai and Rory).

AMEN, SISTER FRIEND

KIRK [*about his new cat*]: I named him Kirk.
LORELAI: Isn't that confusing?
KIRK: Not when you think about it.
LORELAI: No, it's still confusing.
KIRK: I like the name, and whenever I call Kirk's name, I obviously won't be calling myself.
LORELAI: True.
KIRK: Although when my mom calls for Kirk, that may be confusing.

Bio ☺ Todd Lowe (Zack Van Gerbig)

While Zack is a fairly good musician who's pretty slow mentally, Todd Lowe is a wickedly good musician and pretty sharp. And there's also a little bit of Brian Jonestown Massacre frontman Anton Newcombe about him as well. Like Newcombe (and Zack in one of his crazier moments), Lowe has spent much of his career trying to "destroy the system," but with a healthy dose of tongue-in-cheek humor.

Born in a Houston suburb, he spent 10 years in the music-film capital of Austin, Texas, including some time attending the University of Texas. As a post-grad, he helped write and starred in "this I guess shocking at the time" show called *The Tower Massacre Musical*, based on the former Austinite Charles Whitman who killed 14 people on the UT campus in August 1966. It ran for six months at a punk rock bar, "which was unprecedented in Austin for a small theater company." By the end of 1999, he'd moved to LA.

Though theater was the thing that appealed to him first, he's been playing guitar since 16. He fronts a country-rock band called Pilbilly Knights in Los Angeles, and never misses a chance to play. "We'll be tearing shit up soon at some sleazy bar somewhere," he promises. When not playing in front of the cameras on *Gilmore*, "Sebastian [Bach] and I would hang and sing Elvis songs and stupid stuff."

Since *Gilmore*, Lowe has hit it big on another show, HBO's vampire series *True Blood*. When the author caught up with Lowe for this book, he'd just been hired for the role of Terry Bellefleur on the series, which had premiered just a few days prior to the interview. "I hope it's good. My character comes on later in the series. *Gilmore Girls* was established and was pretty much a hit and a good show; it had a loyal fanbase. It's exciting to be working on something new and not know how people will take it. It's also a little scary."

Maybe I can get her to say CatKirk when she's calling Kirk, and HumanKirk when she's calling me.

RORY: That would keep it straight.

KIRK: I'm glad I ran into you. See ya.

LORELAI: See ya, HumanKirk.

RORY: Bye, HumanKirk. He's always been a cat person, he's just never had a cat.

PARIS: Harvard is going to be expecting Thanksgiving shelter work. They'll know I called too late and it will totally impugn my organizational skills. By the way, you know I ultimately do all these things for the good of mankind, right?

[Rory's pager goes off.]

LORELAI: Who's that?

RORY: It's Lane. It just says "Bible kiss bible."

LORELAI: What does that mean?

RORY: I have no idea. Good band name, though.

3.10 That'll Do, Pig

First aired: Jan. 14, 2003 // Written by Sheila R Lawrence // Directed by Jamie Babbit

It's Richard's 60th birthday and his mother has come for another one of those visits that Emily enjoys so much. Meanwhile, Francie continues to undermine Paris as the student council president deals with her blossoming relationship with Jamie. Rory and Dean decide to be friends, and Trix announces she's moving to Hartford.

GINCHY! Trix renting her Hartford house to Korn; Lorelai revealing to Emily how amused she gets at her mother's disapproval; Trix's silent inspection of Lorelai's house and the rest of the family trailing behind her nervously; the interaction between Jess and Dean's sister, Clara.

NOTES *'You really think that by being her friend, you're gonna get her back?'*

Lorelai tells Lane that she and her band can practice in her garage. Paris went to Philadelphia over Christmas and stayed with Jamie and his parents; he told her he loves her. Dean's applied to Southern Connecticut State, thanks to all of Rory's talk about him being able to do more with his life.

Several bits from past episodes get riffed on here. Trix's surprise visit prompts both her and Emily to comment on the gifts Trix has sent them

Behind the Scenes: Emily + Her Maids

Though Emily Gilmore kept her domestic help dancing on the edge of a nervous breakdown, Kelly Bishop frequently found herself taking the actresses playing them under her wing.

"They would be in the makeup chair but they would already be in the maid uniform." Yet the maids still had to wait for the lead actors to get made up, dressed, and to get through their blocking for a scene before they'd even come on. All told, the actresses could be waiting for a good two hours.

"And here'd be this poor young actress. Now we're done with the camera blocking and somebody goes out the door, somebody else gets on their phone and we're all leaving the set, and this person is sitting in a little chair on the side of the stage. No one says anything to them."

It's something Bishop recalls from her own early days in the business. "So I'd walk over and say, 'Listen, you've got about an hour here. You can go back to your trailer, just tell somebody where you're going to be—they'll come get you.' And they go, 'Oh really? Oh, OK.'

"You're going to be there for 12, 14 hours, you have maybe no lines at all, and you're sitting there at attention the whole time. It's terrible. So I would always try to do that because I know how it feels. You're comfortable with your company because you are a series regular. So you have a comfort level that the guests don't have."

over the years (1.18). The prospect of Trix seeing Lorelai's house horrifies Emily, who cites the monkey lamp as a particular problem (1.9). Rory pulling Francie into the restroom for a chat is the mirror image of what happened earlier (3.2).

TODAY'S CELEBRATION The Stars Hollow High Winter Carnival and Richard's 60th birthday.

KIRK OF ALL TRADES Weston's bakery clerk.

OY WITH THE ____, ALREADY! Sookie being clumsy!!!!

LORELAI'S ATTEMPTS AT GIFTS FOR RICHARD

—A high-tech titanium bathroom scale

—Coin sorter

—Silk tie

—Something that lights up and sings.

WHAT LORELAI ENDS UP GETTING HIM

The Complete History of the Peloponnesian War.

Making an Episode 6 Casting

In the making of most US TV productions, there's a certain amount of waiting around punctuated by long, intense periods of action, and to a certain extent it's the same for *Gilmore Girls*. The difference comes in intensity. On *Gilmore*, when your department's up at bat, you're not going to remember the next several hours for how fast you're going to fly.

This was especially true of casting. "*Gilmore Girls* was an interesting situation because the scripts came out so very late we really didn't have the luxury of releasing breakdowns," says Mara Casey who, with partner Jami Rudofsky, handled all of the casting for the show, barring most of the pilot cast. "For the recurring parts, we would have a head's up that something important was going to happen in the near future, so we'd have to pre-read a bunch of people with old material, or material where we've got a good sense of their essence, and then when the material was finally written, have that surplus of people we thought would be right for the actual script."

This means that every week, the pair has to be on the lookout for any actor who might fit *Gilmore*'s quirky nature, because once that final script drops, they will have one day *at the most* to cast the new parts, Casey says. Yet, everyone on the production is used to working under these time constraints. This means that the producers will usually schedule regulars such as Graham and Bledel to shoot their scenes first, followed by recurring actors such as Sean Gunn and Michael Winters shooting their scenes next, affording Casey and Rudofsky every moment possible to find actors to fill new roles for that episode.

"We're just really fortunate to have the same sensibility as Amy Sherman-Palladino," Casey says. "We knew what would make her giggle. It kept us employed for seven years."

RORY'S GIFT *Chuck Berry Live at the Fillmore* LP.

EMILY'S GIFT A cigar humidor once owned by a lieutenant in the army in WWI.

TRIX'S GIFT A humidor owned by novelist Victor Hugo.

AMEN, SISTER FRIEND

LORELAI: You think the couch is terrible. Now, at one point in my life, you saying a couch that I carefully picked out and had to pay off over eight months is terrible might've hurt my feelings, but not anymore.
EMILY: No?
LORELAI: No.
EMILY: Why not?
LORELAI: Because one day I decided that instead of being hurt and upset by your disapproval, I'm gonna be amused. I'm gonna find it funny. I'm even going to take a little bit of pleasure in it.
EMILY: You take pleasure in my disapproval?
LORELAI: I encourage it sometimes, just for a laugh.
EMILY: I don't know what to think of that.
LORELAI: Think, 'Hey, that's brilliant,' because this idea could set you free. Mom, what are you thinking about?
EMILY: That ridiculous Betty Boop head.
LORELAI [*smiling*]: So am I.

RORY [*to Francie*]: I'm finished being your go-between. You're a jerk, and if you wanna play it this way, then fine. All bets are off. I'm no longer your ally. You wanna play rough—fine. I've read *The Art of War*. I can be just as big a pain in your butt as you are in Paris', capiche?

RORY [*at the bottle toss game with Jess*]: Just for the record, I'm a girl and we are supposed to throw like this.

"You look at an episode and you think, Wow, that looks simple. What's so hard about that? It's a couple of wide shots and they're out of the room. But to get it done and to get the actors to perform and block it out, and be able to know where you're going to cut to, for the reverse or the joke, it's hard. Everybody has Final Cut Pro at home today and everybody's an editor. Just like when PCs came out, everybody thought they were Hemingway."

—RAUL DAVALOS, EDITOR

3.11 I Solemnly Swear...

First aired: Jan. 21, 2003 // Written by John Stephens // Directed by Carla McCloskey

---

After all this time, one of Emily's former maids is finally suing her for wrongful dismissal, and Emily is counting on Lorelai to give a deposition in her defense. Francie gets her revenge on Rory, pitting her against Paris in a very un-Yale-like duel. And

Lorelai and Sookie have their hands full with preparing to start their own inn—first order of business, a very unhelpful seminar on doing just that. Fortunately, they run into Joe, an old friend of Sookie's, and his business partner, Alex. Though the pair are preparing to open a chain of coffee shops, it's Lorelai who hopes to get things perking with Alex.

! GINCHY! Emily reading from Lorelai's deposition; the *All the President's Men* homage in the parking garage meeting between Rory and Francie; and Paris and Rory's fencing match.

The 'I'm Rory, don't you want to pet me' face.

NOTES *'Honestly, mom, I doubt they'll be able to find 12 people in the state of Connecticut who haven't been fired by you.'*

* Richard is in London helping Trix prepare for her move to Hartford. Michel went to the Ecole Hôtelière de Genève for his hotelier training. Sookie and Lorelai, on the other hand, are taking a two-hour course through the Learning Center.

* Lorelai's "I'm crushing your head" bit in the seminar is one of the trademark skits from the Canadian sketch comedy TV series *The Kids in the Hall*, telegraphing the appearance of *Kids* alumnus Bruce McCulloch as Tobin (3.18, 4.10).

* It's shocking how disappointing this episode is considering a brilliant situation (Emily being sued by a former maid) and some brilliant lines. Paris' "I'm Rory, don't you want to pet me" remark is one of the best about Rory in the series.

TODAY'S CELEBRATION Lorelai's deposition.

EMILY'S MAID DU JOUR Her present one is Brooke, but Gerta is the one suing her.

AND HERE'S A SHOUT OUT TO OUR INTERNATIONAL FANS Gerta from Hamburg, aka "The Clomper."

OY WITH THE ___, ALREADY! Already Alex is an annoying presence in our lives.

AMEN, SISTER FRIEND

EMILY: If you pay for first class and the airline sticks you in coach, people expect you to be upset. No one calls you demanding or unreasonable. And yet here is this woman whom I pay more than she can get anywhere else in Hartford, whose severance package could finance a summer cruise down the Rhine, dragging me into court saying that I was unfair. Why? Because having paid for one thing, I'm not content with something else? That makes me unfair? Well then, so be it. Let someone else pay first class and ride in steerage, not me.

LUKE: Oh well, I'm going to Doose's because we are out of food.
LORELAI: How can you be out of food?
LUKE: Well, it starts with the words, 'Hey Jess, you do the ordering this week, OK?' And it ends with me selling Kirk a lettuce sandwich.

PARIS [*to Rory during fencing class*]: Don't make that face at me!
RORY: What face? I'm wearing a mask.
PARIS: The 'I'm Rory, don't you want to pet me' face.

EMILY [*reading aloud from Lorelai's deposition*]: "Would you say your mother sets impossible goals which people cannot help but fail to reach, thereby reinforcing her already formed opinion of their deficiencies? Answer: Only for her daughter."

Behind the Music 1 ♪ Hep Alien

Just like members of a real band, those involved with what would become Hep Alien did some real bonding behind the scenes.

"I think Keiko and Todd were really the two I became close to on the show the fastest," John Cabrera says. "Adam [Brody] was only there for a year. I got along well with Adam, but it just never really turned into anything more than a working relationship. But Keiko and Todd and I, we began to frequently hang out outside of the show and became very close."

It was particularly exciting for Keiko Agena, who was about to see her character evolve from simply being Rory's best friend to a multifaceted rock star.

"Even though Keiko was a regular on the show, this was kind of a new thing for her," Cabrera says. "This was going to be a story line that was going to last till the end of the show. Just the idea of having this group of friends there that were going to be a part of something that was created for her character certainly helped create a fun set camaraderie."

What's in a Name?

Names used in the series came from many different places. Take a peek at the writer for this episode and you can gather where Luke's new love interest, Nicole Leahy, got her name.

"Amy put that in as a goof," Janet Leahy says. "I had a tendency toward quiet humility back then; maybe this was her way of throwing a light on me. A little embarrassing, wouldn't you say? It makes it look like the writer put her own name in the script!"

3.12 Lorelai Out of Water

First aired: Jan. 28, 2003 // Written by Janet Leahy // Directed by Jamie Babbit

The band finally has a place to practice now that Lorelai and Rory have cleaned out the garage. Lane is devastated when her plan to go to the prom with Dave backfires, and Paris takes her vendetta against Rory to new depths. Lorelai tells Alex that she's a fan of the great outdoors, which leads to an impromptu fishing lesson from Luke. Luke is perfectly fine with this, as he's met someone, too—Taylor's attorney, Nicole Leahy.

GINCHY! Rory's Hug-a-World; Paris trying to impeach Rory; Mrs. Kim shooting down Dave because "he's not Korean."

NOTES *'Gotta crawl before you can walk.'*

Last week, Mrs. Kim let Dave sit in the Kims' pew. Headmaster Charleston's already sent his letters of recommendation to Harvard for Rory and Paris.

Rory observes that with all of Lane's marrying-age cousins officially married off, the next wedding at Kim's Antiques could be Lane's, which turns out to be the case (6.19).

TODAY'S CELEBRATION The wedding of Lane's cousin, James, and Luke teaches Lorelai to fish.

Character Sketch Emily: Drawing From Experience

Though Emily Gilmore can be a very unsympathetic character at times, Kelly Bishop excelled at betraying just enough of Emily's own vulnerabilities to make us love her more than we otherwise would. Bishop understood Emily on a level that, to some extent, most women automatically do, she says. "I think it happens generation to generation; women seem to understand this. You don't want to be your mother. Yet pretty soon, like 30 years down the line, you're doing exactly what your mother did to you that you swore you'd never do. It's just a mother-daughter thing."

It was a dynamic that Bishop saw firsthand between her mother and her grandmother. "My grandmother was very hard on my mother, and my mother couldn't do anything right her whole life as far as her mother was concerned. I used to watch it with wonder that my grandmother could control her so, even when she was an adult. That she could push those buttons and hurt my mother's feelings in a second. So I kind of used my grandmother as the model for Emily.

"The beauty of that show was showing the three generations and the differences in terms of the hardness on one side and the friendship with her granddaughter on the other. Very complex."

KIRK OF ALL TRADES Beauty supply store clerk.

OY WITH THE ___, ALREADY! Alex. God bless him, he's nice enough, but he's just not *Gilmore*.

TAYLOR OF ALL TRADES Taylor is also the town magistrate.

MEET THE FISH Gomer, Pinky, Cheryl, Pete and Jayne Mansfield.

46 The number of people who've been married at Kim's Antiques over the years.

AMEN, SISTER FRIEND

RORY: Can you imagine marrying someone you didn't know?
LANE: Are you kidding? Used clothes still skeeve me out a little.

Luke hasn't gotten to the part about killing Gomer and company yet.

3.13 Dear Emily and Richard

First aired: Feb. 4, 2003 // Written by Amy Sherman-Palladino // Directed by Gail Mancuso

Discussing their forthcoming backpacking excursion through Europe reawakens some painful memories for Lorelai. Due to her own scheduling "screw up," Sherry's about to go into labor early, and Rory's the only one at the hospital to help her through it. Though there's been a lot of unforgivable things said and done over the years, Lorelai tries to make peace with Emily, and their past.

NOTES *'Life can play some cruel tricks sometimes.'*

This is the first we learn that Dean is working for Tom the contractor. With his perusal of *Hidden Romantic Gems of the Restaurant World*, Luke begins his brief flirtation with books, which will yield slightly better results later (4.20).

Even in Lorelai's flashback (if this actually *is* her flashback), Emily's recently fired a maid. Some interesting reveals here—Richard and Emily were preparing to go on a European jaunt of their own when Lorelai got pregnant, and it was Christopher's idea to backpack through Europe after graduation. We also get to see what happened right before Lorelai's "coming out" photo was taken (1.8). With just a few lines of dialogue, we see how Christopher has always been the type to follow the path of least resistance, and hence, has always been a poor fit for Lorelai.

✱ There's something extremely touching about seeing these short glimpses of events we've already heard about, especially when Emily discovers Lorelai's run away from home. It's nearly impossible not to hear Richard's words to Lorelai all those years later: "Your mother couldn't get out of bed for a month. Did you know that? Did you?" (1.15)

TODAY'S CELEBRATION The birth of GG Hayden, and Luke and Nicole Leahy's first date.

EMILY'S MAID DU JOUR Present day: Leloni, from Honolulu. Flashback: Tina.

YOU'VE ENTERED EMILYLAND [*after reading from a book about backpacking through Europe*] Richard, this book is encouraging them to sleep in a park like a squirrel.

META, META, META Quizzing Rory about Jamie, Madeline asks if he has any datable friends, and puts it this way: "Is there spin-off potential?" In view of the potential spin-off pilot coming up (3.21), it's difficult not to read this as an inside joke.

Bio ☺ John Cabrera (Brian Fuller)

John Cabrera is one of those people who is so intense in person because he is brimming with ideas. Born in Miami, he moved to Chicago in 1993 to attend DePaul University, a prestigious acting school, where he met Sean Gunn.

Prior to his pursuit of an acting career, he'd actually been training for a career in commercial illustration. "In my junior year of high school, I just got burnt out by it. I took a drama class and fell in love with it and started on that path, not really knowing where it was going to lead."

Since meeting at DePaul in 1993, Cabrera and Gunn have been the closest of friends.

"If you had said to us back then in about 10 years you're going to be on a television show together, I think we would've both assumed that it was going to be a show that we both created. Even in school, we were looking for opportunities to direct plays outside of the school system or develop projects. We even formed a little theater company."

AMEN, SISTER FRIEND

CHRISTOPHER [*in flashback*]: Come on, Lor'. Let's get out of here, let's get away from this place. Let's take Myra and just bolt. Leave a note on the dining room table. "Dear Richard and Emily, I don't belong here, I'm going somewhere else, I'll call you when I get there. Love, Lorelai.' How does that sound?

RICHARD [*to Christopher's parents, discussing the future of Lorelai and Christopher*]: They will get married, they will live here, and Christopher will go to work at my company. That is the solution. Now we have a plan so we can all stop talking about it.

3.14 Swan Song

First aired: Feb. 11, 2003 // Written by Daniel Palladino // Directed by Chris Long

Jess is getting increasingly irked by Rory's friendship with Dean, Emily's getting increasingly irked by Trix and her impending move to Hartford, and Lane and Dave's secret is discovered by the rest of the band...kind of. And Emily gets to play her own version of "Guess who's coming to dinner."

GINCHY! Luke's system for going upstairs every 10 minutes to break Rory and Jess up, and Lorelai's response to it; Mrs. Kim telling Dave that Lane has a crush on him; Luke and Jess' talk while hunting the vicious swan; and the band accepting Dave's "devoutness."

NOTES *'It's always best to tell each other major life events so that there's no awkwardness.'*

Rory goes on about *The Holy Barbarians* and how it's written by a Venice Beach beatnik, foreshadowing the emergence of Jess' father, who's more of a Venice Beach bum than a beatnik (3.20).

"What if Dean had sucker-punched me and I had to defend myself," Jess asks Rory after she corners him about his black eye. Rory tells him angrily that Dean would never do that. Yet Dean will do that very soon (3.19).

Jess' victimization at the beak of the swan by Larson's dock gives credence to Michel's own mortal fear of the birds (1.3).

"I was traveling just last month to Mississippi and I had a layover in Chicago where I got in at 1 in the morning, so I had to stay in the terminal. I had a pillow and my carryon and my sleeping bag, and I was wandering around a completely empty terminal looking for a place to just lie down and go to sleep. And these two girls from New Zealand, all giddy with a camera, said, 'Oh my gosh! I'm sorry to interrupt, but it would just be amazing if we could take a picture with you.' So they take a picture and walk off and it's like, that was a very surreal moment."

—TED ROONEY (MOREY)

Lorelai asks Rory to tell her before "it" happens which, naturally, she doesn't (4.22). Come on, Lorelai...ewww.

11 The number of Friday night dinners that have gone by without a mention of Dean by Rory.

Luke and Jess bond during the hunt for the vicious swan.

KIRK OF ALL TRADES Director of Miss Patty's one-woman show.

YOU'VE ENTERED EMILYLAND [*about Wal-Mart*] We've never actually been inside one, but we own the stock.

TODAY'S CELEBRATION Jess meeting Emily, and the test marketing of *Buckle Up, I'm Patty!*

AMEN, SISTER FRIEND

LORELAI [*to Luke*]: 10 minutes. Yeah, that's pretty much the time it took to create Rory. And that included getting dressed and freshening my lipstick.

LORELAI: Mom, hi, listen. Rory kind of explained what happened last night, and how you were really great about it. I just wanted to thank you. I mean, I don't know all the details but I'm sure it all could've been way worse, and you keeping your cool like that was really, really nice. Thanks.
EMILY: How can you let your daughter be with that abominable thug?
LORELAI: Mom–
EMILY: First he arrives late, how disrespectful is that? Then he's rude to Rory, rude to me.
LORELAI: Mom–
EMILY: Oh, and that attitude—I wanted to slap that monosyllabic mouth of his. And God forbid they're in another accident together or his heap of a car breaks down and Lord Jim has decided cell phones are beneath him and they're stranded in the middle of nowhere. How can you let this happen? He had a black eye. He belongs in jail!

3.15 Face-Off

First aired: Feb. 18, 2003 // Written by John Stephens // Directed by Kenny Ortega

Jess still doesn't have this dating thing down yet, and Rory is getting sick of waiting around for him to call. Taylor's family is in town to catch a pivotal Stars Hollow Minutemen hockey game, where Rory discovers that she isn't the only one who's moved on after her split with Dean. After years of being under Trix's thumb, Emily finally thinks she's gotten the upper hand, but as usual, nothing's quite so simple in the Gilmore house.

GINCHY! Dave's mad dash to the hockey game during the band's break; Emily blurting out that she saw Trix kissing a man in front of everybody; and Kirk calling the hockey game.

NOTES *'OK, apparently it's two-for-one flip-out night at the Gilmore house.'* Luke was on the track team, which went to the state finals three times in four years (they won twice). Young Chui, who Mrs. Kim picked for Lane's prom date (3.12), is taking her to the hockey game.

Emily is still having her DAR meetings at the Independence Inn, presumably a continuation of her terms for getting Lorelai the loan (2.11). Lorelai's passion for showing people slides rather than handing them photographs (2.4) finally pays off for Emily when she borrows Lorelai's slide projector for Trix.

TODAY'S CELEBRATION The Stars Hollow Minutemen hockey team plays in the regional semifinals. This is also the first time Lane has ever made a guy jealous before.

KIRK OF ALL TRADES Color commentator for the hockey game.

TAYLOR'S BUTTON "Stars Hollow Hockey, 2003 semifinalists. Go Minutemen! The future is yours. Bring this button to Doose's for 50% off your next purchase of Stove Top Stuffing."

43 YEARS AGO The last time the Minutemen were in the regional semifinals.

AND INTRODUCING...*Lindsay* And Lindsay & Dean as a couple, for that matter.

The Comedy Team of Winters + Gunn

By Season 3, Kirk and Taylor, the two most annoying citizens of Stars Hollow, had become the Abbot and Costello of the town.

"Mike [Winters] was great because Mike's totally old school," Sean Gunn says. "Mike is a professional theater actor and that's what he does. He's got his theater company up in Seattle and he does exactly the same kind of stuff I walked away from in Chicago. From the first time we worked together, we didn't really have to develop any sort of working vocabulary because it was already there.

"I had so many scenes with Mike and yet I don't ever remember having difficulties with us not communicating properly. It would be like, hey, wait half a beat there while I do this. Oh yeah, great, got it. And that's it. We were on the same page from the beginning."

YOU'VE ENTERED EMILYLAND [*about Trix's gentleman caller, who was dressed in a purple jogging suit*] He was dressed like a bookie.

THINGS WE'VE LEARNED In addition to some background work on early episodes of *Gilmore*, Aris Alvarado (Ceaser) recorded a scene as a foreign exchange student in this episode. "There's a scene where Lorelai's on the phone, almost to the end of the episode, and all the tourists are leaving. She finishes the phone call and I was supposed to come into the room and say, 'Where are the Dooses' in Spanish, and she tells me they just left, but they cut that out." A few months later, they called him in to play Ceaser.

AMEN, SISTER FRIEND

KIRK: Well, ladies and gentlemen, much like the Israelites of yore, the Stars Hollow Minutemen languished in the desert for 40 years. But tonight, there was no Promised Land, no New Canaan, only a humiliating 5-to-1 defeat at the merciless hands of the West Hartford Wildcats. So, it's back to the desert for the Minutemen, perhaps for another 40 years. Of course, by then I'll be 70 years old. A lot of the rest of you will probably be dead. Taylor, you'll be dead. Babette, Miss Patty, that man there in the hat.

EMILY [*to Trix*]: Actually, I've had a little experience with being humiliated in front of the people I love, yes. Mom, please believe me, I know how important your pride is to you, and I never had any intention

Character Sketch: No Backstories for Taylor

While some actors are often tempted to create backstories for their characters to better understand their motivations, and ultimately, their actions, it was never something easy to do on *Gilmore*, says Michael Winters. "With Taylor it's hard to make a backstory because they'll put in whatever they need. For example, I had no idea I had a sister. Then there's a sequence where my whole family came to visit. We went to the hockey game and there was a guy who played my brother. Well, I could never have invented that, they did that. And there's this great guy who I happen to know from the local theater who played my brother and we kept hoping he'd come back, because he was Taylor's absolute opposite. I thought there could've been a lot of fun in that, but Amy's imagination was just so full of things that she could throw all of that stuff out and never have to go back to it."

of robbing you of it. I feel terrible that I caused you any pain. I just wish that once in a while you might feel a little bit terrible that you cause me pain. I have pride, too, you know. And my husband travels and is very busy and I miss him and I'm lonely sometimes, just like you.

RICHARD: Do you really think he was wearing a track suit?
LORELAI: I don't–
RICHARD: Well, I wonder if he was wearing Nikes also.
LORELAI: 'Just do it' takes on a whole new meaning, doesn't it?
RICHARD: I guess I've got a new daddy.

3.16 The Big One

First aired: Feb. 25, 2003 // Written by Amy Sherman-Palladino // Directed by Jamie Babbit

Sookie's pregnant, Mr. "four in four" Jackson is freaking, and Rory and Paris are squaring off for one last Chilton competition—a speech to be televised on C-SPAN. Add to that a few college acceptance (and rejection) letters and the return of Lorelai's lost love, and you've got—the big one.

GINCHY! The staff preventing Rory from eating Sookie's sewery meal; Lorelai prank calling Richard from her cell phone; Paris' torturing of Brad; Lorelai's "I've got the good kid" glee; and Paris' address to the audience.

NOTES *'We both have a lot of things to figure out, huh?'*

Though not yet his girlfriend, Nicole has convinced menu-whipped Luke to add three more salads to his menu and to ditch the Monte Cristo sandwich. Lorelai is in for some karmic payback following her eavesdropping on Paris and Rory's discussion about sex (4.22). And Max and Lorelai lock lips.

Lorelai gives Rory a little pre-party advice: "Getting up on a table and performing a song of any kind will haunt you for the rest of your life. Trust me. Been there, done that." Clearly she hasn't learned from her mistakes as she will "done that" again much later (7.20).

TODAY'S CELEBRATION Chilton Bicentennial, Paris and Jamie's first time, and Rory getting into....Harvard!

"I remember one week the producers worked it out for me where I was literally going from the Disney set [for That's So Raven] to the Gilmore set. It was the one where we all got each other's mail. I had an accent in the Disney show, too, and I just had that moment of 'Wait wait wait, I'm not the Spanish teacher.'"

–ROSE ABDOO (GYPSY)

'Pack your chastity belt, Gilmore—you're going to Harvard!'

KIRK OF ALL TRADES Mailman.

EMILY'S MAID DU JOUR The second maid called in sick and the first is busy with dinner.

5 The number of Geller generations who've gone to Harvard. This number has changed (1.6).

OY WITH THE ___, ALREADY! Poor use of Max. Why bother to bring him back if he's just going to stick his head in the door?

WELCOME BACK, BRAD! Announcing Brad Langford's return to Chilton, the teacher says, "He returns to us fresh from Broadway where he's just completed a successful run of *Into the Woods*." In fact, actor Adam Wylie had made his Broadway debut as Jack in *Into the Woods* the previous year.

AMEN, SISTER FRIEND

RORY [*to Kirk the mailman*]: Any chance you could go faster?
LORELAI: Yeah, you got a girl's future in that sack of yours, Santa.
RORY: Thank you for adding the Santa.

BRAD: You can't rattle me.
PARIS: [*sings*] Into the woods at Grandma's house.
BRAD: Look, I'm proud of my part, OK? The New York Times called me winningly naïve.
PARIS: [*sings*] Into the woods, into the woods, into the woods.

PARIS [*about her first time with Jamie*]: We were actually discussing modern day Marxism in America, which is not what I would have deemed a "come and get it" sort of conversation, but nevertheless he came and got it, and I have to figure out what that means to me on a psychological level. So, I thought maybe if you and I could have sort of a healthy debate about it, I could come to some sort of reasonable conclusion about how I should be feeling right about now. So, come on, talk. What do you think?

PARIS [*addressing the assembly, indicating Rory*]: She's never had sex. She'll probably go to Harvard. She's a shoo-in. Pack your chastity belt, Gilmore—you're going to Harvard!

3.17 A Tale of Poes and Fire

First aired: April 15, 2003 // Written by Daniel Palladino // Directed by Chris Long

A fire at the Independence Inn leaves Lorelai and Rory homeless when they loan their own house to the guests who've been displaced, including members of the Edgar Allan Poe Society. Paris has been missing in action for five days since her Chilton freakout, Lane's fake relationship has suddenly become a real one, and Jess appears to be spending a little too much time on that Wal-Mart forklift of his.

GINCHY! "Babette ate oatmeal"; the similar vibe that Rory and Lorelai get from Lindsay and Nicole, respectively—stay away from my man; the tape recording of Paris' Harvard interview; the Yale redecoration job Lorelai does on Rory's room.

NOTES *'You know, you never know how you're gonna react in situations like this until something happens, and I think I did pretty well.'*

It was a bit of a cliffhanger last episode, but now we know Yale and Princeton have also accepted Rory.

Tobin is the one who calls Lorelai to tell her there's been a fire at the inn, but we won't actually see him until next episode. Michel calls The Cheshire Cat Inn for a job; from what we've seen of that place, he probably dodged a bullet there (2.4). Miss Patty tells Michel she was Ricardo Montalban's receptionist for six months. Rory telling Paris "Bed is not a life plan, and you, my friend, need a life plan," is a clever foreshadowing of what we will see their first week at Yale (4.2).

Jess' "I got it under control" is very similar to Luke's own approach to tackling a problem, and equally effective. It's also in this way that Luke and Jess are mirror images of Lorelai and Rory, who frequently talk about "fixing" things that are wrong with their lives, though with slightly better results.

Lorelai finally tells Luke about the dream she had about them as a married couple (3.1).

TODAY'S CELEBRATION Jess Mariano: Wal-Mart Employee of the Month.

"On my second episode, I had a scene with Lauren and that was exciting. That's when I learned about the pace. I took some pauses and she said, 'No no no, you can't take those pauses.' I guess the third episode I did was when I got invited to the table reads, and that's when you got to see the whole cast reading the script and really getting a sense of the pace, the signature style of that show. I loved the table reads. I always thought I did my best work there."

-TODD LOWE (ZACK)

KIRK OF ALL TRADES Purveyor of "daily T-shirts featuring a humorous topical headline of something I witness around town"—all for just $14.95. (Lorelai also suggests he's gone around selling his laundry in the past.) Choose from "Babette ate oatmeal," "Faux Poes foes" and more.

AMEN, SISTER FRIEND

RORY: Look at my wall.

LORELAI: So?

RORY: So, that wall says something.

LORELAI: Yeah, it says the Harvard merchandising department made a nice chunk of change off of us.

RORY: But how can I go to Yale with my wall looking like this?

LORELAI: It's a wall. Look honey, Luke was right. The pro/con lists have to come to an end eventually.

RORY: But Luke also reminded us that it was supposed to be Harvard regardless of a list. Everyone thinks that.

LORELAI: I don't. I don't. I know I'm the one who said no to Yale loudly and a lot, but not anymore. Really, I just want what's right.

What I Kept

One year we got the strangest wrapped gift: They gave us skateboards. I don't understand why we got skateboards. All of us were kind of scratching our heads about that. I went around and got everybody to sign mine, so I have a skateboard from *Gilmore Girls* that everyone had signed. But I still have my *Gilmore Girls* bathrobe.

—George Anthony Bell (dialogue coach)

3.18 Happy Birthday, Baby

First aired: April 22, 2003 // Written by Amy Sherman-Palladino // Directed by Gail Mancuso

While Lorelai tries to get the Independence Inn up and running again after the fire, Rory and the rest of the town plan Lorelai's birthday celebration. Meanwhile, Lorelai comes into a sum of money that threatens to utterly change the relationship she has with her parents, much to Emily's horror.

GINCHY! Richard telling Lorelai that she will not buy 150 pairs of Jimmy Choos.

NOTES *'Everybody in this room named Lorelai is over the moon about the going to Yale.'*

The fire from last episode wiped out five of the upstairs rooms as well as the dining room, and it all needs to be fixed up in 10 days. Sookie's kitchen, too, has been knocked out of commission. Lorelai's hatred of bed and breakfasts probably stems from her own experiences with Rory on their Harvard road trip (2.4).

Bio ☺ Marion Ross (Lorelai "Trix" Gilmore/Marilyn)

Though most casual viewers of *Gilmore Girls* would say its cast is made up of virtual unknowns, more dedicated followers know that part of the show's charm is its brilliant deployment of seasoned actors. While Kelly Bishop and Edward Herrmann are the prime examples, Marion Ross' handful of appearances as Lorelai the First are the standout performances of those episodes.

Born in Watertown, Minn., Ross moved to San Diego while still in high school, and hit the theater circuit right after graduation. Though best known in America as Marion Cunningham on the sitcom *Happy Days* (1974-1984), Ross appeared in dozens of classic television series including *The Donna Reed Show*, *Father Knows Best* and *The Brady Bunch*, to *That '70s Show* and *The Drew Carey Show*.

✱ Madeline is going to Mills College, Louise to Tulane. We also finally discover who the father in *a film by kirk* (2.19) was—Pete the pizza guy!

✱ Lorelai's iffy relationship with pets (1.11) apparently began earlier than we've been told. She was 4 when she was frightened of her pet rabbit, Murray, which Richard and Emily gave away. Jess' "stolen" car won't be mentioned again until next season (4.12).

TODAY'S CELEBRATION Lorelai's 35th birthday!

EMILY'S MAID DU JOUR Teresa, who is designated the birthday candle blower-outer for Lorelai's birthday cake.

LORELAI'S GIFTS Candles, a beret and Joe Strummer's jacket from The Clash's 1979 Pearl Harbor tour, all from Tobin; a fancy journal from Michel; five hours of handyman service from Luke.

KIRK OF ALL TRADES Pizza delivery guy (nearly).

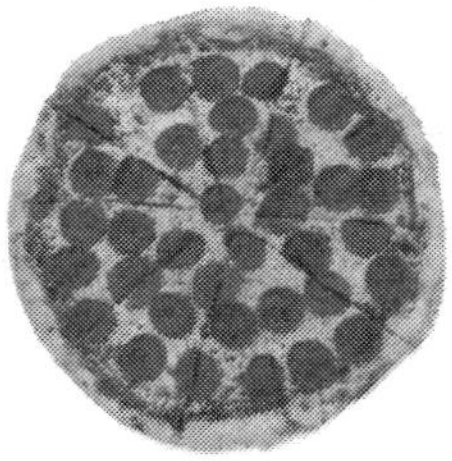

JOHNNY MACHETE Richard's family recipe.

5 The number of years Tobin's been the night manager at the Independence Inn; the number of free handyman hours Luke gives Lorelai for her birthday; and the number of years he's been doing that.

98 FEET The largest pizza in Connecticut, made in Litchfield.

22.8 MILES The distance from Yale to Stars Hollow (according to Jess' Yahoo skills).

$75,000 the amount of the check Richard gives Lorelai as the proceeds from the real estate investment he made in her name when she was born.

OY WITH THE ___, ALREADY! Tobin. Less than a minute in and it's hard to fault Michel for his distaste for the guy.

AMEN, SISTER FRIEND

LORELAI: $75,000. $75,000. Oh my God, that's like 150 pairs of Jimmy Choos.
RICHARD: What are Jimmy Choos?
LORELAI: Shoes.
RICHARD: 150 pairs, that's it?
LORELAI: Dad, they're Jimmy Choos.
RICHARD: For $75,000, you should be able to buy at least three or four hundred pairs of shoes.
LORELAI: Not Jimmy Choos.
RICHARD: But that's ridiculous. You are not going to spend $75,000 on Jimmy Choos when you could buy 400 pairs of less prestigious but I'm sure equally stylish shoes. You will shop around first. Is that clear?

Behind the Scenes: The Giant Pizza

When a 12-hour day is your best case scenario, you find some interesting ways to pass the time. That's a nice way of saying that more than a few pranks were pulled behind the scenes.

"My favorite was the giant pizza," says key set costumer Valerie Campbell. "I know it was only on screen for a split second, but it was just talked about so much, and then when it finally happened..."

Of course what Campbell really remembers is the young crew member who took a dare to do a bellyflop into that pizza.

"It wasn't real pizza, it was made of foam," she says. But the tomato sauce and toppings were real. "So the last day of shooting of that episode, we were all in the backlot. Obviously if something had happened to this pizza, it would've been horrible. But (the crew member) got almost naked, he was in boxers, and he did a bellyflop off the picnic table that was near Miss Patty's at the time. It was just the funniest thing, and we all thought he was crazy. Someone videotaped it, I'm sure."

3.19 Keg! Max!

First aired: April 29, 2003 // Written by Daniel Palladino // Directed by Chris Long

For the first time in years, the girls are not invited to Friday night dinner at the Gilmores, thanks to Lorelai paying them back for Rory's schooling last episode. Jess learns that not being able to take Rory to the Stars Hollow prom is the least of his worries. Lane's band rocks a local party, and an old rivalry turns violent.

GINCHY! Kyle and the party, and Lane's drunken call to her mother.

NOTES *'The charade is over.'*

Lane's band still doesn't have a name, though Brian's suggested "The Harry Potters" and "The We," Dave "The Chops," and Zack "Follow Them to the Edge of the Desert" and "Devil's Advocate." Lorelai has been called back (2.7) to duty as part of the Chilton Booster club; she's elected grad-night treasurer.

The enthusiastic-about-being-21 Rick at Kyle's party is the same Rick (or Rich) Blumenfeld whose hair Lane touched in a fit of hormonal insanity (1.8). Now he's just the keg monkey.

TODAY'S CELEBRATION Lane's band's gig at Kyle's house.

AND INTRODUCING...*Chin-Chin and Pau-Pau* Michel's chows come courtesy of Frank, the Independence Inn employee Michel was supposed to lay off.

OY WITH THE ___, ALREADY! Alex. If Lorelai didn't mention him occasionally, we'd forget she was still going out with him. And oy with Max already, too, come to think of it.

31 The number of days of school Jess has missed; the cutoff is 20.

AMEN, SISTER FRIEND

LANE: [*on the phone to Mrs. Kim, drunk*] Hello, Mama? Hi, how are you doing tonight? It's Lane. Yeah, Lane. Nothing's wrong. In fact, I'm feeling pretty good right now. Had a beer and a half. Nice cold beer. And I just thought I'd tell you, I'm drumming in a band tonight at a party and we rocked. We were The Clash and Rage Against the Machine and Nirvana combined. And I'm in love with Dave Rygalski. He's my guy, not Young Chui. Young Chui's a ship in the night, Mama. Not even a ship, he's a little

"We were very lucky to be on a lot such as Warner Brothers because you see so many different things. The Last Samurai shot on the Warner Brothers lot. They took over an area of New York Street and this other little area that's right behind Stars Hollow. They turned it into 19th century Japan, and it was amazing. You'd go to the commissary and you've got people with bleeding gunshot wounds because they're background and they're going to eat lunch."

–VALERIE CAMPBELL, KEY SET COSTUMER

tugboat tooting along and I'm not gonna go to the prom with him, uh uh. I'm going with Dave because we rock together, Mama. The charade is over.

"I tried to still be funny without stretching outside the limits of what was acceptable. And being 100 percent honest, I don't think I always succeeded at that. There are times when I'll go back and watch something and be like, 'I may have pushed it too far. I may be a little bit too over the top there.'"

-SEAN GUNN (KIRK)

3.20 Say Goodnight, Gracie

First aired: May 6, 2003 // Teleplay by Amy Sherman-Palladino & Janet Leahy // Story by Amy Sherman-Palladino // Directed by Jamie Babbit

There's nothing like a family to screw up a family. A cold wind still blows between Lorelai and Emily, Lane and her own mother are on the outs, Luke and Jess are not getting along, and now there's a new adult who's come along for Jess to rebel against. Poor Rory's trying to process Dean's latest news and her frustrating relationship with Jess. Add to that a death in town that could mean promising things for Lorelai and Sookie, and you have one awkward time.

! GINCHY! The church hand-off between Rev. Skinner and Rabbi Barans; Mrs. Kim's enigmatic quote and Dave's valiant effort to hunt down its source; and that final scene between Rory and Jess on the bus before he slips out of town.

NOTES *'OK, so I guess we're not playing nice anymore.'*

* Amy's love affair with Dorothy Parker continues, this time with a stream-of-consciousness riff about the Algonquin round table and Robert Benchley between Lorelai and Rory.

* Though we've heard nothing more about Fran owning the Dragonfly Inn (2.8), clearly it's never been far from Lorelai and Sookie's minds.

* Jimmy turning up at Luke's Diner to surprise Jess with the news that he's his father will be recreated next season with the appearance of April at the same place (6.9), with far more profound consequences.

TODAY'S CELEBRATION Dean's engagement to Lindsay and the death of Fran. (Maybe celebration isn't the best word here.)

83 How old Fran was when she died.

1893 The year Fran's family opened the Dragonfly Inn.

AND INTRODUCING... *Ceaser 2.0* A big hand for Aris Alvarado, who will see the character through to the end of the series. Also, Jess' dad, Jimmy.

Behind the Music 2
Hep Alien

Stars Hollow's favorite band also happens to be one of its most confusing, with some band members actually playing on screen, and a few named after people who are just a few feet off to the side anytime Hep Alien jams.

Zack: Actor Todd Lowe is an accomplished guitarist, and is pretty much always playing guitar for real on screen.

Brian: John Cabrera doesn't know how to play bass, but he still had to learn the chord changes for every song for the camera. His bass riffs are played by producer Helen Pai's husband, the real-life Dave Rygalski.

Gil: Rock star Sebastian Bach is a killer vocalist, but he isn't a guitarist. His guitar solos were played either by Rygalski or Rygalski's former bandmate Brian Zydiak.

Lane: Keiko Agena took lessons and ended up playing the drums on screen for most of Hep Alien's performances.

Says Lowe, "I was always, 'I'm a musician, I can do it myself.' But it's not going to sound good on TV, trust us, they'd say, so I did. But we would usually rehearse the number a couple of days before. They would rent us a little rehearsal space and we'd go through the stuff and do a couple takes. Helen Pai would send MP3s via her BlackBerry over to Amy & Dan: 'Which way do you like it?' Then they'd pick one and that's the way we'd have to perform it." All of the actors sing during their performances.

In addition to line rehearsals and blocking for their regular scenes, the band had to practice their musical performances for about three hours at a rented studio every time Hep Alien played, John Cabrera says. Pai was always in charge of any Hep Alien story lines, and led all the band rehearsals with her husband.

"On the day of shooting, she would be supervising the band stuff, and Dave was always playing my part just off camera," he says. "My bass wasn't really plugged in. There were a couple of episodes where they actually let me play what I had learned during rehearsal, chord progression wise. It's hard to say if it actually got into the show. I don't think it was terrible, but I'm sure that it didn't compare to Dave's. But I know they also wanted to try to keep the editing of the band stuff down to a minimum because they wanted it to feel like a bunch of young people creating their music. As poor as it might sound, it was beautiful in its own right."

THE WEDDING ANNOUNCEMENT "Mr. and Mrs. Thomas Lister announce the engagement of their daughter, Lindsay Ann, to Dean Forester, son of Randy and Barbara Forester."

AMEN, SISTER FRIEND

LANE [*to Rory*]: Dave dropped me off at home. He wanted to come in, but he's an only child and I saw no reason for his family line to end with him, so I went in and he left.

RORY: OK, well, let's think. Maybe she didn't hear you.

LANE: I was drunk, I could've slurred.

RORY: Exactly. Maybe she thought you said you were at a smarty, playing clock music, drinking fear, and in love with Rave Schmitchalsky.

Jess gets a good look at his future if he doesn't straighten up fast.

DAVE [*to Mrs. Kim*]: A few weeks ago you told me that Lane had a crush on me. Well, I have a crush on her, too. Now, I know you have very strict rules about dating and boys, but I just want you to know that I'm a good person. I don't smoke, I don't drink, I've never gotten a ticket, I'm healthy, I take care of myself, I floss. I never watch more than 30 minutes of television a night, partly because I think it's a waste of time and partly because there's nothing on. I respect my parents, I do well in school, I never play video games in case they do someday prove that playing them can turn you into a serial killer. I don't drink coffee. I hate soda because the carbonation freaks me out. I'm happy to give up meat if you feel strongly about it. I don't mind wearing a tie. I enjoy playing those hymns on my guitar, and I really, really want to take your daughter to the prom. Mrs. Kim? Please don't make me repeat that list again.

MRS. KIM: Let never day nor night unhallowed pass, but still remember what the Lord hath done. *[Later, after Dave tells Mrs. Kim he's read the entire* Bible *and hasn't been able to find the quotation.]*

MRS. KIM: It's Shakespeare, *Henry VI*. I like to goof off now and then, too, you know.

DAVE: Shakespeare.

MRS. KIM: That is a very difficult thing to do, reading the *Bible* in one night. I myself have only done it three times. You need great determination and excellent light. I'm very impressed. All right.

DAVE: All right what?

MRS. KIM: You can go to the prom but you cannot get married.

3.21 Here Comes the Son

First aired: May 13, 2003 // Written and directed by Amy Sherman-Palladino

Lorelai's recent $75,000 windfall may have helped her square things financially with her parents for Chilton, but it's seriously threatening Rory's chances of getting money for Yale. Jess has left Stars Hollow to connect with his father in Los Angeles, and Rory is caving under the pressures of ending one chapter of her life and starting another.

GINCHY! Paris bossing Lorelai around at the grad night ticket table, and then their awkward hug; Rory telling Emily that she's being really stupid; Lorelai (and the rest of us) finding out that Rory's been named valedictorian by reading the inscriptions in Rory's yearbook.

NOTES *'Hey, life's about the spontaneous, right?*

Planning for the great European backpacking trip continues with the girls learning Spanish. Poor Lorelai. Last time around, she was stuck haggling over the tuition for Chilton, this time it's Yale.

Jimmy's hot dog stand is in Santa Monica but he and Sasha live in Venice. This is Jess' first time on the West Coast.

EMILY'S MAID DU JOUR Lupe, who argues with Emily over whether or not dinner is ready.

OY WITH ___, ALREADY! Miss Celine. This has the feeling of one those touches that Amy included strictly for her own amusement, the rest of us be damned.

TODAY'S CELEBRATION Jess landing on his father's doorstep? (I got nothin'.)

PLACES JIMMY HAS LIVED Minneapolis, Chicago, Biloxi, Maine, New Jersey, New York, New Hampshire and now Los Angeles.

AND INTRODUCING...*Sherilyn Fenn* Sure, she's Jimmy's "roomie" Sasha this episode, but Fenn will return (6.11) as April Nardini's mom (and Luke's ex), Anna. Though the actress doesn't get a whole lot of screen time in *Gilmore*, she brings a certain clout that Amy & Dan surely appreciated, especially for her role as Audrey Horne in the David Lynch TV series *Twin Peaks*, and the title character in the odd movie *Boxing Helena* (1993).

"It's still flattering to have someone say, 'Were you Zack?' I get it a lot of times at airports. There's usually kids in that demographic there. I don't spend too much time at malls or anything. I guess if I get really desperate, I can stroll in and out of Hot Topic and wait to be recognized."

—TODD LOWE (ZACK)

Bio Aris Alvarado (Ceaser)

Though initially little more than an explanation for how Luke manages to feed a diner full of people on his own, Ceaser (first played by Christopher Grey in 3.6) would become Luke's lovable foil at the workplace thanks to the wide-eyed, slightly snarky charm of Aris Alvarado.

Born in the Lower East Side of New York City, Alvarado, the class clown in 6th grade, got his start in acting on a dare issued by his teacher: he ended up in his school's production of *The Littlest Angel*. He actually appeared on *Gilmore Girls* twice as an extra (including holding back the throngs of students at the dance when Tristin and Dean go at it in 1.9) before he was approached to play Ceaser.

Since *Gilmore*, Alvarado has appeared in a few indie movies and had a regular role in *Head Case*. Says the actor, "When I was in college, all the acting teachers told everybody don't do this, go to business school. It's very hard. I know this is what I want to do for the rest of my life, so I keep doing it. I'm getting paid to make believe—that's freakin' awesome!"

THE SPIN-OFF THAT DIDN'T Though this feels like one of those episodes where they focused on a single character in a new locale only to give the rest of the cast a chance to take the day off, "Here Comes the Son" actually was an unofficial pilot for a spin-off focused on Jess and his estranged father. Tentatively called *Windward Circle* (after a residential area in Venice Beach, Calif.), it nevertheless died on the vine.

AMEN, SISTER FRIEND

JESS [*to Jimmy*]: You have nothing? I have nothing! I have no place to go. I can't stay at Luke's, I can't stay in Stars Hollow. My mother is a wackjob. I mean, you're saying you're this loser and what, you don't wanna take me off this terrific path I'm headed down right now? I'm not graduating high school. I don't know what I'm gonna do with the rest of my life, but something's telling me I better find out soon or I'm gonna be that guy out there on the boardwalk selling the hemp hats.

3.22 Those are Strings, Pinocchio

First aired: May 20, 2003 // Written by Daniel Palladino // Directed by Jamie Babbit

The inevitable has happened: The Independence Inn has been closed down. With financial aid out of the picture for Yale, Lorelai tells Sookie she can't help buy the Dragonfly Inn after all. But when Rory finds out her college bills are the reason her mother must pass up the opportunity to live out her dream, she swallows her pride and takes drastic action.

GINCHY! Lorelai's impromptu celebration with Sookie and Jackson; Rory's business-like proposal to Richard and Emily; and Lorelai and Rory making faces at each other as Rory walks across the stage at graduation.

NOTES *'Rory grew up here. I grew up here.'*

There's foreshadowing and then there's just "come on!" Luke tells the girls that he's taking Nicole on a cruise to Alaska and Lorelai tells him that's a good place to propose (which Luke says he has no intention of doing). He then has a dream in which Lorelai tells him *not* to propose.

Rory and Lane tried to explain to Dean the logic of calling up the boys they like and hanging up on them without saying anything (3.7), but Rory's clearly grown up since then, flipping out on Jess for doing just that. He has his own growing up to do.

Lorelai stops Rory before she can leave Chilton for her graduation party, urging her to take in her surroundings and see that the place that caused her so much angst over the years is no longer so intimidating. She'll do this again the moment Rory sets foot in her Yale dorm (4.2).

Liza Weil's younger sister, Samantha, plays Bernadette, the girl who drives Paris crazy while she's making her video yearbook entry.

TODAY'S CELEBRATION The closing of the Independence Inn, reinstatement of Friday night dinners, and Rory's graduation.

KIRK OF ALL TRADES Mold spotter.

PICKLEPUSS & SAUERKRAUT Lorelai's names for Richard and Emily. (Presumably this is a step up from Schnickelfritzes.)

THINGS WE DIDN'T KNOW ABOUT CHILTON Author Harriet Beecher Stowe (*Uncle Tom's Cabin*) walked its halls, the banister was donated by poet Robert Frost (*The Road Not Taken*), and the sconce was ceremonially lit for the first time by Thomas Edison.

AMEN, SISTER FRIEND

LORELAI: Rory honey, do you understand the Gilmores do nothing altruistically? Strings are attached to everything.

RORY: There are no strings.

What I Kept

I have everything! I have a robe, I have a sweatshirt, I have many jackets, I have a scarf, I have martini glasses, I have coffee mugs, I have Dragonfly drink stirrers from a party we had. I have a key for the Dragonfly Inn with a Dragonfly hanging off of it. I have a creamer from the Dragonfly, a little cow or a duck or something like that. I think I have a Lorelai scarf – I don't even remember when I got that. It just goes on and on and on.

I've got a journal by my bed that's leather and it says "*Gilmore Girls:* 100 episodes." The bag I carry to work right now daily, that's a *Gilmore Girls* bag that says 100 episodes. The pen in my purse says *Gilmore Girls*. I have so much *Gilmore Girls* stuff, and downstairs in my storage, I have huge plastic containers from Target full of every script from the show, the years I worked on it.

—Patty Malcolm (Lauren Graham's stand—in)

LORELAI: No strings?

RORY: No. I just have to pay them back starting five years after I graduate, and I have to start going back for Friday night dinners.

LORELAI: Um, hello, Pinocchio, those are strings.

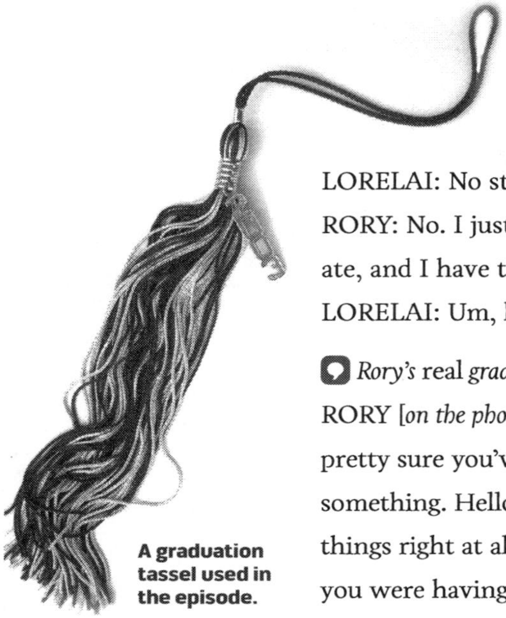

A graduation tassel used in the episode.

Rory's real *graduation speech:*

RORY [*on the phone*]: Jess, is that you? Jess, I'm pretty sure it's you and I'm pretty sure you've been calling and not saying anything but wanna say something. Hello? You're not going to talk? Fine, I'll talk. You didn't handle things right at all. You could've talked to me. You could've told me that you were having trouble in school and weren't going to graduate, and that your dad had been there, but you didn't. And you ended up not taking me to my prom and not coming to my graduation and leaving again without saying goodbye again, and that's fine, I get it, but that's it for me. I'm going to Europe tomorrow and I'm going to Yale and I'm moving on. And I'm not going to pine. I hope you didn't think I was going to pine, OK? I think—I think I may have loved you, but I just need to let it go. So, that's it, I guess. Um, I hope you're good. I want you to be good, and, um, OK, so, goodbye. That word sounds really lame and stupid right now, but there it is. Goodbye.

And there it was. *Gilmore Girls* had withstood the loss of one of its executive producers, yet its popularity with fans continued to hold up, and the critics continued to lament that the series was the best thing on television that most people in America weren't watching. And Amy, who had fought so many battles over *Gilmore*, letting others go when the fate of the series remained in doubt, regained whatever confidence had been lost.

Those Town Meetings

"The cool thing about that town hall meeting place is that all those pictures on the wall are really Liz [Torres, "Miss Patty"] from different Broadway shows."

—ROSE ABDOO

Though viewers might've flocked to *Gilmore Girls* for the witty badinage between Lorelai and Rory, or to see who the girls would end up romantically entangled with that week, it was the series' use of delightfully dotty characters that lent it an extra enticing dimension. One of the show's strokes of genius was the creation of the Stars Hollow town meeting, which brought all of those distinctive personalities together under one roof.

This was hardly new territory. The inmates-running-the-asylum hilarity of the 1960s US sitcom *Green Acres* was fueled by the quirky residents of Hooterville who, on occasion, found themselves thrown together in a town meeting. Yet, with hour-long episodes to play with, Amy & Dan and their stable of writers were able to give even the least-used character a definite personality that went well beyond the one-dimensional mannerism or catch phrase seen on *Green Acres*, or anywhere else.

The meeting scenes were also some of the hardest to shoot.

"They were very complex because there were millions of setups, and they'd last all day long," Michael Winters says. Add to that the fact that the intense lighting necessary to shoot those scenes, combined with California's already warm climate, often made Miss Patty's feel like an oven. Throw in the jackets and sweaters the townspeople wore to reinforce the cold Connecticut location, and "it just got hotter than hell in there," he says.

"It seemed like whenever it was supposed to be winter in Stars Hollow, it would be sweltering in the town hall meetings," Rose Abdoo says. "And whenever it was supposed to be super hot, it was cold—the real weather never matched up with the 'town' weather! You wouldn't think just sitting down and calling out stuff in a meeting would be challenging, but it was."

Those meetings also took a very long time to shoot, as a camera would have to be set up in one position to capture Abdoo's line as Gypsy, for example. Then it would have to be set up again somewhere else and the lighting readjusted to record a retort from Sally Struthers' Babette. Because of this, it often wasn't until well after dark that "they'd send everybody home and turn [the camera] around and I'd have to do all my spiel," Winters says. "I'd either be right on top of it, or exhausted and just hanging on by my fingernails."

That's not quite how Abdoo remembers it, though. "Michael's fantastic. Taylor had these huge monologues.... At least four or five different episodes I remember him having these giant speeches about the deer problem, the pickle problem, everyone getting each other's mail problem, the hay bale maze. And I would be in awe of him. He would just have it all down. That would've been horrible if he wasn't on top of his game—that really would've tortured us."

"I Think I'm Dating Luke"

season **four**

No matter the program, transitioning a character from high school to college is always a gamble, even more so when that character is the super-smart, super-sweet Rory Gilmore.

Ironically, while Rory became an even more interesting character to watch as she navigated her newfound independence this season, Lorelai, so often the engine that drove the series for its first three years, actually sputtered a bit, pulled under by a romantic story line with Jason Stiles that even the writers realized had little chemistry. However, unlike the bland Alex last season, Jason couldn't be so easily dropped from the show thanks to his position as Richard Gilmore's business partner.

This season also brought with it Luke's dippy sister, and Jess' mother, Liz, and her soon-to-be husband, TJ. Initially the pair seemed better suited to sitcom life, but quickly filled an important role: demonstrating Luke's nearly pathological need to fix crises...and people.

Finally, two surprises managed to elevate this season beyond its few shortcomings. The first was more surprising for how it began: the blossoming romance between Luke and Lorelai. Surprise No. 2 was also the most interesting long-term development of the season: the separation of Richard and Emily.

After years of blindly defending high society and the role she played in it, Emily discovered that even her husband had little respect for what she did to keep the Gilmore name so highly respected. This would have ramifications throughout the rest of the series, even forcing Rory's grandparents to realize that they wanted better for her than a life of dinner parties and fundraisers.

4.1 Ballrooms & Biscotti

First aired: Sept. 23, 2003 // Written and directed by Amy Sherman-Palladino

No sooner do Lorelai and Rory return from Europe than they suddenly realize that Rory has to start Yale just a couple of days later. Meanwhile, Jackson doesn't want to know the sex of his baby, Taylor's drafted Rory to be his Ice Cream Queen, and Luke's cruise with Nicole went nothing like he thought it would.

Gifts the Girls Bring Back

—"Pieta" place mat for Gypsy

—Picasso T-shirt for Andrew

—Tower of London nutcracker for Pete

—Castanets for Miss Patty

—Miniature Eiffel Tower for Emily

—A pipe from Copenhagen for Richard

—Biscotti for themselves

—Rosary beads... for Lorelai

—"Fruits de la terre" for Luke (via Jackson's pantry).

! GINCHY! Rory's heartfelt homecoming welcome to her clothes and her sock drawer, and her exasperated speech to the crowd at Taylor's ice cream shoppe; Emily holding Rory hostage by making her watch ballroom dancing competitions; Luke telling Lorelai what happened on the cruise with Nicole; and the girls celebrating their last night together watching those ballroom tapes.

NOTES *'Don't you understand, this is my last night with my daughter!'*

* Rory's reluctance to touch Sookie's stomach may be down to what she went through with Sherry recently (3.13).

* Lorelai's "a single man of a certain age who lives alone" bit with Luke will be echoed by the way Mrs. Kim sums up Lorelai later (6.19): "An unmarried woman of a certain age, unescorted, wearing the clothes you tend to wear; people will think things. *Bad* things."

TODAY'S CELEBRATION The return of the backpacking Gilmores and the opening of Taylor's soda shoppe.

KIRK OF ALL TRADES Mr. Gleason's a busy one this episode. Not only is he putting up posters for Taylor's soda shoppe, he's also still working at the beauty supply store, and even manages to squeeze in some skydiving.

EMILY'S MAID DU JOUR Gerta, maker of tea and time-consuming souffles, and presumably not "The Clomper" from Hamburg (3.11).

AND HERE'S A SHOUT OUT TO OUR INTERNATIONAL FANS Seeing as this is the girls' first day back from their backpacking adventure in Europe, it's pretty much international overload:

- Lorelai laments that "the van ride felt longer than our train ride from Paris to Prague, and we had that group of French boys singing 'Sk8er Boi' and smelling like a soccer field sitting all around us." Also, they saw Notre Dame, the Roman baths, St. Peter's Basilica, and Lorelai touched the Pope's car.

- Rory had dreams about her clothes while she was in Copenhagen. Then there are the consulates that Babette called after the girls failed to return when Rory said they would: that's you, Belgium, Lisbon, Berlin, Paris and The Netherlands. Finally, Lorelai's initial plan to cover the fact that they forgot to get Luke a gift abroad: "We have to just pick up something here and we'll tell him that we got it in Denmark."

- Let's not forget Sookie's "How was Barcelona? Did you see the gaudy apartments? Oooh, did you see a bullfight? Did you see Anne Frank's house? Did you cry? Was Steven Spielberg there?" Lorelai tells Luke that

"There are things that jump out as being extremely unpleasant. This didn't seem that bad, but I had to walk through wearing that parachute, and that parachute was just heavy as hell. I remember that being very uncomfortable."

–SEAN GUNN (KIRK)

Behind the Scenes: Offscreen Angst

One of the greatest challenges any TV series faces is starting a new season, and *Gilmore Girls* certainly had its share of rough starts. Yet this episode is a good example of how to jump back into action. Writer Jane Espenson, who started on *Gilmore* with this episode, is quick to point out one of the series' hallmarks.

"Frequently, major events such as fights between characters happen offscreen, and we only hear about them after the fact. This breaks a cardinal rule of television: you need conflict to establish the drama. But we don't want to see Lorelai hurt, either. We started this season with Luke having married Nicole. And again, we don't see this because it would be hard to watch Lorelai watching this relationship develop."

Rory's Local Event Track Record

—Head pilgrim girl at the food drive table

—Third leprechaun at the St. Patrick's Day festival

—Ticket booth attendant on Groundhog's Day

—Manger procession organizer at Christmas

— Esther at the Purim carnival.

they hung out in Ireland waiting for U2 to show at the Clarence Hotel. Finally, Luke went on a seven-country cruise, though which countries those might be are not revealed.

THINGS WE'VE LEARNED Wild animals around the Warner Brothers lot frequently had a field day in Taylor's Old-Fashioned Soda Shoppe and Candy Store, especially the squirrels, which used to eat the ice cream cones.

AMEN, SISTER FRIEND

TAYLOR [*to Rory, who's apologized for not being his ice cream queen*]: It's my own fault. I should have figured that once you got into Yale, everything would be different.
RORY: That's not fair.
TAYLOR: No, I understand. You're no longer our little Stars Hollow Rory Gilmore. You belong to the Ivy Leagues right now. It's time to cut those small town ties and go off and do something important, like go to drama school or have one of those high-class naked parties with that Bush girl.
RORY: Taylor!
TAYLOR: OK. See you around the quad.

[Later]

TAYLOR [*to kids*]: Now just picture her sitting here just like this, smiling and waving. 'Hello kids, I'm the Ice Cream Queen.'
[Rory storms up and grabs the microphone]
RORY: OK, that's it. I humiliate myself at least six times a year for this town, and just because I'm going to Yale, that's not going to stop. Now the reason I am not the Ice Cream Queen is because Taylor never asked me. I didn't know about it, and that's why I was busy. Now I love this town, I will be back in that ridiculous pilgrim outfit at Thanksgiving, so everybody just get off my back!

4.2 The Lorelais' First Day at Yale

First aired: Sept. 30, 2003 // Written by Daniel Palladino // Directed by Chris Long

Lorelai borrows Luke's pickup and packs Rory off to Yale, but her daughter quickly becomes homesick. Roommates Tana and Paris (!) do little to ease her nerves. Meanwhile, Nicole's lawyers pay a visit to Luke's Diner to sniff out what type of settlement he wants in the divorce.

GINCHY! The (accidental) invention of another catchphrase (copper boom!); Lorelai justifying her actions to the freshman counselor ("A guy told me, I forget his name..."); Luke's wrangling with Nicole's lawyers; the dorm room takeout test ("so we can judge the quality of food, speed of service, cuteness of delivery guys on a scale of 1 to 10"); the boys at Yale howling and the girls howling back; and Lorelai surveying her now-empty house.

Behind the Scenes: Tana's First Day at Yale

Yes, it was Rory's first day at Yale, all right, but she was far from alone when she poked her sweet new hairdo into her new student digs. With just a few minutes of dialogue, Olivia Hack as 16-year-old Tana Schrick brought just the right touch of insanity to the proceedings, actually saving some scenes that might otherwise have toppled under the weight of the "Paris' life coach" story line (which probably worked a lot better on paper than it did in practice). Rory might've been a tad homesick her first day at Yale, but Hack had her own issues to tackle during the shooting of that episode.

Arriving on set just a few days after getting the role, she learned her lines, delivered them verbatim for Tana's first encounter with Rory, and went home at the end of the day to unwind. Around 6 that evening, she received a call from the studio asking her how quickly she could make it back to Warner Brothers because they needed to do some wardrobe tests.

About 20 minutes later, "I show up there and they're throwing different clothes on me and I'm doing the dog and pony show in front of the writers and everyone," she recalls. "And they go, 'OK, we found an outfit and we found a hairstyle. Now let's shoot it.' I'm like, 'Shoot it? What are you talking about?'"

Somebody had watched the dailies and realized that they had actually dressed Bledel "in a French braid and a polo" shirt so that she came across as being the same age as Tana, who was supposed to be a young prodigy who had skipped a few grades to get into Yale. There was nothing else to do but dress Hack even younger and reshoot her scenes, which they did.

"When you go in to work, you're in a certain mindset. When you go in for a costume fitting, you're in a totally different mindset. Especially at 6 o'clock at night. Lauren and Alexis were there for their close-ups and then left. So I think I was just doing that scene with the dialogue coach or something.

"That first episode was my favorite [to shoot] just because there was so much going on. But you can see in one of those first scenes right before Rory walks into the dorm and sees me, that I'm there in the background in my old hair and in my old wardrobe."

Lorelai reminds Rory to be in the moment. Copper boom!

NOTES *'You're gonna be in the moment.'*

✱ Lorelai can't drive a stick shift. Nicole is represented by the law firm of Blodgett, Sage, Albet, Pettruccio, Stein, Lemming and Stein. Rory's freshman counselor is Tess. Paris' father arranged for her to share a dorm with Rory because life coach Terrence felt the girls' "life journey was not complete." Tana is adopted.

✱ Paris is already toying with Jamie, suggesting that effeminate life coach Terrence might be a rival.

TODAY'S CELEBRATION Rory (and Lorelai's) first day at Yale.

AND HERE'S A SHOUT OUT TO OUR INTERNATIONAL FANS Pretty much the entire takeout food delivery scene, and Lorelai and Rory playing at being the scandalous "almost-French Stars Hollow girls." Also, when Rory asks Lorelai to say something to make her hate her, Lorelai says, "Uh, go Hitler." In the German dubs, she says, "I could beat you."

4 HOURS How long before Rory pages Lorelai to return to Yale.

RONNY GILMORE What it says on Rory's Yale ID.

AMEN, SISTER FRIEND

RORY: When did I become one of those girls with dozens of beauty products, none of which are expendable? It used to be a touch of mascara, a dab of Coppertone, zip, bam, boom, out the door.
LORELAI: I heard 'copper' and 'boom.'

[Later]

LORELAI: I want you fully outfitted and settled for your first night or I won't sleep.
RORY: We can get it all later.

LORELAI: No, no. Now go unpack the skimpy amount of stuff I've gotten you so far and I'll be back in a couple of hours. Copper boom!

RORY: What?

LORELAI: It's what you said to me this morning when you were trying to speed me up.

RORY: But you missed a bunch of stuff in between.

LORELAI: I think it's catchy. Go, go, unpack.

RORY: Copper boom!

LORELAI: Copper boom!

LORELAI: [*summing up Luke to the lawyers*] All he likes is fishing and watching baseball, and he's got a reel and he's got a TV, so he's all set.

RORY: It's going to be very hard to be Christiane Amanpour broadcasting live from a foxhole in Tehran with my mommy.

Behind the Scenes — Don't I Know You?

Sometimes it's pretty easy to forget that the film and television community is one of the smallest in the United States. If you've been honing your craft for any length of time in front of or behind the camera, nobody remains a stranger for very long.

When Katie Walder arrived as Janet Billings, she'd already met two of her three dorm mates. Her very first job when she moved to New York City two years before had been recording a public service announcement for the Partnership for a Drug-Free America, where she met Bledel on her first job shooting her own PSA for the organization. Walder had also worked with fellow Philadelphian Liza Weil many years ago on an episode of a local CBS teen talk show called *Rap Around*. "A local newscaster hosted it and it was a bunch of teens from different high schools talking about whatever issue," she recalls. "One week it was drugs, another week it was prom. So it's a very small world."

Walder also knew Lauren Graham from a production of Kaufman and Hart's *Once in a Lifetime* they'd done together the previous July at the prestigious Williamstown Theatre Festival in New York. Even *Gilmore*'s Francie Jarvis, Emily Bergl, had been in that production.

"So I'd met Lauren, and she was so awesome," Walder says. "I just love Lauren. And when I went to the first table read, she was like, 'Oh my God, Katie!' So warm and so welcoming. She wasn't there my first day on the set because we didn't have many scenes together."

Anybody else you knew from before, Katie?

"The one who played Glenn, Ethan [Cohn], we went to camp together," she says with a laugh. "When we were both about 11, we were in a play together at a performing arts camp called French Woods in upstate New York. I have so many connections and I got the part of Janet totally unrelated."

4.3 The Hobbit, the Sofa, and Digger Stiles

First aired: Oct. 7, 2003 // Written by Amy Sherman-Palladino // Directed by Matthew Diamond

While waiting for the Dragonfly Inn renovations to be finished, Sookie talks Lorelai into planning and catering parties, starting with a child's Lord of the Rings *birthday party. At the party, Sookie wonders if she's really ready to be a mother. Jason (aka Digger), the 37-year-old son of Richard's former boss, Floyd Stiles, wants to join forces with him. Finally, after Emily refurnishes Rory's dorm without asking, her granddaughter is determined to politely tell her to "butt out."*

! GINCHY! Lorelai suddenly sensing that Emily's been in Rory's dorm; the glee with which Richard relishes sticking it to Floyd Stiles by partnering with his son; the disastrous *Lord of the Rings* party.

NOTES *'Things are going to be different this year.'*

* Rory subscribes to the Stars Hollow Gazette while at Yale. Sookie's "I can't have it" freakout about her kid at the party fits with her similar reaction to her wedding the night before (2.22).

* Still stewing over her problems with Lorelai, Emily is appalled when she discovers that Jason's prime motivation for partnering with Richard is revenge against his father.

Behind the Scenes: The Naked Guy's Big Break

This episode may be best known for featuring the introduction of an actor who was "plucked from obscurity" in the time-honored Hollywood fashion. Wayne Wilcox was a waiter at the Mercer Hotel in Soho when Dan pointed him out to Amy, she told The New York Times in January 2005. "'He's got that young Tom Hanksy sort of look. Someone like him would be good at Yale. So we said, 'Are you an actor?' And he said, 'Yeah, I am.'"

As Wilcox told TV Guide in November 2006, "I gave them my agent's information and they ended up calling and put me on tape just to see what I could do, and they said, 'We're writing this part for you: Marty.' And I was like, 'Wow, that's weird and great and fast and something completely unexpected.' But the scenes that I read were Dean scenes, so they were thinking along that vein as well."

However, some behind the scenes have said that theater was always Wilcox's first love, and one of the factors that led to his stay on the series being so short.

For those who've straddled that line between working in front of the camera and on stage, that is the real remarkable tale of "the Naked Guy"—an actor knowing what he truly wanted to do, and walking away from television to do it.

TODAY'S CELEBRATION The first Yale party of the year, Aaron Thompson's *Lord of the Rings* birthday party, and Richard's partnership with "Digger" Stiles.

AMEN, SISTER FRIEND

RORY: I came home and all the normal furniture was gone and all this stuff was in here.

LORELAI: What did your roommates say?

RORY: Tana still doesn't know she's at Yale, Paris saw it and said nothing.

LORELAI: Oh, so that's coming.

RORY: Janet's out jogging so I don't know what she thinks, but I have to hope she's pleased 'cause that girl's in shape and can kick my butt.

4.4 Chicken or Beef?

First aired: Oct. 14, 2003 // Written by Jane Espenson // Directed by Chris Long

Home from Yale, Rory finds herself invited to Dean and Lindsay's wedding while work on the Dragonfly Inn runs into a stumbling block in the form of Taylor. Fortunately, a parking space for a "ringy-dingy" ice cream truck could be the key to happy endings all around.

GINCHY! Zack flipping out after hearing how so many rock stars are highly educated; Dean's drunken ramblings about Rory to Luke.

NOTES *'Does our life seem at all ridiculous to you?'*

Dave Rygalski's suddenly gone off to college in California, spurred, no doubt, by actor Adam Brody splitting to play Seth Cohen in *The OC*. Kyle, last seen hosting the party that Dean and Jess trashed (3.19), is now in the Navy, perhaps as a result of that chaos.

Though it's not 100 percent clear, the water over which the town bridge lays may be Potter's Creek.

TODAY'S CELEBRATION Dean and Lindsay's wedding.

KIRK OF ALL TRADES Stars Hollow Security Company rep.

TAYLOR OF ALL TRADES Head of the Stars Hollow Historical Preservation Society.

What *Gilmore* Means to Me

About five years ago, I started watching *Gilmore Girls* on German television. I thought, because of the title, *Gilmore Girls* was something like a suburban housewives drama. Boy was I wrong!

No decent shows were on so I decided to give it a shot, just to pass the time. I was so lucky to catch the show from the second episode of the first season, and was instantly caught by this rather unusual mother/daughter duo. First, the pure physical appeal of Lauren Graham and Alexis Bledel and the effect on their fictional environment. Second, to watch the two dealing with the difficulties of family dynamics, relationships and everyday life in that lunatic town was highly entertaining and wonderful. And when I was watching Rory standing on the stage at her high school graduation, giving that speech, I was touched (crying, too, and I'm not ashamed to admit it). At that point it was clear to me that this was the best show on television ever .

—Zoran Bijelic, Germany

THINGS WE'VE LEARNED The snooty hotel Michel works at was shot in the lobby of a theater on the Warner Brothers lot.

"Gilmore Girls was a very grueling schedule in that you never quite knew how long something was going to take, and they weren't even blowing shit up."

–OLIVIA HACK (TANA)

AMEN, SISTER FRIEND

TAYLOR: Well, the Dragonfly is a historical building, Lorelai.
LORELAI: Yeah, but the whole town is a historical building, Taylor. I mean, George Washington ate, slept or blew his nose all over the damn place.
TAYLOR: He only blew his nose in the park. You've read the sign.

4.5 The Fundamental Things Apply

First aired: Oct. 21, 2003 // Written by John Stephens // Directed by Neema Barnette

Lorelai discovers that the decorator she and Sookie have chosen for the Dragonfly has worked for Emily, Rory is trying to ease herself into dating at Yale, and Luke is still getting over Nicole.

GINCHY! Lorelai using Luke's no-cell-phone rule to get off the phone with Emily; the roommate meeting; Luke the movie virgin watching movies with Lorelai during movie night; and Rory sweetly (but unsuccessfully) trying to ask a boy out in the laundry room.

NOTES *'Never plan for anything more than two days in advance.'*

The uncredited Mike Henry as Ed (the recipient of Luke's Yankee tickets, and his wrath) is the voice of *Family Guy*'s Cleveland Brown and *American Dad*'s Jackson, and hence a member of that whole *Family Guy* circle that includes former Drella/Miss Celine/Sookie (and Jackson Douglas' spouse) Alex Borstein.

Lorelai's initial concern that Rory may be too shy to experience what life has to offer (1.9) showed up again recently (4.3), and finally seems to be recognized this episode by Rory herself when she at first rejects Trevor's advances. Lorelai asking Rory if there's an older professor in her romantic life foreshadows Paris' own fling with Asher Fleming (4.9).

Natalie remodeled Richard and Emily's second floor the year before. Sookie tells Lorelai that their son is going to be called Davey (it would've been Colgate if it was a girl, after Jackson's great grandmother).

Behind the Scenes
From Buffy To Gilmore

Gilmore and Buffy writer Jane Espenson

Buffy the Vampire Slayer, one of The WB's other success stories (though it jumped ship to the UPN for its final season), had ended in May 2003, prompting its writers to seek other opportunities. Jane Espenson, who'd worked in some capacity on more than 80 episodes of that series, soon found herself meeting with Amy & Dan, who were such big *Buffy* fans that they'd regularly held Tuesday night *Buffy* viewing parties. "Here was a place that valued witty dialogue, lots of it, and where I was certain of a warm welcome," Espenson says. "I suspect Amy wanted someone who could help shoulder the burden of the massive amount of dialogue writing that had to be done on the show."

Having worked on two of the shows most identified with their larger-than-life showrunners, Espenson was in a prime position to see two very different ways of running a writers room.

Buffy creator Joss Whedon "and Amy ran very different rooms. We had a hard time making progress in the *Buffy* writers' room if he wasn't there since the ideas really generally came from him and really had to be felt by him before they would go up on the board. And when he spun out a scene or a sequence, it would be with great specificity, although that would be captured in only a few words on the board itself. And nothing actually was written down at all until he saw the whole episode in his head—all of its themes and meanings understood. A broken episode, when it was eventually scrawled on the white board, might just about fill one board. Since we found it hard to make progress without Joss, our time was loosely structured; we would, essentially, wait for him. No one ever minded this top-down approach, since we got to see the genius pour out of him when it happened. It was an inspiration machine over at *Buffy*, and when it was running, there was never anything so lovely.

"Amy spent more time on set than Joss did, and the writers room ran without her a lot of the time, in a much more regulated 10-to-7 schedule than I've even seen on any show before or since. Story ideas often came from the lives of the staff—writers shared their college stories, romance stories, little personal events that made their way into Rory and Lorelai's lives. Amy & Dan would be there for the initial 'break' of the story, in which the scenes were selected to tell the stories, and placed in order. This tended to be a much quicker process than it had been at *Buffy*. The stories didn't rely on unifying themes as much as *Buffy* had. Both Amy and Joss had the ability to make their writing staff feel that someone had a *very* clear vision of the show. This allows a staff to relax and do their best work."

* Luke tells Lorelai that he knows within seconds if he'll be comfortable with someone: "I feel it here. I felt it with Rachel. I felt it with Nicole." First, this should be a big red flag to Lorelai, and second, did he seem all that relaxed when he first met Nicole?

* Again, *Gilmore* namechecks Amy & Dan's beloved documentary *Grey Gardens* (3.9). Lorelai telling Rory that every bad date just becomes a "bad date" story to tell during her next date is an odd lead up to what happens with William, the boy Rory tries to ask out in the laundry room (4.11).

Something of a wet noodle of an episode this, but it does lay the groundwork for the Luke and Lorelai relationship to come.

TODAY'S CELEBRATION Rory's first Yale date, and arguably her first real date, ever.

YOU'VE ENTERED EMILYLAND [*on hearing that Rory let a boy know that she was available for a date*] Rory, you're in Yale, not Amsterdam.

HEY, FAMILY FRIENDLY FORUM! Interior decorator Natalie Zimmermann is played by iconic former American porn star Traci Lords.

AMEN, SISTER FRIEND

LUKE: Oh well, Tom called. The banister on the stairs has to be replaced. It'll be $4,000. Tamsin Cordally called. He needs a deposit on the quartersawn oak. It'll be $4,000. Julio the landscaper called. I have no idea what he said, but it's going to be $4,000. Vicky from Vicky's Horse Supply called. She thinks Pepper and Gunsmoke would suit your needs, but Gunsmoke snores, so the stables can't be too close to the

Bio Olivia Hack (Tana Schrick)

Many *Gilmore* fans probably recognize Olivia Hack from her role as Cindy Brady in the immensely popular movies *The Brady Bunch Movie* (1995) and *A Very Brady Sequel* (1996). Others probably got that nagging sensation that they've heard her voice somewhere before, especially if they have kids, or were kids themselves not so long ago.

Hack has supplied voices for a wide range of animated characters, working on such shows as *Rugrats, Bratz, Hey Arnold!, Blood+ and Avatar: The Last Airbender.*

The daughter of animation voice director Michael (*Dragon Tales, Astro Boy*) and acting coach Mea, Hack began her career at the age of 3, starring in a Minolta camera commercial. And before you say, "Her father's a voice director, that's why-!" No. "I think I'd audition for him every once in a while but I'd never get the part," she says. They worked together for the first time just a few years ago. "Nepotism is kind of disgusting, so it's pretty much all on my own."

Born in Beverly Hills, Hack actually had some behind-the-scenes perspective on *Gilmore* before she ever set foot on set. "I actually had a roommate who was working on the show as an assistant director, years before. He would sometimes work 24-hour days on *Gilmore Girls.* And then once he was done with that, he was shooting *Alias* or something, and the hours were like half what they were on *Gilmore*. They're definitely perfectionists to a certain extent, and it shows in the quality.

"It's a job and a fantastic job and I love my job, but it's merely a job," Hack says. "When you start viewing it in these other terms of 'I'm an actor and an artist,' yes you are. But I don't take it for granted for a second. You see your peers, especially at this age, drop like flies."

guests' bedrooms. Rory's looking for her black Converse and, oh, one last thing—I'm not taking messages for you anymore!

LORELAI: You've been stomping around, barking at people for days.
LUKE: I have not.
LORELAI: Yes, Cujo, you have.
LUKE: I always talk to people like that.
LORELAI: No, Benji, you don't.
LUKE: I'll be fine tomorrow.
LORELAI: Really, Lassie? Why is that?

4.6 An Affair to Remember

First aired: Oct. 28, 2003 // Written by Amy Sherman-Palladino // Directed by Matthew Diamond

Richard and Jason Stiles are officially partners, and Emily hires Sookie and Lorelai to cater the launch party. Though Lorelai loathes working for her mother, she hits the warpath when she discovers that Jason has canceled the party, making her mother feel small in the process. So, how is it she ends up being asked out by him?

GINCHY! Kirk arranging his date with Lulu (and asking how much for Luke's apartment upstairs if the date goes well); Kirk's date with Lulu; Emily telling Lorelai why she's canceling the party; and Lorelai telling Rory to "suck it up" after whining about losing her favorite study tree (amen!).

NOTES *'Important men doing important things.'*

Jason offhandedly labeling the photo session with him and Richard as a "cute idea," and subsequently canceling Emily's launch party, are just two more dings to her dignity that will reach an inevitable conclusion much later (6.9).

Sookie and Lorelai's new company is the Independence Catering Company (imaginative, I know). Jason once tipped over a canoe at camp with Lorelai in it, making him the hero of Cabin 5 for the summer ("green T-shirt, no bra").

TODAY'S CELEBRATION The official cementing of Richard and Jason's partnership, and Kirk's first date with Lulu.

"I tended, in the past, to play really strong characters. On All My Children, I played a teenager that was sort of the leader of the pack, bitch, popular, whatever. I was already used to being quick and bitchy. Maybe it's my voice. I don't know if there's some quality in my voice that makes me sound like a bitch—I don't know. I'm not a bitch! I'll say strong, not bitchy. Strong."

-KATIE WALDER (JANET)

Behind the Scenes Press Ganged Into Being Prof. Bell

Though George Anthony Bell had been helping the *Gilmore* actors conquer their massive scripts as the dialogue coach since Season 3, he was also a seasoned actor in his own right.

"In the script for this episode, there was a role for a professor and they hadn't cast it yet," he recalls. "Somehow they figured George is an actor. Oh perfect, we'll have George do it." Thus Yale's Professor Bell was born. Yet there was a bit more to it than that.

This was the last day of shooting for the episode, the one usually reserved for shooting scenes that had been postponed throughout the week, making for an extremely long day to begin with.

"So we were having a very long day and then it was, 'Oh, by the way, they're going to give you a part as a professor at Yale.' And then I'm being rushed into wardrobe and my agents are being called. So I'm thinking this is great, not realizing that they were going to give me a monologue, which was about a page long with very, very difficult dialogue. I'm thinking they're just going to give me a few lines and no problem. When they finally got me the script, I went, 'Are you kidding me? When am I going to have time to learn this? I'm still working on the show.'

"Then I find out that I'm working the very next day, so I don't even have a couple days. I ask, 'Can you possibly schedule this scene at the end of the day [tomorrow] so I can have some time to learn it?' No way. So when am I supposed to learn this? I'm still doing my regular job dialogue coaching."

Once the camera operator realized what was going on, he sent Bell home early. Though much appreciated, the gesture was just that, as he had been at work for about 12 hours that day already; "my brain was already fried."

After he'd spent several hours trying to learn his lines, Bell's doorbell rang at about 11 that night—he was handed changes to the lines he'd been learning. The next day, barely awake, Bell found himself in the shoes of the actors he'd coached for more than a season, with one important difference—it was a monologue.

"It's not a scene where I can say a line and someone says a line that may help me remember what's coming next; I'm just talking," Bell explains. "I'm like a sociology professor, so I'm using all this terminology that didn't make much sense. But I got through it. It took more takes than I would've liked it to, but it came out great. When I see it, I look so cool, calm and collected on screen, but I was dying on the inside. It gave me an even greater appreciation for what the actors have to go through and made me even more sympathetic to their situation."

Bell with friend and Lauren Graham stand-in Patty Malcolm.

KIRK OF ALL TRADES One-of-a-kind, whimsical mailbox salesman.

AND INTRODUCING... *Lulu* Actually, she's the ex-girlfriend of Kirk's brother, but who can resist Kirk?

$20 How much Rory pays the guy to give her back her study tree.

UMLAUTS Jason's nickname for Lorelai.

YOU'VE ENTERED EMILYLAND [*on learning Jason is taking their prospective clients to Atlantic City*] You cannot be serious. These are dignified men and women. There are mobsters in Atlantic City

AMEN, SISTER FRIEND

LORELAI [*about Kirk*]: Oh, come on, Luke. Give him a break. He wants the date to go well. I mean, it's all any of us wants—to find a nice person to hang out with till we drop dead. Not a lot to ask.

EMILY: Oh, you know, times change, Lorelai. Things that were once considered proper and elegant are now considered stuffy and out-of-date.
LORELAI: Like what?
EMILY: Like canapés and cocktail parties and the people who plan them.
LORELAI: Mom, what are you talking about?
EMILY: Nothing. It's not important.
LORELAI: Mom, come on.
EMILY: Jason decided to take the clients to Atlantic City instead. He thinks that's what they would prefer to do. He's probably right anyhow. What do I know?
LORELAI: Did he know all the work you put into this?
EMILY: It's really not important, Lorelai. I do this for your father. I have done this for your father for the last 36 years. If he thinks that Jason's right, then it's fine with me. And after all, now I don't have to worry about a party. I can just relax and hang out.

"Somehow I was able to say the lines and also pull off a reasonable acting job as a professor. They obviously liked it because they kept bringing me back. All the other times I had more time to prepare, so it wasn't an issue. But that first time was 'Oh my God.'"

—GEORGE ANTHONY BELL, DIALOGUE COACH, ON HIS FIRST TIME PLAYING THE YALE PROFESSOR.

4.7 The Festival of Living Art

First aired: Nov. 4, 2003 // Written by Daniel Palladino // Directed by Chris Long

Lane's band is still auditioning for a Dave replacement, Stars Hollow is hosting a festival in which townspeople reenact famous works of art, Sookie hasn't given birth yet, and Nicole wants to start dating Luke again—in the middle of their divorce. Something's gotta give.

GINCHY! This is Kirk's episode, from his nonchalantly going on about his girlfriend to his harsh treatment of the Troubadour upon learning he's playing Judas to his Christ. Add to that his Christ-like oration when Taylor considers giving up and you have a Kirk Gleason triumph. And finally, the Sookie pager going off in the last scene.

NOTES *'Crazy, doofus town.'*

Lorelai's getting worse at hiding her financial difficulties from Rory, who finds her clipping coupons. The catering gig she lost last episode from Emily didn't help.

Sookie was supposed to have little Davey a week ago. Kirk is calling the same attention to Lulu as he did to his dance marathon trophy (3.8): "My girlfriend and I appreciate it."

Despite the title, the event is actually called the Festival of Living Pictures, and was hosted by Stars Hollow seven years ago. Woodbury was supposed to host it this year, but flooding has made that impossible.

Lorelai flinched seven years ago when she was playing the Renoir girl, so initially she's consigned to working with costumes backstage this year. But Lorelai being Lorelai... Last time, Rory was a Chinese acrobat.

Gil owns a sandwich shop in Salisbury. The baby box Lorelai shows Sookie from 1984 gives us a little more insight into what we've already seen of Rory's birth (3.13), including the fact that Lorelai was listening to a compilation tape including some REM and Thompson Twins, and Nena's "99 Luft Balloons." Considering how handy Lorelai is with a sewing machine, it's kind of neat to learn the very first thing she ever made was a jumper for Rory out of a Bananarama T-shirt.

TODAY'S CELEBRATION The 43rd annual Connecticut Festival of Living Pictures.

KIRK OF ALL TRADES Son of God.

HANK The Taylor Doose of Woodbury.

BUFF OTIS Head of the Connecticut Arts Council.

OY WITH THE ___, ALREADY! Lorelai's lesbian references regarding Buff Otis. Not so much offensive as glaringly out-of-character for *Gilmore Girls.*

THINGS WE'VE LEARNED As this was the first appearance

'Gloria!'

"I'll never forget Sebastian Bach [Gil] coming in and seeing Sally Struthers for the first time," says writers assistant Alison Goodman.

"He didn't know anything about our show, the first episode he did. He walked in, and when he sees Sally Struthers, he goes, 'Gloria! Oh my God, I can't believe it, I love you!' We just all started laughing because he was a rock star. He didn't have any of the PC stuff of 'I'll just walk in and I'll sit down.' He walked in the conference room, he was so loud, and oh my God, it was amazing! And she loved it. She said, 'Come sit down next to me, honey.'"

of rock star Sebastian Bach on *Gilmore*, nobody was quite sure what to expect, or how good he would be. "He memorizes this sucker, a long monologue," remembers key set costumer Valerie Campbell. "We do take 1, perfect, print. Which was like what?! On take 1? We do take 2. Perfect, print. The DP goes up to try and adjust the lights and the director's like, 'OK, print, moving on.' He was like, 'But I want to fix-!' 'Moving on, sorry, we got it.' So if that shot doesn't look quite up to par for *Gilmore Girls*, that's because the acting was so good."

Meet the Living Art

Kirk and the Troubadour: Christ and Judas in "The Last Supper" by Leonardo Da Vinci

Rory: "Portrait of Antea La Bella" by Girolamo Francesco Maria Mazzola ("Parmigianino")

Lorelai: The girl in "Dance at Bougival" by Renoir

AMEN, SISTER FRIEND

TROUBADOUR: Hey, I'm here for a fitting.
LORELAI: Oh, well, you've come to the right place. What are you in?
TROUBADOUR: "The Last Supper."
KIRK: Oh, you must be one of my missing apostles. Still haven't met them all. I'm Christ.
TROUBADOUR: It's gonna be a lot of fun, huh?
KIRK: Definitely. Which apostle are you?
TROUBADOUR: Judas.
KIRK: Judas.
TROUBADOUR: So, uh, where do I go for my fitting?
KIRK: Oh, I think you know where you're going, pal.

4.8 Die, Jerk

First aired: Nov. 11, 2003 // Written by Daniel Palladino // Directed by Tom Moore

Mrs. Kim seems to be nudging Lane down the wedding aisle. Luke's back together with Nicole, which is deeply disturbing Lorelai for reasons she's not yet ready to admit. After a couple of journalistic disasters at the Yale Daily News, Rory

Behind the Scenes

Shooting the "Festival"

A scene from the 2010 "Pageant of the Masters" in Laguna Beach, Calif., the basis for "The Festival of Living Art."

A fan favorite and the only *Gilmore* episode to win an Emmy Award (for makeup), "The Festival of Living Art" features an event modeled after Laguna Beach, Calif.'s "Pageant of the Masters."

"I've never been to it, mainly because the parking down there is so terrible, but apparently it's really amazing," says Michael Winters, who was one of many cast and crew run through the wringer during the making of that episode. "I had to do all the introductions, which had a lot of Italian painters' names in it. They shot it at night, of course. They got to the end of the night and it was my turn. I had sat around outside in a tux all night long. Then I had to get up and do all these intros. The director was very nice and he said, 'I don't want to pressure you or anything, but in about 10 minutes the sun is going to be shining on your face and we have to be finished.' So, I had to do like six or seven of them, one right after the other, at 6 o'clock in the morning or something like that. Just hanging on for dear life."

Winters wasn't the only one. Valerie Campbell, normally just responsible for making sure all the outfits looked right, somehow ended up with the additional task of arranging the actors in precisely the right positions so that they matched the works of art they mimicked. "It was a hard episode but it was fun," she says.

Whether Mike Gandolfi had as much fun in his role as a near naked Andrew sculpture in the gazebo is another story. "They made him wait around all night, and he couldn't put anything on because he had all that makeup on," Campbell explains. "He was freezing his ass off. He said it was retribution. (He and Amy were really good friends.) Michael had taken Amy to one of those yoga classes where they crank the heat up really high. He said, 'She made me freeze outside wearing basically nothing because of that yoga class.'"

Sean Gunn, perhaps the person with the most memorable scenes in the entire episode, really enjoyed the whole Kirk as Jesus riff. "The Jesus stuff was fun, although the makeup was such a nightmare. It was a blast to play those scenes. Another one when I go back and watch it again I feel like almost all of it really works."

finally makes a splash—and an enemy—with a withering review of a ballet performance. And old "Digger" Stiles is determined to woo Lorelai, when he's not introducing the wonders of the World Wide Web to Richard and Emily.

GINCHY! Paris' reaction to the "Die jerk" written on their door; Richard and Emily's relish over Rory's acerbic review of the ballet; and the smooth way Jason discovers Lorelai's restaurant preferences.

NOTES *'People don't write as mean as they talk. Except you.'*

This is the first mention we get of Rory working on the Yale Daily News, though apparently she's been writing tryout articles for a while. It's our first glimpse of the editor, Doyle, and he's already imitating his hero, The Washington Post's Bob Woodward.

Though Rory's said little about Dean's recent wedding, she can't help herself when discussing Lane's "marriage jug": "There have just been enough young people marrying in my life. I don't want any more."

Jason's been sending Lorelai flowers. The summer camp they met at (4.6) was Camp Chateaugay. Apparently Jason bunked with Christopher for a summer, though he's been repressing the memory of Christopher dunking his head in a toilet bowl for years.

TODAY'S CELEBRATION The (almost) presentation of the Kim marriage jug to Dave, and Rory's offending article.

EMILY'S MAID DU JOUR Cora, who is charged with trimming down Emily and Richard's portions if necessary, now that Jason has weaseled his way into staying for a meal.

26 The number of enemies Paris has made (just in their dorm building).

AMEN, SISTER FRIEND

RICHARD: Look at this! I'm walking around and I'm still on the Internet. Emily, I'm going to Google you.
EMILY: You are certainly not going to Google me!

LANE: You told me when I was like six that this was my special marriage jug that you were gonna keep on a special high shelf for the boy I'm going to marry.
MRS. KIM: This thing?
LANE: Yes.
MRS. KIM: It's just a jug.
LANE: What?
MRS. KIM: I probably told you that to make you stop crying. You always cried when you were little. Gave me a headache.

4.9 Ted Koppel's Big Night Out

First aired: Nov. 18, 2003 // Written by Amy Sherman-Palladino // Directed by Jamie Babbit

When the girls join Richard and Emily for their annual pilgrimage to the Harvard-Yale football game, fun flasks and family secrets flow freely. Fuming at her mother, Lorelai decides to go on a date with Jason, and Rory learns something about Paris she will later wish she hadn't.

What I Kept

I have a lot of the banners that they put around the town. Like for the Firelight Festival and all that stuff. I have them in my garage. There was a time when I had them in my editing room. They hung them up on the lampposts and different things. If I ever have an office, I can put them up.

—Raul Davalos (editor)

GINCHY! Richard and Emily taking the girls through their Harvard-Yale-game traditions; the mass boycott of Luke's Diner because of the new waiter, Brendon; Emily's fit after learning about Richard and Pennilyn Lott's tradition; Lorelai and Jason's impromptu shopping spree; and Rory catching Paris kissing Asher Fleming. (Once she's out of the gate, that girl moves fast.)

NOTES *'Apparently everyone has a fun flask.'*

Rory went to junior high with Brendon, Luke's new employee at the diner. "He's the boy who dissected a frog, did not wash his hands, and then ate a sandwich," she says. Greg Sipes, who plays Brendon, shows up

Character Sketch — The Road to Doyle

Beloved by many for his role as the endearingly goofy yet complex Jonathan Levinson on *Buffy the Vampire Slayer*, Danny Strong actually appeared in a couple of episodes of *Over the Top*, a sitcom Amy worked on, several months before he started on *Buffy*.

"Years later I got a call that *Gilmore Girls* wanted to see if I was available for an episode, just completely out of the blue," Strong remembers. "I couldn't do it because I was shooting *Buffy* at the time. I was really disappointed because I would've loved to have done it."

A year later, he received another call from the *Gilmore* casting directors, this time for Doyle.

Amy & Dan "told me they had written Doyle for me. It was just kind of crazy to, 10 years later, have a part written for you. But they were really big *Buffy* fans, which I found out later." Former *Buffy* writer and friend Jane Espenson says she also suggested Strong for the role, which remains a point of pride with her today.

Though he didn't have to audition for the role, Strong still was nervous starting on such a high-profile series. "We did a table read and it was kind of scary because they offered me the part, so I didn't audition. So in a way, you feel like the table read is your audition. Because I'm the editor of the newspaper where Rory works, I'm feeling like, OK, this part could come back, and I'd love for that to happen. But you never know. So you feel just a tremendous amount of pressure at that very first table read. But the part got a lot of laughs and I felt really comfortable when it was all over."

Though everybody was supportive, Strong says Bledel was particularly welcoming on set. "I think my first few episodes were just with her. I always found her quite like her character—that charming and that sweet. She was great to me. All through the entire run of the show, but I think it started from the very first day. Alexis came up to me and said, 'Hey, you did a really great job.' And having the star of the show (who's quite famous at that point) come up to you and tell you that, you instantly feel relaxed."

Danny Strong and Tom Lenk as two-thirds of the Evil Trio in *Buffy*.

Richard and Emily enjoy their Harvard-Yale game outing before things take an ugly turn.

in unaired footage of *Windward Circle*, the *Gilmore Girls* spin-off that wasn't (see notes for 3.21).

✱ Richard and Emily have gone to Harvard-Yale games for the last 32 years. Luke's Diner happens to be one of the "Mrs. Kim-approved" places in Stars Hollow for Lane: "No alcohol, walking distance to the church, and you can see my house from here."

✱ Though Emily and Lorelai remark on how much Rory's like Richard, Rory will soon learn that the comparison stops at academics (4.14). When he sticks up for Brendon, Luke reveals that he wasn't the most popular kid in town either, giving us a better understanding of why he worked so hard to give Jess a break.

✱ On meeting "naked guy" Marty, Richard reveals that he and some of his classmates protested the dress code at Yale by wearing silk ties and nothing else, making us wonder if that's partly why he wears those ties today.

✱ It wasn't so long ago that we discovered Emily stole Richard away from Pennilyn Lott (3.8). At the game, Richard is forced to tell Emily that he's been having lunch with Pennilyn once a year for 39 years. When we remember how guilty Emily felt dancing with Chad in the bar (2.16), it's

"I remember the first time I got a note: 'Don't change there is to there's,' I was just totally taken aback because I had never gotten a note like that before."

–OLIVIA HACK (TANA)

easy to see why she's so shaken. Her first response to the news—lashing out at Lorelai for coming to the game and speaking to Pennilyn—is a sterling example of what makes *Gilmore Girls* a cut above most television, and emphasizes again how essential Richard and Emily are to the series.

We're never quite sure if Lorelai really sees newscaster Ted Koppel at the China Garden restaurant; it's just the sort of smart-ass remark she'd make spotting any man wearing a toupee.

TODAY'S CELEBRATION The Harvard-Yale football game, Lorelai and Jason's first date, and possibly Paris and Asher Fleming's first kiss.

EMILY'S MAID DU JOUR Sandy, who gets yelled at for not cutting enough celery and not displaying Rory's cookies properly at the tailgate party.

AND INTRODUCING...*Asher Fleming* A former classmate of Richard's and the author of a book Paris has read four times. Oh, and so much more, right Paris?

AMEN, SISTER FRIEND

LORELAI [*to Luke about Brendon*]: He doesn't write the orders down, he never brings you food that's hot or yours, he can't distinguish bagels from doughnuts, he hands out butt napkins, and he has worn that Foreigner T-shirt every single day since he started working here and he doesn't know who they are. I asked him.

EMILY: We do not talk to Pennilyn Lott.
LORELAI: Uh, I—
EMILY: We run into her once a year. We say hello, goodbye, and that is it. We do not have conversations, we do not talk about our lives.
LORELAI: But Mom—
EMILY: We do not joke with Pennilyn Lott. We do not refer to Pennilyn Lott as anything but Pennilyn Lott, and I would appreciate you remembering that.
LORELAI: OK, seriously time for the fun flask.

Emily on Campus

Before the *Gilmore* quartet set upon each other in the time-honored fashion, they share a memorable family outing at Yale.

"I was running around in a sweatshirt," Kelly Bishop recalls. "That was one of those times that I thought, 'Emily wouldn't do this. Emily would not wear this sweatshirt.' And there were ridiculous things that Emily did that sometimes might not have made sense, but I went along with it because it was Amy, and she's just sooo good. You can't complain about what she writes; if she wants me to do it, I'll do it."

4.10 The Nanny and the Professor

First aired: Jan. 20, 2004 // Written by Scott Kaufer // Directed by Peter Lauer

Jason and Rory both find themselves having to keep other people's secrets. Lorelai has asked Jason to keep quiet about their romance, and Rory is doing her best to ignore Paris' fling with the 60-year-old Yale professor Asher Fleming.

GINCHY! Luke being stressed out by how good Lane is working at the diner; Michel getting Davey stuck under the bed; Jason's wonderfully trained dog Cyrus; Jason's apartment (especially the guest room); and Richard having a go at the people taking a tour of their house.

NOTES *'You don't find it exhausting, keeping secrets? You have to watch everything you say.'*

Lane's been working at Luke's for a couple of days now. Tobin moved to Utah after the inn burned down, became a Mormon for the job opportunities, but is now Sookie's nanny.

Mysteriously, Emily and Richard seem to have gotten over the whole Pennilyn Lott revelation from last episode.

Jason's dog, Cyrus, was trained by the monks of New Skete in upstate New York, who really do train dogs. Doyle's recently learned that he didn't get the job as the Yale stringer for Time magazine. Rory finds herself taking Asher Fleming's Contemporary Political Fiction class.

"I was trying to go to the Blue Bayou restaurant [at Disneyland] and they said, 'I'm sorry but you should've made a reservation two days ago.' Then someone looks up and goes, 'Oh my God, Mrs. Kim! Here, come in.' I was like, 'Oh, thank you.'"

—EMILY KURODA (MRS. KIM)

Bio Chris Eigeman (Jason "Digger" Stiles)

Described by The New York Observer as an actor who "made his career playing the smartest asshole in the room," Chris Eigeman brought to *Gilmore* a kind of American indie film street cred matched only by Sherilyn Fenn (Sasha/Anna Nardini) and Mädchen Amick.

Born in Denver, Eigeman is known to the New York art house scene for sending up wealthy WASPs like Jason Stiles in the Whit Stillman films *Metropolitan* (1990), *Barcelona* (1994) and *The Last Days of Disco* (1998). Eigeman has since gone on to become a writer/director in his own right with the 2007 indie movie *Turn the River* starring Famke Janssen, inspired by his early years getting hustled in the pool halls of New York. He proposed to his wife, Linda, at the Algonquin Hotel in New York City, where oft-namechecked writer and wit Dorothy Parker held court.

TODAY'S CELEBRATION The gentle hazing of the new reporters at the Yale Daily News (bring your own newspaper hat), and Jason and Lorelai's first night of passion.

EMILY'S MAID DU JOUR Unnamed.

TRUMAN What Michel thought Davey's name was.

1907 When Richard and Emily's house was built, by a protégé of Stanford White.

Behind the Scenes: The Gilmore Mansion

The first rule of any television production: Space must never be wasted, even when you're working on the sprawling Warner Brothers lot. It's a rule *Gilmore Girls* followed faithfully for seven years, nowhere more so than in the evolution of Richard and Emily's stately home.

Here, Kelly Bishop gives us a guided tour through the house, and through the years.

"They tried to copy the Toronto house [in the pilot] at the WB that first year, and they did. We had the living room, and they built a front (including the front door) for the house. And, of course, a foyer for the inside of the house for when I opened the front door, because I was doing that a lot. And the dining room. That's what we had the first year.

"By the second or third year, they started adding on to that soundstage. They added the kitchen, which we didn't go into very often. But suddenly the windows on one side of the house became the patio doors. What were windows on the other side, or possibly a solid wall, became an open archway that went into yet another room.

"I think the fourth year they built the steps that went up to... nowhere. When they had the patio doors, they suddenly had a patio out back with all of the plantings. Then later on there was Richard's office—that had not been there.

"Farther into the house you had the living room on one side and the dining room on the other. But closer to the front door on the interior you had just an open room. It had a desk tucked under the steps. You had the staircase, and then across the hall in the other direction you had a piano room—there was a grand piano there—and a little round writing table. Then if you followed that to the end of what would be the house, that was Richard's office.

"And then when we had the whole pool house, they had to tear out most of the front of the house. There was not much soundstage left by that time. They took a good portion of what would have been the driveway up to the house and built the pool. The pool was amazing. It was an inch and a half of water, but the illusion was amazing. The pool house was beautiful inside. I remember there was a bedroom in the pool house at one point, which really wasn't there—that was on some other stage. But that's the thing I love about crews—they can make magic. I can't believe what they can create in an interior space. That's the quality and the craftsmanship of the people in this industry. In the crew department, they're just awesome. By the time we got later into the years, that whole soundstage was the *Gilmore* house, which made me feel very proud."

AMEN, SISTER FRIEND

LORELAI [*about Asher Fleming and Paris*]: Well, what would the school say if they knew about this?
RORY: Yes, what about that? This guy's risking everything—his job, his reputation.
LORELAI: Yes, well, he'll always have Paris.
RORY: How long have you been waiting with that one?
LORELAI: I just had a feeling the opportunity would present itself eventually.
RORY: Maybe it's a phase. It'll pass.
LORELAI: Oh, yeah. Or he will.

Humiliation of the new Yale Daily Newsers begins.

JASON [*about his dog Cyrus*]: He's incredibly well-behaved. He was housebroken in an hour. He has a two-bark minimum for delivery guys, three for everybody else, but the best thing about him is he doesn't do any of the standard "sit and lie down" commands. I taught him very special commands that only my dog could know.
LORELAI: Like what?
JASON: Like a little to the left.
LORELAI: Shut up.
JASON: Cyrus, a little to the left.
LORELAI: What the hell's that good for?
JASON: Well, what the hell is "sit" good for?
LORELAI: When you sit, you get a cookie.
JASON: Well, when you move a little to the left, you get the satisfaction of knowing you are doing something, but you are not pandering for a dog bone.
LORELAI: Can he move a little to the right?
JASON: No, not yet. We just do a little to the left until he hits the wall, and then I turn him around.

"When I left that job, I told [Amy], 'I didn't want to embarrass myself while I worked for you, but I'll tell you now that you're a hero.' She goes, 'Oh my God, it's not like I'm Moses.'"

-ALISON GOODMAN, GILMORE GIRLS WRITERS ASSISTANT

4.11 In the Clamor and the Clangor

First aired: Jan. 27, 2004 // Written by Sheila R Lawrence & Janet Leahy // Directed by Michael Grossman

Stan Green may have passed away, but his final request, to have the church bells ring out over Stars Hollow, will keep him top of mind for many days to come. Luke's moved into a house with Nicole (guess who handles it badly), Lane's band has a CBGBs gig, and Rory thinks she's the butt of a very embarrassing story making the rounds at Yale. Things are going to get a lot worse before they get better, and some things aren't going to get better at all.

GINCHY! Lane trying to deal with her fellow Adventist college students; Luke and Lorelai wrecking the bells and Rev. Skinner's reaction; Rory confronting William over his crazed-stalker story; and Lane finally coming clean to Mrs. Kim.

NOTES *'Well, here's a newsflash. Some things are not about you.'*

Stan Green made the first lunch reservation for the Dragonfly Inn, though his funeral seems to have put a damper on things. The only people who show up for the CBGBs gig are Brian's parents.

TODAY'S CELEBRATION The passing of Stan Green, the fourth snow of the year, and Lane's band (nearly) playing CBGBs in New York.

20 YEARS How long it's been since the church bells in Stars Hollow "fell into disrepair" thanks to one Mr. Luke Danes.

3 WEEKS AGO When Luke and Nicole moved to a townhouse in Litchfield.

RORY'S YALE ADDRESS 198 Elm Street, Durfee Hall, Suite 5.

6 The age when Lane started living her double life with Mrs. Kim, which was also the day she told Lane the Cookie Monster on *Sesame Street* was Gluttony, one of the Seven Deadly Sins.

META, META, META "We are the witches of Eastwick," Lorelai says when she, Sookie and Rory are speculating on who's will be the next death in Stars Hollow. *Eastwick*, a 2009 ABC series based on *The Witches of Eastwick* book and movie, was shot on the Midwest Street portion of the Warner Brothers lot, previously the home of Stars Hollow. The series was

Jami Rudofsky, casting assistant Sarah Hutchinson "and I would put a dollar in the kitty each casting session and vote on who we thought Amy & Dan would cast, not necessarily who we would cast. We did that for the season and I did win, but I won by like one vote. Sarah was in second place and Jami was in third. That made us giggle, and Dan and Amy knew that we would do that and wanted to know who was winning that session. We managed to always have a really good time."

-MARA CASEY, CASTING DIRECTOR

quickly canceled. (Perhaps Lorelai and Sookie were more powerful than they thought.)

1 AM TUESDAY Hep Alien's CBGBs slot.

AMEN, SISTER FRIEND

PARIS: When you boil it down, isn't the whole Israeli-Palestinian problem a case of sibling rivalry?
FRIEDMAN: Follow up?
PARIS: *The Old Testament*, it's all there. Israelis are descendents of Abraham and Sarah. Arabs are descendents of Abraham and his maid, Hagar. So Israelis and Arabs both have the same dad, and both want the great nation God promised Abraham. They might as well be fighting over who gets the TV remote.

LANE: I don't want to go to Seventh Day Adventist College anymore. I want to be able to play with my band. I want to be a drummer. I will happily go to community college and I will happily live at home and adhere to your curfew, except on the nights when the band plays or practices. This way, I can get what I want and I won't be lying to you or sneaking around. This way we can both be happy.
MRS. KIM: Children do not make the rules. You may move out and live like that somewhere else.

4.12 A Family Matter

First aired: Feb. 3, 2004 // Written by Daniel Palladino // Directed by Kenny Ortega

Lane's moved in with Rory and her roommates at Yale (and has become a servant that even Emily would approve of), Jamie gets dumped by Paris (on his birthday, no less), and Lorelai's wondering who the new woman in Luke's life is. Lorelai's disastrous attempt at telling Emily about Jason, and the return of Jess, culminates in an episode that makes even the most optimistic person think Luke is on to something about families being nothing but trouble.

GINCHY! Lorelai torturing Kirk at Luke's; Liz finding her old pot stash in Luke's apartment; Jason and Lorelai both getting calls from Emily while they're out together; and Paris describing her relationship with Asher (they watch *Frontline* together, how sweet!).

Favorite Scenes: Keiko Agena

The scene in which Mrs. Kim discovers her daughter's life hidden under her floorboards was a pivotal one for both characters and, not surprisingly, one of Keiko Agena's favorites to shoot.

"She walks in and all this stuff that had been hidden for so many years is all out. Being able to film that scene with [Emily Kuroda] was memorable for me because Emily was just so wonderful in it. I kind of felt for both of them. There was this great hope that Lane had that everything would be OK now, and it was clearly not going to be OK."

Ho Cho, Fro Yo & Thou

Though a fair number of Amy & Dan's personal obsessions and eccentricities became those of Lorelai and Rory, many of *Gilmore*'s writers also brought their experiences to the table. Take Lorelai's inexplicable "ho cho" and "fro yo" blatherings this episode.

"A friend of mine used to have the habit of shortening frozen yogurt to 'fro yo' and, even more radical, shortening hot chocolate to 'ho cho,'" says writer Sheila R Lawrence. "Dan Palladino heard that and immediately made it something that Lorelai mocked."

NOTES *'He's always had a problem with your guys.'*

* Liz has a new apartment and a new job, making jewelry that she sells on the Renaissance fair circuit. Luke finally admits (to Liz) that he was the one who stole Jess' car (3.18), a Rambler Ambassador, which he's been keeping in their dad's garage.

* How strange it is to hear Paris call Rory "Mary" when she thinks Rory's being prudish about her relationship with Asher Fleming. It was Tristin who started calling her that when she first started Chilton (1.2). Rory tells Paris that she got lucky having Jamie as her first boyfriend, echoing her own mother's words about Dean when she broke up with him to be with Jess (3.15).

* Luke sarcastically asks Jess if he's written the "great American novel" while he's been on the road; something it seems he might just do later (6.8).

* This is an unusual episode in that Lorelai, who usually helps to lift a show when it's dragging, is actually involved in the least interesting story line this time.

* Once again Rory notices that Lorelai's scrimping—she's discontinued some of her cable channels and magazines and she's actually buying groceries rather than eating out!

* Whatever problems Lorelai (and some fans) may have with Luke in later seasons, this is as close as we come to understanding the man and his approach to family. He's been taking care of himself and everyone in his family since he was old enough to walk, and he's tired of helping people who don't seem to do anything to help themselves.

TODAY'S CELEBRATION The return of Jess Mariano a year after he snuck out of Stars Hollow.

3 YEARS AGO The last time Luke and Liz saw each other.

AND INTRODUCING...*Luke's sister, Liz* Or as Lorelai first describes her to Rory, "A kinda odd, rock-and-roll, hippy chick." And the first mention of Crazy Carrie Duncan.

HEY, FAMILY FRIENDLY FORUM! Rory tells Lorelai that Paris was at Asher Fleming's all night, but claims she was "up all night cramming." Lorelai's response? "Well, she was."

AMEN, SISTER FRIEND

TANA [*after her makeover*]: I am hoping that one boy notices. Chester Fleet.

LANE: Chester Fleet?

TANA: His father was instrumental in conducting research showing that neurons in the brain fire actively during REM sleep, with the exception of nerve cells involved with the transmitter chemicals serotonin and norepinephrine.

Bio Katie Walder (Janet Billings)

Some actors move out to Los Angeles hoping to get that first big break as soon as they get off the plane, but most end up polishing their order-taking skills in one of the city's many restaurants for a good year or two before getting anything substantial. Katie Walder got her foot in Stars Hollow the first month she was in town.

Born in Philadelphia, Walder tackled all the usual school plays and had gone out on a few assignments when she was very young, but decided to concentrate on getting an education instead.

After graduating from Ithaca College in upstate New York, she moved to New York City and landed a role on the ABC soap *All My Children* on her first professional audition. After a year, she moved into doing Broadway theater before realizing she would have to switch coasts if she was going to do more television, and ultimately, movies.

In 2003 she made the move. A few weeks later, she found herself in front of Mara Casey and Jami Rudofsky at Warner Brothers, but it wasn't for *Gilmore Girls*. She got all the way to the screen test phase, the last hurdle, for the Milo Ventimiglia spin-off series, *Windward Circle*. Unfortunately, the Powers that Be decided not to pick up the show, and Walder was back where she started.

Four months later, she was called back to read for a guest star role. "I didn't know that they wanted to see me again to make sure that I was right for Janet," she says. "They didn't even have auditions for that role."

A week later, she was on the Warner Brothers lot, hanging around the brand new Yale set, still trying to take it all in. Fortunately, her first appearance managed to avoid that legendary *Gilmore* dialogue. "I think I was just doing sit-ups or something.

"The funniest part of it was that I really wasn't that athletic at the time. I now have become more athletic because of that role. I was always thin, but they made it out like I was some huge jock, and that's really pretty far from me."

Working on the Yale set at Warner Brothers was an odd experience. The actress had planned to attend the school's drama program for graduate school, but canceled those plans when she landed her role on *All My Children*.

PARIS: I'd forgot the first part of that sentence by the time you finished, but I say jump him.

RORY [*about Asher Fleming*]: My grandfather introduced you to him. Do you see how awkward this is for me?
PARIS: Well, hot men tend to run in packs.

"What was so wonderful about the process, and something I will always be grateful to Dan and Amy for teaching me, is that we never 'discovered' a story in a linear fashion. (In other words, we never pitched the first act, then the second, etc.) We always put up what we knew we wanted to tell in the story, and let the story find itself. This took a great deal of faith that we would find a story, but we usually did. There was an enormous amount of talent in the room; it wasn't long before something great would show up."

-JANET LEAHY, WRITER

4.13 Nag Hammadi is Where They Found the Gnostic Gospels

First aired: Feb. 10, 2004 // Written by Amy Sherman-Palladino // Directed by Chris Long

Liz has brought her new boyfriend, TJ, to meet Luke, and Emily dragoons Lorelai and Jason into "pretending" to be a couple at yet another fundraiser. Jess is still trying to get his car fixed so that he can bail on Stars Hollow (again), pissing Rory off every time he shows his face in her town.

GINCHY! A new personal best for *Gilmore*, as it essentially makes the title of the episode a footnote; Liz's "I'm cool, they're cool, everybody's cool" approach to Luke; her brief conversation with Lorelai at their first meeting; Emily berating the girls and everybody else at the fundraiser; TJ's final dismissal of Luke; and what has now become an Amy signature—a profound closing scene.

NOTES *'Nobody was believing you two as a couple anyway.'*

Apparently Liz showed TJ the same photo of "Butch" Danes that Lorelai found when they went to speak at the school (3.4). TJ tells Jess he'll draw his portrait on an Etch-A-Sketch. Goofy, yes, but a possible nod to Michael DeLuise's own artistic skills as a painter.

Richard proves himself more knowledgeable than Jason about Jason's father, Floyd, when he says he's up to something big (4.18). The Founders Day punch continues to entertain—Liz remembers it was the first booze that made her throw up.

TODAY'S CELEBRATION Liz's 20th high school reunion, the Stars Hollow Firelight Festival, and the rare manuscripts acquisition fundraiser.

KIRK OF ALL TRADES Firelight festival planner.

YOU'VE ENTERED EMILYLAND [*to Lorelai*] I'll see you tonight at 6 o'clock sharp, and don't wear those pantyhose with the seams up the back. You look like 10 cents a dance.

AND INTRODUCING...*TJ* Of course his real name is... Gary.

6 MONTHS How long Liz and Jess have been in touch without telling Luke.

AMEN, SISTER FRIEND

JESS [*to Luke*]: You see, this is your problem. You're going to help people whether they want it or not. You have to fix everything. You have to fix everyone. You think it makes you a good guy, but really it just makes you a pain in the ass. You make it so that when people fail you, you get to feel like the martyr and they get to feel like not only did they screw up, but they also disappointed you. You interfere and you make everything worse. No one is asking for your help. No one wants your help. Focus on your own life and leave everyone else alone!

LUKE: So look, I kind of heard you guys talking, and things seem to be going pretty good for Liz, which is different and a nice change, and I know that you guys are thinking about moving here, and I just wanted you to know it's OK by me.

Character Sketch 'Thanks. You're a Dick.'

When we first meet TJ, we get little indication of whether he's going to be sweet and sympathetic (like Luke) or flat out goofy (hello, Kirk), and Michael DeLuise didn't know much more than we did at the time. "I thought he might be a regular person; I didn't know I was going to be all wacky and fun. So I was trying to do more straight stuff. Over the course of the series I went into more comedic indulgences, but initially I was trying to play it more center of the road."

And leave it to TJ to cap off Luke's horrible day of being trashed by Jess with a line like "You're a dick." Sure, the way he treated TJ was pretty lousy, but still, a dick?

"They made me dub [the line] from the satellite at the end," DeLuise says. "I think the word was a big deal. When we actually filmed it, there was a bonfire behind us and there was gas going to the bonfire underneath fake grass, and I was getting sick off the fumes. That was my first show. My intention was to try to say it from a neutral point of view.

"Also Amy, in order to keep the integrity of her content, would withhold the script until the day before shooting. That kept the network and their suggestions and their involvement—which I hear can be quite extensive—at bay."

TJ: OK. I didn't realize we needed your permission.
LUKE: Oh no, you don't. Maybe you misunderstood me here. I was just trying to say that I assumed because my sister has a history with guys, you know, that you were like the others. But, well, you seem like a pretty good guy.
TJ: Thanks. You're a dick.

RORY: You know, I have actually thought about this moment. A lot. What would Jess say to me if I ever saw him again? I mean, he just took off, no note, no call, nothing; how could he explain that? And then a year goes by. No word, nothing, so he couldn't possibly have a good excuse for that, right? I have imagined hundreds of different scenarios with a hundred different great last parting lines, and I have to tell you that I am actually very curious to see which way this is going to go.
JESS: Could we sit down?
RORY: No. You wanted to talk, so talk. What do you have to say to me?
JESS: I love you.

Uh, Keiko, Glasses

This episode, everybody was nervous for long-time camera operator Steve Clancy, who was being given the opportunity to direct his first episode of *Gilmore*, Keiko Agena recalls. She, Alexis Bledel and the rest of the Yale roommates had just completed their first scene together under Clancy's direction, everybody commenting on how well it had all gone. "Then at the very end we realized that I didn't have my glasses on," she says. "This was when I was wearing them all the time, and we thought maybe can we just get away with it. But as soon as Amy heard about it, it was like no."

After the rest of the episode had been shot, they all had to go back and reshoot that first scene again. "I wasn't focused on it, the prop person was focused on other things, and Steve was focused on his scene, so no one realized I didn't have them on."

4.14 The Incredible Sinking Lorelais

First aired: Feb. 17, 2004 // Written by Amy Sherman-Palladino & Daniel Palladino // Directed by Stephen Clancy

As life accelerates for the girls, they find it impossible to connect, and realize for the first time what it's like to go off into the world without each other's support. Paris pushes Rory to eject Lane from the dorm because she knows about her and Asher Fleming; Rory's told that she's taking too many classes (despite it being the same workload Richard managed at Yale); and Lorelai is forced to approach Luke for financial help with the inn.

GINCHY! Michel's infatuation with Celine Dion when she visits the hotel he's working at; the fight between Lorelai and Sookie (painful to watch, but it lends the episode a sense of realism); Richard's mustache and the argument that develops when Trix rubs his nose in his first financial misstep many years ago; Rory and Lane reminiscing about their childhood plans to live in a house made of cheese; the juxtaposition of Dean comforting Rory and Luke listening to Lorelai as the girls implode.

NOTES *'Everything's falling apart. I thought I had it all under control, but I don't.'*

A lot of firsts for Dean. He tells Rory that Tom's offered him a job working construction on the Dragonfly. He's also going to college on a five-year plan, and finally sprang for a cell phone.

Lorelai's money woes hit the fan when she has to tell Tom she hasn't been able to secure a line of credit. Sookie reminds her that Luke offered to loan her money before (2.11).

Though there's no denying *Gilmore Girls*' oddball sense of humor, this is one of those episodes that proves that, when the series is firing on all cylinders, it excels as much at pulling at the heart strings as tickling the funnybone.

TODAY'S CELEBRATION The first reservation for the Dragonfly Inn (May 8-9 for Mr. Turner).

EMILY'S MAID DU JOUR Jersey.

OY WITH THE _____, ALREADY! Sookie's whininess when Lorelai calls her on being no help with the inn. As Lorelai told Rory earlier (4.6), "Suck it up!"

CLETUS & DESDEMONA The Dragonfly Inn's horses.

MAY 6 The Dragonfly's opening day.

27 How old Richard was when he made an unfortunate investment in Dubliners Paper Corp. He was newly married and had to borrow money from Trix, though he repaid it in two months.

AMEN SISTER FRIEND

RORY'S VOICE MAIL: It's Rory. Talk, please.

LORELAI'S ANSWERING MACHINE: Hey, I've got nothing cute to say for my message. Oh, puppies! There, that's cute. Now leave yours.

SOOKIE & JACKSON'S ANSWERING MACHINE: Hi, this is Sookie. And Jackson. And Davey. And Davey wants to say hello, too. Go ahead, Davey, say hello. Come on, say hi. Say hi. Oh, he's licking the phone. Don't lick the phone. Little peepers. Little peepers, does the phone taste good? I think it tastes like candy. Do you want to say it tastes like candy, huh? Oh he waved! OK, so here comes the beep.

Michel + Celine Dion

The day the author caught up with Yanic Truesdale, the question of whether he shares Michel's love of fellow Quebecois Celine Dion came up.

"I just went to see her last night, actually. She's on tour and she's in Montreal now. But she is not my favorite singer. I think she's an incredible singer, but unfortunately has become a little bit of a caricature of herself. It's a little too much. She's a singer, she's not an artist to me. That's a big difference."

LUKE: What happened?

LORELAI: Um, I just thought I had everything under control but I didn't, and the inn is just falling apart. This has been my dream forever and I have it, and it's here and I'm failing. I can't handle it. I just spend every minute running around and working and thinking. And I thought I would have help, but Sookie has Davey and Michel has Celine, and I'm—I can't do it all by myself. And I don't even have time to see my kid, and hell, forget see her, just even talk to her. And I miss her. And I sat there in my parents' house just listening to my grandmother basically call me a charity case, and I couldn't even argue with her. I couldn't even say anything because I am. I'm running out of money and I don't know what to do about it, and I was gonna ask you for $30,000 at dinner tonight. That's how pathetic I am.

"It's hard to remember the specifics now, but if there's anything humiliating that happened to a character on the show, there's a good chance it came out of my life. Rory had a kind of mortifying job as a meal-card swiper in the dining hall at Yale—that was me at Pomona [where some of the Yale scenes were actually shot]."

-SHEILA R LAWRENCE, WRITER

4.15 Scene in a Mall

First aired: Feb. 24, 2004 // Written by Daniel Palladino // Directed by Chris Long

Phone contact continues to elude Lorelai and Rory, but they've developed a (somewhat unfulfilling) e-mail relationship. Finally, they decide to play hooky for the morning and rediscover the lost joys of window shopping at the mall. Just when they realize why nobody does it anymore, Emily arrives to snap up every luxury item she can find. The feelings that drive this frenzy of retail therapy will leave a longer lasting wound than the minor dent it will make to the Gilmore credit card.

GINCHY! Kirk playing games with the dogs; Lane's cousin Christine's explosion of enthusiasm over Lane moving; and Emily's insane shopping spree!

NOTES *'Richard's right. I buy things, things I don't even want. It's all I have.'* Poor Emily. Between visits from Richard's mother and the new circles Richard has been moving in (dining in the same place as Moby), to say nothing of the scorn with which her husband treats her societal work, it was only a matter of time before she imploded. And she's still fuming about Richard's relationship with Pennilyn Lott (4.9). This time it's expensive "funny glass apples" and absurdly luxurious shoes, next time...a plane (6.9)? We've known Richard for a while now and figure that surely Emily's overreacting, but when he doesn't even realize the glass apples on their table haven't been there all this time, we realize that all is not well in the Gilmore home.

In one of *Gilmore Girls*' subtle-yet-telling touches, Dean, who staunchly defended the virtues of the Donna Reed world where the wife always had dinner on the table and the man earned the living (1.14), is spending an awful lot of time at Joe's Game Gallery. Says Dean, "Lindsay and her mom kind of like me out of the way when they're cleaning up."

TODAY'S CELEBRATION Lane, Zack and Brian move in together.

KIRK OF ALL TRADES Dogwalker.

EMILY'S MAID DU JOUR Lettie, who burned the entree.

BUSTER Lulu's dog.

$30,000 The amount of the check Luke gives Lorelai.

YOU'VE ENTERED EMILYLAND [*after sipping an Orange Julius*] Oh my, that's very good. Your father and I know a man who owns a couple dozen of these stands as part of his holdings. Now I can sincerely tell him I like his product.

AMEN, SISTER FRIEND

LORELAI: Mom, calm down.
EMILY: Why should I calm down? Are you on his side? Do you like that mustache?
LORELAI: I'm not taking sides.
EMILY: I should go to bars! I should hang out with Moby! He'd hate that.
LORELAI: Mom, I'm just suggesting that you slow down on the shopping. This doesn't have to be a whole big thing.
EMILY: Why do I need to slow down? This is what I do, according to Richard. And he's not slowing down. He's got a whole new life. He's got Pennilyn Lott, he's got Digger, he's got a mustache! He's got all that and what do I have? Maybe I should get a job so I can have my own life. I could sell shoes here just as well as Eduardo. I should get an application. [Shouts] Get me an application!

4.16 The Reigning Lorelai

First aired: March 2, 2004 // Written by Jane Espenson // Directed by Marita Grabiak

Luke and Nicole are constantly fighting, Doyle's making Rory the new focus of his abuse (much to Glenn's delight), Trix has suffered a heart attack and died, and then things get bad. While getting the dead woman's affairs in order, Emily discovers a copy of a letter Trix wrote to Richard the day before his wedding, begging him to call it all off. What would Pennilyn Lott do in such a situation?

! GINCHY! Lorelai telling Rory about her great grandparents being second cousins; drunken Emily going on and on about Pennilyn Lott; Doyle telling Rory to finish Trix's obituary ("Everybody should get to know their grandmother"); Rory and Richard's exchange as she helps him tie his tie; and Lorelai putting a Hello Kitty bracelet on Trix.

NOTES *'Find a box, throw her in, we're done.'*

* Lulu taught Kirk to read lips (badly). Trix donated a maternity wing to St. Joseph's Hospital. The funeral's on Friday, with a wake to follow—

Behind the Scenes: It Might Only Be a Cut + Blow-Dry to You

Few will ever truly appreciate the miracles pulled off behind the scenes of *Gilmore Girls*. Though for every panic over pulling off a sticky scene or wardrobe coup, there were dozens of personal milestones, too. Having slaved away in the shadows as Lauren Graham's stand-in, Patty Malcolm finally managed to get her face on screen this episode as Leanne, the hairstylist who never quite gets a chance to get her scissors on Lorelai's wet locks. (She'd first stepped out of the shadows in 4.4, leaving Luke's Diner as Dean's drunken bachelor party was coming in, but blink and you'd miss her.)

"They were shooting a scene and Chris Long, one of our producers, walked by and hands me one of the scripts and says, 'Say thank you.' He opens the script and points at 'Leanne' and says, 'That's you. And it's a tight two shot that can't be cut out so you'll see your face.' I was like, 'Woohoo!'

"I actually went to a hair salon here in LA and asked if I could wash hair so that I knew how, because I've never washed someone's hair in a sink before. It's the star of the show; I do not want to be banging her head around in a sink."

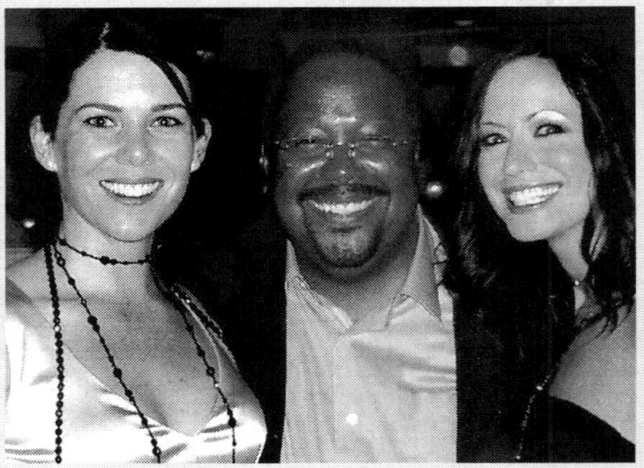

Lauren Graham, dialogue coach George Anthony Bell, and Patty Malcolm.

does that count as a Gilmore family dinner? Apparently the last time Richard saw his mother was during their fight over finances (4.14). Pennilyn Lott continues to be a flashpoint in Richard and Emily's relationship, this time brought up in Trix's correspondence.

✱ Trix and her husband Charles...were second cousins! (Lorelai: I'm sorry but I don't understand how everyone was so OK with this. I mean, what, did they just go, "What a cute couple. They look so much alike.") Trix wants half her ashes to be buried with her husband and the other half to remain in an urn with Richard and Emily, but Richard decides it's best if all of her is buried with Charles. It's not until we hear cousin Marilyn talking about Trix in Egypt and Istanbul that we realize this may be where Rory gets her wanderlust from.

✱ Doyle lost his own grandmother back in December. A drunken Emily goes on to Lorelai about *The Crimson Petal and the White*, a book by Michael Faber which, among other virtues, includes a prostitute called Sugar. The reference slyly suggests that Emily's best friend, Sweetie Nelson, whose funeral Richard skipped at the beginning of this episode, might have a more scandalous reason for her nickname than the one Emily so whimsically made up for her.

TODAY'S CELEBRATION The passing of Lorelai the First.

EMILY'S MAID DU JOUR Hilda, who's given the day off by a drunken Emily.

CHARLES ABBOTT GILMORE Richard's father.

A 'Tennessee Williams' Moment

After nearly four seasons of the straight-laced Emily, her behavior following the discovery of Trix's letter to Richard is as shocking to the audience as it is to the rest of the Gilmore clan.

"It was so crazy, but when [Amy] wrote me those scenes where I was getting drunk and sitting there smoking a cigarette and the whole thing, I kept thinking, 'This is my Tennessee Williams moment,'" Kelly Bishop says. "That episode was just so much fun for me to do. It showed the vulnerability and the deep hurt that she felt. She knew that her mother-in-law was doing to her what she was doing to her own daughter, because the mother-in-law was disapproving of me. But Emily didn't know how deeply that went until she read that letter. She was just really broken by it. Good stuff!"

Escargot Tales

Writing for *Gilmore Girls* was an education from the moment you set foot in the writers room to your very last episode. It wasn't so much the challenge of coming up with high caliber lines and situations as writing for the way the characters spoke, or more accurately, being true to Amy's unique voice for the series.

Writer Jane Espenson recalls her first stab at the opening for this episode in which Richard and Emily serve the girls escargot for dinner. She had Lorelai and Rory going on about the different types of escargot, some that were free-range snails and others that were raised for veal. "But I realized it was my voice," she says. "Not Amy's."

10 How old Richard was when Trix told him, "Life is a battle, and you either enter it armed or you surrender immediately."

86 How old Trix was when she passed away.

AMEN, SISTER FRIEND

LORELAI: I'm Lorelai Gilmore.
REVEREND: Didn't I just bury you?
LORELAI: No, reverend, I'm the one who talked to you on the phone, and I picked you up from the airport.
REVEREND: Oh, really?
LORELAI: Yeah.
MARILYN: That was a different Lorelai. This is her granddaughter. This is the reigning Lorelai.

4.17 Girls in Bikinis, Boys Doin' the Twist

First aired: April 13, 2004 // Written by Amy Sherman-Palladino // Directed by Jamie Babbit

The chronically unhip Rory and Paris head off to Florida to experience spring break first-hand, Jason takes the next step with Lorelai by giving her a key to his place, and Luke ends up in the slammer after attacking the car of the guy Nicole has been seeing in their townhouse.

GINCHY! Paris behind the wheel and perpetually tipping the hotel staff, and basically every scene at The Sea Sprite; and Luke and Lorelai coming to terms with Nicole's cheating outside the townhouse (Lorelai: "Well, at least I finally got to see your house").

NOTES *'We came here to do spring break, and we are going to do spring break.'*
It's never quite clear where spring break is taking place. While the episode namechecks The Sea Sprite in Hermosa Beach, Calif., where it was shot, Paris implies twice that the festivities are in Florida.

If we had to have the customary ratings bait of the girl-on-girl kiss, the peck that the socially desperate Paris gives Rory is just about the best way to pull it off for *Gilmore*, especially with Rory's comeback to Paris after Madeline and Louise suggest they would make a great couple: "You're way too high maintenance for me." Easily one of the season's best episodes.

TODAY'S CELEBRATION Spring break!

KIRK OF ALL TRADES Pedicab driver.

OY WITH THE ___, ALREADY! Jason. Chris Eigeman does wonders with the character, but once you've met his dog, you've gotten all you're going to get out of Mr. Stiles.

4/5: The number of times Paris and Rory have seen *The Power of Myth*, respectively.

MAC & CHEESE Rory's first hangover food.

AND HERE'S A SHOUT OUT TO OUR INTERNATIONAL FANS Rory and Paris spend all of five minutes trying to get fellow Yale students to sign a petition to free Burmese political prisoners.

THINGS WE'VE LEARNED All of the clothes worn by Janet were sponsored by Nike, Katie Walder says. "I remember they had some deal with them. And all of Alexis' stuff during one season was all Marc Jacobs. I remember they would just get all this great stuff."

AMEN, SISTER FRIEND

PARIS: I can't be in a car if anybody else is driving, OK? If I die in a car crash, it's going to be at my own hand.

JANET: I'm gonna go for a run.
RORY: Now?
JANET: Just a short one around the block.
RORY: She looks so normal and then that happens.

MADELINE: We found that if we kiss each other, we can get anything we want from guys.
LOUISE: Free drinks, food...
MADELINE: T-shirts, boat rides, Frisbees...
LOUISE: Earrings, Sea-Doos...

"Most shows now consider a three-page scene to be a long one. Five is massive. Gilmore Girls would have scenes that ran seven or 12 or more pages long. It should've been unworkable...but it worked."

–JANE ESPENSON, WRITER

Rory and Paris discover the joys that await beyond 'The Power of Myth.'

Behind the Scenes
Sea Sprite Memories

Shelly Cole's last episode as Madeline also happens to be her favorite. Shot on location at the Sea Sprite motel in Hermosa Beach, Calif. (check out seaspritemotel.com to see what a contrast it is to the hedonistic spring break atmosphere portrayed in the episode). "I love this episode because it's like, 'What are you guys doing here?' 'Well, we came for spring break a month ago and we just stayed.' This is what Madeline and Louise have been looking for their whole adolescent lives.

"There was this one scene that was just a blast to shoot. Remember where we're all sitting around after the club and we're outside at the Sea Sprite? We're all just drunk and laughing; I think we're drinking some red Kool-Aid punch. We just were so punchy. It was so late in the day and we'd just been there all week, me and Liza and Teal and Alexis. Alexis had a much larger job to do, so I think she actually went home every night. But me and Teal and Liza all stayed at the motel. (Me and Teal had adjoining rooms with a door in between.) We had a blast there. At the end of that day where we're shooting that scene, we're all so tired and punchy and giggly and just like 'Aaaaaa!' Some takes we were just completely useless because we're all laughing so hard."

RORY: OK. Well, that is a good tip.

PARIS: Yeah, maybe later I'll pants you for an Altoid.

LUKE: Anyway, I sat here and watched them go inside. I had all these thoughts rolling around in my head. I mean, how could she do this, you know? In there, in our house. I mean, I put bookshelves up in there.

LORELAI: If it makes you feel any better, I don't think he's using your bookshelves.

4.18 Tick, Tick, Tick, Boom!

First aired: April 20, 2004 // Written and directed by Daniel Palladino

Life stinks. In Stars Hollow, it's down to 59 Easter eggs that were never found (thanks, Kirk) and Lindsay making Dean quit school. In Hartford, Richard and Jason's suspicion that Floyd Stiles has been up to something proves to be right on the money. Yet, the solution Richard comes up with will spell the end of his company as we know it, as well as Jason and Lorelai's relationship.

GINCHY! Emily's snarky attitude regarding Bob Sutton's trophy wife; the mom-like way Lane shops for "the boys"; Rory asking Lane why Lindsay doesn't get a job, and Lindsay overhearing her; the way

Floyd reveals to Richard and Emily that his private investigator discovered that Jason and Lorelai are dating; Luke finding the last 12 eggs and letting Kirk take the credit.

"One scene that took a really long time to shoot for some reason was when Kirk was giving Lorelai and Rory a ride in the pedicab. The weirdest ones took longer to do than you'd think. All the blocking movements were much harder than getting the lines down."

—ROSE ABDOO (GYPSY)

NOTES *'It's like falling 600 feet to your death. You know, it's fun the first 599 feet, but it's just the last foot—total sucko.'*

Initially proud of going to school on a five-year plan (4.14), Dean now admits that he's taking a semester or two off so that Lindsay can get the townhouse she wants by year's end. Rory's angry reaction to this news ("A lot of people who drop out say that it's just temporary. It usually doesn't work out that way") is a delicious piece of foreshadowing for what is to come in her own life (5.22). We learn that dippy Joe, the sometimes pizza boy, is Jewish, when he asks Taylor if it's OK to hunt the rotting Easter eggs that are stinking up Stars Hollow. Another stinky catastrophe will rock the town later on (7.5).

More tales from summer camp: Lorelai sang "Summer Lovin'" from *Grease* with "Crater Face" Cutler, who's now an attorney. We now know that Richard put up his pension as collateral for his new business. Lindsay now knows that Dean and Rory still talk, and has forbidden him from talking to her again, which he promptly ignores. (Essentially, Dean and Rory are a younger version of Richard and Pennilyn Lott.)

TODAY'S CELEBRATION The forthcoming Stars Hollow flower show, a big Yale keg party on Friday, and Richard and Jason's acquisition of Bob Sutton.

EMILY'S MAID DU JOUR Elsa, who incurs her mistress' wrath when she sends Rory to tell Emily that dinner will be ready soon.

KIRK OF ALL TRADES Easter egg hider (300 hidden, 241 found).

5 MONTHS How long Jason and Lorelai have been together.

AMEN, SISTER FRIEND

FLOYD: Our work is wonderful. I've always felt that way. Protective of what I do, protective of what I have.
JASON: I think my cigar is out.
FLOYD: That's why I'm suing you.

JASON: Dad!

RICHARD: You're joking.

FLOYD: I'm not joking. I'm suing your company. My lawyers will be contacting you Monday morning.

RICHARD: Floyd, you're not serious.

FLOYD: Richard, you didn't think I'd let Digger walk away with some of my oldest clients and not respond, did you? Are you that näive?

FLOYD: I'll drop the lawsuit. We'll split the clients evenly. You'll come back to the firm, have your own company under our umbrella.

RICHARD: And Jason is out.

FLOYD: Jason's out. You'll be returning a hero, Richard.

RICHARD: Hmm. Music to my ears.

FLOYD: Beautiful day today.

RICHARD: Beautiful.

4.19 Afterboom

First aired: April 27, 2004 // Written by Sheila R Lawrence // Directed by Michael Zinberg

The Dragonfly Inn's opening is just a few weeks away, but Lorelai has a great deal more on her mind. Luke's getting a divorce (again, or is it still?), and her father has kicked Jason out of the company and rubbished his reputation in the process.

GINCHY! Kirk and Lorelai reveling in TV comedies of yore; Lorelai facing down Richard, and Emily's silent disapproval of it all; Lane feeling like she's being replaced by Kyon; the girls catching Richard and Emily completely off guard when they show up for Friday night dinner; Jason suing Richard, and Lorelai leaving him.

NOTES *'They say people change as they get older. I just didn't think it was all in one week.'*

This is the first time we learn what a player Zack is, something that will have consequences later on (5.2).

Richard's company is under Floyd's Gehrman-Driscoll Insurance Corp., and he's taken all of the clients he and Jason have cultivated with him. Doyle tells Rory that Asher Fleming dates a new student every year, though no one's quite sure who this year's model is.

End of Lorelai + Jason

The Jason/Lorelai story line has run its course, and at least was given a parting bit of melodrama (anyone remember exactly when Lorelai split up with Alex?). It's a testament to Amy's big-picture view of *Gilmore* that she could use even the series' missteps to the show's benefit. As one writer put it, "Amy liked to stick to her plans, but would sometimes bend to accommodate developments." When the Jason/Lorelai "relationship failed to generate sparks, she abandoned plans for a painful breakup story, feeling it wouldn't play."

Making an Episode 7 The Table Read

Once the final script's been approved, copies are circulated to cast and crew so that every department—wardrobe, makeup, lighting, camera, etc.—can start putting together a battle plan for tackling the episode.

On the last day of shooting the preceding episode, every actor slated to be in the next one will cram themselves into a small conference room with Amy & Dan during the lunch hour to read the latest script out loud and in character. After two weeks of hammering out the script, these table reads will be the first time Amy & Dan will actually have an opportunity to see what parts of a script work and what needs retooling.

"Some people come in to a table read and are just saying the words, just to do their part," writers assistant Alison Goodman says. Not actors like Lauren Graham, though. "Lauren always had the most to say. But even in the table reads, she was funny. Lauren would read it and be like, 'Holy shit, how much more do I have to say?'"

Because Herrmann and Bishop both live and work on the East Coast, they occasionally are unable to be at the table reads in person. Ever the consummate professionals, one or both will join the table reads via speakerphone, Goodman says. "They were just as good over the phone as they were in person."

After that day's work is done, the cast will go home for some much-needed rest and preparation for the forthcoming episode.

Yet changes are frequently made to scripts just hours before a scene is set to be shot.

Goodman will often be paged at 3 am on her Nextel beeper saying "I have revisions." She will then make the trip from her place in Santa Monica to Burbank, "all for the love of *Gilmore*."

Once she's worked out which actor has to get revisions ASAP, she will call her production assistant to meet her at the studio. "Then my PA had to drive around LA delivering things to people's offices and putting them under people's doors at home."

As for the script revisions, they could be entirely new scenes, or just one or two new sentences.

Nick Holmes (the Life and Death Brigade's Robert) recalls this is how it went on his second episode.

"I went in for the table read and I didn't have to shoot for four days, and every day a messenger would show up with new pages—sometimes twice a day. Even if it was just a one-word change, I would get messengered a whole new page. And that's just how they were. You had plenty of time between makeup and rehearsal and lighting to work it out, though."

Though never a fan of Jason, Emily is worried that Richard's harsh treatment of him will drive Lorelai and Rory away. Richard points out that Lorelai lied to them both about Jason and that she hardly likes being lied to, a pointed reference to Emily's reaction to the way he tricked Rory into interviewing at Yale (3.8) and his failure to tell her about his annual meetings with Pennilyn Lott (4.9). Emily is pushed one step closer to making a change.

TODAY'S CELEBRATION The dissolution of the partnership between Jason and Richard, Zack gives Lane a compliment for the first time, and Emily leaves Richard!

KIRK OF ALL TRADES Mail Boxes Etc. employee/notary.

EMILY'S MAID DU JOUR Unnamed.

OY WITH THE ___, ALREADY! Sookie's clumsiness!!!!! It's never been funny, and as we see what an interesting actress Melissa McCarthy is, it becomes ever more unnecessary.

AND INTRODUCING...*Kyon* An exchange student from Seoul who's staying with Mrs. Kim for three months.

35 How many years Asher Fleming has been teaching.

GRAFTON HOTEL Where Emily is staying (Room 421).

ASHER'S DEDICATION PAGE FOR 'JAGLON' "To a wise, willful, wonderful woman." But is it Paris?

AMEN, SISTER FRIEND

LORELAI [*to Jason*]: I can't believe my parents are separated. I mean, I dreamed about this as a kid. Of course, my scenario also involved my mother finding her inner Timothy Leary and moving us all out to a commune in Berkeley, but still. I was convinced that these people should

Bio Michael DeLuise (TJ)

For all the thousands of people working in Hollywood today, it's easy to forget sometimes just how small that community can be. Take Michael DeLuise. Sure, he's the son of beloved comic actor Dom DeLuise (*Fatso, Cannonball Run*), but he also is an accomplished actor who's run the gamut from comedy to drama, including roles on *NYPD Blue* (as the son of Dennis Franz's character, Det. Sipowicz), *21 Jump Street* and *SeaQuest 2032*.

It was during one of his earliest jobs, a sitcom called *One Big Family* starring legendary comic actor Danny Thomas, that he first met Daniel Palladino, then a writers assistant, who received a couple of writing credits on the show.

All those years later, when he was working on *Gilmore*, DeLuise had expert help in parents Dom and actress/producer Carol Arthur. "Mom would cue me with my lines," he says. "It took a lot of rehearsal to even attempt to spit it out fast and have some weighted content in it; I didn't want to sacrifice fullness for speed. If I had a three-page scene, it took me three days to learn that. Sometimes you didn't have that much time, so it could be very stressful. If you're in the run of a show, you get good at it."

(Another thing DeLuise has gotten good at over the years: painting. Check out the portrait he painted of his father on the opposite page.)

not be together, but you know what? I was wrong. Richard and Emily Gilmore were made for each other. God, this is so freaky. And I'm not supposed to know, and of course we won't talk about it because we don't do that in our family. We repress everything and we refuse to go to therapy, because why tell a stranger your problems when you can use them to punish those around you? So, what now? Every Friday I'm supposed to pretend that they still live together, and then after we leave, my mother will get in her car and drive back to the hotel? The hotel. My mother's living in a hotel. It's weird. It's just incredibly weird.

4.20 Luke Can See Her Face

First aired: May 4, 2004 // Written by Amy Sherman-Palladino & Daniel Palladino // Directed by Matthew Diamond

Liz and TJ are preparing to get married, Asher Fleming is in the hospital, and Dean and Lindsay's marriage is on the rocks. With the Dragonfly Inn's opening just weeks away, Lorelai and her staff are also drowning in to-do lists. And Luke? After his weird marriage and divorce with Nicole, he's determined to get his love life in order. With the assistance of some self-help audiobooks, he may just see the light, or at least her face.

! GINCHY! Luke's interaction with the self-help audiobook, and his guilting Jess into coming to Liz's wedding; Paris suddenly being aware of how much older Asher is; Lorelai, Sookie and Michel joining Jackson in the zucchini patch and resolving to enjoy the whole inn experience more; and Luke passing along his audiobooks to Jess after he asks Lorelai to go with him to Liz and TJ's wedding.

NOTES *'If you crave love, then you deserve love.'*

Asher Fleming asks Paris to leave with him for Oxford in two weeks. Andrew does not stock porn at his book store. TJ proposed to Liz last week and they're getting married this week. Crazy Carrie Duncan is Liz's maid of honor. Jess is working as a messenger.

The *Gilmore Girls* find-the-loved-one-in-the-hospital-by-following-the-crazy-shouting-woman gag (1.10) continues with Paris' conniption fit over Asher Fleming. Like Richard, Asher appears to be suffering from angina.

"Sometimes dad would listen in, give suggestions and share how great he thought the writing on

Gilmore Girls was. He loved when they mentioned him on the show. We all did. On one show the girls were curled up watching videos as they did and "FATSO" was on—one of dad's best movies!"

-MICHAEL DELUISE, REMEMBERING HIS FATHER AND "FATSO" STAR, DOM DELUISE.

TODAY'S CELEBRATION TJ's bachelor party.

OY WITH THE ____, ALREADY! Lindsay's complaining. Rory's right—get a job!

25 The number of answering machine messages Lorelai leaves herself as she makes her to-do list.

AMEN, SISTER FRIEND

AUDIOBOOK: Whose phone calls or visits are never unwanted or too long? Do you see her face? Who would you most like to have in your life to ward off moments of loneliness? Do you see her face? When you travel, who would make your travels more enjoyable? Do you see her face? When you're in pain, who would you most like to comfort you? Do you see her face? When something wonderful happens in your life—a promotion at work, a successful refinancing—who do you want to share the news with? Do you see her face? Whose face appears to you, my friend? Whose face?

LUKE [*suddenly picturing "her" face*]: Whoah.

Behind the Scenes: Wrestling with Continuity

Like any television show with a following, *Gilmore Girls* comes under some criticism online for errors in continuity, usually of the nitpicking variety. Though crew often lose sleep over mistakes that might've somehow slipped into a scene despite their best efforts, it does happen, even on *Gilmore*.

Yet why it happens is usually not so well understood by those outside the business. Take any show as an example. "People write these books that say 'look at these goofs: he's wearing a tie, and in this shot he's not wearing a tie,'" says *Gilmore* editor Raul Davalos. "It's like dude, we know, we were there. We decided to cut this this way. We noticed he wasn't wearing a tie. What happened was we took out a scene in between where he takes it off that wasn't working because of the performance, lighting, you name it."

Other circumstances can mess with continuity, too. For example, between episodes 1.21 and 2.1, Jared Padalecki had grown about 1½ feet over the three-month hiatus, recalls key set costumer Valerie Campbell. "We were like, 'Oh my God, Jared, you're huge!' And literally the next episode was supposed to be the very next day."

Over a similar summer hiatus between 4.22 and 5.1, Sean Gunn shaved his hair pretty short, meaning he had to wear a wig in that scene where he's recovering from his night terrors.

Finally, you have to realize that many scenes are shot out of order, meaning that great pains have to be taken to figure out what clothing and props will look like after the action in a scene that hasn't yet been shot.

But, as Davalos observes, "At the end of the day, if you're into the story and you're compelled by what's going on, then it works."

4.21 Last Week Fights, This Week Tights

First aired: May 11, 2004 // Written by Daniel Palladino // Directed by Chris Long

Yale is winding down for summer break and Rory is feeling her single status more than ever. Fortunately, Emily is ready to steer an eligible bachelor Rory's way in the form of Graham Sullivan. Liz and TJ tie the knot in the square Renaissance-fair style, Luke asks Lorelai out again, and Jess decides to put his heart on the line by finally talking to Rory. So, why is Dean already with her?

GINCHY! Tana and Paris emphasizing Rory's lack of a boyfriend; Jess reading *You Deserve Love*; Luke and Lorelai struggling not to laugh during the more surreal moments of the wedding; the boys doing their best to impress Mrs. Kim when she comes over and Mrs. Kim flipping out; Lorelai telling her to think of them as girls; Jess finally thanking Luke for everything and asking Rory to run away with him.

TJ and Liz celebrate their love in the square, Renaissance-fair style.

NOTES *'Liz and TJ wouldst enjoy others to join them in their modest wriggles.'*

Emily claims Richard is away on business in Philadelphia. Liz says this is her first wedding that she's ever been sober for; she's been married at least three times. When Liz rips her wedding dress, Lorelai fixes it. Liz already seems to know that Luke has a thing for her.

Though extremely appreciative when Dean comes to her rescue at the bar, Rory soon realizes that he had to lie to Lindsay to be with her.

TODAY'S CELEBRATION Liz and TJ's wedding and the end of classes at Yale.

KIRK OF ALL TRADES Doose's Market cashier and DJ for Liz and TJ's wedding reception. Ka-ching!

EMILY'S MAID DU JOUR Kiki, maker of the raspberry souffle.

AMEN, SISTER FRIEND

SOOKIE [*about the radishes*]: They're puny. They're tasteless.

JACKSON: Puny? These are not puny.

SOOKIE: If they're small enough to shove up our son's nose, they're too small!

JACKSON: No way could you shove one of these up Davey's nose.

SOOKIE: Bet you five bucks.

JACKSON: Get him in here!

LORELAI: Well, do you still have the big door knockers—metal with the chipped red paint? You're a magician, do you know that? Oh, it's great. Isn't it big?

MRS. KIM: And good price, seeing as how it may have belonged to James Madison. It was commonly known that James Madison liked big knockers.

LORELAI: I bet a lot of the founding fathers liked big knockers. I'm sorry for laughing. I'd explain if I could.

MRS. KIM: It's a double entendre. I've been in this country 20 years, I get things.

"At the beginning of the season, we would take any Lauren [clothing] rejects and put them in our extras' stuff, so we had a lot of great clothes for just random people that happened to be her size."

–VALERIE CAMPBELL, KEY SET COSTUMER

4.22 Raincoats and Recipes

First aired: May 18, 2004 // Written and directed by Amy Sherman-Palladino

The Dragonfly Inn officially opens in two weeks, which means this Saturday is all about the test run. In addition to her friends, Lorelai's invited her parents in the hopes of bringing whatever problems they have to a head. She's also still trying to figure out if she and Luke are actually dating. Now if only Jason Stiles would leave her alone, and Rory would hurry back with those CDs. Anyone seen Dean?

GINCHY! Lane hiding food from the boys under the floorboards the way she used to hide things from Mrs. Kim at home; Kirk's impassioned plea to Luke to help him protect Lulu from his night terrors; the guests having to follow their doors to their room; Luke and Lorelai's first kiss and a naked Kirk running out of the inn right after; the bust up between Lorelai and Rory over her sleeping with Dean.

NOTES *'I think I'm dating Luke.'*

Kirk's room at home used to be a bomb shelter. Babette lets Luke in on a little Stars Hollow secret: Miss Patty sometimes gets gossip first because her phone lines sometimes pick up other people's conversations.

* Lorelai sends Rory back to the house to get some CDs in case any of the guests would like to listen to music in their rooms. Luke's never bought a girl flowers before the ones he brings Lorelai. Dean thanking Rory after their lovemaking echoes Rory's "Thank you" the first time she kissed Dean (1.7). Rory bringing up the time that Lorelai slept with Christopher while he was with Sherry (2.22), and that Sherry was pregnant, really rattles her mother.

* Sometimes there's a theme to how much your life sucks. Today, Lorelai is blasted by her parents, and then Luke, for seemingly pretending not to know things she knows. Emily is furious at her for inviting her and Richard to the inn's test run when she knows they've separated, and Luke is exasperated because he feels he's given her all the right signals that he wants to be with her, yet Jason told him he and Lorelai are still dating.

* Reaction to Rory sleeping with a newly married Dean was pretty evenly split. "People are split between praying for her soul and celebrating the fact she's a whore," Amy told The Hollywood Reporter in a February 2005 interview. Added Dan, "The thing is, we didn't exactly rush Rory into sex. She may look 12 but she's 20 in the story, and in her second year of college. She's a normal girl and, in fact, she held off having sex later than most girls in TV do."

TODAY'S CELEBRATION Sookie and Jackson's wedding anniversary, the Dragonfly Inn test run, and Rory losing her virginity...to Dean.

KIRK OF ALL TRADES Firewood provider.

EMILY'S MAID DU JOUR Sriva.

2 WEEKS How long it's been since Lorelai broke up with Jason.

20 The number of years Lorelai says she's been working toward having her own inn.

THINGS WE'VE LEARNED Kirk's night terrors were actually

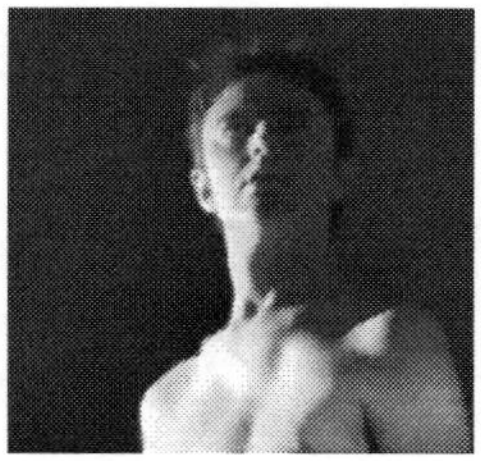

Kirk Au Naturel

Not counting *a film by kirk*, the producers found at least two other reasons to have Kirk appear in various states of undress (4.22, 5.21). Says Sean Gunn, "I told them early on, 'Look, it's your funeral. Anybody who wants to see me with my shirt off gets what they deserve. I'm not going to be the one to feel bad about it.'"

based on the experiences of one of the writers, says writers assistant Alison Goodman. "Him running naked in the final scene, that was also—I'll say 'based on'—a real night terror. But it was great. They loved writing Kirk because some of his funny things really did come from writers' stories."

AMEN, SISTER FRIEND

KIRK: I called the Dragonfly and had them put me and Lulu in the room right next to yours. That way, if you hear anything—screaming or Russian—you can come in and pull me off of Lulu.

LUKE: Oh.

KIRK: Unless, when you come in, it looks like you shouldn't pull me off of Lulu.

LUKE: Kirk.

KIRK: You can use your judgment on that one.

LUKE: Kirk, I don't know about this.

KIRK: Please! This weekend means so much to her. I can't tell her we're not going.

LUKE: Fine.

KIRK: Thank you, Luke, thank you. Remember, anything weird, just jump on in.

LUKE: I got it, Kirk.

KIRK: Just don't touch my bottom or I'll think you have a machete.

RORY: We didn't get around to discussing everything.

LORELAI: You didn't get around to discussing everything?

RORY: It was a crazy night.

LORELAI: You, of all people, the girl who thinks everything through, the listmaker, you didn't bother to discuss those things before jumping into bed with a married guy?

Once again *Gilmore Girls* had managed to end on a cliffhanger that was less to do with plot and more concerned with its emotional impact on the characters.

'Running Naked & Screaming'

Considering it a "quintessential" *Gilmore Girls* episode, Sean Gunn was extremely excited to tackle one of his favorite scenes, but not the one most fans think of.

"I sit down with Luke and I'm explaining about the night terrors and why I'm so nervous and asking him to help me. I love that scene. It's a longer scene with a lot of dialogue and I think it's still insane, really funny, and I hit all the points. I'm really excited about *that* scene when we shoot it. And then when it's coming up, I'm like this is great! I've got this episode where I've got this really great scene. And people remember it, but *everybody* remembers me running naked and screaming like a buffoon at the end, which is something that takes zero preparation and almost zero skill, other than being able to make a funny face. So it's really the most buffoonish stuff that people remember, but it's not really what I remember. When I think of that episode, I think of that scene at Luke's."

The relationship the audience had been waiting for between Luke and Lorelai since the first episode finally seemed to be under starters orders, Rory had finally taken her first heady steps into having an adult relationship. And most unbelievably of all, mother and daughter seemed to be on the verge of a great schism, right after they'd learned just how much they needed each other's support. Yet little did anyone realize just how crazy things would get next season.

Putting (Foreign) Words in Michel's Mouth

Though *Gilmore* fans outside the US have frequently had to put up with odd broadcast times and lengthy delays in seeing the later seasons, they've also enjoyed an added dimension to the weird world that is Stars Hollow: dodgy dubbing.

Take, for example, a throwaway line like Lorelai's "Hate early, must kill early" (5.3). In the Czech Republic, it came out "Ugly alarm, ew," says fan Katka Rylichová. "Isn't that poetic?"

Few in the US may be aware of how dubbing works for shows such as *Gilmore Girls* overseas, and how it can add to (or take away from) the enjoyment of the show for its international fans.

Nobody on the Stars Hollow set was aware of this fact more than Yanic Truesdale (Michel). When he left his native Montreal to study acting in New York around 1998, his own command of the English language was "very, very basic and very, very poor," he admits. Some two years later, he landed his role on *Gilmore Girls*, only to see his fictional alter ego grapple with the same language problems when the show started to air in French-speaking Quebec.

"I should've put in my original contract that I would be the person that would do the French version, which I didn't do. So when it was time to dub it in French, they hired someone who is actually doing a terrible job with my part. But in French, you couldn't do Michel being a French person when everyone else is speaking French around him, so they should've adapted the character and made him British, in my opinion. But they kind of went with a Spanish/Hungarian—a very strange, high-pitched, annoying tone of voice, which is really not the character. It's a very, very weird choice. But by now I've let go of it."

> "Hate early, must kill early," = Ugly alarm, ew..."
>
> —AS DUBBED IN THE CZECH REPUBLIC

Strange Dubbing, Indeed...

Few Americans realize just how important dubbing artists are, not only to the success or failure of a movie or television show, but in their own right.

In Spain, they changed the person who speaks for Lorelai in Season 2, the one who dubs Emily in Season 3, and Luke in Season 4, according to Lourdes Palma Ortiz. Luke's voice man disappeared because he had to go to the hospital. "When he came back, he dubbed some extras. It was really weird to hear the original Luke's voice coming from other characters."

In Germany, pretty much every major Hollywood star has a designated dub artist, explains Zoran Bijelic.

To make a living, voice actors have to work on several series. In Germany, for instance, the actor who dubbed Jared Padalecki as Dean in *Gilmore Girls* also tackled his part on *Supernatural*, Bijelic says. Then the guy who spoke for Milo Ventimiglia's Jess dubbed Jensen Ackles, who plays Padalecki's brother on that show. Says Bijelic, "When I closed my eyes and listened to Sam and Dean bickering, it was like I was listening to Dean and Jess bickering. That was weird."

a little something

Every season, cast and crew received gifts such as a *Gilmore*-embossed bowling shirt (below), skateboard or iPod, as well as a themed coffee mug celebrating an on-set in-joke. Above, we have the "Wolf Girl" from the wedding present Emily gave Lorelai (7.9) pitted against director Lee Shallat Chemel.

Wardrobe!

How Does an Inn Manager Afford all of those Clothes?

While *Gilmore Girls* is one of the smartest, wittiest television programs in recent years, you still have to check your brain at the door for two of its constants: the amount of food these two svelte women put away, and the seemingly endless supply of new clothes they go through, Lorelai especially.

It turns out that one of the main reasons Lorelai went through so many outfits each season wasn't because she was embezzling funds from the Independence Inn, but because of those "Previously on *Gilmore Girls*" montages that led off so many episodes. Since these recaps drew from so many earlier shows, often reaching back over an entire season, the audience saw many of the outfits that Lorelai had worn, all within the space of 30 seconds or less.

Valerie Campbell remembers Graham telling her, "'I was just watching the last episode, and this [outfit] was on at the beginning.' If they hadn't had those 'previously ons,' then we probably would've had a different looking show."

Wardrobe would try to mix up Lorelai's outfits so they didn't look the same as the ones in the episode recaps, Campbell says, but "a lot of times she was wearing something that was so specific, it didn't really mesh well with something else."

Bledel, on the other hand, had a big closet with more clothes than you might expect a girl her age to have, but nowhere near the number of outfits that Graham had.

Baby Got Back...Fix It

Though it comes as little surprise to know that Amy worked long into the night perfecting the language in each script, she was equally exacting when it came to other details, including wardrobe. One of her pet peeves?

"She didn't like to see back," Campbell says. Around the time *Gilmore* began, the trend for waistlines on jeans slipped from the waist to the hips within a matter of months, she remembers. "And then the cropped T-shirts started coming in. You've got actors wanting to wear these kinds of clothes, and it's like, 'It doesn't really make sense for you to wear that.'"

Naturally, even the slightest movements would raise shirt bottoms and pow—instant back shot, which Amy had no interest in seeing on camera. "Think about how many times your shirt comes up in the back on a normal day," Campbell says. "And I would always have to bug them: Tuck your shirt in, because whenever they turned around, the producers didn't want to see the skin coming out of the back of their jeans, and they didn't want to see the top coming up, either. If you watch the episodes during any long scene, you'll see them pulling their shirt down, and that's because I told them to pull their shirt down. It's this weird habit."

Clothing the Gilmore Girls

Naturally, Graham and Bledel were where most of wardrobe's creative energies were concentrated, as whatever either was wearing on the latest Tuesday night episode would invariably be Topic 1 for many girls throughout the US on Wednesday.

When discussing TV wardrobe, you have to realize that getting clothes to fit your actors is like getting them to fit in real life, Campbell points out. "Most things don't fit people right off the rack unless you have absolutely a model's body. So we would have to do a lot of little fixes at the last minute, or just have a lot of clothes."

Bledel was extremely easy to dress because "of her personality for putting clothes on. She'd put the clothes on and most things fit her very well. If not, she had a complete mind about how she wanted things. Like if she wanted something to be fixed, we'd alter it. She'd do a little fitting with me or Brenda [Maben] or whoever."

One of the things that many viewers don't think about is the importance of color when it comes to wardrobe. "If one character was in blue, you would want to have one in red or pink or green," Campbell says. "You don't want to have everyone wearing black or everybody wearing blue. It's really hard not to have everybody wearing the same color, so you have to be aware of it. But if you don't know what your lead actress is wearing because she hasn't picked it out yet, you get into this, 'Oh, please don't put so-and-so in this color.' You never know what someone's going to walk out with."

Daily Trials on the Wardrobe Trailer

Though Graham and Bledel commanded the lion's share of attention when it came to wardrobe, you could hardly leave the rest of the cast to fend for themselves.

Costume designer Brenda Maben, the head of wardrobe on *Gilmore*, was very hands-on and frequently put her considerable skills toward creating unique costumes. For example, "There was nothing off the rack for Sookie," Campbell says. "I'm not saying it didn't come off the rack originally, but Brenda was so talented, she could take two different dresses and put them together to create a dress that was in itself unique, as well as cute. And as the show got more popular and as they were able to buy higher-end clothes, the look of the show progressed."

Yet, regardless of how successful the show became, one thing that never improved was the amount of time there was to get cast members clothed. Normally, the wardrobe department on a television show would prepare clothes for the entire cast the night before shooting. That was seldom possible on *Gilmore Girls*. Whether they hadn't yet been able to pin down an outfit for Graham or casting had only just cast an actor *the day of the shooting*, something always interfered with that plan.

"The Relationship We Have Feared for Some Time has Emerged"

season **five**

For years we've been treated to a fairy tale mother-daughter relationship in a fairy tale town. This season, Lorelai and Rory will fall out over Rory's relationship with a newly married Dean, a precursor to the much more serious rift awaiting them a season later.

Even as Emily wrestles with what might remain of her life without Richard and the social obligations she's always known, Rory suddenly embraces the upper-crust world that her mother ran away from at the earliest opportunity, much to Lorelai's mounting disgust. That also includes the ditching of the awkward Dean for the flashy, well-to-do scion of the Huntzberger empire, Logan.

If Rory is testing her wings and turning her back on her long-sheltered ways, Luke has the opposite planned for his new life with Lorelai, including settling down in one of Stars Hollow's great family homes. But Lorelai seems to have her sights set a little higher, especially after a controversial magazine article brings the Dragonfly Inn to the attention of some powerful business interests.

While Richard and Emily do their best to steer Rory's life in the right direction, Emily takes it upon herself to do the same with Lorelai's, temporarily destroying her daughter's relationship with Luke shortly after repairing her own with Richard.

For all the dramatic flourishes that test Lorelai and Rory, all it takes is a few callous words from an unlikely source to turn Rory's life upside down, and to alienate mother and daughter for a long time to come.

5.1 Say Goodbye to Daisy Miller

First aired: Sept. 21, 2004 // Written and directed by Amy Sherman-Palladino

Kirk is recovering from his night terrors, Sookie is over the moon about Luke and Lorelai's kiss, and Lorelai and Rory are on the outs over Rory's sleeping with Dean. Lorelai's parents finally make a formal split, with Richard moving into the pool house and Emily jetting off to Europe with Rory for the summer. With nothing but problems at home, Rory has decided that maybe the Atlantic Ocean is just the kind of buffer she needs between her and her mother right now.

! GINCHY! Sookie discovering that Luke and Lorelai kissed from Kirk's post-night-terror blatherings; Lane trying to have a heart-to-heart with Rory while the rest of the band's waiting to rehearse; Luke calling Lorelai on his way out of town.

NOTES *'I don't know who you are at all.'*

✱ Rather than "Ginchy" scenes, this episode is anti-Ginchy to the extreme, but in a very Ginchy way. From Richard and Emily's bitter split to Lorelai and Rory's fight and Lindsay's desperate attempts to win some kind of approval from Dean, it's about as cheery as Solzhenitsyn's musings on the Gulag. Whatever internecine struggles went on behind the scenes between Amy and the network, the fact that she was able to begin a season on such a down note is proof that she was still very much in control at this point.

✱ Michel had Sookie call Jason's cell phone and tell him his condo was on fire, presumably getting rid of Digger Stiles once and for all. Despite Lorelai telling Michel not to bring them, Chin-Chin and Pau-Pau are at the inn (and chew up Taylor's shoes). Luke threw the cell phone Nicole got him in the lake after the divorce.

✱ Rory asks Dean to meet her at Miss Patty's dance studio, the place

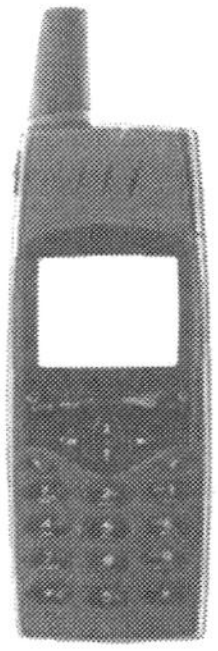

What's That Number Again, Luke?

Not only did our cell-phone hating Luke go over to the dark side, he was happy to share that number with Lorelai... and us. Those die-hard *Gilmore* fans who dialed 860-294-1986 (you know who you are) were put through to a recording of Luke's alter ego, Scott Patterson, doing his bit to drum up some much-needed funds for Johns Hopkins Children's Center—a medical research center in Baltimore. According to an item on Entertainment Weekly's Web site on Oct. 8, 2004, Amy purchased the number and left it up to Patterson to choose the message. What first prompted the idea? "If I hear someone say '555' on television, I'm going to put my own head through a wall," Amy told EW. Amen!

that got them in trouble with Lorelai on their first date (1.9). Back then, Lorelai was furious at her because she thought they had had sex at Miss Patty's. This time, they actually do.

Rory looks forward to putting the Atlantic ocean between herself and her mom.

✱ Liz and TJ each broke an arm and a leg in Maine, so Luke is on his way there to help them run their Renaissance fair booth for a week until they recover—it will take much longer. Luke got another cell phone just in case Lorelai wanted to call him while he's out of town.

TODAY'S CELEBRATION Rory and Emily both leave their miserable social lives behind them for Europe.

OY WITH THE ____, ALREADY! Dean treating Lindsay so badly, especially after he just slept with Rory.

YOU'VE ENTERED RICHARDLAND Only prostitutes have two glasses of wine at lunch.

6½ NARROW Taylor's shoe size

'THE CANDY MAN' Dean and Rory's "song," decided after their first time in bed together.

AND INTRODUCING...*Richard's pool house bachelor pad* He should fight with Emily more often.

AMEN, SISTER FRIEND

RICHARD: Do you know what, Emily? If nothing else, this display tonight demonstrates clearly that you are no longer the woman I married.
EMILY: The woman you married was your partner. You listened to her. You consulted with her. You respected her. So you are right, Richard. I am definitely not the woman you married.

SOOKIE [*to Lorelai about her and Luke*]: I am so glad! You two are perfect for each other. I have always thought that someday, if you just sort of turned around and opened your eyes, that you'd see it, and now that you have, I'm just so damn happy.

RORY: How fast did you tell Grandma that I had nothing to do this summer?
LORELAI: I'm not shipping you off.
RORY: Oh, please!
LORELAI: I'm not. I'm just—OK, maybe I am.
RORY: Ha!
LORELAI: I wasn't planning on it, but maybe in the back of my mind, I just thought–
RORY: Say Goodbye to Daisy Miller.
LORELAI: OK, fine, so maybe I suggested the trip to give you some time to–
RORY: Travel back to the turn of the century?
LORELAI: To think. But you did not have to accept.
RORY: I did, too.
LORELAI: No, Rory, you didn't. You're 19 now, remember? You're all grown up and you can handle your own affairs. Sorry, that's a bad choice of words. You can handle your own life events. So if you didn't want to go to Europe, all you had to do was say you didn't want to go, but you

Bio Arielle Kebbel (Lindsay Lister)

As Lindsay, Dean's Rory-substitute, and briefly, wife, Arielle Kebbel portrayed a girl well aware of the shoes she was filling in the absence of Rory. Sure she was beautiful, but her nervousness around Rory told us all we needed to know: Dean must've waxed poetic about his ex to her at some point.

Growing up in Winter Park, Fla., the daughter of talent agent (and now producer) Sheri, Kebbel occasionally was mistaken for pop princess Britney Spears. Several days after making the move to Los Angeles, she landed the role of Lindsay. Since then, she's appeared on several popular series including *True Blood*, *The Vampire Diaries* and *Grounded for Life*. She's also carved out a pretty impressive film career with starring roles in *The Grudge 2* (2006), *The Uninvited* (the 2009 remake of the Korean horror film *A Tale of Two Sisters*) and *Vampires Suck* (2010).

Behind the Scenes: Huzzah! TJ's Triumph

Throughout the series, the speed of the dialogue continued to be one of the greatest challenges the actors faced. "Scott [Patterson] was evidently not good at it in the first year, and then in the later years he was *really* good at it," Michael DeLuise says. Although he seldom felt completely on top of the material, his mother frequently helped him learn his lines, which led to a personal triumph this episode.

"We were at the Renaissance fair. Scott didn't want to rehearse with all the newbies because a guest actor would come in and they'd want to rehearse—it can be a pain in the neck. You have to go over it and over it and he's got enough to be worried about.

"Anyway, you would say your line and he would say his line right before the period in *your* sentence came, so your brain couldn't even reflex with the next line— you just got stunned! But in that episode, I was faster than him and it pissed him off a little bit. I guess I was just gelling with the material in that particular one. I remember Daniel [Palladino] was directing and he said, 'You're coming back.' So there was a personal pride being quicker on the draw than Scott."

didn't, so I assume you do want to go. [Sees Rory's expression.] You do want to go? How come? I mean, what about Dean? You're just gonna go off and leave now?

5.2 A Messenger, Nothing More

First aired: Sept. 28, 2004 // Written and directed by Daniel Palladino

With a vast ocean between them, Rory and Lorelai finally make up, albeit after Lorelai's driven everybody at the Dragonfly crazy. Rory's sent Lorelai a letter to give Dean in the hopes of straightening everything out. Even Lorelai can count the ways this could go wrong. As if things couldn't get any more confusing, Lane suddenly discovers that she might be falling for Zack.

GINCHY! The Krumholtz children glomming on to Michel; the way Sookie breaks it to Lorelai that she's going a bit mental at work; Zack trying to use what Brian's told him about *The Da Vinci Code* to score with his groupies; the sheer delight that Emily is throughout; Rory playing her home movies of her and Emily from Europe—actually a scene from *A Room With a View* starring Helena Bonham Carter and Maggie Smith.

NOTES *'Want to know the last time I saw staff and maids looking this scared of their boss? Your mother's house.'*

✱ Rory's been sending Lane postcards from her European trip, which Lane's put up on the bulletin board at the diner.

✱ Michel has a profit-sharing agreement with the Dragonfly Inn. Rory revisited the corner of Bark and Cheese in Italy that she and Lorelai came across on their backpacking trip; regrettably there was no little Italian dog there in a basket barking this time. Liz tells Luke that she's had a prophetic dream that he's going to be with Lorelai.

✱ Luke and Lorelai slipping out of his diner on silly pretexts reminds us of when Rory and Jess used to do the same thing (3.8).

✱ Lorelai uses the phrase "Ginchy" again when Luke gives her his bag from the pharmacy (so the author feels duly justified in using it throughout this book).

✱ Lorelai's already wearing the earrings Luke got her when he presents her with the matching necklace he brought from Liz's booth.

Bio ☺ Sebastian Bach (Gil)

"Dude rocks, but dude's too old." With that pronouncement from Zack, it seemed like we'd seen the last of Gil following his Hep Alien audition (4.7). Yet no one told '80s-era rocker Sebastian Bach that he's too old to rock, as he continues to do so to this day with a variety of fellow rock stars and his own band.

Born in Freeport, in the Bahamas, Sebastian Bierk grew up in Peterborough, Ontario, in a family that includes actress sister Dylan Bierk (*Jason X*), father David Bierk, an accomplished Canadian painter, and brother Zac, a retired professional ice hockey player for the Tampa Bay Lightning, Minnesota Wild and the Phoenix Coyotes.

Bach kicked off his professional music career in 1987 when he joined the band Skid Row, which released its self-titled first album in 1989. Since then, Bach has tried his hand at many different forms of performance, from playing with several bands and singers (most notably Guns N' Roses frontman Axl Rose) to nearly touring with a Broadway production of *Jesus Christ Superstar*—the deal fell apart before it could get off the ground.

Bach has also carved out an unusual niche for himself in the world of reality TV, from contributing to VH1's *I Love the '80s* documentary-style series to that network's show *Supergroup*, which dropped him in a house with other longtime rock stars Ted Nugent, Jason Bonham, Evan Seinfeld and Scott Ian. Bach and his wife (both appeared on VH1 special *I Married Sebastian Bach*) have three children, including a son called...Paris!

By this point, a pattern in *Gilmore Girls* writing duties has emerged: Amy writes and directs the most pivotal episodes, which is standard practice for any showrunner. Hers will be the episodes with the most memorable dialogue and where our heartstrings are in the greatest danger of being tugged. Dan, on the other hand, seems to tackle the "shoe leather" episodes that get us from point A to B. They're not much on dialogue, but they deftly get us to where we need to be later in the season. (He will also write some truly sensational episodes later on.)

"It got really difficult for me. When you don't have much material to establish your vision of who that [character] is, it gets very tricky. I'm one who really thinks about the scenes and how to have an angle to it and chooses to show either a side or a little tone difference that we haven't seen. But if it's not in the writing, I have very little to do, so it's very, very challenging."

–YANIC TRUESDALE (MICHEL)

TODAY'S CELEBRATION Parade to mark the opening of the Cider Mill (hey, it *is* Stars Hollow), Luke's return, and Rory and Emily's return from Europe. Oh, and Dean getting kicked out of the house *he* pays for.

AND HERE'S A SHOUT OUT TO OUR INTERNATIONAL FANS Emily's conversation in Italian with the waiter in Rome, as well as her furthering of the Italian-men-are-all-hands stereotype.

518 Emily and Rory's hotel room in Rome, the last stop on their European tour.

5 The number of original songs Lane's band is ready to play live so far.

7 The number of weeks Luke's been at the Renaissance fair helping Liz and TJ.

90% How much of the Dragonfly is booked already.

THINGS WE'VE LEARNED The Renaissance fair queen glimpsed in this episode is wearing the exact same dress Whoopi Goldberg wore to the Oscars, thanks to one of the costumers on *Gilmore*, who had once worked for the dress' designer, Bill Hargate.

AMEN, SISTER FRIEND

MICHEL: Who wants to play some insipid board game with me?
LITTLE GIRL: We want to play an insipid board game!

LINDSAY'S MOM [*to Lorelai*]: All I know is that now my Lindsay is devastated, Dean is back with his parents, lives are destroyed, and you and your daughter can go to hell! [Leaves with Lindsay.]
LORELAI: OK, I have got to know what was in that letter.

"I actually got in a bit of trouble that first episode. I wanted to play larger than life. And they said we want to bring a little bit of energy to the show. So I said well, that's my role here. And [director] Kenny Ortega was just like, 'Bigger, Tanc, bigger, bigger, push the envelope.' And we pushed it. But the creators got back to my agent and they said, 'Tanc, pull it back, will ya? Pull it back.'"

—TANC SADE (FINN)

RORY: Um, I told him that that night was special and that I wasn't sorry that it happened. But he's married and he has to figure out his life. So I was going to make it easier for him and take myself out of the mix.
LORELAI: Well, that was a very good letter.
RORY: I can't believe she found it.

RORY: Hi. I hope this is OK. I wasn't sure where to call, and I just had to—are you OK?
DEAN: Am I OK?
RORY: Yeah, I mean how do you feel? I'm sorry. That's a stupid question.
DEAN: No, it's not a stupid question. Um, let's see. How do I feel? Actually, I feel like an idiot.
RORY: Why?
DEAN: Why? Because I was married, Rory. Married. And I threw it all away for someone who dumped me once and then just bailed on me.
RORY: I didn't just bail. I—
DEAN: I hurt everybody. I hurt Lindsay, I hurt her parents, I hurt my parents, and now I'm back at home and you're in Europe with your grandmother. And what the hell was I thinking? I mean, what am I doing? What's wrong with me?

5.3 Written in the Stars

First aired: Oct. 5, 2004 // Written by Amy Sherman-Palladino // Directed by Kenny Ortega

Richard and Emily's separation has quickly moved from fighting over spending time with Lorelai and Rory to suspicion and jealousy, at least on the part of Emily. Rory's sophomore year at Yale begins with a wake for Asher Fleming, getting reacquainted with Marty, and meeting an obnoxious rich boy who we will get to know much better soon enough. Oh, and the whole town knows about Luke and Lorelai...but don't say anything.

GINCHY! Luke and Lorelai remembering how they first met, and Luke automatically knowing he's going to have to adopt her taste in music; Lorelai suddenly realizing that the entire diner full of customers is looking at her when she stumbles down from Luke's apartment to get coffee; Taylor bringing up Luke and Lorelai's relationship as an official matter at the town meeting; and Emily unburdening herself to Paris at Asher's wake.

Behind the Scenes "Tanc, Where Are You Living Today?"

When Tanc Sade was cast as Logan's Australian pal Finn, he'd only been in LA for about six weeks, and was pretty much living out of his 1992 Toyota Corolla.

"Literally everything I had was in that car and I took it with me everywhere," he says. His agents never knew where to send his scripts next. "I met their courier on random corners or wherever I was staying that night, and I was staying somewhere different almost every night. It was like a running gag. They'd ring me up, go, 'Tanc, where are you living today, where are you going to be living tomorrow?' I'd say hang on, let me grab the address."

Years later, after appearing on everything from the new *90210* to *CSI: NY* and getting his own movies made through his own company (FiveIslandFilms.com), Sade admits that living in LA, there's a lot of pressure to get a fancy car, but he still sticks with his '92 Corolla. "Right now I'd rather not spend that money and be able to take two months off to make movies like *Flowers and Weeds*."

Tanc Sade (left) directing his 2008 short film *Flowers and Weeds*.

NOTES *'Now, as you all know, the relationship we have feared for some time has emerged, and we need to carefully consider whether or not we can support this.'*

✻ Asher Fleming died two weeks ago in Oxford while giving a reading from *A Midsummer Night's Dream*. When he learns Asher didn't die in bed, Marty says he lost the pool. He also happened to learn over the summer that his Uncle Jerry is actually his father.

✻ Marty and Rory are catching up on what they did over the summer when Logan and his friends bump into them; Logan recalls that Marty bartended for one of his parties. (Marty makes a kick-ass margarita.)

✻ Luke eats at Maisy and Buddy's restaurant, Sniffy's Tavern, two or three times a week. Maisy went to school with Luke's mother and Buddy helped Luke convert his father's hardware store into a diner.

✻ Luke and Lorelai's relationship has precedent: flower-shop owner Fay Wellington and candy-store owner Art Brush 10 years ago. Everything was great until Art met Margie, the fudge queen. The whole town split down the middle—you could buy flowers or you could buy candy, not both.

✱ Though Taylor predicts what will happen to the town when Luke and Lorelai have a falling out (5.14), he never refers to Luke's on-the-record promise to close up Luke's Diner and move away if they ever breakup.

TODAY'S CELEBRATION The beginning of Rory's second year at Yale, Asher Fleming's wake, Luke and Lorelai's first date and their first sexual encounter. And who can forget Rory and Logan's first meeting?

YOU'VE ENTERED EMILYLAND I'm not gonna be the one that sits at home alone in the dark like an Italian widow.

EMILY'S MAID DU JOUR Madonna Louise, perhaps the first Gilmore maid to receive a compliment from Emily...for her omelette.

OY WITH THE ____, ALREADY! OK, Logan gets better later, but he's such an arrogant jerk this episode. Boo!

BRANFORD COLLEGE Rory's dorm, which is where Richard stayed when he was at school.

Bio ☺ Matt Czuchry (Logan Huntzberger)

Like Logan, Matt Czuchry is a native New Englander, born in Manchester, NH, though he actually grew up in Johnson City, Tenn.

While he didn't major in drama at the College of Charleston in South Carolina, he took some classes his junior year in the "Meisner technique," an acting discipline developed by Sanford Meisner that encourages actors to marry their ability to improvise a scene with their own emotional experiences. At the time he was majoring in political science and history, and had gone to college on a tennis scholarship, yet quickly decided acting was what he really wanted to pursue.

Czuchry first entered The WB's bright-young-thing factory in its short-lived teen drama *Young Americans* in 2000, followed by an appearance on its family series *7th Heaven* in 2002. It wasn't long before he was noticed by casting directors Mara Casey and Jami Rudofsky, who regularly had him read for *Gilmore* as new characters became available. Amy, too, wanted him on the show; the challenge was finding just the right fit. Finally came the role of Logan, which he signed on to for an initial 13-episode run.

Since *Gilmore*, his loyal fans have followed him to *Friday Night Lights* and *The Good Wife*.

AND INTRODUCING...*Colin, Finn and...Logan!*

AMEN, SISTER FRIEND

PARIS [*about Asher*]: He died two weeks ago in Oxford.
RORY: Oh. Paris, I'm sorry. How?
PARIS: Heart attack. It was quick.
RORY: Heart attack?
PARIS: Yes.
RORY: Um, it wasn't during, um, was it?
PARIS: No, Rory. This great man was not brought down by my vagina, OK?

LUKE [*remembering how they first met at the diner*]: I was with a customer. She interrupts me, wild-eyed, begging for coffee, so I tell her to wait her turn. Then she starts following me around, talking a mile a minute, saying God knows what. So finally I turn to her and I tell her she's being annoying—sit down, shut up, I'll get to her when I get to her.
LORELAI: You know, I bet she took that very well, 'cause she sounds just delightful.
LUKE: She asked me what my birthday was. I wouldn't tell her. She wouldn't stop talking. I gave in. I told her my birthday. Then she opened up the newspaper to the horoscope page, wrote something down, tore it out, handed it to me.
LORELAI: God, seriously. You wrote the menu, didn't you?
LUKE: So I'm looking at this piece of paper in my hand, and under "Scorpio" she had written, "you will meet an annoying woman today. Give her coffee and she'll go away." I gave her coffee.
LORELAI: But she didn't go away.
LUKE: She told me to hold on to that horoscope, put it in my wallet and carry it around with me. [He removes that horoscope from his wallet.] One day it would bring me luck.
LORELAI: Well man, I will say anything for a cup of coffee. I can't believe you kept this. You kept this in your wallet? You kept this in your wallet.
LUKE: Eight years.
LORELAI: Eight years.
LUKE: Lorelai, this thing we're doing here—me, you—I just want you to know I'm in. I am all in.

What I Kept

I have some flannels. I have some clothes. I actually had the original hat [Luke] wore in the pilot in a safe, but about five years ago I was on vacation and somebody broke into the house and stole the safe.... I have other Luke hats that I wore in the series"

—Scott Patterson (Luke), via Movieline.com (10/19/10)

TAYLOR: Think of the consequences. What will happen when the relationship goes sour as, let's face it, most of Lorelai's relationships do?

LORELAI: Hey!

TAYLOR: We'll have to choose. Suddenly you'll either be a "Luke" or a "Lorelai" or, if you're Kirk and you can't make a decision to save your life, you'll be neither.

KIRK: He's probably right.

TAYLOR: That's bad for the economy, bad for the town. I vote against this.

LORELAI: Are they gonna make us break up?

5.4 Tippecanoe and Taylor, Too

First aired: Oct. 12, 2004 // Written by Bill Prady // Directed by Lee Shallat Chemel

As town selectman, Taylor's being a pain in the ass to the people of Stars Hollow, especially to Lorelai over a parking space issue regarding the Dragonfly, and to Jackson over his new greenhouse. In a moment of desperation, Jackson throws his hat in the election ring, and life will never be the same...for a few episodes, anyway. Normally, Rory would savor this kind of Stars Hollow insanity, but Paris has moved Asher's enormous printing press into their common room, and her relationship with Dean is bordering on the depressing. The only glimmer of hope comes from Lane telling Zack how she feels about him, but what Zack thinks of this is anybody's guess. Men!

GINCHY! The glee with which Taylor delivers his tick lecture at the town meeting; Jackson's spontaneous announcement of his candidacy for town selectman; Taylor sitting alone in his soda shop; Hep Alien's rendition of Jackson's favorite song "Believe it or Not"; Lorelai asking a few people to vote for Taylor when she realizes it's going to be a shutout.

NOTES *'Wow, sleeping with you is getting me nothing.'*

Luke cooking Lorelai breakfast in her kitchen is a pretty close approximation of the dream she had about being pregnant with his twins (3.1). Jackson and Andrew went to high school together.

Though it may be hard to see it now, Dean and Rory aren't so very different. This episode, Dean tells her he doesn't want to rub Lindsay's nose in their relationship. Not so long ago it was Rory saying the same

Favorite Scenes: Michael Winters

The humiliating defeat of Taylor Doose as town selectman involves one of Michael Winters' favorite Taylor scenes. "There's this one moment where Lauren is in the diner and looks through the window and I'm sitting in the dark soda shop sort of sad. Then, out of the blue, I pick up the can of whipped cream and just spray a mouthful and put it back down, and I just thought that was so hilarious. So perfect for him."

Taylor's "you *will* have Taylor Doose to kick around again" wasn't the only homage to disgraced President Richard Nixon initially, he remembers. "I did a whole big Nixon thing, and whoever was directing said I don't think he knows he's doing that with the big V (finger signs) and everything, so they made me cut it, so I was a little disappointed with that. But that line was still there."

thing to Jess, worried about Dean's feelings (3.9). How fitting that Jackson's favorite song should usher in his term as town selectman; he will soon discover the irony of such lyrics as "Suddenly I'm on top of the world and it shoulda been somebody else."

TODAY'S CELEBRATION Town selectman elections and Jackson's amazing victory.

KIRK OF ALL TRADES Pollster.

11423-A The official designation for the land under Jackson's greenhouse, which is built 9 ½ feet from the edge of his property.

THE ELECTION RESULTS 1,114 for Jackson; 10 for Taylor.

AMEN, SISTER FRIEND

LORELAI: Hey, Luke?

LUKE: Yep?

LORELAI: You cooking this is so sweet.

LUKE: But?

LORELAI: I just figured, you know, we'd go to Luke's for breakfast.

LUKE: Why?

LORELAI: Because I like Luke's breakfast.

LUKE: I am Luke.

LORELAI: I know.

"Sebastian [Bach] doesn't play the guitar. Sebastian is a singer. However, he's been around guitars so much in his life and has probably played around with them enough, he looks very authentic playing the guitar. He gets the fingering down very quickly and can do some fun stuff with it."

–JOHN CABRERA (BRIAN)

LUKE: This is the same stuff I make at the diner.

LORELAI: I know.

LUKE: So what's the difference?

LORELAI: Well, the difference is, while you are Luke, we're not at Luke's.

LUKE: So?

LORELAI: Well, I have my things, you know? I have certain things. And one of my things is going to Luke's. And just because I now have "dating Luke" doesn't mean I want to lose my "cooking Luke."

LUKE: But I am cooking, and I am Luke.

JACKSON'S VICTORY SPEECH Well, jeez. That was, uh, quite a welcome. Thank you all for coming and supporting me in this thing here. As I stand on this stage, looking at you all, I can't help but think, I have a job. I have a life. I don't have time to be selectman. I have a business. I have a kid, and Sookie and I are trying to have another one. And the doctor has us on this schedule and it's not flexible. And what was I thinking? What the hell am I doing here? I don't want to be selectman.

TAYLOR'S CONCESSION SPEECH Friends and townspeople, today in Stars Hollow, democracy has spoken. The will of the people has prevailed and new leadership has been instated. Your vote has counted. Free elections are a wonderful thing, a thing to be admired and cherished. Here in America, we have something else that is to be admired and cherished: it's called a recall election. I look forward to this other aspect of democracy, which I believe will happen any day now, when sanity and reason have been restored to Stars Hollow. So, in closing, friends, believe me when I tell you, you *will* have Taylor Doose to kick around again. Thank you and God bless.

What I Kept

Ah yes! I got to keep my Chilton outfit. And I got to keep that pink leather jacket I had in the episode where we go to Rory's house for the fire sale and we end up going to the Bangles concert. But the coolest thing I got to keep for sure is my full, head-to-toe Chilton outfit. It's in the back of my closet. I'll never wear it again, it's just neat that I have it. I'm thinking of putting it on eBay — just kidding. Yeah, I think I'll hang on to it for a while and do something really creative with it. I will let it appreciate. After your book it's going to be crazy.

—Shelly Cole (Madeline)

5.5 We Got Us a Pippi Virgin

First aired: Oct. 19, 2004 // Written by Daniel Palladino // Directed by Stephen Clancy

Anxious to get rid of the awkwardness between her, Dean and Rory, Lorelai arranges a double date with Luke. Although Luke is pretty taken with the night's screening of The Adventures of Pippi Longstocking, *the evening soon deteriorates. While Rory stews over her relationship, Zack and Lane finally seem headed for one themselves.*

! GINCHY! Sookie's "I'll forge that for you" when Jackson refuses to sign Lorelai's request for extra parking spaces; Emily's panic room (it'll stop a 9 mm bullet!); the joy that is Kyle (now with chick-magnet prosthetic hand); Zack finally acknowledging Lane's feelings and his own slowness processing them; Lorelai bringing out the Bop It and Luke's "In your face!" to Dean.

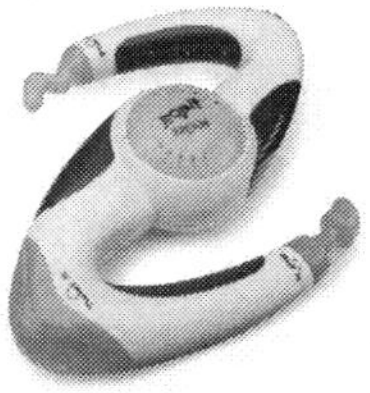

NOTES *'Et tu, former friend?'*

✱ Richard is working with a fellow called Dickie at his new office, whom he loathes. How interesting that Emily has never lived on her own before; she went from home to college to married life.

✱ Dean's now living with Kyle, the kid whose house he trashed when he got in a fight with Jess (3.19), and one of his friends from his bachelor party (4.4).

✱ The first Luke knows of Dean and Rory being together again is when Lorelai pushes him into double dating with them. Lorelai sees Richard reading Proust and tells him she tried once but struck out (1.11).

✱ The Black, White and Read bookstore/movie theater is supposed to be showing *Cool Hand Luke*, but the first reel caught fire, so *The Adventures of Pippi Longstocking* it is. (Dean's seen it with the girls at least three times.)

✱ Desperate to ease the tension between Luke and Dean, Rory quickly

Behind the Scenes: Injury Parade 1

While Zack tells Lane his gums are being eroded because of his vigorous brushing, it was actor John Cabrera who was truly feeling the pain when it came to dental hygiene this episode.

"There's this scene where I keep coming in and out of the kitchen brushing my teeth while Keiko and Todd are doing their little scene, and I'm spitting into the sink," he remembers. "They gave me this tooth-whitening peroxide toothpaste. We had to do like 10 or 13 takes, and by the end of it, my gums were burning so badly from this special toothpaste that it felt like my teeth were going to fall out.

"At one point I was like, hey, can we get another toothpaste here? This is just really painful. The prop guy runs out and then he gets back. 'How's this?' And of course that one also said whitening on it. I was like 'what is going on with all of these whitening toothpastes?' It actually turned my gums white."

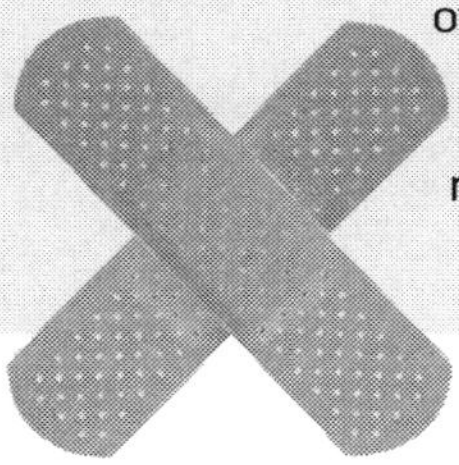

brings up the time they played softball together, but obviously forgets they were at each other's throats even then (1.15).

TODAY'S CELEBRATION Luke and Lorelai's double date with Rory and Dean.

KIRK OF ALL TRADES Black, White and Read ticket taker.

EMILY'S MAID DU JOUR Sarah, who's sent off in search of gin.

2 YEARS How long Lane and Zack have known each other.

AMEN, SISTER FRIEND

[Emily calls Lorelai to give her the code to her new panic room.]

LORELAI: OK, Mom. Give me the code and I will keep the code safe.

EMILY: OK, here goes. Are you ready?

LORELAI: Pen is poised.

EMILY: 1, 1, 1, 1, 1.

LORELAI: Is that the code it came with?

EMILY: Well, I don't know how to change it. The men were supposed to show me, and now it's the code I'm stuck with. Did you write it down?

LORELAI: Barring an aneurysm, I think I'll remember it.

From the Editing Room 3 Making the Cut

Gilmore was hard enough to piece together with two full-time editors; during Season 5, that number was decreased by 50 percent when Raul Davalos went off to work on *The Moguls* (aka *The Amateurs*). Jill Savitt, who had originally been the one to recruit Davalos, was asked to edit the entire season herself. Sure, there were assistants getting the footage ready to edit, but after that, it was all down to her.

"The only reason it worked was because Amy trusted us and she knew that our first editor's cut would be so close to what she wanted, sometimes all she would have to do is edit it down for time. We didn't cut any dialogue out, we let that happen with her," Davalos says. Another reason why it worked is because Amy and the director were the only people the editors had to please. "It didn't have to go through a series of executive producers. Because of that, the whole process was streamlined.

"On a lot of shows, first you work with the director, then you work with the co-producer, then you work with another producer, then you have dueling executive producers. One person will give one set of notes, another person will give another set of notes, and they conflict. 'Well, so-and-so told me to take that out.' 'Well put it back in; he doesn't know what he's talking about.'

"But in our case, it never happened. Not only did we have a good idea of what Amy wanted, but she was the only one who ever sat in the room to lock the episodes with us. But it was still very difficult for one person to edit everything."

LUKE: She can have adventures and be free, she's smart. The whole world's waiting for her.
LORELAI: You're comparing Rory to Pippi Longstocking?
LUKE: Pippi is strong and independent. She can lift a horse above her head. And beat up bullies and build a hot-air balloon. She's unique, like Rory. But I guarantee you, if Pippi had met Dean, there would be no horse, no balloons. He'd drag her down to his level, spend all her gold coins and poof, like that, all her dreams would be gone.

5.6 Norman Mailer, I'm Pregnant!

First aired: Oct. 26, 2004 // Written by James Berg and Stan Zimmerman // Directed by Matthew Diamond

Sookie tries to sell author Norman Mailer on having lunch at the Dragonfly.

Determined to make an impression on Doyle now that she's officially a Yale Daily News staffer, Rory decides to expose a Yale secret society that's operated on campus since the 19th century. Meanwhile, the Dragonfly has to temporarily phase out serving lunch as a cost-cutting measure, something that Sookie takes personally and blames on Norman Mailer only ever ordering iced tea there. Just as Christopher suddenly has to face raising GG on his own, someone else discovers she's going to have another little mouth to feed.

GINCHY! Lorelai saving Christopher's sanity by helping him with GG; the girls going crazy in Richard and Emily's house since they're both gone; Rory discovering the Huntzberger link to the Life and Death Brigade in her research; just having Norman Mailer in an episode!; the final bit of intrigue over IM from Logan; and Rory telling Christopher to leave her mom alone.

NOTES *'What do you say, Ace? You in or out?'*

Lorelai's porch light has been out since Dean and Rory broke up the first time (1.16, and no jokes about Lorelai's porch light being out).

What I Kept

I have a can of Twinings tea that I took from the grocery store, that we still have—we use it little by little. It's just Twinings tea—you can go buy it in the store. But it's in the can, the unpackaged tea, which we like.

—Ted Rooney (Morey)

✱ Paris has the religion beat at the Yale Daily News, Rory is covering features. Billy Joel used to come to the Independence Inn. Doyle tells Rory that Logan (who works at the Yale Daily News—who knew?) took all of last year off and sank his father's yacht off the coast of Fiji. His father, Mitchum, owns at least 12 newspapers. Taylor installed an Icee machine at Doose's Market.

✱ Christopher returned from Seattle on business a couple of days ago to be given a note by GG's nanny from Sherry, which said she'd accepted a job in Paris after putting her career on hold for nearly two years.

✱ There's a distinct possibility that the Rabbi Barans that's changed his number twice to get Paris to leave him alone is Stars Hollow's Rabbi David Barans.

✱ Logan's grandfather, Elias Huntzberger, was a member of the Life and Death Brigade.

✱ Doyle tells Rory to go with her "gut" when pursuing stories, failing to differentiate between good story ideas and bad ones. This season and next, Rory will learn just how unreliable newspaper people's guts are when Mitchum Huntzberger shares some advice from his own (5.21).

TODAY'S CELEBRATION Well, Glenn getting his article about the reprinting of *The Anarchist's Cookbook* picked up by The New York Times is pretty impressive, but we have to give it up for...Norman Mailer at the Dragonfly. (OK, and for Sookie being pregnant...again.)

AND INTRODUCING...*The Life and Death Brigade!* In Omnia Paratus! ("Ready for anything!")

KIRK OF ALL TRADES Giant hotdog promoting lunch at the Dragonfly...in front of Luke's Diner.

EMILY'S MAID DU JOUR Unnamed, but she's good enough to fetch the girls a phone book so they can order pizza to eat at the Gilmore mansion.

70%-75% The occupancy rate at the Dragonfly Inn now that things have settled down.

'KEEP KIRK AWAY FROM THE BUSINESS' The first thing that Lorelai and Sookie agreed on when they formed their partnership.

AMEN, SISTER FRIEND

RORY: No, I'm gonna kick butt. You just wait and see.
DOYLE: You're a reporter now, Gilmore. You've gotta learn to say ass.

DOYLE: The Life and Death Brigade. Yeah, I know these guys.
RORY: Oh, you do?
DOYLE: Well, I've heard of them. They're apparently even more elusive than the Skull and Bones crowd. Of course they've never been linked to masturbating in a coffin, so I automatically like these guys better.
RORY: Well, what do you know about them?
DOYLE: Not much. Paper's tried to track them down before and we've gotten a few leads, but no one's ever gotten close enough to confirm anything. We all know they exist, but we don't know they exist. It's all just too-too. God, I hate those stupid clubs.
RORY: I want to do this story. I want to find this club, track them down, get on the inside. What do you think?
DOYLE: Go with your gut.
RORY: You said that about my downloading story. Hey, you don't trust my gut!

"The hotdog suit sucked, naturally. It was another thing that was like 'You've gotta be kidding me.'"

–SEAN GUNN (KIRK)

Behind the Scenes: Injury Parade 2

"I would say the main thing going through my mind was how much pain I was in because we did that shot over and over and over again," John Cabrera says of the scene in 5.7 where Zack carries Brian out of Lane's room over his shoulder. "In order for it to look just right, they really wanted my butt to be right there in between their faces if they were going to kiss. Kenny Ortega directed that episode and he is just a genius with choreography and blocking and staging. He wanted it to look just right, which required me to be in this really strange position over his shoulder. It ended up looking really great, but I was just in this awkward position and my stomach was jabbed into Todd's shoulder. I'm just hanging there going 'c'mon guys, hurry up, hurry up.' I was very glad that the scene was over when it finally was, but we all knew it was going to be hilarious."

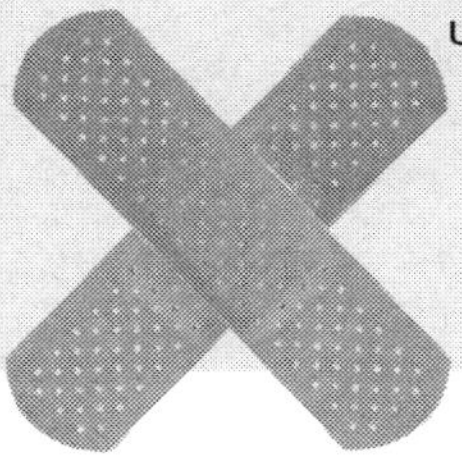

5.7 You Jump, I Jump, Jack

First aired: Nov. 2, 2004 // Written by Daniel Palladino // Directed by Kenny Ortega

Emily and Richard insist on each being "reintroduced" to Luke, now that he's dating Lorelai, with each meeting going about how you would expect. Zack and Lane have their first date, sort of, and Logan whisks Rory away to the Life and Death Brigade's big event. If her relationship with Dean wasn't looking shabby before, now its days are certainly numbered.

! GINCHY! Emily politely tearing Luke to bits at their meeting; Zack and Lane's stay-at-home (with Brian) date; Logan and Rory's "jump"; a drunk Luke calling Lorelai from the club; and Logan returning Rory's camera, complete with images of their jump together.

NOTES *'People can live a hundred years without really living for a minute. You climb up here with me, it's one less minute you haven't lived.'*

✱ Margie, the secretary that Richard was devastated to lose when he left Floyd's company (2.20), is now his secretary again.

✱ Logan's conditions for Rory to attend the event: no photos, no names, no physical descriptions of the participants or the location, and she mustn't interfere with the integrity of the event.

✱ In addition to franchising Luke's Diner, Richard has talked Luke into investing in art. He's supposed to drive to Manhattan to "look at some Diebenkorns." Though Lorelai doesn't know what those are, she and

Behind the Scenes: Shooting the LDB Event

The Life and Death Brigade event, or the "Out of Africa" scenes as many referred to it then, were shot during one day at Griffith Park, just a few minutes drive from the Warner Brothers lot in Burbank, and for two days at the Disney Ranch about 20 miles away.

"It was sort of terrifying," admits Nick Holmes, who plays the paintball marksman Robert. The first time Holmes went in front of the camera for the episode, it was shortly before 11 pm at the top of Griffith Park for an all-night shoot. "I went up and I'm walking past all the big trailers to my little one. When I walked back down to get around the crowd and to see what was up, Matt Czuchry had his guitar out and was strumming it. He was just kind of messing around, so I started singing with him and we made up a song called 'Bacon Sandwich.' Just to have that experience right away was really comforting."

After shooting the tent scenes, they relocated to the Disney Ranch for the next two nights, where they filmed the polo games, the big jump, and the human target shooting. Having spent much of his youth in Kansas entering paintball competitions, he was pleasantly surprised when Amy asked him, "'Have you ever shot a paintball gun?' Oh yeah, I'm the man," he laughs. Now, he was going to have to live up to his words.

Whatever butterflies he was battling on the drive to the Disney Ranch were temporarily dispelled when he saw what they had done with the place.

"You're surrounded by tents with Victrolas and women in ball gowns and men in tuxedos, and your job is to stand there in a tuxedo and shoot people with a paintball gun, also in tuxedos, being launched off a platform."

"You're surrounded by tents with Victrolas and women in ball gowns and men in tuxedos, and your job is to stand there in a tuxedo and shoot people with a paintball gun, also in tuxedos, being launched off a platform."

—Nick Holmes, (Robert)

Earlier, he'd tried to get some time with the paintball gun he'd be using to learn its quirks before filming, but there was no time. "So we got up there to shoot it and everybody was just like, 'Oh well, he'll be fine, he knows what he's doing.'"

At this point, everybody had been working for about 11 hours and they soon would lose the daylight.

"Amy came up, patted me on the back and said, 'Can't wait to see you shoot.' So I had the pressure of the shot, the pressure of doing well, and also thinking about what I had to do as an actor going on, all in a time crunch."

Holmes takes his first couple of shots at the target stunt people. And misses. "Amy's like, 'Don't run the camera, just let Nick practice for a second.' This is my first major television job and this is my second day, so I'm just trying to calm down. It's just a disaster and everybody's like, 'Oh Jesus, this guy's going to screw it up for everybody.'"

Finally, he began hitting his targets, "and then I just start nailing it every time."

Part of the pressure came from the fact that it was all done in one long shot that "starts in front of me, comes behind me, you see me shoot a guy or two, and comes back around in front of me again," he explains. "Every time I worked after that, that moment was what I always got remembered for."

"All that shooting, even Logan's shooting, is Nick with the paintball gun," Tanc Sade says. "Then there's one shot where he's supposed to miss and he gets the guy on the foot!"

As the inebriated Australian show-off Finn, Sade ended up on the other end of that gun, nearly. "I was really anxious to do that but they wouldn't let me. They were all stunt doubles. They built this pneumatic springboard and they had to test it out a few times to make sure it worked. Then they fired people through the air and on to a crash pad."

Sade shot his gun, said his lines, ran off camera and got changed into his formal wear with paint smears on it, and leapt onto a stretcher to be carried back through the scene. "It's literally like a 60-second turnaround."

Rory were confronted with the subject when they visited Yale alumnus Darren Springsteen (3.3).

* After her return from the big event, Rory asks her mother if she takes enough chances in her life. Though Lorelai assures her that she does, this was something she herself was worried about when Rory automatically decided she wasn't going to the Chilton formal (1.9).

* This is one of the best episodes of the series, displaying a sense of wonder that is all too rare on television.

TODAY'S CELEBRATION Lane and Zack's first date, and the 108th assembly of the Life and Death Brigade.

KIRK OF ALL TRADES Delivery guy (according to Emily).

EMILY'S MAID DU JOUR Never named, though Luke does introduce himself to her.

Behind the Scenes: Another 'All The President's Men' Moment

While Doyle yearned to become a big name in the political journalism world, actor Danny Strong rose to prominence in that arena in 2008 with the release of *Recount*, a movie he wrote for HBO about the landmark 2000 US presidential elections, starring Kevin Spacey. The movie was quickly embraced by the nation's political left and Strong found himself on a first-name basis with the real-life people who were Doyle's heroes, including former Watergate-era Washington Post editor Ben Bradlee.

"Oh yeah, we talked all night," Strong recalled of the Washington DC premiere of *Recount*, which Bradlee and his wife Sally Quinn hosted at their house. "Every superstar from the media was there. Tom Brokaw, George Stephanopoulos...the list just goes on and on. A friend of mine who's a DC reporter was there and he said he'd never been in a room with that much DC press star power. Chris Matthews, Bob Woodward, literally everybody.

"But two nights before at the correspondents dinner, I sat next to Ben Bradlee. He was fantastic. He was everything you'd expect him to be. He literally is Jason Robards from *All the Presidents Men*. He's gruff and he's fun; he's got a big personality. I turned to him and said, 'What did you think of *Recount*, Mr. Bradlee?' And he said, 'Danny, I loved it!' He just kind of growled it. And everyone comes over to him because he's Ben Bradlee. Since I was sitting next to him, he introduced me to everyone. The amount of people I got to meet that night sitting next to Ben Bradlee was just fantastic. I looked like his protégé and he would introduce me: 'This is the kid that wrote *Recount*.' That was a lot of fun."

Danny Strong on the set of *Recount*.

85 FEET The estimated height of the LDB jump.

THINGS WE'VE LEARNED Key set costumer Valerie Campbell actually took the photos that appear on Rory's camera of Bledel and Czuchry jumping from the platform.

AMEN, SISTER FRIEND

RORY: Honk if Emily Gilmore views your mind as her personal playground.

LOGAN [*before they make their jump*]: You trust me?
RORY: You jump, I jump, Jack.
LOGAN: I really should have confirmed that those potatoes were OK. [They jump.]
SETH: Oh, thank God.
LOGAN: You did good, Ace!
RORY: Once in a lifetime experience!
LOGAN: Only if you want it to be.

The Dinner Luke Makes Lorelai

—Lamb and artichoke stew

—Penne with pesto and potatoes

—Roasted garlic with rosemary focaccia

—Tomatoes stuffed with bread crumbs and goat cheese

—Ricotta cheesecake with amaretto cookies

5.8 The Party's Over

First aired: Nov. 9, 2004 // Written by Amy Sherman-Palladino // Directed by Eric Laneuville

Ah, family. No sooner does Emily discover that Rory's back together with Dean than she and Richard call a truce long enough to invite her to a "Yale alumni" event at their home, the reasons for which become all too clear to Rory. Lane and Zack are dealing with family troubles, too, as Mrs. Kim makes a discovery of her own—that they're in a relationship. And Luke, the king of cynicism when it comes to families, discovers just what he's in for now that Liz and TJ have moved to Stars Hollow.

GINCHY! Paris thinking all the older professors are lusting after her since Asher died; Richard and Emily's painfully forced phone call to Rory; Lane setting Kyon free from the idea that Mrs. Kim knows about everything she does; and the look on Lorelai's face when Rory comes home with Logan and Co.

NOTES *'They played you, kid.'*

Professor Prady is named after *Gilmore* writer Bill Prady. Emily didn't tell anybody Lorelai was pregnant until her eighth month. ("My mother kept getting numbers for fat farms from her friends.")

TODAY'S CELEBRATION Richard and Emily's "little Yale alumni event," the liberation of Kyon, and Rory and Dean's breakup (again).

EMILY'S MAID DU JOUR Unnamed.

AND HERE'S A SHOUT OUT TO OUR INTERNATIONAL FANS EMILY: Your grandfather bought me these earrings on our first trip to Denmark. He swears he bought them off the ne'er-do-well brother of the king who stole them from the queen.

THINGS WE'VE LEARNED TJ crying at Luke's after his fight with Liz is Michael DeLuise's favorite TJ scene.

AMEN, SISTER FRIEND
KYON: Mrs. Kim does not want me to watch the television!
LANE: And how would she know?
KYON: Because there's a little machine in the television set that will tell her what I watch!

Behind the Scenes Fun With Australians 1

Today we know Tanc Sade as Finn, but when he first interviewed for *Gilmore Girls*, he'd only been in LA a little over a month, and auditioned for Logan. He and Matt Czuchry had the same agent then.

"He's gotta be one of the sweetest guys I've ever met," Sade says. "They'd wanted him on that show for years. What had happened was they had to present a few options to Warner Brothers, so they brought me in."

The day before Sade had arrived at an audition for another show, only to discover four other guys who looked the same as he did, right down to the navy blue T-shirt, jeans and flip-flops he was wearing. "I looked like a clone.

"The next day I was like, OK, I learned my lesson." Sorting through the clothes in his car (see "Tanc, Where are You Living Today?' under 5.3 for the story on *that*), he found a green Pennywise T-shirt and thought he was good to go. Off he went to his *Gilmore Girls* interview. "And I went into that room and there were five other guys, *including* Matt Czuchry, that were wearing blue jeans and green T-shirts."

Sade says Amy and casting directors Mara Casey and Jami Rudofsky were probably "in the room with Matt for about 45 minutes, and then the other guys they brought in for his role, we were all out within about eight minutes."

As he was leaving the audition, another guy with a green T-shirt was coming in to read for the part of Logan. He stuck his head back in the audition room, dropped the American accent he usually used for auditions, and in an Australian twang said, "Guys, you're not gonna believe this..."

LANE: Ha!

KYON: What ha?

LANE: That machine does not exist.

KYON: It does not?

LANE: Nope. It took me 15 years to figure it out, but that's the truth.

KYON: So she cannot know?

LANE: She also cannot smell fast food on you even after you've showered.

KYON: She can't?

LANE: And she can't tell how many times you've opened your *Bible* by staring at your palm.

KYON: My head spins!

LANE: And you don't have to hand out all those religious flyers she gives you. Just post enough of them around her regular route home and she'll think the job is done.

KYON: I think I need to lie down.

LANE: It's a whole new world, Kyon. A world I fought long and hard to figure out, and I'm willing to pass all my knowledge on to you.

Susane Lee (Kyon)

EMILY: Lorelai, I am tired. And the caterers have caked the floor with something sticky and I don't have time for this. We want more for her, period. Now obviously it is too late for you but it is not too late for Rory, and we are going to make sure that she has the life she deserves.

5.9 Emily Says 'Hello'

First aired: Nov. 16, 2004 // Written by Rebecca Rand Kirshner // Directed by Kenny Ortega

Rory has convinced her mother to help get Richard and Emily back together, which fails miserably when Emily decides she's ready to date one of the many men who have expressed interest in her at the club over the years. When Christopher has lunch with Lorelai at the Dragonfly at her request, Rory lets him have it with both barrels, certain he's going to wreck things between her mother and Luke. She may be on to something as Luke wrestles with a bit of jealousy after Lorelai tells him she had dinner with Rory's dad.

GINCHY! Emily telling Lorelai she's ready to date; the town tricking Jackson into chairing the town meeting; Emily's final moments on screen realizing that she's not ready to date after all.

NOTES *'Well, all I know is I helloed him today and now he's taking me to dinner.'*

TJ destroyed the bathroom pipes at their new place after getting mad at a towel rack he was putting up. Michel keeps a written description of all the guests going back to the Independence Inn days.

TJ gave up being a jealous man after it landed him in jail twice, and he realized he couldn't afford any more bail money.

A pretty plodding episode to get through, rather like Friday night dinner at the Gilmore house.

TODAY'S CELEBRATION Emily's first date in nearly 40 years and Ramadan (at least Paris is observing it by fasting).

OY WITH THE ____, ALREADY! Jackson's annoyance with being town selectman; this gag wore itself out about five minutes after he was elected. Sookie's pregnancy-fueled food cravings also are pretty grating.

AMEN, SISTER FRIEND

RORY [*about Christopher*]: It's completely true. He wants you back, and then he disappears or Sherry gets pregnant or he loses his job or he just takes off—whatever. No good reason necessary. And it's been like this forever, and you just let him do it. You can't help it.
LORELAI: Rory, come on.
RORY: You can't just break free of him.
LORELAI: What are you talking about?
RORY: You're engaged to Max, and then suddenly you're not.
LORELAI: Christopher had nothing to do with Max.
RORY: Who was the person you were calling from your bachelorette party?
LORELAI: I was drunk. I tried to call Abe Vigoda, too, if you remember.
RORY: You're just always waiting for him to get himself together.
LORELAI: No, no, hon. I'm not always waiting for him. There have been times when, yes, it would have been nice to actually be with the father of my kid, but not now. I'm with Luke completely.

TJ: We got, like, a rhythm, a groove thing. We can survive in the woods together, start a new civilization, if need be.
LUKE: I think you'd need a woman for that.

"The thing is Lauren understands camera so well. I started out as a dancer—we had blind obedience, that's how we're taught. Lauren would say, 'Why are we shooting this again, because I know you're going to cut to a two shot over there.' And you'd go, 'Jeez, she's right. Of course that's what they're going to do, so there's no reason to do this master again.' She gets it all. I've never seen anybody who was so on top of it."

–KELLY BISHOP (EMILY)

Making an Episode 8 Wardrobe

Normally on a television series, a costume designer will put outfits together the day before a shoot, says key set costumer Valerie Campbell. But most of the time on *Gilmore Girls*, "they'd be getting the scripts right then and there, so [costume designer Brenda Maben] and I would go through our outlines and breakdowns, compare notes, and we'd really double-check each other."

Usually wardrobe will get to work about 4:30 in the morning at the beginning of the week, and end up getting into work on Friday at about 5 in the afternoon, staying up through the night until 7 or 8 Saturday morning, says Campbell, who started *Gilmore* on the last day of shooting for 1.10, and stayed until the end of the series.

The day wardrobe receives the next episode's script, Campbell and costume designer Maben carefully go through it together to see what types of clothes are going to be needed. While there's a certain degree of latitude, so much of what happens in the episode will dictate the types of clothes needed. Is Rory going to a formal dance? Will we see Lorelai in her role as inn manager? Is the Life and Death Brigade up to some sort of sartorial mischief?

Once they know what they need, it's off to the studio's Costume Design Center, which is reasonably close to Midwest Street (where the exteriors of Stars Hollow are shot) on the Warner Brothers backlot, but a pretty healthy bike ride from the soundstages where the interiors are filmed. (Campbell's zipped across the lot by bike more than once to get clothes to the *Gilmore* stars in time for their scenes.)

The main part of the costume center consists of an enormous warehouse filled floor-to-ceiling with costumes from previous Warner Brothers productions, separated by style and time period. The *Gilmore* gang will either rent the outfits they need from here or hit LA's funky shops looking for alternatives. If they still can't find what they're looking for, they might brave LA's traffic to hit its fabric district, where dozens of stores offer every type of fabric imaginable. Once they find what they're looking for, they will make clothes from scratch if necessary.

Once the clothes have been selected for the episode, they schedule quick fittings with the actors before sending the costumes to the studio's tailoring department.

Most shows being shot at Warner Brothers have their own "cage," a chain-link-fence-enclosed area in a large bunker similar to some of the larger self-storage units. Here clothes being used for recent episodes will be stored until they're needed. Clothing that will be used on the episode currently being shot will be taken from here to the wardrobe trailer, which will be set up a short distance from the actors' trailers and the soundstages.

Maben will handle most of the clothes shopping, put the outfits together, and Campbell will steam and set them, then maintain the look of the outfits when they're on set. She's also in charge of continuity, which can be its own little nightmare considering the sheer number of characters and the number of scenes they have to get through in a scant eight-day cycle.

A few other people work in wardrobe, including Cesha Ventre, who handles Graham's wardrobe needs exclusively. "So we all worked together as a team," Campbell says. "But that show was seat of your pants."

TJ: Oh, right. OK, maybe Liz could come, except we couldn't share her 'cause she's your sister and that's a bad way to start a new civilization.
LUKE: How about you and Liz go start a new civilization? I'll stay here in this one.
TJ: No, come on. We could solve this. OK, Lorelai could come. And now *her* we could share.

5.10 But Not As Cute As Pushkin

First aired: Nov. 30, 2004 // Written by Amy Sherman-Palladino // Directed by Michael Zinberg

Headmaster Charleston entrusts Anna, a Chilton student with aspirations of Yale, to Rory's care as she shows her what it's like to go to the Ivy League school. Rory tells Logan she doesn't like the way he's been acting, crushes Marty with the use of the dreaded word "friend," and deals with the fact that Paris and Doyle are now a couple. In Stars Hollow, Lorelai tries to do a nice thing for Luke and ends up pissing him off, on his notorious "dark day," no less.

GINCHY! Luke explaining his "dark day" to Lorelai; Logan, Colin and Finn's prank in Prof. Bell's class; Paris and Doyle bonding over news about the skeletons of small hunters being found during their speed-dating session; Richard and Rory getting Logan back for his prank with one of their own.

NOTES *'Dinner whenever you want. Random sex whenever you want. I can't wait to go to college!'*

Paris' life coach, Terrence, has been in court-ordered rehab. The first Lorelai hears of Logan is when Richard asks Rory about him in front of her. He reminds Lorelai that Mitchum Huntzberger's gone to many of their Christmas parties and that Logan's mother is on the pediatric hospital committee with Emily.

Special commendation must go to Alexis Bledel for memorizing the mouthfuls of Yale history she spouts as she shows Anna around campus.

Behind the Scenes — Fun With Australians 2

A couple of days after auditioning for Logan (and slipping into his native Australian brogue), Tanc Sade's agent told him *Gilmore Girls* had written a part especially for him as Logan's friend. But they wanted him to be Australian.

"And I naively said, 'No, I don't want to play an Australian on American television," he remembers. "I don't want to get known as being Australian."

But Amy & Dan were adamant, he had to be Australian.

"I sat on that for a few days, which again—I was living in my car. Potentially turning down this work, this break on American TV because you wouldn't play an Australian, people thought it was pretty silly. So I caved and did the first two episodes."

Bio Kathleen Wilhoite (Liz Danes)

While Carole King is clearly a singer-songwriter who was dabbling in acting as music store manager Sophie Bloom, it's hard to say if Kathleen Wilhoite is a musician who also acts, or an actor who also plays music. The only certainty, according to many of her *Gilmore* co-stars: she's a trip to have around on and off the set.

Growing up in Santa Barbara, Calif., Wilhoite got into music early, joining the backup singers at a performance of The Carpenters at the Santa Barbara County Bowl when she was only in the third grade. After high school, she enrolled in USC Drama School, and launched her acting career just two months later, making appearances on the major TV series of the '80s, '90s and through to the next millennium: *Family Ties, The Jeffersons, Fame, Twin Peaks, LA Law* and *ER*.

Since leaving Stars Hollow, she's popped up on everything from *Grey's Anatomy* and *Without a Trace* to *Criminal Minds* and *The Mentalist*. Her albums include *Shiva* and *Pitch Like a Girl*.

Rory keeps detailed diaries. When Kirk was in 7th grade, Luke knocked the books out of his hand. (Everybody did; Kirk wore a cape to school.)

For 15 years, Luke's been paying rent on Mrs. Thompson's garage to house the boat his father was building. (His father had paid her for 20 years before that.) Presumably this is where Luke hid Jess' car when he stole it (3.18, 4.12).

Prof. Bell is discussing Joseph Campbell's *The Power of Myth*, the same series Rory and Paris are obsessed with (4.17), and arguably a work that could as easily apply to the heroes' journey undertaken by Lorelai and Rory. This is now twice that Logan has pretended to be in love with Rory (5.8). And "fro yo" returns (4.12)!

TODAY'S CELEBRATION The 40th anniversary of Miss Patty's off-Broadway debut, Paris and Doyle's "first time" and Luke's "dark day."

KIRK OF ALL TRADES Purveyor of Yesterday, Today and Tomorrow bath and shower decals. ("Yesterday's retro designs in today's fashion colors with tomorrow's traction technology.")

NOV 30 Luke's "dark day," the anniversary of his father's death.

AMEN, SISTER FRIEND

ANNA [*about Logan*]: He's cute.

RORY: Yes he is. But not as cute as Pushkin.

What I Kept

They made me these gloves, and knitted them for me and everything. I wanted them and I didn't get to keep them. I've got some pictures like everybody else, but that's about it.

—Olivia Hack (Tana)

'Previously On...'

Though many viewers assumed that those "Previously on *Gilmore Girls*" episode recaps that started off most episodes were there simply to catch us all up on the various story lines, that wasn't really the case, says editor Raul Davalos. "If a show was running a little short, we'd always have a recap. If the show was on time, Amy wouldn't do a recap. Rarely did it happen, as far as I remember, where we were on time in an episode yet we had to take out 30 seconds to make room for a recap."

FINN [*as policeman at the end of the boys' prank*]: All right, that's enough! Break it up, you two! Rory Gilmore, you should be ashamed of yourself, toying with these boys like this! They used to have pride! They used to have dignity! They used to have balls! Dammit Gilmore, give them back their balls.

RORY: I have no words.
LOGAN: It was just a joke.
RORY: Oh no, wait. I found some. Jerk, ass, arrogant, inconsiderate, mindless, frat boy, lowlife, buttface miscreant.
LOGAN: Buttface miscreant?
RORY: Why would you do something like that?
LOGAN: I'm sorry, buttface miscreant?
RORY: Here I am, trying to show Anna what college life is really like.
LOGAN: That *is* what college life is really like.

LUKE [*discovering his father's boat in Lorelai's garage*]: You thought about you. You thought about you and how you'd feel. You didn't think about me or the fact that I said I wanted to get rid of this damn boat. I mean I said it, Lorelai. I said it, you heard it and you ignored it.
LORELAI: Because I didn't want you to–
LUKE: You have no respect for what I wanted! This was my dad. This was his boat and this decision was mine. This was not yours!
LORELAI: I know.
LUKE: This is who I am. I don't want to hang onto things or stare at things.
LORELAI: Except my horoscope, which is absolutely the wrong thing to bring up right now. I'm sorry.
LUKE: I'm getting out of here.
LORELAI: No, I'm sorry. Please, just stay and yell at me.
LUKE: Why? What's the point? You don't listen to anything I say, anyhow.

5.11 Women of Questionable Morals

First aired: Jan. 25, 2005 // Written by Daniel Palladino // Directed by Matthew Diamond

Stars Hollow is adding a historical harlot to its annual Revolutionary War reenactment. It's also the first snow of the season, so Lorelai's gone all doe eyed, until she's forced to face the negative effect snow is having on her new inn and her friends. When a long-haired Jack Russell terrier enters their lives, Richard and Emily call a truce to their predicament, which is more than Christopher can get from Rory, despite his best efforts. With his own father desperately ill, he realizes just how important it is for him to make things right with Rory. When Straub finally dies, Rory realizes whatever faults her father has, he's still a human being.

GINCHY! The harlot tryouts for the reenactment (and Kirk's constant pimping of Lulu); and Luke setting up an ice rink to help Lorelai recapture her love of snow.

NOTES *'Me and snow, we're through!'*

If you're looking for the magical essence of *Gilmore Girls*' appeal, you will find it in little details like Lorelai's wide-eyed obsession with the first snow of the season (1.8). Notice that she can only allow herself to delight in it when her life is relatively stable. (In 4.11, the girls are too busy to mark the first snow of the season.)

However good natured Lorelai's night of drinking tequila with Christopher was, keeping it from Luke is the first step toward torpedo-

Luke reintroduces Lorelai to the magic of snow.

ing a relationship that has only just begun.

Gilmore's dark turn, which began with Rory losing her virginity to Dean (4.22), gains momentum here with Lorelai keeping secrets from Luke, and the sudden collapse of Richard and Emily's truce with the reclaiming of the dog, Princess. Things are only going to get darker from here.

TODAY'S CELEBRATION Revolutionary War reenactment.

KIRK OF ALL TRADES The heroic harlot of Stars Hollow (filling in for a sick Lulu).

AMEN, SISTER FRIEND

TAYLOR: A local historian uncovered new evidence of Stars Hollow's participation in the Revolution. Apparently an English battalion was awaiting the return of their commanding general with plans for a big battle. Our soldiers caught wind of this and blocked the high road so that the general had to travel by the lower road, through town, to reach his troops.
LUKE: So, they kidnapped him.
TAYLOR: No, they were much slyer than that. They had a brave lady of the town use her wiles to draw the general to her rooms and keep him occupied. That delayed the general's arrival, which allowed Lafayette the opportunity to ambush the waiting British troops.
LUKE: A hooker stopped a battle.

LORELAI: I am with you now, buddy, a hundred percent.
LUKE: With me on what?
LORELAI: Snow is nothing but annoying icy frozen water stuff that falls out of the sky at inconvenient times. It's Mother Nature's icy "Screw you, Lorelai Gilmore." It's just stupid stuff you have to shovel out of the way so customers can get into the inn. It's the stuff that melts and leaks through your roof! It's the stuff that stalls your car, it's the stuff that buries your car–
[Snow starts falling again.]
LORELAI: Oh no! No! Don't even try to make up with me now! You and me are through! You stupid—hate you!

What I Kept

I got to keep my glasses. I was very excited about that. Well, what happened with my original glasses was they ended up getting lost, so they had to rebuild a pair. I think some people ended up getting switched, like assistant to props or the actual props person, but the other pair was lost as well. And so they rebuilt another pair and I got to keep those. So that was really cool.

—Vanessa Marano (April)

LORELAI [*as the kids narrate the reenactment*]: Children should shoot us for what we make them do.

5.12 Come Home

First aired: Feb. 1, 2005 // Written by Jessica Queller // Directed by Kenny Ortega

After seeing publicity photos of herself and the band, Lane decides it's time to ditch her glasses, but Zack and Mrs. Kim both hate her new look. Michel is on the trail of a bed mussing, Toblerone-eating rogue employee, and Emily and Richard finally resolve their differences. Now if only Rory could get somewhere with the increasingly intriguing Logan.

GINCHY! Lorelai knowing how to fix Luke's oven because she read the owner's manual the other night when she couldn't sleep; Zack's attachment to Lane's glasses; the band at Mrs. Kim's, particularly Brian and Kyon; Lorelai and Sookie watching *Dark Shadows* at the inn; and Zack and Mrs. Kim bonding over Lane's old look.

NOTES *'Seems inevitable, doesn't it?'*

The shattered state Mitchum Huntzberger leaves Doyle in (because Logan hasn't had a byline in the Yale Daily News all year) is our first indication of just what a son of a bitch Logan's father can be. The detente between Richard and Emily, begun last episode thanks to the dog, ends in a reconciliation.

Richard discovers that his firm's attorney, Simon McLane, dated Emily (5.9). When he finally confronts Emily about it (after hitting her car), she tells him nothing happened, which is exactly what he told her about him and Pennilyn Lott, finally bringing that ugly chapter of their relationship to a close.

Like Kirk, Kyon continues to bring delight completely disproportional to her time on screen.

As subtle as a hammer blow, Emily still points out something that's been glaringly obvious from the beginning—Christopher is an extremely weak individual, but he also has the elder Gilmores' complete support as a partner for Lorelai.

The Extent of the Dragonfly's Sexual Harassment Seminar

"Sexual harassment is bad, so no one touch anyone in any funny places unless specifically asked." Oh, and "Don't touch Michel."

Brian's Penchant for Korean

Brian's transformation from mild-mannered American bass player into Korean-in-training begins here, and ends with Mrs. Kim sending him off to live with a Korean family (7.7). In this episode, he seems to know a great deal of Korean.

"They gave me a CD a couple of days before we were shooting that," John Cabrera says. "I just put the CD in my car and all I'm doing is listening to those words over and over and over again. There were, of course, some Koreans on set, so every chance I could get, while they were lighting a scene or whatnot, I'm standing with the Koreans going, 'Is this how I say it?' I think at one point somebody is telling me to say something and someone else comes up to me and says, 'No, don't say that, that's a bad word. If you say it like that, it's a really, really bad word.' I was like, 'Are you kidding me? Somebody please tell me exactly how to say this, because I'm not going to say something that the Korean community is going to be offended by.'"

TODAY'S CELEBRATION The Dragonfly Inn's first official sexual harassment seminar, Lunar New Year dinner at Mrs. Kim's house, and the reconciliation of Richard and Emily.

KIRK OF ALL TRADES Hotel and kitchen help at the Dragonfly (though nobody actually hired him).

EMILY'S MAID DU JOUR Unnamed.

OY WITH THE ___, ALREADY! Miss Celine!

AMEN, SISTER FRIEND

ZACK [*about Lane's lack of eyeglasses*]: You don't look like you.
LANE: Yes I do. It's just me, my face, without being impeded by a foreign plastic object.
ZACK: But you're the first smart girl I've ever gone out with, and the glasses are a big part of that.
LANE: Well, my IQ is still the same. Contacts don't change that.
ZACK: But you lose that initial impact. Now people will have to talk to you for a few minutes to figure out that you're smart.
LANE: Well then, that's what they'll have to do.
ZACK: OK. I'll try to get used to it.
LANE: Yeah. And you will.
CUSTOMER: I'm sorry, am I supposed to eat my soup without a spoon?
ZACK: Of course she doesn't think that, OK? She's really smart, she's just not wearing her glasses!

EMILY: All right. I'll come straight to the point, Christopher. Now, I have known you a long time. I watched you grow up. You were a charming boy. A weak but charming boy. And to be completely honest, I never thought much of you. I still don't.
CHRIS: Wow. That's great of you to come by and share that with me.
EMILY: However, you have good breeding. You come from an impeccable family and you love Lorelai. You've always loved Lorelai. You would've married her when she got pregnant. I know that. And you would have married her if that girlfriend of yours hadn't gotten pregnant with this. I know that, too. Lorelai's in a relationship now, did you know that?
CHRIS: Yes, I know that.

EMILY: He owns a diner. He's a divorcee. He's uneducated, he's not a proper stepfather for Rory and he's completely unsuitable for Lorelai. My daughter is stubborn but she's capable of greatness. And watching her settle down with a man who could hold her back from that is unacceptable. You, at least, won't hold her back.

CHRIS: OK, Emily, I'm very confused by this speech of yours, and GG needs to be fed.

EMILY: She's getting serious with this man. I've seen it with my own eyes. If you want a chance with Lorelai, you had better do something. And you had better do something now. Timing has never been your strong point, Christopher. You should see if you can change that.

5.13 Wedding Bell Blues (100th episode!)

First aired: Feb. 8, 2005 // Written and directed by Amy Sherman-Palladino

Emily's maid of honor and Richard's best man (Lorelai and Rory to you and me) are forced to give Emily a spur-of-the-moment bachelorette party. Soon, the big day of the vow renewal arrives, bringing love to the couple of honor, and underscoring for Lorelai, Luke, Christopher and Rory their own unsettled social lives. When Logan and Rory are caught during a passionate

Behind the Scenes: Lane's Glasses

Zack's flipout over Lane not wearing her glasses began with a simple suggestion made by Keiko Agena.

"I actually mentioned to Amy at one point, what do you think about me not wearing my glasses? And she said, 'Aw, I'll think about it.' We did a thing where Lane takes off her glasses and Zack doesn't like her without them. After that, apparently when he wasn't around I wouldn't wear my glasses, and when he was around I would wear them, and that's how it went for a little bit. And then I think toward the end I just started wearing them all the time."

Yet Agena's glasses were not just a prop. "I have a light prescription, so it was a little blurry. Those were just my glasses I auditioned with, so it became the character's glasses. We just got duplicates of them and kept them around for all those times," she says. After a moment's thought: "I should've gotten those back! Why don't I have my glasses back? I just thought of that now!"

moment, Christopher comes clean about his own plans to be with Lorelai and who, exactly, has been telling him he will get her in the end.

! GINCHY! Emily drunk at her last-minute bachelorette party; Lorelai rearranging the wedding seating chart while Emily's asleep (getting the wedding planner fired in the process); Rory in her best man tux and awesome hairstyle; Rory taking the initiative with Logan after hearing Christopher's story about how Lorelai kissed him first when they were kids; Luke, Lorelai and Christopher catching Logan and Rory together; and Christopher telling them the real reason he came to the wedding.

NOTES *'You and me, we're done.'*

* Luke's begun work on his father's boat, which is still in Lorelai's garage. Emily greets Lorelai's *Absolutely Fabulous* reference ("sweetie darling") with "Isn't she hilarious? I never have any idea what she's talking about, but she's so entertaining! Like a chimp." This is probably as close as Amy & Dan come to describing their own obscure wit on *Gilmore Girls*.

* Lorelai's brief tirade about rich people like her parents and the Life and Death Brigade is quickly cut short by Rory who, infatuated by the wealthy Logan, insists that she never said anything negative about the LDB in the piece she wrote about them for the Yale Daily News (5.7). Yet after a few bad experiences with the young Huntzberger, she will write an extremely scathing article later on about rich people (7.8).

* As if to underscore what Lorelai said about rich people to Rory, Emily and Richard both fail to notice Luke's presence until he speaks. Lorelai finally tells Luke about comforting Christopher after his dad died, but only because she's afraid he's going to find out anyway. All those who piled on the Luke Danes hate wagon for the way he kept April a secret from her, take note of where this behavior all began.

* "Marry Me Bill," Richard's choice of music for his first dance with

"[Lauren] had a lot on her shoulders there. Of course if she was feeling her way around in terms of how much clout she had within that structure, I think she probably had more than she ever realized."

-KELLY BISHOP (EMILY)

Emily at the reception, contains the lines "but am I ever gonna see my wedding day," a hint at what is to come for Luke and Lorelai (6.22).

✱ While they dance, Rory asks Logan why he hasn't asked her out; he tells her he doesn't do commitment. She proceeds to tell him that she doesn't want commitment, that she just wants to have fun, "no strings attached." Remember this, Rory, when you get what you asked for (5.17).

✱ After a half-season of merely good episodes, this one reminds us why we hung on through those awkward moments.

TODAY'S CELEBRATION Rory and Logan's first kiss and Richard and Emily's second wedding...on their 40th anniversary.

9 Lorelai's boot size.

4 MONTHS How long Luke and Lorelai have been an item.

14 How old Lorelai and Christopher were when they had their first kiss (Lorelai just wanted to see what it would be like).

YOU'VE ENTERED EMILYLAND When a woman gives birth to a crack baby, you do not buy her a puppy.

OY WITH THE ___, ALREADY! Yet again, poor Christopher is saddled with awkwardly saying the name of the show: "Who could not like being kissed by a Gilmore girl?"

AMEN, SISTER FRIEND

LORELAI [*to Rory*]: ...I do know that Dinky Shaw is going to be sitting next to her ex-husband's daughter from his second marriage. This is the daughter whose conception *caused* the second marriage. And everybody should bring an extra roll of film.

LORELAI: These people live in a universe where they feel entitled to get what they want, when they want it, and they don't care who's in their way. I hate that world. Vapid. Selfish. It's like that Life and Death Brigade you wrote about.
RORY: What do you mean?
LORELAI: You know, like a bunch of selfish rich kids, the children of entitlement, blowing off school, drinking for days. Spending thousands on a

stupid and potentially dangerous stunt, knowing full well that they're not going to get in trouble 'cause daddy is important. They're all the same.

RORY: They're not all the same. You don't even know them. And that's not what I wrote. I didn't say all those things about them. You're just reading whatever you want to into it.

LORELAI: OK, sorry.

RORY: Just because you have money, that doesn't automatically make you a jerk.

RICHARD: Focus, please?

LORELAI: I am a camera.

RICHARD [*about 3-year-old Lorelai during her ear infection*]: And so, it fell to Emily to sit with her all night long. She tried everything to calm her down. Finally, she found a song that seemed to soothe her. It was a popular song on the radio and it soon became Emily's favorite. Of course, it drove me crazy. Some woman complaining about how she wanted to marry a man named Bill. Not exactly Cole Porter. Emily would tease me, saying, 'If only your name was Bill, then this could be our song.' Well, Emily, for tonight, and tonight only, my name is Bill, and this is our song.

Gypsy's Night Out

"I think for some reason Gypsy really liked getting to go to the bachelorette party for Emily," Rose Abdoo says. "To Gypsy, it was like 'This is a super special day because I get to go to Lorelai's house.' I think that Gypsy had a little crush on Lorelai, she just wanted to be around her. So when I got to stand on Lorelai's porch, I was like, 'Wow, I'm really at her house.' And I love the line when she goes, 'OK, the party's for Emily.' And I go, 'Great, who's Emily?' Gypsy showed up to the party but she didn't even know why she was there. She just thought, 'Wow, a chance to go in a house and be with people would be fun.'"

5.14 Say Something

First aired: Feb. 15, 2005 // Written and directed by Daniel Palladino

No question about it; Lorelai screwed up royally when she failed to tell Luke that she'd spent the night comforting Christopher over the loss of his father. But Chris' drunken outburst at the wedding last episode spun this whole thing into the unthinkable: the end of Lorelai's brief relationship with Luke. While Lorelai lays in bed, devastated, Rory (with Logan's help) rushes to her side and takes care of her as best she can while Taylor and the town choose sides.

GINCHY! Ceaser dancing alone in the diner; the whole pink ribbons for Lorelai and blue for Luke madness; the way that Rory, Lane and Logan (via Frank the driver) rally to her aid when things fall apart; Luke dropping everything to make sure Lorelai's all right, and Lorelai releasing him from any obligation he feels on her part.

NOTES *'He could have been the one.'*

For a guy who never, ever watched movies (4.5), Luke now turns to them for solace.

Up till now, Dan's name on a script seldom translated into an episode that tugged at the heartstrings, but this one marks an amazing turning point for him and the heart of *Gilmore*.

TODAY'S CELEBRATION The pancake breakfast for the little girls and their dolls at the Dragonfly, and the (first) breakup of Luke and Lorelai.

KIRK OF ALL TRADES Black, White and Read movie theater guy.

META, META, META Commenting on an old movie Luke's watching, Lorelai says, "Man, they sure talked fast in these things." This is another nod to *Gilmore's* own penchant for rapid-fire wit, which was inspired, in part, by those old Hepburn-Tracy movies.

THINGS WE'VE LEARNED When Ted Rooney and his wife adopted a child from Ethiopia, Rooney needed a work reference, he says. "I don't really know that many people closely that I work with, so Sally [Struthers] was the first person I thought of. She said she would do the paperwork only if she could be Abe's fairy godmother, so she's been designated his fairy godmother."

AMEN, SISTER FRIEND

PARIS [*after Rory wakes her*]: Bite me.
RORY: Were there any messages for me?
PARIS: Yes. Four other people called and asked that you bite me.

LORELAI: Luke, I am all in. I'm all in. Please trust me. Let me show you what a great girlfriend I can be. But I can't wait. We can't wait. I need to know what you're thinking right now.
LUKE: Fine. You want to know what I'm thinking right now? That I can't be in this relationship. It's too much.

LANE [*to Rory, both in the limo*]: My compliments to your moxie!
RORY: Oh, I've got moxie coming out of my ears today. [A car honks.]
LANE: They honking at us?
RORY: They better not be. Frank, are they honking at us?

FRANK: I believe so.

RORY: Oh, I am in no mood for this. We are depressed! [Rory pops her head out of the sunroof.] We'll move when we move, so stop-!

[She sees Luke's been the one honking at them.]

LUKE: Oh. Sorry.

RORY [to Luke]: I'm not usually in a limo.

5.15 Jews and Chinese Food

First aired: Feb. 22, 2005 // Written by Amy Sherman-Palladino // Directed by Matthew Diamond

Two weeks after the disastrous post-wedding misery, Lorelai is trying to get on with her life, even transforming her garage into a pretty place for her to spend some alone time, now that Luke has taken his boat out of there. When she and Luke get pulled into helping out with the elementary school's production of Fiddler on the Roof, *they both keep it together for the sake of the kids. Meanwhile, Marty bears his soul to Rory, who makes her preference known.*

! GINCHY! Paris and Doyle, the beginning of an awe-inspiring double act; Luke working with the kids; Lorelai blasting Luke over the way he took his boat back; and pretty much every scene between Rory and Marty.

NOTES *'Little by little it's getting easier to pretend it's easier, which means easier must be right around the corner.'*

✱ Lorelai's now having her breakfast at Weston's (though no one there appreciates her quirkiness). This is the first mention of Paris taking krav maga, but we won't know more about that until later. Christopher sent Rory an e-mail detailing his side of the unpleasantness. Luke snuck his boat out of Lorelai's garage and now has it parked in front of the diner. Crazy Carrie Duncan is the director of the play. Doyle shares an apartment with three roommates. Logan spent a year at a boarding school in Andover, Mass.

3RD GRADE What Lulu teaches at Stars Hollow Elementary School.

3 OR 4 The number of lesbians Luke tells Damon he knows (he's waiting for confirmation on one).

What *Gilmore* Means to Me

As a divorced, single mother, I raised my only daughter on my own. I used to watch *Gilmore Girls* with her, and found the relationships to be some of the best on TV.

My relationship with my daughter was fraught with pain, guilt and deep emotional problems. My daughter was hospitalized many times for depression and I struggled to raise her the best I knew how. When my daughter went to live in a residential facility for over two years, I had plenty of time to reevaluate my life. *Gilmore Girls* became more than a TV show, it became my salvation. I found myself engrossed in the wonderfully complex relationships and gained such comfort in the humor. I made the decision to change the way I treated my daughter. She knew that I loved her and that I would support her through all of the hard times. And just as importantly, I knew that we would be OK. *Gilmore Girls* has taught me so many life lessons, the greatest being to live passionately, love unconditionally and laugh often.

—Lori D., *California*

TODAY'S CELEBRATION Stars Hollow's first Botox party (courtesy of Miss Patty and Babette), Rory and Marty's Marx Brothers film festival night, possibly Rory and Logan's first time (it's never quite clear what happened at the wedding); and the Stars Hollow Elementary School's production of *Fiddler on the Roof.*

KIRK OF ALL TRADES Tevye in *Fiddler on the Roof.*

AMEN, SISTER FRIEND

LORELAI [*to Rory about Richard's possible involvement with the Christopher thing*]: No honey, honestly, the whole thing reeks of Emily. I mean, not that I think he would have discouraged it, but I'm pretty sure she's the one who poisoned the apple and gave it to Dopey to bring to the party.

5.16 So...Good Talk

First aired: March 1, 2005 // Written by Lisa Randolph // Directed by Jamie Babbit

While Luke is taking his frustration over his messed up love life out on his customers, Sookie tries to take Lorelai out for a night of wild fun, and Rory weathers her first Friday night dinner with her grandparents since all the ugliness began. When that ends badly, she tells her mom that she and Logan are now a couple. Not happy with how things have turned out, Emily goes straight to the source of what she sees as the problem: Luke.

Character Sketch 'How Good Should I be?'

This was the question that stumped Sean Gunn when he first discovered that Kirk was going to be playing Tevye in the school-age production of *Fiddler on the Roof*. "Kirk is already kind of a cartoon, and now I'm going to be trying to play a cartoon within a cartoon," Gunn says. "The question was how much should I be sending up how bad Kirk was at doing this? And of course the answer was that I was already bad enough at doing it, I could just do my best and that would still be pretty bad."

Not that he arrived at this decision completely on his own. In fact, this was the only time that Gunn decided to go to another actor for advice. Like many other members of the cast, he "went to Ed Herrmann, who is the actor you'd go to for advice because he's the best. His advice was extremely simple and extremely right, which was just go for it. Have Kirk do his best. So that's what I did. Of course it ends up looking totally ridiculous, but that song that I sing, I'm singing my best. (I can't sing)."

GINCHY! Luke flinging a complaining customer out of the diner and Kirk savoring the horrible food he's been making; Lorelai hanging up on Emily over and over again; Rory blowing up at Emily; Lorelai and Richard switching from an impassioned personal squabble to insurance talk; Lane's sudden realization that she can't have sex with Zack until they're married; and Emily saying her peace to Luke.

NOTES *'This isn't you, this attitude of yours. This is your mother.'*

Last time, it was Rory figuring out that Lorelai was broke from starting the inn. Now Lorelai knows that Rory's broke because of a dearth of jobs at Yale. Richard and Emily brought back a copy of *Leaves of Grass* in Greek for Rory from their honeymoon trip.

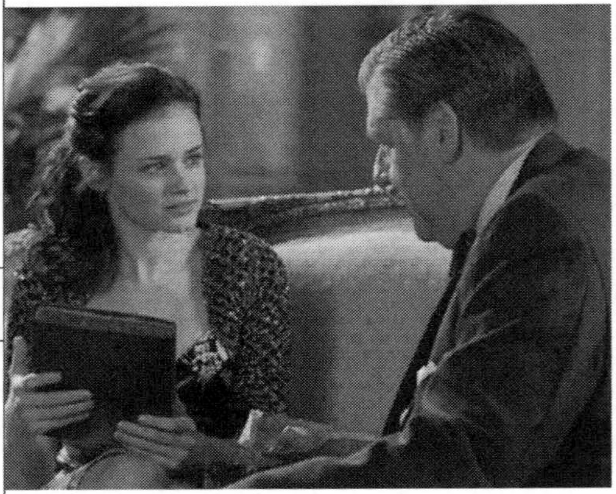

Rory's cold reaction to Emily is in sharp contrast to her enthusiasm toward Richard this episode.

Lane and Zack's sex problems begin here, and only get worse after they're married (7.2).

TODAY'S CELEBRATION Spring break, the return of Richard and Emily from their honeymoon, and the reconciliation of Luke and Lorelai.

YOU'VE ENTERED EMILYLAND Laundry day. Everything young people do sounds like fun to me.

EMILY'S MAID DU JOUR Eliza, who found the first descent strawberries of the season for strawberry shortcake.

AUG. 14 The date Sookie sets for her and Lorelai to go off and party down.

7 How old Lane was when she started listening to rock music.

AMEN, SISTER FRIEND

LORELAI [*to Richard*]: Luke and I have broken up, dad, OK? We are no longer together. And it is a direct result of what mom did. And I know that you could care less, and I know that mom will be thrilled, but I am not thrilled. And Rory is not thrilled. We're both hurt and extremely upset. Now I can stay away and not come to dinner and not see mom, but Rory made a deal with you guys, and Rory never goes back on anything she says, so she went. She was there, and if she was rude or cold, then I'm sorry, but I personally feel she has every right to be, and you and mom will just have to work that out with her yourselves.

ZACK [*about having sex*]: So, what do you think?
LANE: Oh, well, I have to wait until I get married.
ZACK: What?
LANE: I have to wait till I get married?
ZACK: I didn't know that.
LANE: Neither did I.
ZACK: Whoah.
LANE: Yeah, whoah.
ZACK: I don't know if I'm OK with that.
LANE: I'm not sure if *I'm* OK with that, either.
ZACK: What are you doing?
LANE: Cleaning up.
ZACK: I'll do it.
LANE: No, Zack. You're not getting any tonight. The least I can do is clean up.

EMILY [*to Luke*]: My daughter and I aren't speaking. She won't take my calls, she won't come to dinner. She apparently wants nothing to do with me. I'm sure you know that Lorelai and I have had many battles. Most of them have been because I feel that I know what's best for her. But Lorelai has her own ideas about what she thinks will make her happy. She wants you, Luke. She's made her choice. God help her but there it is. It doesn't matter if I agree with it, I can't fight it. You've won. Go back to her. I promise I will stay out of it.

5.17 Pulp Friction

First aired: March 8, 2005 // Written by James Berg and Stan Zimmerman // Directed by Michael Zinberg

Luke and Lorelai are back together, Michel is stuck with a $100,000 motor home courtesy of his recent appearance on The Price is Right, *and Rory and Logan are trying to keep things "casual." When Rory goes to Finn's Quentin*

Tarantino-themed birthday party with Robert, Logan suddenly realizes he has no interest in keeping things casual any longer. Meanwhile, Kirk finally leaves his mother's house and Emily has it out with Luke, and gets a tongue-lashing from her daughter for her trouble.

GINCHY! Luke's crack about Rory ("You have a daughter that looks like she belongs on top of a Christmas tree"); Lorelai's reaction to seeing Logan with another girl; Rory as *Kill Bill*'s GoGo Yubari in her Chilton outfit; and Luke speed-dialing Lorelai in the middle of Emily's tirade.

Logan is suddenly no longer a fan of keeping things casual with Rory.

NOTES *'We're keeping things casual.'*

With Luke and Lorelai a couple again, Kirk collects the ribbons Taylor gave out (5.14). Logan's mother plays canasta with playwright Tony Kushner. While in LA, Michel got Botox and his teeth worked on. Discussing Luke with Emily, Richard says he's not a take-charge fellow, citing his failure to franchise the diner as he'd suggested (5.7).

Though Rory tells Lorelai that her date Robert's last name is Grimaldi, she clearly made it up. (The Grimaldis are the Monacan royal family that Grace Kelly married into.) Luke has his boat back in Lorelai's garage again. (Oooh, dirty.)

TODAY'S CELEBRATION American Travel magazine's photo shoot for an article about the Dragonfly, Luke and Lorelai's "back together date" and Finn's birthday party.

KIRK OF ALL TRADES Ribbon reclaimer.

EMILY'S MAID DU JOUR Olympia, who *mistakenly* set a place for Lorelai at the table.

META, META, META Michel mentions hanging out at the Farmers Market in LA, which is the location of the Gilmore Bank that inspired the name of this series.

AMEN, SISTER FRIEND

EMILY: Why won't you come to Friday dinner? Whatever happened between the two of you, I obviously fixed it, so—

Behind the Scenes
Pulp Friction Separation

Tanc Sade grins and bears it in this scene.

"I had a bad rugby tackle the Sunday before the dancing scene," Tanc Sade says. "I had separated my shoulder. If you watch that scene closely, you'll see my right shoulder is very, very still. I had three reconstructions after that. But it was like two or three days after I'd done that shoulder—I was in so much pain.

"I was supposed to have a gun holster and I couldn't holster the gun. I needed someone to help me dress. I didn't tell them this, I told them I'd hurt my shoulder. They had no idea how serious it was, but I'd popped two Valiums just to get through that *Pulp Fiction* scene. If you can find that episode, watch my right shoulder closely and you'll actually see that it's jacked up about 2 or 3 inches. I'm holding my elbow really tightly to my side.

"Matt Czuchry knew how much pain I was in. And the director of that show, I asked him if he could have me on the left of frame so that I was favoring my left shoulder. I don't know why but he had me the other way around, so of course it's my right shoulder that you see on screen. When I was taken to hospital the next day or whenever I had the surgery scheduled, it hurt to shift gears in the car."

LORELAI: You fixed it? You broke it! Just because Luke and I found a way to repair the damage doesn't erase the fact that it happened!

EMILY: What I did, I did out of concern.

LORELAI: Oh, please!

EMILY: As your mother, I have the right to be concerned. Especially when it looks like you're taking your life down a completely disastrous path. I had to jump in, and—

LORELAI: Mom!

EMILY: Lorelai!

LORELAI: Please hear me. If I want your input in my life in any way, shape or form, I will ask for it. Until then, do us all a favor and shut up!

5.18 To Live and Let Diorama

First aired: April 19, 2005 // Written by Daniel Palladino // Directed by Jackson Douglas

It's been two weeks since Rory and Logan were all "hot and heavy," and Paris, too, is suffering through Doyle withdrawal. To get their minds off their boy troubles, the pair decide to bum around the Hollow with Lane, who thinks Zack's cheating on her. Not that anybody notices, since most of Stars Hollow has turned

out for the unveiling of the Stars Hollow museum, complete with a diorama show. While Luke is making plans for his future with Lorelai, someone else sets him straight on how limited that future might be.

GINCHY! Luke trying to choose which person at the magazine should interview Lorelai for the article; Paris and Kirk joining Lorelai and Rory at breakfast; Rory, Paris and Lane's drunken ranting, and Paris' subsequent hassling of the people in Stars Hollow for change to call Doyle; and finally, Taylor's demented diorama.

NOTES *'I've always said to myself if you're going to have a family and buy a house, then it's got to be this house.'*

* Joshua Twickham's been dying for 20 years and Miss Patty has said goodbye to him 17 times (the town record); Lorelai and Sookie were with him right before he went.

* Lane discovers Sophie Bloom used to be a songwriter (presumably of the Carole King variety). Zack loves shopping for cleaning supplies. Paris' father has been done for tax evasion, meaning "The place in Asylum Hill, the Nantucket cottage—even the crack house in Harlem that we converted into a co-op was sold to one of the *Queer Eye* guys."

* Rev. Ezekiel Jebediah and his family founded Stars Hollow: "Those stars, so bright. This forest, hollow." We get an alternate (and somewhat less probable) story about the founding of Stars Hollow much earlier in the series (1.16). Finn has a Hummer. Stars Hollow made Buff-Rite urinal cakes during WWII.

* Dean probably gets at the heart of what destroyed Luke's relationship with Rachel years before, too, when he tells him that Lorelai "is going to get bored, and you can't take her anywhere. You're here forever."

TODAY'S CELEBRATION The death of Mr. Twickham, the Dragonfly landing a magazine cover story, and the opening of the Stars Hollow museum.

KIRK OF ALL TRADES Twickham memorabilia salesman.

AND INTRODUCING... *Jackson Douglas as director*

2 MONTHS How long Old Man Twickham's will stipulated his house should serve as a museum. A pretty odd stipulation. Hardly seems worth the effort.

$3 Cost of admission to the Stars Hollow Museum.

2 The number of dirty words Lorelai found that rhyme with Emily (for her limerick).

THINGS WE'VE LEARNED Rose Abdoo (Gypsy) is the voice of the mother in the Twickham house diorama. "Daniel [Palladino] let me come in and say, 'But dear, we're just sitting down to breakfast.' I don't remember what the deal was, but that was me as the mom."

AMEN, SISTER FRIEND

SANDRA [*the magazine writer*]: So I'll cross your mother off your list of inspirations.
LORELAI: No, I actually did pick up some valuable lessons on running a staff from my mother.
SANDRA: How so?
LORELAI: Well, I consider what my mother would do in a given situation, then I dial it back. And I have what Mussolini would do, then I dial it back. And I have what Stalin would do, and then I dial that back, and then it starts approaching what a sane person would do.

LORELAI: Now, I don't know what all your plans are, but the grand opening of the Stars Hollow museum is this morning. Any takers?
PARIS: It's always amusing when provincials grasp for legitimacy. I'm in.
RORY: I wouldn't miss it.
KIRK: I helped build it.
PARIS: Bully.
LORELAI: All right. Well, finish up here, grab your jackets and we'll go.
KIRK: I don't need a jacket.
LORELAI: Well, it's chilly, Kirk.
KIRK: I don't want to wear a jacket.
LORELAI: Well then maybe you won't go to the grand opening of the

'It's a Bluegrass Band, OK.'

Zack's secret passion for playing bluegrass was probably the writers' nod to Todd Lowe's own love of playing country music, the actor suspects. "I tried to get my friends in on it but I guess they weren't camera friendly like the guys that I actually play with" in the episode, Lowe says. "They had their own people in mind to do that. But yeah, I play with a country band [Pilbilly Knights], and that's my first love in music. I love all kinds, but I'm best singing and guitar picking country style."

Stars Hollow museum.

KIRK: I'll put on my jacket.

LORELAI: Finish your breakfast first. Kirk, do not turn that TV on.

[We hear the TV turned on again.]

LORELAI: Kirk! I mean it, Kirk!

DEAN: Just go back to your girlfriend.

LUKE: Fine. Whatever.

DEAN: While you've got one.

LUKE: What's that supposed to mean?

DEAN: What do you think it means?

LUKE: I'm not playing games here!

DEAN: Your situation is no different from mine, *buddy*.

LUKE: I've got work to do.

DEAN: Then go. They want more than this. Don't you see that? And all you are is this.

LUKE: Rory was a kid, Dean. She grew up. She moved on. Accept it.

DEAN: You accept it. This town, it's all you are, and it's not enough. She's going to get bored and you can't take her anywhere. You're here forever.

LUKE: It's different.

DEAN: It's not different. You and me. Same thing.

5.19 But I'm a Gilmore

First aired: April 26, 2005 // Written by Amy Sherman-Palladino // Directed by Michael Zinberg

Sookie's been placed on absolute bed rest until the baby's born, but it takes more than a doctor to get that woman to drop her ladle. While Luke drops everything to run the Dragonfly's kitchen, Sookie makes his life hell by constantly second guessing him. Rory's not faring much better. Though she's finally managed to get Logan to commit, her first meeting with Logan's family ends with them saying that she's not a suitable partner for the heir to the Huntzberger fortune. At least Paris and Doyle are happy, now that they're officially an item.

GINCHY! Logan's sudden conversion to being Mr. Commitment; Doyle and Rory pointing out that Paris is pre-med after she says "Sick people freak me out"; Logan defending Rory from his family's attacks;

and Mitchum offering Rory an internship on his newspaper.

NOTES *'Five years of Friday night dinners have prepared me for exactly this moment.'*

Paris attacked a pretzel cart in Stars Hollow during her drunken rampage last episode, requiring police to call for backup for the first time ever.

Apparently Honor, who wired Logan money, was the real hero when Logan sank his father's yacht (5.6).

The speed with which Rory goes from despondency over the way Logan's family treated her to elation because Logan has come back for her worries Lorelai understandably. It also let's us see just how fragile Rory's self-esteem is now, and gives us a hint of what is to come (5.22).

Doyle was dumped two years ago by a girl who slept with his best friend and took the dog.

TODAY'S CELEBRATION Logan's sister, Honor, announces her engagement to the family. Rory and Logan, and Paris and Doyle, become official couples.

AND INTRODUCING...*Logan's parents, grandfather and sister* Whew.

OY WITH THE ____, ALREADY! Sookie! Perfectly fine as Lorelai's best friend, but whenever she's pregnant, she's annoying to the extreme.

3 YEARS How long Honor and Josh have been together.

THINGS WE'VE LEARNED Taylor Doose's name is derived from a real person, according to Michael Winters. "I met members of his family, but he isn't anything like that. They just kind of liked the name, I think. It was from Amy's childhood or young adulthood, I believe. But apparently he isn't like that at all; he wasn't particularly pushy or anything."

AMEN, SISTER FRIEND

SHIRA: Logan, you just haven't thought about this. I mean, I'm sure Rory understands. She wants to work. Isn't that right, Rory? Emily's always talking about you wanting to be a reporter and traveling around doing this and that. A girl like Rory has no idea what it takes to be in this family, Logan.

LOGAN: Oh my God.

SHIRA: She wasn't raised that way. She wasn't bred for it. And this isn't at all about her mother, it's just you come from two totally different worlds.

ELIAS: It would never work. Not for you, and certainly not for us.

LOGAN: OK, this conversation is going to end right now. I am not going to sit here—

ELIAS: You are going to be taking over this company! That's what you are going to be doing! And when you do, you are going to need the right kind of person at your side. This isn't college, Logan!

MITCHUM [*to Rory*]: Say the only reason I offered this to you is because my family behaved badly and I wanted to make up for it. Say I have no interest in furthering your career. This is still an opportunity. Who cares why you got the opportunity? It's here, and life is about making the most of everything you're handed. Well, this is being handed to you. Now, what are you going to do about it?

Life's Short, Talk...Slower?

When asked what their greatest challenge was on *Gilmore*, most actors will tell you it was having to deliver their lines in that now-famous, rapid-fire fashion. Everyone, that is, except for the actress who brought us Logan's sister, Honor: Devon Sorvari.

"In fact when I got the role, I was so excited because I thought that finally I'm going to have a job where they won't tell me to slow down," Sorvari says. "I've been told to slow down in everything I've ever done—and *they* did! I was even too fast for *Gilmore Girls*; I couldn't believe it!"

5.20 How Many Kropogs to Cape Cod?

First aired: May 3, 2005 // Written by Bill Prady and Rebecca Rand Kirshner // Directed by Jamie Babbit

After being trapped under some of his diorama dummies in the Stars Hollow museum, Taylor decides that it may finally be time to sell the Twickham house. Richard hooks Lorelai up with the head of a hotel consortium, and he and Emily have Logan over for dinner. Lorelai swallows her pride to attend the meal and is horrified by how her parents seem to be marrying Rory off to Logan, and by what a jerk Logan seems to be.

GINCHY! Richard and Emily springing in to action to invite Logan to dinner out of social obligation; Rory's first few enthusiastic moments at the newspaper; Emily and Richard briefly daydreaming about having their own place in Cape Cod for the next generation.

NOTES *'Just on those National Geographic shows, people are so sweaty after a mating ritual. But you two are powder dry.'*

✱ Among other accomplishments, Mitchum Huntzberger was short-listed for the Pulitzer prize for his coverage of the Iranian hostage crisis when he was 25, and ran a four-minute mile at Yale.

✱ Emily was kicked off the field hockey team at Smith for elbowing another player in the neck...in the parking lot after the game.

✱ Mike Armstrong is CEO of the Durham Group, a boutique inn company. Twee Silverman is the publisher of American Travel and the one who tipped off Armstrong about the forthcoming article on the Dragonfly in the May issue. Though Lorelai told them to pull the article (5.18), it's coming out anyway.

✱ In a detail beautifully understated, Luke at first discourages Lorelai from meeting with Armstrong, and in the next breath tells her she should meet with him after all. Though Lorelai doesn't give this sudden shift another thought, we know that Luke is sensitive to anything that might tempt Lorelai away from Stars Hollow. While part of this is due to the plans he has for them to move into the Twickham house, he's also clearly stewing over what Dean said about her wanting to leave town at some point (5.18). When Sookie later points out to Lorelai that there's nothing preventing Lorelai from seeing the world, we can see her weighing those options; you can't help but feel slightly hurt on Luke's behalf.

✱ The Kropog unit of measure is based on the height of the fictional Maxwell T. Kropog, Yale class of 1944.

TODAY'S CELEBRATION Rory starts her internship at the Stamford Eagle Gazette, and Richard and Emily have Logan over for dinner/mating rituals.

EMILY'S MAID DU JOUR Beatrice, who Emily berates for her positioning of lilies near dinner, and who she later accuses of stealing her antique sewing box when Logan is the real culprit.

AND HERE'S A SHOUT OUT TO OUR INTERNATIONAL FANS Sookie pictures her and Lorelai topless on a beach in the South of France when Lorelai mentions the business opportunities Mark Arm-

Gilmore's Three Amigos

"Matt [Czuchry], Alan [Loayza, 'Colin'] and I made a conscious effort very early on to spend some serious time together, just to get that rapport, and I think that comes across," says Tanc

Sade (Finn). "The three of us would always jump in the same trailer and we'd swap music and watch movies and hang out. We still do a poker night where we all get together with Nick Holmes [Robert] at his house generally. We have a poker and cigar night and we bring a couple of guitars and just jam away. I don't smoke cigars, and actually I can't play poker, so they're always helping me out. They're some of the closest people I know here, and that was really a testament to that show. In my experience that is rare."

Logan makes a good first impression with Richard and Emily, but Lorelai will see through it all.

strong has suggested. Lorelai adds that she's always wanted to say "I'll be back from Dusseldorf on Friday," like her father used to do.

META, META, META The team works the name of Kelly Kropog, assistant to the line editor, into this episode and its title.

6 ACRES The size of the property the Huntzbergers own at Martha's Vineyard.

90 About the number of Kropogs between Logan and Rory's dorms.

AMEN, SISTER FRIEND

RORY [*to Logan, about her first day at the newspaper*]: I didn't even know if I was supposed to go to lunch when everybody went to lunch, so I just stood in the break room for like 45 minutes. And then I ate an Altoid.

LOGAN [*before swapping out Eleanor Shubick's silver lighter for Emily's little antique sewing box*]: A little Life and Death Brigade business. Every time we're in a rich person's house we take a knickknack. Then I leave the knickknack I took from the last rich person's house. I've been doing this up and down the eastern seaboard for years.
RORY: Logan, no.
LOGAN: Trust me. They never notice.

5.21 Blame Booze and Melville

First aired: May 10, 2005 // Written by Daniel Palladino // Directed by Jamie Babbit

Lorelai is the toast of the town thanks to the American Travel cover story about the Dragonfly, but Emily and the Russian ballet dancer she's sponsoring are not amused by her quotes in the piece. Sookie and Jackson finally have their baby, and Rory thinks her internship is the beginning of her journalism career, until Mitchum Huntzberger gives her a few words from his "gut."

GINCHY! How at-home Rory is at the paper compared with her first day; Sookie's surprise for Jackson at the hospital (but see 7.12 for the punch line); Luke's audience with the town elders; and Lorelai apologizing for a Stalin reference in the article to the ballet dancer Mikhail.

NOTES *'Well I feel like knocking people's hats off.'*

Sookie starts seeing celebrities whenever she's going into labor. When Lorelai was pregnant with Rory, she craved apples, which is one reason she panics after craving apples following her drunken night of fun with Luke.

It was Rosalyn Carter, not former president Jimmy Carter, that Emily had the "bitch fight" with over the hotel room. Rory paraphrases Melville's *Moby Dick* ("when he finds himself growing grim about the mouth and wanted to knock people's hats off, he takes to the sea"), which we actually saw her reading years before (1.1). Mikhail's entire family and everyone in his village were killed by Joseph Stalin.

The last time Rory thought she was doing a good job, she was shattered when told that she had to lighten her Yale course load (4.14). This time around, not only is she told she's not doing well enough, but that she should abandon her lifelong dream of journalism entirely.

TODAY'S CELEBRATION The birth of Sookie and Jackson's baby, Martha, publication of the much-anticipated American Travel article, Honor's engagement party, and the destruction of Rory's journalistic dreams.

KIRK OF ALL TRADES At long last, this joke finally pays off! (And when he loses the Twickham house, he offers to provide lawn services for it.)

"I always loved the long days because that meant overtime. I wasn't a contract player so I was always walking a little bit slower and the crew kind of goes to 80 percent mode, but they'll speed it up when it's time. People like to stretch that out."

–TODD LOWE (ZACK)

EMILY'S MAID DU JOUR Luminista, bringer of marshmallows.

7 YEARS How long it's been since Luke raised the price of his wheat toast.

$247,868 Kirk's net worth; he wants to use it toward buying the Twickham house.

14 Number of hours Sookie was in labor with little Martha Janice-Lori-Ethan-Rupert-Glenda-Carson-Daisy-Danny.

AND HERE'S A SHOUT OUT TO OUR INTERNATIONAL FANS German tourists are shoveling down the chocolate at Taylor's candy store, and Emily trades ballet dancer Pola (from some unnamed land) for Russian Mikhail.

ETHAN/GLENDA OR MARTHA/RUPERT Some last minute name options for the baby, courtesy of Jackson.

AMEN, SISTER FRIEND

KIRK: I've been working for 11 years, Luke. I've had 15,000 jobs. I've saved every dollar I've ever made. That and the miracle of compound interest has created a bounty of a quarter of a million dollars. Again, just under. I don't want to brag.....

LUKE: I don't believe this! You're swimming in cash and you fought me over a 10 cent raise on toast!
KIRK: And you folded like a road map. That might explain the discrepancy in our net worths. So, I think I *will* have those donuts to go. You've got change for a hundred, right?

SOOKIE: You're getting a vasectomy.
JACKSON: What?
SOOKIE: You're getting a vasectomy.
JACKSON: You got me. You got me. You're funny. Dark but funny.
SOOKIE: I'm not joking, sweetie. We're cutting that tube. If it is a tube. I'm not really up on the procedure. The doctor doing it will be, though, so I'm sure he'll know.
JACKSON: You're not kidding.
SOOKIE: I'm not kidding.

JACKSON: Sookie, come on!

SOOKIE: Jackson, we have one of each. We've kept the species going.

JACKSON: But I wanted four!

SOOKIE: And I wanted three. This is a good compromise.

JACKSON: I'm sorry, two is not a compromise between three and four.

[A nurse comes to escort Jackson to his fate.]

SOOKIE: This is Reggie, he's going to take you down and have it done.

JACKSON: I'm having it done today?

SOOKIE: Yep.

MITCHUM: I've worked with a lot of young people over the years. Interns, new hires. I've got a pretty good gut sense for people's strengths and weaknesses. Whether they have that certain something to make it in journalism. It's a tough business. Lot of stress.

RORY: Definitely.

MITCHUM: And I have to tell you, you don't got it. Now, guts can be wrong. Mine's been wrong before. But not often.... Hey, listen. I know this is rough, but I may have just done you a big favor.

TOWN ELDER: We all watched Luke pine for Lorelai for nine long years. He waited for her while she went through her many relationships. He won her. Now he wants this for her. And for the others.

LUKE: Others? What others?

TOWN ELDER: You'll bring children into the house.

KIRK: I'll bring children into the house, too. Maybe not my own.

TOWN ELDER: It's right for Luke to have it. Kirk is young. There'll be other places for him to go. That's what I think.

5.22 A House is Not a Home

First aired: May 17, 2005 // Written and directed by Amy Sherman-Palladino

Things fall apart, just ask the people of Stars Hollow. Lane sees her rock-and-roll dreams fading away as her bandmates find better things to do. Lorelai admits to Luke that she's still considering selling the Dragonfly and taking the job offer being dangled before her. While Luke sees their future crumbling, Lorelai, too, is seeing things fall apart with Rory, who stole a boat last episode and announced that she's quitting Yale in this one. Not knowing what else to

"I'd played these kinds of women before, but not as beautifully written as what Amy did. Because you have the luxury of coming back and playing the same character again, you are able to fill her out a bit as you go. Every once in a while there would be a little shift in the character, and most of the time it was delightful for me because I thought, 'That's exactly what I was thinking,' and I'd see it in the script and I'd go, 'Wow, this is great! This is exactly what I would expect from this character.'"

-KELLY BISHOP (EMILY)

do, Lorelai tries to get her parents to help her convince Rory to stay in school, which succeeds about as well as anything relying on Richard and Emily does. Adrift, Lorelai lays it all on the line with Luke.

GINCHY! Colin and Finn at the police station; Kirk almost towing Lorelai and Rory away; Lorelai going to Richard and Emily for help after Rory quits Yale; and Mrs. Kim launching Hep Alien's first tour.

NOTES *'Everything's falling apart.'*

Lorelai's concern over Rory being "in the system" after her arrest is attributed to an episode of *NYPD Blue* and the fate of Sipowicz's son...who was played by Michael DeLuise (TJ).

When Rory finally tells Lorelai at Weston's that she's not going back to Yale next year, she adds that a lot of college kids take time off—which is pretty rich coming from the girl who gave Dean hell when he said he was taking time off from his own college plan (4.18). Rory also tells her mother that she doesn't understand because she never went to college, a belittling tactic that, until now, has only been used against Lorelai by Richard and Emily. Lorelai tells her parents about how the Huntzbergers treated Rory (5.19), but they don't believe her.

Mrs. Kim calls on her experience in a 27-member, all-girl tambourine band to put together a two-month tour of church-based theaters for Lane's band.

The Sister Kirk Never Had

Amy & Dan wanted to create the role of Kirk's sister for actress Bess Rous, who auditioned for the show. Alas, their schedules never aligned. "She was so damned funny and Amy loved her," casting director Mara Casey says.

TODAY'S CELEBRATION Stars Hollow is the last stop of the 5th annual Connecticut Bike Race, Hep Alien launches its first tour, and Rory quits Yale and moves into Richard and Emily's pool house.

KIRK OF ALL TRADES Tow-truck driver.

EMILY'S MAID DU JOUR Davida, the extremely nervous maid.

AND INTRODUCING...*June 3rd!* This time, it's Rory's court date. Next time it will be Luke and Lorelai's wedding date.

3 How old Rory was when she first wanted to be a journalist.

AMEN, SISTER FRIEND

COLIN [*about Rory and Logan*]: Yes. Maxwell Smart finally found his 99.

LORELAI: I'm just not prepared for this. I mean, Rory never even shoplifted. Not a candy bar, not a lipstick. She forgot to return a library book once, and she was so guilty about it that she grounded herself. I mean, can you imagine? She's just sitting there in her bedroom yelling at me, "Now no one else got to read *The Iliad* this week because of me!"

THE PROPOSAL

LORELAI: Rory dropped out of Yale.

LUKE: What?

LORELAI: She dropped out of Yale and she moved in with my parents, who I went to for help, and they stabbed me in the back. Everything we worked for. All these years. Her whole future. She was supposed to have more than me. She was supposed to have everything. That was the plan. We had a plan.

LUKE: OK, I'm sorry, I have to jump in here. I know you think you have this thing handled but I can help. First off, we call Yale and we tell them something like Rory had a chemical imbalance and she was mentally out of her mind when she told them she was dropping out. And then we get

"John [Cabrera] and I e-mail each other fairly regularly: 'Hey have you gotten a residual check in a while? No? Me neither.' Occasionally I get a crazy text message from Sebastian [Bach] when he's in town."

-TODD LOWE (ZACK)

Behind the Scenes Fun With Australians 3

"I really struggled for the first couple of episodes," admits Tanc Sade. "Their writing, really the cadence and the dialogue, was more fitting for a British character rather than an Australian character, so it took them a little while, in my opinion, to really get the Australian rhythm. It was tough for me because I was trying to play Australian on American television with this British cadence, really, really fast. And on top of that I was getting these things from the Web saying, 'This is the worst Australian accent I've ever heard!'"

Sade had a whole different problem on set. "I would constantly get notes: 'Tanc, we can't understand you. Tanc we can't understand you. What are you saying?' So I'd have to [re-record the dialogue in post-production] to really articulate certain consonants, just to make sure that people understood me. I would say, 'Look, I can't say that word the way you're asking me to say it because it's quite clearly American.' So I had to do this Transatlantic hybrid accent, which is interesting."

Whatever difficulties he had in the beginning, Sade is the first to tell you that he was extremely fortunate to work with a cast and crew who were so down to earth.

"That is not always the case with people in my industry. It was my first job here, so the extent of that didn't really become apparent to me until I went on to work on the next jobs."

her out of your parents' house whatever way we can. We lock her up in her room with you, because you can talk anybody into anything. And if worse comes to worst, we will drive her to school every day and we will follow her to class and camp out there to make sure she goes. I'll take morning classes, you take afternoon classes, or the other way around if it works out better for your schedule. And I know there's a few kinks to work out; the kidnapping thing might be a little problematic. But either way, she is not quitting school. This was her dream. I am not going to let this happen. What?
LORELAI: Luke, will you marry me?

With the end of Season 5, many in the audience were left with the promise of something they'd been clamoring for since the beginning, but presented in such a way as to be something of a sour victory. Rory, whatever you thought of her decision to leave Yale, had asserted some self-sufficiency for the first time, and her mother's response was to propose to the guy she knew would do anything in the world for her. Little did anybody realize that the awkwardness between Luke and Lorelai had only just begun.

Gilmore Stars In the Twitterverse

Actors, with very few exceptions, get into the business for the opportunity to make a living through make believe, and some, certainly, to become the nearest thing America has to royalty. Yet few of today's actors bargained with the broad reach and evaporation of privacy that came with the evolution of the World Wide Web.

"It wasn't like this even five years ago," Lauren Graham told More magazine in a March 2010 cover story, adding that she's not on Twitter or Facebook. "Why would I want to be *more* accessible?"

Gilmore Girls fans—many of whom have grown up without memories of an unwired world—are eager to share their enthusiasm for the show with everybody, including the actors with whom they feel a kinship. Some actors maintain Twitter accounts and will occasionally friend fans on Facebook, or at least keep their own blogs updated. John Cabrera, for example, is extremely accessible online. And though Sean Gunn initially fought the peer pressure to live online, he finally bit the bullet and became something of a Twitter virtuoso starting in 2009.

Other actors have no interest in being this accessible. For some it has to do with a lack of time to engage in such online relationships. Others feel that sites such as Facebook are their only opportunity to keep in touch with other friends in the business that they otherwise wouldn't have time to see. Yet most are just plain uncomfortable for another reason.

On July 18, 1989, rising TV star Rebecca Schaeffer was gunned down at her front door by an obsessed fan, and nothing has ever been the same since. People in the business barely old enough to remember the event admit that the fate of the *My Sister Sam* star remains one of their greatest fears. The stalker in that scenario had to go to the trouble and expense of hiring a private investigator to discover her address. Today, the Web culture has lured a great number of us into casually revealing personal information such as where we're going to be or what we drive in a casual tweet or Facebook update.

"I try to protect the people I have contact with because they're so vulnerable," admits *Gilmore* key set costumer Valerie Campbell. "I can walk down the street, nobody would care. But if I walk down the street with Alexis or Keiko, people do notice them. It can be a little uncomfortable."

For people such as Kelly Bishop, it's more a sense of wanting to maintain some manner of privacy, and having very little time to get online in the first place.

"I have not done Facebook and the Twittering and all that," she says. *(Can't you just see Emily calling it "the Twittering"?)* "It's not only beyond my realm, I don't want to. I do my job, I appreciate the fans and an audience and all of that, but I have a private life. I don't have a publicist. I don't go running around trying to get to openings of things and the right parties—that's not my thing at all. So I have never embraced that. If I am on any of those things, I'm not even aware of it. Who needs it? Of course I'm of another generation, too, aren't I? And Ed [Herrmann] is very much the same way."

Finally, there are some actors who just plain don't feel like dealing with people once they finally manage to get home from the various gigs that keep them on the road most of the time.

"Just think about the people who don't like to answer their phone," Campbell says. "The thing with actors, and it's something that people don't really realize—they're just people."

"Even When I Have a Man, I'm Still the Girl Who Doesn't Have a Man"

season **six**

Rory on a chain gang? Luke faced with a love child from his past? Many could be forgiven for flipping to another channel at this point with a muttered, "You know, I have problems of my own."

This season kicks off uncomfortably with Rory's harsh sentencing for the yacht she stole with Logan last season, her bitter separation from Lorelai, then things got awkward.

Despite this, Season 6, the last for Amy & Dan, is not without its high points. Rory easily masters the DAR life Emily has always claimed so difficult, mother and daughter reunite, Jess returns (in a Ghost of Christmas Future kind of way), and Lane and Zack tie the knot in one of the coolest weddings in TV history.

6.1 New and Improved Lorelai

First aired: Sept. 13, 2005 // Written and directed by Amy Sherman-Palladino

While Luke and Lorelai rejoice over their engagement, the people of Stars Hollow pity Luke for missing his chance to do the proposing. (Kirk's so stunned by the news that he's avoiding Lulu on the phone and in person lest she get the same idea.) Lorelai has given up on Rory for the time being, little realizing that Rory

Now what?

has promised a "new me" that will give Logan's time-wasting skills some stiff competition. Perhaps a lengthy community service sentence will shake some sense into the Yale dropout.

GINCHY! The disturbing way Kirk has built up his ring collection; the surprise "for she's a jolly good felon" party Logan and the gang throw for Rory; and Lorelai waking Richard and Emily in the middle of the night with all of Rory's stuff.

NOTES *'Tough love, baby.'*

Babette had Taylor stocking Zima for a while. Fortunately for Luke and Lorelai, there's a case left over that they use to toast their big news.

Before they call it a night, Luke suddenly begins to defend his blurting of "what about the kids" after Lorelai told him she was still considering selling the inn (5.22). Miss Patty and Babette give us our first mention of rival gossip East Side Tillie. Morey proposed to Babette while they were playing Twister. Though we won't see it again, Emily still has her panic room (5.5) and gives Rory the combination, which hasn't changed.

Behind the Scenes: The Blue Puffy Coats

While it's true that cast and crew spent more time trying to make the warm climes of Hollywood's Warner Brothers lot pass for the nippy environs of Connecticut, there were plenty of cold weather shoots, to say nothing of the times cast members was given precious little to wear. Traditionally, a studio's wardrobe department will keep a few nice coats on hand for the actors for these occasions.

But on *Gilmore Girls*, the coats they had kept disappearing, says key set costumer Valerie Campbell. "Finally we're like, 'We can't just keep buying coats.'" She told costume designer Brenda Maben that they had to "get the ugliest, cheapest, warmest coats you can find; something that can withstand the rain if it's raining."

Maben went out and found six women's "butt ugly" puffy, bright, baby blue long coats, and had "Property of *Gilmore Girls* Wardrobe Department" embroidered in equally bright colors on the back of each one.

"Everybody had to wear these hideously ugly coats down to set," Campbell says. Normally each actor would have a coat that was specifically their own, but there were so many actors on *Gilmore*, they ended up recycling them. "So they'd reach in their pockets and they'd pull out sides from some other character, or some other personal object that they'd left in the pockets."

Soon it was the blue puffy coats that were mysteriously walking off the lot. The following year the wardrobe department brought in some raspberry colored puffy coats to keep up with demand.

According to Paris, Doyle is the tallest one in his family. They're moving in together when school starts. Luke chooses old widow Mason's ring to give to Lorelai. Rory's going to be 21 in October.

TODAY'S CELEBRATION Luke and Lorelai's engagement, and the moment when Lorelai washes her hands of Rory.

KIRK OF ALL TRADES Ring salesman.

EMILY'S MAID DU JOUR Hosanna.

YOU'VE ENTERED EMILYLAND Now the code to the panic room is 1, 1, 1, 1, 1. Don't write it down. And whatever you do, don't tell the maid. They tell their children and then their children grow up and rob you.

OY WITH THE ____, ALREADY! The scorpion and the frog story. This parable has been knocking around American culture alone for a good 60 years at least, and really needs to die now. We get it: Jerky people don't change!

AND INTRODUCING...*David S. Rosenthal* This time around he's executive producer. By 6.3, he will have his first writing credit. Get used to him—he will replace Amy & Dan as showrunner next season.

10 The number of hours of community service attorney Charlie Davenport tells Rory she'll get.

20 The number of hours the prosecutor agreed to.

300 The number of hours the judge orders, to be completed in 6 months, followed by one year's probation. She can petition the court in five years to have the incident removed from her record.

AMEN, SISTER FRIEND

LUKE: Kirk, where did you get all these rings?
KIRK: I befriend really old women.
LUKE: Excuse me?
KIRK: Really old women need companionship, Luke. They are really old. Most people they know are dead. So when someone comes along and they are not dead and they'll listen to their stories and care about their dosage, they are grateful.

"I think back to when I was a kid and I was a big fan of The Andy Griffith Show. Every now and then there'd be a band that would come to town like the Dillards, and they'd get into trouble and Barney would throw them in the jailhouse and they would start up a hootenanny. I always felt like Wow, I'm kind of walking in those footsteps. I think I'm in good company. Stars Hollow was sort of my Mayberry. A childhood dream come true."

–GRANT-LEE PHILLIPS (THE TROUBADOUR)

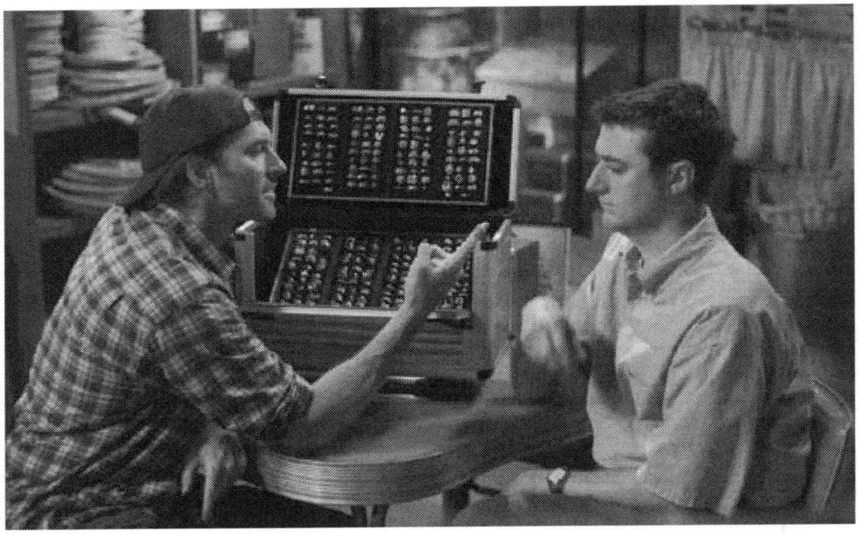

LUKE: Are you serious?

KIRK: Serious as a heart attack. Which is how I got that ring you're holding right now. So what do you think?

PARIS: I need her to be at Yale. Rory has been my only real competition since she showed up at Chilton. She's the only one who's ever challenged me. She's my pace car. She's my Bjorn Borg. Without her I'll get lazy. I'll fall apart. I'll have frosted hair and dragon lady nails. I'll achieve nothing. I'll become my mother.

LORELAI: Paris, listen to me. You are a very smart, driven young lady. You can be anything you want. Except a diplomat. You don't need Rory to push you.

PARIS: Rory is my only friend. She stays in the room until I'm completely done saying something. I need that.

LORELAI: I am calm. I'm fine. You guys must be pretty jazzed though, huh? I mean you finally did it. You finally got a shot at getting the daughter you've always wanted.

RICHARD: I'm too tired to have this conversation.

LORELAI: Rory! Here! Right under your roof. Excellent!

EMILY: You're being ridiculous.

LORELAI: Now you get your do over. A new and improved Lorelai. Congrats. Very well played.

"There was that scene [in 6.2] where I built shelves. Mom was helping me with my lines and Dad said, 'Lean up against the shelf. Wipe 'em off and lean up against them in pride for a second.' And it's just one moment but Dad always gave me really nice little touches in there. He loved comedy."

—MICHAEL DELUISE RECALLING FATHER DOM DELUISE'S SHELF ADVICE.

6.2 Fight Face

First aired: Sept. 20, 2005 // Written and directed by Daniel Palladino

Life goes on. For Rory, that means jumping into her community service and preparing for a new job at the DAR's downtown office. For Lorelai, it's filling the void Rory left with Paul Anka, a shaggy mutt who's nearly as neurotic as she is. For Luke, it's deciding to expand Lorelai's house because he knows she'll never be happy living anywhere else. When Rory stops by the diner to indirectly let Lorelai know that she's doing OK, she's devastated to learn just how much her mother's moved on in the short time they've been apart.

GINCHY! Luke's observations about the whole *Revenge of the Sith* higher-ground conundrum; Liz telling Lorelai, "I want to eat your face"; Rory and Esperanza chatting away in Spanish; Lorelai turning back to find Paul Anka in the Jeep with the door closed; Emily giving Rory pointers about dealing with her fellow felons, including keeping her "fight face at home"; Luke's *Shining*-like reaction when he realizes TJ put the hole in Lorelai's wall; and Rory's reaction to learning that Luke and Lorelai are engaged.

NOTES *'You and Luke getting engaged and not telling me about it, you hurt me.' 'Back at you.'*

Miss Patty brings up Lorelai's bad track record with animals at the pet fair. Not only does she refer to Skippy the hamster (1.11), she adds a rabbit and a turtle to the Lorelai-animal mythos. Luke doesn't like dogs. TJ, Lorelai and Liz mourn the loss of the little boy in Luke.

'You hurt me!'
'Back at you!'

Our worst fears are realized when we find the DAR women discussing which of America's historical gentlemen were the best lovers. TJ almost passed the test to get his contractor's license last month, except he cursed on the written exam, which is what he does when he gets enthusiastic about something.

TODAY'S CELEBRATION Stars Hollow is getting some painting touch ups ("Pardon our spiff, it'll just take a jiff"), Rory begins her community service and Lorelai gets Paul Anka.

EMILY'S MAID DU JOUR Esperanza, replaced by Draguta (from Romania).

3.5 HOURS The length of each community service shift, not counting overtime.

AND HERE'S A SHOUT OUT TO OUR INTERNATIONAL FANS Rory's conversation with Emily's Guatemalan maid Esperanza in Spanish is a nice opportunity to demonstrate Alexis Bledel's fluency in her first language. And let's not forget Emily's new maid, Draguta, from Romania.

AND INTRODUCING...*Paul Anka!* He's as fearless as they come; only scared of popcorn, tissue holders, paperbacks, CDs, framed pictures, lint, bottle openers, stairs, mailboxes, and he freaks out whenever Lorelai drinks something or he's woken up. And that's just this episode.

COCOA Paul Anka's original name.

AMEN, SISTER FRIEND

LUKE: You bought a dog!
LORELAI: Yeah, and he loves me. And he doesn't give his love easily. The only drawback is the name. Cocoa. It's too cutesy. But he's a rescue, so I don't want to freak him out by giving him a new name right away, so I'm gonna get to the name I want to give him in baby steps. For the first week, I'll call him Cocoa to get him acclimated.
LUKE: Acclimated.

But why 'Paul Anka'?

Well might you ask. Here's what Dan told the Chicago Tribune in February 2006: "I was writing the first episode that the dog appeared in, and Paul Anka's record came out at the same time, and I heard it in Starbuck's or something. And it sounded good. He actually pulled off singing "Smells Like Teen Spirit." It just seemed like ... maybe Lorelai would have gone into a coffee place and heard this weird Paul Anka album and would have thought to name her dog Paul Anka. A lot of those decisions we don't really talk about, they come out in the writing and it makes sense."

Making an Episode 9
Shooting Begins

Mindee Clem Forman on the *GG* set with production assistant Danny Giles.

It's 5:30 in the morning and Mindee Clem Forman (then Mindee Clem) whizzes through a dimly-lit Stars Hollow on a bike to get the call sheets and other paperwork that will be needed for the day's shooting. "I would hit more spider webs with my face on that darn bike, because I was the first person there," she laughs.

Like many other trainee assistant directors before her, Forman will help keep the operation running during her two-month stint on Season 4.

Forman is in charge of "base camp," or "actor land" as she calls it, where the actors' trailers are located, as well as those for makeup, hair and wardrobe. As actors arrive for the day's shoot, she greets them, sees to any paperwork necessary with the day players (e.g., actors who are neither series stars such as Graham and Bledel, nor extras), and fetches them food. The trainee AD will also keep track of where each actor is so that he or she can be sent to the appropriate place as soon as they're needed.

The crew prepares for the first scene, dressing the living room of Lorelai's house. The camera department works out the logistics of the shoot, deciding which set walls have to be removed so that they can get just the right angles. Sound is busy tackling its own challenges: will the shot be a close-up of two people talking so that they can dangle a boom mic overhead, or is it going to be a wider shot, which means they will have to plant a mic nearby?

Meanwhile, the actors are in their trailers, going over their lines. While they already have scripts before shooting a scene, that script is always changing. The changes that Amy and the writers have come up with late at night will arrive at an actor's door at all hours in the form of "sides"—detailed, up-to-date script pages for just the scenes that will be shot that day.

Each actor has their own way of absorbing lines, says dialogue coach George Anthony Bell. He'll go to Scott Patterson's trailer and "run the scene over and over until he really feel's comfortable with it," he says. With Alexis Bledel, Bell will either catch up with her in the hair and makeup trailer or on set, or they will go for a walk around the backlot and practice her lines. She's developed a habit of writing out her lines a couple of times before they even meet: "It helps you remember what's coming next," Bell explains. "So that was a little tip that I picked up from Alexis."

When it comes to blowing people away with line learning, all agree that the master is also the person who has the most dialogue: Lauren Graham. Bell is convinced she has a photographic memory.

Forget readthroughs, Graham likes to do "speedthroughs." Bell will sit with her while she's getting her hair and makeup done and, if the character he's reading has a lot of dialogue, he just reads her the first couple of lines and the last line, "and she would know what was coming next before she said her line."

Soon, the AD radios the trainee AD that they're ready to block out a scene. Forman sends Lauren and Alexis to the living room set, where they run through the script, working with the director and the crew to get down exactly where they should be in the room and what they should be doing. Work then begins on lighting while Lauren and Alexis are sent to the hair, makeup and wardrobe trailers. They won't be reporting to set for another hour or two.

One day, an actor fails to show up for a scene where his character is the primary focus. "Usually you call the house, you call the cell," Forman explains. Nothing. The actor's agent is tracked down by phone, but the agent has no idea where his client is, either. "Finally we sent transportation over to his house, and he was just so sound asleep, he hadn't heard his phone." The actor's whisked off to the set, rushed through hair and makeup, and filming begins. Up till that point, "we were just all standing around on set going, 'OK, don't have our actor, can't really do anything else.'"

LORELAI: Second week, I'm gonna call him Cokey. Third week, "Kooky." Fourth week "Tooky."
LUKE: So, you're gonna name him Tooky?
LORELAI: No. I'm gonna name him Paul Anka, but it's gonna take a while to get to Paul Anka.

LORELAI [*to Luke and the workers*]: Wow, I was this close to screaming and siccing the dog on you. (Turns to find Paul Anka is suddenly in the Jeep with the door closed.) How did you get the door closed?
[Later]
LORELAI [*turns her attention back to Paul Anka in the Jeep, tries to open it*]: You locked the door? Dude, come on! I mean, I've got the key, but I'm really curious how you did this.

6.3 The UnGraduate

First aired: Sept. 27. 2005 // Written by David S Rosenthal // Directed by Michael Zinberg

Work has begun on the expansion of Lorelai's house (despite TJ's best efforts as the pretend contractor), Paris is trying to replace Rory by hanging out with

Bio Honorine Bell (LuLu)

Though we never really got to know Kirk's girlfriend, Lulu, it was nice to know that the hapless Mr. Gleason was able to find someone to cushion the blows that frequently befell him in Stars Hollow. Prior to playing the perpetually perky Lulu, Honorine Bell was probably best known as Kasey in the Kirsten Dunst cheerleader comedy *Bring it On* (2000).

Born in Rome, Bell grew up in Zurich, Switzerland with her older brother. "It was very idyllic, a nice place to be a kid. Snow and wild animals and forests; just a beautiful, peaceful place." At 7 she moved to New Orleans, where her father, Battle Bell III, practiced Jungian analysis and worked as an architect until his death in 2006. Her mother, Susan, taught English to adults in Europe, and has taught English as a second language to children since their move to New Orleans.

At 16, Bell moved to New York to pursue acting and modeling, and to Los Angeles a year later. Though not much of a TV watcher, the actress had heard good things about *Gilmore Girls* and frequently hit its casting office to try out for the roles of Rory's friends. "Eventually they thought I was too old to play one of Rory's friends, and so I got a part in the town," she says. When the part of Lulu came up, Bell stuck a flower in her hair and gave it a go. "I think they were just glad I had a little look that I created," she says; they hadn't yet decided what Lulu would be like or even if she'd be hanging around after her first episode. Says Bell, the role " became a little more defined, a little more school teachery, a little more crazy."

Lorelai, and Rory is kicking ass tackling her community service. Yet Lorelai can't commit to a wedding date, and Rory, for all her brave talk, is a bit uneasy trading the promise of Yale for the alien ways of the DAR.

! GINCHY! Everybody pretending that TJ is the contractor to make him feel good; Lorelai breaking it to Luke that five workers saw her naked when she was taking a shower; Emily's sudden delight realizing she now has Rory on the inside of the DAR office to keep an eye on her political enemies; Rory Gilmore sex boat!; the pizza, pizza, salad trick Lorelai teaches Paul Anka; the Dragonfly staff's reaction to Paris' biweekly lunches with Lorelai; and Luke bending over backward to make sure Paul Anka survives his encounter with 3 pounds of chocolate.

NOTES *'I don't want to set a wedding date until things are right with Rory.'*
✱ Add watches to the list of things that freak out Paul Anka. Emily is serving her first term as president of her chapter of the DAR. Poor Rory has another three hours of community service at the nursing home after picking up trash on the roadside.

✱ Last time, Rory was hurt when she learned that Lorelai and Luke were engaged. This time, Lorelai is taken aback when Paris tells her that Rory is working in an office with Emily. Lorelai's dilithium-crystals reference is a subtle dig at Luke's geeky roots (2.8).

✱ Considering how much fuss Lorelai will make over Luke postponing their wedding because he's trying to get himself settled with his daughter (6.22), Lorelai tells him in this episode that *she* can't set a wedding date until she's gotten herself squared away with Rory.

TODAY'S CELEBRATION The last night of Hep Alien's tour (at Whitfield Seventh Day Adventist Church in Massachusetts) and Rory's induction into the DAR.

EMILY'S MAID DU JOUR Unnamed.

AND HERE'S A SHOUT OUT TO OUR INTERNATIONAL FANS Logan's European trip included participating in the Gloucestershire cheese-rolling festival, and Colin falling in love with a milkmaid in Holland (before they went on to Amsterdam).

"I don't know if anybody took as much notice as I did, but every time I had a scene with Lauren, I'd look in those eyes and I would almost forget my lines. I don't know if you can see it on TV but she has the most beautiful blue eyes and they would throw me off."

-BIFF YEAGER (TOM)

META, META, META Michel is horrified when Paris mocks his accent and calls him Canadian. Yanic Truesdale is from Montreal.

MARTHA The name of Gil's van.

125 The number of community-service hours Rory has logged so far.

$9,000 What Hep Alien returns to Stars Hollow with, thanks to Lane fibbing about how much cash they had while they were on the road.

AMEN, SISTER FRIEND

LORELAI: No, look how happy he is strutting around in his tool belt and shiny silver helmet. You know he polishes that thing every night after work?
LUKE: Really?
LORELAI: Yes, really. With real silver polish. That's what he thinks silver polish is for: to polish anything that's silver. I think that's adorable.
TOM: And the good news is he's got terrible instincts. But he combines that with absolutely zero follow-through, so it all works out in the end.

PARIS: Is this about the boat?
RORY: How do you know about the boat?
PARIS: Oh come on. It's out there.

Behind the Scenes: Dealing With Fame in NYC

When you're a beloved actor in Los Angeles, there's a certain amount of staring every once in awhile at Starbuck's or even the local drug store —comes with the territory. But more often than not, people are pretty blasé in Hollywood—there are simply too many actors in the city limits to consider them extraordinary.

In New York City, however, there are the tourists, and the tourists have no problem staring. Kelly Bishop gets recognized when she least expects it. "I mean in a grocery store, when I'm wearing my baseball cap and my sneakers and my jeans. The thing that I found with me, and it surprised me—they recognize my voice. And I don't think of my voice as being that unique. But almost every time I've been found out, it's because I've spoken.

"You can tell when people recognize you because they get this funny little look on their faces, like a half-smile, and of course they keep staring at you. But most people are fine. In New York it's because you're walking all the time; in LA at least you're in your car. But New Yorkers have always been known for giving people their space. If anybody's approached in New York from a fan standpoint, it's usually a tourist from out of town. The New Yorkers, they're far too proud."

RORY: Out there? Why is it out there? How is it out there?

PARIS: I read about it on Rebecca Thurston's blog.

RORY: You're kidding.

PARIS: Dead serious.

RORY: I thought Rebecca Thurston's blog was just about all the guys she has sex with and how much she hates her mother.

PARIS: That's true. But the boat you guys stole belongs to Dr. Daniel Zimmerman, whose son is Jason Zimmerman, who Rebecca Thurston had sex with on her father's boat last semester.

RORY: I can't believe I'm in the blogosphere.

PARIS: Hey, see for yourself. Just Google "Rory Gilmore sex boat."

LUKE [*to vet*]: The dog ate chocolate. And I don't know a lot about dogs, but I do know they shouldn't eat chocolate. And I went to the animal hospital and they were closed, and I called Babette and she told me where you lived, and you've got to do something because this is not my dog. This is my fiancé's dog. She loves him. She named him "Paul Anka," which may, on the surface, not seem like a sign of love, but if you knew her, you'd get it. And believe me there's a lot of ways I could screw up, but I cannot lose her over the fact I killed her dog.

6.4 Always a Godmother, Never a God

First aired: Oct. 4, 2005 // Written by Rebecca Rand Kirshner // Directed by Robert Berlinger

Sookie uses the baptism of Davey and Martha as an excuse to bring Lorelai and Rory together; Zack and Brian use the $9,000 they made from the tour to "buy some magic beans"; and Logan makes a desperate attempt to escape his destiny.

GINCHY! Zack and Brian buying the computer with the tour money; Beau's "Satan can kiss my ass" at the baptism; the ostensibly dramatic (but unintentionally hilarious) *Riding the Bus with my Sister* movie actually being used to highlight Lorelai's misery over her shattered relationship with Rory.

NOTES *'It's not the same.'*

Rory's only just entered the DAR and already Emily is changing her by having the maid get rid of her summer clothes.

Sookie's plan to get Lorelai and Rory back together works...kind of.

✻ Jackson's cousin Rune (1.12, 1.19, 2.10) told Jackson's brother, Beau, that Lorelai is a nymphomaniac. Although Lane and Zack are still not having sex (5.16), she told him he could tell the guys they are.

✻ Though we've received hints along the way, the reason for Logan's reckless behavior (including his exploits with the Life and Death Brigade and his recent European jaunt) are made clear this episode when Logan

Bio George Anthony Bell (Dialogue Coach/Prof. Bell)

If you're an actor on *Gilmore Girls*, some fans ultimately will appreciate how fast you must deliver some real tongue twisters. But what about the guy who has to get the actors to the point where they *can* deliver those lines?

Gilmore had gone through three or four script supervisors who'd pulled double-duty as dialogue coaches before the decision was made that these needed to be two separate jobs. One of the show's first assistant directors, Carla McCloskey, suggested Bell give it a try. After all, the actor had taken jobs as a dialogue coach for the sitcom *Sister, Sister*, and had worked on Steven Spielberg's Peter Pan movie *Hook*.

Bell came by his talent for teaching others to deliver their lines honestly. Born in Shreveport, La., but raised in California from the age of 8, Bell grew up with a father who was a pastor for a very large church in LA, which instilled in him a love of language and song.

One of his proudest moments was his turn as a preacher in *The Ladykillers* (2004). At the audition, the Cohen brothers asked, "Are you sure you're not a minister?" After he told them his father, grandfather and brother were, they replied, "We knew it had to be genetic because that was just too real."

tells Rory that his father insists that he prepare to take a seat in the Huntzberger empire. His impulsive suggestion about going to New York by helicopter is yet another attempt to escape his future. It's this moment that many realize that Logan is, essentially, Lorelai, had she stayed at home.

A deeply unsatisfying episode, like an addict hitting rock bottom. But like an addict, these are the dark places we have to go to on the road to recovery.

TODAY'S CELEBRATION The mixer with the curators of the Gilbert Stuart exhibit, and the baptism of Davey (sponsored by Rory) and Martha (Lorelai)...and Jackson (Beau).

EMILY'S MAID DU JOUR Unnamed.

META, META, META Kirk's characterization of Davey as being The Dandy Warhols to Martha's Brian Jonestown Massacre is a reference to the documentary *DiG!*, which details the rivalry between the two bands, and will get another homage in the Hep Alien breakup scene later on (6.10).

AND HERE'S A SHOUT OUT TO OUR INTERNATIONAL FANS Emily and Richard are stuck in Helsinki, where "the cuisine isn't fit for a stray cat."

OY WITH THE ___, ALREADY! Usually a breath of fresh air, Colin and Finn are extremely annoying when Rory already has her hands full with a brooding Logan. And Jackson's family—arrgh!

THINGS WE'VE LEARNED Todd Lowe (Zack) is a big fan of early 20th century radio/TV comedian Jack Benny. "Two nights ago I followed all of these YouTube clips of him; he's just amazing."

AMEN, SISTER FRIEND

MICHEL [*to Lorelai about Jackson's family*]: They are moochers. They go supermarket-hopping to gorge themselves on free samples and get their perfume from magazine inserts. You can recognize them from the paper cuts on their wrists.

"Lauren was very lucky because she has something of a photographic memory and she could learn the lines. She is very, very smart, and Alexis is good, too. I just think that not many actresses could have done what the two of them did on that show. To learn that amount of dialogue and the number of scenes they were in, day after day, it was just amazing."

–GEORGE ANTHONY BELL, DIALOGUE COACH

LANE: Rory, look at me. You and your mom will talk again. This rift is just nature's attempt to find some equilibrium. You and Lorelai have gone too many years without fighting, so you had to have one big fight to make up for it. Now you've had it, and soon you'll make up and then this will all be just your lost weekend.

6.5 We've Got Magic to Do

First aired: Oct. 11, 2005 // Written by Daniel Palladino // Directed by Michael Zinberg

After Richard speaks with Lorelai about some insurance matters related to a small fire at the Dragonfly, he's forced to confront the reality that the Huntzbergers really did destroy the granddaughter he so loves. Rory, meanwhile, transforms an anemic DAR charity event into a sold-out extravaganza. In Stars Hollow, Luke's insecurities over his relationship with Lorelai are heightened when she urges him to go camping on his own.

GINCHY! Paris' embracing of socialism about five minutes after joining the working classes; Kirk's "The Journey of Man" mime (ew!); Richard and Emily skewering Mitchum and Shira Huntzberger, respectively, and that last shot of Richard looking on as Rory winds up the event.

NOTES *'There's something in the air today.'*

The Dragonfly continues the tradition of inn fires (3.17). Constance Betterton, Emily's longtime DAR nemesis, has only sold half the tables for a fundraiser for the troops at Fort Drum.

Once more (5.22), Lorelai tells Richard how horribly the Huntzbergers treated Rory, and again he doesn't believe her until he confirms it himself with Mitchum at the fundraiser.

The Geller saga continues as the IRS has frozen the assets of Paris' family. Paris speaks Chinese and Farsi (and a smattering of Aramaic). For the first time (but not the last), Paris identifies herself as Rory's best friend.

Rory's anger over Shira Huntzberger's failure to RSVP is a complicated response that goes beyond her loathing of Logan's family for the way they've treated her (5.19). Like Emily, working for the DAR and being under her grandmother's influence is teaching her that the rules of etiquette allow her to sublimate her feelings of anger and resentment by cracking down on others for infractions of those rules. She will show an equal level of ire when Lorelai fails to RSVP for her birthday party (6.7).

Rory transforms a floundering DAR event into a triumph.

✱ One of the most heartbreaking-yet-enjoyable episodes of the season, Richard and Emily defending their daughter at the DAR fundraiser is television at its best.

TODAY'S CELEBRATION The 28th Annual Miss Patty's School Grand Recital and Rory's USO-themed DAR fundraiser.

KIRK OF ALL TRADES Mime.

25 The number of years the DAR has served salmon puffs at all of its events.

100 The number of people at the DAR event.

YOU'VE ENTERED EMILYLAND Give me the seating chart, I'll find someone to bump. There's always someone to bump.

From the Editing Room 4 ⚙ Making It Fit

Editing an episode of *Gilmore Girls* is like jamming toothpaste back into the tube, as you have to fit what amounts to a feature-length script into 42 minutes.

"Let's say we're a minute and 18 seconds long, but Amy likes the performances and everything else, so we have to go through now and find a minute and 18 seconds to take out," says editor Raul Davalos. "So we go through it and she says, 'OK, let's go to the teaser. So we go to the teaser, and if there's a breath of air between Luke saying 'Tomorrow' and Lauren saying 'I'll be here'—if there's like eight frames—I would take it out. That's a third of a second. Then we keep a count like a scoreboard. OK, how many frames and seconds do we have left? So we're down to 36 seconds, so we've gotta find 36 seconds to take out. We go all the way through the show and then back to the beginning.

"If I can overlap some dialogue, I'll do it. People walking toward the door—if I can jump them to the door and cut to the other side and save 20 frames, I'll do it. No one knows. And you can't tell. You can watch the shows now and they play perfectly smoothly.

"It was just a lot of fun. When we're down to like four frames, Amy goes, 'Woohoo! Four frames! Let's find four frames!' She had so much fun doing it, and she would be the final arbiter."

AMEN, SISTER FRIEND

RICHARD: Emily, please. It's Rory. What she tackles, she conquers. This girl could name the state capitals at three. Recite the periodic table at four. Discuss Schopenhauer's influence on Nietzsche when she was 10. She's read every book by every author with a Russian surname and had a

Bell in action on the *Gilmore* set.

Behind the Scenes
Getting Those Lines Out

All of *Gilmore's* dense dialogue would've been for not had the actors been incapable of delivering them correctly. That's why George Anthony Bell was brought in as the show's dialogue coach starting with 3.6.

" I became kind of a safety net for all the actors, and maybe somewhat of a shrink. And the actors really liked me for the most part. They appreciated what I was doing. At times it was very difficult because no one likes to be corrected all the time, and that, essentially, was my job. So you're walking a tightrope. You have to know when to go in to give the correction and when to back off. And there were times I could tell that maybe an actor was really struggling and they were going to lose it, and that I would just back off and say, 'You know what, it's just not worth it. It's close enough.' And I would tell the director.

"I think with many of the guest directors, I was an important ally to them because I knew the actors' behavior and their moods. If they weren't in a good mood or stressed on a particular day, I would tell the director that this is not a good time to do that. If I were you I wouldn't do it now because they're going to go off in a second, because it's very stressful."

Once everybody was ready to shoot a scene, Bell would put on his headphones and follow along in the script while the actors performed their lines. "I have my own kind of shorthand where I knew what they said and maybe I would circle a word. Also what I would try to do, which is even more difficult, is I would try to write what the actor said incorrectly. For some actors, you go up and say this is incorrect, and the first thing they're going to ask is, 'Well, what did I say?' For actors like Lauren, it's better that I knew exactly what she said incorrectly, because then she could make the adjustment. Sometimes you think you're saying the line correctly and you're not. But if I can tell her what she was saying, then she knows what the adjustment should be.

"Other actors like Liz Torres, who is a sweetheart, she'd say, 'Don't tell me what I said wrong,' because she didn't want to lock into that. There were other actors that I wouldn't tell them what they said incorrect, I would just give them the correct line. You know what each person's process was for getting prepared."

4.2 grade point average at one of the toughest schools on the East Coast. If she's excluding salmon puffs, she has a good reason to exclude salmon puffs. And I, for one, have complete confidence in her ability to tackle this job, and so should you.

RICHARD: What did you say to her, Mitchum?
MITCHUM: I did what I do with everyone. I called it like I saw it. I was honest with her. I don't pussyfoot. You know that.
RICHARD: You crushed her.
MITCHUM: And if she's got what it takes, she'll bounce back. No one's ever criticized you, reprimanded you, critiqued you? I find that hard to believe.
RICHARD: This is not about me.
MITCHUM: She was in over her head. She lacked maturity.
RICHARD: She's not even 21!
MITCHUM: Look, just blame me, OK? I felt bad that she had to sit through that disastrous dinner with Shira and pop, going on about marriage and how she can't become a Huntzberger. I don't care about any of that, so I gave her a shot and she wasn't up to it.
RICHARD: You crushed that girl!
MITCHUM: I did what I do.

EMILY [*to Shira Huntzberger*]: Now let's talk about your money. You were a two-bit gold digger, fresh off the bus from Hicksville when you met Mitchum at whatever bar you happened to stumble into. And what made Mitchum decide to choose you to marry amongst the pack of women he was bedding at the time, I'll never know. But hats off to you for bagging him. He's still a playboy, you know? Well, of course you know. That would explain why your weight goes up and down 30 pounds every other month. But that's your cross to bear. But these are ugly realities. No one needs to talk about them. Those kids are staying together for as long as they like. You won't stop them. Now enjoy the event.

6.6 Welcome to the Dollhouse

First aired: Oct. 18, 2005 // Written by Keith Eisner // Directed by Jackson Douglas

When Stars Hollow reverts to its original street names, Lorelai raises hell over the Dragonfly's "Sores and Boils Alley," leading to the inn being dropped from the official historical Stars Hollow map. Hurt that Richard saw Lorelai recently, Emily besieges her daughter with items she was going to leave to her anyway, and finally asks her to pick up her dollhouse. Meanwhile, Rory finds herself falling more in love with Logan just as he seems to be pulling away.

$6,000 to $120,000

The price range for Birkin bags (the high-end ones are made of crocodile skin and include a diamond and white-gold clasp).

! GINCHY! Luke's new zen attitude toward Taylor; Emily's obsession with Rory's Birkin bag; Richard bringing Lorelai her dollhouse, and then telling her they need to talk about Rory.

NOTES *'Let me keep my Zen.'*

* Taylor once tried to attract families to Stars Hollow by driving through other towns offering children candy. (Incidentally, when did Taylor take back the town selectman role from Jackson?)

* Richard and Emily have only been back together a short time and already Richard's keeping things from her again—this time, his meeting with Lorelai at the Dragonfly last episode.

* In the 18th century, the street that the Dragonfly is on was where people went to have their sores and boils lanced (there even may have been a leper colony in the Dragonfly's garage). And Taylor, for some reason, has a collection of antique boil lances (ewww!).

* Logan mentions to Richard a forthcoming trip to Martha's Vineyard he and Rory are taking in a few weeks (6.15). His misunderstanding about Richard hinting at a forthcoming marriage between him and Rory may be partially spurred by the joke Richard and Rory played on him regarding that topic some time ago (5.10).

* Rory tries to ease Logan's mind about him not having to respond after she tells him she loves him, giving him the *Reader's Digest* version of her own experience in the junkyard with Dean (1.16).

TODAY'S CELEBRATION Stars Hollow reverts to street names from its founding days, Rory gets her picture in the paper because of last episode's charity event, Logan gets her a Birkin bag, and Rory tells him she loves him (whew).

KIRK OF ALL TRADES Phineas the cobbler from 1779 Stars Hollow, representative of the Stars Hollow Board of Tourism, and operator of the Stars Hollow Visitors Center.

EMILY'S MAID DU JOUR Consuela, who insists on coating everything with sugar.

26% How much Stars Hollow's tourism earnings have slipped since the last fiscal year.

23 How old Emily was when she married Richard.

SOOKIA Sookie's name in Spanish class.

THIRD STREET The location of the Dragonfly Inn.

AMEN, SISTER FRIEND

EMILY [*searching the pool house*]: Oh don't worry. I used to do this all the time with Lorelai, and the things I found! Once I opened the bottom drawer to her dresser and it was chock full of Tootsie Rolls, hundreds and hundreds, practically spilling out. What could a girl possibly want with a drawer full of Tootsie Rolls?

Behind the Scenes: Drinking Lessons

As Logan's ready-for-anything pal Finn, Tanc Sade appeared intermittently throughout *Gilmore*, which was his first US TV series.

"It was the highest rated show on that network for a long time, and it was a testament to Amy. If she wasn't happy with something, we'd do it again and again. We had one episode where we were all dressed as prisoners standing at the bar. My call time that day was about 11 am I got home about 6:30 the next morning. We were in that bar a long time. Granted that whole time wasn't spent on that one scene, we'd shot others. I think I came out and said something like, 'My, New Haven, you look appealing tonight,' or something like that. So we had that little exterior. But that's Amy. No, we're doing it again.

"I learned a big lesson that day. I was supposed to be drinking something or other and obviously you don't drink alcohol on the set. So, as a double for tequila, I was drinking one of those power drinks. I've gotta say after 15 shots of that stuff, I was bouncing off the walls. I was just working on this job in Australia and they said, Tanc, what do you want to be drinking? Vodka on the rocks. Because Vodka's water."

RICHARD: Perhaps it was what was under the Tootsie Rolls, Emily.

EMILY: Under the Tootsie Rolls! Oh my God, I should have looked under the Tootsie Rolls! Oh, that's going to bother me. God knows what she had in there.

LORELAI [*about Taylor*]: So he thought for a minute, then he stood up and he said to me, 'Lorelai, donate a hundred dollars to the Stars Hollow Historical Society and I will let you back on the map and you can keep Third Street.'

SOOKIE: One hundred dollars.

MICHEL: That's nothing! What did you say?

LORELAI: I said, 'You've got a deal.'

SOOKIE: Oh my God!

LORELAI: And then he said, 'Good girl,' and patted me on the head.

SOOKIE: Oh no.

MICHEL: Don't tell me–

LORELAI: We are on Sores and Boils Alley.

Behind the Scenes Happy Birthday, Little Girl

While many probably have their own ideas about why Rory dreams of Madeleine Albright as her mother, the former Clinton-era US secretary of state (1997-2001) was a major get for *Gilmore*.

Political junky that she and Dan are, Amy would always ring up the casting office and rattle off a few names of high-profile politicos she'd like to see on the show, casting director Jami Rudofsky remembers; Madeleine Albright was one of them. "And every time she said someone like that, I'm like, 'All right Amy, sure.'"

Thinking it was worth a try, she rang up Albright's office and put in her request. Her assistant rang her back almost immediately and said Albright would love to do it. "There was a huge fanbase of all different types, and we were lucky enough to find Madeleine Albright was a fan of *Gilmore Girls*," Rudofsky says. "To call Amy and say, 'All right, she's on board.... It's like we would try to move mountains to get these people that they wanted on the show. Somehow we did it."

6.7 Twenty-One is the Loneliest Number

First aired: Oct. 25, 2005 // Written by Amy Sherman-Palladino // Directed by Robert Berlinger

Rory is officially an adult, despite the fact that she's living with her grandparents and showing no signs of moving forward with her life. Nobody's more horrified by this than Richard, who even begs Lorelai for help. But Lorelai understands Rory well enough to know that she won't do anything until she's ready. When Emily discovers Rory is having sex, she kicks her out of the pool house and installs her in her old room beside her own. Rory invites Lorelai and Luke to the birthday party thrown by Emily, and the girls enjoy their first civil conversation in weeks.

! GINCHY! Madeleine Albright as Lorelai in Rory's dream; Morey and Babette's bizarre hanging demonstration for Halloween; Richard and Emily springing the Rev. Boteright on Rory as a preemptive strike against her sex life, and her response to him; Luke's unintentionally hilarious "What's the DAR"; and Lorelai and Rory finally speaking with each other.

NOTES *'No! We have not failed. We have not failed until that girl comes home pregnant. Then we've failed!'*

✱ This is the first we hear of Richard having set up a trust fund for Rory, which she will receive when she turns 25, the same as Paris (6.5). His insistence that "we can fix this" reveals that this whole mindset of simply "fixing" things extends beyond the three Gilmore women (see "The Fix is In" under 1.18).

✱ Doyle is stepping down as editor of the Yale Daily News at the end of the year, and will write a column called "The World According to Doyle." Paris will be the new editor. Luke corrects Paris at one point, saying he met her a few weeks ago (6.1), but they actually met when Paris went to the diner to expose Stars Hollow's scandals for an article (2.12).

✱ Luke gives Rory a pearl necklace that belonged to his mother. Lorelai tells Rory she and Luke are renovating the house and that she got a dog (and yes, Babette checks to make sure he's fed). Emily notices Lorelai's engagement ring for the first time.

TODAY'S CELEBRATION Rory's 21st birthday party.

Make Yourself a 'Rory'

That's champagne, vodka, pineapple juice and grenadine.

EMILY'S MAID DU JOUR May-May, who waits until somebody has wrung the doorbell three times before answering it.

4:03 AM The time Rory was born 21 years ago.

$40,000 How much Richard paid to convert the pool house into Rory's "sex house."

196 The number of hours of community service Rory has completed so far.

AMEN, SISTER FRIEND

LORELAI [*to Luke about Rory's 21st birthday*]: We were gonna go to Atlantic City. We were gonna sit at a blackjack table at 11:59, we were gonna order martinis, and we were gonna be playing 21 when she turned 21. And then hopefully we'd win, and we'd take our winnings and we'd buy 21 things. And then there was a thing about 21 guys that wouldn't really be appropriate anymore since the engagement, but it was a good plan. She probably doesn't even remember the plan.

REVEREND: You want to give this gift very carefully. It is a gift you can give to only one man. Once you give it, it's gone. You can't re-gift it. If you give it away too soon to the wrong man, then when the right one does come along, you have no gift to give. You'll have to buy him a sweater. Do you understand what I'm saying?
RORY: No.
REVEREND: Think long and hard about when and to whom you want to give the ultimate gift you have to give away.
RORY: Oh.
REVEREND: Yes.
RORY: Oh dear.
REVEREND: Oh dear, indeed.
RORY: Um. Well, listen, reverend. I really appreciate you taking the time out of what I assume is a busy day to come here and talk to me about all of this, but I'm afraid the ultimate-gift ship has sailed.
REVEREND: What?
RORY: A while ago. It's probably in Fiji by now.

What I Kept

I've got a couple things that they gave me. They sent me a Luke's Diner shirt. But nothing that I actually wore during an episode. I had a *Gilmore Girls* bag that they gave me for the 100th episode anniversary party – I have things like that. But I don't have Janet's sweat suit or anything like that.

—Katie Walder (Janet)

RICHARD: Running around with Logan, joining the DAR, planning parties.
EMILY: What's wrong with joining the DAR? We both agreed she needed a job.
RICHARD: Fundraisers and tea parties? It's frivolous and meaningless. She has more to do, more to be. I don't want that life for her.
EMILY: You mean my life. You don't want her to be me.

6.8 Let Me Hear Your Balalaikas Ringing Out

First aired: Nov. 8, 2005 // Written by Daniel Palladino // Directed by Kenny Ortega

Rory has had enough of Emily's constant scrutiny. Yet it takes seeing Jess as a humble, published author and Logan as an arrogant jerk who does nothing but whine about his future for her to realize that she has to jump-start her life. Meanwhile, Lorelai's efforts to socialize Paul Anka lead to the dog falling ill, compounding her feelings of being a "bad mother."

GINCHY! The vicious fieldwork of the little girl soccer team the Bobcats; Jess' modest success as a writer waking up Rory to her own stagnation, and to Logan's; Lorelai keeping a list of all the things that Paul Anka is afraid of on her fridge; and Rory politely but firmly telling Emily that she will no longer be living with her.

NOTES *'You are becoming more like your mother with every passing day.' 'And you are becoming more like my mother's mother with every passing day.'*
Rory has resorted to telling Emily she's sleeping over at Paris' apartment when she stays over at Logan's. Jess is living and working in Philadelphia at a small publishing house on Locust Street.

Logan says that his "life is over" in June, presumably when Mitchum's great plans for him kick in.

TODAY'S CELEBRATION The DAR-sponsored Russian tea party (complete with balalaika players), and with it, Rory's emancipation from Emily and Richard.

KIRK OF ALL TRADES Doggie day care operator (though let's please resist the temptation to blame Paul Anka's illness on the proprietor).

EMILY'S MAID DU JOUR Shandinka has a used SUV.

500 About the number of copies of *The Subsect* by Jess Mariano in print.

AMEN, SISTER FRIEND

LORELAI [*to Luke, after he rejects the little girls*]: Wow, Oliver Twist just kindly asked for a little more gruel and you kicked him right in the junk.

LUKE: Kids usually talk but they don't say anything. You know, they just kind of yammer, so if you don't find them cute, they're just boring.

JESS: What's going on with you?
RORY: What do you mean?
JESS: You know what I mean. I know you better than anyone. This isn't you.
RORY: I don't know.
JESS: What are you doing? Living at your grandparents' place, being in the DAR, no Yale—why did you drop out of Yale?!
RORY: It's complicated.
JESS: It's not! It's not complicated.
RORY: You don't know.
JESS: This isn't you. This, you going out with this jerk with the Porsche. We made fun of guys like this.
RORY: You caught him on a bad night.
JESS: This isn't about him, OK. Screw him. What's going on with you? This isn't you, Rory. You know it isn't. What's going on?
RORY: I don't know. I don't know!

6.9 The Prodigal Daughter Returns

First aired: Nov. 15, 2005 // Written and directed by Amy Sherman-Palladino

Unable to abide living with Emily a moment longer, Rory moves out and crashes at Lane's as she sets out to get her life back on track. When Christopher leaves a message on Lorelai's answering machine, Luke loses it, telling Lorelai that they have to tell each other everything if their relationship is going to work. But when a super-smart (and pretty Rory-like) 12-year-old girl shows up at the diner, he suddenly realizes just how tough honesty can be.

GINCHY! Colin and Finn running into Richard while moving Rory's stuff; Jackson completely missing the fact that Luke and Lorelai are fighting; Lorelai reminding Zack that the band used her garage rent free for years after he asks her to chip in some rent for Rory staying with them; our finally hearing Emily's side of things when Lorelai confronts her in the plane; and every scene that April is in.

NOTES *'We have to tell each other everything.'*

We usually remember how selfish Lorelai was during this season, but seldom do we give her credit for knowing this about herself. While telling Sookie about the furniture Luke's installed in her bedroom, she says, "He has turned his whole life upside down for me. He does everything in his power to make me happy and give me what I want, so can't I just give him this one little thing?"

In addition to Lorelai's riff on "Saturday Night's Alright for Fighting" foreshadowing her own spat with Luke, it will also be reflected in an episode title pretty soon (6.13).

It's been a year since Lorelai last saw Christopher (5.13). His call to Lorelai, which sparks the fight between her and Luke, almost certainly was to tell her about his sudden windfall (6.10).

Bio Vanessa Marano (April Nardini)

Uneasy lies the head that wears the blame for the breakup of Luke and Lorelai; just ask Vanessa Marano. "Yeah, the fans really went after my character a lot. April got no slack. People did not like April."

This was doubly-hard for Marano, who was actually one of the few people on *Gilmore* to have grown up as a fan of the series (watching the reruns on ABC Family). She was just 13 when she started on the series, playing 12-year-old April.

Born in Los Angeles to a college language teacher and an actress/teacher, Marano began her own acting career at 7, and has never looked back. Though her first professional job was on a York's Peppermint Patty commercial, she invariably ended up in the Spanish department of whatever ad agency she was working with. "I didn't speak Spanish, so literally I'd be on set and they'd go, 'Can you say gracias?' And I'd go, 'Ohhhkay, maybe.'"

Since those days, she's had frequent appearances on *Without a Trace* (with sister Laura), *Dexter*, and *The Young and the Restless*. It seems the only slacker in the Marano family is the dog. "She's very lazy," Marano admits. "That's why you don't work with dogs or kids, because the dogs are slackers and the kids will upstage you."

"When I got the breakdown for the role I was like, 'You're giving Luke a daughter! This is going to break them up. Oh my God!' I mean I hated myself. How can my character do this?"

–VANESSA MARANO (APRIL)

✱ April Nardini goes to Martin Van Buren Middle School in Woodbury. According to Brian, the band used Lorelai's garage for rehearsals for three years.

✱ Emily's freakout aboard the plane rips the lid off emotions that have been building for years. Her "It's my fault that Rory dropped out of Yale, it's my fault that she didn't go back..." echoes her telling Lorelai, "Everything that's wrong in your life is my fault, everything that's wrong in your father's life is my fault..." when Richard's mother was about to inspect Lorelai's house (3.10). However, her telling Lorelai, "I lost her like I lost you" this episode is a stunning turnaround on her earlier warning to Lorelai that, "You're going to lose her just like I lost you" about Rory, after she stayed out all night with Dean (1.9).

TODAY'S CELEBRATION Lorelai's housewarming party, April's science fair, Rory gets a writing job at the Stamford Eagle Gazette, and finally comes home.

EMILY'S MAID DU JOUR Sumatra briefly plays go-between when Rory and Emily aren't speaking to each other.

$2,000 How much Luke paid Tom and the guys to finish work on Lorelai's house early.

Behind the Scenes: Finding April's Look

Though Vanessa Marano is extremely intelligent, and was already in college at 16, she'll be the first to tell you that she's not like April. "April's very science and math, and I hate science and math more than anything in my entire life. I would say that April is probably smarter than me.

"I don't wear glasses, even. I actually bought them for the role. My dad and I went to Long's drug store and picked up glasses because the breakdown for the character described her as quirky, very school bookish. So I was like, OK, I'll go in, I'll wear a God-ugly sweater and glasses and put my hair back in a ratty pony tail. So I did that. All they had at Long's drug store were prescription glasses, so my first two days on set, I was seeing two of everything.

"They were reading glasses because I couldn't find anything else. We got the lowest prescription possible, but still everything was a little blurry. Finally the props guy came up to me and said, 'Those real glasses?' I said yes. 'Do you want me to get you clear frames?' I was like, 'Really, could you do that for me? That would be great.' Because before then, I was just taking them off every single take."

Now what was that he told Lorelai about sharing everything?

HEY, FAMILY FRIENDLY FORUM! Lorelai's "I'm not scared of it anymore, Luke" after he tells her to close her eyes.

THINGS WE'VE LEARNED Like April, Vanessa Marano really does say "No prob-lay-mo" in real life.

AND INTRODUCING...*April Nardini* Easily the most controversial character in the *Gilmore* universe, mostly because fans worldwide lay the failure of the Luke and Lorelai relationship squarely on her little shoulders.

"The first scene that I actually shot was when I walk into the diner and I rip the hair out of Luke's head. I didn't rip his hair out, but on the first take I pulled his hair and Scott went, 'You know, it's OK, you don't need to do that.'"

—VANESSA MARANO (APRIL)

AMEN, SISTER FRIEND

EMILY [*about Rory*]: Oh yes. She looked at me just like you used to. With that defiant, "who are you to be telling me what to do?" sort of look. Then she left. Packed her things and moved out when I wasn't even there to see her go. No "thank you," no "goodbye." You would have been very, very proud.

LORELAI: Mom.

EMILY: Just let me buy my plane, Lorelai. Let me be frivolous and shallow, won't you please?

LORELAI: OK. It's not the same, mom, what happened with Rory. It's not the same.

EMILY: I lost her like I lost you. Feels remarkably similar to me.

LORELAI: You didn't lose her like you lost me. She was never supposed to be there in the first place; she was always supposed to be at school. She just went back where she belonged. And you didn't lose me.

APRIL: Well, every year Samuel Polotsky wins the science fair. Now, it's very important that I beat him this year because I hate him. This year I have the perfect project. I'm going to take hair samples from three men, run DNA tests on them, and figure out which one's my father.
LUKE: What?
APRIL: My uncle works for a lab in Hartford, so he's going to oversee me. But I'll be doing all the actual work myself.
LUKE: I'm sorry. Did you say your father?
APRIL: Yeah, see, science fairs have gotten so political lately. It's no longer the simple act of science being appreciated. There's got to be a twist, a gimmick. Something flashy. I figure this is perfect. Real science, DNA testing, with a flash of human drama. "Who's my daddy?" Huh? Catchy, right?

LORELAI: She's back. She's back at home, she's back at school, she got a job, and she did it all on her own. She's at Lane's picking up her things, and then we're going to pull a major all-nighter. We need burgers, fries, onion rings, and anything else you can think of. I'm going to go next door and pick up some ice cream at Taylor's. She's back. We can set the date. We can get married now because Rory's back. Don't skimp on the fries; we don't want to lose her again.

6.10 He's Slippin' 'Em Bread...Dig?

First aired: Nov. 22, 2005 // Written by Daniel Palladino // Directed by Kenny Ortega

It's Thanksgiving, that time of year when families, regardless of their differences, come together to share a meal without killing each other. Yet Rory is separated from Logan (who's told his sister that they've split up), Luke is conflicted over the fact that he has a daughter who doesn't seem to want him in her life, and Christopher is enthused about his inheritance, but has nobody to really share it with, though he's paying Rory's Yale bills. Meanwhile, when Brian good-naturedly writes a song about Lane, Zack goes off the deep end and wrecks the band's shot at the big time.

GINCHY! Rory putting sugar on her toes to get in good with Paul Anka (evil Lorelai!); how happy Christopher is when he tells Lorelai that he's rich; Luke's reversal on the Christopher issue now that he knows he has his own little girl out there.

NOTES *'I'm here to destroy the system so stay out of my way!'*

Hep Alien original songs include "Rebecca in the Morning," "Colleen Francine," "Dear Maureen," "Stella," "Linda Marie," "Lorraine" and "Melissa." (Creatively, Zack is still a player.)

Christopher's grandfather was 98 when he died, leaving him a lot of money. (It's not certain, but we're guessing his name was Deus Ex Machina Hayden.)

Paris suggests driving a forklift being the only thing Rory would be fit for without an education, which probably doesn't have the same connotation of economic desperation for Rory as it does for Paris. Jess, after all, drove a forklift at Wal-Mart, yet it was his minor triumph as a novelist that woke her up to her own squandered potential (6.8). Singer/guitarist Amy Kuney is the folk singer at Rich Man's Shoe, and pops up again as one of the troubadour wannabes in the season finale (6.22).

"Sometimes it was a little difficult to act and actually deliver the music to where it sounds decent enough. Though we weren't supposed to be that great of a band."

—TODD LOWE (ZACK)

Behind the Scenes Injury Parade 3

"I can remember the episode where we all had the fight in the club and I lost it and started yelling at everybody," Todd Lowe says. "Sebastian was so adamant that he didn't need a double—'All it is is just falling to the ground, it's not hard!' So just on the rehearsal, he's going full out. And then the next day he's late coming in and he's got this huge brace on his knee and a limp. He's like, 'Where's my double?' I don't think I ever got physically hurt. It was a really pleasant experience. I have nothing bad to say about working on that show. "

But Bach wasn't the only one to get hurt.

"They called Amy & Dan to the set for them to look at what we'd done, and we'd been practicing and practicing and practicing," John Cabrera recalls. "We all got ready, and action. And we start doing it and Sebastian just knees me in the groin. I just went down. Amy & Dan are watching and I'm just laying there in the fetal position. All I'm thinking is, 'What the-?' In everything we do, I'm the guy who gets injured."

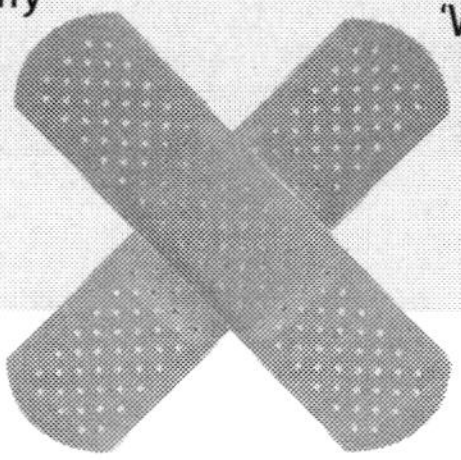

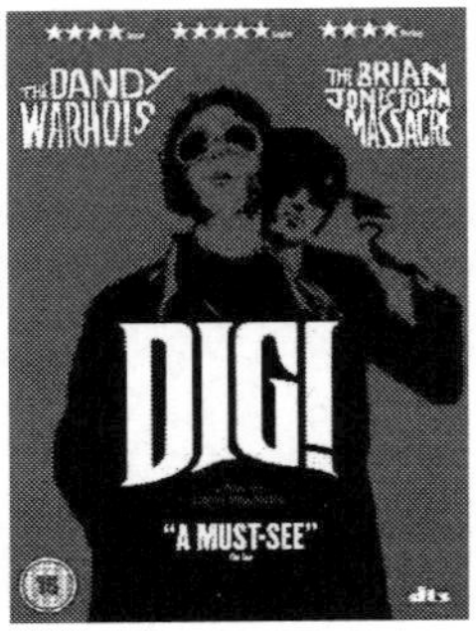

DiG?

Ever the documentary fans, Amy & Dan's violent dust-up between the members of Hep Alien (and the title of this episode) is a reference to the documentary *DiG!* about The Dandy Warhols and The Brian Jonestown Massacre. Adding a little extra oomph to this reference is the inclusion of Brian Jonestown Massacre tambourine player and vocalist Joel Gion as Hep Alien's new addition.

"Amy and I saw [the movie] on DVD when it first came out," Dan told the Chicago Tribune in February 2006. "The second we saw that Viper Room fight scene, we said [Hep Alien] has got to go through that."

"There are too many strings with these people," Rory says of her grandparents, confirming Lorelai's "Those are strings, Pinocchio" line from nearly three years ago (3.22). Lorelai tells Rory that Richard and Emily hit her with a minister, a priest, a rabbi and a Mormon missionary, and had five religious interventions with her when she was a kid, putting Rory's experience with the Rev. Boteright in perspective.

TODAY'S CELEBRATION Thanksgiving, and Hep Alien (nearly) playing a showcase for a music label at the New Deck.

11,000 SQUARE FEET The size of the Huntzberger home.

3 MONTHS How long Rory actually stayed with Richard and Emily.

META, META, META Sookie names her Thanksgiving turkeys Tree, Chuck and Bob, which are actually the nicknames of *Gilmore*'s prop people, Chuck and Bob, and the set dresser, Tree.

AND HERE'S A SHOUT OUT TO OUR INTERNATIONAL FANS Christopher offers to buy Lorelai or Rory a castle in Ireland, Germany, Czech Republic, Scotland...or Narnia.

AMEN, SISTER FRIEND

GIL: I remember once throwing up in that corner, and some dude slipped in it and had to go to the hospital, and I stole the chick he was with and shacked up with her for like a week and a half.

LORELAI [*about Christopher*]: He's come into a lot of money, family money. And he offered Rory and me lots of things we didn't want or need, but Rory took him up on his offer to pay for Yale. It was her idea and I support it. That's it. So he's going to be financing her tuition this year and next year, and we got together today at a diner to finalize it, and that's it.
LUKE : I think that's great.
LORELAI: Really?
LUKE: Yes. I think that's absolutely great.
LORELAI: You heard the part about how I got together with Christopher?
LUKE: Absolutely. You had to, to talk about this. He's her dad. If he's got

something, he should be sharing it. Good for him. He's been gone most of the time, so he owes you. I'm glad he's doing it. He's doing what a dad is supposed to do. He's taking care of his kid. Good.

6.11 The Perfect Dress

First aired: Jan. 10, 2006 // Written by Amy Sherman-Palladino // Directed by Jamie Babbit

The "Rory's back" excitement has worn off and now it's time for mother and daughter's lives to get back on track. For Lorelai, this means hashing out wedding details with Sookie, and happening upon "the perfect dress" that, in retrospect, doesn't seem so perfect. For Rory, it's begging her way back into Yale and dealing with the sudden news that she and Logan haven't just been giving each other space, they've broken up. For Lane, it's living with Mrs. Kim again and trying to get over Zack since his horrible behavior at the club. And for Luke, it's making the decision to be in April's life, even if he can't quite bring himself to tell Lorelai that she, you know, exists.

! GINCHY! Paul Anka wanting to go off with Rory; Lorelai's reaction ("No! No!") to seeing where Rory's living now; Luke logging on to April's Web site (with Kirk's help) and his wistful perusal of it; Mrs. Kim's hidden booze stash; Luke losing the nerve to tell Lorelai about April the moment he sees her in her wedding dress.

Behind the Scenes: April's Bike Helmet

"That was one of the coolest contraptions I've ever seen," says Vanessa Marano about April's helmet. "It was so bizarre and awesome at the same time. And my favorite part of it was that it was pink. I'm in four different scenes taking that bike helmet off and on. You have to keep in mind that we do about a million takes, so that was me taking that thing off and on every time. It was very complicated."

Though we seldom actually see her riding her bike with the helmet on, the actress had to do it anyway. "It's so funny because you never see it, but it's like in the background because you have to do it for continuity reasons. I would have to ride my bike up, park my bike, take my thing off, and then I walk into the diner. "I would've liked to keep the helmet, but I think the prop guy, that was a very special thing to him. He built that actually. He put it on his 10-year-old son's head and built it around that. I think he held that prop very close to his heart."

The helmet also continued a tradition of roles for Marano that required her to be confined by some odd gear. The previous year, she had the title role in *The Brooke Ellison Story*, about a quadriplegic girl whose head is held in place by a "halo" rigging. "Funnily enough, the bicycle helmet, very similar to the halo. Luckily I did that before so I had a little bit of experience. I never had to take that off in a scene, but I had to take it off and on for lunch and stuff like that."

Finding the perfect dress is the least of Lorelai's problems.

"They took some pictures of me for recent shots and they also took some of my own baby pictures and used those. But they also had a little girl on set to be me, too, because they needed a little girl with glasses, and none of my baby pictures have glasses in them."

-VANESSA MARANO ABOUT THE WEB SITE LUKE VISITS THIS EPISODE

NOTES *'Planning a wedding shouldn't be easy because marriage isn't easy.'*

* Kirk informs us that Luke is a Scorpio, which we already knew (5.3). The girls ended up going to Atlantic City as they'd always planned to do for Rory's birthday (6.7). They pretended Rory was turning 21 while they were playing 21, drank martinis, bought 21 things (including shot glasses, pasties and glow-in-the-dark coasters), and got the phone numbers of 21 guys. They were looking forward to seeing Paul Anka in performance there, but ended up seeing Tony Danza instead.

* Rory is now living with Paris and Doyle and is finished with her community service, though she forgot to turn in her vest. Paris hasn't slept through the night since her mother showed her *The Wizard of Oz*. Though she mentioned taking krav maga much earlier (5.15), Paris now says she and Doyle started taking it when they moved into their sketchy neighborhood.

* At last, Lorelai has chosen a wedding date: June 3rd; yes, same as Rory's court date (5.22). She's already booked the church and the reception area, including a carrousel from 1850. Her choice of daisies seems a tad insensitive considering those were the flowers Max bombarded her with (1.21).

* Paris' reign as the editor of the Yale Daily News begins with the posting of "no talking" signs, a ban on decorating people's work areas, the institution of a demerit system and locks on the bathroom doors. Anna

Nardini says she actually saw Luke five years ago at a lumber yard.

Logan finally tells Rory that he loves her (6.6), to no avail. Rory's meltdown at the shrink's results in her having to see him once a week for the next two months, though we'll never hear about it again.

TODAY'S CELEBRATION Rory's return to Yale, and the coming together of Lorelai and Luke's wedding plans.

AND INTRODUCING... *Anna Nardini* Played by Sherilyn Fenn, last seen as Sasha, the girlfriend of Jess' father, Jimmy (3.21).

WENDY & LISA The names Lorelai and Rory used in Atlantic City.

APARTMENT 8 Rory's new digs with Paris and Doyle.

6 WEEKS How long Lane has been living at home since she left Zack.

SAROYAN Doyle's "safety word" during krav maga sparring, presumably after early 20th century playwright and novelist William Saroyan (*The Time of Your Life*, *The Human Comedy*).

AND HERE'S A SHOUT OUT TO OUR INTERNATIONAL FANS PARIS [*to Rory*]: Journalism is an art form, and the best art is created under repression, like Stalin's gulag. You think Solzhenitsyn could have written *One Day in the Life Of Ivan Denisovich* on a yoga retreat?

AMEN, SISTER FRIEND

PARIS [*welcoming the new Yale Daily News staff*]: It's going to be a great term, people, an important term, a term to change the history of the Yale Daily News. The work will be hard. It has to be hard. Nothing less than perfect will be tolerated. Please remember that I am your editor, I am not your mother or your hugger. If you need some love, get a hooker. If you're having a bad day, find a ledge or a way to deal. My door is not open to you ever. You have five minutes to enjoy your cookies. Welcome to the Yale Daily News.

ANNA: We couldn't go to the movies before 10 o'clock at night in case there were kids in the theater.
LUKE: Well, kids talk during a movie and they throw crap around. They run up and down the aisles. They're animals.

Krav Maga, Baby

Though we only see a little bit of Paris and Doyle practicing their krav maga self-defense, Liza Weil and Danny Strong went to the Krav Maga Worldwide Training Center in West Los Angeles twice a week for a month to learn the moves, Strong says. "The instructor was a great guy and he offered to give us this really cheap monthly rate. I told Liza, 'I'm going to do this. This is going to be my thing.' Of course I never went back again. So typical of everything I get involved in. But it was fun, I really liked it, and it's a great workout."

The krav maga scene marked the beginning of a Paris/Doyle double act "where it was what kind of gag are they doing this week," he admits. "One week was krav maga, one week we're doing yoga, one week we're dance training..."

Luke and Anna discuss the finer points of parenting.

"[Sally Struthers] is amazing. You hear people say this in the entertainment industry, but she really is more than anybody I've ever worked with, the person who treats the stand-in and the extras the exact same way she treats the executive producers and the people from the network. Nobody does that. I don't do that. I don't know if that makes her a better person than me or not, but I think it's wonderful."

–SEAN GUNN (KIRK)

ANNA: We would move tables in a restaurant if they seated us near a family.
LUKE: Only if there was something crying or spitting up.
ANNA: You would flip out if you saw a woman breast-feeding in public, you couldn't stand to watch diaper commercials and you had an unnatural hatred of Macaulay Culkin.
LUKE: OK, fine. I hated kids, but I'm not that guy anymore.

RORY [*talking to the Yale shrink about Logan*]: Nothing for weeks, and then he just decides that he loves me. So, what happens now? I get another Birkin bag? And how long until he doesn't love me again, huh? I stole a boat with him! I never stole a boat with Dean!
DR. SHAPIRO: Who's Dean?
RORY: My married ex-boyfriend who I lost my virginity to!
DR. SHAPIRO: Wow.

6.12 Just Like Gwen and Gavin

First aired: Jan. 17, 2006 // Written by Daniel Palladino // Directed by Stephen Clancy

The staff of the Yale Daily News is already planning a coup thanks to Paris' refusal to learn their names, let them write or use the bathroom. Logan throws himself on the mercy of Lorelai to help him get Rory back, and Lorelai finally learns about April when she runs into her at the diner. Everything hits the fan at the winter carnival, especially when Zack sees Lane sharing a laugh with a good looking Korean guy.

GINCHY! "Doo-doo head" Taylor's video address to the town; Logan having a coffee cart follow Rory around all day; April getting all nostalgic over coloring books after Luke mentions them; Rory laughing and changing her mind about Logan while she reads the letter Lorelai gave him to give to her; Paul Anka the doggy swami, with a special round of applause for Zack's "Welcome to the SH, bitch" confrontation with Joe.

NOTES *'Come see the Amazing Doggy Swami. Discover your future...'*

April's learning Morse code and putting. Lorelai has broken many promises to Kirk, including one to attend his birthday party in 2001, to teach him to swim, to bring him a pen and ink set from Colonial Williamsburg, Va., and to put in a good word for him at Al's Pancake World for a batter boy position.

With Luke's call to Anna, we get the first indication of her hard-nosed side, which will

Paris' Magnet System

—On assignment: Red
—In the bathroom: Blue
—At home: Purple
—At your desk: Green
—In class: Orange

Behind the Scenes Talk Fast

Though not one of the most inspiring official television taglines, "Life's short, talk fast" definitely summed up the mainstream image of *Gilmore Girls*. "Anything said quickly can seem wittier than it is," observed *MADtv's* February 2004 parody "Gabmore Girls." Yet if it seemed new to many, those with more of a theatrical background were not quite so taken by surprise.

Too often Kelly Bishop had been told to slow down her line delivery for the stage, until her Lincoln Center performance of *Six Degrees of Separation* under director Jerry Zaks. "That thing flew," she says. "The dialogue was so fast, that real rat-a-tat New York thing. As soon as I got into that, I thought 'I'm home. This is how fast I like to talk.' Then here we go with *Gilmore Girls*, and it had that same kind of energy behind it."

Olivia Hack, who played Rory's child-prodigy dorm mate Tana, points out another aspect of that speedy banter. "The thing about that show is that you think it's really snappy and all of this, and to a certain extent it is. But one of my first days, someone told me it's not about going fast. Because if you watch the show, you think you should just say everything fast. And that's not what it is. Really they do a lot of that in editing. A lot of that snappiness is really on their side. So if you do your job and stay true to your character, they'll edit it so it becomes the tone of the show in that way."

Paul Anka finally starts earning his kibble.

cause a great deal of problems later on (7.10). She tells him that "You're either all in or you're all out" when it comes to being in April's life, pretty much the same words Luke himself used when he first started a relationship with Lorelai (5.3).

TODAY'S CELEBRATION The 126th Annual Stars Hollow winter carnival and the postponement of Luke and Lorelai's wedding.

KIRK OF ALL TRADES Runner of the above carnival (though Taylor isn't too far away).

3:12 AM The time of the emergency town meeting.

AND INTRODUCING...*the Yale Daily News staff* Bill, Sheila, AK, Raj and Joni are some of the ones that actually get names.

5 MONTHS, THREE WEEKS, 16 DAYS How long Lorelai and Rory didn't speak during their fight, according to Lorelai.

2 MONTHS How long Luke has known about April.

Behind the Scenes: Making it Fun

When Lauren Graham had to go off and shoot the movie *Evan Almighty*, cast and crew had to wrap the season earlier than normal to give her the time to do it. The result was crazy call times and starting work on weird days of the week.

"Alexis said, 'I want to make this fun for everybody,'" Valerie Campbell remembers. "'On Saturdays and Sundays we'll have lunch for people and we'll have everybody's families come to the lot.' We had a counting game, like when you have a jar of jellybeans. One of them had licorice in it, one had coffee beans, and one had tampons. I ended up winning the tampons, which got me a free massage."

"We did a scavenger hunt where we had to find all these different items at Luke's. One was a life-size John Travolta, which I think was at the Bat Mitzvah party that [Hep Alien] did. Things were like a Luke's menu, one of the 'I Vote for Taylor' buttons. All these strange items.

"We did an Easter egg hunt because it was close to Easter. There was a talent competition. You could either do karaoke or you could do a scene from the script. The person that won was the craft service girl. She did karaoke and she just wowed them."

SPACE 18 Where Paul Anka the psychic dog has his booth at the carnival.

50 CENTS The cost of a ticket to the carnival.

THINGS WE'VE LEARNED Devon Michaels, the actor who played Yale Daily News reporter/editor Bill, actually ended up on the show partially because he looked like *Gilmore Girls* writer Bill Prady.

AMEN, SISTER FRIEND

BILL: She rewrites our stuff, then rewrites her rewrites.
JONI: And to add insult to injury, the copy gets worse every time.
SHEILA: She used to be good, right? Wasn't Paris good at one point?
AK: Before she was editor.
BILL: Now she's Augusto Pinochet in a pantsuit.

LORELAI: What about June 3rd?
LUKE: It's just so soon.
LORELAI: It's still months away.
LUKE: Well, it feels close. It's everything, you know? It's all piling up. It's all happening so fast.
LORELAI: Well, if it's all happening too fast, you know, we can just postpone.
LUKE: Postpone the wedding?
LORELAI: Yeah, I mean, it's not set in stone. It just happened to work out for a date that soon. I don't want you going into this all jumbled up, you know?
LUKE: And that would be OK with you?
LORELAI: Sure.
LUKE: Well, that'll help. Yeah, that'll really help. That'll give me time to resolve this other thing, and everything will be better later on.

"When I had to do the yo-yo, [Dan] was so worried about it, he showed up on set. And he wasn't worried about anything else that was going on, he was with the props person showing me what to do. It was a team effort to train me to pull off my cat's cradle, which was pretty rusty. I did have some juggling experience, but that's it. If they had to have the Yale Daily Newsers pass juggling balls, that would've been easier, but a lot more surreal than they usually tended to get on that show."

-DEVON MICHAELS (BILL)

6.13 Friday Night's Alright for Fighting

First aired: Jan. 31, 2006 // Written by Amy Sherman-Palladino // Directed by Kenny Ortega

Though Lorelai tries to deal with the fact that Luke now has a daughter (and won't let them talk to each other), her attention quickly turns to ensuring that Rory and her grandparents have some opportunity to reach closure over the events of the last six months. How appropriate that this should be hashed out over a Friday night dinner, which is no longer obligatory now that Christopher is paying for Yale. Meanwhile, Paris so alienates the staff of the Yale Daily News, the latest issue threatens to be the first in the history of the paper not to come out.

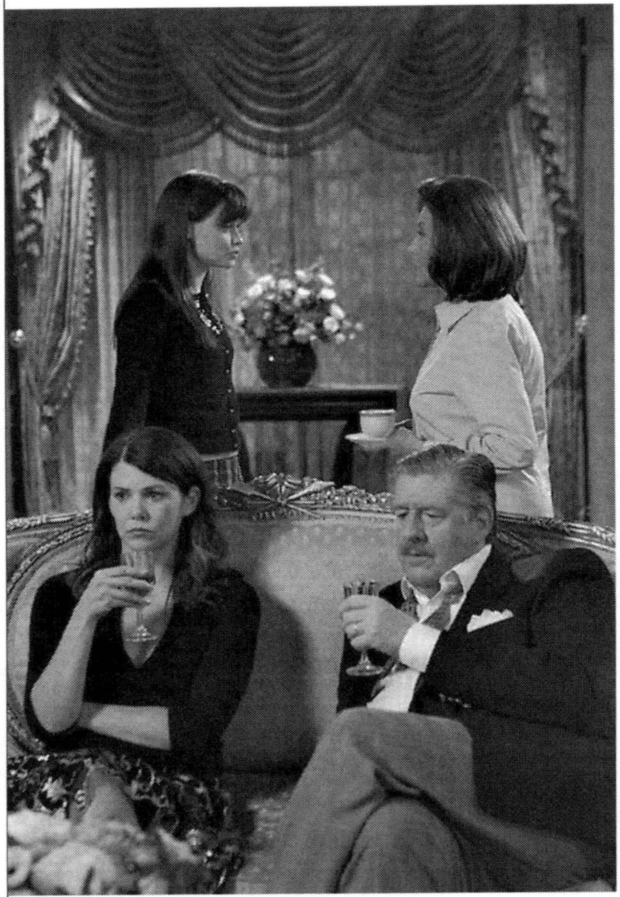

'How's Luke?'
'He has a kid.'

! GINCHY! Sookie suddenly wondering if a local kid is Jackson's "love child"; Paris' Yale Daily News bunker; the formidable team of Rory and Logan managing to get the troubled issue of the paper out in time; the full gamut of emotions let loose over Friday night dinner; Lorelai nonchalantly answering Richard's "how's Luke" with "He has a kid," and her last line of the show: "Well...I think we've officially reinstated Friday night dinner."

NOTES *'Come on, Rory. Friday night dinner: cocktails, Mozart, mind games, good times.'*

* The seemingly hours-long argument at Richard and Emily's puts all of those "previously on *Gilmore Girls*" recaps to shame as we are treated to a spirited summary of the last six months in just a few minutes, including episodes 5.13, 5.22, and pretty much all of Season 6 up to this point, including some pretty entertaining reenactments of scenes we've already seen several episodes back.

* Special kudos go to director Kenny Ortega and crew for the ingenious staging of the fight, from the floating camera and POV shots to placing the bickering characters off screen while the nonbickering ones listen on screen—a tribute to the theater that few other showrunners would have the guts to push through to completion.

TODAY'S CELEBRATION Logan and Rory's first (sort of) date since they broke up, and the reinstatement of Friday night dinners.

KIRK OF ALL TRADES Hot-chocolate-sample hander outer at Taylor's candy store.

EMILY'S MAID DU JOUR Theresa makes excellent passion fruit sorbet, the only respite to a hellish dinner.

YOU'VE ENTERED EMILYLAND Lorelai informs Rory that "cocktail waitress" is Emily's version of the "c word."

90 WORDS A MINUTE How fast Logan types.

AMEN, SISTER FRIEND

LORELAI [*to Rory*]: Hey, listen to me. I'm serious here. I know you and your grandparents are playing "who can freeze out who the longest," which I know can be fun. But if you ever hope to have a relationship with them again, then someone needs to make the first move. I remember the first Christmas after we left Hartford. We were at the Independence Inn and I got an invitation to their annual Christmas party and I didn't go, and that one move defined our entire future relationship. I mean, if I had gone, it would have been awful, but it would have broken the ice, and maybe—and I know this is a big maybe—but maybe we would have been a tad closer than we are now or could ever hope to be.

"She sings like Bonnie Raitt and she talks like a jazz singer or Janis Joplin."

—MICHAEL DELUISE ON KATHLEEN WILHOITE (LIZ)

From the Editing Room 5 What the Eye Doesn't See

Some of the unsung heroes of *Gilmore Girls* are the editors who brought all of those expertly crafted scenes together.

In the first sequence of the insane Gilmore dinner, the camera whips back and forth as it keeps track of who is growling out their grievances that particular moment, making us feel like we're one of the people at the table just trying to keep track of all the action.

"During that initial sequence when they're having the argument and the camera's swishing back and forth, they rehearsed it with the camera multiple times," says editor Raul Davalos. "But then the assistant director, Sean Kavanagh, came in and said, 'Oh my God, you used the whole take! That's really great! We rehearsed this so much.'" The camera operator was going to be extremely happy that all of that rehearsing had paid off, Kavanagh said, and that they'd been able to get all of that frenetic dialogue in a single take. That's when the editor politely pointed out that, "'There are 11 cuts in that scene. I got the best performances out of all those takes.' Then I showed it to him again and I told him where the cuts were and he goes, 'Oh my God.'"

Stylistically, this episode was quite a bit different from what Amy would normally do, he admits, "but she had a lot of fun with that particular episode. That's one of her favorite shows, I think."

LORELAI [*about Paul Anka*]: Uh, he freaks out if he sees his leash. You have to make sure you hide it from him, make sure he doesn't see you putting it on him.
SOOKIE: How is he once he's on the leash?
LORELAI: Oh he's totally fine having his freedom slowly stripped away as long as he's completely unaware that it's happening, just like a true American.

'I Think It Gave Luke Dimension'

Scott Patterson loved the April story line, he told TVGuide in May 2007. "I think it gave Luke dimension. It humanized him more. It showed Luke in a much different light than what we were used to seeing... .I think fans were a little perturbed because it delayed what they considered to be the inevitable, but this is what happens sometimes in life."

6.14 You've Been Gilmored

First aired: Feb. 7, 2006 // Written by Jordon Nardino // Directed by Stephen Clancy

The inevitable has happened and the mighty Paris Geller has been turfed out as editor of the Yale Daily News, replaced by...Rory! As usual, Paris takes the news stoically, which is why Rory finds herself suddenly without a place to live. Moving in with Logan seems the obvious solution, the knowledge of which becomes Christopher's first real test for re-entering Rory's life. Richard and Emily stoke the fires of paranoia in Luke and Lorelai, suggesting that they are only ever a stone's throw away from financial ruin.

GINCHY! The Gilmores trying to get through a few minutes without fighting; Paris' last moments as editor of the Yale Daily News; Michel's little huff over missing out on their monthly handyman list making over cake and coffee at Weston's; Christopher and Logan bonding over their

There may be a reason that Logan and your father get along so well.

Behind the Scenes 'Two Shy People...'

"With Alexis, all I can say about her is she's a very sweet girl, very professional," says Aris Alvarado (Ceaser). "She seems like a shy person, too. You have two shy people, nobody's going to strike up a conversation. There was one scene we were filming where it was Liz Torres [Miss Patty], Rose Abdoo [Gypsy], Honorine [Lulu]—those were the one's talking, and I was just there listening. I was on one side of Miss Patty's dance studio, and Alexis was on the other side waiting to do a scene later. It was just weird because I was quiet and so was Alexis. I'd seen her at parties and said hello to her real quick, told her I liked her in *Sin City*—she said 'Oh, thank you.' Very quiet. It was cool because she's one of those young actresses who's not out there getting crazy."

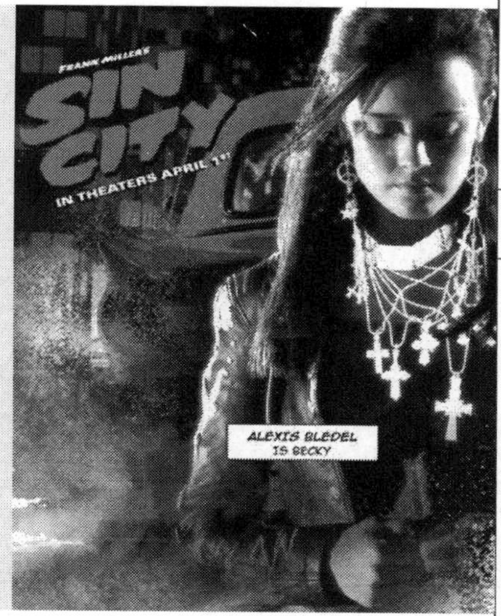

sketchy pasts; Richard and Emily's insurance horror stories, and the anxiety these create in Luke and Lorelai.

NOTES *'You need a place, I got the space. Don't you think it'll be fun?'*

✱ Paris (aka "hotplate Harriet") attributes her competitive streak to her mother being part Viking. She plans on being a surgeon *and* a judge.

✱ Both Christopher and Logan were kicked out of the Groton School (Logan stole a photo of the headmaster off his desk before he left). Christopher continued his education (for a semester) at St. Sebastian's (from which Colin has been banned). Logan lasted a week at St. Mark's, and was even kicked out of Rivers after landing Dean Eldon's Mazda Miata at the bottom of Lake Rutherford. Though Rory is probably relieved on some level that her father and Logan get along so well, the audience sees what Lorelai soon will learn the hard way—Christopher is an older version of the immature Logan, but he's never really grown up.

✱ Lorelai tells Rory that she's never lived with a guy before.

TODAY'S CELEBRATION Rory takes over as editor of the Yale Daily News and moves in with Logan.

EMILY'S MAID DU JOUR Letitia.

EXIT 36-38 The bit of highway Richard and Emily "bought."

26 The Dragonfly Inn's Zagat rating (out of 30), according to Emily.

43% How much real estate in Stars Hollow has shot up in value in the last four years, according to Richard.

FEB. 3, 3:47 PM The exact time Paris evicted Rory from their apartment.

AMEN, SISTER FRIEND

RORY [*at Yale*]: Did you not see those two girls?
CHRISTOPHER: No, what?
RORY: They totally checked you out.
CHRISTOPHER: They did? Cool.
RORY: It's the same way with mom. I swear, I hate having hot parents.

LORELAI [*to Luke*]: If Michel's happy, then I'm happy, and then I take all that happiness and I give it right back to you, tonight, in bed, after you spend four hours with my parents. What do you say?

LUKE: What is this feeling, this tightness in the chest, this anger mixed with paralyzing weakness?
LORELAI: You've been Gilmored. But you know what the weird thing is? They referred to us as family: you, me.
LUKE: Yeah, what was that about?
LORELAI: Well, I think in some twisted way, that may have been them actually validating us as a couple.

RORY: So, what do you think of me moving in with Logan?
LORELAI: I'm sorry, do you remember what happened the last time I piped in with my opinions on your life choices?

"In television, you wake up in the morning and do your scene and you come back at night and it's done. And even if you have another take on it as you're driving home, it's too late. And that is the frustrating part for me. In an ideal world, I would be a movie star, that's what I'd be. I'd travel the world and prepare six months for a part and shoot one scene a day and take 14 hours to shoot it with a brilliant director. And once a year I'd be on stage in Broadway in an amazing play for two months."

-YANIC TRUESDALE (MICHEL)

6.15 A Vineyard Valentine

First aired: Feb. 14, 2006 // Written and directed by Daniel Palladino

The arrival of the zydeco band Buzu Barnes and the Cajun Stompers at the inn only twists the knife for Lorelai, who's already dreading the approach of June 3rd. When Rory and Logan invite her and Luke to stay with them for three days at the Huntzberger place in Martha's Vineyard, it takes some heroics from Logan and a heart-to-heart with Lorelai before Luke manages to calm down and reassure his fiancé that they will get married soon. But just when things are settling down, Mitchum shows up to throw his son on a plane to London, and Lorelai is even more heartbroken over her nonwedding than ever before.

A change in scenery doesn't change Luke and Lorelai's issues.

GINCHY! Bill and Rory going over last-minute newspaper problems; the way that Luke's discomfort while staying at the Vineyard perfectly captures the creepiness of staying at someone else's house for the first time; Logan saving Luke's bacon by giving him the necklace to give to Lorelai; how relaxed Luke is the morning after clearing the air with her about their wedding situation; Lorelai returning home to an answering machine full of well wishes for her forthcoming wedding, thanks to an engagement notice Richard and Emily placed in the local newspaper.

NOTES *'I guess this is the last nail in the coffin of June 3rd.'*

This is Lorelai's first time at Martha's Vineyard. At first, Lorelai simply felt left out of the whole April-Luke bonding thing, but now she's feeling downright neglected by her fiancé, a feeling that's only going to increase as time goes on.

Obviously Lorelai learned nothing from the great Dean-Luke-Bop-It fiasco of '04 (5.5); Luke makes noises about Logan that are similar to those he made about Dean before their infamous double date. Luke claims that Logan "humiliated" Rory by correcting her about the time that Joe's Café opens, similar to the humiliation Taylor says he suffered when Luke contradicted him in front of the staff during the setup of the Stars Hollow museum (5.18).

Lorelai digs cucumber water a lot more at the gym than when she last encountered it at the spa with Emily (2.16). Luke has never had lobster before. Rory tells Lorelai that she and Logan are planning a six week excursion to China, Thailand and Vietnam. But Mitchum reminds Logan that he's going to spend a year in London learning the family business the moment he graduates.

TODAY'S CELEBRATION Valentine's day. Yay?

7 TO 1 The score of the basketball game between Luke and Logan (Logan winning...apologetically).

STAN The raccoon who's been living on the Huntzberger property at the Vineyard longer than the family has.

18 How old Luke was the last time he was at the beach (Harvey's beach, a place Lorelai also used to go when she was a kid).

AMEN, SISTER FRIEND

RORY [*going over the newspaper story schedule*]: I know the boys in the lab can be jerks to women, but don't let that stop you. Girl power, baby! Betty Friedan's dead and we've all got to fill the vacuum.
JONI: You got it.
RORY: Sorry, Bill.
BILL: No problem. Got all the time in the world. Let's see. How about "amphetamine use on campus"?
RORY: Maybe. It would be ironic if my supply dried up based on an exposé I approved.
BILL: Are you serious?
RORY: You leave your sense of humor at home?
BILL: There's another protest over the Yale basic-cable-package fee. They're expecting 80 or so to gather.
RORY: Doesn't warrant a story. Get a photo and tell them all to go home and read a book.
BILL: And Professor Wallace wants a correction to the interview we printed with him. He wants to clarify that he, in fact, referred to his department's problems with the advisory board as an "us-and-them thing."
RORY: What did we print?
BILL: "S and M thing."

LORELAI [*reading Martha's Vineyard facts to Luke*]: "The first people on the island of Martha's Vineyard were Indians of the Wampanoag tribe.

This tribe still makes up a large part of the town originally called Gay Head." Hmm, figures. The Indians survive poverty, disease, then get stuck living in a place called Gay Head.

LUKE: Look, I know I've been preoccupied. I don't like that about myself. It's just who I am. I get in my own head and I forget about the people around me.
LORELAI: I know, that's why I thought this trip would be good for you, get you thinking about something else, but it's been cold here and Logan's been bugging you and the raccoon is noisy and the waves were keeping you up. The trip was a dumb idea.
LUKE: Lorelai, no. It was a good idea. Hey.
LORELAI: What?
LUKE: You know I love you, right?
LORELAI: I really need to hear that once in a while.
LUKE: I love you, and I'm going to marry you, and at our wedding we are having lobster.

6.16 Bridesmaids Revisited

First aired: Feb. 28, 2006 // Written by Rebecca Rand Kirshner // Directed by Linda Mendoza

Caught up in the moment of seeing Rory trounce her fellow journalists during a public forum, Lorelai agrees to babysit 3-year-old GG while Christopher takes his mother to visit his father's grave. The subsequent devastation inflicted on the Lorelai home leads Christopher to admit how angry he is at Sherry for leaving. Rory discovers that Logan took advantage of their time apart to sleep with at least two (and possibly three) of Honor's bridesmaids. After she learns that Paris has kicked Doyle out, Rory shows up at her door to move in. The only people on the road to happiness are Lane and Zack, who are now engaged!

GINCHY! Joel Gion's tambourine solo; the way Rory gets the better of "pompous Princeton guy" Quentin during the panel; Gil and Brian rocking the bat mitzvah; Zack proposing to Lane; Lorelai recounting her travails with GG to Christopher; angry, drunk Rory and sweet, drunk Doyle's brief encounter at the bar; and Paris and Rory burying the hatchet.

What I Kept

Lot of the scripts because I think they're so good. I use them so much as a teaching tool for so many different reasons. The writing's really good. Because the pacing is so quick, it teaches actors to be on their game. There are certain shows written a certain way. On *Gilmore Girls*, the pacing is so fast. And if you don't keep up with that pacing, it doesn't work. It's written to be very quippy and quick and clipped. For me it's been a great teaching tool for actors.

—Jami Rudofsky (casting director)

NOTES *'You're way deep in my bogus bag and it's ziplocked shut.'*

This is Paris' first time at the Yale Daily News under Rory's leadership. She's bought a jazz trumpet. Lane has already started to play Scrabble and Monopoly with April at the diner ("I rule, because she's a kid and hasn't gotten the Monopoly concept. She still thinks Park Place is a good buy.")

Despite the grief that the band gave Zack for his "Gwen Stefani" head mic, Hep Alien is now playing Stefani's "Hollaback Girl" at the bat mitzvah. Paris is still trying to use her craft corner to destress. Lorelai tells Christopher that she keyed his car once.

For all the pain and angst on display in this episode, it contains more touching moments than we're used to. Christopher's anguish over GG's behavior and Sherry's absence, an important emotional scene for the series, is surpassed by the sweet give-and-take between Rory and Doyle, and later, Paris and Rory. Though the episode's writer, Rebecca Rand Kirshner, received her debut *Gilmore* writing credit with "Emily Says 'Hello'" (5.9), this is the first episode where we get a taste of some of the humanity that she brought to *Buffy the Vampire Slayer* in episodes such as "Tabula Rasa." As of this writing, she's the showrunner for The CW's *90210*.

One of the most disturbing aspects of this episode is Zack's frame of mind when he proposes to Lane. His last words to Gil and Brian about getting Lane back in the band were "Leave Lane to me, I'm gonna reason with her." We know he loves Lane, but was it Hep Alien or the prospect of marital bliss that led him to pop the question?

TODAY'S CELEBRATION Rory's young voices of journalism panel, Honor's wedding, Rory and Logan's split, Paris and Doyle's split, and the engagement of Zack and Lane.

17 The number of words Rory used during her panel that were new to Christopher.

THINGS WE'VE LEARNED While the cast were hanging around the set waiting for lighting to be finalized, attention would often turn to Sally Struthers' purse, as actors and crew would take turns guessing what was inside. "Every little thing had a story—her date book, where she got

Zack's Proposal

"I think I started out more as a kind of dolt," Todd Lowe says. "I really liked that episode where I proposed to Lane in the diner. Originally it was going to be Adam Brody, he was going to be Lane's boyfriend, and I guess they were going to follow all of that all the way up to a wedding. I don't know what happened to him. He just disappeared one day. All of the sudden I'm Lane's boyfriend. OK, this is cool. "

it, different receipts she had to take something back," Rose Abdoo recalls. "I think she may have had a wand in there. What I also loved about it was her Babette purse was her real-life purse."

THE SCHOOL NEWSPAPERS AT THE PANEL

—The Harvard Crimson

—The Daily Princetonian

—The Cornell Daily Sun

—The Daily Pennsylvanian (University of Penn.)

—The Yale Daily News

AMEN, SISTER FRIEND

ZACK: I have to talk to you about how it's all feeling wrong. I tried to write a song about it, and I was gonna bring my amp and ax and play it for you. But it was coming out way too emo, so I decided to just say it. I get up in the morning and I don't feel good. I go to work and I don't feel good. I come home and I don't feel good. I brush my teeth and I don't feel good. Then I go to bed and I don't feel good. Then I wake up and I don't feel good. And then I go to work and I don't feel good.

BABETTE: You don't feel good! We get it! Go on!

LUKE: Hey, is something burning down here?

LANE: Luke, shh!

LUKE: OK, sorry.

LANE: Go on.

ZACK: Right. Where was I? Oh, yeah. Lane, will you marry me?

LANE: What?

ZACK: Will you marry me?

LANE: But do you even know what you're saying? I mean, have you even thought about this? [He pulls out a ring.] Oh my god, you *have* thought about this.

ZACK: I got it at the pawn shop. It belonged to like an Elk or a Moose or something. But it looked cool and I could afford it, so I got it.

[Rory's drowning her sorrows at the bar after finding out that Logan slept with Honor's friends while they were apart. A waitress tries to clear away some of the mess in front of her.]

"I remember when Aaron Sorkin left West Wing and he was on Charlie Rose... Charlie Rose was saying, 'Are you still going to watch it?' And he said, 'Absolutely.' I'm thinking, 'Really?! How?! That's your baby!' Believe me, when I leave this show, I ain't watching. I'm sitting in a hole on Tuesday nights, sobbing and drunk for an hour. Jack Daniels."

–AMY, THE AV CLUB (FEBRUARY 2005)

RORY: Don't take what's mine. These came with my drinks. He put them down in front of me. I did not ask you to move them, did I?

WAITRESS: Whatever.

RORY: Snappy comeback. Dorothy Parker know about you? Sick of people touching my stuff.

6.17 I'm OK, You're OK

First aired: April 4, 2006 // Written by Keith Eisner // Directed by Lee Shallat Chemel

Sometimes life is about rolling with the punches. Rory goes back to Logan, not because she really forgives him or has any burning need to be with him, but simply because she's tired of fighting and trying to figure out where else she's going to live, especially now that Paris and Doyle have made up. Lorelai continues to give Luke his space with April, and really tries to ignore the fact that Luke's ex runs a boutique in nearby Woodbridge. As if that wasn't enough, Kirk tells her that Emily and Richard are looking at houses in Stars Hollow! Zack, too, has his own hurdle to overcome if he's going to marry Lane—the formidable Mrs. Kim.

GINCHY! Lane trying to convince Zack that Brian won't be living with them after they're married; Kirk explaining his creepy new career; Zack and Mrs. Kim writing their hit song.

NOTES *'Yep, I'm fine.'*

Apparently Paris' life coach, Terrence, approved of her relationship with Doyle, though he also OK'd a pageboy haircut. April calls Luke for the first time, to ask him to chaperone her math team's trip to Philadelphia for a contest. We finally learn what Zack does for a living: he works at Quest Copying (and is in line for promotion to assistant manager).

Lorelai is as noticeably annoyed by how easily Rory went back to Logan as Rory is by Lorelai's acceptance of the fact that Anna gave Luke a bag from her shop.

This is one of those very few episodes where nothing really happens, no ground is gained, and even the gags feel forced. One senses that Amy & Dan were spending most of their time planning Zack and Lane's wedding, and possibly packing their bags for the end of their reign on *Gilmore Girls*.

What *Gilmore* Means to Me

Around 17 (now I'm 21), I moved out, or I was *moved* out. From then on, I lived in a house with other girls until I got my own flat. There I saw the *Gilmore Girls* for the first time. I thought, 'Wow, what an incredible show.' And they really talked fast, even in German!

But then it became a point in my life that I could hold on to. By watching the show, I came to understand my mother because of Emily. I realized that even if she had been the one to throw me out, she must have also been sad. This hasn't changed anything about our relationship, but I began to understand that everything has two sides and that maybe every mother really cares about her daughter. It also showed me that you can be girly and clever.

It also showed me there is always someone around who cares about you, even if it's "only" the man in the coffee shop.

—S. Brandt, *Germany*

TODAY'S CELEBRATION Rory and Paris reconcile with Logan and Doyle, Richard and Emily see Lorelai's renovated house, and Rory meets Anna Nardini.

KIRK OF ALL TRADES Realtor trainee. ("Your needs are Kirk's needs. Kirk is here for you.")

21 Number of years Lorelai has lived in Stars Hollow

3½ MINUTES Maximum length for a musical hit, according to Mrs. Kim, and it must be radio friendly.

3 HOURS & 14 MINUTES How long Richard and Emily stay at Lorelai's.

AMEN, SISTER FRIEND

PARIS [*to Rory*]: I mean, who are we kidding? I am not cut out to deal with people. I was made to be in a lab or an operating room or a bunker somewhere with a well-behaved monkey by my side.

MICHEL [*to Rory*]: The pink neon Post-It notes are used for guests who are checking in. The green neon Post-It notes are for guests checking out. And the watermelon Post-It notes are for guests who have altered or canceled their reservations. As you can see, the pink neon stack is now woefully out of balance with the green neon stack, creating the illusion that more guests have been checking in than checking out which, of course, is a physical impossibility unless we have begun murdering them.

KIRK: I just need a temporary place to conduct my business and potentially have sex with prospective clients.
LORELAI: What?
KIRK: That's Kirk's other thing, the young, virile eye candy angle for lonely widows and aging divorcées. Works like a charm. I plan on running it by Lulu, of course.

LORELAI [*to Rory*]: I don't know what to do. I moved 30 miles away from my parents for a reason. Those 30 miles act as a buffer so that when my mother says something that makes me want to kill her, I have to drive 30 miles to do it. Ten miles in, I usually calm down or I get hungry

Perhaps Lorelai brought home the wrong Paul Anka.

or I pass a mall—something prevents me from actually killing her. That buffer is my mother's best friend. Take the buffer away and you've got Nancy Grace camping out on Miss Patty's lawn for a month.

6.18 The Real Paul Anka

First aired: April 11, 2006 // Written and directed by Daniel Palladino

Relationships continue to prove challenging for the residents of Stars Hollow and beyond. Luke chaperone's April's school trip to Newark, Philadelphia and Gettysburg, trying to make up for lost time, to April's rising discomfort. Rory continues to punish Logan, this time by being extra hard on him at the Yale Daily News and in front of his friends. Yet when she attends the open house for Jess' book company, she admits to Jess that she loves Logan, despite everything he's done. At least she gets to spend a few minutes getting to know April, which is more than Lorelai's been able to do, and something Emily berates her for not doing. Speaking of Emily, just what are she and Richard doing in Stars Hollow, anyway?

! GINCHY! Lorelai's surreal Paul Anka dream; Kirk taking over the diner the moment Ceaser leaves; Luke's attempts to ingratiate himself to the kids on the bus and April's mounting embarrassment; Luke, April and Rory at the Truncheon Books open house; Lorelai disparaging everything in Stars Hollow to dissuade her parents from buying property there; Emily playing cards with some little girl in the diner because she thought it was Luke's daughter (and constantly referring to her as "it"); and Lorelai ruining the pants part of Lane's wedding dress with a smile.

NOTES *'I know your handiwork when I see it, playing cautious when you should be diving in.'*

Considering how prescient some of Lorelai's dreams have been (3.1), her Dog Paul Anka vs. Real Paul Anka dream may be a premonition of the fight between Luke and Christopher (7.10). The show finally namechecks Washington Depot, Conn., the real-life inspiration for Stars Hollow, when Emily includes it in a list of places she and Richard are scouring for antiques.

This is the first we hear that Taylor is mayor rather than town selectman. Since the town selectman in many Connecticut areas acts as a mayor anyway, the writers may simply have given him this more familiar designation. On the other

Behind the Scenes: the Periodic Table Song

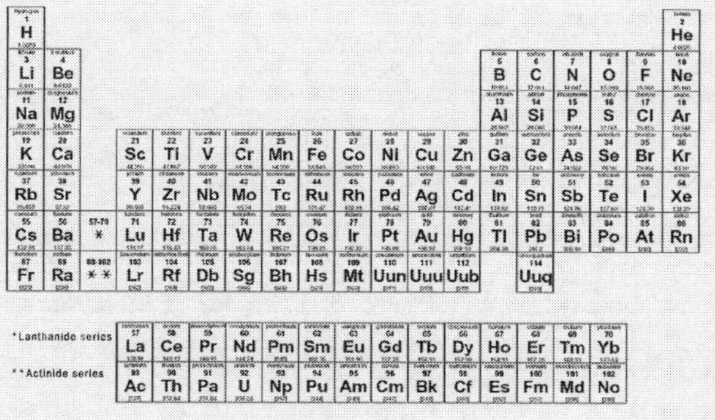

A fan of Tom Lehrer, Dan had to throw in his song "The Elements" (to the tune of the Major-General's Song from *The Pirates of Penzance*), which April and the kids sing on the bus: "There's holmium and helium and hafnium and erbium/ and phosphorus and francium and fluorine and terbium..."

"I have a fairly freakish memory, so memorizing lines wasn't actually that hard for me," Vanessa Marano says. "The hardest, though, was when we had to sing the chemical element song on the bus. I'll tell you one thing, I know all the chemical elements now. I could pretty much recite that song word for word. When I was learning it, I felt so bad for the kids who had to audition with it because you pretty much get the lines the night before when you audition for something. I can just see these kids seeing that and being uh....wow. I think I had a week to memorize it.

"I was actually working on something else at the time, and I had the song on my iPod, so I was listening to it over and over again. My cast members from the other thing I was working on were looking at me like I was insane because I was just shouting out chemical elements in song."

hand, knowing Taylor, it's conceivable that he found a way to oust Jackson from the selectman position, installing himself as mayor.

Rory's obsession with RSVPing (6.5, 6.7) continues when she apologizes for not having done so for Jess' event. Though Rory initially gets Jess' hopes up that they might finally get back together, he again (6.8) proves the more mature of the two, letting it go with a simple "it is what it is."

TODAY'S CELEBRATION April's field trip and the open house for Truncheon Books.

KIRK OF ALL TRADES (Very, very briefly) the proprietor of Luke's Diner. And still a Realtor-trainee.

10 Number of days Luke and his 12-year-olds are on the road.

3,624 FEET (GIVE OR TAKE) The distance from the cliff to the banks of the San Juan River that the Life and Death Brigade intends to parachute during their "ultimate" stunt.

CODE 14/B/14\\\X-8 (est. 1792) "A citizen of Stars Hollow cannot denigrate Stars Hollow while standing on Stars Hollow soil."

DEATH BY 40 MUSKETS The original penalty for violating the above.

28 YEARS AGO When Mrs. Kim married Lane's missing father.

AMEN, SISTER FRIEND

EMILY: You're telling me I played this insipid game for half an hour and it's not even Luke's daughter?
LORELAI: What made you think it was Luke's daughter?
EMILY: Well, it told me it was someone's daughter here.
LORELAI: Well, she must have meant someone in town.
EMILY: Then she's a moron. Why would I play cards if there wasn't a family connection?
LORELAI: I guess she just thought you were being nice.
EMILY: The little idiot kept tipping her cards so I could see them. So I pretended I didn't and specifically asked for what I knew she didn't have. The kid's a moron.

"It was so close, because the schedule changed more than one time, and we were trying to do the schedule around Paul Anka's availability. I don't know if it was Dan or Amy's idea to actually have the real Paul Anka. I think that had been kicking around for a while and we were just fortunate enough that everything worked out."

-MARA CASEY, CASTING DIRECTOR

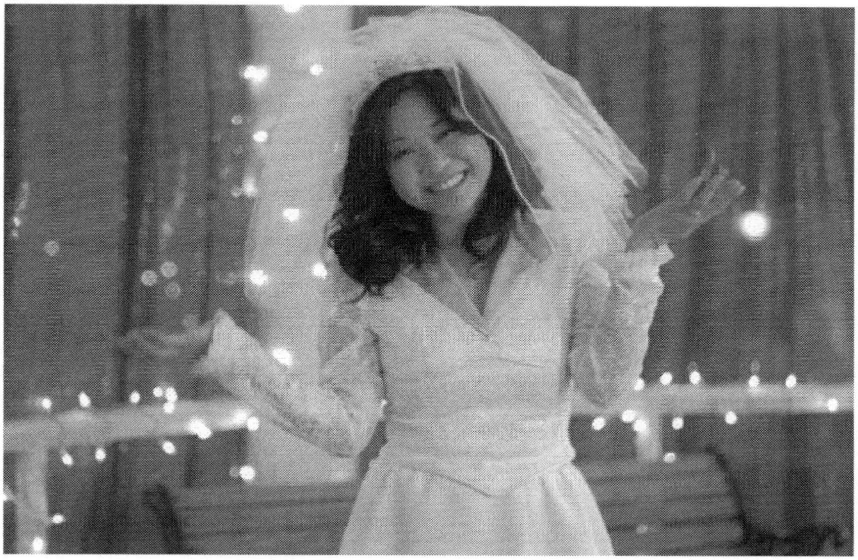

Lane and Zack's wedding brings out the best (and some sadness) in Stars Hollow.

6.19 I Get a Sidekick Out of You

First aired: April 18, 2006 // Written and directed by Amy Sherman-Palladino

Logan's gone off with the Life and Death Brigade, leaving Rory to concentrate on Lane and Zack's wedding. As usual, relationships make things 10 times harder than they have to be. Mrs. Kim insists that Lorelai bring a man to the wedding, so she takes Christopher (Luke's still out of town). Mrs. Kim has enough trouble appeasing her mother who insists on a Buddhist wedding for Lane. Overwhelmed by the two weddings and seeing a 22-year-old girl accomplishing what she could not, Lorelai breaks down at the reception. No sooner do Rory and Christopher get her to bed than an emergency call prompts Rory to take off for a New York City hospital, where Logan's been airlifted after his LDB stunt went awry.

! GINCHY! Paris' "Either way I look at it, I'm right" after being asked to choose a side on the tenure debate; Kyon's defense of Avril Lavigne; Christopher bombarding Rory with messages via the Sidekick he got her; the bachelor and bachelorette parties ending up in Brian's aunt's rec room; the mad dash across town to attend the second wedding ("58 seats and 62 Koreans"); the Hep Alien concert and Lorelai's drunken toast.

NOTES *'This is ridiculous. Even when I have a man, I'm still the girl who doesn't have a man.'*

"Like I told [Amy] on the phone, 'Not only would I hide a body for you, I would chop one up as well.'"

–SCOTT PATTERSON, TVGUIDE.COM, 5/12/07

* Christopher has finally gotten GG under control (6.16). Lane says Mrs. Kim's mother hasn't been out of Korea in 45 years.

* Lorelai sees a picture that Rory and April took together last episode on Rory's camera. Brian says he's known Zack most of his life. Lorelai reminds Christopher that doing an outrageous number of shots is how they ended up with Rory.

* Lorelai's drunken toast at the wedding will be bookended by her equally heartfelt (and equally inebriated) rendition of "I Will Always Love You" a little more than a year later (7.20).

Behind the Scenes: Art Imitates Life Imitates Art

Spending as much time as they did on the set of *Gilmore Girls*, the cast and crew already felt like they pretty much lived in Stars Hollow. But every now and then, Amy and the writers would throw something into the scripts that made some people say, only half-jokingly, "They must be eavesdropping on our lives," Keiko Agena says. "Even as it's happening, it's being written in the scripts."

She should know. But let's allow Emily Kuroda to set the scene. Like many of the cast, Kuroda enjoyed her *Gilmore Girls* role in part because it allowed her time to pursue other creative projects, especially her theater work. Around the time that "I Get a Sidekick out of You" was to be filmed, she was scheduled to appear in a Washington DC play being directed by a friend of hers.

"No, you can't go," Amy told her, hesitant to tell her why. "Everything's really hush-hush," Kuroda says. "Oftentimes we wouldn't get the script until the day before we shot."

After some hemming and hawing, Amy finally came clean about why she really needed Mrs. Kim to be there: Lane and Zack were getting married!

"Amy told me that, and I was like, 'Oh my God!' So I called Keiko and I said, 'Keiko, you're going to get married! Oh my God, oh my God, I'm so excited!'"

What Kuroda didn't know, what nobody knew at the time, was that Agena herself was planning to quietly sneak off with boyfriend Shin to be married.

"I didn't know that she was planning on eloping with her roommate, who is a guitarist," Kuroda says. "And she had no idea that on the show, she was going to marry her roommate the guitarist. So when they actually eloped and she sent me the pictures, she goes, 'I couldn't tell you because it was a secret, but you freaked me out!'" Agena admits, "It was a little bit strange."

Little did anybody know that Keiko Agena was also getting hitched.

This episode just edges out the rest as the author's favorite of the series. Here Amy once again creates the perfect *Gilmore* cocktail: three parts humor to one part drama. Like all true maestros of their craft, she pulls off something here that looks extremely simple. Simple, that is, until others try to attempt the same mix in Season 7, and never quite manage it.

TODAY'S CELEBRATION Zack and Lane's wedding...twice!

KIRK OF ALL TRADES Owner of Yummy Bartenders.

AMEN, SISTER FRIEND

LANE [*to Rory*]: I just discovered today that I am simply the latest link in a chain of Kim women who hide their real lives under floorboards, away from their mothers.

RORY [*texting with Chris as she talks to Lorelai*]: Wow, four tacos. Quite a man, my father. So, what do you think? Should I pull the trigger?
LORELAI: Tell him to bring me a taco.
RORY: Will do. T.P.T.D.I.
LORELAI: What does that mean?
RORY: Totally psyched to do it.
LORELAI: He's making up his own acronyms?
RORY: Yeah, and he just learned how to make the happy face.
LORELAI: Sorry kid, what can I say? He was really hot in high school.

RORY'S TOAST This letter was written in 1995 by one Lane Kim. It was slipped into my hands during a spelling test in Miss Mallon's class. I was so shocked by its contents that I missed the word automobile: o-t-t-o-mobile. That's right, Lane. I remember. I will now share with you the contents of this letter: "Dear Rory, how was your lunch? Mine was bad. Did you have ham again? If you did, I am sorry but mine was worse. I thought you should know that today at recess I decided that I'm going to marry Alex Backus. He has a very nice head, and his ears don't stick out like Roddy Winston's do. I will love him forever, no matter what. See you at Brownies. Love, Lane." I'm sorry Lane, I just thought that Zack should know that in your heart, he will always be second place to Alex Backus and his well-proportioned ears."

The Band Played On

One of the most sublime moments in the entire series takes place immediately after Zack and Lane tie the knot. Hep Alien takes to the stage, Lane still in her wedding dress, Zack still in his traditional Korean silks, and they proceed to rip through The Monkees' "I'm a Believer." There are just a few seconds during this performance when we see Lane banging away at her drums, and an expression comes over Keiko Agena that makes it seem like her character has come to life.

"That was at the end of a very long day, and I just remember thinking honestly, let's just try to get through this without anyone killing each other," she says. "I think by the end of that take, they might've caught a little bit on camera of us really being ourselves in a moment of confusion. There was a little bit of real life in there."

LORELAI'S TOAST Hello, everybody, hello. Some of you know me as Lorelai Gilmore and some of you know me as Cher. But either way, I wanted to say a few words about our girl. I have known Lane forever, and I'm just so incredibly happy that she has gotten married. I mean, I am just so happy that this adorable 22-year-old girl has gotten married, because it's amazing, you know? It's really hard to get married. Believe me, I should know. I mean, seriously, because Lane is married, and next thing it'll be my daughter, and then my granddaughter, but not me. I'm not getting married. No, it ain't for me. It's not in the cards. But hey, do you know what date I'm not getting married? June 3rd. Do not save the date. Do you hear me? Do whatever you want on June 3rd because there's nothing at all happening on that day. If there's anything you need to book or anything, it's totally safe to book it on June 3rd. So, congratulations, Lane and Zack. Who else here had eight shots of Tequila? Anybody? Hands...no? Oh my gosh, who misses the yummy bartenders? I know, me too. They were so great. I was gonna ask them to not work on June 3rd on my not wedding. I just thought that would be so fun.

6.20 Super Cool Party People

First Aired: April 25, 2006 // Written by David S Rosenthal // Directed by Ken Whittingham

Logan survives his brush with death, but not without sustaining some severe damage, much to Rory's horror. While Rory guilts Mitchum into visiting his son, Lorelai finds herself giving the birthday party Luke throws for April some much-needed mouth-to-mouth. Lorelai considers this paving the way for her to have a future relationship with April, but April's mother is livid, and for reasons that Lorelai can easily understand.

GINCHY! Miss Patty telling the town to say that Lorelai sang "Endless Love" at the wedding to save her the embarrassment of explaining to Luke what she really did; Paris calling up the doctors and getting the information about Logan that Rory can't, simply by being Paris; Michel reconfiguring the Dragonfly Inn Web site so it's just a big picture of him; Lorelai transforming April's birthday party from a funereal affair to a smash.

NOTES *'What does Hagrid know about slumber parties?'*

April's birthday party "was a lot of fun. It was kind of like a birthday party because you're in a professional environment and you're doing lines, but we got to put on crazy eyelashes and all the glitter makeup. Not to be a total girl about it, but every now and then it's fun to wear glittery things."

—VANESSA MARANO (APRIL)

✱ Lorelai's "I'm not here to make friends, I want to win" at the party is a shot across the bow of the reality TV shows that nearly always have a contestant who says this. An equally drunk Logan dived off a cliff in Puerto Caldera on Costa Rica's west coast, barely got his parachute open, hitting several rocks on his way down. Honor and Josh were honeymooning on the Greek island of Mykonos when it happened. Logan's taken to Columbia-Presbyterian in Manhattan.

✱ Luke's reasoning for keeping Lorelai out of April's life (see Amen, Sister Friend) is actually pretty much the same as Paris' when she asks Rory to stand in a closet while Jamie picks her up for their first date (3.1). Anna tells him that April and her friends refer to him as Hagrid, after the *Harry Potter* character.

✱ Honor tells Rory that Mitchum refuses to come to the hospital because he disapproves of the whole Life and Death Brigade thing. Anna's explanation of how she doesn't want April getting attached to people who may just disappear one day is extremely similar to Lorelai's own approach with Rory growing up (1.5).

The Further Exploits of Drunk Lorelai

—Posed, strutted and inappropriately gyrated for the videographer

—Started a limbo contest and a poker game (or tried to)

—Crowned herself arm-wrestling champion of the world

—Founded a secret club for "supercool party people" only. ("Supercool party people bid you supercool adieu!")

TODAY'S CELEBRATION April's 13th birthday party and the first meeting of Lorelai and Anna Nardini.

KIRK OF ALL TRADES Stars Hollow video store employee.

10 The number of giant tequila shots Lorelai downed the night before.

AMEN, SISTER FRIEND

LORELAI: I'm just saying that Rory's birthday scavenger hunt of 1998

is still talked about in hushed, reverent tones.
LUKE: Is that the one where all the kids ended up at Taylor's at 11 at night stealing stuff out of his fridge?
LORELAI: Shh! Hushed, reverent tones.

LUKE [*after Lorelai tries to help shop for April's present*]: Because the minute you get involved in her life, it'll be all over for me.
LORELAI: What? That's ridiculous.
LUKE: No, it's not ridiculous. You're colorful and funny. You're practically a cartoon character. Kids love you. I wouldn't hang out with me either after meeting you.
LORELAI: Luke!
LUKE: She'll like you better. That is just a fact.
LORELAI: No, you're her dad.
LUKE: Yes, I am her dad, and this is the way I want it to be.

RORY: Mitchum Huntzberger? Yes, it's Rory Gilmore. I just thought I'd call and remind you that Logan is lying in a hospital bed with a partially collapsed lung and a whole host of other potentially life-threatening injuries. And I'm figuring a guy like you, surrounded by nothing but a bunch of terrified sycophants, might not have someone in his life with the guts to tell him what an incredibly selfish, narcissistic ass he's being, so I thought I'd jump on in. Swallow your pride, get in your car, and come down here and see your son, now!

"The main thing, and I did hear this straight from [Amy], is that they never would tell her that this is going to be the last year or not, until in January or something. It's like, 'Guys, I need more time. I can't just start writing the end of the whole series if you tell me in January and we have to be done by April.'"

-RAUL DAVALOS, EDITOR

6.21 Driving Miss Gilmore

First Aired: May 2, 2006 // Written by Amy Sherman-Palladino and Daniel Palladino // Directed by Jamie Babbit

It's business as usual in the Hollow and beyond. Jackson and Sookie are trying to get rid of a crop of marijuana (sorry, "pickles") the Templeton brothers planted on Jackson's back half-acre before he fired them; Mitchum Huntzberger tells The Wall Street Journal that he gave Rory her start in the journalism business; and Lorelai drops everything to drive a temporarily blind Emily around to take care of several errands, including one that forces her to admit something to her mother that she has refused to face until now.

GINCHY! Paris and Doyle taking care of Logan while watching *March of the Penguins*; Luke going to the bar to punch out TJ, and TJ's reaction; Emily finally revealing why she and Richard have been spending so much time in Stars Hollow.

NOTES *'Look, you have to try to tune in what your partner means as opposed to what she's actually saying.'*

The girls always fight when they have spaghetti and meatballs at Richard and Emily's house (the dish is "just too much excitement," according to Emily). Rory's grandparents decide to donate all the money they're saving from not having to pay for Yale, along with some money from their foundation (?), to pay for what will ultimately become the Rory Gilmore astronomy building.

Liz's new "come what may" philosophy is similar to Luke's zen attitude toward Taylor not so long ago, and look how well that turned out (6.6). If what Liz told Luke about her old pot supplier being the town garbage collector is true (4.12), Jackson could very well have thrown out all that marijuana without any repercussions. Luke's impulse to hunt TJ down to fight him is a side we haven't seen of Luke before, but one we will see again (7.10).

Like mother, like daughter, as Lorelai gives Luke the brush off, even lying about there being a last-minute staff meeting. This is the "grown-up" version of the way Rory punished Logan for sleeping with those bridesmaids just a few episodes back.

TODAY'S CELEBRATION Logan leaves the hospital, Liz has a bun in the oven, Lorelai seems poised to receive an amazing house as a wedding present, and the Troubadour gets a gig to open for Neil Young during some of the musician's East Coast tour dates.

EMILY'S MAID DU JOUR Musepa, though it's doubtful that she survived Emily's "night of the long knives."

YOU'VE ENTERED EMILYLAND [*on Christopher's haircut*] I don't like a man's hair that short. It makes him look like a convict or a masseuse, but I think it works on him.

Logan's Injuries

Internal bleeding, high fever, a partially collapsed lung, six broken ribs, a broken ankle, torn cartilage in both knees, contusions over ⅓ of his body and a severe concussion.

AND HERE'S A SHOUT OUT TO OUR INTERNATIONAL FANS Once again (1.20), the Prague cab drivers get skewered, this time by Emily.

68 POUNDS The amount of marijuana Jackson harvests from his back half-acre.

THE MITCHUM/WALL STREET JOURNAL QUOTE

"I looked for the best and the brightest, even at the intern level. Ben Cochran at Harvard, he helped me out with my Boston paper, as did Frank Williams. And Rory Gilmore, I gave her her first internship at my Stamford paper, and now she's the editor of the Yale Daily News."

14 The number of hours Emily was in labor when she had Lorelai.

3 The number of hours it takes for Jackson to pull the marijuana plants down.

AMEN, SISTER FRIEND

PARIS: Seven up, seminiferous tubules, epididymis, vas deferens, ejaculatory duct, urethra, penis.
LOGAN: What are you doing?
PARIS: Boning up. Pardon the pun. Got my MCATS coming up, medical school.

Behind the Scenes Troubadour Technology

There is a certain dreamlike quality to the way the Troubadour nonchalantly strolls through town singing his songs, belying just how difficult shooting those scenes was. "There was a lot of trial and error," Grant-Lee Phillips says. "It was apparent that the best result would come from me actually performing it live on camera. Which is all well and good except you had a situation where once I walk off camera and I'm out of frame, you still hear the music. There are situations where I'm in the shot and you want to hear the guitar underneath as if I'm in the distance, but to really do that on set, you almost have to mime."

After a little planning, "I think we got really good at it a few shows in," he says. "Sometimes it involved an earbud that I would wear. Nobody could see it but I had a playback system in my ear, so I would be playing to a click or some sort of rhythm. That way, that back and forth between all those shots, it would always remain in sync. It was kind of complicated."

EMILY [*to Lorelai, about the house they're looking at*]: Now, before you get your nose out of joint and accuse me of interfering, hear me out. I think your house is very nice. I know you've put a lot of work into it. But Lorelai, it's too small for the two of you, especially when you have children. If you have children, I mean. A man needs his own space and room, and Luke does not have that at your house. Also, I know you've always wanted horses, so I thought something with a little property might be nice. Now, I know it's not actually in Stars Hollow but it's right on the border. It's only an extra 10 minutes to the inn and an extra five minutes to the diner. Plus, I did a little nosing around and I heard that if you grease the palm of the Stars Hollow zoning commissioner, a man named Taylor Doose, you can get him to change property lines, so we can give you a Stars Hollow address if it's really important to you.

LORELAI: You want to buy us a house?

EMILY: Well, I know you're not going to let me give you a wedding, so I thought a house would do.

LORELAI: All that running around Stars Hollow, you and dad were looking for a house for me?

EMILY: Well of course. You didn't think we wanted to live there, did you? Small-town charm is good for a weekend, Lorelai, but I have no interest in having a next-door neighbor walk in with a pie, wanting to chat. I would kill myself and my neighbors. Now I'm sure Luke will need some convincing. He doesn't look like the kind of man who willingly takes extravagant gifts from people, so I've concocted a few good lies we can tell him. It's for his own good, and once the two of you are in the house–

LORELAI: It's not gonna happen.

EMILY: What? Well, of course it will. If we have to pay more than the asking price, your father and I are totally prepared–

LORELAI: Luke and I, the wedding, it's not gonna happen.

"Neil Young is kind of the ultimate troubadour, so I have a feeling that that's where they were coming from. I was always delighted in how esoteric and how under the radar the music references could be. If you were making a list of all of the bands that were name-checked, all of the musical artists, you would wind up with a very interesting list. A lot of it wasn't very mainstream but very cool."

–GRANT-LEE PHILLIPS (THE TROUBADOUR)

6.22 Partings

First aired: May 9, 2006 // Written by Amy Sherman-Palladino and Daniel Palladino // Directed by Amy Sherman-Palladino

Lorelai wakes up at Sookie's and continues to hide from Luke. She figures she can take some refuge in Friday night dinner, but soon discovers that there are two additional guests: Christopher and Carolyn Bates, the daughter of an old college roommate of Emily's. As disdainful as she and Christopher are about the arrangement, Carolyn proves an excellent sounding board for the limbo Lorelai finds herself in with Luke. Determined, she lays it all on the line with him, with predictable results.

GINCHY! Kirk telling Taylor that Neil Young was one of The Monkees; the troubadours throughout the town and Taylor's increasing annoyance with them; Rory's getup and bad accent at her British-themed goodbye party for Logan; Lorelai's final gambit with Luke, and its utter failure.

NOTES *'I'm not waiting! It's now or never!'*

The "Mrs. Harris" that Taylor says good morning to right after the opening credits is played by Lauren Graham's stand-in, Patty Malcolm.

It's been a week since the Troubadour was "discovered." Richard and Emily are adding the settlement money they received for Emily's botched lasik surgery to the money earmarked for constructing a science building in Rory's name: The Rory Gilmore Astronomy Building. Richard shows the girls a model of the structure, which begins construction this summer, with an opening date of around Christmas. Richard and Emily are going to be in Europe for the next two months.

Last episode, Emily was floating ideas for a suitable match for Christopher while Lorelai chauffeured her around town. This time, she's invited Carolyn. Those who don't know Emily as well as we do might suggest she's trying to genuinely help Christopher, but time and again she's made it clear that she wants to see him and Lorelai together.

Mary Lynn Rajskub's troubadour mutters "Can you say BTK" after Taylor's rant, which is the same thing Lorelai said as an aside to Richard and Emily after Taylor berated her for disparaging the goods in Doose's Market (6.18). Both references, of course, are to Dennis Rader,

"Before I read the script, I would look through it, not even to see what my lines were, but to see if there were any complicated words that I had to say, and there always were. I had a little Web site on my computer that told me how to pronounce things. I would type them in and I would listen and I would say them over and over again."

-VANESSA MARANO (APRIL)

better known as the BTK (bind, torture, kill) killer, who killed at least 10 people in Kansas before his 2005 arrest. (And yes, there's a very slight physical resemblance.)

* During their impromptu therapy session, Lorelai admits to Carolyn that she didn't really love Max. Lorelai tells Luke a) that she talked to Anna, and b) she said everything would be fine with April once they were married, which is not quite what Anna said. ("I need to know he's sticking around first. And then, when you're married, we'll deal with that then," is what actually she said.)

* Logan's told Rory that he loves her before (6.11), but this time it's not about his trying to get back into her good graces; this time it means the world to her.

TODAY'S CELEBRATION Logan's Yale graduation and his farewell party, Christopher's "date" with Carolyn, Lorelai's ultimatum to Luke, and she and Christopher sleeping together.

EMILY'S MAID DU JOUR Gerta, who Emily meant to fire, but forgot to because "everything's off tonight."

$700 How much the Troubadour made from his Neil Young gig (and he got booed).

THE FEATURED WANNABE TROUBADOURS (IN ORDER OF APPEARANCE)

Thurston Moore & Kim Gordon of Sonic Youth (with daughter Coco) jam in the Hollow.

1. Joe Pernice (singing "Amazing Glow"). Indie rocker most associated with the band the **Pernice Brothers**.

2. Ron & Russell Mael (singing "Perfume"). They make up the 1970s band **Sparks**.

3. Dave "Gruber" Allen. Stars Hollow's rival troubadour (1.21) turned produce seller (2.17).

4. Mary Lynn Rajskub. The stylish girl singing about her '89 Volvo (and ultimately interrupted by Taylor) is an actress best known for her role as Chloe on *24*, though she was also Kirk's girlfriend in *a film by kirk* (2.19).

5. Ira Kaplan, Georgia Hubley & James McNew. Together, they are the band **Yo La Tengo**, singing, appropriately enough, "The Story of Yo La Tengo." They're best known to *Gilmore* fans for their rendition of "My Little Corner of the World."

6. Kim Gordon & Thurston Moore (performing "What a Waste"). Husband and wife team behind the band **Sonic Youth**, appearing at right with their daughter Coco Gordon-Moore in front of the Stars Hollow sign.

7. Daniel Palladino. Sings "The Beaver Ate My Thumb" song with "thumbless bassist" Dave Rygalski (producer Helen Pai's husband and the namesake of Lane's guitarist boyfriend from Season 1) and "thumbless guitarist" Brian Zydiak, a friend and former band partner of Rygalski's.

8. Sam Phillips (singing "Taking Pictures"). The music composer for *Gilmore Girls* appears here with violinist Eric Gorfain as a sorrowful Lorelai walks by, closing out this bummer, bummer of an episode.

AMEN, SISTER FRIEND

LORELAI: I feel so stupid. I really had myself believing it was gonna happen. I bought that stupid dress, and now it's just hanging there, mocking me. And the crazy thing is, I am ready to get married. I am ready to start the next phase of my life. I want another kid and I don't want to wait anymore. I don't want to be patient. I've been patient long enough. I'm not happy and I feel crappy all the time. And I just think I've had it.

'I've been waiting for a long time and I don't want to wait anymore.'

CAROLYN: So, what are you gonna do? Only you can make you wait. Nobody else can. You need to decide what you want and what you're willing to give up to get it, and then you've got to be OK with that, or you've got to be OK with waiting.

LORELAI: I could lose him if I push too hard.

CAROLYN: You don't really seem to have him now, at least not the way you want to have him. You won't get anything unless you ask for it. And if you ask for it and you don't get it, maybe it wasn't worth having in the first place. Some things are just never meant to be, no matter how much we wish they were.

LORELAI: ...I've been waiting for a long time and I don't want to wait anymore.
LUKE: I have to think this through.
LORELAI: No!
LUKE: I have April!
LORELAI: You're gonna have to figure out how April fits into our lives, not the other way around.
LUKE: I'm trying.
LORELAI: Well, try married!
LUKE: Just wait!
LORELAI: No! I'm not waiting! It's now or never!
LUKE: I don't like ultimatums!
LORELAI: I don't like Mondays, but unfortunately they come around eventually.
LUKE: I can't just jump like this.
LORELAI: Well, I'm sorry to hear that. And I have to go.

The Fall of *Gilmore's* Saigon: The Departure of Amy & Dan

Though Amy & Dan publicly praised The WB for the creative freedom they'd been given, things had been getting desperate behind the scenes for a while. To some it appeared that comments such as Amy's from the following February 2005 Hollywood Reporter piece were actually meant to convince network execs to give them more time to wind up the series:

"The network has allowed us to make this show our way, which is to draw out our stories slowly. One of the problems today in TV is that everything has to be so instant. I watch other shows where the lead characters have slept together by Episode 4, broken up by Episode 6, are back together by Episode 8—I mean, by the end of the season, what do you have left?"

However, by April of the following year, the Palladinos would officially announce their departure. What happened?

Throughout the run of the series, Amy would begin the year asking studio executives if *Gilmore Girls* would be coming back the following year, says editor Raul Davalos. "She'd say, 'I have to start writing shows and doing an arc of 22 episodes, and I'd like to be able to end [the series] a certain way. But if I start the season and I don't know it's going to be the last year, then it's very hard for me to get to the place I want to get to.'"

Though some would paint Amy's requests for advance information about the cancellation of the show as the demands of a prima donna, the television landscape is riddled with the burnt out wrecks of great series that met horrible ends precisely because they weren't given enough notice to wind up properly.

Amy told Ken Tucker at Entertainment Weekly that she'd had executives telling her that whatever season she was working on would be its last since Season 4. She and Dan went to negotiate with the network around the Christmas holiday, "but we got frozen out. It was like *Footloose*, when they're revvin' up the tractors, playin' chicken. It took too long and before everyone knew it, we were loading our desks on a truck and driving off the lot."

In addition to a two-year commitment, they also had wanted to have a dedicated second unit to shoot additional scenes involving other actors, potentially granting Lauren and Alexis some relief from their 14-plus-hour days, Davalos says. The WB's unwillingness to grant this and other requests would have grave ramifications for the series the following season. For now, though, it effectively drove a stake through the heart of Stars Hollow.

"I remember Amy was in my room and she got a call from" a network executive who seemed to want to continue negotiating, Davalos says. "The movers were coming in to take her furniture from her office that morning. In fact they might've already been there."

The executive asked her what he had to do to see that Amy & Dan stayed. As many would find out in published interviews later on, Amy had been telling the Powers That Be what she needed since January at least, and more generally, for as long as she'd been making *Gilmore*.

As the movers methodically disassembled the office, there could've been no doubt anywhere, from the *Gilmore* writers room to the network board room, that whatever came next, they and their millions of viewers were leaving the real Stars Hollow for good.

40 winks

'I Loved My Job, But I Wasn't a Big Fan of the Hours'

Those who toil away in front of and behind the camera in Hollywood are no strangers to working long hours on just a few hours sleep; Haskell Wexler's 2006 documentary *Who Needs Sleep* demonstrates how endemic to Hollywood, and detrimental to those who work there, the problem is.

Yet those on *Gilmore Girls* were particularly estranged from their beds for long stretches, even by Hollywood standards. Tell your new co-workers on another series that you'd done time on *Gilmore*, and they knew you could handle whatever they had to throw at you. Many still joke about the odd 21-hour day that was put in on the Warner Brothers backlot.

This usually wasn't too much of a problem for the cast who had their own trailers where they could catch 40 winks, but the crew was another matter. Lorelai's bedroom, living room, the inn (whichever inn) all had one very big attraction to members of the crew—beds and couches, says Lauren Graham's stand-in, Patty Malcolm.

"We would race for those and we'd be peeling out around the corner as soon as they called lunch to get to a couch before any of the other crew members got there. There were some couches you knew that certain people had dibs on like the sound department. You'd race around and they'd already be there, shoes off, a big blanket over them, half asleep. It was get in, get some sleep and get out."

A lot of scenes were shot on Stage 18, which contained the interiors of Lorelai's house and the Dragonfly Inn, Malcolm says. "So there were a lot of couches in the inn, there was a couch in Lorelai's house, Rory's bed, and the last season we actually built the interior of Lauren's bedroom on that stage. She had a big bed, so we were thrilled about that."

The fact remained that, like "58 seats and 62 Koreans," there were more exhausted crew members than reclining surfaces, meaning that many ended up sleeping in their cars, which were conveniently parked along the street in Stars Hollow, alongside the cars of day players such as Rose Abdoo (Gypsy).

"A Ring is No Guarantee"

season **seven**

Whether the timing was coincidental or not, Amy & Dan had left the series with guns blazing at the end of Season 6. Lorelai had broken up with Luke and ended up in bed with Christopher, and if the dialogue wasn't pouring out of your TV speakers like machine-gun fire, you'd swear you were watching *Neighbours*, *Dawson's Creek* or some other soap. Entertainment Weekly reviewer Ken Tucker dubbed the final season *Gilmore Ghosts*, and he wasn't far wrong.

Gilmore Girls also found itself on a new network, kind of. After more than 11 years of duking it out with each other, UPN and The WB networks merged to form The CW (from CBS and Warner Brothers, the parent companies of each company, respectively).

With their work cut out for them, the *Gilmore* writers, under the command of *Gilmore Girls* writer and new showrunner David S Rosenthal, set about extricating the characters from the tight spots Amy & Dan had dropped them in.

7.1 The Long Morrow

First aired: Sept. 26, 2006 // Written by David S Rosenthal // Directed by Lee Shallat Chemel

Picking up immediately after the final moments of the last episode of Season 6, Lorelai leaves Christopher's place shaken, Rory's wondering if Logan will remain faithful now that he's in London, and Taylor has installed Stars Hollow's very first red-light camera...right in front of Luke's Diner. (Never mind the fact that there hasn't been an accident at that corner in 15 years.) Meanwhile, Paris is using the Yale Daily News offices to tutor students (and to terrorize their parents) for the SATs, and Rory's trying to decipher the meaning behind a model rocket ship Logan gave her.

! GINCHY! Sookie psyching out Michel at arm wrestling, Lorelai and Rory's racquetball date and their attempts to figure out what the rocket means ("Hey, maybe it's code. Like I'm his rocket, right? Like I'm his rock, E.T. I'm his rock in the eastern time zone."), Paris' SAT prep course, Luke and Rory waving at each other sadly at the red-light camera test, and Kirk turning Luke's into a "drive-through."

NOTES *'There is no us. There's you and there's me. It's over. It was over last night and it's over now. It's over.'*

* Just like the last time they were apart (5.16), Luke is taking his feelings out on the customers. Taylor calls himself town selectman rather than mayor this time around. Stars Hollow is so small that it doesn't even have its own police force, according to Taylor, who must lay awake

From the Editing Room 6 ⚙ The New Boss

Though Amy & Dan had left *Gilmore*, the show had to go on, says Raul Davalos. David Rosenthal, the new showrunner, had been there the previous season as a writer, so he knew what to do in terms of story. "In fact, we'd been there for so long, it was easy to work with David on the shows. He was clear about what he liked and what he thought was working or wasn't working.

"He was very accommodating, very nice, and very smart about what he was doing. So, there's no sudden procedural change. We're pros, we've done this before, I've been on it from the pilot, so it wasn't like we had to go in a whole new direction or we had to recut the whole episode or something like that. With him it was 'is it working, is it funny, does it fit the *Gilmore Girls* model that Amy created?' He had a lot on his plate; the last thing he needed to worry about was post-production."

at night worrying about his prized 1964 Ford Thunderbird, which we see for the first (and last) time. The Bop It (5.5) is now on the toss pile, along with everything else that reminds Lorelai of Luke. Rory finally figures out (with the help of an online geek) that the rocket model Logan left her is a romantic reference to an episode of *The Twilight Zone* ("The Long Morrow") that they watched when they were first dating. It's about an astronaut who avoided suspended animation during a space journey, just so he would be the same age as the woman he loved back home. "That's true love," Logan said at the time.

"Everything I did in that episode, they had to shoot in one day. It was 105 degrees and we were outside and they had to shoot everything because there were scenes in front of the diner with me in it, then the car wreck (which was very complicated), then scenes after it. We started at sunrise and went till it got dark."

—MICHAEL WINTERS (TAYLOR)

✱ Lorelai tells Sookie that she doesn't want Luke to ever know she slept with Christopher the night before, but she blurts it out at the end of the episode to convince Luke that their relationship truly is over. Luke's delay in finally deciding to run away with Lorelai is reminiscent of Zack's slow processing of his own feelings toward Lane (5.5).

✱ Luke's impassioned plea to Lorelai to run off and get married, followed by Lorelai's rejection, is probably this season's finest hour in terms of making us care about these characters. If you don't feel for Luke by the time the credits roll, please avoid human contact from now on.

TODAY'S CELEBRATION The installation of Stars Hollow's first red-light camera and Logan's first day at work in London.

KIRK OF ALL TRADES Taylor's red-light camera tester.

AND HERE'S A SHOUT OUT TO OUR INTERNATIONAL FANS Logan proposes that Rory come to Europe for two weeks around Christmas: a week in London, four days in Rome and three days in Paris.

$15/HOUR What Paris is paying her tutors.

1999 The vintage of the undeveloped film lurking in Lorelai's freezer.

RATINGS *Gilmore Girls*' Season 7 debut (also its CW network debut) attracted 4.5 million, a nearly 2 million drop-off from the last season, according to the Sept. 28, 2006 edition of The Washington Post.

AMEN, SISTER FRIEND

PARIS [*to Kaitlin's mother*]: She's got a "C" average, which means she's either lazy or stupid. I can work with either. Frankly, sometimes stupid is easier. I can scare the stupid out of you, but the lazy runs deep.

LORELAI [*to Sookie*]: No, you don't get it. I need it to be over. I need it to be over because I can't take this anymore. Yes, I love Luke and yes, I wanted to marry Luke. But I didn't want a life separate from Luke, and that's all he could give me. I don't want that. If I'm gonna be with Luke, I want to be with Luke, and he didn't get it, and I waited. I mean, God, I waited. It's like Luke is driving a car, OK, and I just want to be in the passenger's seat. But he's locked the door, and so I have to hold onto the bumper, you know? I'm not even asking him to open the door for me. Just leave it unlocked and say, "Come in." But no, he didn't do that, so I'm hanging onto the bumper and life goes on and the car goes on, and I get really badly bruised and I'm hitting potholes. And it hurts. I mean it hurts. So yesterday I had to let go of the bumper because it hurts too much.

LUKE [*to Ceaser about Lane's honeymoon*]: Seven days seems like plenty of time to sit in some mountain cabin together and realize you've just chained yourself to another human being for all eternity.

LUKE [*rather tellingly, to tow-truck driver*]: Look, do not pressure me, OK? I do not like being pressured. It's not one or the other. I need to think. Will you people just give me some time to think?

7.2 That's What You Get, Folks, for Makin' Whoopie

First aired: Oct. 3, 2006 // Written by Rebecca Rand Kirshner // Directed by Bethany Rooney

Lane and Zack return from their honeymoon in Mexico, both sick with "parasites"—Zack from drinking the water, and Lane...pregnant. Since Rory and Logan's Asian trip had to be canceled, Lorelai recreates Asia in their house. But when Rory discovers that her mother slept with Christopher right after she broke up with Luke, she's furious. Luke tries his best to hide his hurt over the breakup, helped in part by Liz and TJ. In the end, though, he tells Lorelai that they were just never right for each other.

GINCHY! Luke punching out Christopher; Lorelai calling Rory "loin fruit"; Kirk's outdoors diner; Lorelai recreating Asia for Rory in their

aerie

The Aerie Girls

Billed as the first experiment of its kind, The CW teamed up with American Eagle Outfitters to produce 30-second ads promoting the store's Aerie line of "intimates and dormwear" targeted at girls 15 to 25. The ads ran from Oct. 3 to Dec. 5, 2006 around episodes of *Gilmore Girls* and *Veronica Mars*. Both shows received promotion in 818 American Eagle Outfitters stores.

The commercials featured young Aerie customers discussing the story lines of each episode of both series, relating them to their own experiences. The result was as awful as it sounds, and only made the show's move to The CW that much more challenging. Six years spent building an audience used to quality were quickly squandered by what struck many as a desperate cash grab by execs who already knew both shows' days were numbered. It also prompted some to wonder if Amy & Dan had foreseen what The CW had in mind for their series as soon as the dust settled from The WB/UPN merger.

Behind the Scenes 8 Days a Week

"We shot so much stuff outside that when it rained, chaos would ensue," Michael Winters says. "Eight days was just enough time to shoot an episode. If one of those days got lost…

"And then there were the wild fires up on the hills that one time in the last season that sent smoke down over the sets and everything. That was really difficult. There were a few times where there would be two crews shooting because they had missed a day or two. That was very rare because it was so expensive. But they'd miss a day or two for some reason, rain or something, so they'd start the next episode. And in the meantime they're shooting the last few scenes of the previous episode someplace else on the lot.

"And when we shot in the diner, they'd shoot everything facing the windows first so if we went overtime, which we often did, then they could light it to make it look like the sun was still shining. But you wouldn't see outside that it was getting dark out the windows."

house; Rory and Lane letting off steam by daydreaming about play dates with celebrities' bizarrely-named children; Luke finally making some sort of peace with Lorelai at the market.

NOTES *'You don't get to 'Rory' me. You slept with dad.'*

For their first time, Lane and Zack had sex on the beach a la *From Here to Eternity*. Lorelai's Asian food includes sushi made with fried chicken, a Tootsie-Roll-marshmallow-Twizzler roll, a Butterfinger-Junior-Mints-chocolate-chip-Jujubes roll and Oreo-Red-Hots sashimi.

What's the trouble? Kirk offered to hire Luke.

✱ Rory's reaction to hearing Christopher on the answering machine is similar to Luke's (6.9), but for a completely different reason. This time Christopher as good as says he and Lorelai slept together, which angers their daughter immensely. Not only is she offended by the fact that she felt stupid for worrying about her mother's recent depression and what the one-night stand will do to her relationship with her father, it also hits her where she hurts most—bringing up all the feelings she had over Logan sleeping with Honor's friends not so long ago (6.16).

Lorelai recreates Asia for Rory.

✱ As rough a time as fans give Season 7, it's difficult to see how Amy & Dan could've pulled the good ship *Gilmore* back from the brink without a few awkward episodes. (Of course some might argue that this is why they split up Luke and Lorelai before they left.)

TODAY'S CELEBRATION Lane and Zack return from their honeymoon in Mexico and Lorelai recreates Asia for Rory. Stateside, this episode marked the premiere of the Aerie girls commercials (see the "Aerie Girls" sidebar, p. 400).

KIRK OF ALL TRADES Proprietor of Kirk's diner, right across the street from the demolished Luke's Diner. (Considering that Kirk's has a liquor license suggests that all the years that Kirk kissed up to Taylor finally paid off.)

23 The number of miles from the ocean that Lane and Zack's lodgings were in Mexico.

AND HERE'S A SHOUT OUT TO OUR INTERNATIONAL FANS Rory's plans for the now-aborted Asian excursion: "We were going to see the terra-cotta soldiers in Xi'an. And we were going to go to Peking for the opera and the duck. I want to see Tibet. I want to snorkel off the An Thoi islands in Vietnam. I want to see the crazy teenage fashions in the Harajuku district of Tokyo." Lane and Zack's tales of honeymooning at "Pedro's Paradise" probably didn't do much for Mexican tourism. Finally, Lorelai's admirable attempt to reproduce Asia in the Gilmore home.

Lane tells Rory she's uncovered the great sex conspiracy.

AMEN, SISTER FRIEND

RORY: I can't believe you didn't tell me this. I mean, first of all, you say you don't want to talk. So I figure you're going through some hard emotional time and you need some space. That's fine, but what you didn't tell me is that you slept with dad. No, instead you're going around joking about, you know, origami and marshmallow sushi, like I'm some idiot 5-year-old.

LORELAI: Rory, I was gonna tell you. I just wanted–

RORY: You know what, mom? If you're heartbroken, rent *An Affair to Remember*, have a good cry and drown your sorrows in a pint of ice

Behind the Scenes Good Eats

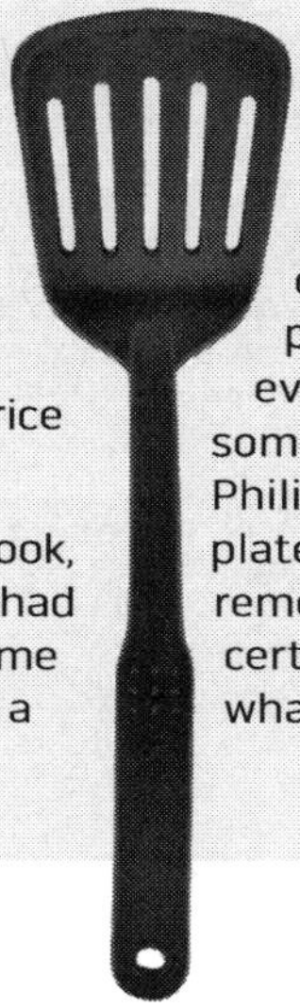

One of the George Foreman grills used by Kirk for his outdoors diner ended up on the wardrobe trailer, a dangerous instrument in the hands of key set costumer Valerie Campbell. "So now I had a rice cooker, a grill, and I had full-on kitchen utensils on the trailer. I would make pasta, all sorts of stuff. I'd make omelettes in my rice cooker in the morning with vegetables.

"On normal shows you don't have time to cook, you're not waiting around, but because we had 14-page oners, it would take them a long time to figure out how they were going to shoot a scene. We had some good food on that trailer."

Sometimes, second assistant camera Mark Sasabuchi, the resident practical jokester of the *Gilmore* crew, would tease other people around the craft services area, where everybody got their meals. "Sasi would cook something or he would get something from Philippe's or somewhere and he'd put it on his plate, and walk into craft service," Campbell remembers. "All the sudden you would see certain people run bolting to craft service to get what he had."

cream. You get a hideously unflattering breakup haircut. You don't sleep with dad.

LUKE [*to Lorelai*]: It's not your fault. It's not my fault. It's just, we're not right together, you know? You're you, I'm me. I just want to stop pretending we're something else. You don't belong with me. You belong with someone like Christopher. And I just—let's just stop fighting it, OK? And you go back to being Lorelai Gilmore. I'll go back to being the guy in the diner who pours your coffee.

What I Kept

Brenda [Maben] the costume lady was so fun, and Gypsy had a long underwear shirt with bugs on it, and I took a liking to it. She let me keep it.

—Rose Abdoo (Gypsy)

7.3 Lorelai's First Cotillion

First aired: Oct. 10, 2006 // Written by Rina Mimoun // Directed by Lee Shallat Chemel

As usual, romance in Stars Hollow is a sticky, awkward affair. Lane finally tells Zack she's pregnant and he seems to ignore it. Paris suggests that Rory send Logan sexy text messages to rekindle their lost intimacy, and Christopher tells Lorelai she's the one for him, no matter how long he has to wait. Meanwhile, Lorelai takes Michel to a cotillion Emily has arranged for young girls, and begins to wonder how much of her decisions have been based on doing what her parents would hate her to do most.

GINCHY! Lorelai rethinking Pop-Tarts and the rest of her life decisions; Paris' phone-sex pep talk with Rory; Zack and Brian's reaction to Lane's pregnancy news; the fact that Rory instantly goes to Henry Miller to find ideas for phone-sex talk; and how closely Lorelai identifies with dorky little Caroline.

NOTES *'I feel like the more I try to connect, the more disconnected I feel.'*

Rory tells Richard that she's working part time for Paris' SAT prep course, which is "kind of like the Princeton review but meaner." Last November, Michel looked after Paul Anka at his house and the dog pooped in his Prada loafers. Lorelai told him she owed him a big favor in return.

While Babette and Miss Patty take turns trying to guess what's new at Luke's Diner, Rory notices right away that he's changed his baseball cap. A similar change will cause a great deal of confusion later on (7.20).

This is the episode that contains both the seeds of the Lorelai/Christopher marriage and its destruction. Christopher's impassioned declaration

Making an Episode 10 The Stand-Ins

Cast and crew put in a ridiculous number of hours on *Gilmore Girls*, no question. Yet when co-stars and guest stars are catching a quick movie in their trailers, or Graham, Bledel and Patterson are running through their lines for the next scene, the stand-ins are on set helping the lighting department get their lighting just right. And that's just the beginning.

Because of the length of the scripts and Amy's insistence on word-perfect delivery, just about every second of the stars' time is accounted for. This means that any opportunity to move them on to prepare for their next scenes is taken. Those Friday night dinners, for example: Whenever you see Richard or Emily on camera talking to Lorelai or Rory, occasionally they're speaking not to Graham and Bledel, but to stand-ins Patty Malcolm and Inger Jackson, respectively. The same goes for those shots of the girls in the Jeep during their commute when you can't quite see their faces.

The stand-ins watch the actors rehearse a scene, making notes on their copies of the day's script (or "sides") about how the actress they're covering stands and sits, after what line she picks up her coffee, everything. If a stand-in holds her head at a different angle, it affects how the actress will be lit later; cross the room on the wrong line and the camera operator has no idea where to aim the camera. After that, the stand-ins rehearse the scene so the camera and other departments can make all the modifications they need to without eating into any more of the actors' time.

Finally, with the sides on the table in front of her for the dinner scene, Malcolm doesn't just read Graham's lines aloud, but performs them the way any actor would. This is when the camera operators are shooting close-ups of Herrmann or Bishop. The sound department is recording the couple because they're miked, "but they're also picking up my voice," Malcolm says. "You can hear it slightly, because when I've looked at the dailies, I've heard myself in the background. Since I'm not miked and the boom isn't on me, it's not as prominent. When they go to edit it, they edit my voice out and Lauren's voice is put there instead."

With Lorelai and Rory in nearly every scene, shooting an episode could easily take 12 days rather than the eight allotted for the entire production if they had to be present every moment for every single scene they're in.

of love combined with Rory getting along with her father paves the way for what comes next in France (7.7), while Lorelai's questioning of what she wants out of life will ultimately lead her away from him. For as long as she can remember, Richard and Emily have pushed her toward making a family with Christopher—how could she ever consider him her own choice?

TODAY'S CELEBRATION The reopening of Luke's Diner, Lane telling

Lorelai vanquishes a few childhood anxieties at Emily's cotillion.

Zack that she's pregnant, and Lorelai taking Michel to Emily's cotillion.

EMILY'S MAID DU JOUR Charlotte, age 10.

YOU'VE ENTERED EMILYLAND [*about peanut butter and jelly sandwiches*] This is a proper tea, Sookie. I'm not interested in circus food.

AND HERE'S A SHOUT OUT TO OUR INTERNATIONAL FANS Rory suggests talking about American companies outsourcing their customer care to Bangalore as a way of deflecting Richard and Emily's questions about the Luke-Lorelai breakup at Friday night dinner. Emily has a go at the table manners of Russians and mentions the recent surge in renovations of paradores in Spain to get them all off the subject of Lorelai's breakup.

THINGS WE'VE LEARNED Edward Herrmann is a great fan of old time radio, especially Fred Allen, Jack Benny, and especially Bob & Ray, who are, in his words, "magically bizarre."

AMEN, SISTER FRIEND

LORELAI: I mean what if I don't like what I like because I like it, but because my mother doesn't like it and doesn't want me to like it? What if I don't actually like the music that I like, or the movies, or the clothes or the men? What if I don't like what I seem to like?
RORY: Ah, hence the Pop-Tart.
LORELAI: Yes, hence. I can remember the first time I had a Pop-Tart. It was at my friend Erica Katcha's house and she said, "Do you want a Pop-Tart?" And I knew my mother would recoil at the very idea of me having a Pop-Tart. I could just picture her. "A Pop-Tart?!" And so I had one. And I opened the little silver wrapper and I took a bite, and I thought nothing had ever tasted so good. I thought it tasted like freedom. It tasted like I was my own person. The Pop-Tart tasted like freedom and rebellion and independence.
RORY: Wow, that's some Pop-Tart. What flavor was that?

LORELAI: But now I think I don't know if I like Pop-Tarts. What if I don't like Pop-Tarts? Would I like Pop-Tarts if Richard and Emily had served me Pop-Tarts on a silver platter and demanded I eat every bite? I don't know.

RORY: Hey, where are all the Pop-Tarts?

LORELAI: I've been experimenting.

RORY: You ate all the Pop-Tarts?

LORELAI: If it makes you feel any better, I don't know if I like them.

RORY: Well, I hope you didn't eat all the Froot Loops.

RORY [*after Paris suggests phone sex with Logan*]: What? You mean... I can't do that, I talk to my mother on that phone.

PARIS: OK, what about texting?

RORY: No. No, thank you.

PARIS: Why not? You say stuff when you're together, don't you?

RORY: Yeah. I guess. Sometimes.

PARIS: So, text it. Texting is great. And you can do it while you're doing other things. Doyle and I are doing it right now.

RORY: What? [*Glances horrified at Paris' phone*] Oh my God!

7.4 'S Wonderful, 'S Marvelous

First aired: Oct. 17, 2006 // Written by Gayle Abrams // Directed by Victor Nelli Jr.

While Rory and Sookie are urging Lorelai to be careful dating Christopher, April slyly convinces Luke to decorate his apartment in the hopes that he will have a lady friend over. After seeing five bad movies in a row, Christopher surprises Lorelai with a barnside projection of Funny Face. *But not even this Lorelai favorite can top the evening's highlight—bailing Emily out of jail! Meanwhile, Rory continues to try to put Logan out of her mind, this time by covering an art exhibition for the paper, where she meets artist Olivia and actress Lucy.*

GINCHY! Nearly a ginchy-free episode, with the (somewhat lame) exception of Christopher's big date surprise and the fan-service scene of Emily being jailed for driving while intoxicated.

NOTES *'I feel I may have gotten overshadowed a bit. I mean how's my little barn movie supposed to compare with your mom in jail?'*

"They used [Warner Brothers' Midwest Street] in so many things—The Music Man, the Dukes of Hazzard. I didn't know that until I'd been working there, and Dukes of Hazzard was one of my favorite TV shows as a kid. And I was like, 'Aw yeah, the General Lee used to go on two wheels around this whole block.'"

—TODD LOWE (ZACK)

What *Gilmore* Means To Me

I started to watch the show because I got to tour the Warner Brothers studio. Early on, it was like the people from the show could be your friends, and I found myself pulling for each character to realize their dreams.

A year later, my sister moved back to town. When she fell in love with the show, we had a common thing to do together. We still get together and watch the DVDs. *Gilmore Girls*

has made us so much closer as siblings.

I started sending letters to actors from the show to say thanks for their work and to ask for their autograph. It was so great getting personal replies from the great people that made us fans of this wonderful series. I will be a fan of the show and the great cast members for the rest of my life. Thank you *Gilmore Girls*!!!

—Chas Demster, *Warsaw, Indiana*

Anna will be in New Mexico for two weeks following her mother's back surgery. Luke continues to impress with the list of things he's never done. In Season 1 it was not having seen any movies; now he's never been to a Target department store.

Doyle is a fact-checker at the Hartford Courant. When Lorelai and Christopher go to pick up Emily from the police station, it's almost certainly where she had to pick up Rory (5.22).

A disappointing episode on a number of fronts. Even the inclusion of Richard and Emily barely tickles the enjoyment meter, mostly because Richard says nothing memorable and Emily is used more as a pantomime dame than the multidimensional character we're used to.

TODAY'S CELEBRATION April has an extended stay with Luke, Rory begins her senior year of Yale, Richard becomes a visiting lecturer in economics there, and Emily gets arrested for driving while intoxicated.

AND INTRODUCING...*Lucy and Olivia* Perhaps competing with the Aerie girls commercials for most annoying additions, but points go to them for at least recognizing the "genius" that is Paris Geller.

6 WEEKS How long Lorelai and Christopher have been dating at this point.

AMEN, SISTER FRIEND

PARIS: Dormitory renovations—that's quaint. I recently had the opportunity to be a fly on the wall at the Hartford Courant as the editor selected their lead story. It was down to the wire and I was on the edge of my seat when, right at the last second, a local-corruption story broke. It was thrilling. It made this place look like a joke.
RORY: Your point, Paris?
PARIS: Oh, I thought I was clear. Compared to the Courant, this place is a joke.

EMILY [*to officer about to administer a Breathalyzer test*]: Young man, I don't know where that's been, but I can say with absolute certainty it won't be going anywhere near my mouth.

LORELAI: I'm just so glad you were with me tonight. I mean,

anybody else who would have seen me laughing as I bailed my mother out of jail would have just thought I was completely deranged.

CHRISTOPHER: Well, I know you're deranged but for completely different reasons.

LORELAI: I mean, you just get it, and you make everything fun, and it's so nice to be with someone who understands you and makes you...[*They kiss.*]

Rory picks up two new Yale friends: Lucy (Krysten Ritter, left) and Olivia (Michelle Ongkingco).

7.5 The Great Stink

First aired: Oct. 24, 2006 // Written by Gina Fattore // Directed by Michael Schultz

A train full of Ohio pickles derails in Woodbridge, causing a horrible stink to blow through Stars Hollow. Logan returns to New York with his team—Nick, Bobby and Philip—and succeeds in acquiring a social networking Web site. At first proud of him, Rory quickly becomes insecure when she meets Bobby, a stunning, Oxford-educated British woman who sees far more of Logan than she does. Things are no less complicated for Lorelai. Sherry wants GG to spend a couple of months with her in Paris. Christopher and Lorelai fight over the idea of sending the 4-year-old to France with her nanny until Christopher asks Lorelai to go with him and GG to Paris instead, in two weeks time.

! GINCHY! Logan's rooftop surprise visit; the fawning way that Nick, Philip and Logan praise the way Bobby stood up, literally, to the owners of the Web site they wanted to buy; the delight with which everybody (including Richard) gathers around Lorelai's phone as she shows them pictures of Emily in jail.

NOTES *'Chris is open to me. Christopher is not Luke.'*

* Rory seems to have a knack for picking boyfriends who think it's particularly clever to phone her up and pretend they're somewhere else when they're extremely close by. Dean used to do it, but his resources never made his appearances this dramatic.

* The Web site Logan & Co. acquire is essentially Facebook—MySpace but by invitation only—which is pretty much how Facebook operated around the time this episode aired.

Christopher and Sherry's divorce is final; she's dating her yoga instructor. Lorelai continues to try to talk herself into her relationship with Christopher, complimenting him on showing her the letter from Sherry requesting a place in GG's life, suggesting it's an improvement on the way Luke hid April from her—never mind that they're pieces of information of staggeringly different magnitudes.

Richard's anecdote about teaching an economics class at Yale includes his surprise discovery that the students are discussing Franz Ferdinand the band, and not the archduke whose assassination sparked World War I—the second "how out of touch older people are" joke about the same band (5.21).

Last time Lorelai and Christopher went to dinner at Richard and Emily's, Christopher was trying to get away from the woman Emily was trying to set him up with (6.22); this time, he's fighting with Lorelai over sending GG to Paris. As usual (2.14, 6.16), Lorelai tries to say something nice to him ("you leaving Rory when you were 16 is not at all the same as Sherry, a grown woman, packing up and leaving GG"), and he takes it the wrong way.

TODAY'S CELEBRATION Paul Anka's first night at Christopher's, Logan's team buys a Web site, and the great pickle train crash.

EMILY'S MAID DU JOUR Hildegard.

3.5 TONS The amount of pickles and pickle brine that was scattered along the tracks three days ago when the train derailed in Woodbridge, east of Stars Hollow.

$2,500 The cost of cleaning up the pickles.

AMEN, SISTER FRIEND

RORY: Do you think I like feeling this way? I mean, I haven't seen you for months and months, and now you're in town for what, 26 hours? And in that time, I can't just get happy and act like a fruit fly?
LOGAN: Mayfly.
RORY: I can't just live in the moment and enjoy the 26 great hours ahead of me? I have to be sulky and miserable while all the other fruit

flies share private jokes with my boyfriend? You think I like this about myself? Wrong. I hate myself for being this way. I hate Bobby for her professionally tweezed eyebrows and her oh-so-incredible ability to stand up at a moment's notice. And most of all, I hate the fact that in a few seconds you'll be in that car leaving me again.
LOGAN: That is a hell of a long way to go just to say, "I miss you."

7.6 Go Bulldogs!

First aired: Nov. 7, 2006 // Written by David S Rosenthal and Rebecca Rand Kirshner // Directed by Wil Shriner

Christopher nudges Lorelai into attending parents weekend at Yale with him, where they discover that Emily and Richard have been going to it since Rory's freshman year. Anxious to make up for lost time, Christopher takes Rory's Yale Daily News co-workers to lunch at Chez Zinjustin, the swankiest restaurant in town (where the creme brulee is to die for). Meanwhile, Luke goes out on a date with April's swimming coach, Susan Bennett, who's not exactly his ideal dinner companion.

GINCHY! Lorelai pretending the phone isn't working when she calls Emily; Kirk upset by Lulu's constant presence; and the Yale Daily News staff getting hammered at lunch.

NOTES *'Is there anyone who's not a little tipsy? Thanks for lunch, dad.'*

Last episode, it was Bill and Paris fighting over who would be in charge of the Yale Daily News while Rory was away; this time, it's Michel and Sookie fighting over the reins for when Lorelai is in Paris.

Who knew Christopher was so knowledgeable about astrophysics? Add Marlene Dietrich to the list of pop culture references lost on Luke. Luke is the third single dad that swimming coach Susan Bennett's dated.

The first truly awful episode in a long, long time. The double byline only seems to confirm the feeling that this script was completed during the shoot, with the actors waiting for some sort of direction while the writers banged it out.

TODAY'S CELEBRATION Parents weekend at Yale and student war protestors take over President Stewart's office.

Amy's 'Sense of the Romantic'

"Amy's sense of romance and her sense of the romantic—there's nobody that does that better for television," says Scott Cohen (Max). "It's almost sentimental but not quite. It's not like a *Desperate Housewives* or *Grey's Anatomy* type of romance, it's romance that's from another era; it's so deep."

Amy claimed that she modeled *Gilmore*'s rapid-fire wit after the romantic films of Katherine Hepburn and Spencer Tracy of the '40s and '50s. It's obvious that she also borrowed the occasionally combative relationships from movies of this era, too. Whether it was Luke and Lorelai's constant sparring over her cell phone abuse or Rory and Jess' fights over Dean, you could always tell the most passionate relationships by the sparks that flew. Lorelai and Christopher, on the other hand, had more in common with a bathrobe that is extremely comfortable, but hardly likely to set anybody's heart on fire.

OY WITH THE ___, ALREADY! The final iteration of the "creme brulee to die for" joke could easily have been lifted from any cookie-cutter sitcom. And the "Sookie cheated on Jackson by accepting produce from another man" gag has been done before, and to much greater effect (3.11).

LORELAI'S NAME TAG "Zinf" (as in "Zinf and "Del"...zinfandel).

CHRISTOPHER'S NAME TAG "Hello, I'm Rory Gilmore's dad, Christopher."

AMEN, SISTER FRIEND

KIRK: Everywhere I go, there she is. I'm sitting at the movies. Who's sitting next to me? Lulu. I go out to dinner. Who's sitting across from me? Lulu. I'm hanging out on the couch, watching TV. Who's right there next to me?

LUKE: Your mother.

KIRK: And Lulu. And at least mother respects my personal space. Sometimes when you're watching *Antiques Roadshow*, you just don't want somebody tickling your arm.

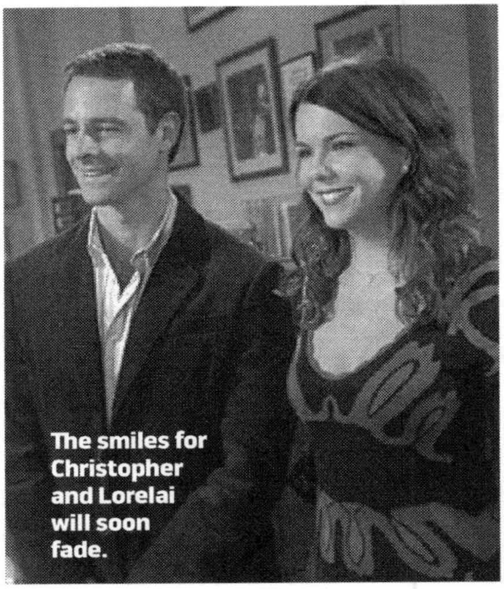
The smiles for Christopher and Lorelai will soon fade.

[Later]

KIRK: You inspired me. I look at you and I think this guy's doing it right. Slave to no master. You come home at 3 in the morning—no one cares. You want to eat dessert for dinner—no one cares. You walk around in tube socks and tighty-whities—no one cares. No one cares what you do or where you go. So, what do you say, Luke? You want to be my wingman, Goose to my Maverick? [Sings into a ladle] You never close your eyes anymore when I kiss your lips and there's no tenderness...

LUKE: Listen, you pinhead, you should be kissing the ground that Lulu walks on. Why that sweet girl lets you within a hundred miles of her is beyond me, but she does. You are the luckiest man on the planet to have

Behind the Scenes Lunch With Christopher

While the series regulars had long since found their place in *Gilmore*, those playing the Yale Daily News staffers never quite knew when their time would be over. The scene where they had dinner with Christopher and Lorelai felt something like a "going away present" to Devon Michaels (Bill), though they still had one more episode to go.

"That was one of our longest days because of the way they had to shoot everything," he says, especially because of the attention to detail necessary to keep the continuity of how the food appeared on the table. "Just keeping track of everyone's amounts and everything, I'm sure glad that wasn't my job."

Also, because of the configuration of the table, they couldn't just film the people on one side, then film those on the other side. "They actually had a couple of different tables. One had a big hole in the middle where the camera was. It looked like it was part of the table, and it was remote controlled by one of the camera operators. And then there was a regular table where they shot a bunch of other angles and had a few of us move. We were there late into the night."

a girl like that looking out for you and caring about you. And if you say so much as one unkind word to her, I will personally break every bone in your body. You got me?

7.7 French Twist

First aired: Nov. 14, 2006 // Written by David Babcock // Directed by Lee Shallat Chemel

Zack and Lane discover they're having twins, meaning it's way past time that they told Mrs. Kim about the future addition, er, additions to their family. Mrs. Kim is overjoyed...and expects them to move in with her immediately. After dropping GG off with Sherry, Lorelai and Christopher stay in Paris and give in to the romantic city's charms (and a lack of early morning food options) in a way that will (briefly) complicate both their lives. Rory's not doing much better at home. With Logan away and her days as editor of the Yale Daily News officially over, she realizes for the first time that she has no idea what the next year will bring. And why the heck is her old pal Marty pretending not to know her?

! GINCHY! Zack thinking the sonogram means they're having conjoined twins; Christopher getting himself and Lorelai into L'Arpege when it should've been closed; Mrs. Kim packing off Brian to live with a Korean family; and Lucy's "Boyfriend" turning out to be Marty.

NOTES *'The first day is hard. Then it just gets worse.'*

"Many actors ask the writer, 'Can we change that line to this, it'll just come out more naturally that way.' Sometimes that benefits the project because this person is having a hard time getting it, we need to move on. But it is taking away some of the challenge because there's a way to make anything sound natural and believable and real."

-JOHN CABRERA (BRIAN) ON BREAKING FROM GILMORE'S TRADITION OF VERBATIM LINE DELIVERY IN SEASON 7

✱ Kirk was born at Woodbury Memorial Hospital. According to the markings in the Gilmore home, Rory went through a growth spurt in 1992.

✱ The "Aerie girl" influence (see 7.1) continues with Rory hanging out with Olivia and Lucy in Stars Hollow. Dyeing their hair and making Rice Krispies treats? Really? The final scene with the girls gives the story line some much-needed heart, leaving Lorelai and Christopher's "French twist" the least interesting development of the episode. What saves it all: Zack's half-assed prenatal parenting and the quick shot of Brian being sent to live with a Korean family.

TODAY'S CELEBRATION Rory hands over the reins of the Yale Daily News to Bill; Olivia, Lucy and Rory hang out in the Hollow; and Christopher and Lorelai get married in Paris.

THE FORBIDDEN FJORDS Lucy's suggestion for the name of the Norwegian girl band she and Olivia want to start based on their dyed hair.

MARCO & POLO Zack's baby name suggestions. ("Whenever we call for Marco, Polo would answer with his name, so we'd always know where *he* was.")

AND HERE'S A SHOUT OUT TO OUR INTERNATIONAL FANS Paris (the French city, not Ms. Geller) gets a pretty even shake from this episode, where the hotel staff are rude, but restaurateurs are easily bribed. Norway, on the other hand, gets credit for little more than the Vikings and Edvard Munch.

32½ the number of hours Lorelai's been awake since they left for Paris.

104 The number of fleur-de-lis stenciled on the ceiling of Lorelai and Christopher's Paris hotel room.

AMEN, SISTER FRIEND

PARIS: You really shouldn't be alone at a time like this. Why don't you call your "girls gone wild" friends? They seem delightful in a "get crazy-drunk in Cancun and flash your breasts" kind of way.
RORY: Your take on Lucy and Olivia is so not them.
PARIS: Whatever. Later. Oh, and Lexapro is fast-acting, but side effects

Nothing will ever be the same after Paris.

are weight gain and a noticeable drop in sexual appetite. Of course with Logan gone, that's moot.
RORY: Always a pleasure, Paris.

RORY: Everything is just ending. I just feel like everything is gonna be over. I'm done at the paper. Soon I'm gonna be done at Yale, and it's just like I'm standing on this cliff, looking out into this huge, foggy-
LUCY: Abyss?
RORY: Like a huge, foggy abyss, and in my whole life there's never been an abyss. It's been abyssless. I've always known exactly what is in front of me, and I've always known exactly where I'm going, and now I don't know what's out there.

7.8 Introducing Lorelai Planetarium

First aired: Nov. 21, 2006 // Written by Jennie Snyder // Directed by Lee Shallat Chemel

Two days after the fact, Lorelai and Christopher tell Rory they got married in Giverny, pissing her off because she wasn't able to be there. At the prelaunch party for Logan's new Web site, Rory meets the editor of an online magazine for which she writes "Let Them Drink Cosmos," a piece skewering the rich people at the party. Naturally, Logan doesn't think too much of Rory's view of him and his associates, and reminds her that she's hardly one to talk. Luke gets on the

The Wedding Ring

"When Lorelai ran off to Paris and got married, I didn't even know it because I was behind a few episodes," Michael Winters says. "One of the background people said to me, 'She's got her wedding ring on. Do you think that's a good idea she has a wedding ring on?' I said, 'Gee, I don't know why she does.' And it wasn't until later in that episode that I realized they'd gotten married in the episode before, and it hadn't aired yet."

bad side of April when he prevents her from going to a birthday party after she develops appendicitis.

GINCHY! Luke attentively following April's school gossip; Logan's reaction to Rory's piece about the party; and Luke discovering that Lorelai's married when the doctor calls attention to her wedding ring.

NOTES *'I really do hate everyone today, including myself. Great. The circle's complete.'*

Considering Lorelai wanted nothing to do with snails when Emily served them (4.16), it's odd that she would go so far as to cook them now. Rory's reaction to the news that Lorelai and Christopher got married is similar to the way she behaved when she discovered that the two of them slept together right after Lorelai bailed on Luke. She does not trust the man-child type to protect her feelings, or those of her mother, something she's made clear on several occasions over the years. Ultimately, she will apply this defensiveness to Logan when he makes his own intentions known (7.21).

Logan's friend Hugo, who happens to be starting an online magazine described as "Slate meets The New York Times' lifestyle section before they sold out," spent two years working at the Times, two at Slate.com, and worked for the Paris Review under legendary journalist George Plimpton.

Sen. Barack Obama came to speak at Yale a couple of weeks ago and Rory interviewed him. When asked if he planned to run for president in 2008, "Standard answer—'no current plans.' But I saw a twinkle in his eye," she says. She'll get to see a lot more of him soon (7.22).

Christopher stole Lorelai's Police *Synchronicity* T-shirt 22 years ago; Lorelai thought Emily had gotten rid of it.

Once again, Rory manages to offend people with her writing unintentionally (4.8). Luke calls Lorelai in a panic over April's illness, and she comes to the hospital to be with him, just like he came for her when she needed him most (5.14). Lorelai makes it clear to Rory that she's not taking Christopher's name.

The title of this episode highlights one of the problems with Season 7—insertion of place names and cultural references simply for the sake of it. Unless there's something the author is missing (certainly not unheard of), the only reason for "Introducing Lorelai Planetarium" is because of a bad play on words Lorelai makes relating to New York City's Hayden Planetarium, strictly because it has Hayden in its title. What makes this particularly annoying is that this is the episode many go to expecting to find the episode describing the Rory Gilmore Astronomy Building Richard and Emily plan to build.

TODAY'S CELEBRATION The prelaunch launch party for the Web site Logan & co. bought, April's first boy-girl party (though she doesn't actually get to go), and Rory learns about Christopher and Lorelai getting married.

HENRY The name of Logan's suit of armor.

AMEN, SISTER FRIEND

LOGAN: What, I'm a rich trust-fund kid. I'm not ashamed of it.
RORY: No and you shouldn't be. That's not what I meant. I mean, the point, or the point I was trying to make, was that people use connections to get ahead.
LOGAN: Oh give me a break. You act like making connections is something nefarious. It's just people meeting people.
RORY: Well, it's certain people meeting certain people. It's not like anyone's meeting Joe bus driver.
LOGAN: And you're Joe bus driver.
RORY: Well, no, but—
LOGAN: Exactly. I mean where do you get off acting all morally superior?
RORY: That is not what I intended to say at all.
LOGAN: You clearly think you are. Why? Because you read *Ironweed*? 'Cause you saw *Norma Rae*?
RORY: Logan—
LOGAN: Wake up, Rory. Whether you like it or not, you're one of us. You went to prep school. You go to Yale. Your grandparents are building a whole damn astronomy building in your name.
RORY: That is different, OK? It's not like I live off a $5-million trust fund

my parents set up for me.
LOGAN: Yeah well, you're not exactly paying rent, either.
RORY: Screw you, Logan.

LORELAI: No. No. Hayden? No. I don't want to be Mrs. Hayden Planetarium for the rest of my life. I'm Lorelai Gilmore, OK? Lorelai Gilmore without the Gilmore is like, Gil-, you know, -less.

7.9 Knit, People, Knit

First aired: Nov. 28, 2006 // Written by David Grae // Directed by Lee Shallat Chemel

Liz gives birth to her baby at home and Anna tells Luke that she and April are moving to New Mexico to be with her mother. Rory moves back in with Paris and Doyle, and even manages to dispel the awkwardness between her and Marty, temporarily. And despite Christopher's eagerness to get moving on his new life with his new wife, Lorelai realizes it's going to take a bit of doing to get Stars Hollow used to Christopher. The Knit-a-thon seems the perfect opportunity—a typical, crazy town tradition. How could Christopher possibly mess it up?

GINCHY! Emily playing the answering machine message Lorelai left telling them she and Christopher got married...twice; the dancing duo of Paris and Doyle; Christopher's awkward man date with Jackson; and the simple way Rory defuses the awkwardness with Marty.

NOTES *'Well honey, you married an outsider.'*

Around the age of 8 or 10, Lorelai told Richard that she was going to marry US Speaker of the House Tip O'Neill.

The Knit-a-thon is to rebuild the Old Muddy River bridge that has been the focus of so many charitable benefits over the years (1.13; 2.5; 2.8; 3.7). This may also be the bridge from which Luke pushed Jess (2.5), and where Jess took Rory for their picnic (2.13). According to Lorelai, it was rebuilt *again* a couple of years ago (roughly Season 5), this time out of Japanese maple, but was ravaged by beetles.

Lorelai explains to Christopher that she doesn't want to seem like they're flaunting their marriage. What she doesn't say is she doesn't want to flaunt it in front of Luke, which is exactly what Rory told Jess when they were together about Dean (3.9). As part of her duties as town chairwoman, Miss Patty is supposed to greet all newlyweds with the Stars Hollow Welcome Wagon.

TODAY'S CELEBRATION Rory moves back in with Paris and Doyle, Lucy's 21st birthday party (the theme is "2002"), the Stars Hollow Knit-a-thon, and Liz and TJ have their baby. (Only those two could name their baby Doula.)

KIRK OF ALL TRADES Free-knitting-needle guy.

LORELAI'S MR. "LONG SENTENCE OF WORDS STRUNG TOGETHER" THING

1. Mr. Favorite Son-in-law Happy Smiley Face
2. Mr. I Remember Stuff from English Class in High School
3. Mr. Doesn't Understand the More Annoying You Tell Me a Bit is, the More I Want to do it
4. Mr. Doesn't Seem Like he Knows What he's Talking About But is Actually Pretty Wise.

$30 How much Rory pledges for Lorelai in the Knit-a-thon.

$2,200 How much was raised for the bridge before Christopher became so generous.

$10,000 The goal for rebuilding the bridge.

AMEN, SISTER FRIEND

CHRISTOPHER: Lor' come on. How great did our walk through town go? You were worried about that and everybody was nice.
LORELAI: They were nice.
CHRISTOPHER: It went great.
LORELAI: Eh.
CHRISTOPHER: Didn't it?
LORELAI: Nah.
CHRISTOPHER: What are you saying?
LORELAI: I'm saying it didn't go so great. They were cordial, they were polite.
CHRISTOPHER: But the wagon–
LORELAI: Was full of cleaning supplies and shoe trees. When Claude and

"There were running gags about how many takes some directors would do. Some would do 20 or 22 takes on one shot, and that makes your day really long. And things can fray, it's just natural. And some people were doing three or four scenes before that."

-MICHAEL WINTERS (TAYLOR)

What's With All the Knitting?

By Season 7, one of the ways that several people dealt with the time spent waiting to film was by knitting.

Wardrobe's Brenda Maben and Valerie Campbell, some of the hair and makeup people, and even director Lee Shallat Chemel, all knitted regularly on set, Campbell says. "That's why they did that episode, I think."

On this episode, knitting needles were busy to ensure that Taylor Doose had himself a nice blue sweater.

"So I'd be doing my job *and* knitting, and Brenda said, 'Here's some yarn, knit some more.'"

When Maben finally put it all together, the sweater was enormous "because we didn't have any direction as to how to knit," Campbell says. "She actually cut it as if it were a piece of fabric and put that thing together. She had enough left over that she knit him a hat, too. It was crazy."

Michele Davies got married, they got handmade clothing and homemade baked goods, and the pizza guy whittled them bookends in the shape of Senegalese tigers. That's a welcome wagon. We got a "we're tolerating that you're here" wagon. Sorry.
CHRISTOPHER: So, going out with Jackson is important because-?
LORELAI: Jackson is loved. Jackson is respected. If you're in with Jackson, you're in with Stars Hollow.

7.10 Merry Fisticuffs

First aired: Dec. 5, 2006 // Written by David S Rosenthal // Directed by Jackson Douglas

While Emily is trying to enlist Lorelai's help in planning their wedding party, Christopher grows increasingly annoyed at how Lorelai seems to be saying no to everything he wants: a new place to live, another child, even the exchanging of vows at the party. Luke's week's been no better, with Anna refusing to let him see April and his lawyer telling him he has little legal recourse. Fuming, Luke and Christopher duke it out. Meanwhile, after Rory tells him about how weird Marty's been, Logan tells Lucy that Marty and Rory have known each other since freshman year. Not to be outdone, Emily warns Lorelai that she's going to wreck her marriage if she doesn't start compromising with Christopher.

! GINCHY! Pretty depressing, ginchy-less episode all around.

NOTES *'Boys suck.'*

* The complexity that is Lorelai continues. Though she once again manages to convince her significant other to stay in her house rather than get a new one (6.2), there remains the sense that Dean was right when he told Luke that Lorelai wanted more than Stars Hollow (5.18).

* Randall Farber has been the designer-in-residence for the Connecticut Opera House for 15 years. Taylor's niece, Bonnie, is an extremely slow Doose's Market cashier and couldn't care less about her job. During Luke's briefing with the lawyer, he tells him about the time he was arrested for beating up the car of Nidaisi's boyfriend (4.17). Marty has four jobs: tutoring, landscaping, the bookstore and Finnegan's.

TODAY'S CELEBRATION Rumble in the tinsel as Chris and Luke beat each other up.

KIRK OF ALL TRADES Christmas-wrapping-paper seller.

11 DAYS How old Doula is.

11 POUNDS, 4 OUNCES Doula's weight.

10 The number of days Emily expects Lorelai to help her plan the wedding party.

AMEN, SISTER FRIEND

LORELAI: I have no idea. Mars and Venus, you know?
RORY: Yeah, see, I don't think that's right. Because Mars and Venus are both planets, right? So they have something in common. I think it's more like Mars and a bowl of soup.
LORELAI: Venus and a bowl of soup.
RORY: What?
LORELAI: Venus is the woman. Venus and a bowl of soup.... sorry boys suck.
RORY: Yeah, stupid bowls of soup.

EMILY [*to Lorelai*]: I think he's good for you. But it's not going to be perfect. He's not perfect, and God knows you're not perfect. But marriage is not about always being happy, and often it's about not

Behind the Scenes Take That!

On most one-hour shows, each scene usually only requires three or four takes before you move on to shooting the next one. *Gilmore*, however, was notorious for wracking up an enormous number of takes. While this invariably was down to ensuring the best quality possible, it did take its toll on cast and crew at times. Fortunately, they knew how to take the pressure off.

"Whenever we would do those long oners, there was a record book that was kept of how many takes it took to shoot and how many times it took the directors to get and print the gates," says key set costumer Valerie Campbell. "I know at one point somebody had 34 takes to get a shot. We were shooting this forever. And usually it was a big long walk and talk. Now sometimes it was camera's fault, sometimes it was the actors' fault, sometimes it was a combination. Obviously there was some reason why we kept shooting."

Second assistant camera Mark Sasabuchi "would take a deck of cards around the crew. Randomly you would buy a card, and if it matched the number of takes that scene took, then you won whatever the pool was. There was another game that had to do with wrap time. They would pick a time and you would go high or low. I think it was a dollar or something. Basically it was the same dollar going back and forth."

being happy at all. It's about compromise, which is not your strong suit. Marriage is about swallowing your pride sometimes, about doing what he wants. It's not about winning an argument, which may make you sad, because that's what you love. But I don't want to see you ruin this. Marriage is serious business, Lorelai, and if you don't take this very seriously, then this whole thing could fall apart faster than you could possibly imagine. And he'll be gone and you'll be alone again. A ring is no guarantee.

"I always wanted [the Luke/Lorelai/Christopher triangle] to be as complex as it could be so that there wasn't an obvious choice. It's like when you go see some romantic comedy movie and you're like, 'Well, obviously she shouldn't be with that guy.'"

-LAUREN GRAHAM, TV GUIDE, 5/7/07

7.11 Santa's Secret Stuff

First aired: Jan. 23, 2007 // Written by Rebecca Rand Kirshner // Directed by Lee Shallat Chemel

Talk about post-Christmas blues. Rory returns from London, still in a quandary over Lucy not speaking to her. Determined to assert his parental rights over April, Luke asks Lorelai to write a character reference for him to submit to the court. Trying to maintain the delicate peace between herself and Christopher, Lorelai finally manages to write and mail it without Christopher any the wiser. Meanwhile, April sneaks over to the diner to exchange Christmas presents with Luke: an April mask for Luke; another rock tumbler for April, before they exchange it for a microscope. Lane, sick of all the baby talk at work and at home, tries to get the band back together.

! GINCHY! Maybe Rory's airy "Peppermint" when Lorelai goes on about her coffee having the vaguest whisper of peppermint, but that's about it.

NOTES *'Why are you lying to dad?'*

✱ Usually it's Luke being rude to the customers after he's had a fight with Lorelai; this time it's Lane working out her hormones on them now that she's pregnant.

✱ Lorelai gets Babette a needlepoint pillow containing a sassy saying, Michel and Emily the same cologne (because they'll both return whatever she gets them anyway), and whatever it is Williams-Sonoma sold her for Sookie. She very nearly gets Christopher a telescope to go along with his sweater and large book.

✱ During Luke's "monogram" phase of gift giving with Rory, he gave her monogrammed towels, pencils, a mug, backpack and a belt.

A chance encounter with Luke and April inspires Lorelai to write the character reference he needs.

Traditionally the injection of a cute kid into the TV mix is pretty horrendous, but GG's brief contributions may be the only interesting thing in this episode. Paul Anka 2.0?

TODAY'S CELEBRATION Christmas after Christmas.

MACON Gil's youngest child.

7 The number of Christmas trees in the Gilmore home.

'OUR TRADITIONS ARE IMPORTANT TO US'

1. Mistletoe on the ceiling-fan blades
2. Leaving cookies out for Santa on Christmas Eve
3. Red and green M&Ms in their cereal Christmas morning
4. Stockings hung on the banister
5. Weston's for a cup of candy-cane coffee
6. Putting on Christmas music, drinking eggnog, and pretending to bake cookies bought at Weston's (though they make their own frosting).

AMEN, SISTER FRIEND

RORY [*about Lorelai's trouble writing Luke's character reference*]: Sounds like you're over thinking this. Maybe if you just put pen to paper.
LORELAI: I tried that. I thought, "I'll just sit down and write whatever comes—no judgment, no inner critic." Boy was that a bad idea.
RORY: Really? Why?

LORELAI: Because my brain is a wild jungle full of scary gibberish: "I'm writing a letter. I can't write a letter. Why can't I write a letter? I'm wearing a green dress. I wish I was wearing my blue dress. My blue dress is at the cleaners. The Germans wore gray. You wore blue. *Casablanca. Casablanca* is such a good movie. *Casablanca*. The White House. Bush. Why don't I drive a hybrid car? I should drive a hybrid car. I should really take my bicycle to work. Bicycle. Unicycle. Unitard. Hockey puck. Rattlesnake. Monkey, monkey, underpants."

RORY: Hey, remember the year you got me the unicorn marionette with the purple horn?
LUKE: You didn't like the unicorn marionette?
RORY: I've never really been that into unicorns.
LUKE: I thought you loved that.
RORY: I know, because I was being polite.
APRIL: Being polite can be dangerous.
RORY: Yes, it totally backfired because for the next five years, I only got unicorn items—unicorn sweatshirt, unicorn pencil case, bumper sticker—"I brake for unicorns." No, but you were always so nice. You never forgot my birthday. And every holiday, there was a monogrammed unicorn item.
APRIL: Dad, for the record, I'm not really into unicorns, either. [*Watch 3.12 for the same story told by Sookie about frogs*].

LANE [*to Zack*]: I'm sick of being told what to eat and what I shouldn't and what side I should sleep on. I'm a person, Zack. I'm an adult. I don't want to be hiding things under the floorboards and behind cushions again.

Technology Bytes

Edward Herrmann and Kelly Bishop both were reluctant adopters of technology during *Gilmore*, Bishop admits. She, at least, had a cell phone. "He didn't have a cell phone for the first three or four years of that show, and he didn't do any e-mail. One day, after the show was over, we were all over at ABC going up for some pilot and I saw him there. I was like, 'Oh hello, it's wonderful to see you,' and all that. And he said, 'I have an e-mail address!' 'You finally did it?'" And they've been e-mail friends ever since.

7.12 To Whom It May Concern

First aired: Jan. 30, 2007 // Written by David Babcock // Directed by Jamie Babbit

Rory agonizes over Lucy, Paris redoubles her efforts to finish Yale with a bang, Luke squares off against Anna in court over visitation rights with April, Jackson reveals why he's been so protective of Sookie lately, and Christopher finds a copy of Lorelai's character reference for Luke. While some dramas come to a happy end, a whole new one begins for Richard.

GINCHY! Paris' "Operation Finish Line"; Richard's pep talk with Rory over her misunderstanding with Lucy; Jackson not telling Sookie that she's pregnant because he didn't get the vasectomy after all (5.21); Paris diffusing the whole Rory-Lucy rift by being Paris; Lorelai's letter read out in court, and Luke's face when he hears it.

NOTES *'I can't handle being your second choice.'*

Though we knew Richard was teaching economics at Yale last semester, this is the first we learn that Rory took the class.

There's an obvious change in the editing of this episode as we jump back and forth between Christopher at home and Luke floundering in court. The fact that Christopher only discovers the letter Lorelai wrote because he was looking for a spirit level to adjust the flat-screen TV he selfishly installed (after Lorelai said she didn't want it) is telling. The legal decision means Luke can see April at least one weekend each month, half the summer, and every other major holiday.

Not surprisingly, Lucy broke up with Marty. With Lorelai's own relationship troubles playing themselves out in alternate scenes, we immediately get the sense that Lucy was, in some respects, the Christopher to Marty's Lorelai—Rory has always been Marty's first choice; Lucy was the rebound girl.

Sookie's pregnancy was written in to the show to accommodate Melissa McCarthy's own with daughter Vivian, who was born on May 5, 2007.

After several subpar episodes, this one is a refreshing surprise. Lorelai and Christopher's relationship, which has been horribly awkward from the start this season, comes to a merciful end. Luke, who's scrambled through this season like a wounded dog finally experiences a bit of justice, not just with the legal decision, but also being able to hear some kind words from the woman he still loves. Finally, it rekindles the relationship between Richard and Rory that took such a beating last season. "Rory, you're a person of great heart and great character," he tells her. Though Rory later thanks Paris for praising her

"I see Scott Patterson on occasion. He has said to me that people have literally stopped him in the grocery store and would just be like, 'Why are you and Lorelai fighting?' They'd just talk to him as if he were Luke. He would be at a loss."

–KATIE WALDER (JANET)

Lorelai's Character Reference

Jan. 9, 2007

To whom it may concern,
In the nearly 10 years that I have known Luke Danes, I have come to know him as an honest and decent man. He's also one of the most kind and caring persons I have ever met.

I'm a single mother, and I raised my daughter by myself, but once Luke Danes became my friend in this town, I never really felt alone. Luke and I have had our ups and downs over the years, but through it all, his relationship with my daughter, Rory, has never changed. He's always been there for her no matter what. He was there to celebrate her birthdays. He was there cheering her on at her high school graduation. Luke has been a sort of father figure in my daughter's life. With his own daughter, Luke wasn't given the opportunity to be there for her first 12 years, but he should be given that opportunity now.

Once Luke Danes is in your life, he is in your life forever. I know from personal experience what an amazing gift that is, and not to allow him access to his daughter would be to seriously deprive her of all this man has to offer, and he offers so much. Thank you for your time.

Sincerely,
Lorelai Gilmore

to Lucy by saying "it's just nice to hear sometimes," a part of her is really commenting on her grandfather's words.

TODAY'S CELEBRATION Luke wins his custody battle, Rory and Lucy reconcile, and Sookie's pregnant again!

EMILY'S MAID DU JOUR Bridget, maker of the quail Mazatlan.

AND INTRODUCING... *Lauren Graham as producer*

5 MONTHS How long Rory and Paris have before they graduate.

AMEN, SISTER FRIEND

SOOKIE [*about Jackson ducking out of his vasectomy*]: I mean what am I supposed to do—start watching him brush his teeth? Does he want me to start cutting his meat?
LORELAI: I don't think he wants his meat cut at all.

7.13 I'd Rather Be in Philadelphia

First aired: Feb. 6, 2007 // Written by Rebecca Rand Kirshner // Directed by Lee Shallat Chemel

As Richard is rushed into emergency surgery following his heart attack last episode, the Gilmores and their friends rally. Logan comes into town by chopper to be with Rory, Luke drops everything to make sure the family is fed, and Emily follows a plan she and Richard hatched the last time this happened. The only one missing is Christopher.

GINCHY! The enthusiastic way Zack takes to filling in for Lane at the diner; Luke showing up at the hospital as soon as he learns about Richard; and Emily revealing why she's been so businesslike the whole time she's been at the hospital.

NOTES *'Mom, it was awful. He just fell down.'*

After his heart attack, Richard is taken to John Skinner Medical Center. Last time Richard was in the hospital, Emily showed a similar inordinate amount of concern for the pillows he had (1.10). Richard drives a green 2006 Jaguar.

Logan originally took the prospect of buying this Internet company to his father, but Mitchum rejected the idea. This will only add to the pain to come (7.15).

A remarkable episode, mostly for the lengths it goes to undo much of the damage inflicted by Season 7 up to this point. Luke, who acted like such a jerk early on, now is the ideal man, making sure that Lorelai and her family have everything during their crisis, even putting up with Emily's snarky remarks without complaint. Richard and Emily, mostly marginalized this season, are allowed to become a loving couple once more. Finally, we seem to be through with pretending that Christopher is anything but a selfish, emotionally stunted young man. The danger now is allowing that pendulum to swing too far in the other direction. Whatever you think of Christopher and Lorelai, he was never the seething ball of anger we're now left with.

TODAY'S CELEBRATION Richard survives his heart surgery.

EMILY'S MAID DU JOUR Soledad.

B10 Richard's hospital room.

$5 MILLION How much Logan needs to buy the Austin geek's interactive media platform. (Logan's kicking in $3 million from his trust fund.)

AMEN, SISTER FRIEND

LORELAI: Are you OK, dad? I mean how are you feeling, considering everything? You look OK.
RICHARD: Well, all in all, I think I'd rather be in Philadelphia.
RORY: Ronald Reagan.
RICHARD: Quoting WC Fields.
RORY: Oh, I didn't know that.

LORELAI [*leaving Christopher a voice mail*]: Hi, it's me again. Um, dad's out of surgery and it went well and he's doing fine, so it's good news. I just, I wanted you to know... because... I don't know why. 'Cause you haven't returned any of my calls. But I just thought I would tell you what's going on because I'm your wife and I think that's what I'm supposed to do. No idea how to be your wife but I'm trying. You're my husband, you know, and it seems like you should be here or call me back. I mean, I'm pretty sure that's what married people do, is be there for each other. But I know you're upset and I know we had a fight, but this is just bigger than that, you know? It's my dad, and he's had a heart attack. And everybody's been here. I mean, I've talked to Sookie and even Michel and Patty and Babette, and they've all been here for me, but my husband's not here. That's not OK, Chris, you know? It's not OK.

7.14 Farewell, My Pet

First aired: Feb. 13, 2007 // Written by Jennie Snyder // Directed by Jamie Babbit

Richard is on the mend, but the same cannot be said for Lorelai's relationship with Christopher. Though she floats the idea of blocking Luke out of her life completely to prove her loyalty to her husband, in the end it's Christopher who has to make the final decision. Devastated by the death of his beloved Chin-Chin, Michel guilts Lorelai and Sookie into arranging a funeral service for the chow. Rory develops a crush on Tucker, the TA filling in for Richard at Yale, and Paris tells her that they've both managed to "break" Logan and Doyle.

GINCHY! Paris redacting her "History of Feminism" notes because she doesn't want to share her insights into the material; Rory's self-flagellation as she tells Logan about her crush on the TA who's filling in for Richard; the brief instant when Lorelai waves at Luke, all the while contemplating the prospect of cutting him out of her life completely.

NOTES *'You're just gonna have to dig a little deeper.'*

Christopher finally tells Lorelai about his fight with Luke (7.10). The only one who puts any thought into Chin-Chin's funeral is Zack who, while brainstorming music to play at the service, suggests "I Will Always Love You." "It's got the cheese factor, but it's still at least a legitimate..." he says before he's cut off by Lorelai, who finds the sheet music for "My Heart Will Go On," the Celine Dion song Michel had his heart set on. This is a clever little set up for Lorelai's karaoke rendition of "I Will Always Love You" later on (7.20).

Despite his aversion to Luke's unhealthy menu, Michel, in a moment of "insanity," bought a burger there last year after dealing with a group of mimes at the inn. Though he didn't eat it, Chin-Chin did, which is why Michel will eat one in his honor. (Or, for the ultra cynical, this is merely an excuse for the writers to get Lorelai close enough to the diner to see, and be seen by, Luke.)

A Frankenstein's monster of an episode, with part of it trying to erase the insanity of Lorelai's marriage to Christopher, and the other justifying it in the first place—when did we ever think that he was the one she would "want to want"? In the end, all of Liz's talk about Lorelai and

What I Kept

I said to wardrobe, "This is a really great robe [from the spa in 2.16]; is there any way I can keep this?" They said, "We're not going to use it for anything else and it's not going to go into stock because it's got the spa name on it, so no, take it." So I have that, but it's hanging in the closet. I've never worn it. That's probably why I don't take things. Isn't that terrible?

—Kelly Bishop (Emily)

Michel mourns the loss of his beloved Chin-Chin.

Luke being out of phase (7.2) with each other actually applies more to Lorelai and Christopher.

TODAY'S CELEBRATION The memorial for Chin-Chin and the end of Lorelai and Christopher's marriage. This time for sure.

KIRK OF ALL TRADES Grayson's flower delivery guy. (Actually, he's volunteering.)

AMEN, SISTER FRIEND

PARIS [*about Logan*]: What I'm trying to say is, he's changed. You changed him. It's amazing. I'm rarely this wrong.

RORY: Well, thanks.

PARIS: Don't get me wrong. Doyle was quite the ladies' man, as well. Now he's down for the count. The other night, he wanted to play "let's think up baby names" in bed.

RORY: Really?

PARIS: Yeah. I mean, let's face it. We took two wild stallions and we broke them.

Behind the Scenes When a Pet Is More Than a Pet

The death of a chow story idea had actually occurred to Yanic Truesdale during a press tour for *Gilmore Girls* when a journalist asked him which episode had been the most emotional for him. At the time, he couldn't think of any. "And I told Amy that they asked me that, and I think it would be interesting to see Michel vulnerable, to see a different side. I said what about the chows? He loves the chows; what if he loses a chow?"

No dice. Again and again he pitched the idea to Amy, but it just wasn't something she saw being a fit for the series. Obviously actors are all for suggesting episodes focused on their characters, even when that means additional work on an already exhausting series. But the actor had other reasons for suggesting it, he says.

"Most of the time, things were happening to other people and [Michel] would comment on what was happening. But that's why we need to have stuff happening to him, so we can learn more about who he is and see different sides of him."

The actor gets at an aspect of *Gilmore Girls* that few casual viewers ever really understand. They watch an episode and see right away that Stars Hollow is populated by several quirky characters who spend most of their time acting as comic foils to whatever dramatic plotline is unfolding for Lorelai, Rory and their immediate family. Yet throughout the series, Amy & Dan kept each character three dimensional, not by painting complex backstories for them, but merely by adding a human touch here and there.

Yet up until this point, even the little character-defining details that had been given to Michel had mostly been for comedic effect, from his buddy-like relationship with his mother to his Celine Dion addiction. Seven years into the series, Michel was finally able to show his emotions, even if he covered his hurt with his usual acerbic wit.

RORY: I don't think I really "broke" Logan.

PARIS: Oh you broke him. You broke him hard. You can open the gate and he's not going to bolt. You can kick him with a spur and he's not going to spook. You own him.

RORY: Paris, stop. That's ridiculous. I think I'm gonna go work on my résumés.

PARIS: Hey, let's make them go out and get tattoos. It'll be like we branded them.

LORELAI: You've always been this possibility for me, this wonderful possibility. But it's just not right. And I'm so sorry. I'm so sorry.

CHRISTOPHER: Yeah. I guess I should have known, huh? It took me 20 years to get you to say yes.

LORELAI: I need you to know that you're the man I want to want.

CHRISTOPHER: I know.

7.15 I'm a Kayak, Hear Me Roar

First aired: Feb. 20, 2007 // Written by Rebecca Rand Kirshner // Directed by Lee Shallat Chemel

Richard's convalescent diet is driving him crazy, Richard is driving Emily crazy, and Lorelai's need to tell her parents that she and Christopher are no longer together is driving her crazy, especially as plans continue to move forward for their wedding party. Liz, TJ and Doula move in with Luke for a short stay to get away from their moth problem, and Lorelai and Emily share a rare moment of mutual understanding while tackling Richard's business affairs. Rory does her best to shower Logan with affection on his birthday, and even Mitchum seems more generous than usual on the occasion. Unfortunately, Logan's latest business acquisition threatens to prove every negative thing his father ever said about him.

GINCHY! Paris and Doyle getting sucked into yoga when all they intended to do was make fun of it; Rory trying to recreate all of her birthdays for Logan; Lorelai helping Emily take care of Richard's business filings, and Emily's canoe/kayak talk.

NOTES *'Yep, all they've got to do is find the right wormhole.'*

After years of Emily frightening the maids, it's now Richard's turn with poor Aurora. Liz's jewelry business continues to flourish, with TJ

"Amy & Dan were just so terrific to work with. To me it didn't feel like I was going to work; I was going to the studio to play. Then you'd go in and you'd read the script and realize what they were doing. They're doing a festival of living art—this is going to be cool! Then you start seeing it coming together and you start getting dailies. There are a lot of shows on the air now I wouldn't dream of wanting to work on. But you get a show like this, somehow everything gels."

–RAUL DAVALOS, EDITOR

talking about being a stay-at-home dad now.

✱ Mitchum's changed his tune about Rory, going so far as to tell her that journalism needs "an infusion of bright, talented people like you." And the even more startling "You've been a real asset to Logan and to our family."

✱ Richard and Emily own a rental building, some stocks, and a couple of windmills in Palm Springs. Luke lies awake in bed listening to Liz and TJ discuss his loneliness and pining for Lorelai, just as Lorelai did when she was staying with Sookie and Jackson (6.22).

✱ When Rory confides in Logan about the disturbing way she found herself agreeing with Mitchum over dinner, Logan tells her she's been "Huntzbergered," a riff on Season 6's "You've Been Gilmored" (6.14).

✱ Prism Active in Palo Alto, Calif., is poised to sue Logan and his company over patent infringement related to the new company they just purchased. "They were just waiting for someone with deep pockets to buy in before they sued," Philip explains.

✱ Rory applies for the James Reston journalism fellowship, which will play a small role in her future just a few episodes later (7.18).

✱ Emily's heart-to-heart with Lorelai about kayaks and canoes is the closest we've come to recapturing some of the finer moments of *Gilmore* episodes past, finally giving Bishop and Graham scenes worthy of their talents.

TODAY'S CELEBRATION Logan's 25th birthday.

EMILY'S MAID DU JOUR The emotionally shattered Aurora.

THE HEN AND THE BEAGLE Babette and Miss Patty's code for Lorelai and Christopher when they're talking about them in Luke's Diner. (Luke is "the rooster.")

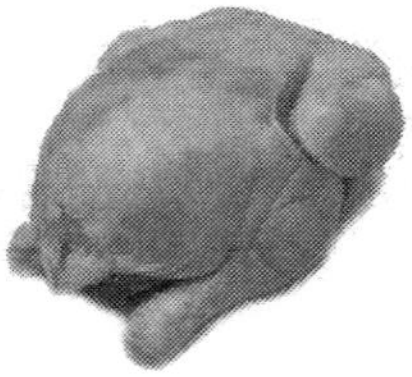

400 The number of Cornish game hens whose lives hang in the balance if Lorelai doesn't fess up to her breakup with Christopher soon.

RORY'S BIRTHDAY PARTIES

6TH Outer space birthday with space suits made out of garbage bags, Tang and freeze-dried ice cream

Making an Episode 11 Shooting + Editing

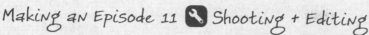

About two or three hours after rehearsals, it's time to shoot a scene. The cast is run through wardrobe, makeup and hair, each department keeping an eye out for continuity. Wardrobe's Valerie Campbell will take dozens of photos of the actors and make notes to not only record what clothes they're wearing in that scene, but also how they're wearing them (e.g., sleeves rolled up, coat zipped). The director runs everybody through the blocking one more time, sound makes its adjustments, sometimes changing the placement of microphones on the set, and "last looks" or "pictures up" is called, to ensure everything looks perfect before cameras roll.

Despite all the nuances involved in editing a program bursting at the seams with dialogue, the *Gilmore* editing team consists of just two editors and two or three assistant editors. Editors Jill Savitt and Raul Davalos, with the show from pilot to the final episode, each have a room in the production offices. Though theoretically this is to be close to Amy, the showrunner is seldom in her office as she whizzes around the giant Warner Brothers backlot.

The assistant editors log and transfer footage to Savitt and Davalos' hard drives, and away they go. At any given moment, each editor is juggling two episodes: finishing up one and cutting the dailies from the one being shot that week.

Say Davalos is nearly done editing Episode 2, and is just waiting for Amy to come in and go through it one more time with him. Meanwhile, he may be editing the dailies—the raw footage from today's shoot—for Episode 4. (Savitt will be editing Episode 3 and prepping for 5, which shoots next week.)

Gilmore **editor Raul Davalos, A.C.E.**

"When Amy comes into the room, I just switch over to Episode 2 and we go through it," Davalos says. "Let's say she gets a phone call and she has to go to a meeting and she can only give me an hour and a half, and we can only get through the teaser in Act 1. Then I put that away and I go back to cutting dailies on Episode 4."

Usually, the episode's director will receive a DVD of the editor's cut and approve it by phone. "For example, Kenny Ortega did a number of shows. I'd get a call from Kenny, who says, 'I love the show, I don't need to come in today. Just take a look. Didn't I do a shot of Rory reacting to this?' Then I'd look and say, 'Yeah, you have a medium shot and a close shot.' 'OK, just change it to the close shot,' and that would be it. He'd come in the next day and we're done with the director's cut.

"What's fun is that a lot of time we'll cut a scene and there are no changes in it. So the way we cut it the first time as an editor's cut goes on the air because the director didn't want to make any changes and Amy didn't want to make any changes. We just move on to whatever scene Amy feels we need to work on." Once Amy OKs Episode 1, it's "locked" for picture; next the sound editors drop in sound effects, and composer Sam Phillips the music (and yes, those "lah lahs").

Despite the popularity of deleted scenes on DVD, they're usually an afterthought, Davalos admits. "At the end of the season, we compile all complete scenes that were deleted for story reasons, not just a section of a scene. If it was a completed scene, we'd show it to Amy and then she would decide if it would be included in the DVD. Sometimes the scenes were deleted for good reason, so those weren't included. If it was taken out just because of time, or the story was weighted a little too much toward one story line rather than another, she'd make that decision. Although she liked the scene, we had to take it out. The DVDs, once they started coming out, were just fun to see what they decided to put into the bonus features."

7TH Fiesta birthday with piñatas, tacos and freeze-dried ice cream

8TH Teddy bear tea party birthday. Also the birthday when they arrested the clown (see 1.6).

12TH Ice skating in Central Park. Though she also apparently visited Mark Twain's house in Hartford (7.20).

AMEN, SISTER FRIEND

LORELAI: Mom, you know how to do things by yourself. You are totally capable.

EMILY: Sure, I went to Smith and I was a history major, but I never had any plans to be an historian. I was always going to be a wife. I mean, the way I saw it, a woman's job was to run a home, organize the social life of a family, and bolster her husband while he earned a living. It was a good system and it was working very well all these years. Only when your husband isn't there because he's watching television in a dressing gown, you realize how dependent you are. I didn't even know I owned windmills.

LORELAI: Mom, now you know, and you know how to right-click.

EMILY: But you. You provide for yourself. You're not dependent on anyone.

LORELAI: Hmm.

EMILY: You're independent.

LORELAI: I am kayak, hear me roar.

EMILY: I mean, look at you. For all these years, you've done very well without a husband.

LORELAI: Maybe so, but I still wanted it to work out.

EMILY: You know, the way I was raised, if a married couple split up, it was a disaster because it meant the system had fallen apart, and it was particularly bad for the woman because she had to go out and find herself another rich husband, only she was older now. But with you, it's not such a disaster, is it?

LORELAI: I guess not.

EMILY: I mean it's really not such a horrible thing that you're going to get a divorce, not really. Oh, you're going to be fine.

7.16 Will You Be My Lorelai Gilmore?

First aired: Feb. 27, 2007 // Written by Gayle Abrams and Gina Fattore // Directed by David Paymer

While Lorelai is brokering peace between Mrs. Kim and Lane and figuring out how to throw Lane a baby shower when she's been placed on complete bed rest, Logan finally tells Rory about his company's legal troubles over the new Internet acquisition. The disaster pushes him back to his old Life and Death Brigade ways with Colin and Finn (hello, Las Vegas). Meanwhile, Luke finally comes to a decision about his father's old boat after Liz and TJ try to sell it.

GINCHY! Lorelai getting Lane and Mrs. Kim over their differences; Lane's bed-bound adventure through Stars Hollow; (as usual) Gil; and Luke buying a new boat.

NOTES *'Hey, less Rory, more Lane.'*

Hugo, the editor of the online magazine Rory met at Logan's party (7.8), put her in touch with the assistant managing editor at The New York Times. This is the first we hear that Mitchum's money was tied up in Logan's doomed Internet deal.

Mrs. Kim gives Lorelai a door knob once owned by President John Adams.

Rush frontman Geddy Lee (second from left, with daughter) and Hep Alien (minus Lane).

Behind the Scenes
What's The Rush?

You never know who's a fan of *Gilmore Girls*, as the cast found out when Rush's frontman, Geddy Lee, showed up with his daughter.

"His daughter was a huge fan," Todd Lowe says. "I was walking out of my trailer and a WB tour person came up and said, 'Todd, this is a fan—I don't know her name, but I know her dad.' I was shell-shocked. And then I told Sebastian [Bach] and he ran around trying to find Geddy Lee. It was the episode with Lane's baby shower where we wheeled the bed down the street, and he's actually in that scene as an extra, just kind of standing there smiling. We had to sing a song in that and Sebastian was trying to get him to help us with the harmony."

✱ An episode that should've worked but ends up feeling forced, the "would you be their Lorelai Gilmore" being a large part of that (right up there with saying the name of the show in the dialogue).

TODAY'S CELEBRATION Lane's baby shower, Luke's new boat, and Rory's meeting with the guy from The New York Times.

KIRK OF ALL TRADES Aspiring yachtsman.

60 The number of Onesies Lorelai and Rory get.

128 The number of days Sookie has left (give or take) before her next baby is due.

$600 How much Luke sells his boat to Kirk for (Lulu loves waterskiing). It's now called the S.S. Lurk, for Lulu and Kirk.

AMEN, SISTER FRIEND

LIZ [*about the boat*]: How many generations are gonna cart this thing around town? Look, get rid of it for your own sake, before you end up like dad.
LUKE: What does that mean?
LIZ: Oh, OK. OK, forget it.
LUKE: No, I want to know. What does that mean?
LIZ: He was stuck, Luke.
LUKE: He was happy.
LIZ: He was stuck doing the same thing at the same time the same way every day of his life.
LUKE: So? He did the things that made him happy.
LIZ: Dad didn't do stuff 'cause it made him happy. He did stuff because he was afraid to do anything else.

What I Kept

From the opening of the Dragonfly Inn, I have one of the little dragonflies. It has a light in it, nice purplish-blue. I haven't put a battery in it for about a year. I specifically asked for it because I thought that was nice, and I did want a souvenir, so the prop guy gave me one. [No tools?] I have too many damn tools that I don't use. I would've liked to have had that power saw, but they wouldn't give that up.

—Biff Yeager (Tom)

7.17 Gilmore Girls Only

First aired: March 6, 2007 // Written by David Babcock // Directed by Lee Shallat Chemel

Anxious to get away from Logan's display of self-pity and Richard's moping around the house, Rory and Emily go with Lorelai to Mia's wedding in Charlotte, NC. (Actually, Emily only wanted to go to the Valentine Resort there, but gets roped into the reception, too.) Lane and Zack ask Luke to be the godfather to their boys, and Logan takes a big step toward becoming his own man.

GINCHY! Emily preventing Lorelai from opening the car window with the child lock; Zack and Luke discussing fatherhood in the middle of the mad rush at the diner; and Emily having a "thing" for Will Smith.

Lorelai and Rory at Mia's wedding reception, where Emily 'doesn't play well with others.'

NOTES *'Road trips are so fun.'*

In addition to The New York Times, Rory has also applied to The San Francisco Chronicle, The Seattle Times and The Detroit Free Press. Mia invited Lorelai to her wedding two months ago; she'd intended to take Christopher then.

Emily's encountering the same frustration with Richard as she did the last time he was around all the time, when he briefly retired (2.12). He's moved on from merely watching old professional golf games to installing a putting green in the backyard. Emily finally confirms that she was, in fact, hit with a driving while intoxicated (DWI) charge (7.4).

Mia tells Lorelai about the time Emily came to see her (2.8). This time around, Mia is played by Kathy Baker. Last time, it was Elizabeth Franz, who wasn't available when this episode was made.

Though not a terrible episode, it's not a good one, either, and a pretty sad choice when you consider the next new one wouldn't come for more than a month.

TODAY'S CELEBRATION Mia's wedding, Logan leaves the Huntzberger Group, Luke agrees to be godfather to Lane and Zack's twins, Steve and Kwan, who are born this episode.

EMILY'S MAID DU JOUR Emily mentions there are now two maids, but no names are given.

YOU'VE ENTERED EMILYLAND [*at the prospect of going to Mia's in Lorelai's Jeep*] Oh, and we'll take my car. I have no intention of driving 800 miles in an army vehicle.

META, META, META Zack tells Luke "It's pretty obvious you played some ball" after he catches something Zack nearly knocked off a table in the diner, a reference to Scott Patterson's former career as a minor league baseball player.

META, META, META 2 Emily's "thing" for Will Smith, especially her "I think that he's very charming" remark, may be a nod to Kelly Bishop's role in the 1993 movie *Six Degrees of Separation*, in which Smith plays a con artist.

AMEN, SISTER FRIEND

MIA: Everything OK?
LORELAI: Yeah, it's fine. I just always seem to forget my mother doesn't play well with others.

LOGAN: I am officially not working for the Huntzberger Group anymore.
RORY: Oh my God.
LOGAN: Yeah, and it feels really good. I mean, it felt great finally standing up to my dad.
RORY: How did he take it?
LOGAN: He tried to put up this cool, detached front, you know, but I think I actually saw steam coming out of his ears. Basically, he told me to hit the road.
RORY: And you took him literally.
LOGAN: I just needed to see you. The thing is, even though he was mad, I swear I saw the slightest glimmer of pride in his eyes, you know, just for a second. I mean no one walks out on Mitchum Huntzberger.

7.18 Hay Bale Maze

First aired: April 17, 2007 // Written by Rebecca Rand Kirshner // Directed by Stephen Clancy

After Taylor pleads with the people of Stars Hollow to fulfill his childhood dream of having a hay bale maze at this year's Spring Fling Festival, he goes overboard, using up the festival's entire budget to create a town-wide maze. Rory goes for a job interview with the Providence Journal Bulletin. Logan advises her to pursue her dreams rather than worrying about financial security, something that rubs Lorelai the wrong way considering how reckless Logan's been lately. Yet it's within the maze that Luke and Lorelai finally clear the air and face the challenges of life's maze, at least for the moment, together.

GINCHY! Logan and Lorelai coming to an understanding in the middle of the night; Luke and Lorelai apologizing to each other in the maze.

NOTES *'No running in the maze!'*

Rory goes to a job interview for the (real life) Providence Journal Bulletin. April continues to be very much like a young Rory, carting around several books on her visit to Luke, including Herman Melville (1.1., 5.21).

Taylor insists on ripping out the gazebo to accommodate his maze.

The Reston fellowship (7.15) that Rory decides to hold out for is a six-week paid internship.

TODAY'S CELEBRATION The Spring Fling Festival and hay bale maze, Rory's interview for the Providence Journal Bulletin, and Logan's first real visit to Stars Hollow. More importantly, the burying of the hatchet between Luke and Lorelai.

KIRK OF ALL TRADES Minotaur for Taylor's town meeting demonstration, and the maze guard.

THINGS WE'VE LEARNED Robert Lee (who plays the fairly silent busboy in Luke's Diner) is also a dab hand at repairing and troubleshooting Mac computers, one of the reasons he was so beloved by the assistant directors.

AMEN, SISTER FRIEND

APRIL: Growing up in New England, it's like you're told over and over that you live in this old place where houses are 300 years old and there's all this history, right?

LUKE: Right.

APRIL: Well, some of these pueblos, like the Aztec Ruins National Monu-

"It was enormous; it took over the whole town square on the Warner Brothers backlot. We shot scenes that included most of the cast members, and I seem to remember that there were a lot of family and friends visiting set that day, too. It was toward the end of our seventh season when everybody was saying their goodbyes for the summer, not sure if we would return for another season in the fall."

—ALEXIS BLEDEL ON WHY HAY BALE MAZE WAS HER FAVORITE EPISODE TO SHOOT. (Post Grad Web site, 8/11/09)

ment, or the Casamero Pueblo Ruins—I mean, people were living there in 1100 AD It's like, "Suck it, New England."

LUKE: It's like what?

LORELAI: This was not a silver-spoon household. This was spork city all the way.

LOGAN: I get that, and I respect that because I just spat out a whole place setting of sterling silver royal Danish. I left my dad's company, I left that world because I have my own values.

LORELAI: I understand that.

LOGAN: I thought you would because that's what you did. You left the world of privilege to do things your way.

LORELAI: I guess I never thought of it that way.

LOGAN: And you did it when you were younger and had a baby to take care of. It was really impressive.

LORELAI: I don't need you to be impressed by me. I just need you to know it wasn't easy.

LOGAN: I know that.

LORELAI: I didn't get anything like "boom," you know? I worked hard for everything I got.

LOGAN: I want to work. I'm ready to work. And I want to work hard.

LORELAI: I messed up. That night I went to Christopher—I'm sorry.

LUKE: Yeah.

LORELAI: I mean I never admitted it to you that it was wrong what I did, and it was, and I'm really sorry.

LUKE: OK. Thanks.

LORELAI: I don't know why I didn't say this before.

Sean Gunn tackles the 3-foot stilts as the maze guard.

Behind the Scenes
Trials of the Maze Guard

It's no secret that many cast members were less than thrilled with the final season of *Gilmore*. While a drop off in the quality of scripts and story are often cited, Sean Gunn had another reason: those stilts he wore as the maze guard.

"I was proud that I learned how to do it. Eventually, I walked on 3-foot stilts, but they were trying to get me to walk on 5-foot stilts. Professional stilt walkers were like, 'You don't just learn how to walk on stilts and immediately go to 5 feet in two days.'

"At that point, I was over a lot of it on the show, anyway. The head writers were gone and I was unhappy about the way my character was handled in the last season. I was like, I don't know about this. And they kept saying just try it, pushing me to do something that is pretty dangerous. I did try it and I was actually able to walk a few feet on the 5-foot stilts, but we didn't shoot it. I didn't feel comfortable enough. I could do this in a controlled environment with all these pads around and a few people, but I'm not doing it on set.

"Then, thank God, Lee Chemel was there and she was great. So when she finally walked in and they're like, 'Well, he's not sure,' she says, 'he's the boss. You ask him if he wants to do it.' I say, 'I'm not going to do it.' She says, 'Great, then you're not doing it.' But I still had to do it on the 3-foot stilts."

Toasting the future, but is everyone seeing the same future?

LUKE: Ah. You know, I'm sorry too, 'cause, I don't know, it's just... Now that I've had April, it's—I've learned a lot, and I was crazy to think that I had to fix everything in my relationship with April before I could really be with you. And that's just not how you fix things. I mean things just don't stand still. They're always changing.

LORELAI: Yeah.

LUKE: I guess I was compartmentalizing, if that's what you call it. I mean I should have opened my compartments. I should have gotten your help.

LORELAI: I wanted to help.

LUKE: I know. And I'm sorry. And I'm sorry, also, because I think I kind of used April to push you away.

7.19 It's Just like Riding a Bike

First aired: April 24, 2007 // Written by Jennie Snyder // Directed by Lee Shallat Chemel

Poor Jackson. As if Martha and Davey having the chicken pox wasn't enough, Sookie drops him off at Lorelai's to stay (he's never had it) and warns him not to make a mess or annoy her while he's a guest at her house—she's still mad at him over his lying about the vasectomy. Lorelai's 1999 Jeep Wrangler finally kicks the bucket, which presents the perfect opportunity to enlist Luke's help in car shopping—maybe it will help them get over this weird patch they've hit recently. Paris breaks up with Doyle to prevent him from influencing her choice of graduate school, and Rory learns that the one job opportunity she's been counting on is not going to come through.

GINCHY! Paris' manic opening of grad school letters; the spectacle of Lorelai on her bike; Sookie and Jackson resolving their differences after Jackson's "accident"; Paris and Rory's "factoring each other in" discussion when it comes to their respective boyfriends; Luke being Luke, finding a solution to Lorelai's crazy Jeep hang-up; and Doyle refusing to leave Paris.

NOTES *'Everything can be fixed, huh?'*

Paris is accepted to Harvard Medical School, Yale Law School, the University of Pennsylvania Medical School, Columbia Medical School, Washington University Medical School and Duke University Medical School. Lucy and Olivia have signed a lease on an apartment near Manhattan that they've dubbed "Glenda" (now that their brief story line has played itself out). Michel drives a Volkswagen Golf.

Luke has a big boat trip planned with April in June. Lorelai and Rory made a pact never to have matching cars. Jackson breaks the dollhouse that Richard delivered to Lorelai after Emily threatened to get rid of it (6.6).

TODAY'S CELEBRATION Lorelai finally returns to Luke's Diner, Paris gets accepted to several grad schools, and Luke solves Lorelai's Jeep dilemma.

MAY 22, 2006 The last time Lorelai was at Luke's Diner, according to Kirk, which very nearly tracks with real time.

10 How old Rory was the last time she and Lorelai rode their bikes.

AMEN, SISTER FRIEND

LUKE: OK, here's the deal. I borrowed Kirk's computer and Zack got me on this craigslist thing, and I found a 1999 Jeep Wrangler for sale. The guy actually doesn't live too far from here, so I went to see it. It looks like it's in pretty good shape. So I ran the VIN number. It's got a clean history—no accidents, no failed emissions. And the guy said he kept it up pretty good, and there's nothing really wrong with it. So I took it for a test drive and it drove fine. So if you want to keep your

"I loved the episode with the little twins, although I was really nervous before shooting that scene. The director came up to me before (it was about 6 am) and she said, 'You've handled a baby before, right?' Um, yeah. 'You've got to be really careful about their heads. They have very weak, loose heads.' I'm like, 'Oh my God!' Then I couldn't stop thinking the entire day that I would pick up one of these babies and their heads would fall off."

-JOHN CABRERA (BRIAN)

old car, for whatever crazy feeling it gives you, then buy this guy's car, send it to Gypsy. She'll take the engine out, put it in the old car, which makes absolutely no sense because you'd basically be paying the same amount of money to fix your old car as you would be paying to get into a new one.

LORELAI: But I'd still have my car.

LUKE: Yeah, Gypsy said it'll take about two weeks to finish. Here's the number of the guy, Larry. That's his name. I already negotiated him down 1,500 bucks. Tell him you're Lorelai, Luke's friend. He'll know.

LORELAI: Thanks, I will.

LUKE: It's still a completely ridiculous idea.

"As you can tell, there's a ton of phone calls throughout the show. When she's on her bicycle, I'm on a truck in front of her, and we're miked to each other, and I'm saying the line [that she's responding to] through my little mic, and she's got an ear piece."

—PATTY MALCOLM, Lauren Graham's stand-in

PARIS [*to Rory, about why she chose medicine*]: It's as close to being God as you can get.

7.20 Lorelai? Lorelai?

First aired: May 1, 2007 // Written by David S Rosenthal // Directed by Bethany Rooney

It's a weird time in Stars Hollow. Many are anticipating a round of karaoke at a local bar, Rory is devastated by her first setbacks to break into journalism, and Luke is bummed that April can't go on the boat trip they've been planning. Yet all is not gloom and doom. Zack has landed an awesome gig as lead guitarist for Vapor Rub during their two month tour, and Logan has found a good position with a startup technology company in Palo Alto, Calif. While Lorelai discovers an unusual way to get through to Luke, Logan has some surprises of his own for her...and Rory.

GINCHY! Rory's horrible dream; Babette and Miss Patty's rendition of "Fever" at karaoke; Lane pushing Zack to go on tour without her; Kirk singing "Do You Really Want to Hurt Me"; Lorelai's heartfelt "I Will Always Love You" to Luke; the real reason Luke was wearing Lorelai's hat (or was it?); and the reason for Logan's visit.

NOTES *'Honey, it's another embarrassing moment for your diary.'*

Richard and Emily bought a small two-bedroom apartment in New

York's Upper East Side in anticipation of Rory getting the internship at the Times. Luke is wearing the baseball cap Lorelai bought him years ago (1.10). After she gets rejected by the Chicago Sun-Times, Rory tries to get the job at the Providence Journal Bulletin she blew off before, but it's already been filled.

Luke is planning a six-week excursion for his boating adventure with April, which gets scuttled when April is accepted for the Metropolitan Museum Science Camp. After years of pushing various food stuffs on the sly—frozen bananas, "Ceaser" salads—Ceaser (with Luke's approval) finally gets to experiment with chilaquiles, which prove extremely popular.

After several episodes of thrashing around trying to find its way, *Gilmore*, with this episode, seems on the verge of turning a very difficult corner. For the first time we're seeing most of the characters mature, especially Luke, Lorelai and Rory.

TODAY'S CELEBRATION Final exams at Yale, karaoke night, and Zack getting the two-month gig as lead guitarist for Vapor Rub.

AND INTRODUCING...*Steve and Kwan!* This time, in the flesh.

EMILY'S MAID DU JOUR Alexandra.

$1 The cost of Lorelai's coffee at Luke's. (Bargain!)

11 POUNDS How much weight Richard has lost while exercising.

8 WEEKS, 25 CITIES, 40 SHOWS Zack's Vapor Rub tour. (Opening for Tokyo Police Club during the Philadelphia and DC dates.)

AMEN, SISTER FRIEND

LOGAN: So, the thing is—as you can imagine, I'm pretty excited about all this.

LORELAI: Yeah.

LOGAN: But it does mean a move to San Francisco—Palo Alto, actually.

LORELAI: Oh wow.

LOGAN: Yeah.

LORELAI: That's big. That's funny that Rory didn't mention it.

LOGAN: Well actually, I haven't told her yet.

LORELAI: And you're here 'cause you want me to tell her for you?

LOGAN: No, no. I'm gonna tell her. I just, I wanted to talk to you first about it.

LORELAI: OK. That's...thoughtful.

LOGAN: Look, I love Rory. She means the world to me, and I want her to come with me to California.

LORELAI: Oh.

LOGAN: But not just as my girlfriend, which is why I'm here. I'm here to ask your permission—your permission to ask Rory to marry me. Lorelai? Lorelai?

7.21 Unto the Breach

First aired: May 8, 2007 // Written by David Babcock and Jennie Snyder // Directed by Lee Shallat Chemel

Yale's been one of the roughest experiences of Rory's life, but at least she can look forward to graduation. Little does she know that she has one more test, the results of which will determine her life for a long time to come. Meanwhile, a simple misunderstanding over Lorelai's karaoke performance from last episode hardens Luke's heart to her, making Lorelai doubt her own feelings about him.

GINCHY! Rory taking pictures of Paris and Doyle packing up the apartment ("I need a picture of Doyle. He's packing up the toaster. Oh, no toast tomorrow, that's so sad."); the town bullying Lorelai into reenacting Rory's graduation in a week; Richard and Emily's graduation song; and Paris and Rory's brief interaction before receiving their diplomas.

NOTES *'She's waiting for you to make a move.'*

Paris has definitely decided to go to Harvard Medical School, though, after the hell she went through with Harvard before (3.16), was there ever any question? Paris and Doyle are going to India after graduation.

Luke gets earrings for Rory and a necklace for Lorelai from Liz, but after he overhears Lorelai saying she wasn't serenading Luke at karaoke, he only gives Lorelai the earrings for Rory.

TODAY'S CELEBRATION Rory and Paris' graduation from Yale, Kirk's "Kirk in a Box" performance, and Logan proposes to Rory.

What *Gilmore* Means To Me

I was having a really hard time adjusting to college and caught *Gilmore Girls* on ABC Family and loved it. I made my mom and sister watch it and they fell in love with it, too. We watched the series finale the night before I moved back to college. When my parents left me at school the next day, I was upset and we went through the whole "Why didn't you socialize me properly" banter. This year I moved away to grad school and we watched a *Gilmore* my first night in my new apartment. Even though I'm a few hours away from home, my mom and I still like to 'watch' *Gilmore Girls* together by texting while we watch. We even made my mom a *Gilmore Girls* cake for her birthday one year.

—Beth Williams, *Cincinnati, Ohio*

KIRK OF ALL TRADES Performance artist.

MILAN KUNDERA The author of *The Unbearable Lightness of Being* author is the speaker at Rory's graduation (hence her lame "I'm unbearably light on him" line).

RICHARD + EMILY'S GRADUATION SONG

You're the top, you have graduated.
You're the top, your grandparents are elated.
Newspaper editor. Phi Beta Kappa wow!
You're a revelation. A huge sensation.
You should take a bow.
You are done. No more school for you.
There is nothing, now that you can't do.
You'll make us proud, we'll sing it loud.
It's true!
'Cause now, Rory you're a Bulldog through and through.

THINGS WE'VE LEARNED John Cabrera is an award-winning filmmaker in his own right. In particular, *Gilmore* fans are strongly encouraged to Google *The Man Who Invented the Moon*, a whimsically touching short movie he directed starring longtime friend Sean Gunn. "This was something I couldn't really have done if I hadn't gotten the role on *Gilmore Girls*. That obviously gave me a lot of freedom to start to dabble in my own films."

Underage Acting

Part of being a child actor in Hollywood is dealing with the restrictions that are placed on the number of hours you can actually work on set. This can be especially problematic on a workaholic, round-the-clock show like *Gilmore*.

Vanessa Marano was only allowed to work an 8½-hour day, with three of those hours having to be spent working on school work, she says. "We had a school room set up on set, and we had a different trailer for school as well. If April ever had friends (my character very rarely had friends), I would be schooled with them."

Behind the Scenes: Amy + Dan + Barack

In a post-post-post-modernist twist that could only happen in the era of reality TV and Twitter, the creators of *Gilmore Girls* contributed to Entertainment Weekly's PopWatch blog in August 2008 during the Democratic National Convention in Denver. In 10 witty posts, the duo, boosters of then-presidential candidate Barack Obama, turned a critical eye on the whole election process. Amy, for example, characterized her financial support of the Democratic party this way: "[2004 Democratic presidential candidate John] Kerry is when I started 'panic check writing.' I'd see Bush speak—I'd panic and write a check. I'd see Bush wave—I'd panic and write a check. I wrote so many checks, senators started calling me at home. I had Tom Daschle, Chuck Schumer and Bill Nelson on a conference call one Tuesday night at 9 saying 'we're all in a hotel room and we just finished watching *Gilmore Girls*.' Flattering? Yes. Disturbing? Completely. But Kerry didn't win."

By series end, every member of the Gilmore clan had graduated in one way or another.

AMEN, SISTER FRIEND

LOGAN [*about getting married*]: Remember when we were in the Life and Death Brigade and we stood on top of that tower, and we held hands and we jumped? Let's do that again, Rory. Let's jump.

RORY: Logan, I'm sorry, I can't. I love you. You know how much I love you. I love the idea of being married to you, but there are just a lot of things right now in my life that are undecided. And that used to scare me, but now I kind of like the idea that it's just all kind of wide open. And if I married you, it just wouldn't be.

Behind the Scenes What A Doll!

During the last year of production, the crew had a doll-making contest where everybody chose a person or character to reproduce in doll form, says Valerie Campbell. "I picked Kirk; I didn't win. *[Modesty seems to prevent Campbell from adding that she reproduced hay-bale-maze guard Kirk, complete with uniform.]*

"Some people would grab Barbies or embroidered faces on the dolls. Someone actually printed a photo and ironed it on the doll, but then you had to make clothes for it. They had to do all these different things. The person that won was a guy named Isaac, and the character that he picked was this guy named Robert Lee."

Robert Lee, as in the Luke's Diner busboy we frequently see cleaning up tables. "You know those little chips that you can record someone's voice? They had Robert Lee start laughing and they recorded him, and they sewed that into the doll. It was dressed like Robert Lee at Luke's, so it's a Tickle Me Elmo doll, but it's a Tickle Me Robert Lee doll. There were some really great dolls that people made."

LOGAN: So what? I go to San Francisco, you stay on the East Coast and we see each other occasionally?

RORY: Well, we can try long distance. We've done it before.

LOGAN: You really think that's gonna work?

RORY: I think it would be hard but—

LOGAN: I don't want to do that, Rory. I don't want to go backwards. If we can't take the next step—

RORY: What?

LOGAN: I mean—

RORY: Does it have to be all or nothing?

LOGAN: Yeah, it does.

RORY: But we could at least try.

LOGAN: What's the point?

RORY: So...

LOGAN: So... [Rory returns the engagement ring to him.] Goodbye, Rory.

7.22 Bon Voyage

First aired: May 15, 2007 // Written by David S Rosenthal // Directed by Lee Shallat Chemel

Lorelai and Rory plan on riding roller coasters at various amusement parks for a month, but a sudden job opportunity lands in Rory's lap: a chance to cover Barack Obama's presidential campaign, starting in Iowa, for the online magazine Hugo runs (7.8). Though it also scuppers Rory's Yale graduation reenactment party, it gives Luke another idea: a surprise going-away party for Rory.

! GINCHY! Rory finally meeting Christiane Amanpour...in her pajamas; the town's secret meeting in Miss Patty's studio; everybody stealthily setting up the town square for her party; the ultimate Luke-being-Luke moment: sewing together all of those tarps and raincoats; Luke and Lorelai's kiss; and the nice bookending of the final scene with the final scene of the pilot.

NOTES *'Mom, you've given me everything I need.'*

✱ Other famous guests of the Dragonfly Inn include newswoman Jane Pauley, Harry Belafonte and Marisa Tomei (whose mother's best friend is Lorelai's hairdresser's cousin's roommate).

Adventures Through the TV Glass

"Oh yeah, I was annoying on set," admits *Gilmore* fan-turned-star Vanessa Marano. "I was taking pictures of everything. Not even taking pictures of the actors, but taking pictures of the set. I was taking pictures of Doose's Market, Luke's Diner, the gazebo. I was just running around, I was so excited. I think that's a big reason why I did get the part. I knew the pacing of the show so well because I watched it religiously."

'I think this party's a testament to you, Lorelai, and the home you've created here.'

"I don't know if you notice but a lot of the background are the same people over and over and over. You'll see the same faces in the back of Luke's or even the ones who were at Chilton or the ones who were at the college. They always had the same group of people for each set, so they did keep a lot of continuity. On some shows, it's always different people all the time. On this they tried to keep that feeling of a town."

-VALERIE CAMPBELL, KEY SET COSTUMER

* Though Rory's salary for the online magazine assignment is small, her food, travel and lodging expenses will be covered. Lane admits that Dave Rygalski wasn't her first kiss, it was Billy Fink.

* Robert Lee, who's been Luke's silent busboy all these years, finally gets a couple of lines as they're setting up the party: "Hey Luke, I got the turntable. What's next," and "OK, will do."

* Luke finally gives Lorelai the necklace Liz made (7.21).

TODAY'S CELEBRATION Rory lands a job covering Obama's presidential campaign for Hugo's online magazine, and the town's surprise going-away party for her.

KIRK OF ALL TRADES Official town sash maker and presenter.

ROOM 7 Christiane Amanpour's room at the Dragonfly.

74 The number of résumés Rory prepares.

200 The number of people Luke expects to show at the party.

THINGS WE'VE LEARNED

After standing-in for Lauren Graham since the end of Season 2, Patty Malcolm was given the chance to appear on screen for the series finale. "Lee Shallat Chemel says you're going to say a line, what do you want to say. I'm like, I don't know. And Lauren comes up and says, 'Oh, oh, oh, say where's the bratwurst,'" continuing the joke about Luke's meat supplier trying to sell him bratwurst for the party. "And the first thing out of my mouth is, 'No bratwurst?' And Lauren's like, 'No, you've gotta say something else.' And Lee's like, 'Yeah, say something else.' So I step off Lauren's mark, I step on to my own mark that they just created. Wardrobe comes on a bicycle from a trailer, throws a sweater at me, I throw it

Behind the Scenes Christiane Amanpour Reporting Live... from Stars Hollow

It's hard to decide which is crazier—convincing the respected correspondent to swing by the Warner Brothers studio for the short time she happened to be in the United States, or that producers would think that a significant number of viewers would have the faintest idea who Amanpour was. Yet her appearance is also evidence that, despite the guff the Season 7 producers would take, they were determined to remain true to the series as best they could. They might not have been able to duplicate Amy & Dan's vision for the series, but they could at least bring Rory's odd career obsession full circle by having her meet her longtime idol.

"The only unfortunate part of that was that it was Amy's baby," says casting director Jami Rudofsky. "As you know, [Amy & Dan] are really involved with politics and they're very savvy. She's someone they loved, and I think they reflected that in the scripts because they wrote her as Rory's idol. It was always Amy's goal to get her on the show. Of course Christiane Amanpour's schedule is amazingly hectic. It took us a few years, but we finally made it happen. That was really exciting."

However, it was an appearance that nearly didn't happen at all. "The Christiane Amanpour thing was such a complicated situation that I was actually having nightmares about it until she was actually physically on the set," says casting director Mara Casey. "I mean I was dreaming of her in her khaki with her hat on the set and all this crazy shit. I was literally holding my breath and panicking until the moment she drove onto the set."

For starters, CNN's foreign correspondent didn't have an agent, work visas had to be arranged, and "we were on a holiday on a Monday, and she was to shoot on a Tuesday," Casey recalls. "So pretty much nothing was in my favor. But a lot of people joined forces with me at the last minute and helped me get all the paperwork together. It took a lot of higher-ups to help me out, so I can't take the final credit for her actually being on the show. She only had 4 to 6 hours to commit to us. It was just a lot of work, but of course well worth it."

Amanpour's appearance was seven years in the making.

on. Hair walks by and brushes the back of my hair. Makeup never even took a look at me. And we shot it. ["No bratwurst? Just corn then."] And as soon as we shot it, I stepped off of my mark, back on to Lauren's mark to stand in for her. And that was my last ever part on the show."

AMEN, SISTER FRIEND

LUKE [*to Taylor*]: I don't know what your problem is, but the town wants to throw this party and you're either gonna join us or you're gonna stay home and comb your beard.

LORELAI: I can't believe they did this for her.
RICHARD: I don't think this is all for Rory. I think this party's a testament to you, Lorelai, and the home you've created here. I regret that you needed—
EMILY: Richard.
RICHARD: Now let me finish, Emily. I regret it, and we've—recent experience has taught me—
EMILY: Oh, please don't become one of those "I had a heart attack, let me express my every thought" types.
RICHARD: Not every thought, dear, just this one. It takes a remarkable person to inspire all of this.
LORELAI: Thanks, dad.
EMILY: OK, that's enough. It's not as though the two of you are saying goodbye.

LORELAI [*after Emily tries to loan her money for improvements to the inn*]: Mom, why don't we just talk about it Friday night at dinner?
EMILY: Oh, so our Friday night dinners are going to continue, then?
LORELAI: Well, we might as well. I've kind of gotten used to it.
EMILY: All right. That sounds fine. But don't be late and don't wear jeans.
LORELAI: When have I ever worn jeans to dinner?
EMILY: Well I don't know, it could very well be Rory who enforces the dress code. I'm just saying I don't think that jeans are appropriate.

And with that, it was over

Yes, the series had come full circle, but *Gilmore* fans and those involved in the series' making shared the same sense of being left high and dry, with everyone asking the same question: "Is this all there is?" As one cast member put it, "I'd just as soon forget about the final season." This was the type of rushed ending that Amy & Dan had struggled to avoid during their multiyear push for advance notice on the series' cancellation.

Under the leadership of David Rosenthal, the writers, cast and crew had worked tirelessly to keep the spirit of *Gilmore Girls* alive, complete with such hallmarks as Stars Hollow's over-the-top community events (the hay bale maze), surprise guest stars (CNN journalist/Rory Gilmore hero Christiane Amanpour being a particularly brilliant coup), and some truly memorable scenes (Kirk's outdoor diner and Luke sewing that gigantic tent for the final episode).

Rosenthal "did a great job trying to match it, but he knew it would be hard to fill those shoes," editor Raul Davalos says. "It would be hard for anybody to."

Adds Sean Gunn, "I don't mean any disrespect to David Rosenthal or the writers of the final season—they are all talented people who had a difficult mountain to climb. But I don't think they quite got there in terms of finding the perfect tone for the show. Amy Sherman-Palladino's vision was singular and proved super tough to recreate."

Though Rosenthal and company never quite managed to make it all ring true, they did much better than anybody could've hoped for, and better than most hardcore fans (including, it must be said, the author) are usually willing to admit. While Season 7 may get its fair share of drubbing from the *Gilmore* faithful, particular scenes from that season are greatly embraced by many.

Lorelai's impassioned karaoke serenade and Christopher's movie date with Lorelai hit just the right notes for the romantics, while Emily's roadside arrest provided a chuckle or two as the unflinching pride of Emily Gilmore finally hit the immovable force of law and order.

Still, however good a series Season 7 was, it was a shadow of its former self. In a sense, it was a slick production of 22 fan-fiction pieces. And like those fan works, there was always something missing: Amy & Dan.

"Right now, I know what the series-finale show should be," Amy told The AV Club in February 2005. "I don't know if I'll be here to do it. But hopefully, whoever is writing the show at that point will give me a call and I can fill them in." Sadly, that didn't happen.

"I don't know what went on in the writers room during that year, but obviously they all loved the show and they wanted to make it work, but it was a difficult task to undertake," Davalos says. "Ultimately, Amy has a very unique voice, and try as you may, you can't really duplicate it—just the turn of a phrase or the references she picks to highlight some point. She's typing away and it just comes to her. You can't bottle it. I think they did a very stand-up job, but I think she probably would've done things differently and taken things in a different direction."

Many cast members, too, let the mask slip on occasion when it came to their feelings about the final season. Herrmann and Bishop, speaking with a candor borne of years of experience and respect in the field, made it clear that it hadn't been their favorite season. Whatever riff on the St. Crispin's Day speech the venerable actors delivered to each other prior to the series finale, they played their parts well, and only hinted at the disappointment they must have felt in a few interviews.

"I see a series of dots after the last scene of the show, rather than a period, or better yet, an exclamation point," Bishop told The Washington Post. Added Herrmann in the same piece, "You don't have the emotionally satisfying moments. After seven years, each of those story lines needs its own episode, almost."

Two years later, Herrmann related an experience from his home life to the author that reflected beautifully fan reaction around the world.

"Emma, my youngest, was too young to really get [*Gilmore Girls*] for a while, until a year or two years ago when she started watching it," he says. Once the then-11-year-old dipped into *Gilmore Girls*, she was hooked. "She would pop in and say, 'How can you be so mean?!' Then she'd come back, 'Oh Dad, you are so funny!'

"But she was sobbing in the dark one evening when I came home. When I asked the trouble, she said 'It's *over*. It just is *over* and nothing is settled! Does she marry Luke? What *happens*? You guys have to get together and make the ending. Can't you just make a movie about it?'

"The explanation that the series didn't belong to us didn't mollify her. It still hasn't. I have the feeling millions of kids (and mothers) feel the same way."

Last Minute Meltdown

It wasn't just the lack of closure in the series finale that had the talent in front of and behind the camera on edge. As is so often the case, the deal making and last-minute wrangling behind the scenes between cast and the network had toppled the series, and had done so with the worst possible timing.

The previous year, Amy & Dan had been lost because the studio couldn't make the numbers add up enough to give the team enough notice on series cancellation. This time out, attempts to keep series stars Graham and Bledel also broke down, according to many accounts.

"We left thinking the girls were negotiating," Yanic Truesdale says. "I had been reassured by the other cast members and the girls that it was a tough negotiation, but they would go back and we would go back."

At the wrap party for Season 7, many were told that the series was coming back for half a season, 13 episodes. "So no one said goodbye at the wrap party," Patty Malcolm says. Producer Lee Shallat Chemel told her not to go looking for work because she would be standing in again for Graham. "And me and Lauren didn't even say goodbye. I said, 'Have a nice break, and she's like, 'It's going to be 13 episodes and it's going to be easy. We're not going to work as long hours.'"

But three or four weeks into their break, cast and crew saw reports online that *Gilmore* would not be returning for another season. Recalls Malcolm, "It spread like wildfire.

"That whole season, we were prepared that it was going to be over because we knew that Lauren and Alexis probably were ready to do other things. So we were prepared for it, but then at the end with the 13 episode thing, it was like oh, we are coming back." When *Gilmore's* end was made official, there were a lot of heavy hearts in Hollywood.

So What Happened?

Lauren Graham told Michael Ausiello (then at TV Guide) that a couple of months before the idea of doing 13 episodes was floated, she had informed the Powers That Be "that I didn't see it coming back, and they had asked to just give them some time to figure something out that would make it work. Both Alexis and I felt tired, and also creatively like the show was in a place where we were either at the end or very close to it. We really couldn't imagine another season."

The real problem, she added, was that the 6-7 days an episode both she and Alexis were working was running them ragged, something that Amy & Dan had reportedly tried to put an end to in their own negotiations the previous year. Those who were in a position to know say that Graham and Bledel had agreed to come back for two more seasons after Season 6 if Amy was retained, but when the Palladinos left at the end of last season, it was over.

There it was. Finished. Even as Graham and Bledel became reacquainted with the little snatches of free time that most take for granted, the shock of post-*Gilmore* life rippled through the entertainment world.

Scott Patterson was on the set of the horror film *Saw 4* when he found out that he was going to be putting up his baseball cap for good, he told TV Guide in May 2007. He turned on his cell phone and noticed there were about 15 voice mails. "I was like, 'Ooooh, that's either really good or really bad.'" The actor had actually inked a deal with Warner Brothers just a few months before to come back to the show.

"I walked around the lot three days after we got cancelled," Malcolm says. "I went through the sets. I got to say my goodbyes. I came in not even a month later and I went into the sets and they were completely gone. They were already building the *Chuck* set on one of our stages. But it's like out with the old and on to the new."

Emily Kuroda returned to the Warner Brothers lot in 2008 for a project. "On my lunch hour, I went and walked around where Stars Hollow used to be." Granted, it had all been there for seven years, which is a long time for sets to remain standing. Yet, "to see it gone now, with new facades and everything, it was sad."

Malcolm visited the lot again in 2009 to say goodbye to the people who worked on *ER*, which was ending that year. "I wanted to go say goodbye because, for all these years, we worked against them. It was always who's still on the lot: it's either *Gilmore Girls* or *ER*, because we worked so many hours."

By then, the iconic gazebo, where bands played and Kirk slept and speeches were made, had been relegated to the parking lot. "When I went into Stars Hollow, they were shooting *Ghost Whisperer* back there," Malcolm says. "It was just not Stars Hollow anymore."

Gilmore Girls...The Movie?

Edward Herrmann's youngest hadn't been the only one to suggest that the seven-year tale of Lorelai and Rory could be sewn up "the right way" on the big screen.

"Amy did say at a certain point that she wanted to do a feature," Davalos says. "In the feature, she would end the series the way she would have, and we're all waiting for her to come up with that." How this idea would line up with her earlier insistence that she needed a certain number of episodes to get to where she wanted to go plotwise remains unclear.

When Amy was asked if she and Dan had watched the final episode of the series, she told The Star-Ledger newspaper in New Jersey in July 2007, "I think I just got very drunk that night and sat in a corner, and

[Dan] read in a corner, and then we just got quiet and went to bed. I couldn't watch it because it wasn't my ending, it wasn't going to be what I had in my head forever, and I was going to do something crazy, homicidal, suicidal, something with an '-idal' in it." When asked what the two-words were that she had always planned to end the series with, Amy replied, "You're adopted." Dan quickly jumped in to assure everyone she was kidding.

A couple of months earlier, Amy told Entertainment Weekly writer and all-around *Gilmore* booster Michael Ausiello that the reason she'd never revealed the final words that were to end the series was because she was planning on putting together a two-hour TV movie.

In January 2009, Graham told Ausiello that she was open to the idea of a *Gilmore Girls* movie, but added her own interesting spin:

"But for me, when you have a bad breakup, going back and dating the guy again is not really going to change the breakup. It didn't end in the way I think any of us would have liked—and that is a disappointment for me as well. When the reruns come on now I think about the path it took, and it makes me sad. I wish we would have known it was the end when we shot the final episode, quite simply. But we can't go back and change that. And I'm not sure a movie would help."

By July of that year, Graham was telling Moviehole.net that "What's really funny is, no one actually involved with the production of that show has ever brought it up. It is only an Internet rumor..."

If it was a rumor, it was one that dogged everyone involved in the original series. "I keep hearing odd comments regarding a *Gilmore* film from teenagers at market checkout counters," Herrmann admits.

Other cast members continue to innocently fan the flames in interviews, abetted by journalists anxious to be the ones to reveal that a movie is in the works, even if it isn't. Scott Patterson and Alexis Bledel have regularly been backed into a corner this way, politely replying that they would be interested in reading a script, which translates into "the movie is coming, queue up now" after reporters get done with it.

Kelly Bishop says she's still urging Amy to come up with a movie. "There's so much that needs to be resolved in her voice, the way it should've been. People still love it so much, and they do want an ending. I want one, too. You always have that situation where you're never sure if the show is going to be picked up, but that year it looked pretty much like it wasn't going to be. But it just kind of faded. Nothing really happened. There's total room for that to be rectified, if I can just talk Amy into doing it.

"I think we'd all love getting together again. Approaching the work again with a little bit of space in between the exhaustion and just the sheer joy of being together and doing some good work. Let's hope so. We'll see what we can do."

"It only can come from Amy," Davalos says. "Any news you hear is just hearsay until you hear it from her. I did hear it from her that she wanted to [make that movie], but in her own time. It could be true, but it could be true three years from now..."

...and so we wait.

Gilmore Girls Around the World

Like GG Hayden during her terrible tyke stage, *Gilmore Girls* has always shown a penchant for laughing in the faces of its critics, gleefully knocking down every stereotype and insult hurled its way: "You can't get young people to watch a dialogue-heavy show. Every actor on your series has to be *GQ/Vogue* beautiful. A woman can't be a showrunner."

In fact, the only real certainty about *Gilmore Girls* seemed to be the idea that no matter how well written it was, an hour-long show depicting life in a small American town, packed with obscure American pop culture references and boasting more dialogue than most two-hour movies couldn't possibly find an audience outside of the United States. This attitude was summed up perfectly by a reader comment on the Entertainment Weekly Web site responding to a foreign reader who'd been confused by a joke about the long-rumored *Gilmore* movie:

"What country do you live in that you don't understand sarcasm and how can you possibly enjoy *Gilmore Girls* if you don't get sarcasm?"

It's not too hard to see a similar attitude prevailing at Warner Brothers when the idea of exporting the show was first debated.

Yet today, three years after the series ended, some of the show's most dedicated fans can be found in India, Germany, Austria, Scotland, England, Argentina, and pretty much anywhere else you can think of. Despite unpredictable broadcast schedules, dodgy dubs, and the exorbitant prices charged for *Gilmore Girls* DVDs overseas, their devotion has never wavered. Some are content to write and share fan fiction, others haunt various online forums to debate the merits of Chris over Luke (or vice versa, or doubtless in the case of some fan fic, as a couple themselves), but nearly all maintain a love for the show and a respect for one another.

The following are a few of those people who keep the memory of *Gilmore Girls* alive abroad today.

Italy

***[Author's note:** There are a great many Gilmore fans in Italy. One group has taken to regularly posting information about the references on* Gilmore. *They even have plans to share parts of* The Gilmore Girls Companion *in Italian. Here's why.]*

"We're talking about having something like a weekly date in which we could explain things to people of our fan page as a "goodnight fable." This is because, and for me this is a very bad thing to say, there are a lot of people who cannot read so good in their home language, so you can imagine they could not read a book in English. We try to reach everyone. In Italy, it is a period of bad things, especially for culture, not only for university but also for school in general. This is the reason why we tried to explain some references about Rory's books or famous people in the fiction, to spread culture (in our little funny way).— *Eleonora Baggio*

India

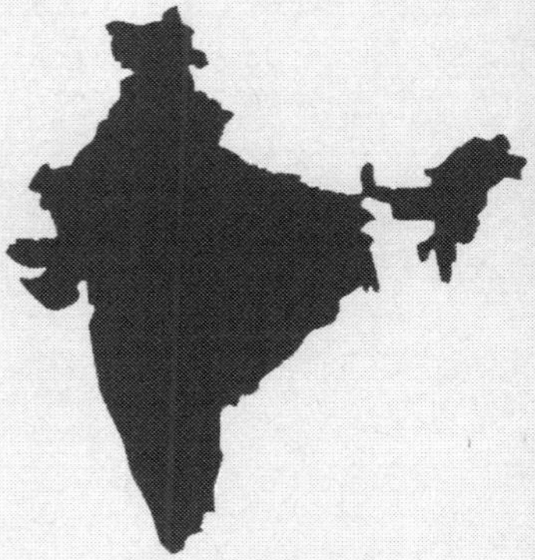

"It's on English TV, so it's not dubbed and Michel is French. Also, only Disney shows are dubbed in Hindi for some reason, and some movies, but the 'grown-up' TV is in English. When I started watching *GG*, I was Alexis Bledel's age (18), so yeah, I grew up with Rory. But I cannot for the life of me relate to her personality. I can relate more to Lorelai's... To me, it went beyond being fiction. They were my escape, and also like my good friends who went through pretty much the same thing. I really hope it doesn't sound creepy but I just relate to this show more than anything else." —*Saroma Srinidhi (Romy Skye)*

Scotland (U.K.)

"I got hooked last summer after watching just Season 1 and bought the entire series on DVD. I seriously don't think I would have been able to wait watching it in real time, although I probably would have enjoyed that I was a similar age to Rory throughout! The show isn't overly popular here, but I think that has more to do with when it is aired rather than the content of the show itself. I guess the audience is made up of students and housewives." *—Claire Mcloughlin*

***Note:** In July 2009, Claire had the opportunity to catch a production of* Guys & Dolls *starring Lauren Graham in New York City.*

Spain

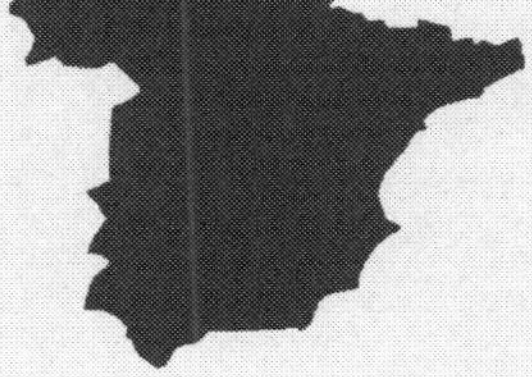

"It's not the most popular show, mostly because they are always playing with its schedule, but it's popular enough to have almost 1,300 users in our *Gilmore Girls* Spanish Forum. It's played dubbed and yes, Michel is still French." *—Lourdes Palma Ortiz*

Czech Republic

"The show has quite a big fan base here but, because of the airing time, they are usually young teen girls. I think our dubbed version is really good, but I agree that lots of jokes get lost in translation. I myself watch *GG* in English—nothing can be better than the original. And yes, Michel is French in our version." *—Katka Rylichová*

Germany

"When *Gilmore Girls* aired for the first time here in Germany, I was about Rory's age. It was one of the things that amazed me. Finally, I had somebody on TV who was my age and I could relate to this person and her problems and everything. Rory's character helped me a lot to get through my teenage years. In her, I always could see how everything could be for me if I worked hard enough." *—Myriam Meinzer*

The Netherlands

"I was happy we had subtitles; I'm so glad I could just hear the voice of everyone instead of the dubbing, even though the translation did annoy me from time to time. They always tried to translate the pop culture references as well, but most of the time you just can't. Some things just aren't translatable. And they tried anyways. Therefore some of the translation was really weird." *—Denise Bergshoeff*

"That'll Do, Pig"

after *gilmore*

Three years after the last episode of *Gilmore* aired, the series lives on in syndication on the US cable channel ABC Family and SOAP-net. And the drumbeat continues for some type of closure to the series.

While this was initially viewed as the daydreams of fans alone, it now seems that the conditions are right for some sort of ending to take place. Part of the reason for that: Amy & Dan have not yet found their Next Big Thing. Their *Untitled Wyoming Project* pilot for The CW, about a horse trainer who must take over his parents' ranch after their death, pretty much died before it left the gate, or landed a proper title. Though Amy had a couple of other projects cooking, neither sounded particularly viable. With Amy at a loose end, and the recent success of the *Sex and the City* movies, it's not difficult to understand the appeal of a *Gilmore* movie to Warner Brothers.

Though Lauren Graham has made no secret of her desire to leave *Gilmore* behind, the actress may be softening her stance against revisiting Stars Hollow. As Edward Herrmann puts it, "It is rare that an actor likes what he's first famous for. Actors get these roles that define them to the public and the industry, and then they spend most of their time trying to break that mold."

"I walked by our apartment set [on the Warner Brothers lot] and it's all gone, they've taken everything out of there. What did I expect? It's not going to be a museum forever."

-TODD LOWE (ZACK)

Yet, since *Gilmore*, Graham has proved to the industry, and more importantly to herself, that her breakout role was not a fluke. Not only has she upped the quality of her cinematic choices with such movies as *Flash of Genius* and *Cloudy with a Chance of Meatballs*, but she also made her Broadway debut as Miss Adelaide in *Guys and Dolls* in 2009; a singing role, no less, and wowed critics and audiences alike.

More importantly, in March 2010, Graham threw herself back into series television as single mom Sarah Braverman on NBC's *Parenthood*, stepping in to replace Maura Tierney shortly before the series premiere. (Tierney had to bow out to pursue treatment for breast cancer.) In just a few months, her bold performance revealed two things many had already guessed—the fanbase Graham had built on *Gilmore* would follow her anywhere, and she was far from a one-hit wonder. Becoming a success on a smaller network such as The WB or The CW was one thing, carrying a series on a full-fledged network such as NBC was another. After years of slagging off mentions of a *Gilmore* movie in the press, she finally admitted to Vanity Fair in September 2010 that it was actually possible. "What's funny to me is that in all these years, no one ever talked about it except the fans. But now people with power, people who could actually make it happen, are talking about it. I think it could be good, but I wonder if we've waited too long. I don't want to be walking around the town square with a cane."

That other integral part of any *Gilmore* movie, Alexis Bledel, has avoided series television for a string of predictable rom-coms, the exceptions to this being 2010's *The Conspirator*, in which she plays the wife of a soldier who defends the one woman arrested in the murder of Abraham Lincoln, and *Violet & Daisy*, which casts her as one of two teenage assassins. The only obstacle to her reprising her part for a *Gilmore* movie is the question of whether she really wants to relive the role that made life so hard for her in those early years?

Since taking the role of Sarah Braverman on *Parenthood*, Lauren Graham has continued to grow her fanbase the world over, landing several magazine covers in the process.

Of course to have a *Gilmore* movie, you must have Luke, if only to answer once and for all that "will they or won't they" question. Fortunately, Scott Patterson has never seemed too against the idea of revisiting Stars Hollow. September 2010 saw the premiere of NBC's *The Event*, a *Lost*-style series predicated on a mystery so confusing, even the actors had trouble figuring it out while shooting it, Patterson told AOL News that month.

When you get down to it, if Amy & Dan are on board, chances are excellent for the making of a movie. Whatever differences cast and crew had over the years, many admit they formed a family during their time in Stars Hollow, dysfunctional though it sometimes appeared.

When Kelly Bishop went to Graham's final performance of *Guys and Dolls* on Broadway, she spent some time catching up with Graham's father at the after party while Lauren got her things.

"I'd met him several times; he's a lovely man," Bishop says. "We had a chance to really just sit and chat for a bit in a way we never had before."

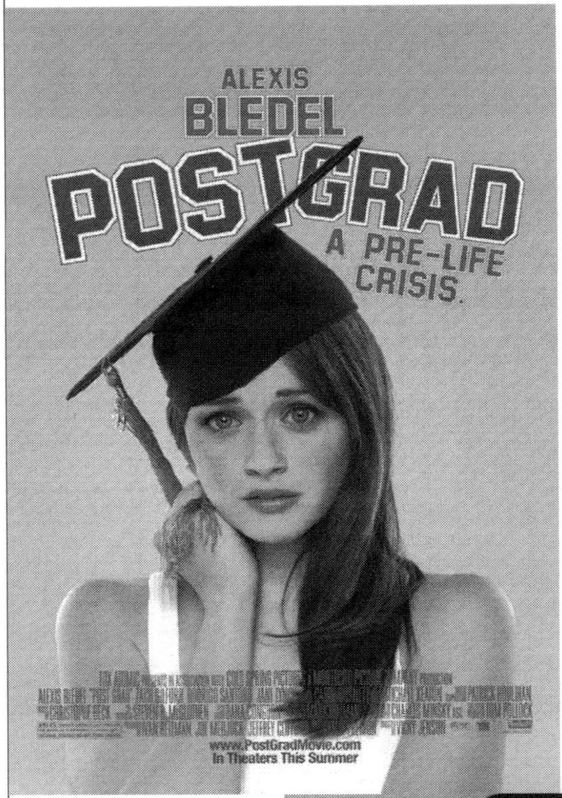

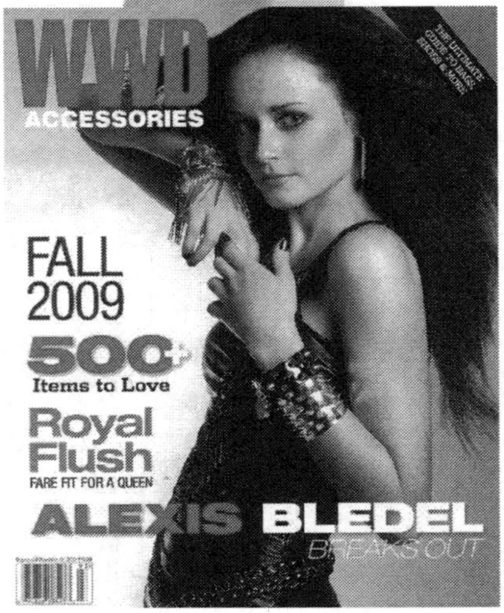

Alexis Bledel is seldom out of the spotlight, with a movie or two opening each year.

Graham's mother, Donna Grant, had passed away in 2005 during the filming of *Gilmore*. Bishop told Lawrence Graham that Lauren "'Kind of feels like a daughter to me.' And he said, 'Well, in a way, you're kind of her mother.' That was wonderful. I was so glad that he said that to me; it made me feel very good. I'm very proud of her."

"You're always looking to get to that next level where you're recognized or you have a certain amount of respect or you have a certain amount of clout, and it changes all the time," Scott Cohen says. "One side of it becomes a business, so you become really business minded, and the other side of it is artistic. Lauren's an extremely talented woman. She just needed to find her niche. And she did."

Meanwhile, Herrmann and Bishop have continued to wow theater audiences when they aren't appearing on series such as *Grey's Anatomy* (the former) and *Army Wives* and *Mercy* (the latter).

Though everyone's gone on to something else since *Gilmore* ended, many say that, despite the long hours and energy-sapping work, they still get nostalgic for the good old days in Stars Hollow.

"I think we all realize that we'll never have that dynamic again," Patty Malcolm says. "We were really having a good time and we didn't even realize it. It's the only show I've ever worked on where I'd be off and I'd actually come visit after working 60 hours. I'd get a day off and I'm like, 'What are you guys doing for lunch?' Now, I work on another TV series and when I'm wrapped, I'm like the wind, I'm out of there."

"It was still hard work and there were a lot of frustrating times and loneliness and all the other things that go with the territory," Kelly Bishop says. "But it was just a blessing to me. It was absolutely wonderful. Not the least of which is it helped my SAG pension insurance, so my SAG pension is much better than it would've been without *Gilmore Girls* —I can promise you that. I would be delighted if I had something half as good again. At least I've had it."

And that was *Gilmore Girls*, from the first germ of an idea until the final curtain. At the time of this writing, it is the 10th anniversary of *Gilmore's* first episode, and the Web is awash with praise for this series we can't seem to get out of our minds.

With all this recent talk about a *Gilmore* movie or a Season 8, the truth is that whatever new iteration of *Gilmore* arrives, it will be the original series that endures in our hearts, and lingers in our memories. To paraphrase Lorelai's words about Luke to the family court, once *Gilmore Girls* is in your life, it is in your life forever.

"I've been with Criminal Minds since Gilmore ended, and yeah, I'm kind of close to everyone. But we don't do anything with each other outside of work. Gilmore Girls, we would work a 70-hour week and we'd still hang out till the sun came up on Friday nights singing karaoke. Who does that?"

-PATTY MALCOLM (LAUREN GRAHAM'S STAND-IN)

Super Cool Party People: [top, l to r] Jenny Yang, Shin Kawasaki and Keiko Agena (Lane); [Bottom] Valerie Campbell and Biff Yeager (Tom); [Above, right] Campbell and Michael DeLuise (TJ)

ACKNOWLEDGMENTS

When I first suggested this book to publisher Ben Ohmart at BearManor Media, I laid out this grand idea for a book that would get at the very heart of the creative process in Hollywood. After all, here was a television show loved worldwide and lauded for its writing, yet very little has ever actually been published about its making. Suddenly realizing that there might be a reason for that, I quickly added "or worse comes to worst, we can publish a program guide." Little did I know that nearly three years later, *The Gilmore Girls Companion* would turn out to be a bit of both.

All told, there were 40 people from the world of *Gilmore* who agreed to speak with me, answering my often naïve questions with candor and, frequently, humor. Many went out on a limb for the sake of this book, taking a chance that I would not somehow land them in it with future bosses in Hollywood. The names of those brave souls can be found here. One, however, went so far beyond the call of duty, she rates special mention here.

About 10 people into the interview process, I realized that nine had mentioned Valerie Campbell, the key set costumer from *Gilmore*. "She's kind of like our glue, keeping us together," Emily Kuroda explained. When I finally got in touch with Valerie, I realized why everybody was so fond of her. Not only is she one of the most positive people I've met, she and her husband, Colin, actually put me up at their place for a week when I was in LA, and bent over backward to ensure that I saw the Warner Brothers backlot, met some *Gilmore* people at a large party they threw, and even took me to a show where Keiko Agena was playing with her band in Japantown. Thanks, Valerie.

Thanks, too, must go to all of the online *Gilmore* fans who helped me through this adventure over the years. In these pages you will find some of their personal stories, artwork and observations, whether they watch *Gilmore* in California, Austria or Czech Republic. They kept me sane. Cheers to Claire, Zoran, Cira, Katka, Eva Pfeffer (who also created the fine illustrations throughout this book), Ele, Denise, Lori, Eleonora, Romy, Myriam, Susan and all the rest (literally hundreds) who joined me in debating everything from their favorite episode to the best saying to come out of seven years of *Gilmore*.

My appreciation for photographer Mark Lipczynski's efforts for this project is immense. Not only did he drive from Arizona to LA, but he also set up a photo booth and spent the better part of a day and night photographing different *Gilmore* people at the aforementioned party.

Finally, I really must get a rubber stamp made for the following sentence: Without Pamela Norman Berman's patience, love, support, keen eye for design, and all around awesomeness, this book would not have been possible.

Thanks also go to interviewees:

Edward Herrmann (and for the foreword he wrote to this book), Kelly Bishop, Keiko Agena, Emily Kuroda, Liz Torres, Yanic Truesdale, Michael Winters, Sean Gunn, Rose Abdoo, Scott Cohen, Ted Rooney, Shelly Cole, Danny Strong, Vanessa Marano, Todd Lowe, John Cabrera, Honorine Bell, Alan Blumenfeld, Devon Sorvari, Devon Michaels, Nick Holmes, Tanc Sade, Grant-Lee Phillips, Olivia Hack, Katie Walder, Aris Alvarado, Biff Yeager, Michael DeLuise, Sheila R Lawrence, Gavin Polone, Jane Espenson, Janet Leahy, Raul Davalos, Patty Malcolm, Mara Casey, Jami Rudofsky, Jeff Block, Alison Goodman, George Anthony Bell, Mindee Clem Forman and Casey Kasemeier.

BIBLIOGRAPHY

Abel, Olivia. "Out of the Bullpen," People magazine, Jan. 28, 2002

Ausiello, Michael. "Exclusive Q&A: Lauren Graham on Broadway, *Gilmore* movie, and her big TV comeback." EW.com, Jan. 23, 2009

Ausiello, Michael. "It's Here: Lauren Graham's Final *Gilmore Girls* Interview," TV Guide, May 7, 2007

Ausiello, Michael. "*Gilmore* girl Lauren Graham on her big TV comeback," http://ausiellofiles.ew.com/2009/10/16/exclusive-gilmore-girl-lauren-graham-on-her-big-tv-comeback/

Ausiello, Michael. "Exclusive Q&A: *Gilmore Girls*' Scott Patterson," TVGuide.com, May 12, 2007

Blackman, Lori. "Gilmore Girl Lauren Graham," CNN.com, Jan. 10, 2001

Cherkezian, Megan. "Marty's Back! Wayne Wilcox Talks about Being the *Gilmore Girls* Nice Guy," TVGuide.com, Nov 21, 2006

Daniels, Susanne and Cynthia Littleton, "Season Finale: The Unexpected Rise & Fall of The WB and UPN." HarperCollins Publishers, 2007.

Fine, Audrey. "Getting to Know: Chad Michael Murray," Seventeen magazine, www.seventeen.com/entertainment/features/chad-michael-murray

Fretts, Bruce. "Happy Gilmore," Entertainment Weekly, Sept. 29, 2000

Frey, Hillary. "'90s Boy Grows Up," The New York Observer, Oct. 16, 2007

Frey, Jennifer. "Is This Really Goodbye, Girls?" The Washington Post, May 15, 2007

Garske, Monica. "*The Event* Cast Completely Confused by Own Show," AOL News, September 2010

Grossberg, Josh. "Networks: We Are Family (Friendly, That Is)," E! Online,

Nov. 14, 2000

Hart, Hugh. "The Gift of Gab," Los Angeles Times, April 9, 2001

Hart, Hugh. "A *Roseanne*, *Gilmore Girls* Connection," Los Angeles Times,

April 9, 2001

Heffernan, Virginia. "The Gilmore Noodge," The New York Times, Jan. 23, 2005

Hochman, David. "Graham Belle," More magazine, March 2010

Ichikawa, Anne. "Miss Blue Eyes Bledel," Elle Girl, Nov. 29, 2005

Katz, Jesse. "How a Pathologically Blunt Producer Makes It in Suck-Up City," The New York Times Magazine, Feb. 9, 2003.

Kaufman, Joanne. "A Comic's Quarter Century of Smooth Sailing," The Wall Street Journal, Feb. 22, 2006.

Kizis, Deanna. "The Geek Shall Inherit the Earth," Elle magazine, May 2004

LaTempa, Susan. "The Best of Friends," April, 29, 2002.
www.gilmoregirls.org/news/211.html

Midler, Caryn. "The Gilmore Guy: David Sutcliffe," People magazine, Sept. 25, 2006

Miller, Julie. "Scott Patterson on *The Event* and the Possibility of a *Gilmore Girls* Movie," Movieline.com, Oct. 19, 2010

Pfefferman, Naomi. "Nice, Jewish Maidel: Amy Sherman-Palladino turns *Gilmore Girls* into a homage to the Catskills," Jewish Journal, March 27, 2003

Richmond, Ray. "Producers Dialogue," The Hollywood Reporter, Feb. 8, 2006

Rosen, Steve. "Art Imitates Strife," Denver Post, Aug. 10, 1998

Ryan, Maureen. "They're slippin' 'em Paul Anka, dig?" Chicago Tribune, Feb. 11, 2006

Sansing, Dina. "The *Gilmore Girls* You Love to Hate," Seventeen magazine, January 2003.

Schweber, Arieanna, "*Gilmore Girls* may get 2 Hour Movie," May 23, 2007, www.gilmoregirlsnews.com/2007/05/23/gilmore-girls-may-get-2-hour-movie/

Sepinwall, Alan. "Lorelai's last words (but not really)," The Star-Ledger, July 23, 2007

Stepakoff, Jeffrey. "Billion-Dollar Kiss: The Kiss that Saved Dawson's Creek and Other Adventures in TV Writing." Gotham Books, 2007.

Spitznagel, Eric. "*Parenthood's* Lauren Graham is Not Afraid to Hump a Chair to Get a Movie Role," Vanity Fair, Sept. 10, 2010

Tobias, Scott. "Interview: Amy Sherman-Palladino," The AV Club, Feb. 9, 2005

Tomczak, Sarah. "*Gilmore Girls*' Liza Weil," YM magazine, Jan. 24, 2002

Tucker, Ken. "*Gilmore Girls*," Entertainment Weekly, May 11, 2007

Tucker, Ken. "Town Meeting," EW.com, April 24, 2006

Tucker, Ken. "Mailer Call," EW.com, Oct. 15, 2004

Post Grad interview with Alexis Bledel, Aug. 11, 2009, http://origin.foxsearchlight.com/postgrad/blog/?p=168

"Insanity in Denver." Amy Sherman-Palladino and Daniel Palladino's blog posts for Entertainment Weekly.

"Exclusive Interview: Lauren Graham," www.moviehole.net/200919911-exclusive-interview-lauren-graham

PHOTO CREDITS

Chapter openers/front cover swirl illustrations: Aleksandar Velasevic

Front cover coffee cup illustration: Ayse Nazli Deliormanli

Warner Bros./The WB
Front cover, 2, 27, 37, 39, 41, 44, 48, 49, 51, 56, 59, 61, 62, 67, 71, 76, 79, 82, 83, 84, 85, 86, 87 , 91, 93, 95, 99, 104, 115, 117, 118, 119, 120, 124, 128, 129, 134, 139, 140, 143, 147, 155, 158, 164, 170, 175, 178, 180, 182, 190, 193, 196, 200, 204, 207, 208, 213. 216, 219, 220, 231, 234, 235, 238, 239, 246, 251, 253, 256, 261, 263, 271, 281, 285, 288, 299, 303, 304, 310, 312, 313, 314, 319, 320, 326, 330, 332, 333, 334, 340, 343, 344, 348, 355, 360, 362, 364, 366, 368, 371, 374, 378, 381, 382, 285, 391, 392

The CW
278, 317, 397, 401, 402, 403, 406, 409, 412, 415, 423, 430, 437, 442, 444, 448, 450, 451

Mark Lipczynski
(marklipczynski.com) Back cover (author photo), 266, 468, 474

Shelley Cole 93, 169

Yanic Truesdale 98

Michael Winters Back cover, 77, 127, 478

Patty Malcolm Back cover, 23, 228, 250, 340, 405, 473, 476, 478

Eva Pfeffer 50, 88, 94, 139, 464, 470, 472, 474, 475, 476, 477, 479

Vanessa Marano 8, 57, 353, 449

Rose Abdoo Back Cover, 145, 475

Grant-Lee Phillips 171 (photo by Denise Siegel), 388 (photo by Kenneth Scott)

Michael DeLuise 258, 259, 273

ABC 21, 109

Tanc Sade 277, 347

Fox 185, 363

Other credits
8: Fred DeRuvo, 46: Raysonho, 47: Mara Casey, Jami Rudofsky, 52: Signe Hammar, 72: Michael Valdez, 78: rzelich, 91: Mango Pop, 98: Yanic Truesdale, 100: Nick Schlax, 105: George Peters, 113: Sheila R Lawrence, 115: Dieter Spears, 131: Robert Lehmann, 146: Dieter Spears. 155: -M-I-S-H-A-, 156: Biff Yeager, 166: 179, 477: Valerie Campbell, Barbara Boxer, 194: John Cabrera, 203: Vasko Miokovic, 210: Aris Alvarado, 225: Jane Espenson, 230: CBS, 232: The Festival of Arts, 237: Nancy Campbell, 252: Arpad Benedek, 270: Sergey Peterman, 271: Cristian Baitg, 274: Sebastian Bach, 283, 287, 557: Aleksandar Jocic, 290, Danny Strong, 293: Susane Lee, 292, 296, 325: Andrea Venanzi, 297: Kathleen Wilhoite, 298: Ming Kai Chiang, 305: Vicki Reid, 315: David H. Lewis, 318: Devon Sorvari, 322: Creativeye99, 327: More magazine, 335: Mindee Clem Forman, 336: Honorine Bell, 338: Joshua Haviv, 349: Jesus Ayala, 361: Israeli Krav Maga Association, 369: Dimension Films, 372: Eric Isselée, 385: pixhook, 388: Scott Cramer, 403: Susan Trigg, 409: Chas Demster, 410: GH01, 412, 445: DNY59, 415: Damian Palus, 417: Alexander Podshivalov, 420: felinda, 433: Raul Davalos, 446: Beth Williams, 461: Claire Mcloughlin, 465: Redbook magazine, 465: NBC, 466: WWD magazine, 466: Fox Searchlight, 479: Sean Gunn

index

H

I

J

K

L

M

N

O

P

Q

R

S

POLICE WOMAN
WONDER WOMAN 1977-1979
SALEM'S LOT
MOVIOLA
THE THORN BIRDS

T

U

V

W

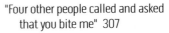

X

Y

Z

Quotes + Phrases

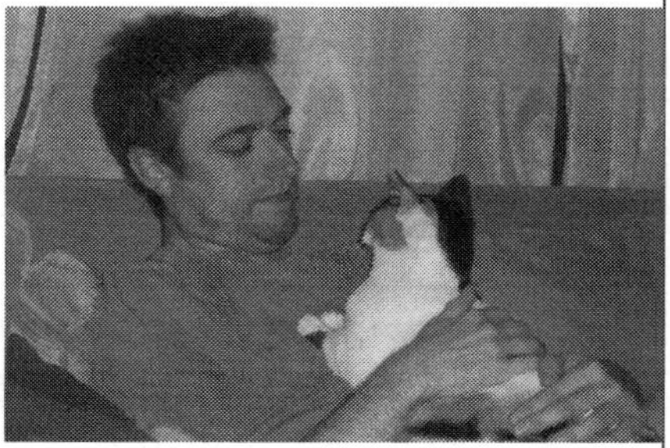

27126042R00268

Made in the USA
San Bernardino, CA
08 December 2015